Running
Microsoft®
Excel 4

Running
Microsoft®
Excel 4

The Cobb Group

Douglas Cobb and Judy Mynhier with
Craig Stinson, Mark Dodge, and Chris Kinata

THIRD EDITION

Microsoft
P R E S S

The Authorized Edition

PUBLISHED BY
Microsoft Press
A Division of Microsoft Corporation
One Microsoft Way
Redmond, Washington 98052-6399

Library of Congress Cataloging-in-Publication Data
Stinson, Craig, 1943 –
    Running Microsoft Excel 4 / Douglas Cobb and Judy Mynhier
with Craig Stinson, Mark Dodge, and Chris Kinata. -- 3rd ed.
      p.   cm.
    Includes index.
    ISBN 1-55615-488-7
    1. Microsoft Excel (Computer program)   2. IBM microcomputers-
-Programming.   3. Business--Computer programs.   I. Dodge, Mark.
II. Kinata, Chris.   III. Title.
HF5548.4.E93S75   1992
650'.0285'5369--dc20   92-3201
                                                     CIP

Printed and bound in the United States of America.

    456789 AGAG 76543

Distributed to the book trade in Canada by Macmillan of Canada, a division
of Canada Publishing Corporation.

Distributed to the book trade outside the United States and Canada by Penguin Books Ltd.

Penguin Books Ltd., Harmondsworth, Middlesex, England
Penguin Books Australia Ltd., Ringwood, Victoria, Australia
Penguin Books N.Z. Ltd., 182–190 Wairau Road, Auckland 10, New Zealand

British Cataloging-in-Publication Data available.

PostScript is a registered trademark of Adobe Systems, Incorporated. Apple, Macintosh,
and TrueType are registered trademarks of Apple Computer, Incorporated. HP and LaserJet
are registered trademarks of Hewlett-Packard Company. AT and IBM are registered trademarks of International Business Machines Corporation. Lotus, 1-2-3, and Symphony are
registered trademarks of Lotus Development Corporation. Microsoft, MS-DOS, and Power-
Point are registered trademarks and Autosum and Windows are trademarks of Microsoft
Corporation. OS/2 is a registered trademark licensed to Microsoft Corporation. Q+E is a
trademark of Pioneer Software Systems Corporation. Ami is a registered trademark of
Samna Corporation. Paintbrush is a trademark of ZSoft Corporation. All other trademarks
and service marks are the property of their respective owners.

Acquisitions Editor: Marjorie Schlaikjer
Project Editor: Peggy McCauley
Manuscript and Technical Editors: Editorial Services of New England

Contents

CHAPTER 6 *Worksheets, Windows, and Workbooks* 225

CHAPTER 7 *Worksheet Graphics* 271

CHAPTER 8 *Built-in Functions* 293

CHAPTER 9 *Date and Time* 373

Acknowledgments

Once again I'd like to thank the editorial and production team that conceived and designed this book and then did the necessary pushing and pulling to get it completed: Marjorie Schlaikjer, Peggy McCauley, Sally Brunsman, Mary DeJong, Bill Teel, and Tara Powers-Hausmann of Microsoft Press; and Michelle Neil, Justin Cuyler, Debra Marvin, Sean Donahue, Carla Thompson, Liz Sutherland, Karen Segal, and Joan Goldsworthy of Editorial Services of New England. And thanks again to J. T. Aldridge for performing the technical edit.

I also want to thank the three University of Oregon students who helped me at home while this book was being written: Margy Grassmeyer, Shannon Maerki, and Gina Papachristopoulos. Thanks, above all, to my wife Jean and son Russell for their patience and encouragement.

— *Craig Stinson*

Thanks to all the folks at Editorial Services of New England for diving into the pool of a thousand dangling participles, made triply murky by the dreaded three-headed author. Thanks to Marjorie Schlaikjer for the afterthought that created said dread' author. Thanks to Mary DeJong and Bill Teel for sweating the details of a zillion screendumps. Thanks to Will Sibbald, Melissa Mullineaux, and Tom Grismer for the space in time. And thanks to Vicki and M. J., for allowing my mental absence and enduring my physical presence as I danced the deadline boogie.

— *Mark Dodge*

I'd like to thank Marjorie Schlaikjer for being at the forefront of the solution to the maximum-cortex-per-square-inch conundrum; to Peggy McCauley, for suffering the patter of gnome's feet that delivered shoes ere dawn's light; to Michelle Neil of Editorial Services of New England; and to J. T. Aldridge, who walked the walk.

— *Chris Kinata*

Preface

Bigger, better, faster, stronger — these are the buzzwords for every new generation of personal computing software. With the latest generation, we can add two new terms to the list: intuitive and easy to learn.

Microsoft Excel version 4.0 meets all these qualifications — and more. The program's intuitive graphical interface, made possible by Microsoft Windows, features drop-down menus, dialog boxes, and icons that enable even computer novices to get their systems up and running quickly and easily. With Excel 4, you don't have to think like a computer to get the most out of your software.

Don't confuse ease of use with lack of depth, however. Excel 4 is the most sophisticated and powerful spreadsheet available on any platform today. The program's vast array of built-in functions is only the beginning. You'll also discover sophisticated three-dimensional business graphics, a powerful macro facility, fantastic formatting capabilities, customization features, and presentation-quality output. These features, combined with the ability to run Excel concurrently with other Windows applications, set a new standard for integrated business software on the PC.

So even though you'll find it easy to come up to speed on Excel, you'll also find that you have a lot of exploration ahead of you as you delve into this powerful application. We hope this book helps you realize the full potential of Microsoft Excel.

What is Microsoft Excel?

Microsoft Excel is an integrated spreadsheet and graphics software package. It features three work environments — spreadsheets (which can also be used to design databases), graphics, and macros — all bundled into one easy-to-use package. This combination of features makes Excel a powerful tool that lets you perform a variety of tasks for business, science, and engineering.

Although Excel's business graphics and macro capabilities are very powerful, Excel is first and foremost a spreadsheet program. As you'll discover in Chapter 1, the first thing you see when you load Excel is a worksheet.

Excel's worksheet is an electronic replacement for traditional planning tools: the pencil and eraser, the accountant's ledger sheet, and the calculator. The electronic spreadsheet is to these tools what a word processor is to a typewriter. In addition, the Excel worksheet can be used as a database manager. Now you can store information within easy reach, only a worksheet away.

Because Excel stores your reports, analyses, and projections in your computer's memory, making changes to them is as easy as typing a few characters and pressing a key or two. In fact, one of the most important reasons for building a projection in Excel or another spreadsheet program is that you can play "what-if" games, varying assumptions and measuring their effects on the bottom line.

In addition to this powerful spreadsheet, Excel offers the best business graphics available in an integrated program. Excel's chart-customizing commands allow you to create hundreds of varieties of charts in two or three dimensions. You can display and print your charts as separate documents or integrate them with worksheet data to create presentation-quality documents.

Finally, Excel enables you to create macros to automate routine tasks or create sophisticated application programs in the Excel worksheet. Probably the most exciting aspect of Excel's macros is that they enable you to create user-defined functions — your own supplements to Excel's extensive library of built-in functions — as well as your own menus and dialog boxes. With these powerful features, the possibilities are almost limitless.

What's new in Microsoft Excel version 4.0

If you have been using an earlier version of Microsoft Excel, you'll be pleased to know that almost every part of Excel 4 incorporates an impressive variety of new features. Here is a partial list of the important improvements in Excel 4.

Ease-of-use improvements

Direct cell manipulation. You can now move and copy cells and ranges by dragging them with the mouse. You can also use the mouse to insert and delete cells, ranges, or entire rows and columns.

New, customizable toolbars. Excel 4's nine built-in toolbars provide mouse shortcuts for many of the program's most commonly used commands. You can position toolbars at any edge of the application window, or you can make them float within the window. Simple customizing procedures let you create your own toolbars, so that the commands *you* use most often are only a click away.

Shortcut menus. When you press the right mouse button (or press Shift-F10) in any context, Excel displays a *shortcut menu*, listing the commands available in the current context. For example, if you use the right mouse button to click a cell, the shortcut menu offers formatting and editing commands for that cell.

AutoFill. At the lower right corner of the current cell boundary, Excel displays a small dark square. By simply dragging this *fill handle*, you can copy cell contents into adjacent ranges or create series. If you drag the fill handle on a cell containing the label *Jan*, for example, Excel creates labels automatically for the remaining months of the year.

Easier formula entry, more readable formulas. A number of new features make it easier than ever to enter and edit formulas. If you forget the arguments for a function, simply press Ctrl-A on the formula bar to make the argument names appear. If you forget a function's right parenthesis, Excel supplies it. You also can add tabs and returns to formulas to make them easier to understand and edit.

Display of names in the reference area. When you select a cell or range to which you've assigned a name, Excel now displays that name in the reference area to the left of the formula bar.

An enhanced Goto command. Excel 4 "remembers" the last four places you went to with the Goto command. These cell addresses appear in a dialog box when you choose Goto (or press F5), making it easy for you to find your way back.

Analytic features

Named worksheet views. A View Manager add-in lets you assign names to combinations of window and printing settings, for easy re-use.

Named scenarios. A Scenario Manager add-in lets you specify any number of input cells in a model and then assign names to various combinations of the values of those inputs. You can cycle through all your named scenarios to test their impact on specified output cells, or you can use a simple command to create a new worksheet table summarizing the impact of each scenario on the bottom line.

Workbooks. Excel 3's workspace feature has been replaced with a more versatile form of document association called a *workbook*. Member documents of a workbook can be either *bound* (incorporated into the workbook) or *unbound* (associated with the workbook but saved as separate files). Excel automatically creates a table of contents for each workbook and provides simple mouse navigation buttons.

The Analysis ToolPak. The Analysis ToolPak add-in brings to Excel a massive assortment of sophisticated engineering, statistical, and financial functions, many of which are not available in any other spreadsheet program. The ToolPak also includes commands for creating histograms and performing distribution analysis, generating non-uniformly distributed random numbers, producing descriptive statistics, performing analysis of variance and other statistical tests, creating moving averages and exponential smoothing, and more.

A faster, more powerful Solver. The Solver, Excel's nonlinear optimizer, is both faster and more versatile than before. Among other things, it is now the only spreadsheet optimizer that lets you specify problems with integer constraints.

The Crosstab ReportWizard. The Crosstab ReportWizard lets you crosstabulate an Excel database in three easy steps. You pick one or more fields to appear in the row dimension of the crosstab table, one or more fields to appear in the column dimension, and one or more fields to be tabulated. Excel populates the table by summing, averaging, counting, or applying one of the other statistical functions to your tabulation fields. Because the resulting table is automatically outlined, you can click level buttons to see the forests, the trees, or something in between.

Formatting and presentation features

The AutoFormat command. With a single mouse click or menu command, you can apply built-in formats automatically to the current worksheet region. Excel looks at your worksheet and applies heuristic reasoning to come up with a combination of fonts, colors, shading, and borders that works for your data.

Centering across columns. No more adjusting column widths to make a label appear centered across two or more columns. Simply select the column range, type the label, and click the Center Across Columns tool.

Vertical alignment. Excel now can display labels and values vertically as well as horizontally. You can make your letters and numbers read top to bottom or bottom to top, or you can stack the characters. Excel automatically expands the row height to accommodate the vertical entry.

Sound annotation. If your computer has the appropriate audio hardware, you can attach sound annotations to worksheet cells. Because Excel 4 fully supports Object Linking and Embedding (OLE), you can also link or embed sound files created in OLE server applications.

A spelling checker. You now can proofread your documents electronically before you commit them to paper.

Slide shows. A new slide-show facility lets you turn a set of worksheets and charts into a polished presentation, complete with transitional effects.

Worksheet zoom. A Window Zoom command lets you shrink or magnify your worksheets from 25 through 400 percent.

Enhanced tiling. New Arrange options let you tile worksheets horizontally, vertically, or both; they also let you synchronize scrolling in two or more windows.

Printing features

Named reports. With the new Report Manager add-in, you can assign names to combinations of named views (created with the View Manager) and named scenarios (created with the Scenario Manager) and turn them into easily reproduced reports.

Control of pagination. If your worksheet is both wider and deeper than a single printed page, you can specify either vertical or horizontal pagination.

Easier headers and footers. No more need to remember codes for inserting the date and time, page numbers, and the name of your file or for specifying header and footer fonts and alignment options. A simple dialog box offers a point-and-shoot setup of headers and footers.

Scale to fit, on any printer. Excel 3 could squeeze or expand a printout to make it fill a single page — provided you were using a PostScript printer. Excel 4 extends these capabilities to all printers and also lets you scale a report to fit multiple pages.

Charting features

The ChartWizard. Like the Crosstab ReportWizard, the new ChartWizard steps you through the process of creating a chart, taking the last vestiges of mystery out of Excel's superb charting module.

New chart types. Excel 4 offers three-dimensional surface and wireframe graphs, in addition to the three-dimensional bars, ribbons, and pies that were introduced with Excel 3. The program also includes a new radar chart type.

Changing 3-D orientation with the mouse. Now you can rotate, flip, and otherwise manipulate a three-dimensional chart by grabbing its corners with the mouse.

Macro features

A global macro sheet. You can record or write macros on a global macro sheet. This macro sheet is loaded automatically as a hidden file at the start of every Excel session. Thus, you can create a set of macros that will be available every time you use Excel.

New ON functions. The new functions ON.ENTRY and ON.DOUBLECLICK let you run a macro whenever the user enters data in a specified document or double-clicks any cell, object, or chart element in a specified document.

The Add-in Manager. You can use the Add-in Manager to specify which of the numerous add-ins supplied with Excel should be available at the start of any session. You can also add your own add-in (XLA) macros to the Add-in Manager's list.

A PAUSE function. A new PAUSE macro function interrupts the execution of a macro, much like the {?} command in Lotus 1-2-3. While the macro is paused, you can enter data, choose commands, open and close worksheets, and so on. You can also begin execution of a second macro. To resume execution of the paused macro, you can either click the Resume tool or choose the Resume command from the Macro menu.

Improved support for 1-2-3

A 1-2-3 macro interpreter. Excel 4 includes a 1-2-3 macro interpreter that will run most macros written for Lotus 1-2-3 Release 2.x, without requiring you to use the Macro Translation Assistant.

Support for FMT and FM3 files. Excel's routines for importing 1-2-3 worksheets now recognize formatting assigned via the Lotus WYSIWYG add-in or PC

Publishing's Impress add-in. In addition, export routines translate Excel formatting into information that the WYSIWYG add-in can use.

Alternate Formula Entry and Alternate Expression Evaluation. Two new calculation settings give you the option of making Excel behave more like Lotus 1-2-3.With Alternate Formula Entry on, for example, you can type an entry such as *5/16* and have Excel treat it as a formula instead of a date label. With Alternate Expression Evaluation on, Excel uses Lotus 1-2-3's approach to evaluating text entries within statistical-function arguments, text indices into lookup functions, and other matters. The Alternate Expression Evaluation option allows 1-2-3 macros that depend on functions and arithmetic expressions to work correctly. The Alternate Formula Entry lets you import 1-2-3 worksheets into Excel and use them there, exactly as you would use them in 1-2-3.

About this book

This book is a user's guide and tutorial for Microsoft Excel. It is designed to help you, the Excel user, gain the deepest possible understanding of Excel in the shortest possible time.

The book has six sections and two appendixes. The first section, Chapter 1, provides an introduction to Excel. Here we cover the basics of starting and using Excel, give you a tour of the Excel screen, and show you how to save and open files.

The second section, Chapters 2 through 12, covers the Excel worksheet. It begins by showing you how to make entries in the worksheet. It covers such topics as formatting entries; using functions; editing the worksheet; using graphic objects; using the Analysis ToolPak, the Scenario Manager, and the Solver; and preparing polished printouts and slide shows.

The next section, Chapters 13 through 15, covers Excel's charting capabilities. Chapter 13 introduces the ChartWizard. Chapter 14 shows you how to customize the appearance of your charts. And Chapter 15 explains how to edit chart data.

The fourth section, Chapters 16 through 18, discusses Excel's database capabilities. A brief discussion in Chapter 16 of the general principles of database management is followed by a discussion in Chapter 17 of Excel's query and extract capabilities. In Chapter 18, we turn our attention to the Crosstab ReportWizard, Excel's new built-in report manager.

The fifth section, Chapters 19 through 21, explains macros. Here you'll learn what macros are and how you can use them. Chapter 20 provides an overview of Excel's macro functions, and Chapter 21 shows you how to use the macro language to create applications with custom menus, dialog boxes, and toolbars.

The sixth section, Chapters 22 and 23, addresses the interaction of Excel with other Windows and non-Windows applications. Chapter 22 discusses the use of

Dynamic Data Exchange (DDE) and Object Linking and Embedding (OLE). Chapter 23 covers the ins and outs of file exchange with other spreadsheet, text, graphics, and database software.

The two appendixes provide easy access to basic reference material. Appendix A covers the new Excel tools and toolbars, and Appendix B lists the program's 30 most valuable keyboard shortcuts.

Using this book

In this book, when you see a key combination written with a hyphen, like this:
    Ctrl-A
it means "Hold down the key on the left side of the hyphen, and then press the key on the right side." For example, Ctrl-A means "Hold down the Ctrl key and press A." When you see two key names separated by a comma, like this:
    Alt, F
it means "Press and release the first key, and then press the second."

This book assumes that you have a working knowledge of Microsoft Windows. Section 5, "Macros," assumes that you have installed the optional Dialog Editor utility.

Two of the add-ins shipped with Excel, the Solver and the Analysis ToolPak, are so rich in features that they warrant their own books. To keep the current volume within manageable dimensions, we have not covered these topics exhaustively. Instead, we have concentrated on the features that we believe are most valuable in a business context, omitting those that require expertise in statistics or engineering. Where appropriate, we have provided suggestions for additional reading.

INTRODUCTION

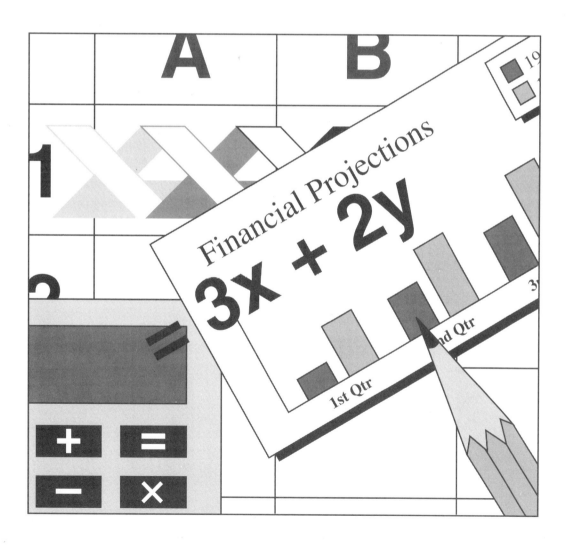

1

Introducing Microsoft Excel

*I*n this chapter, you'll learn how to get started with Microsoft Excel. We'll start by describing the program's hardware requirements. Then we'll walk you through the installation process. Next, we'll show you how to load the program and take you on a brief tour of Excel's working environment. Along the way, we'll introduce you to Excel's system of drop-down menus and show you how to issue commands with a mouse and from the keyboard. You'll learn how to use dialog boxes, how to open and save files, how to use Excel's extensive Help system, and how to quit the program.

If you're a first-time Excel user, we recommend that you read this chapter carefully before you move on. The next few pages introduce crucial terms and concepts that are used throughout the book. Even if you've used Excel before, we suggest that you read the section "A brief tour" to ensure that you're familiar with the terminology we use.

If you've worked with earlier versions of Excel but are new to version 4, be sure to read the sections entitled "Add-ins," "The toolbars," and "Shortcut menus." Excel 4 offers an expanded selection of tools and toolbars and provides shortcut menus, which are a new feature.

Hardware and software requirements

Microsoft Excel runs under Windows version 3 or later on an IBM PS/2, an IBM PC/AT, or an IBM PC/AT-compatible computer that uses the Intel 80286, 80386, or 80486 microprocessor. In addition to Windows itself, your system must include MS-DOS (version 3.1 or later), a minimum of 2 megabytes (MB) of memory, one 5 ¼-inch or 3 ½-inch floppy-disk drive, a hard disk with a minimum of 5 MB of free space, and a Windows-compatible monitor.

Optional components

Several additional components can help speed your work in Excel. These are optional; the choice depends on your personal requirements.

Printers and plotters

You have a number of printer choices, including the Hewlett-Packard LaserJet, the Apple LaserWriter (or any PostScript-compatible printer), the IBM ProPrinter or Graphics printer, the Epson FX 80, and a number of other printers compatible with Microsoft Windows version 3 or later. You might also want to use a plotter to print high-quality color charts and graphs. Excel supports the Hewlett-Packard 7470A plotter and all other plotters compatible with Windows version 3 or later. (See the *Microsoft Windows User's Guide* for more information on printer support.)

A mouse or other pointing device

Excel uses a graphical interface, taking advantage of drop-down menus and icons to let you make selections quickly and easily. Although a mouse is an optional accessory, a few of the most advanced formatting options require one. For example, none of the tools on the toolbars can be accessed from the keyboard.

Many mouse-driven applications require that you use a two-button mouse. Excel requires only one button, but if you do use a two-button mouse, you can take advantage of Excel's new shortcut menus (discussed later in this chapter).

You can use a track ball or other pointing device as a substitute for a mouse if you prefer.

Networks

You can install Excel on a computer attached to a network so that two or more users can share data stored on a common network drive. Networking also allows two or more users to share printing resources.

Excel supports any network compatible with Microsoft Windows version 3 or later, but your network might need a version of MS-DOS later than 3.1. Check with your dealer for details about your network system.

Additional memory

Although Excel can run with as little as 2 MB of memory, it runs more efficiently if your system has more than that amount. With additional memory, you can build larger worksheets and carry out commands and calculations more quickly.

Math coprocessor

A math coprocessor can speed your work by enabling Excel to perform certain calculations — particularly those involving financial and trigonometric functions — faster. Excel supports the Intel 80287 and 80387 math coprocessors.

Installing Microsoft Excel

To install Microsoft Excel, start Windows and make Program Manager the active application. Insert the Excel Setup disk in drive A. Then pull down the File menu, choose the Run command, type A:SETUP, and press Enter. The Setup program then prompts you for information about your computer system, tells you when to change disks, and copies the appropriate files from each floppy disk to your hard disk.

Add-ins

The Excel Setup program can install several macro sheets that contain auxillary programs called *add-ins*. These macro sheets add functions and commands to Excel that appear to be part of the program itself. (You can also create add-ins, allowing you to customize Excel for your own needs. We explain how to create add-ins in detail in Chapter 21.) If you select the Full Installation option from the main Setup screen, Setup installs the following add-ins on your hard disk:

Add-in name	Filename	Commands or functions added	See Chapter
Add-in Manager	ADDINMGR.XLA	Add-ins command (Options menu)	Chapter 19
Analysis ToolPak	ANALYSIS.XLA	Analysis Tools command (Options menu), plus a number of financial and engineering functions	Chapters 8 and 10
Crosstab	CROSSDEF.XLA	Crosstab command (Data menu)	Chapter 18
Report Manager	REPORTS.XLA	Print Report command (File menu)	Chapter 12

(Continued)

Add-in name	Filename	Commands or functions added	See Chapter
Scenario Manager	SCENARIO.XLA	Scenario Manager command (Formula menu)	Chapter 11
Solver	SOLVER.XLA	Solver command (Formula menu)	Chapter 11
View Manager	VIEWS.XLA	View command (Window menu)	Chapter 6

A number of add-in macro sheets are also included in the LIBRARY directory that the Setup program creates in your Excel directory. These add-ins are described in Chapter 19.

If you choose the Custom or minimum installation options from the main Setup screen, the XLA files listed in the table above might not be available on your hard disk. You can install them later by rerunning Setup, selecting the Custom Installation option again, and selecting only the Macro Library and Microsoft Analysis ToolPak options.

If, after installation, any of the add-in commands do not appear on your menus, choose the Add-ins command on the Options menu and click the Add button to find the missing file in your LIBRARY directory. (If the Add-ins command is not available, choose Open from the File menu and select the ADDINMGR.XLA file in the LIBRARY directory.)

Starting Microsoft Excel

You can start Microsoft Excel either from the MS-DOS command line (before you start Windows) or from within Windows. To start Excel from the MS-DOS command line, follow these steps:

1. Use the CHDIR command, if necessary, to access the directory in which Excel is stored.

2. Type *excel* at the MS-DOS prompt and press the Enter key. This command starts both Windows and Excel.

To start Excel from the Windows Program Manager:

1. Open the Program Group window that contains Excel.

2. Double-click the icon labeled Excel. (Or use the arrow keys to highlight that icon, and then press Enter.)

When you run Excel, a copyright box appears briefly, followed by a screen like the one shown in Figure 1-1. Excel creates a new, blank worksheet file, ready for your input. This document is called Sheet1. (Of course, you can save the document under any name you like. See "Saving files," later in this chapter.)

FIGURE 1-1.
*When you start Excel,
your screen initially
looks like this.*

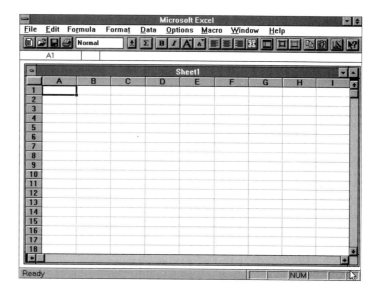

A brief tour

Windows are much like portholes through which you view information. You perform all your work in Microsoft Windows in one of two basic types of windows: application and document. An *application window* holds a program, such as Excel or the Windows File Manager. *Document windows* hold worksheets and other data that you create in Excel.

In Figure 1-1, Excel's application window fills the screen. The application window encloses one document window, titled Sheet1.

The Microsoft Excel application window

As Figure 1-2 on the following page shows, the Excel application window contains five main elements: the application window title bar, the menu bar, the toolbar, the formula bar, and the status bar.

At the top of your screen is the application window's *title bar,* which identifies the program you're working in. Below the title bar is the *menu bar,* where

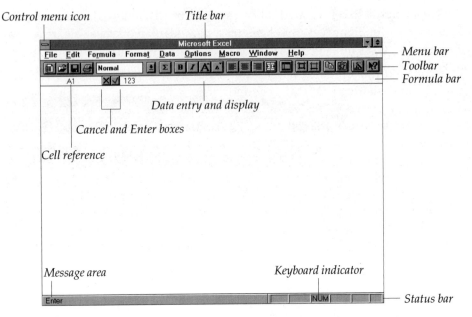

FIGURE 1-2. *The application window provides your working environment for Excel.*

you select the commands you need to manipulate the information you enter in your worksheet. Below the menu bar are any number of toolbars, which let you use your mouse to select frequently used commands. Below the toolbar or toolbars is the *formula bar,* where you enter and edit information in your Excel documents.

The formula bar is split into three portions. On the left is the *reference area.* When a worksheet is open, this area displays the active cell reference. When you activate the formula bar by clicking it, pressing F2, or typing a new cell entry, the middle area displays a set of Cancel and Enter boxes. You use these boxes to lock in worksheet entries or to cancel entries and revert to the previous contents of the cell. Most of the formula bar is taken up by the data-entry and display areas, where you make your entries into the worksheet and view the contents of cells.

At the bottom of the application window is the *status bar.* The left portion of this bar, the *message area,* brings you information about current menu and command selections. The right side of the bar, the *keyboard indicator area,* displays information about the current state of certain keys on the keyboard, such as Caps Lock or Excel's Extend key (F8). For example, you might see NUM in this area, which indicates that the Num Lock keyboard setting is in effect.

The toolbars

Excel also gives you the option of displaying toolbars below the menu bar. Excel 4 includes nine different toolbars. When you first start Excel, the Standard toolbar is displayed, and the top of the application window looks like Figure 1-3. Toolbars provide handy shortcuts for many common actions, but you must have a mouse or other pointing device to take advantage of them. If you do not have a mouse, you can free up some screen real estate by suppressing the display of the toolbar. To do this, press Alt-O, and then press O to choose Toolbars from the Options menu. Use the arrow keys to select Standard from the Show Toolbars list, and press Alt-I to choose the Hide button. If the first button in the Toolbars dialog box is Show, instead of Hide, scroll down the list of toolbars until the button changes to Hide.

The Standard toolbar contains tools that are useful in most of your day-to-day operations. Some other toolbars are displayed automatically when you need them. For example, the Chart toolbar appears whenever you are working on a chart. We discuss the Chart toolbar in Chapter 13.

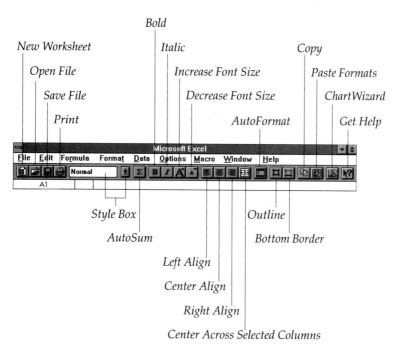

FIGURE 1-3. *The Standard toolbar. Toolbars provide shortcuts for editing, formatting, drawing, charting, and other common activities.*

You can display another toolbar at any time using the Toolbars command on the Options menu. You can have as many toolbars active as you want — at the expense, of course, of your worksheet's visible window size. To display another toolbar, follow these steps:

1. Click the mouse on the Options command, near the middle of the menu bar.

2. In the menu that drops down, click the Toolbars command. A dialog box appears.

3. In the Show Toolbars list, click the name of the toolbar you wish to display; for example, Formatting.

4. Click the button labeled Show.

As a shortcut for selecting the name and clicking the Show button, you can display a toolbar by double-clicking its name in the Toolbars dialog box.

You can hide a toolbar by following these steps again. Choose the Toolbars command and click the word *Formatting* again, but this time, instead of clicking the Show button, click the Hide button to remove the Formatting toolbar from the application window.

Excel also allows you to relocate your toolbars within the application window. When you first start Excel, the Standard toolbar is located at the top of the screen and is said to be "docked." You can undock a toolbar by double-clicking it or by dragging it to another location. (Be careful not to click one of the tool buttons by mistake.)

If your toolbar looks different

Perhaps you are using a computer that was used previously by someone else or that is shared with others. Because Excel 4 has so many toolbars that can be customized so many ways, the copy of Excel you are using might have already been modified. You can use the Toolbars command on the Options menu to redisplay the Standard toolbar if it is not currently active. If the Standard toolbar has been modified, you might want to make some modifications of your own. If so, see Appendix A for details on customizing the toolbars.

When you relocate a toolbar, its appearance changes slightly. For example, after you drag the Standard toolbar from its default location to the middle of the screen, the toolbar looks like a miniature window, complete with a title bar and what appears to be a little Document Control menu icon in the upper left corner. Actually, this indicator is a Close button — when you click it, the toolbar disappears. When you undock a toolbar, you can also resize it by dragging one of its borders, as shown in Figure 1-4.

Excel remembers the size and location of the toolbar. The next time you start Excel, the toolbar will appear as it did the last time you quit the program. You can redock a toolbar by dragging it all the way to the top, bottom, left, or right of the screen, or by double-clicking the toolbar. (Be careful to avoid clicking a tool.) If you drag the toolbar shown in Figure 1-5 on the following page to the bottom of the screen, it reshapes itself into a single row of tool buttons, and the title bar and Close button disappear. The borders of the toolbar merge with the application window, as shown in Figure 1-5. If you want to undock the toolbar again, it will take on the last shape it had before you docked it. Each time you double-click the toolbar, it will alternate between its most recent docked and undocked locations.

FIGURE 1-4.
You can change both the shape and the location of toolbars.

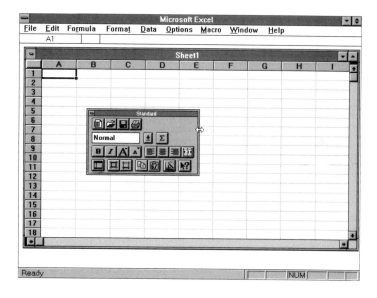

FIGURE 1-5.
*You can "dock" a
toolbar at the bottom
of the screen as well as
at the top.*

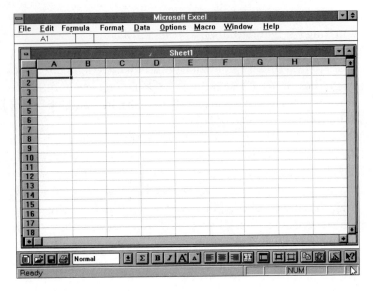

We'll discuss the other tools and toolbars throughout this book. Appendix A lists all the tools and toolbars available and explains how you can customize and even create toolbars containing the tools you use most often.

Document windows

Excel uses five kinds of document windows — for worksheets, charts, macros, workbooks, and slides. The document window that makes up most of the screen in Figure 1-5 is a worksheet window.

Initially, as you become acquainted with Excel, you'll work only with worksheet files. Later you'll learn to plot your worksheet data in a chart window and to use macros to automate your work. At some point, you will undoubtedly find it useful to combine documents into groups as workbooks and perhaps create on-screen slide show presentations. (See Chapter 6 for information on Workbooks and Chapter 12 for information on slides.)

Document windows, like application windows, have title bars that identify their contents. When you start Excel without specifying a particular document, the program automatically opens a blank worksheet titled Sheet1. This worksheet is illustrated in Figure 1-6.

As Figure 1-6 shows, document windows can also have scroll bars. With the aid of your mouse, scroll bars enable you to move quickly from one part of a worksheet to another. Chapter 2 discusses the use of scroll bars and how to scroll through the document with the keyboard.

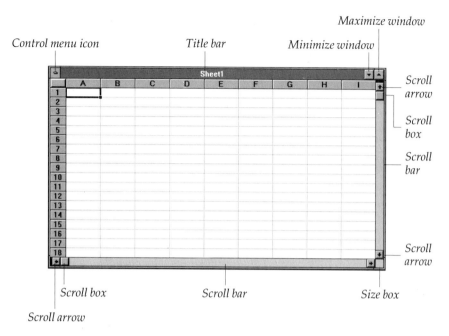

FIGURE 1-6. *Document windows include their own title bars and can also have scroll bars.*

The Microsoft Excel worksheet

Like a paper accounting ledger, the Excel worksheet is a grid made up of columns and rows. Letters ranging from A through IV identify a total of 256 columns. (After column Z comes column AA, after AZ comes BA, and so on to IV.) Numbers from 1 through 16384 identify the rows. The intersection of each column and row is a *cell*.

Cells are the basic building blocks of every worksheet. Each cell occupies a unique location on the worksheet where you can store and display information, and each cell is assigned a unique pair of coordinates called a *cell reference*. For example, the intersection of column Z and row 100 has the cell reference Z100.

With 256 columns and 16,384 rows, each worksheet contains a total of 4,194,304 individual cells! Before you try to unravel the mysteries of the universe on a single worksheet, however, keep in mind that the memory capacity of your computer limits the number of cells you can use at any one time. Even though the program uses a sophisticated sparse matrix system for efficient memory management, you probably won't be able to fill all the cells in one worksheet.

If you were to lay an entire worksheet out like a paper ledger, it would measure more than 21 feet wide by 341 feet long! Because the worksheet is so large, you can see only a small portion of it on your screen at any given time. In the worksheet in Figure 1-1, only 162 cells are visible. Thus, the worksheet window is like a porthole that lets you look at a limited portion of the worksheet document.

With a large worksheet, you might soon find it tedious to move the window back and forth across the "page" every time you want to see a different set of cells. Fortunately, you can create multiple windows to get different views of the same worksheet. You can also move the windows independently to compare different parts of the worksheet simultaneously. Chapter 6 explains how to do this.

Menus, commands, and dialog boxes

Microsoft Excel uses *drop-down* menus. That is, under each name in the menu bar is a list of related commands from which you can choose. When you open a menu, you'll notice that some commands are dimmed to indicate that they are not currently available. The program monitors the status of your workspace and allows you to choose only those commands applicable at any given time.

If you use a mouse, you can choose a command by pointing to the menu name and pressing the left mouse button. The menu drops down to show a list of available commands. Without releasing the mouse button, drag the arrow-shaped mouse pointer through the list of available commands. As you highlight each command, a brief description of the command appears on the left side of the status bar at the bottom of your screen. When you find the command you want, release the mouse button to choose that command.

When you pull down a menu, that menu stays active until you choose a command, click elsewhere on your screen, or click the menu name again. Therefore, if you don't need the descriptive messages to help you find the right command, you can click a menu, release the mouse button, move the pointer to the command you want, and click again.

You can also use the keyboard to choose commands. To access a menu from the keyboard, simply press Alt to activate the menu bar, and then choose the menu you want to use. (The F10 function key and the slash key [/] serve the same purpose as the Alt key.) Notice that one of the letters in each menu name in Figure 1-5 is underlined. After pressing Alt, you can choose a menu by entering the letter that represents the menu name. For example, to access the Edit menu, press Alt and then press E.

Alternatively, after pressing Alt to activate the menu bar, you can use the Left and Right arrow keys to highlight the name of the menu you want to use. After highlighting the menu name, press the Down arrow key to pull down that menu. For example, to access the Format menu, press Alt, press the Right arrow key three times, and then press the Down arrow key.

When you use the mouse or the keyboard to pull down the File menu, you'll see a menu like the one in Figure 1-7. Again, one letter in each of the command names on this menu is underlined. To choose that command from the keyboard, simply type the appropriate letter. (At the bottom of the menu, you'll find the names of the four files you used most recently. To select one of these files, type the under-lined number that precedes the filename.) Alternatively, after you pull down a menu, you can use the Up and Down arrow keys to move through the list of avail-able commands. Using the arrow keys is much like using the mouse to move through the list of commands in the active menu — as you highlight each command name in turn, you'll see a brief description of that item at the bottom of your screen. When the command you want is highlighted, press Enter to execute it.

FIGURE 1-7.
*When you pull down
the File menu, you see
a list of available
file-management
commands.*

If you want to access another menu after you've already pulled one down, you can press Esc followed by another menu's underlined letter, or you can use the Left and Right arrow keys to move to adjacent menus. To deactivate the menu bar with-out issuing a command, press the Alt key.

In some cases, you can bypass the menu bar altogether and use keyboard short-cuts to issue commands. For example, to issue the Save As command, press F12 or Alt-F2; to issue the Copy command, press Ctrl-Ins or Ctrl-C. After you learn the keyboard shortcuts, you'll find them a timesaving convenience. But they're optional, of course. Use the normal menu commands if you prefer. Appen-dix B lists all of Excel's keyboard shortcuts.

Shortcut menus

New in Excel version 4 are *shortcut menus*. Shorter menus provide a handy way to get at the commands you need with a minimum of mouse movement. You access shortcut menus by clicking the right mouse button or by pressing Shift-F10. If you click the right mouse button, the menu pops up adjacent to the location of the mouse pointer, as shown in Figure 1-8 on the following page. If you activate the shortcut menu by pressing Shift-F10, the shortcut menu appears in the upper left corner of the document window. Shortcut menus are identical in function to regular menus — simply choose the command you want with the mouse or keyboard.

FIGURE 1-8.
*Clicking the right
mouse button
activates the shortcut
menu.*

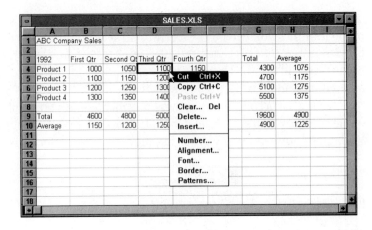

The shortcut menu contains only those commands that are directly applicable to the item indicated by the position of the mouse pointer when you activated the shortcut menu. (Although if you use Shift-F10 to activate the shortcut menu, the commands that appear apply to the document window in general.) This means that the shortcut menu can contain many different combinations of commands, depending on the position of the pointer and what type of document you are working on. For example, if you click the right mouse button when the pointer is on the toolbar, the shortcut menu that appears looks like the one in Figure 1-9. This shortcut menu includes commands that allow you to display or hide any of the built-in toolbars and to access both the Customize and Toolbars dialog boxes. Excel has over 20 shortcut menus, each one offering the commands most likely to be useful at the pointer's current location.

FIGURE 1-9.
*This shortcut menu
appears when you
click the right mouse
button while the
pointer is on the
toolbar.*

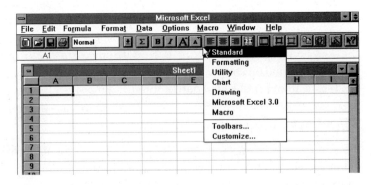

Dialog boxes

Some command names on the File menu in Figure 1-7 are followed by ellipses (...). The ellipses indicate that Excel needs additional information to carry out the command. You provide this information in a special window called a *dialog box,* which Excel displays after you choose the command. For example, when you choose the Clear command from the Edit menu, you see a dialog box like the one in Figure 1-10.

FIGURE 1-10.
*Dialog boxes ask you
for additional
command information.*

Notice that one item in this dialog box has a dark button beside it and is encircled with a dotted line. This item is the *default* option in this dialog box. A default option (or default entry) is the choice that Excel uses automatically, unless you override it by making another choice.

Nearly all dialog boxes have two kinds of elements: one or more places for you to enter information or choose options, and one or more *command buttons.* For example, the Edit Clear dialog box shown in Figure 1-10 offers four options, labeled All, Formats, Formulas, and Notes. And it has three command buttons, labeled OK, Cancel, and Help.

You can move between elements of a dialog box most easily with a mouse, but pressing Tab also moves you from one element to the next. Pressing Shift-Tab moves you back to the previous element.

Most dialog boxes have a command button that you choose after you fill out the dialog box to your satisfaction and another that you choose if you want to back out without making an entry. In many cases, these buttons are OK and Cancel. But you might see other buttons, such as Save, Accept, Yes, No, or Close.

Some dialog boxes, such as the Save As dialog box accessed from the File menu, include command buttons with ellipses, such as the Options button in Figure 1-11 on the following page. Choosing one of these buttons either brings up an additional dialog box or adds options to the current one.

Dialog boxes include a variety of devices for gathering information or letting you choose options. The next several paragraphs describe those devices.

Text boxes

A *text box* is a place for you to type something. In Figure 1-11, for example, the box below the words "File Name" is a text box. You use this box to specify the name under which you want to save a new file. Text boxes sometimes have default entries. The default entry in this example is SHEET1.XLS.

FIGURE 1-11.
You use a text box when you enter a file name.

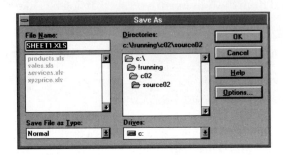

List boxes

A *list box* presents a set of options in the form of a list. In Figure 1-11, the section of dialog box marked Directories is a list box. Typically, the options in a list box are mutually exclusive, but they might not always be.

  If the list contains more items than can be displayed at once, a scroll bar appears at the right side of the list box. You can move through the list one item at a time by clicking the arrows at the top and bottom of the scroll bar. You can also move through a list box by pressing the Up and Down arrow keys, PgUp, or PgDn. A quick way to move to the first item in a list that starts with a letter is to press the key that corresponds to that letter.

Drop-down list boxes

A *drop-down list box* is an ordinary list box displayed in a more compact space. It appears as a single item with a downward-pointing arrow to its right. In the dialog box shown in Figure 1-11, the element labeled Save File as Type is a drop-down list box.

  To open a drop-down list box, click the mouse on the downward-pointing arrow or press Alt-Down arrow. Sometimes, when a drop-down list box is too close to the bottom of the screen, the list will "drop up," so that the entire list will be visible. If the list is very long, a scroll bar appears in the box, indicating that more choices are available in the indicated direction.

Option (radio) buttons

Option buttons (sometimes called *radio buttons*) always come in groups, have circles beside them, and present a set of mutually exclusive options. The four choices shown in Figure 1-10 — All, Formats, Formulas, and Notes — make up a group of option buttons.

To select an option button, click the item you want to select. If you don't have a mouse, press Tab until a dotted line appears around one of the options, and then press the arrow keys until the option you want has a darkened circle. If an option has an underlined letter, choose it by holding down Alt and pressing that letter.

Check boxes

Check boxes appear either in groups or one at a time and are marked by squares instead of circles. Figure 1-12 includes a check box.

FIGURE 1-12.
The small square next to Read Only is a check box.

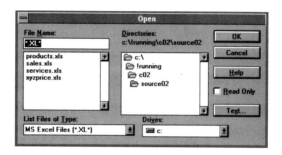

An X in a check box means you accept the option. An empty check box means you decline it. To select (put an X in) a check box, click the mouse on the box or the associated text. To deselect (remove the X), click again. To select and deselect a check box with the keyboard, press Tab until the option is encircled by a dotted line. Then press Spacebar. If the option's text includes an underlined letter, you can select or deselect it by holding down Alt and pressing that letter.

Alert boxes

In addition to dialog boxes, you'll sometimes see another kind of window called an *alert box*. Figure 1-13 on the following page shows the alert box that appears if you type an invalid option in the Font dialog box's Size text box. (The Font command is on the Format menu.) These alert boxes contain informational messages, warnings, and prompts for further information. They also contain command buttons that you use to acknowledge a warning or message, cancel an operation, issue further instructions, or go directly to the on-line Help reference for that particular alert box. (Most dialog boxes have a Help button in them. We'll discuss the Help system later in this chapter.) You choose the command buttons in alert boxes just as you do in dialog boxes.

FIGURE 1-13.
Alert boxes carry informational messages and warnings.

The Control menus

In addition to the menus you access through the menu bar, every application and document window includes a special menu called a *Control menu*. You can open the Application Control menu by clicking the bar at the left end of the Excel title bar, or by pressing Alt, Spacebar. You can open a Document Control menu by clicking the shorter bar at the left side of the document window's title bar, or by pressing Alt, Hyphen.

Control menus offer commands for sizing, moving, and closing windows. We'll discuss those commands in Chapter 6. You'll also find a Switch To command on the Application Control menu. This command invokes the Windows Task List utility, which allows you to switch to another application running under Windows. You can also invoke the Task List at any time by pressing Ctrl-Esc.

The Application Control menu also offers a Run command you can use to access the Clipboard, Control Panel, Macro Translator, and Dialog Editor applications. Clipboard and Control Panel are general-purpose Windows utility programs, described in your *Microsoft Windows User's Guide*. Macro Translator and Dialog Editor are Excel features and are described in Chapter 23 and Chapter 21 of this book, respectively.

File management

You use the File menu commands to create new files, save new files, open and close existing files, and exit the program. We'll begin our discussion of file management by showing you how to create and save new files. Next, we'll show you how to retrieve files from disk and delete files. In this chapter, we use worksheet files as examples. But the techniques discussed here apply to chart, macro, workbook, and slide files, which are also types of documents. Workbooks are actually collections of documents. Workbooks are discussed in Chapter 6.

The File menu also contains commands that control printing tasks and let you access linked documents. File linking and printing are discussed in Chapter 6 and in Chapter 12.

Creating a new file

When you load Microsoft Excel without loading a document, you see a new, blank worksheet called Sheet1. To create a new document at any other time, simply choose New from the File menu. In this case, you see a dialog box like the one shown in Figure 1-14.

FIGURE 1-14.
Select the type of
document you want to
create from the New
dialog box.

Notice that the Worksheet option is already selected in this dialog box. Whenever you issue the New command, Excel looks at the type of document window currently active and suggests the same file type for your new document. If you want to create another type of document, simply select another option before you choose OK, or press Enter to execute the New command. You can also create a new document quickly by clicking the New Worksheet tool on the Standard toolbar.

If you select the Worksheet option, Excel displays a new, blank worksheet window on your screen. If another document is already open, the new window appears on top of the existing document. If the previous worksheet was Sheet1, the new worksheet is named Sheet2. Subsequent worksheets are numbered sequentially — Sheet3, Sheet4, and so forth.

Saving files

After you invest time and energy in creating a worksheet, you'll probably want to save it so you can retrieve it later. When you save a worksheet, you save the settings you assigned to that worksheet — including the window configurations and display characteristics, formulas, functions, formats, fonts, and styles — in addition to its alphanumeric contents.

On the File menu, you'll find three commands — Save, Save As, and Save Workbook — that let you save your Excel files. Each of these commands works in a slightly different way. Generally, you use the Save As command to save a document for the first time or to modify the way Excel saves your document, and the Save command to save changes to existing documents. However, the program also asks if you want to save your changes when you choose the Close or Exit command, to ensure against accidental loss of your work. You can also save the current document quickly by clicking the File Save tool on the Standard toolbar.

When you save a document with one of the Save commands, that file remains open. When you close a file or quit Excel with the Close or Exit command, however, Excel removes the file from the screen.

Saving a file for the first time

Before you can save a document for the first time, you must assign a name to the file and indicate where you want Excel to store it. To name your document, first choose Save As from the File menu. You'll see a dialog box like the one shown in Figure 1-11.

The suggested filename — SHEET1.XLS in this example, because we haven't yet assigned a new name to the document — appears in the File Name text box. This filename is already highlighted; to change the filename, simply type a new name. The original contents of the text box disappear as soon as you begin typing. After you press OK to save the file, the worksheet's new name appears in the document-window title bar.

Filename rules

File naming in Excel follows the same basic rules you use in other Windows or MS-DOS applications. Filenames can have as many as eight characters and can include any combination of alphanumeric characters, as well as the special characters &, $, %, ', (,), -, @, [,], ~, !, and _. Blank spaces are not allowed. Even though you can use any combination of uppercase and lowercase letters, keep in mind that Microsoft Excel does not distinguish case in your filenames. For example, the names *MYFILE*, *MyFile*, and *myfile* are identical as far as Excel is concerned.

In addition to the eight-character filename, you can append a three-character file extension to help identify your document. Usually, you'll want to use the following default extensions:

Document type	Extension
Add-in macro	XLA
Backup	BAK
Chart	XLC
Macro sheet	XLM
Slides	XLS
Template	XLT
Worksheet	XLS
Workbook	XLW

Occasionally, however, you might want to create your own file extensions to flag special files. To do so, simply type the filename, a period character, and then the extension. For example, you might create a file called MYFILE.EXT.

If you want to accept the program's default file extension, simply type the filename with no period character or extension name. If you don't want any file extension at all attached to the filename, type a period character alone after the filename.

Unless you specify otherwise, Excel saves your file to the current directory, which appears on the line to the right of the text box. To save your file to a different directory, you can specify the directory along with your filename in the text box, or you can select the directory you want from the Directories list box.

The Directories list box lists all subdirectories of the current directory, in alphabetic order. The Drives list box lists all the disk drives connected to your system. If you want to save a file to another disk, specify the disk drive using the Drives list box.

File formats and other options

In addition to providing the filename and location, you can specify a number of additional options in the Save As dialog box. Click the downward-pointing arrow to the right of the Save File as Type drop-down list box. The list expands to reveal the 18 formats in which you can save your files.

The default format is Normal, and you'll almost always use this option. If you want to export some or all of your Excel files to another program, however, you can use one of the other options to convert the file into a format that is readable by that program. Excel's export formats are described in Chapter 23.

To access additional options, choose the Options button. Another dialog box appears, as shown in Figure 1-15. If you select the check box labeled Create Backup File, Excel creates a duplicate copy of your file on the same disk and in the same directory as the original. This duplicate file carries the same filename as your original, but the file extension changes to BAK. If this is the first time you've saved the file, the backup file and the worksheet file are identical. If you saved the file previously with the Create Backup File option selected, Excel renames the last saved version of your file, giving it a BAK extension, and overwrites the existing BAK file.

FIGURE 1-15.
Choosing the Options button allows you to access additional file-management options.

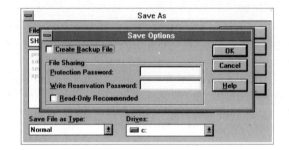

CAUTION: *Keep in mind that Excel always uses a BAK extension when creating backup files, regardless of the file type. Suppose you save a worksheet named MYFILE.XLS and a chart named MYFILE.XLC and select the Create Backup File option for both. Because only one MYFILE.BAK can exist, the most recently saved file is saved as the BAK file, and Excel overwrites the other file's backup, if one exists.*

The remainder of the Options dialog box provides measures for protecting your work against deletion, alteration, or unwanted inspection by other users. Those features are described in Chapter 2.

Resaving a file

After you save a file for the first time, you need not use the Save As command again unless you want to resave the file under a new name or to choose one of the file options discussed in the previous section. To save your changes to a file that you have already saved, simply select Save from the File menu. Excel overwrites the last saved version of the file with the current contents of the worksheet and leaves the window open in the workspace.

If you choose the Save As command again, you can save a file under a new name. When you choose Save As to store a previously saved file, you'll see the same Save As dialog box shown in Figure 1-11, except that Excel displays the name under which you last saved the file. If you type a new name before pressing Enter or clicking OK, Excel saves the current worksheet under that new name and leaves the previous version of the file intact under the old name. If you don't change the name before choosing OK, Excel asks you whether you want to overwrite the existing file. If you choose to overwrite the old version and the Create Backup File option is active, Excel creates a BAK file or updates the existing BAK file.

Retrieving files

To retrieve a file from disk, choose the Open command from the File menu or click the Open File tool. Excel displays a dialog box, like the one shown in Figure 1-16, that contains a list of the Excel files (files with the extension XL*) stored in the current directory.

FIGURE 1-16.
Use the Open dialog box to retrieve files.

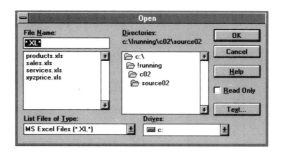

As when you save a file, you must provide two pieces of information: the name of the file and its location. The current directory is indicated by the open file-folder icon in the Directories list box. The Files list box on the left lists the files available in that directory. To change directories, select the directory you want from the Directories list box. The selected directory remains open until you make a new selection.

The File Name text box near the top of the dialog box determines which files are available for selection. The default entry is *.XL*, which tells the program to display only Excel files in the Files list box — that is, only those files whose extensions begin with the characters *XL*. You can display specific types of files or display all files by selecting an option from the List Files of Type drop-down list box. For example, to show all documents in the current directory, select All Files (*.*) from the List Files of Type list box. To display only Lotus 1-2-3 files, select the Lotus 1-2-3 Files (*.WK) option.

You can click the filename in the Files list box, or you can type the full filename in the File Name text box. If that file is located in the current directory, Excel opens it when you choose OK. If you want to retrieve a file in another directory without changing the current directory, you can type the full pathname for the file you want.

You can use the Read Only check box on the right side of the dialog box to prevent changes to the saved version of the file on disk. If you have turned this check box on, you can view and even edit the file, but you can't save it under its current name. Instead, you must use the Save As command to save the edited file under a new filename.

The Read Only option is most useful when you're working on a network. If you open a file without selecting the Read Only option, others on the network must select the Read Only option to view that file. Naturally, you can still save your changes, but the other users would have to use the Save As command to save their changes under a new filename. If other users try to open the same file *without* using the Read Only option, they'll get an error message.

Finally, the Save dialog box includes a Text button that allows you to save your file in various text formats. These options are discussed in Chapter 23.

Reopening a recently opened file

Near the bottom of the File menu, you'll find the names of the four files you've worked with most recently, even in previous sessions. To reopen one of these files, simply choose its name from this menu.

Deleting files

You can also delete files or erase files from a disk while you're working in Excel. To delete a file, choose Delete from the File menu. The program displays a dialog box like the one in Figure 1-17. Select the directory and the name of the file you want to delete, just as you would select a file you want to open.

FIGURE 1-17.
Use the Delete dialog box to erase a file from a disk.

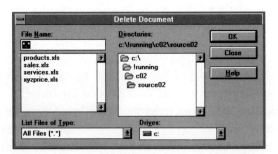

Because you cannot recover a file after it has been deleted, Excel asks you to confirm your choice when you select a file for deletion. If you're sure you want to delete the specified file, choose Yes; if you're not sure, choose No.

Starting Microsoft Excel with particular files

There are several ways to start Excel with one or more files already open.

If you start Excel from the MS-DOS command line, you can supply the name of the file you want to open directly after the word *excel*. For example, to open a worksheet called PAYROLL.XLS, you could type

    EXCEL PAYROLL.XLS

at the MS-DOS command line.

If Windows is already running, you can use the Run command on the Program Manager File menu. In the dialog box that appears, type the word *excel* followed by the names of any files you want to open. If those files are not stored in the current directory, be sure to include their full pathnames.

To start Excel with the worksheet files C:\REGIONS\NORTH.XLS and C:\REGIONS\SOUTH.XLS, you could pull down the Program Manager File menu, choose the Run command, and then fill out the dialog box as follows:

    EXCEL C:\REGIONS\NORTH.XLS C:\REGIONS\SOUTH.XLS

You can also use this method of starting Excel with the Windows File Manager.

If you have a set of files you work with regularly, you might want to store them in a special directory called XLSTART. This directory must be a subdirectory of the directory that contains your Excel program files. (Microsoft Excel's Setup program automatically creates the XLSTART directory for you when it installs Excel on your hard disk.) Use Save As to save worksheet, chart, macro, or workbook files you want automatically loaded when you start Excel in the XLSTART subdirectory.

Starting Excel with no file

You might prefer not to see Sheet1 every time you start Excel. To do this, you can add /e to the command line, like this:

    Excel /E

You can add this switch to a Program Manager program item using the Properties command. (See your *Microsoft Windows User's Guide* for details.) Alternatively, you can choose Run from the Windows File menu and type *EXCEL /E*. (The /E startup option is undocumented and might not be supported in all future versions of Excel.)

NOTE: For compatibility with earlier versions, Excel also automatically starts any file named START.XLS, START.XLC, START.XLM, or START.XLW that is stored in the same directory as your Excel program files. In fact, Excel will automatically load any file whose name begins with the letters start — STARTUP, STARTLE, *or even* STARTREK!

Finally, if you frequently start Excel with a particular file, you might want to create a Program Manager program item icon for it. (See the *Microsoft Windows User's Guide* for details.)

Closing files and exiting Microsoft Excel

When you finish your work on a document, you'll probably want to remove that document from your screen and then either exit from Excel or work on another file. To close a single document, choose Close from the File menu. To simultaneously close all the documents currently open in the workspace, hold down the Shift key as you access the File menu. This combination changes the Close command to Close All. Close All lets you clear the entire workspace without leaving the program. Then you can open another file or create a new document to work with.

To close all files and exit from the program, choose Exit from the File menu. After all the active files are closed, Excel removes itself from memory.

Alternatively, you can close all files and exit from Excel by pressing Alt-F4 or by double-clicking the Application Control menu icon on the Excel title bar.

No matter which command you choose, if you've changed any open files since you last saved them, an alert box asks whether you want to save your changes for each altered file. Choose Yes to save the new version of the file before closing it. If you choose No to close the document without updating the file on disk, any changes you made since you last used the Save or Save As command will be lost. Choose the Cancel button to cancel the Close or Exit command and return to Excel.

In addition to the File menu commands, you can use the Document Control menus to close individual document windows and to exit from the program. These menus are discussed in Chapter 6.

Getting help

If you forget the procedure for performing a task or need a reminder of the arguments for a particular function, help is only a few keystrokes or mouse clicks away. Microsoft Excel provides a complete on-line reference facility to help you learn the program and get quick reminders on specific topics.

Because the program gives you step-by-step instructions on how to use this facility when you issue a Help command — there is even a "Help" topic to teach you how to use the Help facility — we won't cover the Help window in great detail here; we'll simply show you how to access the Help application window and give you an overview of the available options.

You can access the Help facility in two ways: by choosing a command from the Help menu or by pressing F1. The Help menu offers eight commands: Contents Search, Product Support, Introducing Microsoft Excel, Learning Microsoft Excel, Lotus 1-2-3, Multiplan, and About Microsoft Excel. When you click on the Contents command, you see a listing of the general categories of the available Help topics. If you want information about a specific topic, use the Search command which provides alphabetical access by topic. The Product Support command gives you instant information about Microsoft's extensive product support services, including phone, fax, and on-line services. It also contains a list of the 20 most commonly asked questions about Excel. If you're new to Excel or want to learn about a feature you haven't used before, you can use the Introducing Microsoft Excel and Learning Microsoft Excel commands to access self-paced tutorials. The About Microsoft Excel command tells you which version of Excel you're using and displays the copyright notice. It also tells you how much memory is available and whether or not you have a math coprocessor installed. We'll discuss the Lotus 1-2-3 and Multiplan commands later in this chapter.

Before you call product support

We encourage you first to use the Excel documentation, the on-line Help system, and this book to find the answers to your questions. (Be sure to scan the Commonly Asked Questions Help topic by choosing the Product Support command on the Help menu.) When you have exhausted these resources, it's time to call Microsoft Product Support. But first, open the file named CHECKUP.XLM, located in the C:\EXCEL\LIBRARY\CHECKUP directory on your hard disk. When you open this file, a dialog box appears that lists your computer's current system configuration, various Excel workspace options, and other information. You can choose to print the information in a report, if you like. When you get in touch with Product Support, having this information at your fingertips will help the representative diagnose your problem and will save you both some time.

You can also get information about a specific command or action by using the program's context-sensitive help capabilities. To get context-sensitive help, choose a command or a dialog-box option, and then press F1 to get more information about that topic. Alternatively, press Shift-F1 to access the Help facility and then choose the command you want to learn about. When you press Shift-F1, a question mark appears next to your pointer. Use the mouse or keyboard techniques described earlier in this chapter to select the command you want to learn about. If you use a mouse, you can also press Shift-F1 and then click an object on the screen, such as the scroll bar, to get information about that object. As mentioned earlier, you can also click the Help buttons that are located in dialog boxes to get an explanation of the dialog box's function and a complete description of each element it contains.

The on-line Help system window includes four buttons — Contents, Search, Back, and History — as you can see in Figure 1-18. The Contents button takes you directly to the Help contents screen. The Search button allows you to search for Help topics using keywords. The Back button takes you back to the previous screen. The History button allows you to view a list of all the Help topics you have accessed during the current Excel session, making it easy to return to an item you already looked at, even if you forgot where you found it.

FIGURE 1-18.
The on-line Help
system gives you
instant access to a
wealth of information.

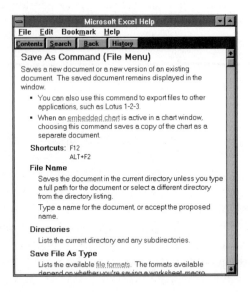

Looking at a typical on-line Help topic, you will notice that some of the text is a different color than the rest. The different colored text indicates *hot spots* that you click on with the mouse for more information. There are two kinds of hot spots, *pop-ups* and *jumps*. A pop-up is colored text with a dotted underline. When you click it, a small window appears that gives you further information. Usually, pop-ups are used to define terms. A jump is colored text with a solid underline. When you click it, Excel takes you to a different Help topic that relates to the particular item you jumped from. To get back to the original topic after a jump, simply click the Back button at the top of the window.

Help for Lotus 1-2-3 and Multiplan users

The Lotus 1-2-3 and Multiplan commands let you type the command sequence for a Lotus 1-2-3 or Multiplan command to issue the equivalent command sequence for the Excel program. The Lotus 1-2-3 command provides you with the options of having the equivalent Excel commands carried out for you in a demonstration or presented as instructions. If you choose the Instructions option, the equivalent Excel commands are placed on the worksheet in a floating text box, which you can delete when you are finished.

If you choose the Demo option, you can specify the speed at which Excel carries out the equivalent action, so that you can watch and learn at your own pace. To adjust the speed of the presentation, click the Faster or Slower button in the Help Options section of the Help for Lotus 1-2-3 Users dialog box (shown in Figure 1-19). Clicking the More Help button takes you to the on-line Help window and presents the main Lotus 1-2-3 Help screen.

FIGURE 1-19.
*The Help for Lotus
1-2-3 Users dialog box
gives you complete
instructions on how to
accomplish similar
tasks in Excel.*

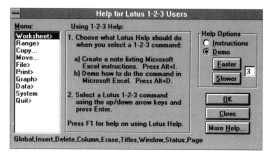

You can also use the Workspace command on the Options menu to change the way Excel responds to the slash (/) key. The slash key normally activates the menu bar, allowing you to choose Excel commands with the keyboard. The Workspace dialog box includes an Alternate Menu or Help Key option that allows you to reassign the slash key to the Help for Lotus 1-2-3 Users feature. Then you can enter Lotus 1-2-3 commands as you would normally, using the slash key. Excel either carries out the equivalent Lotus 1-2-3 command or presents a set of text instructions automatically, depending upon the option you set in the Help for Lotus 1-2-3 Users dialog box. If you find the slash key awkward, you can use the Workspace dialog box to specify a key other than the slash key for this command.

S E C T I O N   T W O

WORKSHEETS

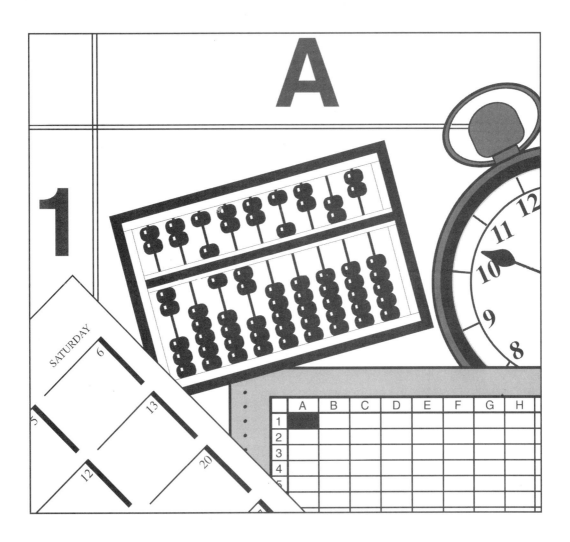

2

Worksheet Basics

*I*n this chapter, you'll learn how to select cells and move around in the worksheet, make cell entries, and perform some basic editing tasks. The chapter also discusses how Microsoft Excel makes calculations. If you're a new user, we suggest that you try the examples in this chapter, experimenting as you read. When you feel comfortable with the basic techniques described here, you'll be ready to move on to the more advanced worksheet topics in Chapters 3 through 11.

Cell selection and navigation

Before you can do anything with the cells in your worksheet, you must indicate the cell or range of cells with which you want to work. After you make your selection, you can enter data or formulas; copy, move, erase, and format entries; or otherwise manipulate the contents of your worksheet.

When you select a single cell, that cell becomes the worksheet's active cell. Only one cell can be active at a time. You can identify the active cell in two ways. First, the cell reference box at the left end of the formula bar always displays the reference of the active cell; second, a heavy border appears in the worksheet around the active cell.

Although only one cell can be active at a time, you can often speed up data entry, formatting, and editing by selecting groups of cells called *ranges*. When you select a range, you can move through the individual cells in that range (and not those outside the range) without changing your range selection. You can make entries in a range one cell at a time or all at once.

As you know, only a small portion of the worksheet is visible in the document window at any given time. To select and view different cells and ranges, you must move the document window. This process is called *navigation*. Often, the processes of selection and navigation overlap. For example, if A1 is the active cell and you want to make an entry in G100, you can bring G100 into view and select that cell. However, if you simply want to view another area of the worksheet, you can also use a technique called *scrolling* to change your view without changing your selection.

In this chapter, we include selection and navigation instructions for mouse users and for those who feel more at home at the keyboard. In subsequent chapters, we don't differentiate between the mouse and the keyboard when giving instructions; instead, we only tell you, for example, to select a cell or to click OK.

Using the mouse

To select a single cell with the mouse, point to the cell and click. When you do this, the active cell border appears around the cell and the cell's reference appears in the reference box on the left side of the formula bar.

To select a range of cells with the mouse, point to one corner of the range, press the mouse button, drag to the opposite corner of the range, and then release the mouse button. When you select a range, the first cell you select always becomes the active cell when you release the mouse button.

For example, to select the range from A1 through B6 of your worksheet, point to cell A1, press the mouse button, and drag to cell B6. As you drag the pointer down and to the right, Microsoft Excel highlights the cells in your selection. In the cell reference box on the left side of the formula bar, the size of the selected range appears as you drag; when cells A1:B6 are highlighted, you see the notation 6R x 2C (6 rows by 2 columns) in the cell reference box. When you release the mouse button, cells A1 through B6 are selected and A1 is the active cell, as shown in Figure 2-1.

FIGURE 2-1.
The selected cells are highlighted as you drag through a range.

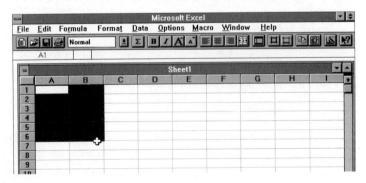

Excel always uses references to the cells at the upper left and lower right corners of a range to describe the range. For example, Excel identifies the range we just selected as A1:B6.

The active cell — the first cell you select — is the pivot point for your selection. That is, this cell always occupies one corner of the selected range. To test this for yourself, click on a cell near the center of your worksheet and, while holding the mouse button down, drag your mouse pointer in a circular pattern around the active cell. As you drag, notice that the active cell always anchors one corner of the highlighted range.

Extending a selection

Instead of dragging through all the cells you want to work with, you can indicate any two diagonal corners of the range. This technique is known as *extending a selection*. To begin, select a cell in any corner of the range you want to select. Now you can either hold down Shift or press F8 to enter Extend mode. (When you press F8, you see the EXT notation at the right side of the status bar.) Finally, click the cell at the opposite corner of the range.

For example, to select the range A1:C12, click C12, press and hold down Shift, and then click cell A1. Cell C12, which you clicked to begin defining the range, becomes the active cell in this range. Alternatively, you could select the range A1:C12 by clicking one corner of the range, pressing F8 to enter Extend mode, and then clicking the opposite corner. To leave Extend mode, press F8 again or make a cell entry.

It doesn't matter which diagonal corners of the range you use to make your selection. In the example above, you could just as easily have used cells A12 and C1 to define your range. However, Excel still identifies this selection by the upper left and lower right corners — A1 and C12 — even though you did not actually click those cells.

Selecting beyond the window borders

Often, when you need to select a large range of cells, some of those cells are hidden from view. When this occurs, you can drag the mouse pointer past the window border to bring additional cells into view as you highlight them. Alternatively, you can scroll the cells you need into view and then use the range extension technique already described to make your selection. (For more details, see "Scrolling the window," later in this chapter.)

If your selection is relatively small, you can move beyond the borders of the current window by dragging to the edge of the window. For example, suppose you want to select the range A14:A25. Click on cell A14, and then drag the pointer to the bottom of the screen. When the pointer reaches the horizontal scroll bar at the bottom of the window, the window begins scrolling down one row at a time. When cell A25 comes into view, highlight it and release the mouse button. Figure 2-2 shows the screen at this point.

Now suppose you want to select the range A3:A11, beginning from the screen shown in Figure 2-2. To do this, click cell A11 and then drag the pointer up to the title bar. This time, the window scrolls up one row at a time. When cell A3 comes into view, highlight it and release the mouse button. Excel selects cells A3:A11 and makes cell A11 the active cell.

You can also drag past the left and right borders of the screen to bring additional columns into view as you make your selection.

When you need to select large ranges, the dragging technique can be too time-consuming. For example, suppose you want to select the range A1:M38. Instead of dragging to highlight the cells, you can click cell A1 and then use the scroll bars to move the window until cell M38 is in view. (A1 will be out of sight.) Then hold down Shift or press F8, and click on cell M38. As soon as you click on M38, Excel highlights the range A1:M38; A1 is the active cell. Alternatively, you can select cell A1, press F5 (Goto), type M38, and then hold down the Shift key and click OK.

Selecting nonadjacent ranges

Excel lets you include several separate ranges in a single selection. Multiple-area ranges are also called *nonadjacent ranges,* because they are not extensions of a single rectangle. To select a nonadjacent range with the mouse, use Ctrl. For example, suppose you've selected the range A1:B6 and you want to add cells C7:E10 to this range without eliminating cells A1:B6 from the selection. Hold down Ctrl and drag through cells C7:E10. Excel adds a new area to your selection without deselecting

FIGURE 2-2.
You can drag past the window borders to bring additional cells into view as you make your selection.

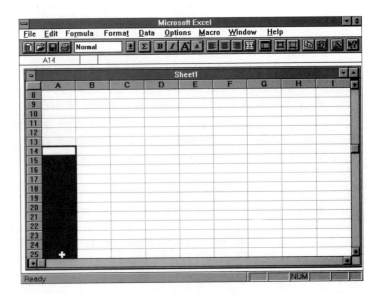

the original range. As you can see in Figure 2-3, when you hold down Ctrl and drag through a new area, the first cell you click in the new area becomes the active cell.

FIGURE 2-3.
Hold down Ctrl while
selecting nonadjacent
cell ranges with the
mouse.

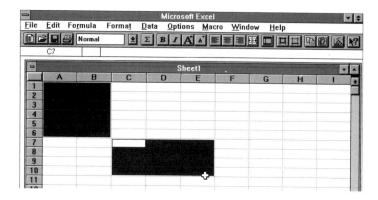

You can also select a nonadjacent range by using Add mode. For example, if cells A1:B6 are selected, you can add cells C7:E10 to your selection by first pressing Shift-F8 to enter Add mode. When you see the ADD notation at the right side of the status bar, drag through cells C7:E10 to add that range to your nonadjacent selection. Press Shift-F8 again to leave Add mode.

Selecting rows and columns

When you want to insert, delete, format, or move an entire row or column of data, select the entire row or column of cells by clicking the row or column header. When you click a row or column header, the first cell in that row or column that is visible in the window becomes the active cell. For example, if you click row header 6 when columns A through I are visible on the screen, Excel selects cells A6 through IV6 and cell A6 becomes the active cell.

Similarly, if you click on the header for column B, Excel selects cells B1 through B16384, and cell B1 becomes the active cell. If cell B1 is not in view when you select the header, Excel makes the first visible cell in the column the active cell.

You can select more than one adjacent row or column at a time by dragging through several row or column headers. Alternatively, you can click the row or column header that will form one edge of the range, press F8 or Shift, and then click the header for the opposite side of the range. For example, to select columns B, C, and D, begin by clicking the column B header. Then press F8 to enter Extend mode and click the column D header.

To select entire nonadjacent rows or columns, use Ctrl or Shift-F8 as already described.

You can even select entire rows *and* columns at the same time. For example, suppose you enter a series of identifying labels in column A and rows 1 through 3 of your worksheet and you want all these entries to appear in bold for emphasis. To select all these cells at once, click on row header 1 and drag down to row header 3; then press Ctrl and click column header A. As you can see in Figure 2-4, Excel highlights all of column A and all of rows 1, 2, and 3.

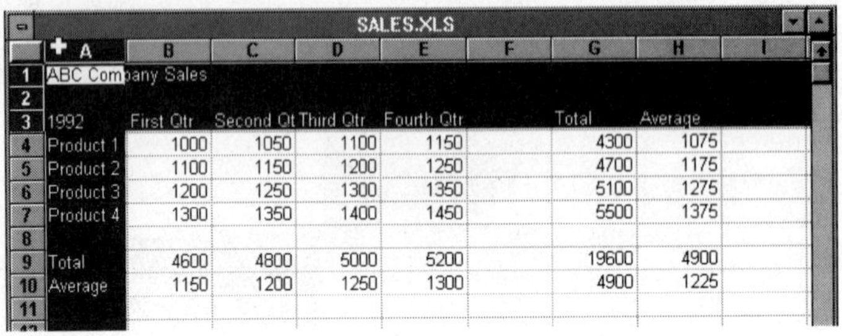

FIGURE 2-4.
You can select an entire row and an entire column at the same time.

You might want to select all the cells in the worksheet to change a default format or to copy the contents of one document to another. Fortunately, you can do this easily, without much clicking and scrolling. Simply click the box that appears near the upper left corner of your document window, where the row and column headers intersect.

Selecting and navigating regions

Excel 4 has a new feature that lets you directly manipulate cells in the worksheet. This feature makes working with large blocks of cells, called *regions,* much easier.

A region is a range of cell entries bounded by blank cells. For example, in the worksheet in Figure 2-5, the range A3:E7 is a region, as are the ranges G3:H7, A9:E10, and G9:H10.

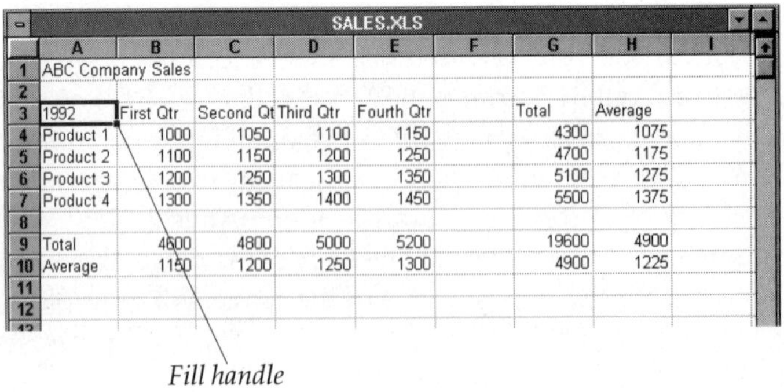

FIGURE 2-5.
The small square at the lower right of the cell-selection rectangle shows that direct cell manipulation is active.

Fill handle

To select or navigate regions, you must first activate the direct cell manipulation feature.

1. Choose the Workspace command from the Options menu.

2. Select the Cell Drag and Drop option. (An X appears in the check box.)

3. Click OK.

The Cell Drag and Drop option provides other capabilities that we explain in detail in Chapter 5. Notice in Figure 2-5 the small square at the lower right corner of the cell selection rectangle. This is called the *fill handle*. It became visible when you activated the Cell Drag and Drop option.

The dark border around the cell is the *cell selection rectangle*. When you move the mouse pointer over the edge of a cell selection rectangle, the normal Excel shaded-cross cursor changes to an arrow. With the arrow pointer visible, double-click the bottom border of the cell selection rectangle. The cell selection rectangle moves to the bottom edge of the current region or, if the cell selection rectangle is currently at the bottom edge of a region, to the top edge of the next region, as shown in Figure 2-6. Double-clicking on the borders of the cell selection rectangle moves you to the next edge of region in that direction. For example, double-clicking the right border of the selection rectangle in Figure 2-6 moves the selection to cell E7. Next, double-clicking the top border moves the selection to cell E3. Finally, double-clicking the left border moves the selection back to cell A3.

FIGURE 2-6.
Double-click the
bottom border of the
cell selection rectangle
to move to the top
edge of the next region.

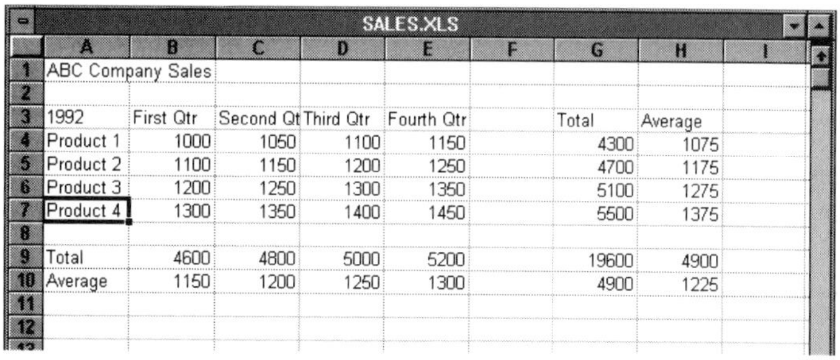

If you hold down Shift as you double-click the border of a selection rectangle, the selection moves to the cell at the next edge of a region and selects all the cells in between. For example, with cell A3 active, double-clicking the bottom border of the selection rectangle while holding down Shift results in the selection of the range

A3:A7, as shown in Figure 2-7. Then, if you double-click the right border of the selection rectangle while holding down Shift, the range A3:E7 is selected, as shown in Figure 2-8.

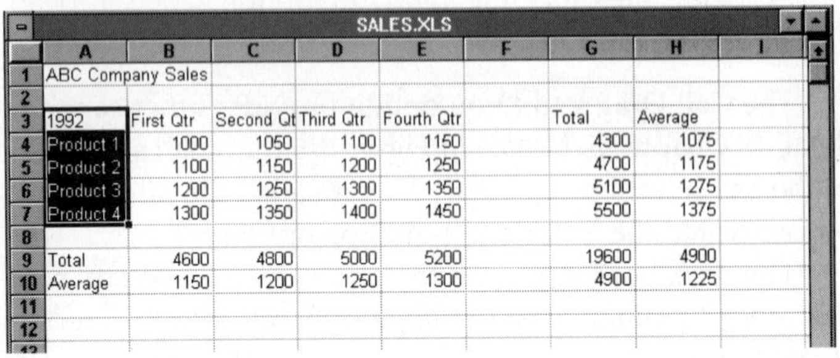

FIGURE 2-7.
Holding down Shift while double-clicking a cell selection rectangle border extends the selection in that direction to the region's edge.

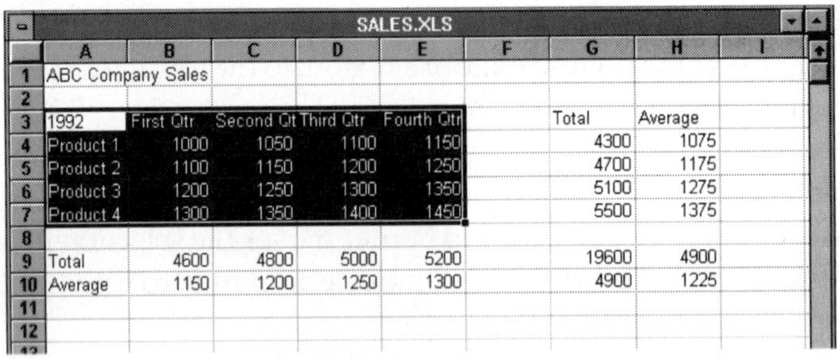

FIGURE 2-8.
You can select large blocks of cells with a few mouse clicks.

This technique comes in handy especially when you are working on large worksheets with many rows and columns of data. Simply selecting the top cell in a long column of numbers and double-clicking the bottom border selects the entire column, without your needing to scroll down the page.

Using the keyboard

You can also use the keyboard to navigate and make selections in your worksheet. The simplest way to select a single cell with the keyboard is to use the arrow keys to activate the desired cell. For example, if cell A1 is currently active, you can select cell A2 by pressing the Down arrow key once. When you do this, the active-cell border appears around cell A2 and the cell reference A2 appears in the cell reference box. Similarly, to move from cell A1 to cell C5, press the Right arrow key twice and the Down arrow key four times.

You can also use Tab and Shift-Tab to move the active cell. Tab activates the cell immediately to the right of the currently active cell. For example, if cell B2 is active, pressing Tab activates cell C2. Pressing Shift-Tab activates the cell immediately to the left of the currently active cell.

Of course, if you need to move through several rows or columns of a worksheet, these Tab and arrow key techniques could soon become tedious. Fortunately, you can use keyboard shortcuts to move around more rapidly in your worksheet. We'll discuss some of these shortcuts next.

Moving between cell regions

You can use Ctrl in conjunction with the arrow keys to move through cell regions in your worksheet.

Suppose cell A3 is the active cell in Figure 2-9. If you then press Ctrl and the Right arrow key, cell E3 becomes active. Press Ctrl-Right arrow while E3 is selected and cell G3 becomes active. Press Ctrl-Right arrow once more and H3 becomes active. Similarly, if you press Ctrl-Down arrow while cell A3 is selected, cell A7 becomes active.

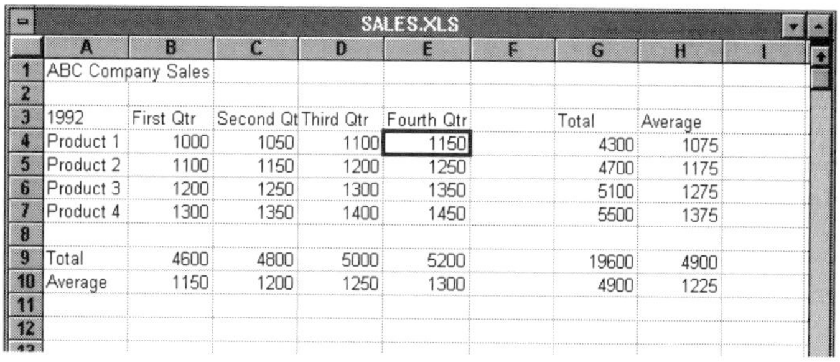

FIGURE 2-9.
You can use Ctrl and the arrow keys to move between cell regions.

	A	B	C	D	E	F	G	H	I
1	ABC Company Sales								
2									
3	1992	First Qtr	Second Qt	Third Qtr	Fourth Qtr		Total	Average	
4	Product 1	1000	1050	1100	1150		4300	1075	
5	Product 2	1100	1150	1200	1250		4700	1175	
6	Product 3	1200	1250	1300	1350		5100	1275	
7	Product 4	1300	1350	1400	1450		5500	1375	
8									
9	Total	4600	4800	5000	5200		19600	4900	
10	Average	1150	1200	1250	1300		4900	1225	
11									
12									

SALES.XLS

If a blank cell is active when you use a Ctrl-arrow key combination, Excel moves to the first cell in the direction of the arrow that contains a cell entry. For example, if cell D12 is active when you press Ctrl-Up arrow, cell D10 becomes active.

Using Home and End

Home and End are also valuable navigational and selection tools. Home lets you move to the first cell in the current row, and pressing Ctrl-Home lets you move to cell A1, the first cell in the worksheet. Pressing Ctrl-End moves the highlight to the last cell in the active area. The *active area* of the worksheet is defined as a rectangle that encompasses all the rows and columns in the document that contain entries. For example, in Figure 2-9, if you press Ctrl-End while any cell is active, Excel moves you to cell H10. Then, if you press Home, the active cell becomes A10, the first cell in the current row. (You can change these keys so that they operate similarly to the Lotus 1-2-3 navigation keys by changing the Alternate Navigation Keys option, which we explain in the next section.)

End, in combination with the arrow keys, lets you move between cell regions. Press End to activate End mode; press it again to deactivate End mode. When you activate End mode, END appears in the keyboard-indicators area of the status bar.

Pressing End followed by the Right arrow key moves the selection to the right, to the end of the current region (or the beginning of the next region). Pressing End followed by the Down arrow key takes you down to the end of the current region — and so on. For example, in Figure 2-9, if you press End and then the Right arrow key while cell A7 is active, Excel moves you to cell E7. Pressing the same key combination again moves you to cell G7. Pressing it again moves you to cell H7. And pressing it again moves you to cell IV7 (the last possible cell in row 7). Press Home to return to A7, the first cell in the row.

When you turn on Scroll Lock, navigation actions take place relative to the window rather than the active cell. When you press Scroll Lock, SCRL appears in the keyboard-indicators area of the status bar. To activate the first cell in the current window, press Scroll Lock, and then press Home. Similarly, to activate the last cell in the current window, press End with Scroll Lock activated. To deactivate Scroll Lock, press Scroll Lock again.

Alternate navigation keys

Excel also offers an alternative set of navigation keys, similar to those used by Lotus 1-2-3, Quattro Pro, and other spreadsheet programs. To use these keystrokes, you must first change a dialog box setting, as follows:

1. Choose the Workspace command from the Options menu.

2. Select the Alternate Navigation Keys option. (An X appears in the check box.)

3. Click OK.

The following table lists keystrokes, the action associated with each keystroke in Excel, and the action of the keystroke when the Alternate Navigation Keys option is selected:

Keystroke	Excel action	Alternate action
Ctrl-Left arrow	Moves to edge of region on the left	Moves left one screen
Ctrl-Right arrow	Moves to edge of region on the right	Moves right one screen
Home	Moves to first cell in current row	Moves to cell A1
Ctrl-Home	Moves to cell A1	Moves to first cell in current row
Ctrl-End	Moves to last cell of active area	Moves to last active cell in current row
F6	Moves to next pane	Moves to next window of active document
Ctrl-Pg Up	Moves left one screen	Moves to next worksheet in workbook

(Continued)

Keystroke	Excel action	Alternate action
Ctrl-Pg Down	Moves right one screen	Moves to previous worksheet in workbook
Tab	Moves right one cell	Moves right one screen
Shift-Tab	Moves left one cell	Moves left one screen

When Scroll Lock is activated, the keystrokes have the following effects:

Keystroke	Excel action	Alternate action
End	Moves to last visible cell	Activates End mode
Home	Moves to first visible cell	Moves to cell A1
Ctrl-End	Moves to last cell in active area	Moves to last visible cell
Ctrl-Home	Moves to cell A1	Moves to first visible cell

The Alternate Navigation Keys option also affects the way the Find command on the Data menu acts when a database table is active. For more information, see Chapter 17.

Navigating with the Goto command

Another invaluable way of moving from one part of a worksheet to another is the Formula Goto command. This command lets you select a cell anywhere on the worksheet in one jump. (See "The Goto command," in Chapter 3.)

Extending a selection

As with the mouse, you can extend a keyboard selection by using Shift or F8. To select a range with the keyboard, hold down Shift and use the arrow keys to draw the rectangular range. (You can't extend a selection with Tab.) To select the range of cells from A1 through B6 of your worksheet, begin by selecting cell A1; then, while holding down Shift, press the Right arrow key once and the Down arrow key five times. When you release Shift, your screen should look like Figure 2-1.

Or suppose you want to select the range A1:C12. To do this, select C12, hold down Shift, and press the Left arrow key twice and the Up arrow key 11 times. Cell C12, the first cell you selected to begin defining the range, is the active cell in this range.

You can also use F8 to extend a selection. To select the range A1:C12, first select cell A1. Next, press F8 to put Excel in Extend mode. (Watch for the EXT indicator in the status bar at the bottom of your screen.) Now press the Right arrow key twice and the Down arrow key 11 times to select cells A1:C12.

You can also use the keyboard to extend a selection beyond the window border. Suppose you want to select the range A1:C40. Select cell A1, hold down Shift, and then press the Right arrow key twice to select cells A1:C1. Then (assuming your worksheet window is sized to display 18 rows at a time), to extend the selection through row 40, continue to hold down Shift and press PgDn twice. Cells A1:C37 are now highlighted. Complete your selection by pressing the Down arrow key three times as you continue to hold down Shift. Excel selects the range A1:C40, with A1 as the active cell.

Selecting nonadjacent ranges

To select multiple, or nonadjacent, ranges with the keyboard, use Add mode. Suppose, for example, you selected the range A1:B6 and want to add cells C7:E10 to this range without eliminating cells A1:B6 from the selection. First, enter Add mode by pressing Shift-F8. (You'll see ADD in the status bar.) Then use the arrow keys to select cell C7. Now you can add this second group of cells by selecting the same way you selected the range A1:B6 — to extend the selection, hold down Shift and use the arrow keys, or press F8 and use the arrow keys.

Selecting rows and columns

You can select an entire row or column from the keyboard simply by selecting a cell in the desired row or column and then pressing Shift-Spacebar to select the row or Ctrl-Spacebar to select the column.

To select several entire adjacent rows or columns from the keyboard, first highlight a range that includes the rows or columns you want to work with and then use Ctrl-Spacebar or Shift-Spacebar. For example, to select columns B, C, and D, you can select any range that includes cells in these three columns, and then press Ctrl-Spacebar.

Finally, to select the entire worksheet from the keyboard, press Ctrl-Shift-Spacebar.

Scrolling the window

All the selection and navigation techniques we've described so far select cells and ranges. Often, however, you might want to view different areas of your worksheet without changing your selection. For example, you might want to compare the results of a formula you just entered with the results of a similar formula in a remote area of the worksheet. To change your view of the worksheet without changing your current selection, you must use a technique called *scrolling*. You can scroll through the worksheet with either the mouse or the keyboard.

To scroll through the worksheet with your mouse, use the scroll bars that appear on the right side and at the bottom of your document window. By clicking the scroll arrows that appear at either end of the scroll bars, you can move up, down, left, or right one row or column at a time. By clicking the shaded area of the scroll bar, you can move a new screenful of information into view.

The distance you cover when you click the shaded area of the scroll bar depends on the size of the document window. If you resized the document window so that only 5 rows are visible, clicking the gray area of the vertical scroll bar brings the next 5 rows into view; if 20 rows are visible, the next 20 rows scroll into view.

To move long distances in the worksheet rather than a line or a screenful at a time, you can drag the scroll boxes to the desired positions. The position of the scroll box in the scroll bar gives you an idea of your relative position in the active area of your worksheet. Thus, in a worksheet whose active area is only 30 rows deep, dragging the scroll box to the middle of the vertical scroll bar brings row 15 into view. If the active area is 200 rows deep, however, dragging the scroll box to the middle of the vertical scroll bar brings row 100 into view. As you drag the box in the vertical scroll bar, Excel displays the current row position in the upper left corner of the screen. Similarly, as you drag the horizontal scroll bar's box, Excel displays the current column position. In a large worksheet, dragging the scroll boxes to the bottom and right side of the scroll bars brings the end of the active rectangle into view at the upper left corner of the window.

To scroll the worksheet window with the keyboard, press Scroll Lock and then use the arrow keys, PgUp, or PgDn. The SCRL indicator appears in the status bar when Scroll Lock is in effect. As you might guess, the arrow keys let you scroll up, down, left, and right one row or column at a time; PgUp and PgDn let you move a new screenful of data into view. To scroll down through your worksheet a screen at a time without changing your selection, press Scroll Lock and then press PgDn. To scroll left and right a screen at a time, press Scroll Lock and then press Ctrl-PgDn to move right or Ctrl-PgUp to move left.

When you scroll through the worksheet, you can lose sight of the active cell. To quickly bring the active cell back into view, press Ctrl-Backspace, choose Show Active Cell from the Formula menu, or begin typing the cell entry.

Making cell entries

Microsoft Excel accepts two basic types of cell entries: *constants* and *formulas*. Constants fall into three main categories: text values, numeric values, and date and time values (which are represented as a special type of number). We look at text and numeric values in this section. We discuss techniques for building formulas in Chapter 3 and discuss date and time values in Chapter 9.

Excel also recognizes two special categories of constants: logical values and error values. We address error values in "Correcting errors in entries," later in this chapter and save logical values for the discussion of functions in Chapter 8.

Simple text and numeric values

In general, any entry that includes only the numerals 0 through 9 or one of a select group of special characters is a *numeric value*. For example, 123, 345678, 999999, and 1 are all numeric values. An entry that includes almost any other character — that is, any cell entry that can't be interpreted as a number — is treated as a *text value*. The entries *Sales, Hello, A Label*, and *123 Main Street* are all text values. (Text values are also referred to as *labels* or *strings*.)

The distinction between numbers and text is important. Although you can create formulas that link number cells to number cells and text cells to text cells, you can't create a formula that links a number cell directly to a text cell. Any formula that attempts to do this produces a #VALUE! error. However, the distinction between text and numeric values is less important in Excel than in some other spreadsheet programs because you can perform the same mathematical operations on numeric text entries that you can on numbers.

If you aren't sure whether Excel will treat a value as text or as a number, check the way the value appears in the cell after you press Enter. Unless you use a formatting command to change the cell display or have altered the Normal style, numbers are always aligned to the right side of the cell and text entries to the left side of the cell. (See Chapter 4.)

Making numeric entries

You can enter a number in your worksheet simply by selecting a cell and typing the number. For example, suppose you want to enter the number 100 in cell C5. First select cell C5 and then type *100*. As you type, the number 100 appears in the formula bar and also in cell C5.

Notice the flashing vertical bar that appears in the formula bar when you begin typing. This bar is called the *insertion point*. The insertion point moves in front of the characters as you type, to show your current position. Later in this chapter, you'll see how to move this insertion point to edit cell entries.

Locking in the entry

When you finish typing, you must "lock in" the entry to store it permanently in the selected cell.

You can lock in an entry in several ways. The simplest way is to press Enter. When you press Enter, the insertion point disappears from the formula bar, and

Excel stores the entry you typed in the active cell. When you select a single cell, pressing Enter does not deselect the cell.

If you press Tab, Shift-Tab, or one of the arrow keys after you finish typing the entry, Excel locks in the entry and simultaneously activates an adjacent cell. For example, pressing Tab to lock in the entry activates the cell immediately to the right of the cell into which the entry was made; pressing Shift-Tab locks in the entry and activates the cell to the left.

When you begin typing an entry, two new icons appear on the screen: the *Enter box* and the *Cancel box*. These icons are illustrated in Figure 2-10. The Enter box, which contains a check mark, is another way to lock in your entry when you finish typing. For example, to lock in the entry in cell A1 and keep cell A1 active, you could click the Enter box with the mouse instead of pressing Enter. Or, to cancel the entry, click the Cancel box, which contains an X.

FIGURE 2-10.
You can lock in an entry by clicking the Enter box or cancel an entry by clicking the Cancel box.

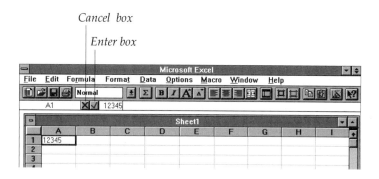

The Cancel box allows you to cancel an entry before you lock it in. If you make a mistake while typing in the formula bar, you can click on the Cancel box with the mouse to delete the information you typed. If the cell originally contained another entry, Excel restores that entry. To use the keyboard to cancel an entry, press Esc.

Other numeric characters

In addition to the numerals 0 through 9, numeric values can include the following characters:

$+ - E e \$, . \% ( ) /$

You can begin any numeric entry with a plus sign (+) or a minus sign (−). If you begin a numeric entry with a minus sign, Excel interprets that entry as a negative number and retains the minus sign. If you begin a numeric entry with a plus sign, Excel simply drops the plus sign.

The characters E and e can be used to enter a number in scientific notation. For example, if you select a cell and enter 1E6, Excel interprets that entry as the number 1,000,000 (1 times 10 to the sixth power).

Excel interprets numbers enclosed in left and right parentheses as negative numbers. This notation, common in accounting, is to ensure that negative cash amounts are not overlooked. For example, if you make the entry (100) in a cell, Excel interprets that entry as −100.

You can use the decimal point as you normally do. You can also use commas to separate the hundreds from the thousands, the thousands from the millions, and so on, as you normally would in numeric entries. When you do this, the number appears with commas in the cell. If you look in the formula bar, however, the number appears without commas. For example, if you enter 1,234,567.89, Excel interprets that entry as the number 1234567.89, and it is displayed as such in the formula bar. Meanwhile, the cell displays the number as if you had applied one of Excel's built-in number formats. (Formats and formatting commands are discussed in Chapter 4.)

If you begin a numeric entry with a dollar sign, Excel assigns one of its currency formats to the cell. For example, if you select a cell and enter the number $123456, Excel assigns a special dollar format to that cell and displays the number as $123,456. Note that in this case Excel also adds the comma.

Similarly, if you end a numeric entry with a percent sign (%), Excel interprets the entry as a percentage and assigns one of its percentage formats to the cell that contains the entry. For example, if you type 23%, Excel interprets and displays that number in the formula bar as 0.23 and assigns a percentage format to the cell.

Finally, if you enter a numeric entry with a slash (/) and that string cannot be interpreted as a date (such as 14/2), Excel interprets the number as a fraction. For example, if you enter 11 5/8, Excel interprets and displays that number in the formula bar as 11.625 and assigns a fraction format to the cell. The worksheet shows 11 5/8.

To enter a fraction that could be interpreted as a date (such as 1/2), you must either use a decimal fraction, such as 0.25 for 1/4, and apply a formatting command, or precede the fraction with a zero and a space (such as 0 1/2). (See Chapter 4.)

Displayed values vs. underlying values

A cell entry in Excel can include as many as 1024 characters. Because the standard column width in Excel is only 8.43 characters, the program clearly needs some rules for displaying long entries. If you enter a number that is too wide to appear in the cell, Excel converts the number into scientific notation to display it in a single cell. For example, if you select cell A1 and enter the numeric value 1234567890123, Excel displays this number as 1.23E+12, as Figure 2-11 shows, rather than letting the number overlap into the next cell. If you look at the formula bar, you see that Excel stores the number the way you entered it. Although Excel changes the appearance of the entry in cell A1, the actual contents of A1 stay the same.

FIGURE 2-11.
*The number
1234567890123 is too
long to fit in cell A1,
so Excel displays it in
scientific notation.*

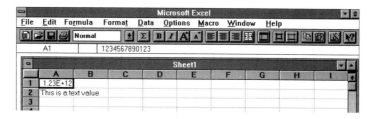

Like the previous example of using commas in numeric entries, this comparison of displayed and input values illustrates an important Excel concept: What you see in a cell and what is actually in the cell can be entirely different things. The values that you see when you look at the worksheet are called *displayed values*; the values that appear in the formula bar are called *underlying values*. Keep in mind that, unless you tell it otherwise, Excel always remembers the underlying values in your cells, no matter how it displays those values. When you build formulas, Excel uses the underlying values rather than the displayed values so that your calculations are always correct.

The number of digits that appear in a cell depends on the width of the column. If you change the width of a column that contains a long entry, Excel changes the displayed value according to the width of the cell. Remember, however, that the column width affects only the displayed values of numbers on your worksheet; it has no effect on the actual numbers stored in the cells.

We'll come back to this concept again in Chapters 4 and 5, where you'll learn to control the way cell entries are displayed by changing the formats and column widths assigned to cells.

Making text entries

The process of making a text entry is nearly identical to that of making a numeric entry: All you need to do to enter a text value into a cell is select that cell and type. When you finish typing, lock in the entry by using any of the techniques discussed in "Locking in the entry," earlier in this chapter. If you make an error, you can cancel the entry by clicking the Cancel box with the mouse or by pressing Esc.

Long text entries

We've seen that Excel converts long numbers into scientific notation for display purposes. Excel treats long text values somewhat differently. If you create a label that is too long to be displayed in a single cell, Excel lets that label overlap into adjacent cells. For example, we entered the label *This is a text value* in cell A2 of the worksheet in Figure 2-11. Notice that this text entry spills into cell B2.

Don't let this ability to overlap mislead you, however. The entire label is stored in cell A2. If you select cell B2 and look at the formula bar, you can see that it is still empty. The characters that seem to be contained in cell B2 are really in cell A2 and overlap B2 only for display purposes.

Now, select cell B2 and type *This is another text value*. As you can see in Figure 2-12, this new entry makes it impossible for Excel to display all of the long text value in cell A2. Again, this change affects only the way the label is displayed and has no effect on the contents of either cell. If you move back to cell A2 and look at the formula bar, you'll see that Excel stored the entire label.

FIGURE 2-12.
When the cell to the right contains an entry, a long text value cannot spill over and appears truncated.

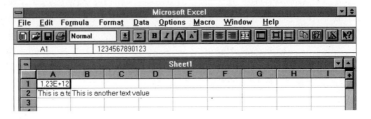

Using word wrap for long text entries

By applying a formatting command to a cell, you can create long text entries that wrap onto two or more lines within the same cell, rather than being truncated or spilling over onto adjacent cells. To accommodate the extra lines, Excel simply increases the height of the row that contains the affected cell. This formatting feature is described further in Chapter 4.

Annotating worksheets with text boxes

If you use a mouse, you can use the Text Box tool on the Utility toolbar to create text boxes on your worksheet. You can size and move a text box independently of the underlying worksheet cells. A text box can hold up to 64,000 characters. Text boxes are discussed further in Chapter 7.

Numeric text entries

At times, you might want to create text entries that are made up partly or entirely of numbers. If you want to enter a text value like *1234 Main Street*, you need only select a cell, type the entry, and press Enter. Because this entry includes non-numeric characters, Excel assumes it is a text value.

Sometimes you can create text entries made up entirely of numbers, however. For example, suppose you're developing a price list like the one shown in Figure 2-13. Column A contains a series of part numbers. If you want Excel to treat these part numbers as text rather than as numbers, you must either enter them into the worksheet as *literal strings* or use *text prefix characters* to simultaneously format the entry as text and align the entry in the cell. To activate the text prefix characters feature, choose the Workspace command from the Options menu and select the Alternate Navigation Keys option. For example, you can enter part number 1234 in cell A4 in two ways. First, as a literal string:

    ="1234"

or using the left text-alignment prefix character:

    '1234

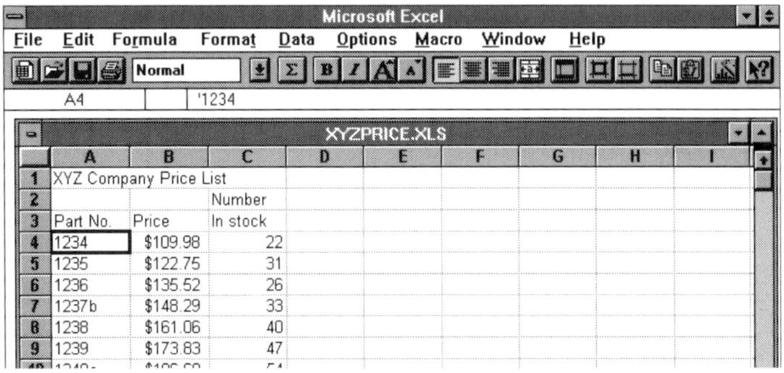

FIGURE 2-13.
The part numbers in column A were entered with left text-alignment prefix characters rather than as numeric values.

In most cases, using a text prefix character for data entry is quicker and more convenient. (You cannot use text prefix characters in formulas, however, because they convert the contents of the cell to text.) Unless you enter all the part numbers using one of these methods, Excel left-aligns those that include text (1237b, for example) and right-aligns those that are purely numbers.

The following table lists text-alignment prefix characters and their effect:

Character	Effect
'	Left-aligns characters
"	Right-aligns characters
^	Centers characters
\	Repeats characters to fill cell

NOTE: *If you use the backslash (\) prefix, any characters you type in the cell will be repeated as necessary to fill the cell but will not overlap into the next cell, even if the next cell is empty. If you change the width of the cell that contains the repeated characters, the number of characters will also change so that the cell is always filled.*

Making entries in ranges

If you want to make a number of entries in a range of cells, select those cells before you begin making entries. Then you can use Enter, Tab, Shift-Enter, and Shift-Tab to move the active cell within the range. When you're working in a selected range, Excel restricts movement to that range. When you reach the end of a column or row, you automatically move to the next column or row in the range. Because Excel does not allow the active cell to move out of the range of selected cells, you can devote your attention to making entries, without worrying about the location of the active cell.

For example, suppose you want to make some entries in the range B2:D4. To begin, select the range. (Select from B2 to D4, so that cell B2 is the active cell.) Then type *100* in cell B2 and press Enter. When you press Enter, cell B3 becomes the active cell. If you type *200* and press Enter again, cell B4 becomes the active cell. If you now type *300* and press Enter yet again, cell C2, the first cell in the next column of the range, becomes the active cell, as shown in Figure 2-14. You can continue this way until you fill the entire range.

FIGURE 2-14.
You can lock in your entry and move to the next cell in a range automatically.

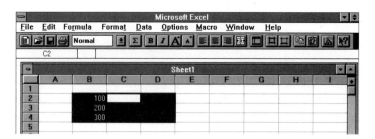

Pressing Enter activates the cell below the currently active cell. As you might expect, pressing Shift-Enter activates the cell above the currently active cell. For example, if cell B3 is active and you press Shift-Enter, B2 becomes the active cell.

Pressing Tab activates the cell one column to the right of the current active cell. If cell C2 is the active cell and you press Tab, cell D2 becomes active. If you press Tab again, however, the active-cell border moves to cell B3, because Excel restricts the movement of the active cell to the range of selected cells. If you press Shift-Tab, the cell one column to the left becomes the active cell.

When you work with a discontinuous range, you can move between selected areas in two ways: You can use Tab, Shift-Tab, Enter, and Shift-Enter to move from the last cell in one area to the first cell in the next, or you can press Ctrl-Tab or Ctrl-Shift-Tab to jump directly to the first cell in another area.

NOTE: *Don't use the arrow keys when you're making entries in a range. If you do, Excel deselects the current range and activates the cell in the direction you specify.*

Making an entry in all selected cells at once

A simple procedure allows you to enter the same value into many cells at once. First select the cells. Then type your entry and hold down Ctrl while you press Enter or click the Enter box.

Correcting errors in entries

No matter how good a typist you are, you'll sometimes make errors in cell entries. Fortunately, Excel makes it easy to fix mistakes.

Correcting errors before you lock in the entry

If you make simple errors as you type an entry, you can correct them by pressing Backspace. For example, suppose you selected cell A1 and are entering the text *This is a label*. As you make the entry, however, you type *This is ala*. To correct this error, press Backspace twice to erase the *a* and the *l* and then type the space you forgot the first time and complete the entry. Each time you press Backspace, Excel erases the character to the left of the insertion point. When you finish making the entry, press Enter to lock it in.

Using Backspace is a good way to correct errors if you catch them quickly. If you discover an error before you lock in an entry but have typed too much text to use Backspace, you can simply reposition the insertion point in the entry and erase, insert, or replace characters.

For example, suppose you enter the text *This is a label* in cell A1 of your worksheet. Before you lock in the entry, you realize you want to add the words *rather long* before the word *label*. To add characters to an entry, use the mouse to point to the position in the formula bar where you want the characters to appear and click. (The pointer becomes an I-beam when positioned over the formula bar.) Then simply begin typing. Excel pushes the insertion point — and any characters after it — to the right as you type. To add the words *rather long* to the entry in cell A1, point in front of the first letter *l* in the word *label* in the formula bar. When you click the mouse button, the insertion point moves to the indicated spot in the entry — in this case, in front of the letter *l*. Now type *rather long*, followed by a space. If the entry is now correct, press Enter to lock it in.

You can also delete characters to the right of the insertion point by pressing Del. (Backspace erases one letter to the left; Del erases one letter to the right.) If you want to delete several adjacent characters, you can drag across all the characters you want to delete and press Del or Backspace. For instance, to erase the word *rather*, position the pointer before the first *r* in *rather*, press the mouse button, drag to the right until the entire word plus one space is highlighted, and press Del once.

If you prefer to use the keyboard, you can activate the formula bar by pressing F2. When you press F2, two things happen: The status bar at the lower left corner of the screen changes from Enter to Edit, telling you that Excel is ready for editing, and the insertion point appears at the end of the cell entry. Use the arrow keys to position the insertion point to the right of the letter or letters you want to remove, use Backspace to erase the letters, and then type the correction. To move quickly from one end of the formula bar to the other, press Home or End. You also can hold down Ctrl and press the Left or Right arrow key to move through an entry one word at a time. When you finish, lock in your changes by pressing Enter or selecting another cell with Tab or Shift-Tab.

To use the keyboard to replace several characters, position the insertion point in front of or behind the block of characters you want to work with and use Shift in conjunction with the Left and Right arrow keys to extend your selection in the formula bar. Then erase the characters by pressing Del or Backspace or overwrite them by typing the new characters. Excel deletes the selected characters as you type the replacement characters. When you finish making the change, press Enter.

You can also replace characters in the formula bar by entering Overwrite mode. Generally, when you activate the formula bar and type new characters, they appear to the left of the insertion point marker. If you want to replace the characters to the right of the insertion point, press Ins before you begin typing. The OVR indicator appears in the status bar at the bottom of the screen indicating that you are in Overwrite mode. To cancel Overwrite mode and go back to Insert mode, simply press Ins again or deactivate the formula bar by pressing Enter or selecting another cell.

Correcting errors after you lock in the entry

If you've locked in an entry but haven't left the cell, you can erase the entire contents of the cell by pressing Backspace once. You don't have to create an insertion point to do this. If you press Backspace accidentally, click the Cancel box with the mouse or press Esc to restore the contents of the cell.

If you've already locked in the entry and left the cell, you must select the cell again before you can correct an error. When you select a cell that already contains a value or formula, the formula bar is not active; that is, no blinking insertion point appears in the bar. To activate the formula bar, click it or press F2.

If you want to replace the entire contents of a cell with another entry, select the cell and type. Excel erases the previous entry as soon as you begin typing. For example, suppose you want to enter the word *Sales* in cell A1, which currently contains the word *Purchases*. To make this change, simply select cell A1, type *Sales*, and press Enter. If you decide you want to retain the original contents of the cell, click the Cancel box with the mouse or press Esc to revert to the original entry.

Document security

Two basic sets of features allow you to secure your documents against unwanted inspection, alteration, or deletion. You can assign a password to any file so that users without the password cannot access the file. Or you can protect individual elements within the file — particular cells, particular graphic objects, or the size and position of windows.

Protecting files as a whole

To restrict access to a worksheet or any other type of document, you can use the Save As command and click the Options button. Figure 2-15 shows the dialog box that you see.

FIGURE 2-15.
*Excel lets you assign
two passwords to a file.*

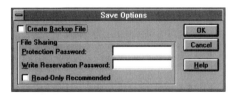

As the figure shows, Microsoft Excel lets you assign two kinds of passwords to a file. A *protection password* prevents anyone without the password from opening the file or accessing it via file-linking formulas. Files protected this way are also encrypted, making them difficult to read with utility programs such as Lotus Magellan and the Norton Desktop for Windows. You'll want to assign a protection password to particularly sensitive documents — for example, worksheets that contain information unauthorized persons must not see.

A *write reservation password* doesn't restrict access to the file but prevents users without the password from deleting the file or saving it under its current name. A write reservation password is useful for protecting documents that must remain unchanged but that are not necessarily for authorized eyes only.

You can use these two kinds of passwords separately or together. Note that a protection password does not prevent a file from being deleted from disk!

Entering and removing passwords

To assign either kind of password, select the appropriate text box in the dialog box shown in Figure 2-15, and then type your password. Excel displays asterisks in the text box while you type. After you press Enter, Excel asks you to repeat the password — to confirm that you typed it correctly.

Be sure to type your password *exactly* as you mean to type it. Excel distinguishes capital letters from lowercase letters in passwords. And be sure to remember the exact form of your password. (You might want to write it down in a safe place away from your computer.) If you forget or lose your password, you'll be out of luck.

To remove a password from a document, open that document and choose the File Save As command. Click the Options button, select the entire password you want to remove, press Del, and then click OK.

The Read-Only Recommended option

As Figure 2-15 shows, you can also assign "Read-Only Recommended" status to a file. You might find this option useful if you work with Excel on a network. When two or more users on a network open the same file, the network software assigns "read and write" privileges only to the user who opens the file first. All subsequent users have read privileges only; that is, they can work with the file but cannot save any changes to it.

Any user can choose to open a file in Read-Only mode, however, by selecting the Read-Only check box in the File Open dialog box. If the first user on the network to open a particular file opens it in Read-Only mode, then the next user is granted read and write privileges.

If you know that several users need a file but you want to discourage most users from changing the file, you can save the file with the Read-Only Recommended check box selected. Then, whenever someone opens the file, the dialog box in Figure 2-16 appears.

FIGURE 2-16.
*This dialog box
appears when you
open a file saved with
the Read-Only
Recommended option.*

This dialog box provides no formal protection against unwanted changes to the document. But it encourages users to voluntarily open the file in Read-Only mode.

Protecting cells, graphic objects, and windows

In addition to offering password protection for whole files, Excel lets you protect individual cells, graphic objects, or windows from alteration. By default, Excel "locks" (protects) all worksheet and macro sheet cells and any graphic objects you create. But the protection does not take effect until you use the Option menu's Protect Document command. When you choose that command, Excel presents the dialog box shown in Figure 2-17. As the figure shows, you can enable protection separately for cells, objects, or windows; or you can turn it on for any combination of the three elements. Note that the protection status you set applies to the current document only.

FIGURE 2-17.
The Options Protect
Document command
lets you enable or
disable protection.

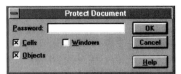

When a cell is locked and you've used the Protect Document command to turn cell protection on, you won't be able to edit the contents of the cell or replace them with a different entry. If the locked cell is blank, you won't be able to make an entry in the cell. If you try to edit or make any other change to a locked cell, Excel will return the error message *Locked cells cannot be changed.* Similarly, when a graphic object — such as a chart drawn on the worksheet or a text box — is locked and protection for objects is enabled, you won't be able to move, size, format, or even select that object. (You can move or size an object if you formatted it to move and size with underlying cells. See Chapter 7 for more details.)

When protection for windows is enabled, you cannot move, size, open, or close individual windows into a document. You can still open or close the document itself, however.

Most of the time, you won't want every cell in a worksheet to be locked. Although you might want to protect every cell that contains an important formula, you'll probably want to leave a few cells unlocked so that you can change variables or enter new information. For this reason, you'll usually use the Format Cell Protection command to unlock a few cells before you use the Protect Document command. When you choose the Cell Protection command, you'll see a dialog box like the one in Figure 2-18.

FIGURE 2-18.
The Cell Protection
command lets you set
the status for
individual cells.

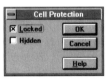

Unless you use the Info window (discussed in Chapter 5) to monitor the status of the cells in your worksheet, Excel has no constant on-screen indication of the protection status of a cell. However, if you use the Display command from the Options menu to deactivate gridlines in the worksheet, Excel continues to display a horizontal gridline below every unlocked cell in the worksheet.

Hiding cells

As mentioned, all cells are locked by default. Excel lets you apply a second kind of attribute, called *Hidden*, to individual cells. When you assign the Hidden attribute to a cell that contains a formula, the formula won't appear in the formula bar when you select that cell. However, unless you've also used the ;;; format described in Chapter 3 to hide the formula display, the result of the formula will be displayed in the spreadsheet.

To apply the Hidden attribute, select the cells you want to hide. Then choose the Format Cell Protection command and select the Hidden check box.

Using a password to protect cells, objects, and windows

As Figure 2-17 shows, the Protect Document command gives you the option of assigning a password. If you choose to do this, follow the same steps as you would to assign a password to the file as a whole. (See the section "Entering and removing passwords," earlier in this chapter.)

Removing protection from cells, objects, and windows

If you pull down the Options menu when a worksheet is protected, you'll see that the Protect Document command has changed to Unprotect Document. When you choose this command, Excel removes protection from all of your document's cells, objects, and windows.

If you supplied a password when you protected the worksheet, Excel will not unprotect the worksheet until you type the password. If you type the wrong password, you'll see the message *Incorrect password*. The password you type must match the worksheet's protection password in every detail, including case.

3

Building Formulas

Microsoft Excel offers you a rich environment in which to build complex formulas. Excel provides you with a number of features that will help you get to the bottom line quickly and easily. Armed with a few mathematical operators and rules for cell entry, you can turn your worksheet into a powerful calculator.

Creating formulas

Let's walk through a series of rudimentary formulas to see how they work. Begin by selecting a blank cell, A20, and typing the simple formula

=10+5

Notice that the formula begins with an equal sign (=). The equal sign tells Microsoft Excel that a formula follows. If you forget to begin the formula with an equal sign, Excel interprets the entry as text unless it's a simple numeric value.

As soon as you press Enter, the value 15 appears in the active cell. If you look at the formula bar, however, you'll notice it displays the formula that you typed. What appears in the cell is the displayed value; what appears in the formula bar is the underlying value. Similarly, if you type

=10−5

you see the displayed value 5 in the active cell. Now enter the formulas

=10*5

and then

=10/5

Excel displays the values 50 and then 2.

Each of the preceding formulas uses one of Excel's mathematical operators: the plus sign (+), the minus sign (–), the asterisk (*) for multiplication, and the slash (/) for division.

Precedence of operators

As you begin to use complex formulas that contain more than one operator, you'll need to consider the precedence that Excel assigns to each operator. The term *precedence* refers to the order in which Excel performs calculations in a formula.

Excel multiplies and divides before it adds and subtracts. For example, the formula

=4+12/6

returns the value 6. When Excel evaluates this formula, it calculates the value 12/6 first and then adds 4.

If two consecutive operators have the same level of precedence, the order in which they're calculated is insignificant. For example, the formula

=4*12/6

returns 8 regardless of whether Excel multiplies 4 by 12 and then divides by 6 or divides 12 by 6 and then multiplies by 4.

You can change the order in which Excel calculates operations by using parentheses. Excel processes expressions within parentheses first. For example, each of the following formulas uses the same values and operators, but the placement of the parentheses differs:

Formula	Result
3*6+12/4–2	19
(3*6)+12/(4–2)	24
3*(6+12)/4–2	11.5
(3*6+12)/(4–2)	15

If you're not certain of the order in which Excel will process a sequence of operators, you can use parentheses to ensure that Excel follows the order you want, even if the parentheses aren't actually necessary.

Using cell references in formulas

Although simple formulas like the ones you've built so far are convenient for quickly calculating values, Excel's real magic lies in its ability to use cell references in formulas. When you create a formula that contains cell references, you link the formula to other cells in your worksheet. The cell that is pointed to by the cell reference is the *source cell.* As a result, the value of the formula always reflects the values in the source cells. You'll find this capability enormously valuable when you begin using your worksheet for financial planning or other extensive calculations.

For example, suppose you've entered the formula

=10*2

in cell A1. If later you select cell A2 and type the formula

=A1

cell A2 also displays the value 20. So why not simply type the value 20 in A2? To see why, select A1 and change the entry to 100. Now look at the displayed value in A2. When you change the value in A1, Excel updates A2 as well. The formula in A2 links A2 to A1 so that the value in A2 always equals the value in A1.

Now select cell A3 and type the formula

=A1+A2

Excel returns the value 200. Of course, you can create much more complex formulas in Excel using references to cells or ranges. In Chapter 6, we discuss a number of applications for cell references.

Pasting cell references

You can save time and avoid typographical errors by clicking the cells you want Excel to include in your formulas rather than typing their references. This technique is called *pasting a cell reference* into a formula.

Suppose you want to create a formula in cell A26 that totals the values you entered in cells A20:A24. To do this, select cell A26, and then type an equal sign (=). Next click cell A20, and then type a plus sign; next click cell A21, and then type another plus sign. Then click cell A22, and so on. (Notice that Excel surrounds each cell with a flashing border as you select it. This border is called a *marquee.*) Your finished formula is

=A20+A21+A22+A23+A24

Of course, you can use operators other than the plus sign.

When you finish entering a formula, be sure to lock in your entry by clicking the Enter box or by pressing Enter or Tab before you select another cell. Whenever you click a cell while the formula bar is active, Excel assumes you want to paste the cell reference.

A cell does not have to be visible in the current window for you to make an entry in that cell. You can scroll through the worksheet without changing the currently selected cell and point to cells in remote areas of your worksheet as you build formulas. Suppose you want to enter a formula in cell M50 that calculates the sum of your first-quarter and second-quarter sales. You know that the totals for first-quarter sales are located somewhere in column G of your worksheet, but you don't remember the exact cell reference. After you select cell M50 and enter an equal sign, you can scroll through your worksheet, find the correct cell, and click it. Excel adds the reference to the formula in cell M50.

Relative and absolute references

The cell references we've used in the sample formulas so far are called *relative references*. Relative references refer to cells by their position in relation to the cell that contains the formula.

Excel also lets you create *absolute references* to other cells in your worksheet. Absolute references refer to cells by their absolute, or fixed, position in the worksheet. You specify absolute references in your formulas by typing a dollar sign ($) before the column and row coordinates. For example, to enter an absolute reference to cell A1, type

    =$A$1

You can also use the Reference command on the Formula menu or press F4 to define absolute and relative references quickly. To enter an absolute reference to cell A1, type

    =A1

and then press F4 before you press Enter. Excel changes the reference nearest the insertion point to an absolute reference, and the formula appears as

    =$A$1

If you press F4 again, Excel changes your entry to a mixed reference, with a relative column coordinate and an absolute row coordinate:

    =A$1

If you press F4 a third time, the reference changes to

    =$A1

Here, the column coordinate is absolute and the row coordinate is relative. Press F4 one last time to return to the original relative reference to cell A1.

Absolute and mixed references are important when you copy formulas from one location to another in your worksheet. We'll return to this concept in Chapter 5.

Editing formulas

You can edit formulas the same way you edit text entries, using either the mouse or the keyboard.

To delete a cell reference or other character from a formula using the mouse, drag through the reference in the formula bar and then press Del. Alternatively, you can click the portion of the entry you want to replace, point to the replacement cell, and click. As soon as you click the new cell, Excel replaces the old reference with the new one.

If you want to undo your changes and you haven't locked in the new formula, click the Cancel box or press Esc. If you locked in the entry but haven't issued another command or typed in another cell, you can use the Undo command on the Edit menu.

You can also insert additional cell references in a formula. Simply click the desired insertion point and then select the cell you want to add to the formula. (Of course, you can also type the cell reference.) For example, suppose you want to change the formula

    =A1+A3

to

    =A1+B1+A3

To do this, place the insertion point after the reference A1, type +, and then either type *B1* or click cell B1.

To delete a cell reference or other character from a formula with the keyboard, press F2 to enter Edit mode. The insertion point appears at the end of the formula. Use the arrow keys to position the insertion point, press Backspace to erase the incorrect reference, and then type the correction. If you locked in the entry but haven't issued another command or typed in another cell, you can undo your changes with the Undo command on the Edit menu.

To insert additional cell references with the keyboard, select the cell that contains the formula and press F2 to enter Edit mode, use the arrow keys to position the insertion point, and then type the cell reference.

Using numeric text in formulas

Unlike most other spreadsheet programs, Excel allows you to perform any mathematical operation on numeric text values, as long as the numeric string contains only the characters

    0 1 2 3 4 5 6 7 8 9 . + − E e

In addition, you can use the / character in fractions. You can also use the five number-formatting characters

    $, % ( )

with numeric text, but if you do, you must enclose the numeric string in double quotation marks. For example, if you enter the formula

    =$1234+$123

Excel displays an alert box that states *Error in formula*. However, the formula

    ="$1234"+"$123"

produces the result 1357. In effect, Excel translates the numeric text entry into a numeric value when it performs the addition.

Text values

Throughout this section, we've referred to text entries as text "values." The concept of using alphabetic characters as values may seem a bit confusing until you begin using formulas to manipulate text entries.

Excel lets you perform many of the same manipulations on text values that you perform on numeric values. For example, suppose cell A1 contains the text *abcde*. If you enter the formula

    =A1

in cell A10, that cell also displays *abcde*. Because this type of formula treats a string of text as a value, it is often called a *string* value.

You can use a special operator, &, to *concatenate*, or join, several text values. For example, suppose cell A2 in the same worksheet contains the text *fghij*. You can use the formula

    =A1&A2

to produce the text *abcdefghij*. You can also include a space between the two strings by changing the formula to

    =A1&" "&A2

to create the string *abcde fghij*. Notice that this last formula uses two concatenation operators. The formula also includes a literal string, or *string constant* — a space enclosed in double quotation marks — to separate the two halves of the string value. To use a literal string in a worksheet formula, you must place double quotation marks before and after the string.

You can also use the & operator to concatenate a string of numeric values. For example, suppose cell A3 contains the numeric value 123 and cell A4 contains the numeric value 456. The formula

    =A3&A4

produces the string *123456*. This string appears left-aligned in the cell, indicating that Excel considers it a text value. (Keep in mind that you can use numeric text values to perform any mathematical operation, as long as the numeric string contains only the numeric characters listed in the preceding section, "Using numeric text in formulas.")

You can also use the & operator to concatenate a combination of numeric and text values. For example, if cell A1 contains the text *abcde* and cell A3 contains the numeric value 123, the formula

    =A1&A3

produces the string *abcde123*.

The string values we've created so far are meaningless, but the concatenation operator has many practical applications. For example, suppose cell A1 contains the first name of a client, Gena, and cell B1 contains her last name, Woods. You can use the formula

    =A1&" "&B1

to produce the string *Gena Woods*. Alternatively, you can use a formula like

    =B1&", "&A1

to produce the string *Woods, Gena*.

Using functions: a preview

The formulas we've built so far perform relatively simple mathematical calculations. Chapter 8 describes in detail a special set of operators, called functions, that can help you build more sophisticated formulas.

Many of Excel's functions are shorthand versions of frequently used formulas that would take you a long time to type into the worksheet if you had to construct them yourself. For example, earlier in this chapter you learned how to calculate the

Making Excel behave more like Lotus 1-2-3

If you're moving to Excel from Lotus 1-2-3, you don't have to change your keystroke habits to enter formulas in Excel. For example, you can begin an Excel function with an @ sign, use the 1-2-3 range operator (..) in place of the Excel range operator (:), and use a + sign to begin a formula that references another cell. Excel always translates these Lotus 1-2-3 characters into the equivalent Excel characters.

Excel also has two options — Alternate Formula Entry and Alternate Navigation Keys — that let you choose to make Excel behave like Lotus 1-2-3 in other ways.

The Alternate Formula Entry option causes Excel to handle range names the way Lotus 1-2-3 Release 2.3 (but not Release 3.1 or 1-2-3 for Windows) does. When you open a Lotus 1-2-3 worksheet (with the extension WK1 or WK3) in Excel, this option is turned on automatically. You can turn it on manually by choosing the Calculation command from the Options menu and selecting Alternate Formula Entry in the dialog box. (The Calculation command is examined in "Calculating the worksheet," later in this chapter.)

If Alternate Formula Entry is on and if you enter a formula that references a named cell or range, Excel immediately substitutes the name of the cell or range for its row and column coordinates. (For more information about name definitions, see "Naming cells and ranges," later in this chapter.) If you subsequently press F2 to edit the formula, the name changes back to the cell reference. If you delete a range name, any references to that name revert to references to cells by their row and column coordinates. When you turn on Alternate Formula Entry, Excel also applies any defined cell or range names to the formulas you've already created.

With Alternate Formula Entry on, you can spell the average function AVG (as Lotus 1-2-3 does) instead of AVERAGE (as Excel would otherwise require). And you may omit the empty parentheses after functions that require no arguments. For example, typing @RAND in Lotus 1-2-3 produces a random number. The equivalent Excel formula is =RAND(). With Excel's Alternate Formula Entry option turned on, you may enter a random-number function without typing the empty parentheses.

Excel normally ignores the Lotus label-prefix characters — the apostrophe, the caret, the double-quotation mark, and the backslash — even if you turn Alternate Formula Entry on. If you want Excel to recognize these label-prefix characters, you must pull down the Options menu, choose Workspace, and then select Alternate Navigation Keys.

sum of a range of cells by pasting each cell reference individually into a formula. This is fine when you're adding the values in only 2 or 3 cells, but imagine pasting 20 or 30 cells into a formula! Excel's SUM function lets you add a series of cell values by simply selecting a range. For example, compare the formula

=A1+A2+A3+A4+A5+A6+A7+A8+A9+A10

with the formula

=SUM(A1:A10)

Obviously, the SUM function makes the formula a lot shorter and easier to create. (Excel's standard toolbar includes the AutoSum tool, which simplifies entry of the SUM function. This tool is described in Chapter 8.)

Other Excel functions perform extremely complex calculations that would be difficult, if not impossible, to perform with standard mathematical operators. For example, Excel's NPV function calculates the net present value of investments.

Using functions and references to cell ranges rather than building formulas with references to individual cells offers other advantages, too, as you'll see in Chapter 8.

Parentheses matching

When you use parentheses in your formulas, be sure you include a close parenthesis for each open parenthesis. If you do not, Excel displays the message *Parentheses do not match* in an alert box. To help you match open and close parentheses, Excel highlights the matching open parenthesis whenever you enter a close parenthesis. This is of particular value when you are entering long formulas that contain several sets of parentheses.

In addition, Microsoft Excel 4 includes an enhanced parentheses-matching feature that will automatically add the close parenthesis if you forget to type it in, as long as it is obvious to Excel where the parenthesis is supposed to go. Generally speaking, Excel adds the missing close parenthesis only when you are entering built-in worksheet functions. (See Chapter 8 for more information about worksheet functions.) For example, if you enter the incomplete formula

=A1+(A2*A3

and press Enter, Excel displays a dialog box that informs you the parentheses do not match. While it may seem obvious to you where the missing parenthesis should go, as far as Excel is concerned, it could go in one of two places: after *A2* or after *A3*. However, if you incorrectly enter the SUM function as follows:

=SUM(A1:A3

Excel adds the close parenthesis automatically when you press Enter. This works with both worksheet and macro functions. (We'll discuss macro functions in Chapter 20.)

On the other hand, if you want to multiply the total of cells A2 and A3 by the value in cell A1, and you enter the following incomplete formula

    =SUM(A2:A3*A1

Excel adds the close parenthesis after *A1*, in this case incorrectly assuming that the parentheses that follow the SUM function should encompass all of the subsequent entries. When you press Enter, a #VALUE error appears because you can't multiply a cell range by a single value in this manner. (We'll explain more about error values later in this chapter.)

The best advice we can give you about entering parentheses in formulas is to enter them yourself and double-check that you have placed them correctly. Relying on Excel's parentheses-matching feature can produce unpredictable results, unless you use it strictly with formulas containing only a single worksheet function.

Formula bar formatting

Excel provides a feature that helps make your formulas more readable in the formula bar. This is particularly useful when you are entering long formulas or formulas that have repetitive components. In most spreadsheet programs and in previous versions of Excel, you must enter formulas in one continuous string, such as

    =A2+A3+A4+B2+B3+B4+C2+C3+C4

In Excel, you can enter spaces, tabs, or return characters in a formula to make it easier to read, without affecting the calculation of the formula. To enter return characters in the formula bar, press Alt-Enter. For example, in Figure 3-1, we typed the above formula into cell A1, except that we added return characters in the formula bar just before *B2* and *C2*.

FIGURE 3-1.
You can add return characters in the formula bar to make long formulas more readable.

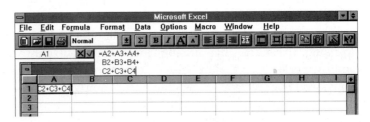

Similarly, you can insert tab characters in the formula bar by pressing Ctrl-Tab. In Figure 3-2, we added tab characters between three sections of a multiplication formula.

FIGURE 3-2.

You can add tabs in the formula bar to set off sections of your formulas for added clarity.

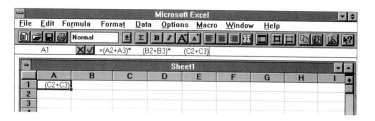

Naming cells and ranges

So far, you've seen how to build formulas by using references to cells in the worksheet. Microsoft Excel also lets your assign names to cells and use those names in your formulas.

To name a cell, first select it and then choose the Define Name command from the Formula menu. Excel looks at the selected cell, the cell immediately to its left, and then the cell immediately above to see if one of them contains a label that can serve as a cell name. If it finds a label, Excel displays it in the Define Name dialog box. For example, suppose you want to assign a name to cell B4 in Figure 3-3. First, select cell B4 and choose Define Name from the Formula menu. The Define Name dialog box is shown in Figure 3-4.

FIGURE 3-3.

We'll use this worksheet to demonstrate naming procedures.

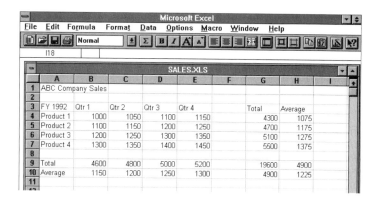

FIGURE 3-4.

Excel suggests a name for a cell or range.

Notice that the name *Product_1* appears in the Name box and that Excel highlights the name. Notice also that Excel has added the underline character (_) to indicate a blank space in the name, because it does not allow spaces in reference names.

The coordinates of the selected cell appear in the Refers to box, in the form of an absolute reference. (Excel assumes you want to use absolute references when you name cells in your worksheet.)

If you want to accept Excel's suggested name, select OK. Notice that the name now appears in the reference area of the formula bar. The name of the range appears in the reference area any time you select a range, as long as you select the entire range. The next time you open the Define Name dialog box, the name appears in the Names in Sheet box, which contains a listing of all the defined names for that worksheet. Of course, you can type your own cell name or edit Excel's suggested name. To enter your own cell name, simply type the name you want. When you begin typing, Excel deletes the existing contents of the Name box. For example, you might want to use the name *Qtr_1* instead of *Product_1*. To do this, type *Qtr_1* and then press Enter or click OK.

You can edit the cell reference in the Define Name dialog box as you would edit the contents of the formula bar. Begin by selecting the Refers to text box. When you enter a new reference in the Refers to text box, be sure your entry begins with an equal sign (=). You can then use the techniques described earlier to add, delete, and replace characters. You can also use the mouse to point to the cell you want to name.

In addition to letting you name individual cells, Excel lets you assign names to adjacent and nonadjacent ranges. For example, to name the range B4:B7 in Figure 3-3, select cells B4:B7, and then choose Define Name from the Formula menu. The Define Name dialog box is shown in Figure 3-5.

FIGURE 3-5.
If you select cells B4:B7, the Define Name dialog box looks like this.

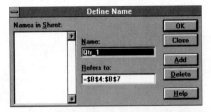

Notice that the Refers to text box contains the reference of the range you selected, not just the reference of the active cell, and that Excel suggests the name *Qtr_1* for the range. To accept Excel's suggested name, click OK.

When you click OK after you define a name, the Define Name dialog box disappears from the screen. If you want to name several cells or ranges at once, click Add instead of OK. Excel then leaves the dialog box on the screen so you can define another name.

Rules for naming

Cell and range names must comply with a few rules. First, the name must begin with a letter. You can use numbers and some special symbols in the name, but Excel won't accept a name that *begins* with a number, period, dollar sign, or any other special character. Excel also returns an error message if you enter blank spaces in a name like *1st Quarter* or *Region A*. To indicate a blank space in your range name, use an underline.

Excel displays an alert box if you specify a name that looks like a cell reference. For example, the program does not accept names like *A1* or *R2C1*. (*R2C1* is not acceptable because it's an alternative way of referring to A2 — the cell in *Row* 2, *Column* 1. This alternate naming convention is discussed in Chapter 4.) In addition, although you can use single-letter names such as *A, B,* and *Z,* you cannot use the single letters *R* and *C*.

Using names in formulas

You can use range names in formulas the same way you use cell references. For example, if you assign the name *Region_1* to cell A10, you can create the formula

=Region_1–21

This formula evaluates in the same way as

=A10–21

Editing names

Use any of the editing techniques already described to edit the contents of the Refers to text box in the Define Name dialog box when you name a range. To change the cells associated with a range name, choose the Define Name command, and select the name of the range whose reference you want to edit from the Names in Sheet list box. Then in the Refers to text box, either select the characters you want to change and type over them, or select the entire contents of the Refers to text box and drag through the cells you want to use. Excel pastes the new cell or range reference into the Refers to text box, the same way it pastes references into the formula bar. If the cells you want to select are hidden behind the dialog box, use the mouse to move the dialog box by clicking anywhere on the title bar and dragging it. (For more on dragging windows, see Chapter 6.) You can also use the keyboard to move the dialog box: Press Alt-Spacebar-M, and then use the arrow keys to reposition the dialog box. After you type your changes or select the cells you want, press Enter to lock in the new range reference.

To delete a range name, select the name from the Names in Sheet list box and then click Delete. Excel deletes only the name you select from the Names in Sheet list box. Be careful! If you delete a range name, any formula in the worksheet that refers to that name returns the error value #NAME? (unless you turned on the Alternate Formula Entry option).

Creating names from text cells

The Create Names command lets you name several individual cells or adjacent ranges at once. This command uses the labels in the upper or lower row or the left or right column of the range (or some combination of these) to name the other cells in the range.

For example, the sample worksheet in Figure 3-3 contains a series of labels in column A and row 3. To assign names to each of the values in columns B through E that correspond to the labels in column A, select cells A4:E7 and choose the Create Names command from the Formula menu. You'll see the dialog box shown in Figure 3-6. Excel selects the Left Column option by default, so click OK. Excel assigns the name *Product_1* to the range B4:E4, the name *Product_2* to the range B5:E5, and so on. (If you have already used one of these names in this worksheet, Excel asks whether to replace the existing definition.)

FIGURE 3-6.
Use the Create Names
dialog box to name
several cells or ranges.

Similarly, you can use the labels in cells B3:E3 to name cells B4:E7. Simply select cells B3:E7 and then choose Create Names from the Formula menu. When you select Top Row in the Create Names dialog box, Excel assigns the name *Qtr_1* to cells B4:B7, *Qtr_2* to cells C4:C7, and so forth.

If you select both Top Row and Left Column in the Create Names dialog box, Excel uses the label in the upper left corner of the range to name the entire group of cells. The range begins with the cell one row down and one column over from the top left cell. In this example, if you select cells A3:E7 and then select the Top Row and Left Column options, Excel assigns the name *FY_1989* to cells B4:E7 and applies the labels in row 3 and column A to the columns and rows as well.

The names you create with the Create Names command appear in the Names in Sheet box that appears when you use the Define Name command. You can delete or edit these names just as you would names created with the Define Name command.

Naming constants and formulas

You can assign names as long as 255 characters to formulas and constants, independently of the cells in your worksheet. Suppose you often use the value 5% in your worksheet to calculate sales tax on products sold by your company. Instead of typing 5% or *.05*, you can use a name — for example, *Tax* — in your calculations. Choose the Define Name command, type *Tax* into the Name box, and type *.05* or 5% directly in the Refers to box. Excel assigns the name *Tax* to the constant value 5%. After you create this name, you can use the formula

=Price+(Price*Tax)

to calculate the cost of items with 5% sales tax.

If you enter a formula in the Refers to box that refers to a cell in your worksheet, Excel updates that formula whenever the value in the cell changes. In other words, Excel treats named formulas in the same way it treats formulas you enter directly into the worksheet. For example, if you select cell E5 in the worksheet shown in Figure 3-7, you can enter the formula

=C5–($B$2*C5)+D5

in the Refers to box and the name *Amount_Billed* in the Name box in the Define Name dialog box. This formula calculates the purchase amount, subtracts a 10% discount for preferred customers, and adds shipping charges to calculate the total invoice amount. Notice that the reference to cell B2 is absolute, so Excel always refers to cell B2 for the correct discount rate. The remaining references are relative, however, which tells Excel to draw the billing information from the appropriate row each time you enter the formula

=Amount_Billed

in column E of the worksheet. Thus, when you enter this formula name in cell E8, Excel uses the formula

=C8–($B$2*C8)+D8

to calculate a total billing amount of $429.34.

FIGURE 3-7.

You can increase your efficiency by defining names for values and formulas that you frequently use.

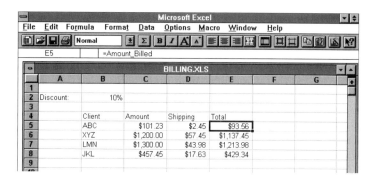

Whenever you create a named formula that contains relative references, keep in mind that Excel interprets the position of the cells that are being referenced in relation to the cell that is active when you use the Define Name command. Thus, when you create the named formula *Amount_Billed*, be sure that cell E5 is the active cell, so when you enter

=Amount_Billed

in cells E6 through E8, Excel adjusts the relative references in your named formulas to refer to the corresponding cells in columns C and D.

The Paste Name command

After you define one or more names in your worksheet, you can use the Paste Name command from the Formula menu to paste those names in your worksheet formulas. For example, suppose you assign the name *Discount* to cell B2 and the name *Amount* to the cells in C5:C8 of the worksheet shown in Figure 3-7. You can use these values in a formula like this:

=Discount*Amount

To create this formula, type *Discount* and *Amount* directly in the formula bar. Alternatively, use the Paste Name command to paste the names in the formula. Paste Name not only saves time when you need to enter several names, it also helps reduce typographical errors and serves as a memory aid when your worksheet contains many name definitions.

To use the Paste Name command, first select the cell in which you want to enter the name. If you want the name to appear at the beginning of the formula, use the Paste Name command or press F3 to access the dialog box shown in Figure 3-8.

FIGURE 3-8.
Use the Paste Name dialog box to enter names in your formulas.

Then select the name you want to paste and click OK. Excel enters an equal sign in the formula bar, followed by the name you selected. The formula bar remains active so that you can type the remainder of the formula. If you want the name to appear in the middle of a formula, select the cell that will contain the formula, type an equal sign and the first portion of the formula, and then, at the spot where you want the name to appear, issue the Paste Name command and double-click the name you want. This name appears at the current insertion point, and the insertion-point marker moves to the right of the name so that you can continue typing the formula. You can also paste names into an existing formula by placing the insertion point at the spot where you want the name to appear and then issuing the Paste Name command.

Microsoft Excel 4 includes a Paste Names tool that you can use instead of the Paste Name command or the F3 key to access the Paste Name dialog box. The Paste Names tool is in the Formula tools category and is not located in any of Excel's predefined toolbars. You can, however, customize a toolbar to include the Paste Names tool, if you want. (For details about customizing toolbars, see Chapter 21 and Appendix A.)

The Paste List option

The Paste List option in the Paste Name dialog box can help you keep track of the names you create in your worksheet. When you choose Paste List, the program places a list of the names in your worksheet, like the list shown in columns G and H of Figure 3-9. Column G contains the names and column H contains the definitions. The cell that is active when you choose the Paste List option becomes the first cell in the list.

FIGURE 3-9.

Use the Paste List option to create a list of the names and definitions in your worksheet.

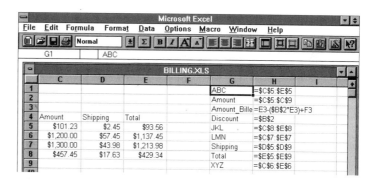

When it pastes names and definitions from the list to your worksheet, Excel overwrites any data that lies in its way. If you accidentally overwrite existing data, use the Undo command on the Edit menu to remove the list. For more about the Undo command, see Chapter 5.

Applying names to formulas

Excel does not automatically apply the names you create to formulas in your worksheet, unless the Alternate Formula Entry option is activated. (See the sidebar "Making Excel behave more like Lotus 1-2-3," earlier in this chapter.) With regard to the sample worksheet shown in Figure 3-7, suppose you enter a series of formulas like

=$B$2*C5

and

=$B$2*C6

in cells F5:F8 and then use the Define Name command to assign the name *Discount* to cell B2. The formulas in cells F5:F8 will not automatically change to read

=Discount*C5

To substitute the named reference *Discount* for $B$2 in your formulas, you must do one of three things:

- Edit the formulas and type over the current reference to cell B2 with the name *Discount*

- Select the characters $B$2 in the formula bar and use the Paste Name command to paste the name *Discount* over the cell reference

- Use the Apply Names command on the Formula menu to instruct Excel to replace the reference with the appropriate name.

You are already familiar with the first two techniques; let's look now at the Apply Names command.

The Apply Names command searches through the formulas in your worksheet and locates cell and range references for which you defined names. If you've selected a range in your worksheet, Excel applies those names to the selected cells only. However, if only one cell is selected when you issue the command, Excel applies the names throughout the worksheet.

When you issue the Apply Names command, you see a dialog box like the one in Figure 3-10.

FIGURE 3-10.
Use the Apply Names command to substitute names for cell and range references in your formulas.

All the cell and range names you define in the worksheet appear in the Apply Names list box. (Named values and formulas do not appear in this list.) You can apply any or all of these names to your worksheet formulas. To select more than one name, hold down Shift while you click each name you want to apply. If you work without a mouse, use the arrow keys to move to the first item you want to select, hold down Ctrl, move to the next item, and press Spacebar. Continue until you select all the names you want to apply.

Use the Ignore Relative/Absolute option to indicate whether you want to replace references with names regardless of the type of reference — relative or absolute — you used in your name definitions or in your worksheet formulas. Generally, you'll want to leave this check box selected, because most of your name definitions will use absolute references (the default when you use the Define Name and Create Names commands), and most of your formulas will use relative references (the default when you paste cell and range references into the formula bar). If you deselect this option, however, Excel replaces absolute, relative, and mixed references in your worksheet with name definitions only, using the corresponding reference style.

To understand the Use Row and Column Names option (and the other choices that appear if you click the Options button), you need to know a little more about how Excel handles range names. In particular, you need to know about Excel's *intersection operator*.

In the worksheet in Figure 3-3, we assigned the name *Qtr_1* to the range B4:B7. We also assigned the name *Product_1* to the range B4:E4. If at cell I4, we enter the formula

=Qtr_1*4

you might expect Excel to give us an error message. It appears that we asked Excel to multiply the values in cells B4:B7 by 4 and deposit the result in a single cell, I4. This is a request the program cannot possibly fulfill.

Instead of giving us an error message, however, Excel assumes that we want to use only one value in the range B4:B7 — namely, the one that lies in the same row as the formula that contains the reference. Because we entered that formula in I4, Excel gives us the value in B4. Thus the formula =Qtr_1*4, when entered in I4, is equivalent to the formula =B4*4.

If we copy this formula into I5:I7, each cell in that range would still contain the formula =Qtr_1*4, but at I5 that formula would reference B5, at I6 it would reference B6, and so on.

You can use the same technique to reference individual cells in a named row. For example, because we assigned the range B4:E4 the name *Product_1*, a formula at B12 can use the name *Product_1* to reference the value at B4. A formula at C12 can use the same name to reference the value at C4, and so on.

But what if we enter the formula

=Qtr_1*4

at I15, instead of I4? This time, no cell within the range named *Qtr_1* lies on the same row as the referencing formula, so this formula returns an error value. In this case there is still a way to reference B4 by name, though. We can do that with the help of Excel's intersection operator. The intersection operator is the space character you get when you press Spacebar. (Now you know why Excel won't let you use space characters *within* a range name.)

If at I15 we write the formula

=Qtr_1 Product_1*4

Excel knows that we want to reference the value that lies at the intersection of the range named *Qtr_1* and the range named *Product_1*. In other words, it knows we want to reference cell B4.

What does all this have to do with the Use Row and Column Names option of the Apply Names command? You might find typing range names tedious. You might find it especially tedious to type range names in formulas that require inter-section operators. But if you leave the Use Row and Column Names option selected (its default state), Excel does all this work for you.

For example, if you enter the formula =B4*4 (without names) in cell I4, use the Apply Names dialog box, and select the Use Row and Column Names option, Excel changes the formula to read =Qtr_1*4. If you use Apply Names and deselect the Use Row and Column Names option, Excel does not apply any names to this for-mula. Similarly, if you enter the formula =B4*4 in cell I15, and then use the Apply Names command, Excel makes that formula read

=Product_1 Qtr_1*4

Excel does this only if you leave the Use Row and Column Names option selected, which you will want to do under most circumstances.

Other options in the Apply Names dialog box

If you click the Options button in the Apply Names dialog box, Excel expands the dialog box to reveal additional choices, as shown in Figure 3-11.

FIGURE 3-11.
Clicking the Options button makes additional choices available.

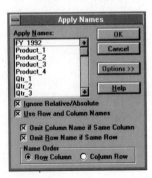

To see what the Omit Column Name and Omit Row Name options do, refer once more to Figure 3-3. If we enter the formula

=B4*4

in cell B12, and then use the Apply Names command, Excel ordinarily makes the formula read =*Product_1**4. It applies a row name — *Product_1*. But it doesn't apply the column name, *Qtr_1*. Because of the way Excel handles range names, the column name is superfluous. You can include the column name if you want it. To include it, deselect the Omit Column Name if Same Column check box. Similarly, by deselecting the Omit Row Name if Same Row check box, you can make Excel apply both a row name and a column name to a formula. You may find these two options a convenient way to clarify the origin of data referenced in your formulas.

Finally, the Name Order selection lets you control the order in which row and column components appear when Excel applies two names connected by an intersection operator.

The Goto command

Microsoft Excel's Goto command on the Formula menu lets you move around your worksheet and select cells quickly. Suppose cell A1 is selected and you want to select cell M50. Instead of scrolling over and down to cell M50, click Goto on the Formula menu. Excel displays a dialog box like the one shown in Figure 3-12. In the Reference box, type *M50* and then click OK. Immediately, Excel moves the window so that cell M50 appears in the lower right corner and is now the active cell.

FIGURE 3-12.
Use the Goto dialog box to select a cell or range quickly.

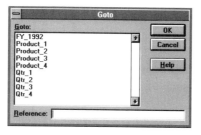

As you can see in Figure 3-12, if you create range names in your worksheet, those names appear in the list at the left side of the Goto dialog box. To go to one of these ranges, click the range name in the dialog box. For example, suppose you assign the name *Subtotals* to cells C5:F5 in your worksheet. When you choose *Subtotals* from the list of your worksheet's named ranges, Excel highlights cells C5:F5 and makes the first cell in the range, C5, the active cell.

You can also use the Goto command to move to another open worksheet. To do this, select Goto and type the name of the worksheet, followed by an exclamation point and the name or reference. For example, to go to cell D5 in a worksheet called Billing, type *Billing.xls!D5*.

Each time you use the Goto command, Excel remembers the cell or range that you moved from and lists it in the Reference box. Excel also keeps track of the last four locations in the worksheet from which you used the Goto command. These locations appear at the top of the list in the Goto dialog box. Thus, you can toggle between two points in your worksheet simply by repeating the Goto command, and you can use the Goto command to return to any of your four prevous locations. Figure 3-13 shows the Goto dialog box with four previous locations listed.

FIGURE 3-13.
The Goto dialog box keeps track of the last four locations from which you used the Goto command.

Error values

If you enter a formula that can't be resolved, Microsoft Excel displays an *error value* as the "result" of your formula. Excel uses seven error values — #DIV/0!, #NAME?, #VALUE!, #REF!, #NULL!, #N/A, and #NUM! The particular error value that appears can help you understand why your formula cannot be evaluated.

One of the most common error values is #DIV/0!, which indicates that you attempted to divide a number by zero. This error usually shows up when you create a division formula with a divisor that refers to a blank cell. For example, suppose cell A1 contains the formula

=32/A2

As long as a numeric value other than zero appears in cell A2, Excel can resolve the formula correctly. If A2 is blank, however, Excel can't resolve the formula. To correct the problem, you must either edit the formula or enter a value in cell A2.

The #NAME? error value indicates that you entered in a formula a name that Excel can't find in the Define Name dialog box list. If you see this error, check to see if you mistyped the name reference or included a reference to a deleted name. You also see this error value if you do not enclose a text string in double quotation marks. For example, suppose you create the string formula

=My name is &A1

You intend this formula to combine the string *My name is* with the contents of cell A1. However, unless you enclose the text string in double quotation marks, Excel treats it as a name and returns the #NAME? error value. To correct the problem, enter the formula like this:

="My name is "&A1

The #VALUE! error value usually means you entered a mathematical formula that refers to a text entry. For example, if you enter the formula

=A1*A2

in your worksheet and cell A1 contains a text string, the formula returns the error value #VALUE!

The #REF! error value appears if you use the Delete command to eliminate a range of cells whose references are included in a formula. For example, suppose you enter the formula

=A1+A2+A3

in cell A5 of your worksheet. If you then delete row 3 from the worksheet, the formula changes to

=A1+A2+#REF!

and cell A5 displays the value #REF! Note that Excel does not let the formula reference the value that formerly resided in A4, because it can't assume that is what you want. The program has to play it safe and assume that you made a mistake when you deleted row 3.

The #N/A error value indicates that no information is available for the calculation you want to perform. If you're building a model for which you do not have complete information yet, you can enter #N/A into those cells that are still awaiting data. (To do this, simply type *#N/A* or *#n/a* and press Enter.) Any formulas that reference cells that contain the #N/A value return #N/A as well.

The #NUM! error value often indicates that you've provided an invalid argument to a worksheet function. For example, if you use a negative argument in a SQRT function, you receive a #NUM! error value. The #NUM! value also appears if you create a formula that results in a number that is too large or too small to be represented in the worksheet.

The last, and least common, error value is #NULL! This value often appears when you enter a formula in the form

=SUM(A1:C1 A6:F6)

The blank space between the two sets of references tells Excel to find the value of the cell at the intersection of the range A1:C1 and A6:F6. Because these two ranges have no common cells, Excel returns the #NULL! error value.

Arrays

Arrays are special calculating tools you can use to build formulas that produce multiple results or to operate on groups of values rather than on single values. If this definition seems confusing, bear with us. When you see arrays in action, their function will become clearer.

First, let's briefly define a few terms. An *array formula* takes much the same form as a standard worksheet formula, except that it acts on two or more sets of values, called *array arguments*, to return either a single result or multiple results. An *array range* is a block of cells that share a common array formula. An *array constant* is a specially organized list of constant values that you can use as arguments in your array formulas.

Using arrays

The easiest way to learn about arrays is to look at a few examples. Typically, the formulas you enter in your worksheet produce a single result. For example, suppose cells A1 and A2 contain the values 10 and 15. To determine the sum of these two values, you can enter the simple formula

= A1+A2

This formula evaluates to a single value, 25, that occupies a single cell in the worksheet.

Now suppose you enter several groups of values in rows 1 and 2 of your worksheet, as shown in Figure 3-14. Typically, to total the values in each of these columns, you would create five separate formulas, as we've done in cells A3:E3. The formula in cell A3 calculates the total of the values in cells A1 and A2, the formula in cell B3 calculates the total of the values in cells B1 and B2, and so forth.

But here's an alternative: Using arrays, you can calculate the sum of each column of values in Figure 3-14 with a single formula. To begin, select cells A3:E3 and type

= A1:E1+A2:E2

To lock in this formula, press Shift-Ctrl-Enter. Figure 3-15 shows the results.

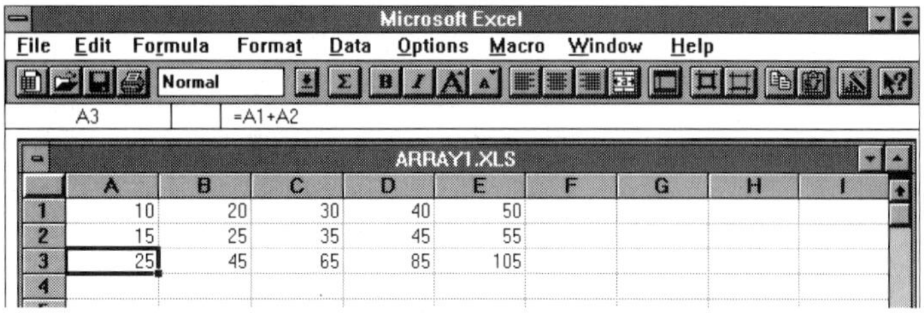

FIGURE 3-14.
We used five formulas to calculate the totals of the values in columns A through E.

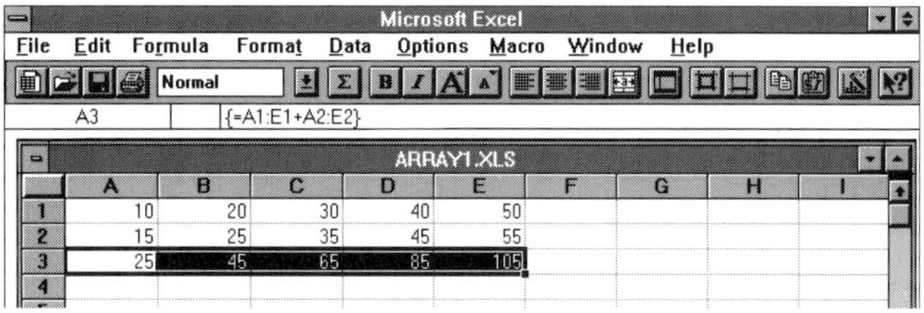

FIGURE 3-15.
We used a single horizontal array formula to total the values in each column.

As you can see, a single array formula computes the sum of each group of values: A1:A2, B1:B2, C1:C2, D1:D2, and E1:E2. Cells A3:E3 serve as the array range in this simple example, and the array formula

{=A1:E1+A2:E2}

is stored in each cell of the array range. (Microsoft Excel adds the braces automatically when it distributes the array formula throughout the cells of the array range.) In this example, the array arguments are the range references A1:E1 and A2:E2.

The array formula in Figure 3-15 occupies a horizontal array range. Let's look at a similar example that uses a vertical array range. Suppose you want to calculate the product of each pair of values in columns A and B of Figure 3-16 on the following page. Simply select the range C1:C7 and type

= A1:A7*B1:B7

Figure 3-16 shows what happens when you lock in this formula as an array by pressing Shift-Ctrl-Enter.

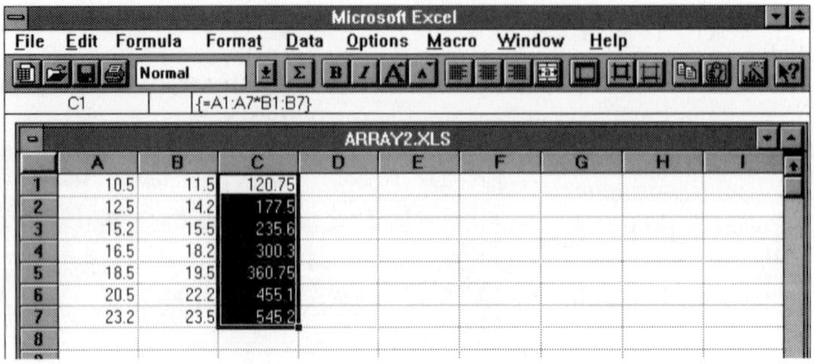

FIGURE 3-16.
In this worksheet, a vertical array formula calculates the products of the values in each row.

Now suppose you want to compute the average of the products of each pair of values in this worksheet — that is, the average of A1*B1, A2*B2, A3*B3, and so on. With an array formula, you can reduce this calculation to one step using the AVERAGE function. (Worksheet functions are explained in detail in Chapter 8.) Select cell D1 (or any blank cell), and type

     = AVERAGE(A1:A7*B1:B7)

and press Shift-Ctrl-Enter. Figure 3-17 shows the result. Notice that, instead of producing multiple results, this array formula operates on multiple arguments to produce a single result.

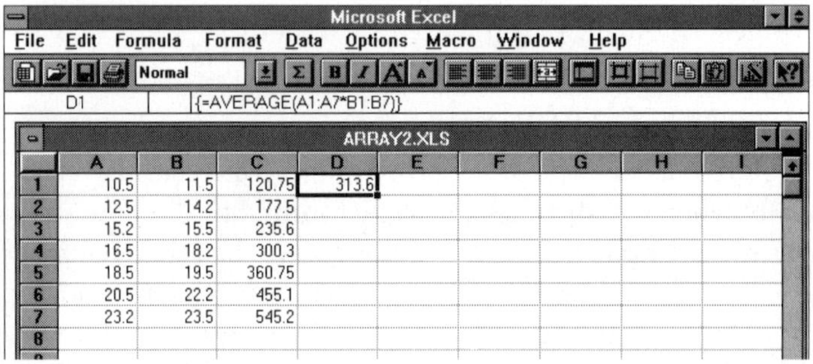

FIGURE 3-17.
We used an array formula in cell D1 to compute the average of the products of the pairs of values in columns A and B.

Two-dimensional arrays

In the previous examples, the array formulas resulted in a horizontal, a single-cell, and a vertical array range. These array ranges are one-dimensional. You can also create two-dimensional array ranges.

For example, suppose you want to calculate the integer values (whole numbers only) of each of the entries in cells A1:C7 of Figure 3-17. First, select a range the same size and shape as the range you want to work with. In this case, you would select a range with seven rows and three columns, such as E1:G7. Next, enter the formula

= INT(A1:C7)

and press Shift-Ctrl-Enter. (The INT function simply changes a number to its integer value. See Chapter 8.) As you can see in Figure 3-18, each cell in the range E1:G7 displays the integer value of the corresponding cell in the range A1:C7. In fact, Excel has entered the array formula

{=INT(A1:C7)}

in each cell in the range E1:G7.

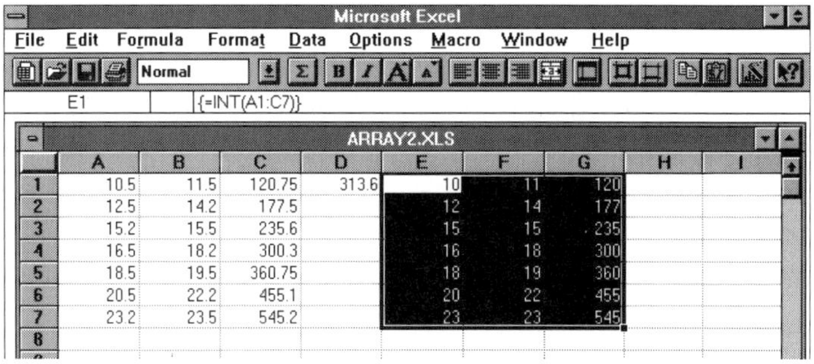

FIGURE 3-18.
We used an array
formula to compute
the integer value of
each of the entries in
cells A1:C7.

Array formula rules

As demonstrated in the previous examples, array formulas can return either single or multiple values. Either way, you enter array formulas by first selecting the cell or range that will contain your result or results. If the formula produces multiple results, you select a range the same size and shape as the range or ranges on which you perform your calculations. In the preceding example, we selected a range with seven rows and three columns to hold the array-formula results.

You must press Shift-Ctrl-Enter to lock in an array formula. When you do this, Excel places a set of braces around the formula in the formula bar to indicate that it is an array formula. Don't type the braces yourself; if you do, Excel interprets your entry as text.

Because array formulas are specially structured, the rules for editing array ranges differ slightly from the rules discussed earlier in this book. You cannot edit, clear, or move individual cells in an array range, nor can you insert or delete cells.

You must treat the cells in the array range as a single unit and edit them all at once. For example, if you try to clear cell E1 in Figure 3-18, Excel displays the message *Cannot change part of an array* and prevents you from clearing the cell.

To edit or clear either a single-cell or multiple-cell array formula, first select any cell in the array, and then activate the formula bar. When the formula bar is active, the braces around the formula disappear. Now edit or clear the formula as needed and press Shift-Ctrl-Enter to lock in your changes. Excel reinserts the braces and distributes your change to all the cells in the array range or clears the array range.

To move or clear the contents of an array range, first select all the cells in the range. If the array range is large or if you are unsure of the dimensions of the range, you can select any cell in the range and then press Ctrl and the slash (/) key to select the entire array. (Or you can use the Select Special command on the Formula menu to select the entire array range. We discuss Select Special in Chapter 5.) Then you can use the Cut or Clear command to move or clear the selection.

Even though you can't cut, clear, or edit part of an array, you can assign different formats to individual cells. You can also copy a single cell from an array range and paste it in another area of your worksheet. Excel adjusts any relative references in the pasted array formula just as it does when you copy and paste any standard worksheet formula.

Using array constants

Array constants are to arrays what literal values are to cell references. Array constants can consist of numbers, text, or logical values. You must enclose an array constant in braces ({ }) and separate its elements with commas and semicolons.

The best way to understand array constants is to look at an example. Suppose you want to compute the integer values of the three numbers 123.456, 1.234, and 12345.678. You can perform these three computations with a single array formula by selecting any horizontal three-cell range, typing the formula

    = INT({123.456,1.234,12345.678})

and pressing Shift-Ctrl-Enter. Notice that the argument of the INT function is made up of the three numbers enclosed in braces. In this case, you type in the braces shown above to indicate that the enclosed values make up an array constant.

Figure 3-19 shows the results of this formula. Each cell in the range B2:D2 contains the array formula

    {=INT({123.456,1.234,12345.678})}

The value displayed in each cell, however, is the result of the INT function for the element of the array constant that corresponds to the position of that cell in the range. For example, cell B2, the second cell in the range, displays the result of INT for the value 1.234, the second element in the array constant.

FIGURE 3-19.
*We used an array
constant as the
argument for this
array formula.*

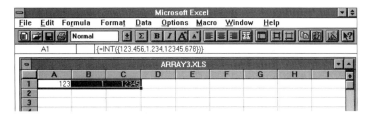

You can also create vertical array constants. In a vertical array constant, the elements in the array are separated by semicolons instead of commas. For example, the array constant

{123.456;1.234;12345.678}

is a three-row vertical array. As you might expect, you must enter formulas that refer to vertical array constants in vertical ranges. For example, if you want to compute the integer values of the three numbers in this vertical array constant, you can select the range A1:A3, type the formula

= INT({123.456;1.234;12345.678})

and press Shift-Ctrl-Enter. Figure 3-20 shows the result.

FIGURE 3-20.
*In a vertical array
constant, the elements
in the array are
separated by
semicolons.*

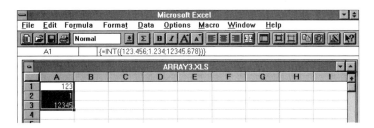

Just as you can create two-dimensional variable arrays, you can also create two-dimensional array constants. In a two-dimensional array constant, commas are used to separate the elements in each row of the constant, and semicolons are used to separate the rows that make up the constant. For example, suppose you want to calculate the square roots of a series of 12 values and display them as a block rather than as a list. Instead of entering each value in an individual cell in the worksheet, you can use the SQRT function with an array formula like this:

=SQRT({4,9,16,25;36,49,64,81;100,121,144,169})

To enter this formula in your worksheet, you must first select a range with four columns and three rows — we used A1:D3 — and type the formula with the array constant in braces. When you press Shift-Ctrl-Enter to lock in the formula, Excel supplies the outer set of braces for you. Figure 3-21 on the following page shows the resulting array of square-root calculations. (The SQRT function is described in Chapter 8.)

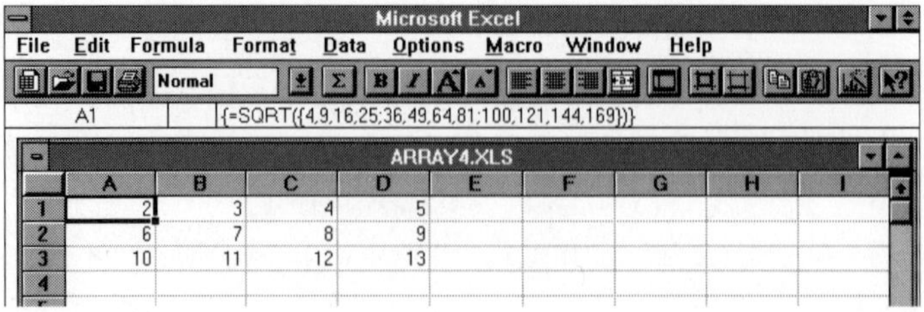

FIGURE 3-21.
This array formula uses a four-column-by-three-row array constant.

Notice that the commas and semicolons in the array argument correspond to the row and column positions of the resulting square-root calculations. Thus, the argument {4,9,16,25;36,49,64,81;100,121,144,169} represents an array constant shaped like this:

4 9 16 25

36 49 64 81

100 121 144 169

You can also mix array-constant arguments with cell references, in much the same way that you mix constant values and references in a standard worksheet formula. But before we show you this technique, we need to introduce array expansion.

Array expansion

When you use arrays as arguments in a formula, all your arrays should have the same dimensions. If the dimensions of your array arguments or array ranges don't match, Excel often expands the arguments as required to complete its calculations. For example, suppose you want to multiply all the values in cells A1:B5 of your worksheet by 10. You can accomplish this with a simple array formula like

{=A1:B5*10}

or you can use array constants in a formula like

{={1,2;3,4;5,6;7,8;9,10}*10}

Notice that these two formulas are not balanced; we have 10 values on the left side of the multiplication operator and only 1 value on the right. Fortunately, Excel can expand the second argument to match the size and shape of the first. In the preceding examples, the first formula is equivalent to

{=A1:B5*{10,10;10,10;10,10;10,10;10,10}}

and the second is equivalent to

{={1,2;3,4;5,6;7,8;9,10}*{10,10;10,10;10,10;10,10;10,10}}

When you work with two or more sets of multi-value arrays, each set of arguments must have the same number of rows as the argument with the greatest number of rows, and the same number of columns as the argument with the greatest number of columns. Single-value arguments are repeated as needed to match the dimensions of the other arguments in your array formula. If you use a one-row or one-column array argument, Excel repeats that row or column of values as needed to match the dimensions of the other arguments. For example, the formula

{={1,2,3;4,5,6}*{7,8,9}}

is equivalent to

{={1,2,3;4,5,6}*{7,8,9;7,8,9}}

and results in an array range like this:

7 16 27

28 40 54

Excel doesn't expand an array when you use cell references as your array arguments. For example, in the formula

{=A1:A6*B1:B3}

you might expect Excel to repeat the argument B1:B3 to match the size and shape of the argument A1:A6, like this:

{={A1;A2;A3;A4;A5;A6}*{B1;B2;B3;B1;B2;B3}}

Instead, the preceding formula results in this array:

{={A1;A2;A3;A4;A5;A6}*{B1;B2;B3;#N/A;#N/A;#N/A}}

However, whether you use array constants or cell references, if you select a result range that is larger than the array argument, Excel attempts to expand the array formula to fill the selection. For example, in the worksheet in Figure 3-15, we used two one-row-by-five-column array arguments and a corresponding one-row-by-five-column result range. If we selected cells A3:E7 rather than A3:E3 when we entered the array formula, the worksheet would look like the one in Figure 3-22. In effect, the formula in the range A3:E7 produces a five-by-five array by repeating the one row, A3:E3, five times.

FIGURE 3-22.

When you select a result range larger than the array arguments, Excel repeats the array formula to fill the selection.

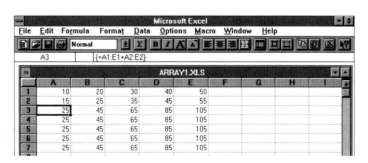

If the array range is not a multiple of the same dimensions as the array arguments, however, Excel returns #N/A error values. For example, in the worksheet
shown in Figure 3-18, if we entered our INT function in the range E1:H8 rather than
E1:G7, our worksheet would look like the one in Figure 3-23. Notice that the #N/A
error values appear in row 8 and column H because the array argument, A1:C7, is
only three columns wide and seven rows deep.

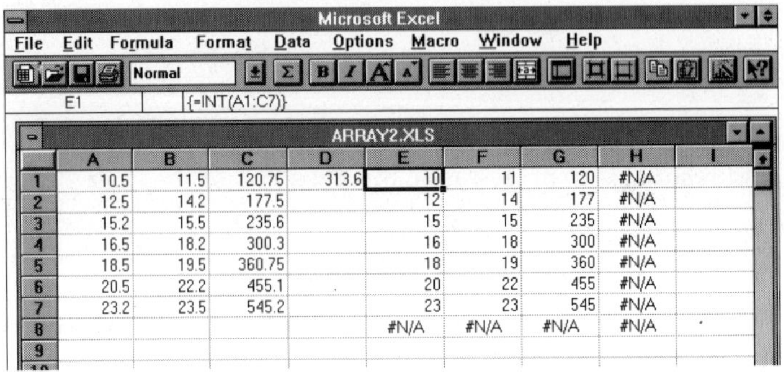

FIGURE 3-23.
*If the array range is
not a multiple of the
same dimension as the
array arguments,
Excel returns #N/A
error values.*

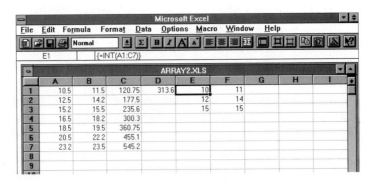

Finally, when you select a result range smaller than the argument range, Excel
simply fills the available rows and columns, beginning with the upper left corner
of the result range. For example, continuing with the sample worksheet in Figure
3-18, if we selected the range E1:F3 rather than E1:G7 to enter our INT function, our
worksheet would look like the one in Figure 3-24.

FIGURE 3-24.
*If you select a result
range smaller than the
argument range,
Excel fills only the
available rows and
columns.*

Calculating the worksheet

As you've already seen, you can enter formulas into your worksheet that refer to
other cells in the worksheet. When you change the values in the cells that these
formulas refer to, Microsoft Excel updates the values of the formulas as well. This

updating process is called *calculation* or *recalculation*. (Because Excel uses the underlying values in cells, not their displayed values, when it performs calculations, you can format a cell without affecting the calculation.)

Excel performs "smart" recalculation. That is, when you add or edit a cell in Excel, the program recalculates only those cells affected by the entry. For example, if you enter the formula

    =A1*B2

in cell C1 and then make a change to cell A1, Excel automatically recalculates cell C1, but not the other cells in your worksheet. However, if other formulas in the worksheet refer to cell A1 or to cell C1, then Excel recalculates those cells — and only those cells.

Even with smart recalculation, there may be times when Excel has to recalculate a large number of formulas. At such times, the word *Recalc,* followed by a number, appears in the left section of the formula bar. The number, which indicates how many cells remain to be recalculated, rapidly drops to 0. While the recalculation continues, the mouse pointer might assume an hourglass shape, which normally means you have to wait before you can use another command or make a cell entry. You can interrupt Excel's recalculation, however. Even if the mouse pointer is an hourglass, you can still use commands or make cell entries. Excel simply pauses in its recalculation and then resumes when you're done.

Manual recalculation

When you work with a large worksheet that contains many interdependent formulas, or when you work with charts, Excel might need several seconds to recalculate your worksheet and redraw any open charts. Despite Excel's background recalculation, you might prefer to change the method of recalculation to Manual while you enter data.

To set calculation to Manual, choose Calculation from the Options menu. Excel displays a dialog box like the one in Figure 3-25. Next, select the Manual option in the dialog box, and then click OK.

FIGURE 3-25.
*The Calculation
Options dialog box
controls worksheet
calculation and
iteration.*

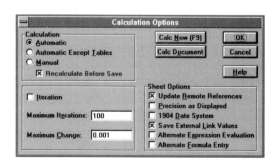

If you make a change that normally initiates recalculation, Excel displays "Calculate" in the status bar. When you want to see the effects of your cell entries, simply press Ctrl-= or F9. Excel calculates all the cells in the worksheet that are affected by the changes you've made since you last recalculated, and then Excel updates all open charts.

You can also initiate calculation by clicking the Calc Now or Calc Document buttons in the Calculation Options dialog box. Clicking the Calc Now button is equivalent to pressing Ctrl-= or F9, and recalculates all open worksheets. If you want Excel to recalculate only the active worksheet, click the Calc Document button in the Calculation Options dialog box or press Shift-F9. Yet another way to recalculate all open worksheets is to use the Calculate Now tool, which is located on the Utility toolbar. You can customize the Standard toolbar to include the Calculate Now tool, if you like. For information about customizing toolbars, see Chapter 21 and Appendix A.

Even if you choose manual recalculation, Excel normally recalculates your entire worksheet when you save it to disk. If you don't want Excel to recalculate your worksheet when you save a file, deselect the check box labeled Recalculate Before Save in the Calculation Options dialog box.

You can also tell Excel to automatically recalculate all the cells in your worksheet except your data tables by selecting Automatic Except Tables in the Calculation Options dialog box. (Data tables are discussed in Chapter 11.)

Changing formulas to values

You can use the Ctrl-= or F9 key to change one or more of the cell references in your formulas into values. For example, suppose A6 contains the formula

    =A1+A2+A3

Cell A1 contains the value 100, cell A2 contains the value 200, and cell A3 contains the value 300. If you select A1 in the formula bar and press Ctrl-= or F9, Excel converts the formula to

    =100+A2+A3

If you select the entire formula or activate the formula bar without making any selection and then press Ctrl-= or F9, Excel computes the sum of the values and displays 600, with no equal sign, in the formula bar.

You can then click the Enter box or press Enter to lock in the change, or press Esc to return the formula to its original state. Keep in mind, however, that unless you immediately choose Undo Entry from the Edit menu, you can't retrieve the original cell references after you lock in the entry. This means, in this example, that after you change the cell references to values with Calculate Now, Excel no longer links the formula in cell A6 to the values in the range A1:A3.

Circular references

Circular references occur when a formula depends, either directly or indirectly, on its own value. The most obvious type of circular reference occurs when you create a formula in a cell that contains a reference to that same cell.

For example, if you enter a formula like

=C1–A1

in cell A1 of your worksheet, Excel displays an alert box with the message *Cannot resolve circular references.* When you click OK to acknowledge the error, the formula returns the value 0.

Why can't Excel solve this formula? Because each time it arrives at a value for the formula in cell A1, the value of cell A1 changes. When it evaluates the formula in A1 using the new value in A1, the value in cell A1 changes again. Obviously, the program could continue to go around this circle forever.

Unlike the previous example, many circular references *can* be resolved. For example, look at the simple series of formulas in the worksheet in Figure 3-26. We formatted this worksheet to display the underlying formulas in each cell. As you can see, cell A1 contains the formula

=A2+A3

cell A2 contains the value 1000, and cell A3 contains the formula

=0.5*A1

FIGURE 3-26.
This worksheet contains a circular reference.

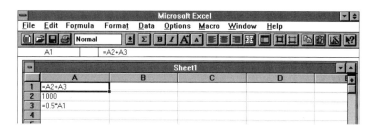

This set of formulas is circular because the formula in A1 depends on the value in A3, and the formula in A3 depends on the value in A1. In fact, Excel identifies the first circular reference it finds in the status bar at the bottom of the screen: *Circular: A1.* (Depending on the order in which you enter the formulas, the message might identify A3 as the circular cell, instead of A1.)

You can use the Iteration option in the Calculation Options dialog box to resolve this kind of circular reference. When you choose Iteration, Excel recalculates all the cells in open worksheets that contain a circular reference a specified number of times. Each time Excel recalculates the formulas, the results in each cell get closer and closer to the correct values.

To resolve the circular reference in our example, click OK in the *Cannot resolve circular references* alert box, and then choose Calculation from the Options menu. Next, select the Manual and Iteration options in the Calculation Options dialog box and click OK.

When you select the Iteration option in the Calculation Options dialog box, Excel sets the Maximum Iterations option to 100 and the Maximum Change option to 0.001. These settings tell Excel to recalculate the cells involved in the circular reference up to 100 times or until the values in these cells change less than 0.001 between iterations, whichever comes first. Excel lets you set Maximum Iterations as high as 32,767! You'll probably find that the default 100 iterations is enough to resolve most intentional circular references in your worksheet, however. Similarly, you can set Maximum Change to any number greater than 0, although the 0.001 default is adequate in most cases.

Begin the calculation by pressing Ctrl-= or F9. Table 3-1 shows how the values in cells A1 and A3 in our example from Figure 3-26 change as Excel recalculates the circular reference. Notice that the values change less with each iteration as Excel closes in on the correct answer. The final results in cells A1 and A3 are very close to correct — 999.999 is almost exactly half of 1999.999. The recalculation stops after 21 iterations because the change in the values in cells A1 and A3 in that iteration is less than 0.001.

Unfortunately, Excel does not repeat the *Cannot resolve circular reference* message if it fails to resolve the circular reference within the specified number of iterations. Instead, it displays the values of the formulas at the last iteration. You must rely on your common sense to determine whether the value produced by Excel is really the answer you're looking for.

The process we just described is called *convergence*, meaning that the difference between results becomes smaller with each iterative calculation. Sometimes circular references are resolved through a process called *divergence*, meaning that the difference between results becomes larger with each iterative calculation. In this case, Excel ignores your Maximum Change setting and continues its calculations until it completes the maximum number of calculations you specify in the Calculation Options dialog box.

Excel's ability to perform smart recalculation is a real time-saver when it comes to using the Iteration option. Because Excel recalculates only those cells needed to resolve the circular reference, Excel can perform 100 iterations in a matter of seconds. However, when you use iterative calculation, be sure the Calculation option is set to Manual, or Excel recalculates the circular references every time you press Enter. The following table illustrates the resolution of a circular reference in cells A1 and A3.

Iteration number	A1	A3
0	(=A2+A3)	(=0.5*A1)
1	1000	0
2	1500	500
3	1750	750
4	1875	875
5	1937.5	937.5
6	1968.75	968.75
7	1984.375	984.375
8	1992.188	992.188
9	1996.094	996.094
10	1998.047	998.047
11	1999.023	999.023
12	1999.512	999.512
13	1999.756	999.756
14	1999.878	999.878
15	1999.939	999.939
16	1999.969	999.969
17	1999.985	999.985
18	1999.992	999.992
19	1999.996	999.996
20	1999.998	999.998
21	1999.999	999.999

Although you may occasionally build circular references into your worksheet intentionally, Excel's circular-reference warning usually indicates that you made an error in one of your formulas. Sometimes it takes a little detective work to track down these errors.

To correct the problem, first click OK in the alert box, and then look back at the formula you just entered. Did you inadvertently include the formula cell in your calculation? When you calculate the sum of a series of values, it's easy to select one cell too many and accidentally include the total cell itself in the formula. This kind of error is easy to correct: Simply edit the formula to remove the formula cell reference.

If the circular reference is not immediately obvious, check the cells that the formula references. Do those cells contain references to the formula cell itself? As you've already seen, this type of circular reference is impossible to resolve, no matter how many iterations you specify. One way to quickly find the cells a formula refers to is to double-click the cell that contains the formula. When you do this, all the cells the formula in that cell directly refers to become highlighted, as shown in Figure 3-27. (We formatted this worksheet to display the underlying formulas in each cell.)

FIGURE 3-27.
*When you
double-click a cell that
contains a formula,
any referenced cells
are highlighted.*

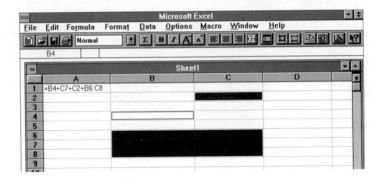

Precision of numeric values

Excel stores numbers with as much as 15-digit accuracy. If you enter an integer that is longer than 15 digits, Excel converts any digits after the fifteenth to zeros. If you enter a decimal fraction that is longer than 15 digits, Excel drops any digits after the fifteenth. In addition, as described in Chapter 2, Excel displays numbers that are too long for their cells in scientific notation.

Thus, if you enter a number like 123456789123456789 in a cell, Excel displays that number as 1.23E+17 but retains only the first 15 digits of the number in the cell. The remaining digits are converted to zeros without rounding, like this:

123456789123456000.

Here are several other examples of how Excel treats integers and decimal fractions longer than 15 digits when they are entered into cells with the default column width of 8.43 characters:

Entry	Displayed value	Underlying value
123456789012345678	1.23E+17	123456789012345000
1.23456789012345678	1.234568	1.23456789012345
1234567890.12345678	1.23E+09	1234567890.12345
123456789012345.678	1.23E+14	123456789012345

Notice that each of the displayed values in the table is eight characters wide, to fit the standard column width in your Excel worksheet. If you change the column width (using the Column Width command, described in Chapter 4), Excel changes the displayed value to fill the width of the cell. Keep in mind that the column width affects only the displayed value of numbers on your worksheet; it has no effect on precision. In other words, Excel stores and calculates numbers with as much as 15-digit accuracy, no matter what the displayed value.

Excel can calculate positive values as large as 1.798E+305 and as small as 2.225E–307. If you create a formula that results in a value outside this range, Excel stores the number as text and assigns a #NUM! error value to the formula cell.

With 15-digit accuracy and the ability to use extremely large numbers, you should be able to perform almost any kind of calculation in your Excel worksheets. In fact, you'll generally want to use numbers less precisely than Excel's standards. For example, when you perform financial calculations, you probably need to round numbers to two decimal places. In Chapter 4, you'll learn how to format the cells in your worksheet to display currency, percentages, fixed decimal places, and other numeric formats.

The Precision as Displayed option

Sometimes, your worksheets can appear erroneous when you use rounded values. For example, the values 1.4 plus 3.2 equal 4.6. But if you round off each of these three values to the nearest whole number, the equation reads 1 plus 3 equals 5. While the underlying values still have their 15-digit precision intact, their appearance in the worksheet might be unacceptable for a particular purpose, such as preparing a presentation. Excel provides an option in the Calculation Options dialog box called Precision as Displayed. When you choose this option, Excel actually discards the underlying values and retains only the displayed values. If you do this, Excel displays a warning message: *Data will permanently lose accuracy,* and offers a chance to cancel the operation. Needless to say, be sure that you won't again need the full precision of your data before you use this option.

The Alternate Expression Evaluation option

Excel interprets text and logical values differently from Lotus 1-2-3. In Excel, if you average a column that contains both numbers and text entries, the text entries are ignored. In contrast, Lotus 1-2-3 treats cells that contain text as zero values. For example, the average of 4, 6, and 8 is 6, while the average of 4, 6, 8, and 0 is 4.5. Quite a difference, and an important factor in the design paradigm used when building your worksheets. When you open a Lotus 1-2-3 worksheet in Excel, the Alternate Expression Evaluation option in the Calculation Options dialog box is automatically activated. With Alternate Expression Evaluation active, Excel interprets text as zero values. It also interprets TRUE as 1 and FALSE as 0 when these values are referred to in formulas.

4

Formatting the Worksheet

*I*n Chapters 2 and 3, you learned to make entries in the worksheet. You may have noticed that all the entries you've made so far have the same format: All numbers (and the numeric results of formulas) are right-aligned and have what is called the General format; all labels are left-aligned. In this chapter, you'll learn to use Microsoft Excel's formatting features to change the formats, alignments, and fonts of text and numeric cell entries. You'll also learn to use borders and to change column widths and row heights. (We'll save the Justify command on the Format menu for Chapter 5. We discussed the Cell Protection command in Chapter 2.)

We'll also examine Excel's new AutoFormat feature, which may become the most important formatting tool you will use. Later in the chapter, we'll explain Excel's worksheet outlining features. This chapter also introduces the concepts of styles and templates.

A *style* is a named combination of format settings that you can use in many different contexts. Styles make it easy not only to assign formatting characteristics, but also to change your mind about them. If all your headings are formatted in one font and you want to change them to a different font, styles let you do that with a single command.

A *template* is a file that you can use as the basis for creating other files. A template can include text and numbers, as well as formatting information. For example, if you create a particular kind of report at the end of every month, you can store the information that's common to each month's report in a template.

Finally, in this chapter you'll learn how to change the overall appearance of the worksheet window and workspace with the Display, Color Palette, and Workspace commands on the Options menu.

Why use formats?

Formatting your worksheets gives them a professional appearance and makes them easier to read and use. Look at the unformatted worksheet in Figure 4-1. Although this worksheet provides much valuable information, the information is difficult to interpret. Important totals and key headings blend into the background, columns look misaligned, and some entries are truncated.

Now look at the formatted worksheet in Figure 4-2. The contents of this worksheet are identical to those of the worksheet in Figure 4-1, but the formatted one looks better and is easier to read.

FIGURE 4-1.
All entries in this worksheet carry default formats.

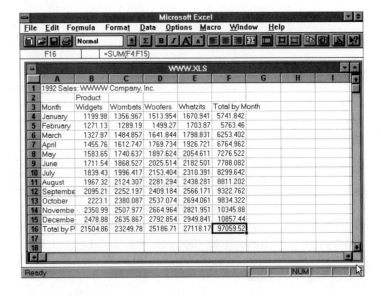

FIGURE 4-2.
*Formatting makes
the worksheet easier
to read.*

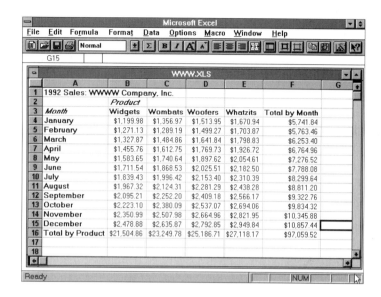

Assigning and removing formats

Formatting is easy: Simply select the cell or range you want to format and choose the appropriate Format menu commands. You can select a single cell, an adjacent range of cells, a nonadjacent range of cells, a named range of cells, an entire column or row, or the entire worksheet. You can even assign a format to empty cells, although the format might not have any visible effect until you make entries in those cells.

For example, to add a dollar sign and commas to the values in cells B4:F16 in Figure 4-1 and round each value to two decimal places, simply select cells B4:F16, choose Number from the Format menu, select Currency from the Value Type list, and select the $#,##0.00_);($#,##0.00) option from the Number Format dialog box. As you can see in Figure 4-2, Microsoft Excel changes the numbers in those cells to display currency values.

After you format a cell, the cell remains formatted until you apply a new format or use the Clear command to remove the format. When you overwrite or edit an entry, you need not reformat the cell.

To remove all assigned formats, select the cell or range of cells whose formats you want to delete and then press Del or choose Clear from the Edit menu. When the Clear dialog box appears, select the Formats option to return the selected cells to their default formats. The values in the cells will not change unless you select All from the Clear dialog box to erase both the contents of the cells and the assigned formats. (If you choose Formulas, values and formulas are removed but the formatting remains unchanged. The Clear command is discussed at length in Chapter 6.)

The Group Edit command on the Options menu allows you to assign formatting characteristics to a common set of cells in two or more worksheets at once. We will examine this feature in detail in Chapter 6.

Formatting with toolbars

As shown in Figure 4-3, the Standard toolbar provides mouse shortcuts for 11 common formatting actions — bold, italics, increase and decrease font size, left, center, and right alignment, center across columns, AutoFormat, outline border, and bottom border. You can also apply styles from the Standard toolbar. These shortcuts are described in detail under their appropriate headings later in this chapter.

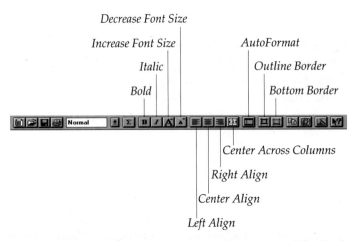

FIGURE 4-3. *You can select 11 formatting options and any defined style from the Standard toolbar.*

To display the Standard toolbar on your screen, choose the Toolbars command from the Options menu. In the Show Toolbars section of the dialog box, select Standard. (A keyboard shortcut for the command to display the Standard toolbar is Ctrl-7. Press this combination a second time to remove the Standard toolbar.) For more information about toolbars, see Chapter 21 and Appendix A.

The Formatting toolbar

Excel provides another toolbar, called the Formatting toolbar, designed specifically for formatting. To display this toolbar, choose the Toolbars command from the Options menu and select Formatting from the Show Toolbars list. A faster alternative to the Toolbars command is to use the shortcut menu (explained in Chapter 1). To display the Formatting toolbar using the shortcut menu, click the right mouse button while the pointer is on any toolbar. From the menu that appears, choose Formatting. The Formatting toolbar appears on your screen below the Standard toolbar, unless you already changed the default toolbar display. Figure 4-4 shows the Formatting toolbar.

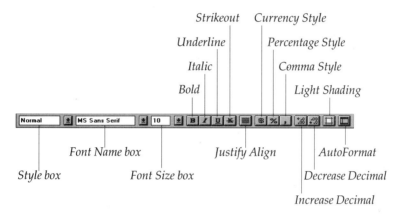

FIGURE 4-4. *The Formatting toolbar.*

As Figure 4-4 shows, the Formatting toolbar increases the set of tools available on the Standard toolbar. The Formatting toolbar provides tools for underline and strike-through font formats; for currency, percent, and comma number formats; to increase and decrease decimal places; to apply light shading to cells; to justify text in cells; and to change fonts and font sizes. The Formatting toolbar also duplicates several tools found on the Standard toolbar, in case you don't want to display them both at the same time. To use a tool, simply select the range of cells you want to format and click the appropriate tool. After it applies the format, the tool changes to its "depressed" appearance. You can remove the format by clicking the depressed tool.

We'll refer to the menu-command and keyboard-command methods of applying formats as we go through this chapter, and to the toolbar methods whenever appropriate.

Using the AutoFormat feature

The AutoFormat tool appears on both the Standard and Formatting toolbars. This tool corresponds to the AutoFormat command on the Format menu, except that the tool applies only to the last-selected format from the AutoFormat dialog box. Excel's automatic formats are predefined combinations of formats: number, border, text alignment, font, pattern, column width, and row height. This gives you a clue to the amount of time you can save by using the AutoFormat command!

To use the AutoFormat tool, you must first enter data into your worksheet. The AutoFormat tool feature works best when you have created a worksheet, complete with formulas, headings, and labels to which you are ready to apply formatting. While you enter your worksheet data, don't bother to add any formatting if you plan to use the AutoFormat feature, because the AutoFormat feature will probably write over any pre-existing formats.

After you enter all the values, labels, and formulas for your worksheet, you are ready to use AutoFormat. First, select any cell in the group of cells you wish to format to define the current region. (The *current region* is the largest contiguous block of cells that contains the active cell, surrounded by blank rows and columns. Excel formats the current region only.) Next, choose the AutoFormat command from the Format menu. The cell selection expands to include the entire current region, and a dialog box like the one in Figure 4-5 appears. (We clicked Options to reveal the Formats to Apply area at the bottom of the dialog box.)

Format before you copy!

When you copy a cell entry, you copy both the contents and the formats assigned to that cell. If the cell you're pasting into is already formatted, the format of the cell you're copying replaces the old format. You can take advantage of this by formatting your source cell before you choose the Copy and Paste commands, the Fill command, or the Series command. For example, suppose you've entered 123 in cell A1. You want to format this cell to display currency with no decimal places, and you also need to copy this value to several other cells. Assign the special format before you use the Copy and Paste commands. Then, when you copy cell A1, the pasted cells will assume identical formats. (We'll talk more about the Cut, Copy, Paste, Fill, and Series commands in Chapter 5.)

FIGURE 4-5.
The AutoFormat dialog box offers a selection of predefined formats you can apply to your worksheet data.

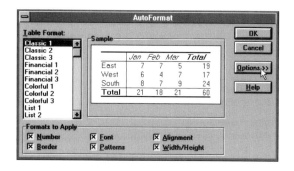

The Table Format list contains 14 predefined formats from which you can choose. Each predefined format appears in the Sample area when you select it from the list. If you click Options, the dialog box expands to reveal the Formats to Apply box, which allows you to select the types of formats currently used in the chosen table format. If you click one of the check boxes to deselect a type of format, the Sample display adjusts so you can see what effect the removal of that format has on the selected table format. In this way, you can customize a vast number of different combinations using the predefined formats as a basis.

Using the worksheet in Figure 4-1, select Colorful 2 from the Table Format list and press Enter. The worksheet now looks like the one in Figure 4-6.

FIGURE 4-6.
In seconds, you can transform a raw worksheet into a presentation-quality piece with the AutoFormat command.

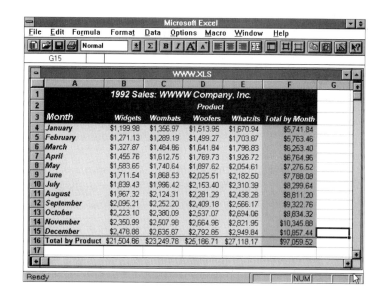

The AutoFormat feature uses the existing formulas and text labels to determine the way formatting is applied. You can use other formatting commands after you use the AutoFormat feature to adjust the overall appearance. If you don't like the way something looks, choose Undo AutoFormat from the Edit menu. Then try adding blank rows to set off areas you don't want AutoFormat to change, or manually select portions of your data for AutoFormat to affect.

Another way to use the AutoFormat feature is to click the AutoFormat tool on either the Standard or Formatting toolbar. When you do this, the last-used automatic format is applied to the current region. If you hold down Shift while repeatedly clicking the AutoFormat tool, Excel cycles through each of the formats in the Table Format list.

The Number command

The Number command on the Format menu controls the display of numeric values. You can also use it to modify the way Microsoft Excel displays text entries. When you choose this command, you'll see a dialog box like the one in Figure 4-7. This box contains a list of 27 built-in numeric formats, divided into 7 categories, plus the self-explanatory All category. You can use these formats to display numbers and formula results as integers, currency, percentages, fractions, dates, times, or exponents.

FIGURE 4-7.
Microsoft Excel offers
27 built-in numeric
formats.

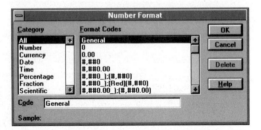

When you select an item from the Category list in the Number Format dialog box, the Format Codes list displays all the formats available in that category. In this chapter, we'll look at the 18 built-in numeric formats in the table on the following page.

Four of the formats in the table include *[Red]* in their codes. These are identical to the formats that precede them in the list, except that negative values are displayed in red. (The remaining built-in formats apply only to date and time values and are discussed in Chapter 9.) We'll also show you how to design your own numeric and text formats and how to change the color of cell entries.

Category	Format Codes
All	General
Number	0
	0.00
	#,##0
	#,##0.00
	#,##0_);(#,##0)
	#,##0_);[Red](#,##0)
	#,##0.00_);(#,##0.00)
	#,##0.00_);[Red](#,##0.00)
Currency	$#,##0_);($#,##0)
	$#,##0_);[Red]($#,##0.00)
	$#,##0.00_);($#,##0.00)
	$#,##0.00_);[Red]($#, ##0.00)
Percentage	0%
	0.00%
Fraction	#?/?
	#??/??
Scientific	0.00E+00

Keep in mind the difference between underlying and displayed worksheet values. Numeric formats do not affect the underlying values in your cells. For example, when we assigned the currency format to cells B4:F16 in Figure 4-2, we did not change the underlying values in those cells. Although cell C4, which contains the number 1356.967, appears as $1,356.97, Microsoft Excel still uses the underlying value, 1356.967, in its calculations.

Also, remember that the Number command's built-in numeric formats do not affect text values. You can assign a numeric format to a range that contains both text and numbers without affecting your text entries. But if you later overwrite a text entry with a number or with a formula that results in a numeric value, the number will take on the format you assigned. (As you'll see in a few pages, you can work with text when you create your own custom formats.)

The General format

The General format appears when you select the All category in the Number Format dialog box. This format usually shows you exactly what you've entered in a cell. If you enter the number 123.45 in a cell with the General format, that cell displays the number 123.45; if you enter the number −654.3, the cell displays the number −654.3.

This rule has three exceptions. First, if a number is too long to appear in its entirety, the General format displays the number in scientific notation or displays only a portion of the number, depending on the type of number and the cell width. In a standard-width cell, integers (numbers with no decimals) with nine or more digits appear in scientific notation. For example, if you enter 12345678901234, the General format displays it as 1.23E+13. Long decimal values, however, are either rounded or displayed in scientific notation, depending on cell width. For example, if you enter 123456.7812345 in a standard-width cell, the General format displays the number as 123456.8.

Second, if you enter a number with trailing zeros, the General format does not display the trailing zeros. For example, if you enter 123.0 in General format, that value will be displayed as 123. To display trailing zeros, choose one of the other built-in numeric formats.

Finally, if you enter a decimal fraction with no number to the left of the decimal point, such as .123, Excel displays that number with a single 0 to the left of the decimal point, as in 0.123.

The number formats

The next eight options in the Number Format dialog box are in the Number category. These options let you display numbers in integer, fixed-decimal, and punctuated formats.

The 0 format displays numbers as integers. For example, if you enter the number 1234.567 in a cell and then assign the 0 format to that cell, Excel rounds the displayed value to 1235.

The 0.00 format displays numbers with two decimal places. If you enter 1234.567 in a cell that has the 0.00 format, the value appears as 1234.57. Notice that the number is rounded to two decimal places. If the number has only one decimal place to start with, Excel adds a zero to the number for display purposes. For example, 1234.5 appears as 1234.50. If the number is an integer, Excel adds a decimal point and two trailing zeros.

The #,##0 and #,##0.00 formats are similar to the 0 and 0.00 formats except that they display numbers with commas between the hundreds and thousands, thousands and millions, and so on. For example, 1234.567 appears as 1,235 under the #,##0 format and as 1,234.57 under the #,##0.00 format. Like the 0.00 format, the #,##0.00 format adds zeros to the number, if needed, to achieve the indicated number of decimal places. You can also apply the #,##0.00 format using the Comma Format tool on the Formatting toolbar.

The #,##0_);(#,##0) and #,##0.00);(#,##0.00) formats are similar to the previous pair of formats, except that negative numbers are displayed in parentheses. Both formats also leave a blank space (the width of a close parenthesis) on the right side of positive values, which is indicated by the _) in each format. This blank space ensures that decimal points align in a column of similarly formatted positive and negative numbers. The last two formats in the Number category are identical to these formats, except that the code *[Red]* appears after the semicolon to indicate that the negative values will appear not only in parentheses, but also in red.

The currency formats

Four built-in currency formats are available in Excel — $#,##0_);($#,##0) and $#,##0.00_);($#,##0.00), — along with their counterparts, which display negative numbers in red, $#,##0_);[Red]($#,##0) and $#,##0.00_);[Red]($#,##0.00). These formats are identical except that the first displays the number with no decimal places and the second displays the number with two decimal places. All four formats place a dollar sign in front of the formatted number and use commas to separate hundreds from thousands, thousands from millions, and so on. You can also apply the $#,##0.00_);[Red]($#,##0.00) format using the Currency Format tool on the Formatting toolbar.

The currency formats have two parts, separated by a semicolon. The first part of each format applies to positive numbers, the second to negative numbers. Both currency formats tell Excel to enclose negative numbers in parentheses. For example, if you enter 1245.22 in a cell that carries the $#,##0.00_);($#,##0.00) format, Excel displays the value $1,245.22; if you enter –1245.22, Excel displays ($1,245.22).

Both formats also leave a blank space (the width of a close parenthesis) on the right side of positive values. This blank space ensures that decimal points align in a column of similarly formatted positive and negative numbers.

The percentage formats

The 0% and 0.00% choices in the Percentage category of the Number Format dialog box display numbers as percentages. When you select one of the percentage formats, the decimal point of the formatted number shifts two places to the right and a percent sign appears at the end of the number. For example, 0.1234 appears as 12% under the 0% format and as 12.34% under the 0.00% format. You can also apply the 0% format by clicking the Percentage Format tool on the Formatting toolbar.

The fraction formats

The two formats in the Fraction category, # ?/? and # ??/??, display fractional amounts as fractions rather than as decimal values. These formats are particularly useful for entering stock prices. The first fractional format uses a single-digit numerator and denominator, while the second uses up to two digits in both the numerator and the denominator.

The scientific (exponential) format

The last category in the Number Format dialog box comprises the single scientific format, 0.00E+00, which displays numbers in scientific, or exponential, notation with two decimal places. For example, the exponential format displays the number 987654321 as 9.88E+08.

The number 9.88E+08 is 9.88 times 10 to the eighth power. The symbol *E* stands for the word *exponent*, a synonym here for the words *10 to the nth power*. The expression *10 to the eighth power* means eight 10's multiplied together ($10 \times 10 \times 10 \times 10 \times 10 \times 10 \times 10 \times 10$), or 100,000,000. Multiplying this value by 9.88 gives 988000000, an approximation of 987654321.

You can also use exponential format to display very small numbers. For example, this format displays 0.000000009 as 9.00E−09, which is 9 times 10 to the negative ninth power. The expression *10 to the negative ninth power* means 1 divided by 10 to the ninth power, or 1 divided by 10 nine times, or 0.000000001. Multiplying this number by 9 gives our original number, 0.000000009.

Typing cell entries in a numeric format

Often, you can format numbers as you enter them. If you include special formatting characters such as dollar signs, percent signs, commas, or fractions when you enter a number in a cell, Excel assigns the appropriate numeric format to that cell.

For example, if you type *$45.00*, Excel interprets your entry as the value 45 formatted as currency with two decimal places — $#,##0.00_);($#,##0.00). Only the value 45 appears in the formula bar, but the formatted value appears in the cell. Similarly, if you enter the number 1 3/8 (with a single space between the 1 and the 3), Excel assigns it the # ?/? format and displays it the way you entered it.

Sometimes Excel has to guess which format you want. If, for example, you enter the number $4444 in a cell, the program assigns the $#,##0_);($#,##0) format to that cell, even though the number you typed lacks a comma. If you enter the number 4,444.4 in a cell, however, Excel assigns the #,##0.00 format to that cell, because no additional characters (such as $ or %) tell it otherwise.

Moreover, if you enter a fraction such as 3/8, without an integer and a space, Excel interprets it as a date; for example, 3/8 is read as March 8 of the current year. To make your intentions clear in this case, enter 0, a space, and then 3/8. Excel ignores the 0 for display purposes but recognizes that you're asking for a fraction, not a date.

Creating your own numeric formats

Excel lets you create custom display formats and save them along with your worksheets. The formats you design can be variations on the built-in formats, or they can be radically different. You can even format worksheet entries to appear in different colors! You use the Format Number command to create a custom format by typing special formatting symbols into the Code text box. New formats are added to the bottom of the Format Codes list. Excel determines the category in which to include your format, based on the codes you use to create it. For example, if you create the 000% format, you will subsequently find it listed in the Percentage category as well as the All category. To create your own formats to add to the list in the Number Format dialog box, select from the symbols in the following table.

Symbol	Meaning
0	Digit placeholder. Ensures that a specified number of digits appears on each side of the decimal point. For example, if the format is 0.000, the value .987 is displayed as 0.987. If the format is 0.0000, the value .987 is displayed as 0.9870. If a number has more digits to the right of the decimal point than 0s specified in the format, the number is rounded. For example, if the format is 0.00, the value .987 is displayed as 0.99.
#	Digit placeholder. Works like 0, except that extra zeros do not appear if the number has fewer digits on either side of the decimal point than #s specified in the format. This symbol shows Excel where to display commas or other separating symbols. The format #,###, for example, tells Excel to display a comma after every third digit to the left of the decimal point. If you want Excel to include commas and display at least one digit to the left of the decimal point in all cases, specify the format #,##0.
?	Digit placeholder. Follows the same rules as for 0, except that space is left for insignificant zeros on either side of the decimal point. This placeholder allows you to align numbers on the decimal points. For example, 1.4 and 1.45 would line up on the decimal point if both were formatted as 0.??.
.	Decimal point. Determines how many digits (0s or #s) appear to the right and left of the decimal point. If the format contains only #s to the left of this symbol, Excel begins numbers smaller than 1 with a decimal point. To avoid this, use 0 as the first digit placeholder to the left of the decimal point instead of #.
%	Percentage indicator. Multiplies by 100 and inserts the % character.

(Continued)

Symbol	Meaning
/	Fraction format character. Displays the fractional part of a number in a nondecimal format. The number of digit placeholders that surround this character determines the accuracy of the display. For example, the decimal fraction 0.269 when formatted # ?/? displays as 1/4, but when formatted # ???/??? displays as 46/171.
,	Thousands separator. Uses commas to separate hundreds from thousands, thousands from millions, and so forth, if the format contains a comma surrounded by #s, 0s, or ?s. When this symbol follows a placeholder without being surrounded by placeholders, it is used as a scaling factor. For example, the format 0, scales by a thousand. The format 0,, scales by a million. The format 0.0, displays 1200 as 1.2.
E− E+ e− e	Scientific format characters. Displays the number in scientific format and inserts E or e in the displayed value if a format contains one 0 or # to the right of an E−, E+, e−, or e+. The number of 0s or #s to the right of the E or e determines the minimum number of digits in the exponent. Use E− or e− to place a negative sign by negative exponents; use E+ or e+ to place both a negative sign by negative exponents and a positive sign by positive exponents.
$ − + ( ) space	Standard formatting characters. Enter these characters directly in your format. To display a character other than , $, −, +, (,), or space, use a backslash (\) before the character or enclose the character in double quotation marks (".").
\	Literal character demarcator. Each character you want to include in the format (except for , $, −, +, (,), and space) must be preceded by a backslash. Excel does not display the backslash. To insert several characters, use the quotation-mark technique described in the "Text" table entry.
_	Underline. Leaves space equal to the width of the next formatting character. For example, _) leaves a space equal to the width of the close parenthesis. Use this formatting character for alignment purposes.
"Text"	Literal character string. Works like the backslash technique except that all text can be included within one set of double quotation marks without separate demarcators for each literal character.
*	Repetition initiator. Repeats the next character in the format enough times to fill the column width. Use only one asterisk in a format.
@	Text placeholder. If the cell contains text, the placeholder inserts that text where the @ appears in the format.

A complete set of date and time formatting symbols is also available in Excel. For more information, see Chapter 9.

Editing existing formats

Often, you can use a built-in format as a starting point for creating your own format. To build on an existing format, select the cells you want to format and choose the Format Number command. Select the format you want to change from the Format Codes list box, and then edit the contents of the Code text box the same way you edit a cell entry in the formula bar. The original format will not be affected by your changes. The new format is appended to the list of numeric formats in the Format Codes list box.

For example, to create a format to display percentages with three decimal places, select the 0.00% format, place the insertion point between the last 0 and the % sign in the Code list box, and add another 0. Then click OK or press Enter. Excel applies the new format to the selected range in your worksheet. When you choose the Number command again, your new format appears at the end of the listing in the Number Format dialog box so you can assign this custom format to other cells in the worksheet without having to re-create the format each time.

Building new formats from scratch

To create a new numeric format from scratch, select the cells you want to format and choose the Format Number command. Next, instead of selecting an option in the Format Codes list box, select the contents of the Code text box at the bottom of the dialog box and type the format. When you begin typing, the highlighted characters in the box disappear and the characters you type appear. When you finish, click OK. The contents of the selected range appear in the new format and your custom format is appended to the list in the dialog box.

For example, suppose you're creating an inventory worksheet and you want all the entries in the range A5:A100 to appear in the format *Part XXX-XXXX*. To create this format, first select the range A5:A100 and choose the Number command. Next, instead of selecting one of the standard options, select the contents of the Code text

---

Check the Sample line!

Formatting symbols are not the easiest Excel feature to understand. While you're learning to use them — and even after you've mastered them — you'll find the Sample line at the bottom of the Number Format dialog box invaluable. As you scroll through the list of built-in formats, the Sample line shows you how the value in the active cell appears in each format.

box, type *"Part" 000-0000,* and click OK. Now begin making entries in column A. (You might have to widen the column. Choose the Column Width command on the Edit menu and select Best Fit.) Simply type the numbers for each part; Excel will add the word *Part* and the hyphen. For example, if you select cell A10 and enter *1234567,* Excel displays the entry as Part 123-4567.

Similarly, to create a telephone number format for your worksheet, you can use the format *(000) 000-0000.* Then, when you enter *2125551212* in a cell with that format, Excel displays the entry as (212) 555-1212.

Using formats in this way lets you evaluate the numeric values of the entries, if you want. In contrast, if you type *123-4567* directly in a cell, Excel treats it as text because it is in an unfamiliar numeric format.

Formatting positive, negative, zero, and text entries

Excel assigns different formats to positive and negative currency values in your worksheet. You can also specify different formats for positive and negative values when you create custom formats, and you can specify how you want zero and text values to appear.

You can create custom formats with up to four parts, with the portions separated by semicolons, like this:

Positive format;Negative format;Zero format;Text-value format

---

Displaying selected zero values

When you use the Options Display command to deselect the Zero Values option, Excel suppresses the display of every zero value in your worksheet unless you explicitly instruct otherwise. If you want some zero values to remain in view in your worksheet, you can use the Number command on the Format menu to build a three-part custom format to display those cell entries.

As explained earlier, the third set of instructions you enter in the Format text box applies to zero values. Thus, if you want to create a currency format that displays zero values as $0.00, you enter the following instructions in the Format text box of the Number dialog box:

$#,##0.00_);($#,##0.00);$0.00

If your custom format includes only one part, Excel applies that format to positive, negative, and zero values. If your custom format includes two parts, the first format applies to positive and zero values; the second format applies only to negative values. Unless you explicitly include text-value formatting in a custom format, your instructions have no effect on text in cells that use that custom format. Text-value formatting instructions must be the last element in the format specification.

For example, suppose you're creating a billing statement worksheet and you want to format the entries in the Amount Due column to display different text, depending on the value in each cell. You might create a format like this:

"Amount Due: "$#,##0.00_);"Credit: "($#,##0.00);"Let's call it even.";"Please note: "@

The following table shows the effects of this format on various worksheet entries:

Entry	Display
12.98	Amount due: $12.98
−12.98	Credit: ($12.98)
0	Let's call it even.
This is not a bill.	Please note: This is not a bill.

If you want to specify a custom label format without changing the formats for your positive, negative, and zero values, enter only the text-value element of the format specification. The @ symbol alerts Excel that the format applies only to labels.

Adding color to your formats

In addition to controlling the display of numeric values, the Number command can change the color of selected cell entries, giving you tremendous flexibility for emphasizing selected areas of your worksheet. For example, you can use different colors to help distinguish the categories of information in a worksheet model, or you can apply a color to the Total cells to make them stand out from the rest of your worksheet data. You can even assign colors to selected numerical ranges so that, for example, all values above or below a specified threshold appear in a contrasting color. Of course, the colors you assign don't appear on printed worksheets unless you have a color printer.

NOTE: *You can also use the Format Font command, described later in this chapter, to change the color of a cell entry. But the colors specified with the Format Number command take precedence over the colors specified with Format Font command.*

To change the color of an entry, type the name of the color you want, in brackets, in front of the definition of the format. For example, suppose you want the totals in row 16 of the worksheet shown in Figure 4-2 to appear in blue. If you also want these values to appear in currency format with two decimal places, you can simply edit Excel's built-in $#,##0.00_);($#,##0.00) format to create a custom format, like this:

[Blue]$#,##0.00_);($#,##0.00)

This format tells Excel to display positive and zero values in blue. Text and negative values appear in Excel's default color, black.

Even if you want to use Excel's default General format to display your work-sheet entries, you can specify color options for different types of entries by typing the colors you want to use in the Format text box. For example, the custom format

[Blue];[Red];[Yellow];[Green]

tells Excel to display positive values in blue, negative values in red, zero values in yellow, and labels in green. Of course, you can add color to your custom formats as well.

You can specify the following color names in your formats: BLACK, BLUE, CYAN, GREEN, MAGENTA, RED, WHITE, and YELLOW. You can also specify a color as COLORn, where n is a number between 1 and 16. If you use the COLORn syntax,

---

The "hidden" format

If you want to ensure that certain sets of values do not appear in your worksheet, you can "hide" those values by assigning them a null format. To create a null format, enter only the semicolon separator for that portion of the format, with no other formatting symbols. For example, if you want positive and text values to appear in your worksheet but you want to hide negative and zero values, use a format like this:

$#,##0.00;;

This format tells Excel to display positive numbers in the currency format. The two semicolons instruct the program to hide negative and zero values. Because we did not include a third semicolon separator for text entries, Excel displays those entries.

To hide all the entries in a cell, create a custom format that consists only of three semicolons, like this:

;;;

Excel selects the corresponding color from your worksheet's current 16-color palette. If that color happens to be a *dithered* color (a color achieved by mixing dots of two or more solid colors), Excel uses the nearest solid color for your format.

For more information about Excel's color palette, see "Customizing the color palette," later in this chapter.

Conditional formatting

Earlier you learned how to create different formats for positive, negative, zero, and text entries. Excel also provides a way to make the format dependent on the value of the cell. You can add a condition to the first two parts of the standard four-part custom format, replacing the standard positive and negative formats. The third format becomes the default format for values that don't match the other two conditions.

For example, if you are tracking Accounts Receivable balances in Excel and you want to show accounts with a balance over $50,000 in blue, you might create a format like this

[Blue][>50000]$#,##0.00_);[Red][<0]($#,##0.00);$#,##0.00

This format displays values over $50,000 in blue, negative values in red, and all other values in the default color.

Conditional formatting can be a powerful aid if you need to scale numbers. For example, if your company produces a product that requires a few milliliters of a compound for each unit and you make thousands of units every day, when you budget the usage you will need to convert from milliliters to liters and kiloliters. Excel can make this conversion with the following numeric format:

[>999999]#,##0,,_m"kl";[>999]#,_k_m"l";#_k"ml"

The following table shows the effects of this format on various worksheet entries:

Entry	Display
72	72 ml
24680	25 l
7286957	7 kl
5876953782	5,877 kl

As you can see, using a combination of the conditional format, the thousands separator, and the proportional space indicator can improve both the readability and effectiveness of your worksheet, without increasing the number of formulas you need.

Deleting custom formats

To delete a format from the Number dialog box, simply select the format you want
to remove and then click Delete. You can delete only those formats you create; you
cannot delete any of the built-in selections.

The Alignment command

The Alignment command controls the positioning of text and numbers within the
boundaries of a cell. You can also use this command to create multi-line text labels
or to repeat a series of characters within one or more cells. You can also format text
vertically in cells. As you can see in Figure 4-8, Microsoft Excel offers seven mutually
exclusive alignment options: General, Left, Center, Right, Fill, Justify, and Center
across selection. You can select the Wrap Text check box with any of the alignment
options. The Vertical text options give you control over both orientation and vertical
alignment.

FIGURE 4-8.
Excel offers many
alignment options.

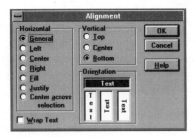

General is the default alignment option. When you use the General format, cells
that contain numeric values are always right-aligned and cells that contain labels
are always left-aligned.

The Left, Right, and Center options

The Left, Right, and Center options align the contents of the selected cells to the left,
right, or the center of the cell. For example, look at the entries in the worksheet in
Figure 4-9. The entries in cells B1 and C1 have the General alignment. Therefore, the

FIGURE 4-9.
Use the Alignment command to change the alignment of cell entries.

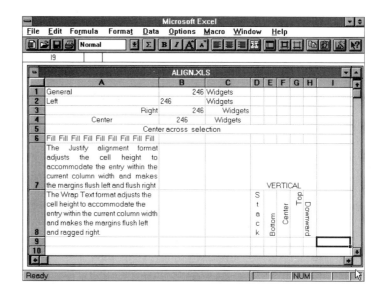

number in cell B1 is right-aligned and the label in cell C1 is left-aligned. The entries in cells B2:C2 are left-aligned, those in B3:C3 are right-aligned, and those in B4:C4 are centered.

Centering text across columns

If you have a single heading that you want to center over three equal columns, it is easy to type the heading above the center column and format it with Center alignment. But what do you do if you have four columns, or if the columns are not equal? Excel's Center across selection alignment option provides the solution.

Before we used the AutoFormat command on the worksheet in Figure 4-2, the *Product* heading was in column B, above Widgets. But in Figure 4-6, *Product* appears incorrectly centered over all five columns that contain numbers. In this case, part of the AutoFormat process was to apply the Center across selection format to cells B2:F2, a common location for a main table heading. As a result, the contents of cell B2 appear centered across all the cells to the right that have the same format.

The Center Across Columns tool on the Standard toolbar appears depressed when you select a cell with the Center across selection format. If you select cell F2 in Figure 4-6, and click the Center Across Columns tool, the label *Product* adjusts to become correctly centered over columns B through E, as shown in Figure 4-10 on the following page.

FIGURE 4-10.
*You can use the
Center Across
Column tool to
make a title span
several columns.*

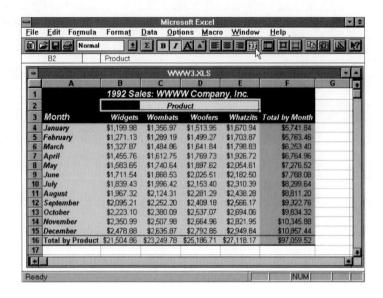

Month	Widgets	Wombats	Woofers	Whatzits	Total by Month
January	$1,199.98	$1,356.97	$1,513.95	$1,670.94	$5,741.84
February	$1,271.13	$1,289.19	$1,499.27	$1,703.87	$5,763.46
March	$1,327.87	$1,484.86	$1,641.84	$1,798.83	$6,253.40
April	$1,455.76	$1,612.75	$1,769.73	$1,926.72	$6,764.96
May	$1,583.65	$1,740.64	$1,897.62	$2,054.61	$7,276.52
June	$1,711.54	$1,868.53	$2,025.51	$2,182.50	$7,788.08
July	$1,839.43	$1,996.42	$2,153.40	$2,310.39	$8,299.64
August	$1,967.32	$2,124.31	$2,281.29	$2,438.28	$8,811.20
September	$2,095.21	$2,252.20	$2,409.18	$2,566.17	$9,322.76
October	$2,223.10	$2,380.09	$2,537.07	$2,694.06	$9,834.32
November	$2,350.99	$2,507.98	$2,664.96	$2,821.95	$10,345.88
December	$2,478.88	$2,635.87	$2,792.85	$2,949.84	$10,857.44
Total by Product	$21,504.86	$23,249.78	$25,186.71	$27,118.17	$97,059.52

Selecting alignment from the toolbars

If you have a mouse, you can select Left, Right, Center, or Center across selection alignment by clicking the corresponding tools on the Standard toolbar. The tools for these commands are shown in Figure 4-3. Also, the Formatting toolbar provides the Justify alignment tool, which is shown in Figure 4-4.

Note that the alignment tools are three-dimensional. When you "turn on" one of these alignment options, the appearance of its button changes to show that you have pressed the button. You can always glance at the toolbar, therefore, to see whether one of these three alignment options applies to the active cell.

To turn an alignment option off (and return the active cell to General alignment), click the button a second time.

Vertical text in cells

Excel's new vertical alignment options let you enter text or numbers in cells with three vertical orientation options and three vertical alignment options. You can format your entries to read from top to bottom, from bottom to top, or vertically in line. Figure 4-9 shows these variations, as well as the bottom, top, and center vertical alignment options.

The Fill option

The Fill option repeats your cell entry to fill the width of the column. For example, suppose cell A5 contains a formula that totals the entries in cells A1 through A3. You can enter a row of hyphens in cell A4 to separate the values in cells A1:A3 from the total in cell A5. To do this, enter a single hyphen in cell A4 and then choose the Alignment command. When you select the Fill option in the Alignment dialog box and click OK, Excel repeats the hyphen across cell A4, as shown in Figure 4-11.

FIGURE 4-11.
Use the Fill option to repeat a character across a cell.

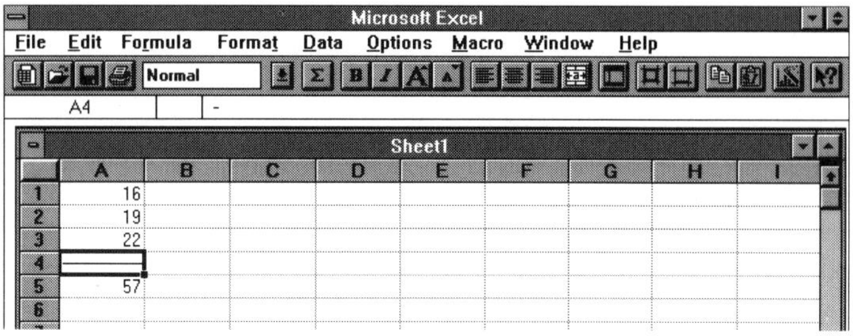

Although cell A4 seems to contain 12 hyphens, the formula bar reveals that the actual entry in the cell is a single hyphen. Like the other Format menu commands, the Alignment command's Fill option affects only the appearance, not the underlying contents, of the cell.

Although the entries you repeat with the Fill alignment option will usually be single characters such as a hyphen (-), an asterisk (*), or an equal sign (=), you can use this command to repeat multi-character entries as well.

You might think it would be as easy to type the repeating characters as it is to use Fill. However, the Fill option offers two important advantages. First, if you adjust the column width, Excel increases or decreases the number of characters in the cell to accommodate the new column width. In addition, the Fill option lets you repeat a single character across several adjacent cells in your worksheet. For example, in the sample worksheet shown in Figure 4-12 on the following page, we created a series of hyphens across cells A4:D4. To create this line, we entered a single hyphen in cell A4; next we selected cells A4:D4 and assigned the Fill alignment format to that range. Excel repeats the hyphen characters across the entire range, with no breaks between cells. Although they appear to contain entries, cells B4:D4 are empty.

The Justify command vs. the Justify format

Do not confuse the Justify alignment format with the Justify command on the Format menu. The Justify alignment format wraps text within a cell and adjusts the row height as necessary, displaying the cell contents with flush left and right margins. In contrast, the Justify command redistributes a text entry in as many cells below it as necessary, actually dividing the text into separate chunks. See Chapter 5 for more information about the Justify command.

FIGURE 4-12.
*You can also use the
Fill option to repeat a
character across
several adjacent cells.*

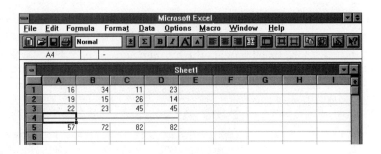

The Fill Alignment option has one hazard: Because it affects numeric values as well as text, it can cause a number to look like something it isn't. For example, if you apply the fill alignment to an eight-character-wide cell that contains the number 3, it will appear to contain 33333333.

The Wrap Text and Justify options

If you enter a label that's too wide for the active cell, Excel extends the label past the cell border and into adjacent cells — provided those cells are empty. If you select the Alignment command's Wrap Text check box, however, Excel displays your label entirely within the active cell. To accommodate the entire label, Excel increases the height of the row in which the cell is located and then "wraps" the text onto additional lines. Figure 4-9 includes an example of a multi-line label formatted with the Wrap Text option.

Similarly, the Justify option wraps text in the active cell and adjusts the row height accordingly. But instead of allowing the right margin of the text in the cell to be ragged, the Justify option forces the text to align flush with the right margin, as shown in Figure 4-9. See "The Justify command vs. the Justify format," earlier in this chapter.

If you create a multi-line label, and then subsequently deselect the Wrap Text or Justify option, you must return the cell to its original row height manually; see "Row height with the Wrap Text and Justify formats," later in this chapter.

You may find multi-line text entries a convenient way to document your worksheets and macros. Excel also provides two other important annotation tools: notes and text boxes. Notes are described in Chapter 5 and text boxes are described in Chapter 7. For more lengthy annotations, you can embed text created in a word processing application that supports object linking and embedding. Object linking and embedding (OLE) is described in Chapter 22.

Text alignment prefix characters

Using text alignment prefix characters, you can specify the alignment of text entries as you type them into cells, as you can with Lotus 1-2-3. As you type, precede each cell entry with one of the text alignment prefix characters shown in the following table to specify the left, right, center, or fill alignment formats. Because these characters convert the contents of the cell to text, you cannot use them when you enter formulas or numeric values. For more information about this feature, see Chapter 2.

Character	Action
'	Left-aligns characters
"	Right-aligns characters
^	Centers characters
\	Repeats characters to fill cell

The Font command

The Font command lets you select the typeface, size, character style, and color of your cell entries. You can use as many as 255 fonts in a single worksheet. You might select different typefaces and sizes to emphasize major headings, or you might use bold, italic, underline, and regular type styles to distinguish different kinds of information.

To specify a font for a cell or range, select that cell or range and then choose the Font command from the Format menu. You'll see the dialog box shown in Figure 4-13. To return to the font and size defined by the Normal style, just click the Normal Font check box. (We'll discuss styles later in this chapter.)

FIGURE 4-13.
The Font dialog box lets you assign typefaces, sizes, character styles, and colors to your words and numbers.

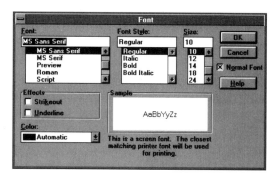

Selecting a typeface

Technically, the term *font* refers to a combination of typeface, size, and character style. In Microsoft Excel's Font dialog box, however, the word is used to refer to a typeface. In the list box labeled Font, you'll find the names of the available typefaces. To specify a typeface, click its name.

Below the Sample area in the dialog box is a message that informs you whether the selected font is a screen font, a printer font, or a TrueType font. Screen fonts and printer fonts are a complicated topic. Suffice it to say that because the mechanics of printing and screen display are so different, separate fonts are usually needed to optimize the display and the printed output. If you select a printer font, Excel uses the closest screen font available for the display. If you select a screen font, Excel uses the closest printer font to print out. TrueType fonts are dual-purpose fonts that are designed to more closely correlate the display with the printed output.

Selecting a size

When you select a typeface in the Font list box, the numbers in the Size list box change to show the sizes at which Excel can print that typeface optimally. To specify one of those sizes, simply select it.

In the text box directly below the Size list, you can specify an unlisted size if you want. For example, when you select the MS Sans Serif typeface, the Size list shows six sizes from 8 to 24 points. If you want to use another size — say, 19 — type that number in the box directly below the Size list.

Some of the fonts listed in the Fonts dialog box take on a distorted, "jaggy" appearance if you try to use them at unlisted sizes. TrueType fonts, however, are designed to be scalable. You can get good results with these fonts at virtually any size. (Excel will accept sizes from 1 to 409 point.) TrueType fonts are identified with the prefix TT in the Fonts dialog box.

Selecting font styles and effects

Excel offers four font styles for most fonts: Regular, Bold, Italic, and Bold Italic. In addition, you have two Effects options: Strikeout and Underline. For any given typeface and size, you must select one of the font styles, normally the Regular font style, and either or both of the Effects options. Select the option from the Font Style list and select the check box next to the effect you want to use.

Selecting font formats with the toolbar

If you have a mouse, you can apply several font format options using tools located on the Standard or Formatting toolbar. Between them, the two toolbars include the following tools: Bold, Italic, Increase Font Size, Decrease Font Size, Font Name box, Font Size box, Underline, and Strikeout. You can use these choices singly or in combination. To remove a tool-applied format from a cell or range, select it and click the tool again to turn it off. See Figure 4-3 for the Standard toolbar and Figure 4-4 for the Formatting toolbar.

Selecting a color

In the lower left corner of the Font dialog box, you'll find a drop-down list labeled Color. To see your color choices, click the downward-pointing arrow beside this list or press Alt-C followed by Alt-Down arrow.

If you choose Automatic (the default color option), Excel displays the contents of your cell in the color assigned to "Window text" in the Windows Control Panel. That color is black unless you change it to another color. (For information about the Windows Control Panel, consult your *Microsoft Windows User's Guide*.)

The other 16 color choices offered in the drop-down list represent your current color palette. If you don't see the color you want there, you can customize the palette. See "Customizing the color palette," later in this chapter.

The Border command

The Border command lets you add borders and shading to cells in your worksheet. These can be effective devices for dividing your worksheet into defined areas or for drawing attention to important cells.

NOTE: Borders often make a greater visual impact when worksheet gridlines are removed. The Options Display command, described later in this chapter, lets you remove gridlines from your worksheet.

As you can see in Figure 4-14 on the following page, the dialog box that appears when you choose the Border command lets you specify the style of line you want to use, the color of the line, the placement of your borders, and whether you want to apply shading. Although the shading option appears here in the Border dialog box, you can use this option with or without borders.

FIGURE 4-14.
The Border command
on the Format menu
lets you assign seven
styles of borders in 16
colors.

Selecting a line style

Microsoft Excel offers seven border-line styles: three kinds of broken lines, three solid weights, and a double line. The last is particularly useful for underscoring columns of numbers above a total. To select a line style, click the box that contains the type of line you want to use.

Selecting line color

The default color for borders is called "Automatic." This choice displays the border in the color currently selected in the Display Options dialog box. (See "The Display, Color Palette, and Workspace commands," later in this chapter.)

To select a color other than Automatic, click the downward-pointing arrow in the lower right corner of the dialog box. (With the keyboard, press Alt-C, then Alt-Down arrow.) The drop-down list box unfolds, revealing the current 16-color palette. You can use one of these colors, or you can modify the palette to change these choices. (For details about modifying the palette, see "Customizing the color palette," later in this chapter.)

Selecting border placement

After you select a line style and color, tell Excel where you want to put your border. The placement options are Outline, Left, Right, Top, and Bottom. If you select Outline, Excel puts a line around the perimeter of the current selection, whether it is a single cell or a block of cells. If you select Left, a line is drawn along the left edge of each cell in your selection — and so on.

To select a placement option, click the box to the left of that option. Excel responds by displaying a sample of the border line in the adjacent box. If the line sample is not satisfactory, click a different Style option, and then reselect your placement option.

Applying two or more borders at once

You can apply more than one kind of border to a cell selection. For example, you can apply a heavy outline border to a block of cells and, at the same time, apply a set of light-weight border lines to the right border of each cell in the selection. The worksheet in Figure 4-15 shows another possible combination of border styles. Excel lets you mix and match border styles in any way that pleases your eye.

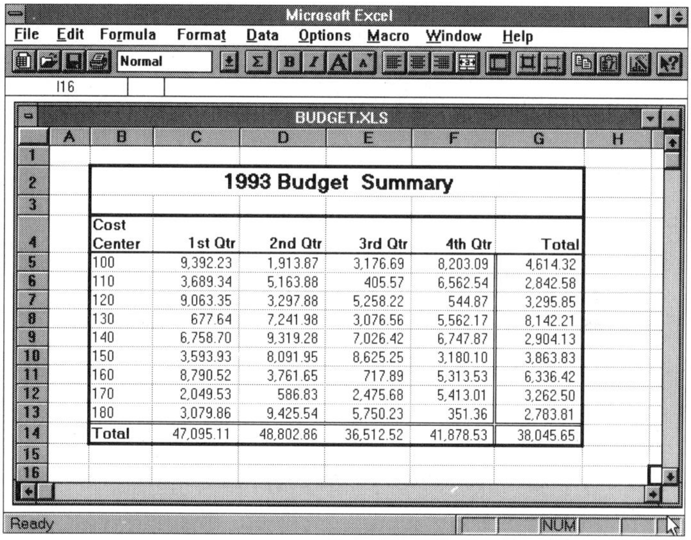

1993 Budget Summary					
Cost Center	1st Qtr	2nd Qtr	3rd Qtr	4th Qtr	Total
100	9,392.23	1,913.87	3,176.69	8,203.09	4,614.32
110	3,689.34	5,163.88	405.57	6,562.54	2,842.58
120	9,063.35	3,297.88	5,258.22	544.87	3,295.85
130	677.64	7,241.98	3,076.56	5,562.17	8,142.21
140	6,758.70	9,319.28	7,026.42	6,747.87	2,904.13
150	3,593.93	8,091.95	8,625.25	3,180.10	3,863.83
160	8,790.52	3,761.65	717.89	5,313.53	6,336.42
170	2,049.53	586.83	2,475.68	5,413.01	3,262.50
180	3,079.86	9,425.54	5,750.23	351.36	2,783.81
Total	47,095.11	48,802.86	36,512.52	41,878.53	38,045.65

FIGURE 4-15.
This budget worksheet makes use of several border styles.

Adding shading

You can also use the Shade option in the Border dialog box to add emphasis to selected cells in your worksheet. For example, you might use shading to set apart worksheet totals or to draw attention to cells in which you want the user to make an entry in a worksheet template. Figure 4-16 shows how you can use shading to create a "banding" effect. In this case, the shading helps the reader follow a row of numbers while reading from left to right. Banding is particularly useful when you want to print wide reports without gridlines.

FIGURE 4-16.
Shading can be used for emphasis or, as in this example, to help distinguish rows of numbers.

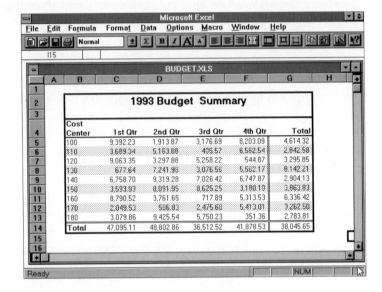

When you apply shading by selecting the Shade check box in the Border dialog box, Excel fills the selected cells with the default shading pattern — a black-on-white dot pattern of medium density. You can choose a different pattern, or different foreground and background colors, by choosing the Patterns command from the Format menu. (See "The Patterns command," later in this chapter.)

Changing or removing borders

If you change your mind about a border style, simply reselect the cell block and choose the Border command again. The dialog box will show what border styles have already been applied. For example, suppose you want to change a solid bottom border to a double line. When the dialog box appears, you'll see a solid line next to the word Bottom. To make the change, first select the double-line style, and then select Bottom again. The double line replaces the solid line. Now click OK.

In the same example, if you want to remove the solid bottom border, you can do either of two things. You can select Bottom without selecting another style, which makes the solid line disappear from the box. Or you can select the "null" line style (the empty box in the Style section) and then reselect Bottom.

Sometimes you might see solid gray in the box to the left of one or more of the placement options. This means that the cells in your selection do not all share the same border style for the placement option in question. For example, if you select cells B2:G14 in the worksheet shown in Figure 4-16, and then choose the Format Border command, you will see the dialog box shown in Figure 4-17.

FIGURE 4-17.
Solid gray next to an option means that the format applies to some, but not all, of the selected cells.

In this case, the cells in column B have a heavy border on their left. Those in column C do not have a heavy left border. Therefore, Excel displays gray instead of either line style in the box next to the word Left. The Right, Top, and Bottom placement options and the Shade check box are marked with gray for the same reason.

In this example, to change all the left borders to the same style — a dotted line, say — first select the dotted-line option in the Style section, and then reselect the Left placement option. Excel replaces the gray with a dotted line. To remove all left borders from all the cells in the selection, click the Left option twice (until the box next to Left becomes empty), or select the null line style and then reselect Left.

Removing shading

To remove shading from an area, select that area, choose the Format Border command again, deselect the Shade check box, and then click OK or press Enter.

If, when you redisplay the Border dialog box, you see gray in the Shade check box instead of an X, it means one of two things:

- Shading is now applied to only some of the current cell selection.
- A shading pattern has been assigned by means of the Patterns command.

When you select this check box again, the gray is replaced by an X. Now the default shading is applied to the entire selection. When you select the check box one more time, the X goes away, leaving the check box blank. If you now click OK or press Enter, your cell selection is redrawn with all shading removed.

Selecting border formats with the toolbars

If you have a mouse you can apply several frequently used combinations of border formats using tools located on the Standard or the Formatting toolbar. Between them, the two toolbars include the following tools: Outline Border, Bottom Border, and Light Shading. You can use choices singly or in combination. To remove a format from a cell or range that was applied with one of these tools, select the cell or range, and click the tool again to turn it off. The exception to this rule is the Outline tool. Because the Outline Border format is really a combination of the Left, Right, Top, and Bottom Border formats, you must remove each format individually using the Border command. Figure 4-3 shows the Standard toolbar, and Figure 4-4 shows the Formatting toolbar.

The Patterns command

The Patterns command on the Format menu lets you apply a variety of shading styles to a selection of cells. (To apply Microsoft Excel's default shading style, you'll probably find it easier to use the Format Border command. See "Adding shading," earlier in this chapter.)

The Format Patterns dialog box includes three drop-down list boxes, labeled Pattern, Foreground, and Background, as shown in Figure 4-18.

FIGURE 4-18.
The Format Patterns command lets you choose styles and colors.

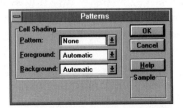

The Pattern drop-down list includes 18 options you can use to add shading patterns to your cells and one option to specify no patterns. The options offer black, 5 gray shades, 12 patterns, and None, which is the default option. Figure 4-19 shows the 18 shading patterns available.

The Foreground and Background drop-down boxes each open to reveal Excel's current 16-color palette. You can choose among 18 styles of shading in any of these colors or modify the palette to create different choices. (For details about modifying the palette, see "Customizing the color palette," later in this chapter.) Whatever

FIGURE 4-19.
Each of these 18 cells has been assigned a different pattern using the Patterns command.

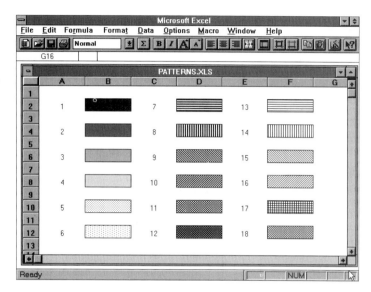

combination of pattern and colors you pick, the Sample box at the lower right corner of the Patterns dialog box lets you see how your selections will appear when applied to the worksheet.

To return the Patterns settings to their default state (a medium density black-on-white dot pattern), select the pattern labeled None.

Controlling column width

Microsoft Excel's default column width is 8.43 characters. This does not mean that each cell in your worksheet can display only 8.43 characters, however. Because Excel uses proportionally spaced fonts (such as MS Sans Serif) as well as fixed-pitch fonts (such as Courier), each character may take up a different amount of space in the worksheet. However, a default-width column can hold 8.43 numbers in most 10-point fixed-pitch fonts.

Often, the standard column width is not wide enough to display the complete contents of a cell. When a label is too long, it runs over into adjacent cells; if the adjacent cell contains an entry, the label is truncated. When you enter a long number into a narrow column that has the General numeric format, that number appears in scientific notation. If, when you assign a numeric format to a cell, its entry is too long to fit in that format, a series of pound signs (#) appears.

To display the entire contents of the cell, change the width of the column or columns that contain the long entries. Excel offers several ways to control the width of cells in a worksheet.

Using the mouse to change column widths

A simple mouse maneuver allows you to change the width of one column at a time. To use this feature, place the mouse pointer in the column-header area, on the divider line that divides the column you want to change from its neighbor to the right. For example, to widen or narrow column A, you put the pointer in the column-header area, on the divider line separating column A from column B. When you do this, your mouse pointer changes to a double-headed arrow. Now hold down the mouse button and drag the column divider to the left or right. While you are doing this the width of the column is displayed in the left portion of the formula bar. When you've changed the column's width to your satisfaction, release the mouse button.

To change the width of more than one column at a time, click on the column headers of the columns you want to change. (You can choose nonadjacent columns by holding down Ctrl as you select the columns.) Next, change the width of one of the columns as previously described. When you release the mouse button, all of the columns change simultaneously to exactly the same width.

Using the keyboard to change column widths

You can also change the widths of columns using the keyboard. Simply select cells in each of the columns you want to change. (You can select nonadjacent columns by holding down Ctrl as you select the columns.) Then choose the Column Width command from the Format menu. To change the widths of all columns in the worksheet, click one of the row headers at the left edge of the worksheet (or select any cell and press Shift-Spacebar) before you choose the Column Width command.

When you choose the Column Width command, you'll see a dialog box like the one shown in Figure 4-20. If all the columns you select are the same width, that width appears in the dialog-box text box; if the columns you select are different widths, the text box is blank. Either way, type a number from 0 through 255 in integer or decimal-fraction form. (The old width setting disappears as soon as you begin typing.) When you click OK, Excel redraws your worksheet and adjusts the selected columns.

FIGURE 4-20.
Use the Column
Width dialog box to
change the widths of
columns.

If you want to restore the default width of one or more columns, select any cells in those columns, choose the Column Width command, and select the Use Standard Width check box. As soon as you select Use Standard Width, the standard column width appears in the Column Width box. Then simply click OK. You can change the Standard Width setting to any size you choose by simply typing a new value in the Standard Width text box. All columns currently set to Standard Width in your worksheet will adjust to the new setting.

Automatically fitting a column to its widest entry

Excel can automatically adjust the width of a column so that it accommodates the column's widest label or numeric entry. If you have a mouse, you can take advantage of this feature by double-clicking the column's column divider. For example, to make column F in Figure 4-1 wide enough to fit the label "Total by Month" (the widest entry in that column), move the mouse to the column-header area and double-click the divider line between column F and column G.

If you don't have a mouse, you can adjust a column's width automatically by choosing the Column Width command from the Format menu and pressing Alt-B to select the Best Fit button.

If you select multiple columns and then use either method to activate the Best Fit command, Excel sizes each of the columns to its own best width.

Be aware that if you add a longer entry to a column after automatically adjusting its width, you will need to use the automatic-adjustment feature again. Also, depending on which font you are using, characters that appear to fit within the column on screen may not fit within the column when you print the worksheet. Excel includes a Print Preview command, however, that lets you make any necessary column-width adjustments before you print a worksheet. (Print Preview is discussed in Chapter 12.)

Hiding a column

You may, on occasion, want to hide certain information in your worksheet. For example, suppose you're developing a departmental budget and need to list employee salaries and benefits in your worksheet in order to forecast next year's personnel expenditures. You may want to display overall salary information without revealing sensitive information about individual employees.

Excel doesn't offer a built-in way to completely hide selected cells in your worksheet. On the one hand, you can use the Hide option in the Cell Protection dialog box to hide formulas, but not the displayed values of the cells; on the other hand, the null Number format hides the cell display but not the formulas. You can use the Options Workspace command to suppress the display of the formula bar, but then you won't see formulas for any cell on any worksheet. You can, however, conceal sensitive information by hiding an entire column.

To hide a column with the mouse, drag the column separator to the left until it crosses into the next column. For example, to hide column G, put the mouse pointer on the line that separates columns G and H in the column-header area. Drag the column separator to the left until you reach column F, and then release the mouse button.

To hide a column with the keyboard, select the column, choose the Column Width command from the Format menu, and then press Alt-H to select the Hide button.

To redisplay a hidden column with the mouse, position the mouse pointer to the right of the column divider for the next column to the left, and then drag the column divider to the right until the column reaches the described width. To restore the column width to its previous setting, select a range of cells that spans the hidden column, and then use the Unhide button on the Column Width dialog box. For example, if column G is hidden, select the cells in columns F through H. Then choose the Format Column Width command and click Unhide.

Controlling row height

Microsoft Excel automatically adjusts the standard height of a row to accommodate the largest font used in that row. For example, when the largest font used in row 1 is 10-point MS Sans Serif, the standard height for that row (on a system with a VGA display) is 12.75. If you apply 12-point Times New Roman to a cell in row 1, however, the standard height of the entire row automatically becomes 15.75. (Like font size, row height is measured in points. One point equals $\frac{1}{72}$ of an inch. Thus, a row with a height of 12.75 is a little over $\frac{1}{6}$ inch tall.)

If you don't make any row-height adjustments yourself, Excel generally uses its standard row height. The exception to this rule is that Excel does not automatically reduce a row's height if you delete words from a cell formatted with the Wrap Text feature. See "Row height with the Wrap Text and Justify formats," later in this chapter. Thus, you don't usually need to worry about characters being too tall to fit in a row.

If you want, however, you can override the standard height of any row. Adjusting the height of a row is similar to adjusting the width of a column. In the row header, point to the line under the number of the row you want to change. When the pointer takes on the double-arrow shape, hold down the mouse button, drag the line that divides the rows to the new position, and then release the mouse button.

To change the width of more than one row at a time, click on the headers of the rows you want to change. (You can choose nonadjacent rows by holding down Ctrl as you select the rows.) Then change the width of one of the rows as described above. When you release the mouse button, all of the rows change simultaneously to exactly the same height.

As with the Column Width command, you can use the Row Height command to change the heights of several adjacent or nonadjacent rows at once. Simply select at least one cell in each of the rows you want to change and use the Row Height command to access the dialog box shown in Figure 4-21. If you want to change the height of all the rows in the worksheet, click one of the column headers (or select any cell and press Ctrl-Spacebar) before you use the Row Height command. If all the rows you select are the same height, that height appears in the dialog-box text box; if the rows are of different heights, the text box is blank. Either way, you can change the height of all the selected rows by entering a new row height and then clicking OK.

FIGURE 4-21.
Use the Row Height
dialog box to change
the height of selected
worksheet rows.

To restore the standard height of a row, select any cell in that row, choose the Row Height command, and select the Standard Height box. As soon as you select Standard Height, Excel displays the standard row height for the font you're using in the Row Height text box. Then simply click OK.

Hiding a row

The procedures for hiding rows are analogous to the procedures for hiding columns. See "Hiding a column," earlier in this chapter.

Row height with the Wrap Text and Justify formats

When you create a multi-line text entry using the Wrap Text or the Justify alignment options, Excel adjusts row height to accommodate your multi-line entry. (See "The Wrap Text and Justify options," earlier in this chapter.) If you subsequently make that entry longer (either by adding words or increasing the point size), Excel adjusts the row height again — so that your text never spills out of the cell in which it's entered. If you reduce the size of a multi-line entry, however, Excel does not readjust the row height.

Fortunately, if you have a mouse, you can easily adjust the row height yourself. Simply put the mouse pointer in the row-header area, then double-click the line that separates the row you want to adjust from the row below it. You can also reapply the Wrap Text or Justify alignment format to re-establish the height of the row. Note that the Justify command is different from the Justify alignment format. See "The Justify command vs. the Justify format," earlier in this chapter.

Formatting with styles

Microsoft Excel's Style feature allows you to assign names to combinations of formatting attributes. You can then apply those attributes by selecting the name from a list. Styles not only help you achieve consistency in your formatting, both within a given worksheet and across worksheets; they also make it easy for you to modify the formatting characteristics of many cells at once.

Every new Excel worksheet comes with six predefined styles: Normal, Comma, Comma [0], Currency, Currency [0], and Percent. These six predefined styles have the same characteristics on each new worksheet. But you can change them for any worksheet, and you can add styles of your own. When you save a worksheet, all its style definitions are saved along with the rest of your data.

As Figure 4-22 shows, the Normal style that is supplied with every new worksheet has the following six characteristics:

- The numeric format is General.

- The font is 10-point MS Sans Serif.

- The alignment is General and bottom-aligned.

- No borders are assigned.

- No custom shading patterns are defined.

- The protection status is "locked." (Excel's worksheet and cell-protection features are described in Chapter 2.)

FIGURE 4-22.
Excel's predefined
Normal style includes
these attributes.

Styles can have fewer than six attributes, but not more. The predefined Currency style, for example, has only one attribute: the numeric format $#,##0.00_);[Red]($#,##0.00).

The predefined Normal style has one important characteristic: It is automatically applied to every cell on every new worksheet. Thus, if you want a cell to have the standard set of formatting attributes, you don't need to do anything. If, however, you want to change the attributes that Excel applies to all cells by default, you can change the definition of the Normal style. (See "Modifying a style," later in this chapter.)

The difference between the Comma and Comma [0] formats is that the Comma format uses two decimal places, while the Comma [0] format rounds to the nearest integer value. The Currency and Currency [0] formats differ in the same fashion.

Applying a style

To apply a defined style (either one of Excel's six predefined styles or one that you create yourself) to a cell or range, first select that cell or range. Then do either of the following:

- Click the downward-pointing arrow near the left edge of the Standard or Formatting toolbar, and choose from the list that unfolds.

■ Choose the Style command from the Format menu, open the drop-down list labeled Style Name, choose from the list that unfolds, and then click OK.

For example, the predefined Currency style uses a numeric format with two decimal places and parentheses for negative values. If you want to change the dollar values in Figure 4-15 to appear with two decimal places, you can select C5:G14, open the Style list on the toolbar, and choose Currency. (You might have to widen the columns to make room for the extra digits.)

If the Standard or Formatting toolbar is displayed, you can tell which style has been applied to any cell on your worksheet by making the cell in question the active cell. When you do this, the name of the cell's style appears in the style window at the left side of the toolbar.

Defining a style

You can define a style in either of two ways: by providing an example of the style attributes you want or by choosing the Style command from the Format menu and filling out the Style dialog box. After you define a new style, you can use it anywhere in the current worksheet. You can also copy it to another worksheet. (See "Merging styles from different worksheets," later in this chapter.)

Style by example

If you have already used commands on the Format menu to apply formatting attributes to a cell or range, you can easily assign a new style name to those attributes. For example, the heading "1993 Budget Summary" in Figure 4-15 was formatted with Center across selection alignment and 14-point MS Sans Serif Bold font. Suppose you want to make that combination of attributes a new style called Heading. You can do it easily with style by example.

First, select the cell that contains the heading. Then, with the Standard or Formatting toolbar displayed, simply click the toolbar's style list box, type the word *Heading*, and press Enter.

If you don't have the Standard or Formatting toolbar displayed, or if you prefer to work with the Style dialog box, select the cell that contains the heading. Then choose the Style command from the Format menu, type the word *Heading* in the box labeled Style Name, and click OK.

The safest way to create a style by example is to select only one cell — one that you know has all the attributes you want to assign to the new style. If you select two or more cells that are not formatted identically, the new style assumes only those attributes that the cells in the selection have in common.

Style by definition

To create a new style without first applying individual Format menu commands, start by choosing the Style command. In the box labeled Style Name, type the name of the style you want to define, and then click Define. Figure 4-23 shows how the Style dialog box looks if you are in the process of defining a new style called *Heading*.

FIGURE 4-23.
When you click Define, the dialog box expands, letting you assign as many as six formatting attributes to your new style.

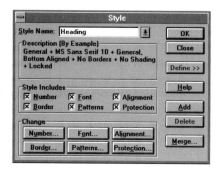

As already mentioned, a style can specify up to six formatting attributes. These attributes are the numeric format, the font, the alignment, borders, custom shading patterns, and protection status. When you click Define in the Style dialog box, the dialog box expands to include one check box and one command button for each of these attributes. To assign a formatting attribute to your new style, make sure its check box is selected, and then choose the corresponding command button.

For example, suppose you want to assign your Heading style the 14-point MS Sans Serif Bold font. First make sure the check box marked Font has an X in it, and then click the Font command button. Excel responds by presenting the Font dialog box, as shown in Figure 4-24.

FIGURE 4-24.
The Font button in the Style dialog box takes you to the Font dialog box. Excel applies changes made here to the current style.

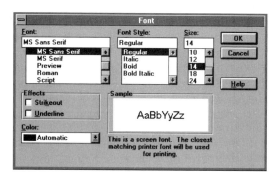

As you can see, the dialog box that appears when you choose the Font button is similar to the one you saw earlier in this chapter, in the discussion of the Font command. (Compare Figure 4-24 with Figure 4-13.) However, the changes you make here apply to your new style definition, whereas changes made with the Font command apply only to the current selection of cells.

The other five command buttons — Number, Alignment, Border, Pattern, and Protection — also bring up familiar dialog boxes.

After you assign all the formatting attributes you want to your new style, simply click Add. Your new style takes its place among the others defined for the current worksheet, and you can apply it at any time from either a toolbar's Style window or the Style dialog box's Style Name list.

Modifying a style

A major advantage to formatting with styles is that, if you change your mind about the appearance of some element of your worksheet, you can revise every instance of that element at once by changing the definition of the style. For example, if you decide you'd like the font in your Heading style — which is now 14-point MS Sans Serif Bold — to be italic as well as bold, you can simply redefine the Heading style.

To modify a style's definition, reopen the Style dialog box, choose the name of the style you want to redefine, and then click Define again. To add italics to the definition of Heading, for example, choose the Style command, select Heading in the Style Name list, and then click Define. Next, click Font, select the Bold Italic font style, click OK to return to the Style dialog box, and then click OK to confirm your changes.

You can also redefine a style using the style-by-example procedure. To do this, select a cell that includes the current definition of your style and make the format changes you want. Then click a toolbar's style box and press Enter, or choose the Style command and press Enter. Excel asks you to confirm that you want to change the existing style.

Overriding a style with local formatting changes

What if you want only some of your headings to be italic? You have two choices: You can define a separate style for those headings that you do not want to italicize, or you can simply use the Format Font command to override the style's definition in those particular cases.

You can always use the formatting commands discussed earlier in this chapter — the Number, Alignment, Font, Border, and Pattern commands — to change the appearance of any cell or range on your worksheet, whether or not you've also applied a style to that cell or range.

If you override a style with a local formatting command and subsequently modify the definition of that style, Excel applies the new style's definition but retains the formatting change you made locally. For example, if you decide you want to underline one particular heading, you might use the Font command to apply the underlining. If you subsequently change the definition of the Heading style so that it uses Courier instead of MS Sans Serif, all your main headings — including the underlined one — will change to Courier. But your underlined heading will remain underlined.

Merging styles from different worksheets

To help maintain formatting consistency across a group of documents, you can copy style definitions between worksheets. (You can also achieve consistency by using templates. See "Using template files" later in this chapter.)

To copy a style from one worksheet to another, both the source worksheet (the one you're copying from) and the destination worksheet (the one you're copying to) must be open. Start by making the destination worksheet the active window. Choose the Format Style command, click Define, and then click Merge. Excel responds by displaying a list of all other open documents, as shown in Figure 4-25. Select the name of the document you want to copy styles *from*, and click OK.

FIGURE 4-25.
When you copy styles
from one document to
another, you see a list
of all the open
documents.

If a style in your source document has the same name as one already in your destination document, Excel presents an alert box asking you whether you want to use the source document's style or stick with the one in the destination document. You will receive this warning and choice only once, however, no matter how many duplicate style names exist.

Deleting a style

To delete a style's definition, use the Style command, select the style in the Style Name list, click Define, and then click Delete.

Any cells that had the deleted style will revert to the Normal style. (You cannot delete the Normal style.) But any local formatting commands you have applied are retained.

Using template files

A *template file* is a model that can serve as the basis for many separate worksheets. A model might include both data and formatting information. Template files are great time-savers. They're also an ideal way to ensure a consistent look among reports or models. Figure 4-26 shows an example of a template file.

To create a template file, fill out a worksheet with all the data and formatting instructions that are common to all uses of the template. Then choose the Save As command from the File menu and supply a filename. Don't include an extension; Microsoft Excel supplies the extension XLT. Before clicking OK to save the file, open the Save File as Type drop-down list and select Template. Then click OK to save the file. If you make changes to the template that you want to keep, be sure to specify the Template file format each time you save your change.

To use a template file, open it like any other Excel file. Excel recognizes that the file is a template, rather than an ordinary worksheet, and brings a *working copy* of the file to the desktop, leaving the original intact on disk. The copy is given a temporary name made up of the original template name plus a number. If the template file is named EXPENSES.XLT, for example, the working copy appears under the name Expenses1. When you save it, of course, you can use Save As to assign it any name you please, and the new worksheet will have an XLS file extension.

FIGURE 4-26.
This template file
serves as the basis for
creating specific
expense reports.

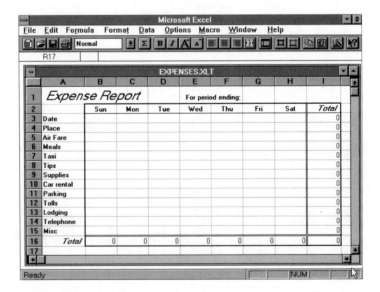

NOTE: A good place to store a template file is in the XLSTART *subdirectory of your Excel directory. As Figure 4-27 shows, you can choose an* XLT *file stored there with the New command from the File menu. After you save a template file in the* XLSTART *directory, its name appears in the New dialog box in your next Excel session.*

FIGURE 4-27.
The File New command lists the template files stored in your XLSTART directory.

Modifying a template file

If Microsoft Excel always gives you a copy of your template file instead of the original, how do you modify the original? By holding down Shift when you open the template file. After you make changes, resave the template, specifying the Template file format in the Save As dialog box.

The Display, Color Palette, and Workspace commands

In addition to the formatting commands available on the Format menu, the Options menu offers three other important commands that let you control the way your documents appear on screen: the Display command, the Color Palette command, and the Workspace command.

The commands on the Format menu affect only selected worksheet cells, while those on the Options menu are global in scope. The Display command controls the overall appearance of the current window. The Workspace command controls certain aspects of the appearance of all open windows. The Color Palette command allows you to modify the set of 16 colors currently available for any given worksheet.

The Display command

The Display command on the Options menu controls the appearance of formulas, gridlines, column and row headings, zero values, outline symbols, automatic page breaks, and graphic objects in your worksheet. (We'll discuss outlining and outline symbols later in this chapter. Automatic page breaks are described in Chapter 12, and graphic objects are described in Chapter 7.) When you use the Display command, you'll see the dialog box shown in Figure 4-28 on the following page.

FIGURE 4-28.
Use the Display
Options dialog box to
control the appearance
of your worksheet.

The options you select in the Display dialog box affect only the active worksheet window; they do not change the display of other windows in the workspace. Thus, if you've used the New Window command on the Window menu to create two or more windows to view the same worksheet, you can use different display options in each. For example, you can view formulas in one window and see the results of those formulas in another window. See Chapter 6 for more information about Window commands.

The Formulas option

Normally when you enter a formula in a cell, you see the results of that formula, not the formula itself. Similarly, when you format a number, you no longer see the underlying (unformatted) value. You can see the underlying values and formulas only by selecting individual cells and looking at the formula bar.

The Formulas option lets you see all the underlying values and formulas in your worksheet at once. For example, to see all the underlying numbers and formulas in the worksheet shown in Figure 4-2, choose the Display command, select the Formulas option, and click OK. As you can see in Figure 4-29, the underlying contents of each cell appear and all cells are now left-aligned. (Excel ignores any alignment formatting when you select the Formulas option.)

In addition, notice that the width of each column in the worksheet changes so that the underlying formulas can be better displayed. When you select the Formulas option, all columns in the worksheet expand to twice their actual width setting, plus one character. Thus, a column 3 characters wide becomes 7 characters wide when you select the Formulas option. When you deselect the Formulas option, Excel restores all the columns to their former widths.

The Formulas option is particularly helpful when you need to edit a large worksheet. You can see all your formulas at a glance without having to activate each cell and see its contents in the formula bar. You can also use the Formulas option to document your work: After you select Formulas, you can print your worksheet for archiving purposes. (See Chapter 12 for information on printing.)

FIGURE 4-29.
Use the Formulas
option to view
underlying values and
formulas.

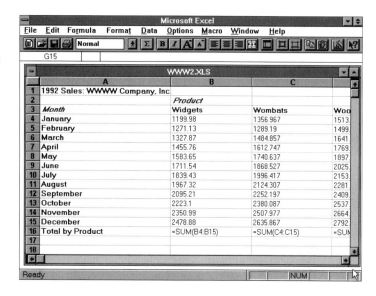

The Gridlines option

Typically, Excel uses a gray grid to mark the boundaries of each cell in the worksheet. Although this grid is usually helpful for selection and navigation, sometimes you would rather not have it in view. To suppress the display of these gridlines on your screen, issue the Display command and deselect the Gridlines option.

You can increase the effectiveness of your border formats dramatically by eliminating the gridlines in your worksheet. The worksheet we created in Figure 4-16 shows a worksheet with borders but without gridlines. The borders are much more prominent in this worksheet than they are in Figure 4-15.

The Row & Column Headings option

The third option in the Display dialog box is Row & Column Headings. If you deselect this option, the column letters and row numbers you usually see at the top and left edges of the worksheet disappear. Figure 4-30 on the following page shows a worksheet without column and row headings or gridlines. (We also clicked the Maximize document button to fill the screen.) When Row & Column Headings is deselected, you must use the Column Width command on the Format menu to change the width of a column.

The Zero Values option

Normally, zero values are displayed in your worksheet, but you can deselect the Zero Values option to hide them. With Zero Values deselected, any cell containing zero or a formula that results in zero values appears blank. The underlying entries

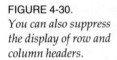

FIGURE 4-30.
You can also suppress the display of row and column headers.

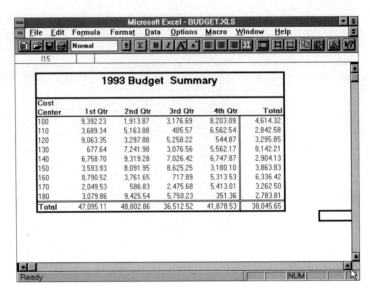

are unaffected, however. If you edit an entry or if the result of a formula changes so that the cell no longer contains a zero value, the value immediately becomes visible.

Changing the color of your gridlines and headers

You can also change the color of the gridlines and the row and column headers in your worksheet windows. Select the color option you want from the Gridline & Heading Color portion of the Display dialog box and click OK. Select the Automatic option to change back to the default screen colors (the color currently defined for Window Text in the Microsoft Windows Control Panel).

Customizing the color palette

The Font, Border, Patterns, and Display commands all offer a choice of 16 colors. The 16 colors presented in these drop-down lists constitute your default color palette. With the help of the Color Palette command on the Options menu, you can modify any color in the palette.

The dialog box that appears when you choose the Options Color Palette command presents samples of each color in the current palette. To substitute a different color for one of the current colors, select that color and then click Edit. You'll see a new dialog box like the one shown in Figure 4-31. (This dialog box is not available if you are using a monochrome monitor.)

FIGURE 4-31.
*Excel lets you edit the
colors in its default
palette.*

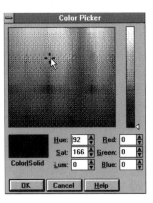

Colors displayed on your screen are defined by three parameters — their red, blue, and green values. An alternative system of specification uses three different parameters, called *hue, saturation,* and *luminosity.* You can specify a new color by modifying the values of any of these parameters. (Click the arrows, or type new values in the various boxes.)

If you have a mouse, you can define a new color more directly by dragging either or both of two pointers. The first pointer is a cross-like shape in the large square that dominates this dialog box. This pointer controls hue and saturation. The second pointer is the arrowhead beside the vertical scale to the right of the large square. This pointer controls luminosity. By experimenting with these two pointers and looking at the samples that appear in the Color/Solid box (in the lower left corner of the dialog box), you can come up with new colors without having to know anything about the parameters that define them.

Depending on your computer system's display hardware, you can probably display a maximum of either 16 or 256 solid colors. Any colors you define that are not among your system's repertoire of solids are achieved by a mixture of dots from solid colors. Such "blended" colors, which are said to be *dithered,* work well for shading. But for text and lines, Excel always uses the nearest solid color in preference to a dithered color. When you define a color that can be achieved only by dithering, the Color/Solid box shows you both the dithered shade and the solid alternative that Excel uses when necessary.

When you have finished editing the color palette, click OK to save it. Your customized palette then becomes a permanent attribute of the current worksheet; it will be there each time you open this worksheet, but not other worksheets.

To achieve a consistent look among worksheets, however, you may copy a custom palette. To do this, you must have both the destination worksheet (the one to which you're copying) and the source worksheet (the one from which you're copying) open. Make the destination worksheet active, choose the Color Palette command from the Options menu, and then open the drop-down list box named Copy Colors From. Excel presents a list of all open documents; choose your source document and then click OK.

The Custom Palettes command

Excel also provides an add-in command called Custom Palettes. After you load this add-in, you can choose among 12 predefined coordinated palettes included with the Excel program. To install this add-in, choose the Add-ins command from the Options menu, and click Add to display the Open dialog box. Switch to the EXCEL\LIBRARY\COLOR directory. From the File Name list, select PALETTES.XLA and click OK. Close the Add-In Manager dialog box by clicking Close. Now when you open the Options menu, you will notice a new command — Custom Palettes — just above the Color Palette command.

When you choose the Custom Palettes command, you see a dialog box containing a list of palette names, including Autumn, BlackWht, BlueRed, Blues, Dusk, Pastel, Rainbow, Reds, Summer, Sunset, Winter, Yelgreen, User1, and User2. When you select a name from the list, that palette replaces the default palette. If you have used the default colors in the current worksheet, you can click Apply in the Custom Palettes dialog box to test the effects of different palettes on your worksheet without dismissing the dialog box. When you find a combination you like, click OK to make that palette the active palette for the current worksheet. Other worksheets are not affected.

At first, the custom palettes named User1 and User2 are the same as the default palette. But you can modify a User palette and save it so that you can select your custom colors from the Custom Palettes dialog box. To open the User1 palette, choose Open from the File menu, and then choose User1 from the EXCEL\LIBRARY\COLOR directory. The custom palettes are hidden files, so you must choose the Unhide command from the Window menu, select User1 from the list, and click OK. Next, maximize the User1 window by clicking the upward-pointing arrow in the upper right corner of the window. Now you can choose the Color Palette command, select each color you want to edit, click Edit, and modify each color as described earlier in this chapter.

When you are finished, you should save the User1 document as a hidden file. First, hide User1 by choosing Hide from the Window menu. You must have another worksheet open. If you do not, you must open one. Making sure to save any changes you made to the other worksheet, hold down Shift and choose Close All from the File menu. A dialog box appears, asking if you want to save changes made to the User1 document. Click Yes. Now your custom color palette is ready to use.

The Workspace command

The Workspace command on the Options menu is similar to the Display command in that it affects the overall appearance of your worksheet window, not just a selected cell or range. Unlike the Display command, however, the Workspace command applies to *all* open windows. When you use the Workspace command, you'll see a dialog box like the one in Figure 4-32. In this chapter, we'll look at many of the options provided by this command. Because the Ignore Remote Requests option applies only if you're sharing data with another program, we'll save that for Chapter 22. The Cell Drag and Drop and Info Window options will be explained in Chapter 5. We discussed the Lotus 1-2-3 Help and Alternate Navigation keys options in Chapter 2.

The options you choose with the Workspace command are saved when you quit Excel and remain in effect in your next session.

FIGURE 4-32.
The Workspace command affects all open windows.

The Fixed Decimal option

The Fixed Decimal option is handy when you enter long lists of numeric values. For example, suppose you're entering data in an accounting journal. All your entries must contain two decimal places. Instead of typing the decimal point for each entry, select the Fixed Decimal option and, in the Places text box, indicate the number of decimal places you want to use. After you type each numeric value in your worksheet, Excel adds a decimal point at the specified position. For example, if you select

Fixed Decimal and use the default Places option of 2, and then enter the number 12345 in a cell of your worksheet, your entry will be converted to 123.45; if you enter a single-digit value, such as 9, it will be converted to 0.09.

The Fixed Decimal option does not affect existing entries in your worksheet; it applies only to entries you make after you select the option. Thus, you can select or deselect the option at any time or change the number of decimal places without altering existing data. When you choose the Fixed Decimal option, FIX appears at the right side of the status bar.

The R1C1 option

Worksheet formulas usually refer to cells by a combination of column letter and row number, such as A1 or Z100. If you use the R1C1 option, however, Excel refers to cells by row and column *numbers* instead. The cell reference R1C1 means row 1, column 1, so cell R1C1 is the same as cell A1. When you choose this option, all the cell references in your formulas change to R1C1 format. For example, cell M10 becomes R10C13, and cell IV16384, the last cell in your worksheet, becomes R16384C256. Figure 4-33 shows a worksheet in R1C1 format.

When you use R1C1 notation, relative cell references are displayed in terms of their relationship to the cell that contains the formula rather than by their actual coordinates. For example, suppose you want to enter a formula in cell R10C2 (B10) that adds cells R1C1 and R1C2. After selecting cell R10C2, type an equal sign, and then select cell R1C1, type a plus sign, select R1C2, and press Enter. Excel will display

=R[-9]C[-1]+R[-9]C

FIGURE 4-33.
Use the R1C1 option to refer to cells by row and column numbers.

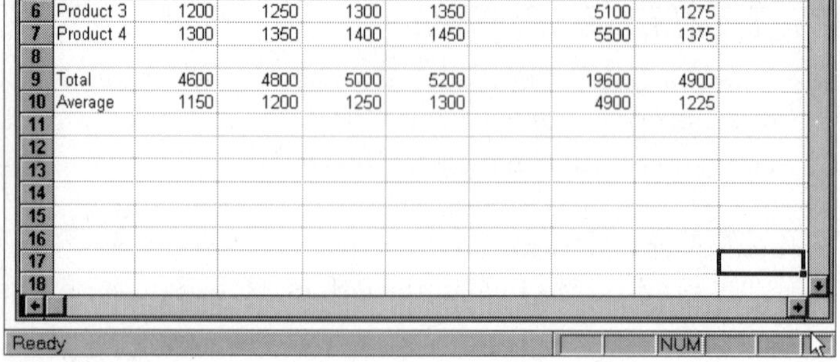

Negative row and column numbers indicate that the referenced cell is above and to the left of the formula cell; positive numbers indicate that the referenced cell is below and to the right of the formula cell. So, this formula reads *Add the cell nine rows up and one column to the left to the cell nine rows up in the same column.*

To type a relative reference to another cell, you must include brackets around the numbers in the reference. If you don't include the brackets, Excel assumes you're using absolute references. For example, the formula

=R9C1+R8C1

uses absolute references to the cells in rows 8 and 9 of column 1.

The Status Bar, Scroll Bars, and Formula Bar options

The next three options in the Display portion of the Workspace dialog box let you suppress the display of the status bar, scroll bars, and formula bar. Figure 4-34 shows how your worksheet looks if you deselect these three options and maximize the document window. Because you need the status bar, scroll bars, and formula bar to navigate and edit your worksheet, you'll deselect these options only when you complete a worksheet and want to hide these objects for display purposes.

The Note Indicator option

Excel lets you attach text and sound notes to particular cells, explaining their purpose, how their data was derived, or whatever else you like. The content of these notes does not appear within the cell itself, but you can display the notes in a separate window, print them along with your worksheet, or, in the case of sound notes, play them back, using the techniques described fully in Chapter 5.

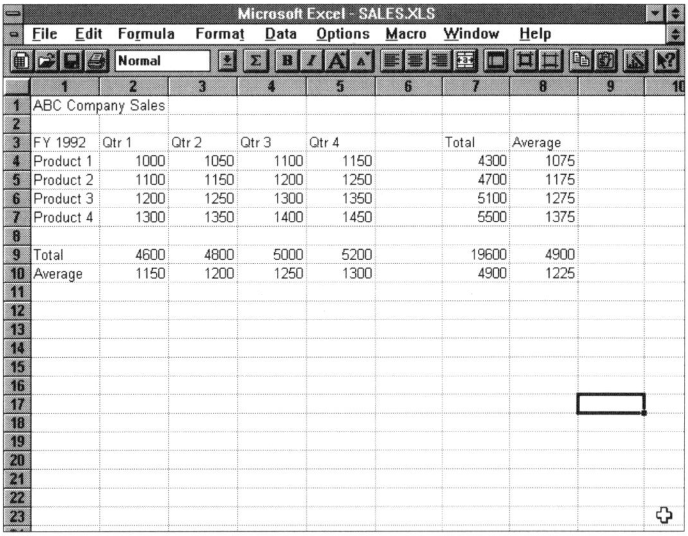

FIGURE 4-34.
You can suppress the display of the status bar, scroll bars, and formula bar.

Unless you deselect the Note Indicator option, cells to which you have attached notes are marked by a small dot in their upper right corners.

The Alternate Menu or Help Key option

As explained in Chapter 1, you can use the slash (/) key to access the menus directly from the keyboard. If you like, you can use another key on your keyboard to activate the menus. Simply select the Alternate Menu or Help Key text box and type the key you want to use.

The Move Selection after Enter option

When you select a block of cells and then begin entering data, Excel moves the active cell step by step through the selection each time you press Enter. When you select a single cell, however, pressing Enter does not move the active cell. If you prefer to have Excel move the active cell down to the next cell in the column after each data entry, even when you have not selected a multi-cell block, select the Move Selection after Enter option.

Using Lotus 1-2-3 keystrokes

If you're familiar with Lotus 1-2-3, you'll be glad to know that you can use many of Lotus 1-2-3's cell-entry procedures in Microsoft Excel. For example, if you type the label

   "Totals

with the Alternate Navigation Keys option in effect, Excel enters the label *Totals* and right-aligns it. If you type \-, Excel fills the active cell with hyphens — and so on.

Whether or not you choose the Alternate Navigation Keys option, you can begin formulas with +, instead of =. You can also begin function names with @ if you wish (Excel simply removes the symbol from your formula) and use one or two periods, instead of a colon, when you specify ranges. For example, instead of typing

   =SUM(A1:A10)

you can type @SUM(A1..A10). Excel accepts these Lotus-style entries, whether or not you select the Alternate Navigation Keys option (described in Chapter 2).

Outlining your worksheets

Many typical spreadsheet models are built in a hierarchical fashion. For example, in a monthly budget worksheet, you might have a column for each month of the year, followed by a totals column. For each line item in your budget, the totals column adds the values in each month column. In this kind of structure, you can describe the month columns as subordinate to the totals column, because their values contribute to the outcome of the totals column. Similarly, the line items themselves might be set up in a hierarchical manner, with groups of expense categories contributing to category totals. Microsoft Excel can turn worksheets of this kind into outlines.

Figure 4-35 shows a table of sales figures prior to outlining. Figure 4-36 on the following page shows the same worksheet as an outline, and Figure 4-37 on the following page illustrates Excel's outlining capability. After you outline a worksheet, you can use simple commands to change the level of detail displayed.

The only difference between the worksheets shown in Figures 4-36 and 4-37 is that the detail rows and columns (the individual team members and months) are hidden in Figure 4-37. Without outlining, you would have to hide each group of rows and columns manually; with outlining, you can change the level of detail instantly.

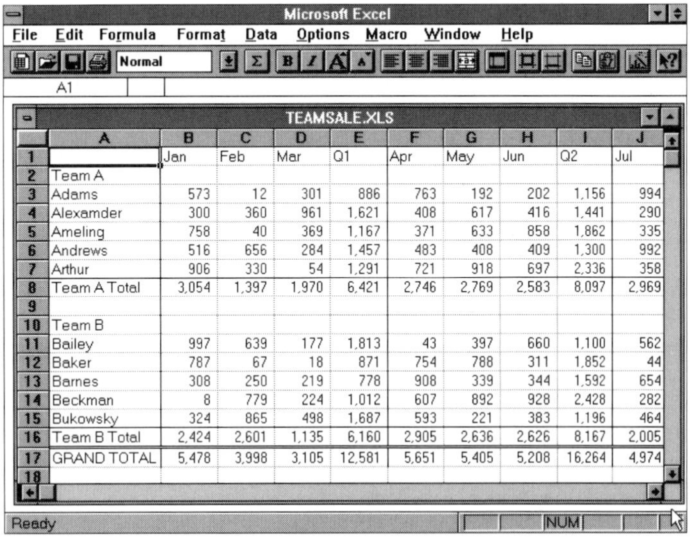

FIGURE 4-35.
This worksheet is an excellent candidate for outlining.

	A	B	C	D	E	F	G	H	I	J
1		Jan	Feb	Mar	Q1	Apr	May	Jun	Q2	Jul
2	Team A									
3	Adams	573	12	301	886	763	192	202	1,156	994
4	Alexamder	300	360	961	1,621	408	617	416	1,441	290
5	Ameling	758	40	369	1,167	371	633	858	1,862	335
6	Andrews	516	656	284	1,457	483	408	409	1,300	992
7	Arthur	906	330	54	1,291	721	918	697	2,336	358
8	Team A Total	3,054	1,397	1,970	6,421	2,746	2,769	2,583	8,097	2,969
9										
10	Team B									
11	Bailey	997	639	177	1,813	43	397	660	1,100	562
12	Baker	787	67	18	871	754	788	311	1,852	44
13	Barnes	308	250	219	778	908	339	344	1,592	654
14	Beckman	8	779	224	1,012	607	892	928	2,428	282
15	Bukowsky	324	865	498	1,687	593	221	383	1,196	464
16	Team B Total	2,424	2,601	1,135	6,160	2,905	2,636	2,626	8,167	2,005
17	GRAND TOTAL	5,478	3,998	3,105	12,581	5,651	5,405	5,208	16,264	4,974
18										

FIGURE 4-36.
Outlining symbols in this worksheet show that team-member figures are subordinate to team totals, team totals are subordinate to grand totals, monthly figures are subordinate to quarterly totals, and quarterly totals are subordinate to the annual total.

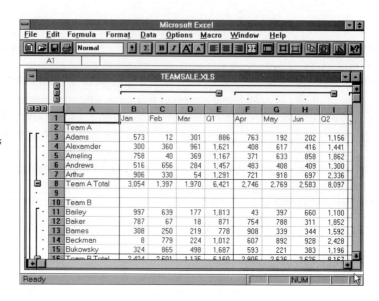

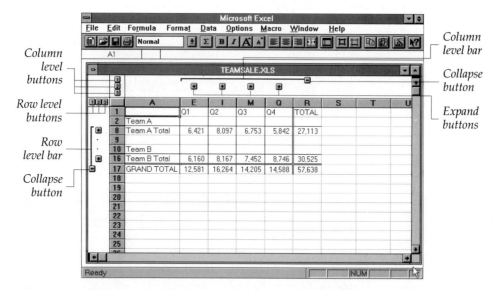

FIGURE 4-37. *Two clicks of the mouse button transformed the worksheet in Figure 4-36 into this quarterly overview.*

Outlining has two additional benefits. First, you can more easily reorganize an outlined worksheet than one that is not outlined. In Figure 4-37, for example, if you hold down Shift while clicking the Expand button at the top of column E, and then use editing procedures to move that column, the subordinate columns B, C, and D automatically move as well.

Second, in an outlined worksheet you can easily select only those cells that share a common hierarchical level. For example, if you want to graph the quarterly sales totals in Figure 4-36 (omitting the monthly details), you can first adjust the detail level, as shown in Figure 4-37. Then you can select columns E, I, M, and Q (the quarterly totals) without selecting the intervening columns. (Again, you can accomplish this by hiding columns individually. But in most cases outlining is considerably faster.)

The outline in Figure 4-37 is a simple one. It uses three levels each for the column and row dimensions. You can create much more complex outlines. Excel can handle up to eight levels in each dimension.

Creating an outline automatically

To outline all or part of your worksheet automatically, select the worksheet area that you want to outline, and then choose the Outline command from the Formula menu. If you want to outline your entire worksheet, select only one cell.

Excel responds with the dialog box shown in Figure 4-38. Excel assumes that your worksheet is set up so that summary cells (totals, for example) appear below and to the right of the detail cells. If that's not the case on the worksheet you are outlining, deselect the appropriate check boxes in this dialog box.

FIGURE 4-38.

When you choose the Formula Outline command, this dialog box appears.

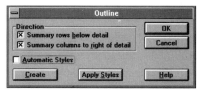

To create the outline, select the Create button. In a moment or two, depending on the complexity of your worksheet, your outline will appear.

Creating an outline with the Utility toolbar

If you're using a mouse, you can take advantage of some toolbar shortcuts for working with an outline. Figure 4-39 shows the Utility toolbar. The four tools it contains allow you to promote and demote the current selection, display or hide outline symbols, and select visible cells only.

FIGURE 4-39.
These tools on the
Utility toolbar are
used in outlining.

Promote

Demote

Show Outline Symbols

Select Visible Cells

The easiest way to display the Utility toolbar is to use the shortcut menu. Move the mouse pointer over the Standard toolbar, or any other toolbar, if one is currently visible. Click the right mouse button to display the toolbar shortcut menu, and choose Utility. Alternatively, or if no toolbars are currently visible on your screen, choose the Toolbars command from the Options menu and select Utility from the Show Toolbars list. To hide toolbars, you can use either method described and select the name of the toolbar you want to hide. For more information about tools and toolbars, see Appendix A.

To create an outline with the Utility toolbar, select the range you want to outline. Then click the Show Outline Symbols tool. Excel presents an alert box that asks if you want to create a new outline; click OK. Excel creates your outline using the current settings in the Formula Outline dialog box.

Using automatic styles

If you want, Excel can automatically apply a predefined set of styles to cells at the various levels of your outline. Figure 4-40 shows the same outline as Figure 4-36, with automatic styles applied.

As the figure shows, these automatic styles have names like RowLevel_1, Col-Level_1, and so on. When you apply automatic styles, Excel adds the names of these styles to the drop-down style list at the left side of the Standard toolbar (and to the corresponding lists on the Formatting toolbar and in the Format Styles dialog box). You can then work with these styles — and modify their definitions — the same way you work with any other styles.

If you know before creating an outline that you want to use automatic styles, select the Automatic Styles check box in the Formula Outline dialog box. If you create an outline without automatic styles, and then change your mind, first select

FIGURE 4-40.
*Excel can
automatically apply
predefined styles to
the summary levels of
an outline.*

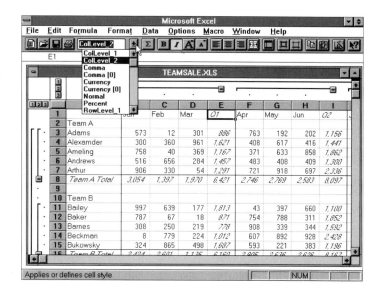

the area of your worksheet to which you want to apply automatic styles. Then reopen the Outline dialog box and click Apply Styles.

Extending the outline to new worksheet areas

At times, you might create an outline and then add more data to your worksheet. You might also want to recreate an outline if you change the organization of any area. To include new rows and columns in your outline, simply repeat the procedure you followed to create the outline in the first place, but be sure to use the Outline command on the Formula menu. Excel will present an alert box that asks you to confirm that you want to modify the outline.

Suppressing the outline display

When you outline a worksheet, Excel displays some additional symbols above and to the left of the row and column headings. These symbols indicate the structure of your outline and allow you to change the level of detail displayed.

You don't have to look at these symbols all the time when you work with an outlined worksheet. The symbols take up screen space. To remove them, simply click Show Outline Symbols on the Utility toolbar, or choose the Display command from the Options menu and deselect the Outline Symbols check box.

When you need to redisplay the outline symbols, click Show Outline Symbols a second time, or reselect the Outline Symbols check box in the Display dialog box.

Collapsing and expanding outline levels

When you first create an outline, the areas above and to the left of your worksheet are marked by one or more brackets that terminate in minus-sign symbols. The brackets are called *level bars,* and the minus-sign symbols are *collapse buttons.* Each level bar indicates a range of cells that share a common outline level. The collapse buttons appear above or to the left of each level's summary cell.

For example, if you translate columns B through E in Figure 4-36 into a traditional outline, it would look like this:

I.   Q1 (column E)

    A.   January (column B)

    B.   February (column C)

    C.   March (column D)

Excel indicates this structure by drawing a level bar across columns B through D, terminating the level bar in a collapse button above column E.

To collapse an outline level so that only the summary cells show, you simply click that level's collapse button. For example, if you no longer need to see the sales numbers for January, February, and March in Figure 4-36, you can click the collapse button above column E. The worksheet then looks like Figure 4-41. Note that the collapse button above the Q1 column is replaced by an expand button. To redisplay the monthly details that are now hidden, you can click the expand button.

FIGURE 4-41.
We have hidden the details for January through March by clicking on the collapse button above Q1. Excel now displays an expand button above Q1.

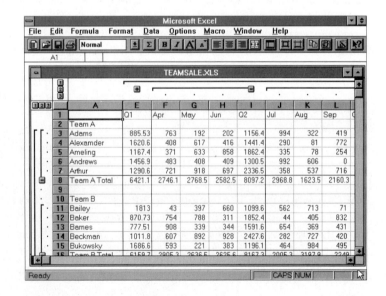

Displaying a specific level of detail

If we want to collapse each quarter in Figure 4-36 so only the quarterly totals and annual totals appear, we can click on three more collapse buttons (the ones above Q2, Q3, and Q4). But the *level buttons* — the little squares with numerals inside them at the upper left of the worksheet — provide an easier way. An outline usually has two sets of level buttons, one for the column dimension and one for the row dimension. The column level buttons appear above the worksheet, and the row level buttons appear to the left of the worksheet.

Level buttons let you set an entire worksheet dimension — either columns or rows — to a specific level of detail. The worksheet in Figure 4-36 has three levels each in its column and row dimensions. By clicking on both of the number 2 level buttons in the upper left area of the worksheet, you can transform the outline shown in Figure 4-36 to the one shown in Figure 4-37. By clicking on the number 1 level buttons above the worksheet, you can reduce the dimensions to make it show only the top summary level — the grand total sales figure for the year.

Selecting cells at a specific detail level

When you collapse part of an outline, Excel hides the rows or columns that you don't want to see. In Figure 4-37, for example, columns B–D, F–H, J–L, and N–P, as well as rows 3–7 and 11–15, are hidden. Normally, when you select a range that crosses hidden cells, those hidden cells are included in the selection. If you drag the mouse from E3 to Q3 in Figure 4-37, for example, Excel selects the entire range, including the hidden cells. If you copy and paste these cells to a different location, the hidden data reappears. By clicking the Select Visible Cells tool on the Utility toolbar, however, you can restrict a selection to only the visible cells within a range.

Suppose you want to add formulas in column S to compute the averages of your four quarterly sales figures. To do this, make S3 the active cell and type

=AVERAGE(

Then drag the mouse from E3 to Q3. The formula bar now reads

= AVERAGE(E3:Q3

Before entering the close parenthesis, click the Select Visible Cells tool. Excel changes the formula in the formula bar to read

= AVERAGE(E3,I3,M3,Q3

Type a close parenthesis and press Enter, and you have your quarterly average for row 3. Now you can use the Copy or Fill Down commands on the Edit menu to replicate the formula in the remaining rows of your worksheet. (We'll explain these editing features in Chapter 5. To read about the AVERAGE function, see Chapter 8.)

The Select Visible Cells tool is ideal for copying, plotting, or performing calculations on only those cells that occupy a particular level of your outline. But you can use it with any set of visible cells in an outline, even if they're not all at the same hierarchical level. You can also use the Select Visible Cells tool with columns or rows that have been hidden "manually" — without outlining. The command works the same way in this case; it excludes any cells in hidden rows or columns from the current selection.

If you don't have a mouse, you can use the Select Special command on the Formula menu to restrict a selection to a range of visible cells. The Select Special command is discussed in Chapter 5.

Promoting and demoting rows and columns

In most cases, Excel's automatic outlining procedure reads the structure of your worksheet correctly and sets up your outline with the right levels in the right places. If the default outline doesn't give you the structure you expect, however, you can make adjustments by promoting or demoting particular rows or columns.

To demote or promote a column or range of columns, first select the entire column or columns. Then click the Demote or Promote tool on the Utility toolbar. (With the keyboard, press Alt-Shift-Left arrow to promote or Alt-Shift-Right arrow to demote.) To demote or promote a row or range of rows, first select the entire row or rows. Then use the tools or the equivalent keyboard procedure.

Note that you cannot demote or promote a nonadjacent selection, and you cannot promote a selection that's already at the highest hierarchical level. If you want to bump a top-level column or row a level higher, to display it separately from the remainder of the outline, you have to demote all the other sections of the outline instead.

Removing an outline

You can remove either the column dimension or the row dimension of an outline (or both) by promoting all the outline's levels to the top level. If your outline is many levels deep and your worksheet is large, this can be a laborious process. Another way to make your worksheet behave as though it is not outlined is to display all levels of detail (by clicking on the highest numbered level button in each dimension), and then suppress the display of Excel's outlining symbols. You can do this by clicking the Show Outline Symbols tool on the Utility toolbar or by using the Display command on the Options menu and deselecting the Outline Symbols check box.

5

Editing the Worksheet

*T*he Edit menu commands take the place of old-fashioned erasers, scissors, and paste. Among other things, these commands let you erase, copy, and move cells and ranges on your worksheets. In this chapter we discuss the Edit menu commands: Undo, Redo, Repeat, Clear, Delete, Insert, Cut and Paste, Copy and Paste, Insert Paste, Paste Special, and Fill. We explain the importance of relative, absolute, and mixed references, which were introduced in Chapter 3. We also examine some other important editing and auditing features, including the Find, Replace, Note, and Select Special commands, as well as the Info window. Finally, we look at the Series, Justify, Parse, and Sort commands.

In addition to the editing procedures described in this chapter, Microsoft Excel lets you make changes to two or more worksheets simultaneously. Those *group editing* procedures are described in Chapter 6.

The Undo command

The Undo command on the Edit menu lets you recover from editing mistakes without having to reenter data or patch information back in place. If you catch your mistake before you use another command or make another cell entry, you can simply choose Undo to reverse the previous command.

You can use Undo to reverse the effect of any command on the Edit menu and to restore any entry in the formula bar. For example, if you accidentally delete a range of data, you can choose Undo or press Ctrl-Z to paste the entries back in place. If you edit the contents of a cell and subsequently discover that your changes are incorrect, you can use Undo to restore the original cell entry. In addition, you can use Undo to reverse formatting operations and many of the commands on the Formula and Data menus.

The Undo command changes its name to indicate the action it's currently able to reverse. For example, suppose you just chose the Clear command to erase the contents of a range of cells. When you pull down the Edit menu, the Undo command appears as Undo Clear. If you just entered a formula in a cell, the Edit menu displays Undo Entry.

There are many commands that Undo can't reverse. After you choose one of these commands, you'll see the dimmed command Can't Undo on the Edit menu.

If you're working with a large range, you might find that Excel cannot undo your mistakes because not enough memory is available. For example, suppose you try to use the Cut and Paste commands to move all the cells in column A (cells A1:A16384) into column C (cells C1:C16384). You might see the alert message *Selection too large. Continue without Undo?* If you click OK, Excel disables the Undo command and attempts to carry out the requested operation (although sufficient memory still isn't guaranteed). A better choice is to select Cancel and then perform the editing task in smaller chunks — by using two or more sets of Cut and Paste commands, for example. By breaking the command into more manageable portions, you can achieve the desired effect and still use the Undo command.

Actions that don't affect Undo

As we mentioned earlier, you can undo an action only if you haven't used another command or made another cell entry. However, you can take several actions in the worksheet without affecting the Undo command. For instance, you can use the cell

An extra precaution

A few commands have irreversible effects. For example, you cannot reverse the Delete command on the File menu. If you're not sure whether you need a file, open the file and take a look before you delete it. Similarly, you can't reverse the Delete and Extract commands on the Data menu. It is a good idea to save your worksheet before you use these commands. If you later find that you've deleted or extracted the wrong cells, you can always retrieve your original worksheet.

pointer and scroll bars to move through your worksheet and activate other cells. (After you activate a cell's formula bar, however, the Undo command becomes Can't Undo and is dimmed.) Also, commands that move the cell pointer, discussed in Chapter 2, do not affect Undo. For instance, you can use the Goto and Find commands on the Formula menu without affecting Undo. And you can move to other windows by selecting their names from the Window menu or by clicking the window itself.

The Redo command

After you use the Undo command, the command name changes to Redo. The Redo command reverses the Undo command, restoring the worksheet to its condition before you used the Undo command. For example, when you pull down the Edit menu after you use the Undo Clear command, the command appears as Redo Clear. If you choose this option, Excel again clears the contents of the selected range and changes the command name back to Undo Clear.

You can take advantage of the Undo/Redo combination to see the effects of an editing change in your worksheet. Suppose you edit a cell that is referenced in several formulas throughout your worksheet. To see the effects of your change, you can scroll through the worksheet and view the other cells. If you don't remember what a cell looked like before the change, you can use the Undo and Redo commands to get a "before and after" view. An easy way to do this is to repeatedly press Ctrl-Z to toggle the display back and forth between the before and after versions of the worksheet.

The Repeat command

The Repeat command lets you repeat an action — a great time-saver when you need to perform the same action in several areas of your worksheet. Repeat is particularly handy with commands like Insert and Delete, which you cannot perform on non-adjacent cell or range selections.

In some ways, the Repeat command is similar to Undo. Like Undo, the text of the Repeat command changes to reflect your last action in the worksheet. For example, suppose you issue the Clear command and select the Formats option in the Clear dialog box. When you access the Edit menu, you'll see that this command appears as Repeat Clear. If you select another cell or range and select the Repeat Clear command, Microsoft Excel assumes that you want to apply the same set of dialog-box options — the Formats option in this case — to the new selection.

Also like Undo, the Repeat command applies only to the last command you used and changes to reflect the name of that command.

Unlike Undo, Repeat works with almost any command on any menu. The only exceptions are those commands that can't logically be repeated. For example, if you use the Workspace command on the Options menu to change the appearance of your workspace, that command applies to all open documents and windows; you need not repeat it.

The Clear command

The Clear command lets you erase the contents of a cell or range, the format assigned to that cell or range, or both. You can also use the Clear command to erase cell notes and charts. (Notes are discussed later in this chapter; charts are discussed in Chapters 13, 14, and 15.)

To clear the contents or format of a cell or range, simply select that cell or range and choose the Clear command from the Edit menu. Alternatively, you can bypass the Edit menu and press Del. Either way, you'll see the dialog box shown in Figure 5-1.

FIGURE 5-1.
Use the Clear command to erase cell formats, formulas, and notes.

NOTE: *If you're working in the formula bar, pressing Del erases only the characters you selected. The Clear dialog box does not appear.*

The Clear dialog box offers four options: All, Formats, Formulas, and Notes. The All option erases the contents of the selected cells and any formats (other than column width and row height) and notes attached to those cells. The Formats option removes the formats from the selected cells but leaves their contents and notes in place; the selected cells then revert to the default General format. (If you assigned a style other than Normal, the cleared cells revert to the Normal style.) The Formulas option erases the contents of the selected cells (whether or not the cells contain formulas), but leaves their formats and notes alone. Finally, Notes removes any notes from the selected cells but leaves their contents and formats in place.

You can also use the mouse to clear cell entries, formats, and notes directly. See "Direct cell manipulation," later in this chapter.

The Delete command

The Delete command lets you remove cells from your worksheet. Unlike Clear, which erases the contents, formats, or notes in a cell but leaves the cell in place,

Delete removes the selected cell or range from the worksheet. In other words, Clear works like an eraser and Delete works like a pair of scissors.

You can also use the mouse to delete cells and cell ranges directly. See "Direct cell manipulation," later in this chapter.

Deleting entire rows and columns

You can use the Delete command to remove entire rows and columns from your worksheet and eliminate wasted space. For example, consider the worksheet in Figure 5-2. Three blank rows appear between the last items in the lists in columns A through G and the totals in row 13. To delete these blank rows from the worksheet, select cells B10:B12 (or any number of cells as long as you include one in each row you want to delete), and then choose the Delete command from the Edit menu. You'll see the dialog box shown in Figure 5-3.

As Figure 5-3 shows, Microsoft Excel needs more information before it can carry out the Delete command. To delete all of rows 10 through 12, choose the Entire Row button and click OK. (Alternatively, you can select all of rows 10 through 12 before

FIGURE 5-2.

Three extra rows appear above the totals row in this worksheet.

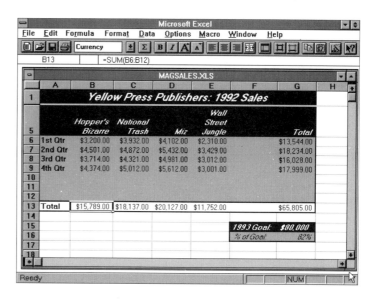

FIGURE 5-3.

The Delete command deletes specific cells as well as entire rows and columns.

you choose the Delete command. In that case, Excel does not display the dialog box because it's clear what you want to do.)

As you can see in Figure 5-4, after you delete rows 10 through 12, every entry in the rows below the deleted rows is shifted up so that the totals that were in row 13 now appear in row 10.

In addition to deleting a row from the worksheet, Excel adjusts the formula in row 10 to account for the deleted row. Before we deleted the extra rows, the formula in cell B13 (now in cell B10) was

=SUM(B6:B12)

However, cell B12 now contains the formula

=SUM(B6:B9)

You can also use Delete to remove columns from the worksheet. Select any cell in the column you want to delete and choose the Delete command. Next, select Entire Column in the Delete dialog box. Your column disappears from the work-sheet and all subsequent columns shift one cell to the left. Again, Excel updates any formulas affected by the deletion.

You can't delete nonadjacent rows or columns in one operation. For example, if you select A1 and F4 in your worksheet and issue the Delete command, you'll see the alert message *Cannot do that command on a multiple selection.*

FIGURE 5-4.
When we deleted rows 10 through 12, the remaining rows in the worksheet moved up to fill the gap.

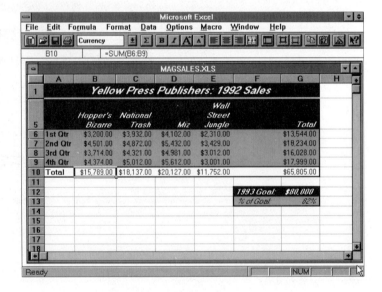

Deleting partial rows and columns

Excel lets you delete partial rows and columns — in fact, you can delete a range as small as a single cell. Select the cells you want to delete and choose the Delete command. Only the selected portion of the column or row is affected.

For example, to delete cells F6:F10 from the worksheet in Figure 5-4 without changing the remaining cells in column F, select cells F6:F10 and then choose Delete from the Edit menu. Next, in the Delete dialog box, select Shift Cells Left. Excel deletes only the selected range — F6:F10. It then adjusts the worksheet so that cells that occupied G6:G10 move to F6:F10, those that were at H6:H10 move into G6:G10, and so on. Figure 5-5 shows how the worksheet looks after this deletion.

If you selected F6:F10, used the Delete command, and then selected Shift Cells Up, Excel would still remove only the range F6:F10. But it would then adjust the worksheet by moving the remainder of column F — the entire range F11:F16384 — upward five cells.

When you delete a partial row or column, it's easy to misalign data. For example, in Figure 5-5, the label *Total* in column G did not move left with the other data in that column. As a result, the heading for column F now appears in the wrong column. We could have avoided this problem by selecting cells F5:F10 instead of F6:F10 before choosing the Delete command.

FIGURE 5-5.
The Shift Cells Left option deleted cells F6:F10.

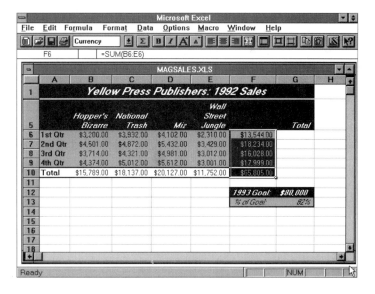

The Insert command

The Insert command lets you add a cell or range to the worksheet. For example, suppose you created the worksheet in Figure 5-6. As you're putting on the finishing touches, your boss tells you that your company has added a new product line. Fortunately, with the Insert command, you can add a new row or column to your worksheet without a lot of shuffling and recalculation.

NOTE: *If you just used the Cut command or Copy command from the Edit menu to transfer some information from your worksheet to the Windows Clipboard, the Insert command on the Edit menu is replaced by Insert Paste. To perform a normal insert under these circumstances, close the Edit menu, and then press Esc to clear the Clipboard's contents. Next reopen the Edit menu and use the Insert command. (See "Using Insert Paste with the Cut command," later in this chapter.)*

To insert a column for a new product line in the sample worksheet, simply select one or more cells in column B, C, or D (we'll use D) and choose Insert from the Edit menu. Microsoft Excel presents the dialog box shown in Figure 5-7. Choose Entire Column, and the contents of columns D and E will move into columns E and F, leaving column D blank and ready for new information. The newly inserted cells take on the same formats as the selected cells, and the formulas in cells F4:F16 are adjusted to account for the expanded range. (Alternatively, you can select *all* of column D before you use the Insert command. In that case, Excel does not display the dialog box because your intentions are clear.)

FIGURE 5-6.
This worksheet sets annual sales goals by product and by month.

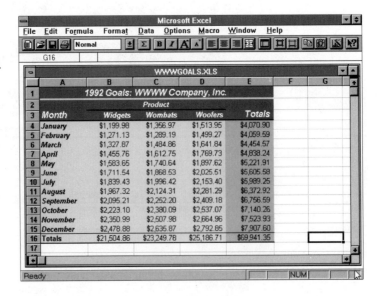

FIGURE 5-7.

When you select a partial row or column before choosing Insert, this dialog box appears.

You're now ready to enter the new product line's sales goals and to add these goals to the totals in column F. Figure 5-8 on the following page shows the finished worksheet with the data for Whatzits in column D.

Similarly, suppose you want to insert an extra row in the worksheet in Figure 5-8 so that you can add some space to separate the monthly sales data in rows 4 through 15 from the totals that appear in row 16. Simply select one or more cells in row 16, choose Insert from the Edit menu, and select the Entire Row option.

The insert and delete tools

Excel provides six tools you can use to insert and delete cells, rows, and columns. The Delete, Delete Row, Delete Column, Insert, Insert Row, and Insert Column tools are not located on any toolbar, so to use them you must either create a custom toolbar or modify an existing toolbar. For more information about tools and customizing toolbars, see Appendix A.

You won't see the Insert or Delete dialog box when you use the Insert tool or the Delete tool. Instead, when you use these tools, Excel uses common-sense rules to determine the direction in which to shift the surrounding cells. If the selection is wider than it is tall (2 cells wide by 1 cell high, for example), the Insert tool automatically shifts cells down, and the Delete tool automatically shifts cells up. If the selection is taller than it is wide (1 cell wide by 2 cells high, for example), the Insert tool automatically shifts cells right, and the Delete tool automatically shifts cells left.

The Insert Row, Insert Column, Delete Row, and Delete Column tools are equivalent to choosing the Insert or Delete command and selecting the Entire Row or Entire Column option. These commands operate as you might expect, performing the appropriate operation on entire rows or columns when you click on the tool. You need not select entire rows or columns when using these tools, however. Simply select one or more cells in each row or column you want to delete, or select one or more cells to the right or below each row or column you want to insert.

(Alternatively, select *all* of row 16 before you use the Insert command. In that case, you can bypass the dialog box.) Cells A16:F16 move down one row, as shown in Figure 5-9.

Often, you'll need to insert only a partial row or column in the worksheet. For example, suppose rows 22 through 35 in the sample worksheet in Figure 5-6 include information that would be damaged if you insert a column all the way down the

FIGURE 5-8.
The Insert command added a column for a new product line.

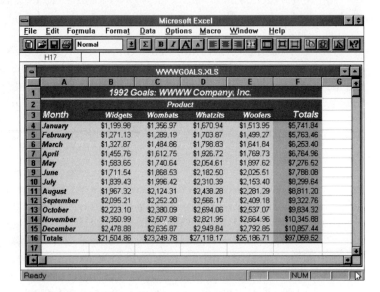

FIGURE 5-9.
The Insert command created a new row to set off the totals.

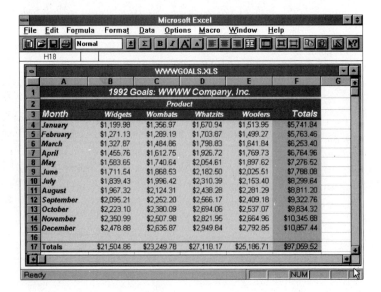

worksheet. You therefore need to insert cells in column D between rows 1 and 17 only. Select cells D1:D17, choose Insert from the Edit menu, and then choose the Shift Cells Right option.

Again, be careful not to misalign data when you're adding partial rows and columns. All cells to the right of the selected range move when you select Shift Cells Right in the Insert dialog box; similarly, the Shift Cells Down option affects all cells below the range you select. You can easily misalign many entries with the Insert command. For example, if you select only cells D1:D16 in Figure 5-6 and then choose Insert, the product totals for the last two columns are no longer aligned with their associated columns of values.

Deletion pitfalls

Although you can generally use the Undo command to cancel a deletion, here are a few pitfalls to avoid.

First, before you delete an entire row or column, scroll through your worksheet to be sure you're not erasing important information that is not visible in the current window.

Second, if you delete a cell upon which formulas in other cells depend, you'll see a #REF! error message in those formula cells. For example, suppose cell A6 in your worksheet contains the formula

=A1+A2+A3+A4+A5

If you delete row 5, this formula shifts to cell A5 and becomes

=A1+A2+A3+A4+#REF!

The result of the formula is also #REF!

Clearly, the results of deleting a row that contains cells referred to by formulas can be disastrous!

Interestingly, functions behave differently from pure formulas in this regard. When you delete a row or column referred to by an argument of a function, Excel modifies the argument, if at all possible, to account for the deletion. For example, if cell A6 contained the formula

=SUM(A1:A5)

and you deleted row 5, the formula (now in cell A5) would change to

=SUM(A1:A4)

This adaptability is a compelling reason to use functions instead of formulas where possible.

Finally, as with Delete, you can't choose a nonadjacent range when you use the Insert command. If you attempt to do so, you'll see the alert message *Cannot do that command on a multiple selection.*

The Cut and Paste commands

The Cut and Paste commands on the Edit menu let you move entries from one place to another on your worksheet. Unlike the Delete and Clear commands, which simply remove cells and cell entries from your worksheet, the Cut command places your selection on the Windows Clipboard, where it is stored until you paste it in another location.

The Cut command puts a dotted-line marquee around any entries you select and places a record of the number of rows and columns within the marquee on the Clipboard. When you select the range to which you want to move the cut cells, the Paste command pastes them in their new location, clears the contents of the cells within the marquee, and erases the marquee.

Microsoft Excel offers keyboard shortcuts for the Cut and Paste commands. Instead of using commands on the Edit menu, you can press either Ctrl-X or Shift-Del for the Cut command and Ctrl-V, Shift-Ins, or Enter for the Paste command. You can also use the mouse to cut and paste cells and cell ranges directly. See "Direct cell manipulation," later in this chapter.

When you use the Cut and Paste commands to move a range of cells, Excel clears both the contents and the formats of the cut range and transfers them to the cells in the paste range. For example, to move the contents of the range A1:A5 in Figure 5-10 to cells C1:C5, select cells A1:A5, and then choose Cut from the Edit menu. When you choose Cut, a marquee appears around the cells you selected. Next, select cell C1 and choose Paste from the Edit menu. Figure 5-11 shows the results: Both the contents and the formats assigned to cells A1:A5 are transferred to cells C1:C5, and cells A1:A5 are blank. Now if you make an entry in cells A1:A5, you'll see that those cells reverted to their default formats.

FIGURE 5-10.
You can use the Cut and Paste commands to move the contents of the range A1:A5 to cells C1:C5.

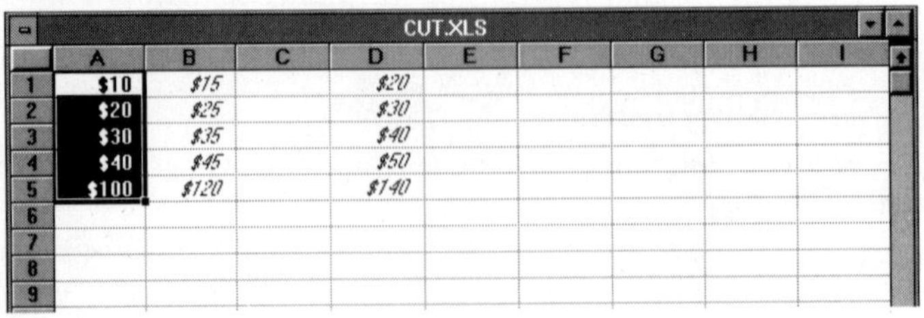

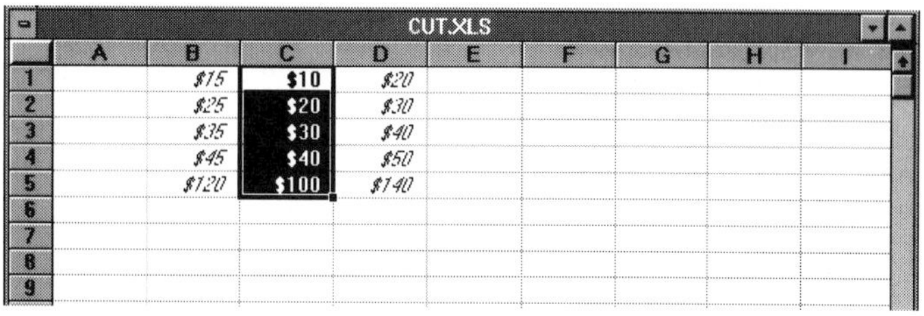

FIGURE 5-11.

The contents and formats of cells A1:A5 now appear in cells C1:C5.

Cut and Paste rules

You need to remember a few rules as you use the Cut and Paste commands. First, the cut area you select must be a single rectangular block of cells. If you try to select a nonadjacent range, you'll see the message *Cannot do that command on a multiple selection.*

Next, you can carry out cutting and pasting operations only once for each range of selected cells. In other words, you can specify only one paste area after you use the Cut command. The contents of the cells, when moved, disappear from their original locations and cannot be referred to for further pasting. If you want to paste the selected data in two or more locations, use the Copy command and then use Clear to erase the contents of the original cell or range.

You don't have to select the entire paste range before you issue the Paste command. When you select a single cell as your paste range, Excel extends the paste area to match the size and shape of the cut area. The cell you select becomes the upper left corner of the paste area. However, if you do select the entire paste area, be sure the range you select is the same size and shape as the cut area. If the cut and paste areas are not identical in size and shape, you'll see the alert message *Cut and paste areas are different shapes.* To correct the problem, click OK in the alert box and select a new paste area.

Finally, remember that Excel overwrites the contents and formats of any existing cells in the paste range when you use the Paste command. If you don't want to lose existing cell entries, be sure your worksheet has enough blank cells below and to the right of the cell you select as the upper left corner of the paste area to hold the entire cut area.

Using overlapping cut and paste ranges

Suppose you want to move cells A1:B5 in Figure 5-10 into cells B1:C5 to fill the empty column, C. You could select cells A1:A5 and choose the Insert command, but this would shift all the cells in rows 1 through 5 one column to the right.

Fortunately, there's a way around this problem. We mentioned earlier that Excel overwrites any existing entries in the cells in the paste range when you use the Paste command. But, because the program transfers the contents of your cut area to your paste area before it erases them from the cut area, you can specify overlapping cut and paste areas without losing information in the overlapping cells.

In the worksheet shown in Figure 5-10, select cells A1:B5 as your cut area and cells B1:C5 as your paste area. As you can see in Figure 5-12, the entries that were in cells A1:B5 in Figure 5-10 are now in cells B1:C5, but the entries to the right of column C in rows 1 to 5 have not moved.

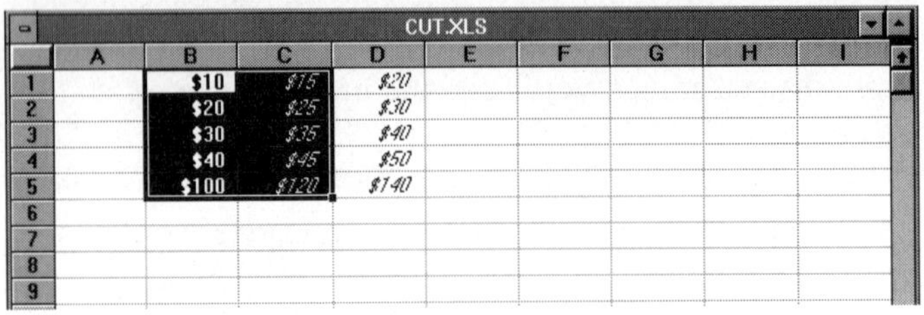

FIGURE 5-12.
You can use overlapping cut and paste areas when moving information.

Using Insert Paste with the Cut command

When you use the Paste command, Excel copies the Clipboard's contents to the selected area of your worksheet. If the selected area of your worksheet already contains data, that data is replaced by the data that you paste.

Under some circumstances, you can insert material from the Clipboard *between* existing worksheet cells, instead of pasting it *over* existing cells. To do this, use the Insert Paste command instead of the Paste command. Insert Paste, like Paste, is located on the Edit menu, but it appears only after you have cut or copied data to the Clipboard. You can also use the mouse to perform an Insert Paste operation on cells and cell ranges directly. See "Direct cell manipulation," later in this chapter.

Figure 5-13 provides an example of a situation in which you might want to use Insert Paste. Suppose you want to rearrange the names of the months in that figure so that they start at September and end at August. To do that, first select A10:A13 and use the Cut command. Then make A2 the active cell and use the Insert Paste command. Excel puts the data that occupies A10:A13 into cells A2:A5, and then moves the rest of column A downward to accommodate the insertion.

As Figure 5-14 shows, the Cut and Insert Paste command transferred four month names from the end of the sequence to the beginning of the sequence. The rest of the worksheet is unchanged.

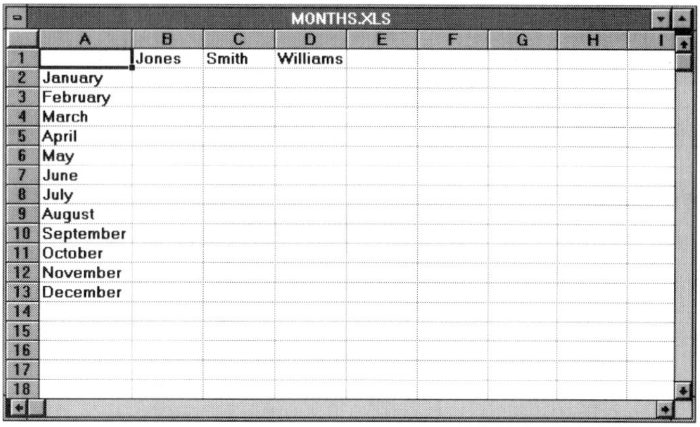

FIGURE 5-13.
We want to rearrange the sequence of months in this worksheet.

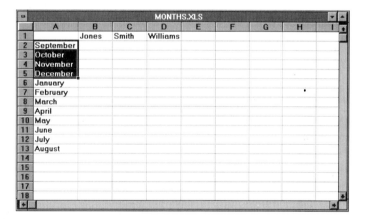

FIGURE 5-14.
Using the Cut command with the Insert Paste command, we transferred four months from the bottom of the list to the top without changing the rest of the worksheet.

Inspecting and saving data stored on the Clipboard

The Windows Clipboard holds data temporarily when you use the Cut or Copy command. Windows also includes an application called the Clipboard Viewer that allows you to inspect the contents of the Clipboard. To access the Clipboard Viewer, choose the Run command from the Application Control menu. Then select the Clipboard option.

If you open the Clipboard Viewer after cutting cells A1:B5 in Figure 5-10, you see the window in Figure 5-15.

FIGURE 5-15.
The Clipboard's default display format shows only the size and shape of the area you cut or copy.

As you can see in Figure 5-15, the Clipboard Viewer initially shows only the size and shape of the worksheet area you cut or copied. But you can use commands on the Clipboard's Display menu to see the data itself. More importantly, you can use commands on the Clipboard's File menu to store the Clipboard's contents in a disk file and to reload a previously saved Clipboard file. These commands make it easy to copy an area of one worksheet into many other worksheets at different working sessions.

For more information about the Windows Clipboard and the Clipboard Viewer, consult your *Microsoft Windows User's Guide.*

Moving formulas

When you move a cell, Excel adjusts any formulas inside or outside the cut area that refer to that cell. For example, in Figure 5-10, cell A5 contains the formula

=SUM(A1:A4)

When we moved cells A1:A5 into cells C1:C5 (Figure 5-11), the move had no apparent effect on the cell contents. However, the formula in cell C5 now reads

=SUM(C1:C4)

Similarly, if we had moved only cells A1:A4, leaving cell A5 behind, the formula in cell A5 would change to

=SUM(C1:C4)

The Copy and Paste commands

You can use the Copy and Paste commands to duplicate the contents and formats of selected cells in another area of your worksheet without disturbing the contents of the original cells. You use the Copy command to indicate the range of cells you want to copy and the Paste command to indicate where you want the copies placed.

Microsoft Excel offers keyboard shortcuts for the Copy and Paste commands. After you select the copy range, instead of opening the Edit menu and choosing Copy, you can press Ctrl-C or Ctrl-Ins. After you select the paste range, you can press Ctrl-V or Shift-Ins to paste the copy. You can also press Enter instead of choosing the Paste command, but only if you want to paste a single copy. Pressing Enter after you choose the Copy command pastes one copy and then cancels the Copy command.

You can also use the mouse to copy and paste cells and cell ranges directly. See "Direct cell manipulation," later in this chapter.

The Paste command copies everything in the cell — entries, formats, and notes. If you want to paste only certain properties, use the Paste Special command. (See "The Paste Special command," later in this chapter.)

Copying a single cell

Suppose cell A1 of your worksheet contains the value 100 formatted to display currency with no decimal places. To copy the contents of cell A1 into cell C1, which is in General format, select cell A1, and then choose Copy from the Edit menu. A marquee appears around the selected cell to show your copy selection. Now select cell C1 and choose Paste from the Edit menu. Figure 5-16 shows the result.

FIGURE 5-16.
A duplicate of cell A1,
including its format,
appears in cell C1.

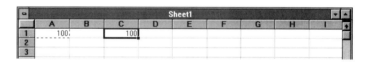

The marquee around cell A1 does not disappear after you use the Paste command. This marquee indicates that your copy area is still active. As long as the marquee appears, you can continue to use the Paste command to create additional duplicates of the cell. You can even use the commands on the Window menu and the Open and New commands on the File menu to access other worksheets and windows without losing your copy area. For example, you might copy a cell into another area of your worksheet, and then use the Open command on the File menu to access a second worksheet and paste the cell into that new worksheet as well.

By specifying paste areas of different sizes and shapes, you can create multiple copies of the contents of the copy area. For example, if you specify the range C1:F2 as the paste range, Excel copies the contents of cell A1 into all the cells in the range C1:F2, as shown in Figure 5-17.

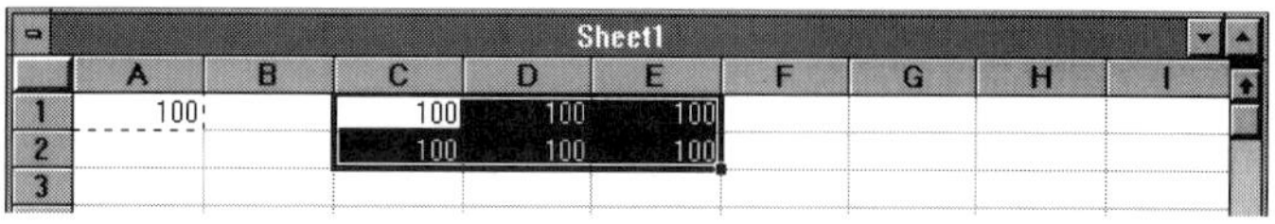

FIGURE 5-17.
You can create
multiple copies of a
single cell.

You can also specify multiple nonadjacent paste areas. For example, to copy the contents of cell A1 into cells C1, C3, and D2, select cell A1 and choose the Copy command. Next, click cell C1 and, holding down Ctrl, click cells C3 and D2. When you choose the Paste command, your worksheet looks like the one shown in Figure 5-18.

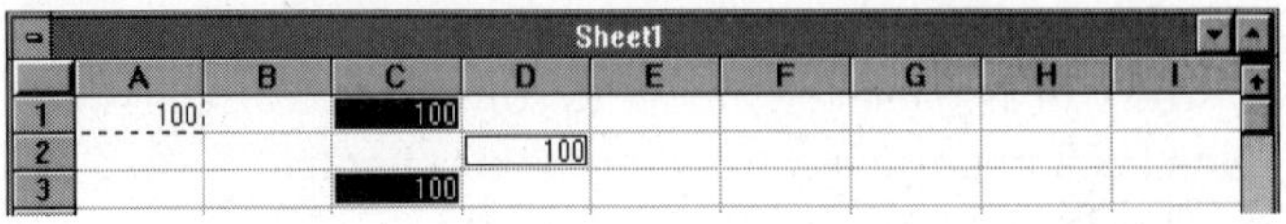

FIGURE 5-18.
*You can select
multiple nonadjacent
paste areas.*

Copying ranges

You can use the Copy command to copy ranges as well as single cells. For example, to copy the contents of cells A1:A3 into cells C1:C3, select cells A1:A3, and then choose Copy from the Edit menu. A marquee appears around the range of cells to be copied. Now select cell C1 and choose Paste from the Edit menu to copy A1:A3 into C1:C3.

As with the Cut and Paste commands, you don't have to select the entire paste area when you copy cells. You need only indicate the upper left corner of the range by selecting a single cell.

You can also create multiple copies of the copy range. For example, you can select C1:D1 as the paste range to create two copies of A1:A3, side by side, in columns C and D. You can achieve the same result by selecting the range C1:D3. Not every paste range works when you're copying ranges, however. For example, if you copy cells A1:A3 and then designate the range C1:C2, C1:D2, C1:C4, or C1:E5, the alert message *Copy and paste areas are different shapes* appears. In other words, you must either select only the first cell in each paste area or select one or more paste ranges of exactly the same size and shape as the cut area.

You can also use the mouse to copy and paste cell ranges directly. See "Direct cell manipulation," later in this chapter.

Using overlapping copy and paste ranges

With one exception, you cannot specify overlapping copy and paste ranges. For example, if you select the range A1:A3, choose the Copy command, select cell A2, and then choose the Paste command, you'll see the message *Selection is not valid.*

The exception to this rule is that you can specify a paste range that contains the entire copy range. Generally, it serves no purpose to specify a paste range that exactly overlaps the copy range, because the contents of the selected cells don't change. When you're using the Paste Special command, however, this technique can be quite useful. You'll see why in a moment.

Using Insert Paste with the Copy command

When you use the Paste command, Excel copies the Clipboard's contents to the selected area of your worksheet. If the selected area of your worksheet already contains data, that data is replaced by the data that you paste.

With the help of the Insert Paste command, you can insert material from the Clipboard *between* existing worksheet cells, instead of pasting it *over* existing cells. To do this, use the Insert Paste command instead of the Paste command. Insert Paste, like Paste, is located on the Edit menu, but it appears only after you have cut or copied data to the Clipboard.

The Insert Paste command works the same way with a copied selection as it does with a cut selection. (For more information, see "Using Insert Paste with the Cut command," earlier in this chapter.) If Excel needs more information from you about how to adjust the worksheet after carrying out an Insert Paste, it will present a dialog box. Select Shift Cells Down or Shift Cells Right, and then click OK to finish the operation.

You can also use the mouse to perform an Insert Paste operation on cells and cell ranges directly. See "Direct cell manipulation," later in this chapter.

Copying relative, absolute, and mixed references

As you learned in Chapter 2, Excel uses two types of cell references: relative and absolute. These two types of references behave very differently when you use the Copy command.

Relative references

When you copy a cell that contains relative cell references, the formula in the paste area doesn't refer to the same cells as the formula in the copy area. Instead, Excel changes the formula references in relation to the position of the pasted cell.

Returning to the sample worksheet in Figure 5-5, suppose you enter the formula

=AVERAGE(B6:E6)

in cell G6. This formula averages the values in the four-cell range that begins five columns to the left of cell G6. Of course, you want to repeat this calculation for the remaining categories as well. Instead of typing a new formula in each cell in column G, select cell G6 and choose Copy from the Edit menu. Next, select cells G7:G10 and choose Paste from the Edit menu. The results appear in Figure 5-19 on the following page.

Because the formula in cell G6 contains a relative reference, Excel adjusts the references in each copy of the formula. As a result, each copy of the formula calculates the average of the cells in the corresponding row. For example, cell G7 contains the formula

=AVERAGE(B7:E7)

FIGURE 5-19.
We copied the relative references from cell G6 into cells G7:G10.

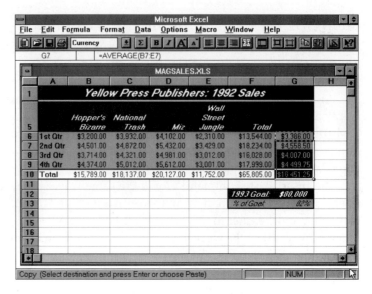

Absolute references

When you want to ensure that cell references do not change when you copy them, use absolute references instead of relative references.

For example, in the worksheet in Figure 5-20, cell C5 contains the formula

=B2*B5

Cell B2 contains the hourly rate at which employees are to be paid.

FIGURE 5-20.
The entry in cell C5 is a formula that contains relative references.

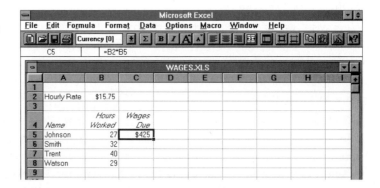

Suppose you want to copy this formula into the range C6:C8. Figure 5-21 shows what happens if you copy the existing formula into this range. The formula in cell

C6 returns the value 0 and cell C7 contains the error value #VALUE! If you look at the formulas in cells C6:C8, you'll see that none of them refers to cell B2. The formula in cell C6 is

=B3*B6

Because cell B3 is empty, the formula returns a 0 value. Similarly, cell C7 contains the formula

=B4*B7

Because cell B4 contains a label rather than a value, the formula in cell C7 returns an error value.

FIGURE 5-21.
We incorrectly copied the relative formula in cell C5 into cells C6:C8.

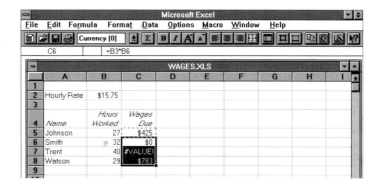

Because the reference to cell B2 in the original formula is relative, it changes as you copy the formula through the worksheet. To apply the wage rate in cell B2 to all the calculations, you must change the reference to cell B2 to an absolute reference before you copy the formula.

You can change the reference style in three ways: by typing a dollar sign ($) in front of the row and column references, by using the Reference command on the Formula menu, or by pressing F4 to insert dollar signs for you. The $ symbol tells Excel to "lock in" the reference. For example, on the worksheet in Figure 5-20, you can select cell C5 and insert the $ symbol before the B and the 2 in the formula bar so that the formula becomes

=$B$2*B5

Alternatively, you can select the cell reference B2 in the formula bar and then choose Reference from the Formula menu or press F4 to have Excel change the relative reference to an absolute reference. The reference to cell B5 is not affected.

When you copy the modified formula into cells C6:C8, the second cell reference, but not the first, is adjusted within each formula. In Figure 5-22, cell C6 now contains the formula

=$B$2*B6

FIGURE 5-22.
We created an
absolute reference to
cell B2.

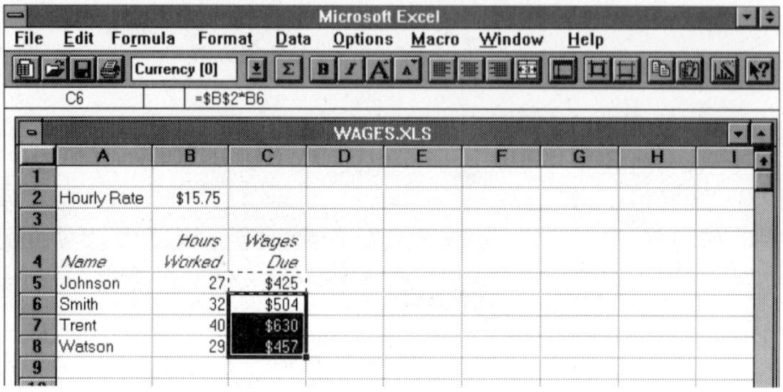

Mixed references

You can also use mixed references in your formulas to anchor only a portion of a cell reference. In a mixed reference, one portion of the reference is absolute and the other is relative. When you copy a mixed reference, Excel anchors the absolute portion and adjusts the relative portion to reflect the location of the cell you copied to.

In a mixed reference, a dollar sign appears in front of the absolute portion of the reference but not in front of the relative portion. For example, the references $B2 and B$2 are mixed references. $B2 uses an absolute column reference and a relative row reference; B$2 uses a relative column reference and an absolute row reference.

To create a mixed reference, you can type the $ symbol in front of the row or column reference, or you can use the Reference command (or press F4) to cycle through the four combinations of absolute and relative references — from B2 to $B$2 to B$2 to $B2. (You must repeat the entire command to see the next selections.)

The loan payment table in Figure 5-23 shows one situation in which mixed references are convenient. Cell C5 uses the formula

=PMT($B5,10,C$4)

to calculate the annual payments on a $10,000 loan over a period of 10 years at an interest rate of 10 percent. We copied this formula into cells C5:E8 to calculate payments on three different loan amounts using several different interest rates.

FIGURE 5-23.

This loan payment table uses formulas that contain mixed references.

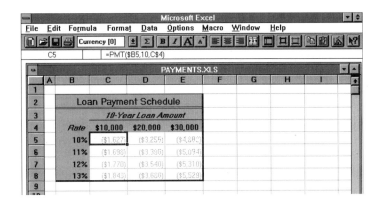

The first cell reference, $B5, indicates that we always want to refer to the values in column B. The row reference remains relative, however, so that the copied formulas in rows 6 through 8 refer to the appropriate interest rates in cells B6 through B8. Similarly, the second cell reference, C$4, indicates that we always want to refer to the loan amounts displayed in row 4. In this case, the column reference remains relative so that the copied formulas in columns C through E refer to the appropriate loan amounts in cells C4 through E4. For example, cell E8 contains the formula

=PMT($B8,10,E$4)

Without mixed references, we would have to edit the formula manually for each column or row of the calculations in cells C5 through E8.

Using Cut, Copy, Paste, and Clear in the formula bar

You can also use the Cut, Copy, Paste, and Clear commands to edit entries in the formula bar. Often, it is easier to simply reenter a value or formula, but the Edit menu commands are convenient when you're working with a long, complex formula or label. For example, to add another *very* to the label

This is a very, very long label.

you can place the insertion point to the left of the space before the word *long,* type a comma and a space, and then type the word *very.* Alternatively, you can select the first instance of the word *very,* the comma, and the space after the comma in the formula bar and issue the Copy command. Then you can place the insertion point in front of the *v* in the second *very* and choose Paste from the Edit menu. Your label now reads

This is a very, very, very long label.

You can also use this capability to copy all or part of a formula from one cell to another. For example, suppose cell A10 contains the formula

=IF(NPV(.15,A1:A9)>0,A11,A12)

and you want to enter

=NPV(.15,A1:A9)

in cell B10. Select cell A10 and select the characters you want to copy — in this case, NPV(.15,A1:A9). Then choose Copy from the Edit menu and press Esc. Now select cell B10, type =, and choose the Paste command to insert the contents of the copy range in that cell's formula bar. The formula's cell references are not adjusted when you cut, copy, and paste in the formula bar.

The Paste Special command

At times, you may want to copy the value in a cell without carrying over the underlying formula on which the value is based. Or you may want to copy the formula but not the format of a cell. The Paste Special command on the Edit menu offers a convenient way to copy only a selected aspect of a cell.

For example, cell F4 in Figure 5-24 contains the formula

=AVERAGE(B4:E4)

FIGURE 5-24.
We want to use the value from cell F4 in cell G4.

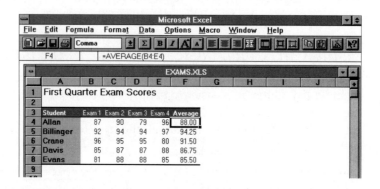

To use the value from cell F4 in cell G4 of your worksheet without copying the formula from cell F4 to the new location — that is, to make the pasted entry a constant value — select cell F4 and choose Copy. (You must choose Copy to use the Paste Special command. When you choose Cut, Paste Special is dimmed.) Then select cell G4 and choose Paste Special. You'll see the dialog box shown in Figure 5-25.

FIGURE 5-25.
The Paste Special dialog box lets you paste formulas, values, formats, or notes.

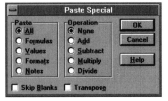

The Paste Special dialog box lets you selectively paste the formulas, values, formats, or notes from the copy range into the paste range. (Cell notes are discussed later in this chapter.) If you select Values in the Paste Special dialog box, Microsoft Excel copies only the value of the formula in cell F4 into cell G4. After the copy operation is complete, cell G4 contains the number 88. As you can see in Figure 5-26, Excel does not copy the formula and numeric format of the original cell, so if you later change any of the values in cells B4:E4, the value in cell G4 will remain unchanged.

FIGURE 5-26.
We used Paste Special to copy the value of the formula in F4 into G4.

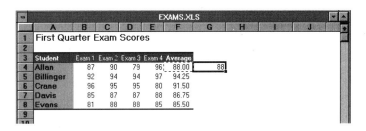

The Formulas option transfers only the formulas from the cells in the copy range to the cells in the paste range. Any formats or notes in the paste range remain unaffected.

The Paste Formats and Paste Values tools

The Paste Formats tool on both the Standard and Utility toolbars and the Paste Values tool on the Utility toolbar provide easier ways to access these often-used Paste Special command options. Clicking one of these tools is equivalent to choosing the Paste Special command on the Edit menu, selecting the corresponding dialog-box option, and pressing Enter. For more information about tools and toolbars, see Appendix A.

You can select Formats from the Paste Special dialog box if you want to copy the formats in the cells in the copy range to the paste range without copying the values assigned to those cells. This command has the same effect as selecting a range of cells and choosing the appropriate options from the Format menu. For example, in Figure 5-24, cells A3:A8 are formatted with several different pattern and font formats, while cells H3:H8 are not formatted. If you copy cells A4:A8 into cells H3:H8 using the Paste Special Formats option, the worksheet looks like Figure 5-27. The formats in cells A4:A8 have been copied to cells H3:H8, but the contents have not. Now anything you enter in cells H3:H8 will assume the same font, alignment, and number formats as you assigned to cells A3:A8.

FIGURE 5-27.
We copied only the formats of cells A3:A8 to cells H3:H8 using the Formats option of the Paste Special command.

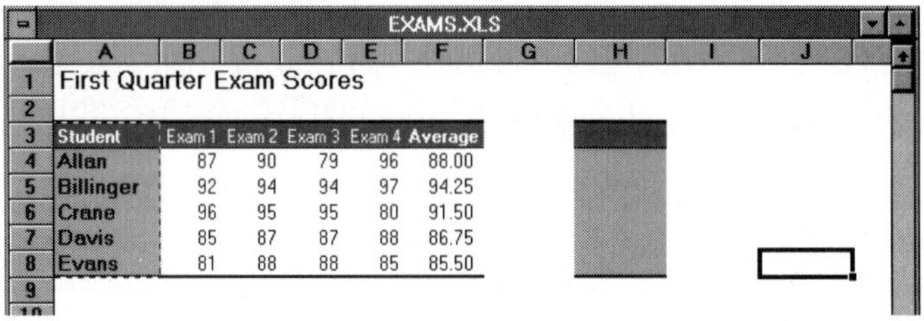

If you select All in the Paste Special dialog box, the values, formulas, formats, and cell notes from the copy range are all copied to the paste range. Because selecting All has the same effect as selecting the regular Paste command, you may wonder why Excel offers this option. That question brings us to our next topic — the Operation options.

The Operation options

The Operation options in the Paste Special dialog box let you mathematically combine the contents of the copy area with the contents of the paste area. When you select any of these options other than None, Excel does not overwrite the paste range. Instead, it uses the specified operator to combine the copy and paste ranges.

For example, suppose you want to add the average exam scores and bonus points in columns F and G of Figure 5-28 to calculate each student's final score. First, select cells F4:F8 and choose Copy. Then select cell H4 and choose Paste Special. Click the Values option and OK in the Paste Special dialog box to copy only the values in cells F4:F8 into cells H4:H8. (Because the pasted cells are still selected, you can now choose Number from the Format menu, or simply select Comma from the Style drop-down list in the Standard toolbar, to give them the 0.00 format.) Next, select the range G4:G8 and choose Copy again. Then select cell H4 and choose Paste

Special. Select the Values and Add options in the Paste Special dialog box, and then click OK. As you can see in Figure 5-29, Excel adds the values in cells F4:F8 to the values in cells G4:G8.

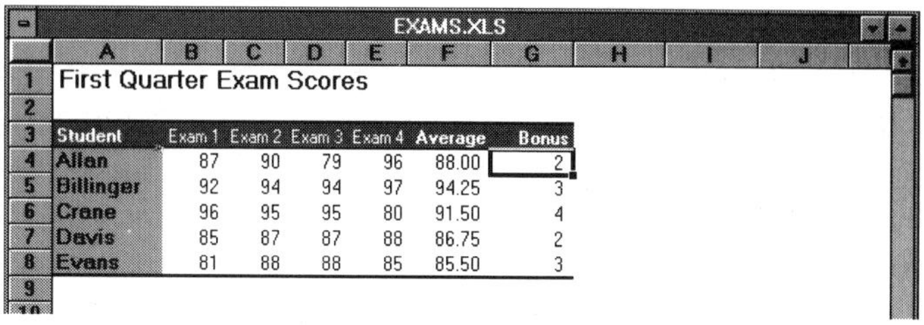

FIGURE 5-28.
This worksheet contains average exam scores and bonus points.

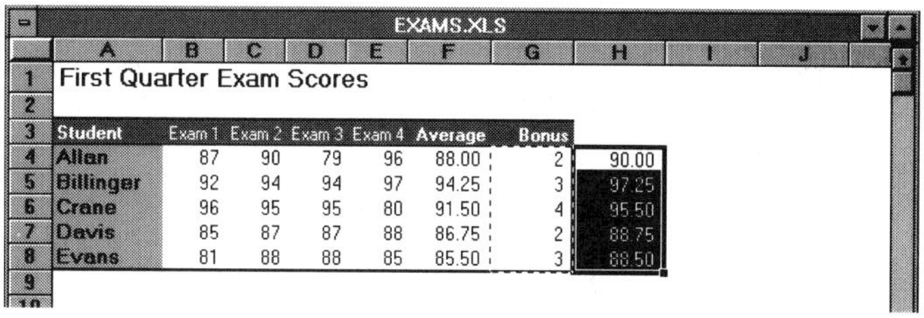

FIGURE 5-29.
We used the Values and Add options in the Paste Special dialog box to combine the average scores with the bonus points.

The other Operation options combine the contents of the copy and paste ranges using different operators. The Subtract option subtracts the contents of the copy range from the contents of the paste range, the Multiply option multiplies the contents of the ranges, and the Divide option divides the contents of the paste range by the contents of the copy range.

You'll usually choose the Values option from the Paste portion of the Paste Special dialog box when you take advantage of the Operation options. As long as the entries in the copy range are numbers, you can use the All option, instead of Values, to copy the numbers and the formats from the copy range to the paste range. If the copy range contains formulas, however, you might get unexpected results using All.

For example, suppose cell A1 contains the value 10, cell A2 contains the formula

=A1

which returns the value 10, and cell B2 contains the value 2. If you select cell A2 and choose the Copy command, select cell B2 and choose the Paste Special command, and then select All and Add, Excel combines the formula from cell A2 — adjusted because it is a relative reference — with the entry in cell B2. The result is the formula

=2+(B1)

The same occurs if the cells in the paste range include formulas, even if you select the Values options.

As a rule, avoid using the All option with any of the Paste Special Operation options when the copy range includes formulas. In fact, you'll probably want to avoid the Operation options altogether if the paste range contains formulas.

If the copy range contains text entries and you use Paste Special with an Operation option, Excel does not copy those text entries into the paste range. Blank spaces in the copy range are assigned the value 0, regardless of which Operation option you select. For example, suppose you use the Multiply option to copy the values in cells B1:B7 into cells A1:A7 in Figure 5-30. As you can see in Figure 5-31, cells A2, A4, and A6 contain zeros because Excel assigns the value 0 to blank cells and the result of multiplying any number by 0 is 0.

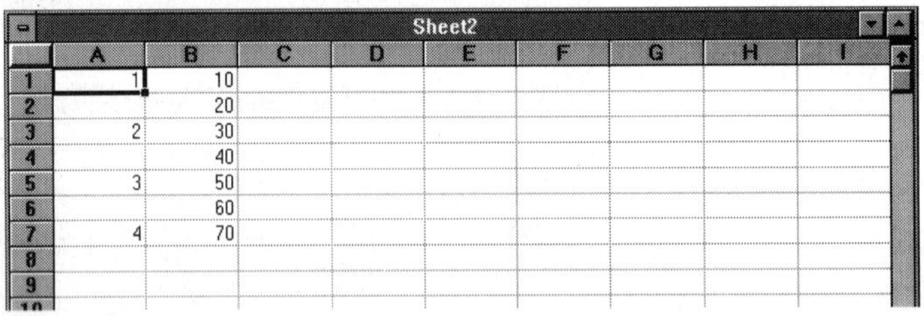

FIGURE 5-30.
The range A1:A7 contains some blank cells.

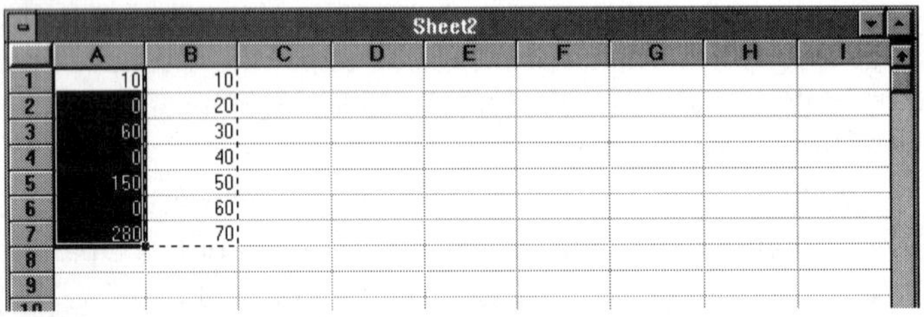

FIGURE 5-31.
After we copy the values in B1:B7 into A1:A7 with the Multiply option, Excel displays a 0 in cells A2, A4, and A6.

Skipping blank cells

At the lower left of the Paste Special dialog box is a Skip Blanks check box. Use this option when you want Excel to ignore any blank cells in the copy range. Generally, if your copy range contains blank cells, Excel pastes those blank cells over the corresponding cells in the paste area. As a result, the contents, formats, and notes in the paste area are overwritten by the empty cell. When you use the Skip Blanks option, however, the corresponding cells in the paste area are unaffected.

For example, let's use the Skip Blanks option to copy cells A1:A7 into the range B1:B7 in Figure 5-32. As you can see in Figure 5-33, the blank cells A2, A4, and A6 don't affect the entries in cells B2, B4, and B6. Instead, the entries from the two ranges are interwoven.

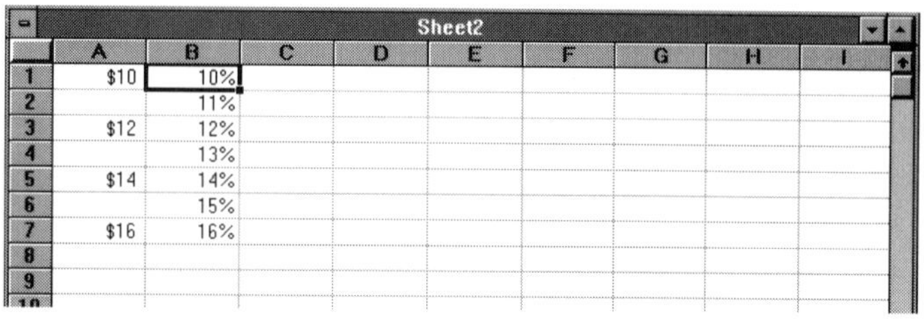

FIGURE 5-32.

Cells A2, A4, and A6 contain blank cells.

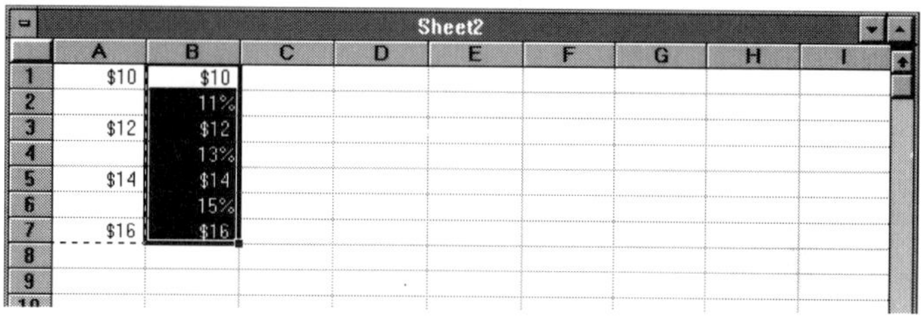

	A	B	C	D	E	F	G	H	I
1	$10	10%							
2		11%							
3	$12	12%							
4		13%							
5	$14	14%							
6		15%							
7	$16	16%							
8									
9									

FIGURE 5-33.

When we use the Skip Blanks option, the empty cells in the copy range don't affect corresponding cells in the paste range.

	A	B	C	D	E	F	G	H	I
1	$10	$10							
2		11%							
3	$12	$12							
4		13%							
5	$14	$14							
6		15%							
7	$16	$16							
8									
9									

Transposing entries

The last option in the Paste Special dialog box is Transpose, which lets you reorient the contents of the copy range in the selected paste range. When you use the Transpose option, entries in the top row of the copy area appear in the left column of the paste range; entries in the left column appear in the top row. To illustrate, let's use the Transpose option to paste the contents of cells A1:B7 in Figure 5-32. If we specify cell A10 as the upper left corner of our Paste Special range, our worksheet looks like the one in Figure 5-34.

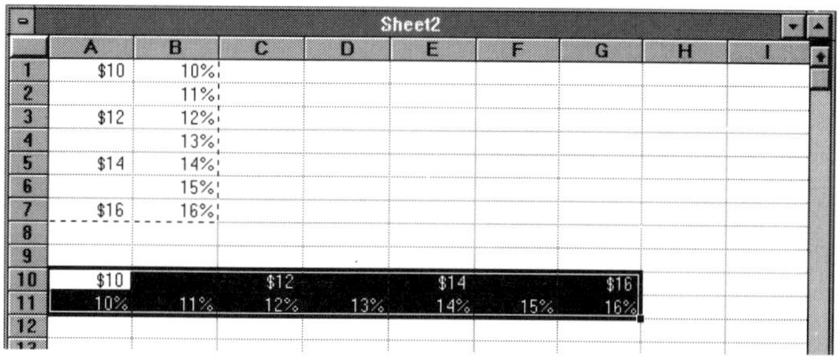

FIGURE 5-34.

The Transpose check box reorients a pasted selection.

	A	B	C	D	E	F	G	H	I
1	$10	10%							
2		11%							
3	$12	12%							
4		13%							
5	$14	14%							
6		15%							
7	$16	16%							
8									
9									
10	$10		$12		$14		$16		
11	10%	11%	12%	13%	14%	15%	16%		
12									

Excel transposes the values as well as the formulas and adjusts cell references as necessary.

Using Paste Special with arrays

As with any other formula, you can convert the results of an array formula into a series of constant values by selecting the array range, choosing the Copy command,

and — without changing your selection — issuing the Paste Special command. When you use the Values option in the Paste Special dialog box, Excel overwrites the array formulas with constant values. Because the range now contains constant values rather than a formula, Excel no longer treats the selection as an array.

The Fill commands

The Fill Right, Fill Left, Fill Down, and Fill Up commands are handy shortcuts when you want to copy one or more cells into an adjacent set of cells. Fill Right copies the entries in the leftmost column of a range into the rest of the cells in the range; Fill Down copies the entries in the top row of a range down into the rest of the cells in the range. If you press Shift before accessing the Edit menu, Microsoft Excel changes the Fill Right and Fill Down commands to read Fill Left and Fill Up. As you might have guessed, Fill Left copies the entries in the rightmost column of a range into the rest of the cells in the range, and Fill Up copies the entries in the bottom row of a range up into the rest of the cells in the range.

You can also use the mouse to fill cell ranges directly. See "Direct cell manipulation," later in this chapter.

For example, in Figure 5-19, we used the Copy and Paste commands to copy the formula in cell G6 into cells G7:G10. We could also have used the Fill Down command to copy this formula. To use Fill Down, type the formula you want to copy in cell G6, select cells G6:G10, and choose Fill Down from the Edit menu. The resulting worksheet looks like the one in Figure 5-19. As with the Copy and Paste commands, any relative cell references in the filled cells are adjusted.

Similarly, you can use the Fill Right command to copy a series of cells across your worksheet. Let's use the simple worksheet in Figure 5-35 as an example. To copy the contents of cells A1:A4 into cells B1:E4, select cells A1:E4 and choose Fill Right from the Edit menu. The results appear in Figure 5-36.

FIGURE 5-35.
This simple work-
sheet contains entries
in cells A1:A4, B1,
and B3.

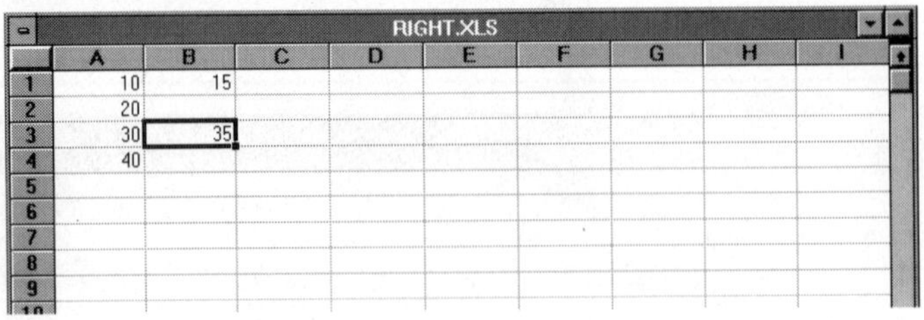

FIGURE 5-36.
We used the Fill Right command to copy the entries in cells A1:A4 into B1:E4.

Notice that the contents of cells B1 and B3 were overwritten as a result of the Fill Right command. Whenever you use a Fill command, any existing cell entries in the fill range are replaced with the values that reside in the leftmost or top cells of the range.

The Series command

The Series command on the Data menu is similar to the Fill commands. It lets you quickly create a regular series of numbers in your worksheet. You supply a starting value, the range to be filled, an interval, and, if you wish, a maximum value for the range.

You can also use the mouse to create series of numbers and dates directly. See "Direct cell manipulation," later in this chapter.

Let's look at the Series command in action. Suppose cells A1 and A2 contain the values 10 and 20. If you select cells A1:A10 and choose Series from the Data menu, Microsoft Excel displays a dialog box like the one in Figure 5-37.

FIGURE 5-37.
Use the Series dialog box to create a regular series of numbers.

To create a data series, first tell Excel whether you want to create the series in rows or in columns. Like Fill Right, the Rows option tells Excel to use the first value in each row to fill the cells to the right; like Fill Down, the Columns option tells Excel to use the first value in each column to fill the cells below. In this case, because our selection is taller than it is wide, the Columns option is already selected.

Next, choose the type of data series you want to create: Linear, Growth, or Date. Excel uses the Type option in conjunction with the start values in cells A1:A2 and the value in the Step Value text box at the lower left corner of the dialog box to create your data series. The Linear option adds the value specified in the Step Value text box to the values in your worksheet. The Growth option multiplies the first value in the selection by the step value. If you select the Date option, you can specify the type of date series you want to create from the options in the Date Unit box.

The Date options of the Series dialog box are described in more detail in Chapter 9. For now, we'll accept the suggested value of 10 in the Step Value box and click OK. Next, we'll enter the same two starting values (10 and 20) in cells C1 and C2, select the range C1:C10, then choose the Series command again, this time using the Growth option with the suggested Step Value of 10. The resulting two series are shown in Figure 5-38.

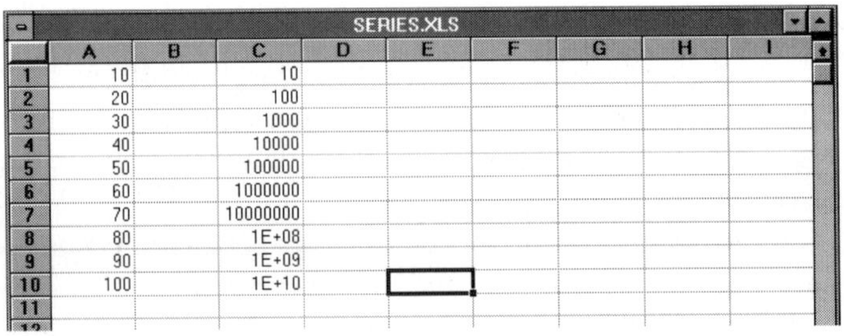

FIGURE 5-38.
Starting with identical values in both columns, we created a Linear series in column A and a Growth series in column C.

The AutoFill option is a powerful way to create data series. You can enter one or more values as an example and AutoFill extends the series using the interval between the selected values. Figure 5-39 shows some examples of series created using AutoFill with various selected values. The values to the left of the bold border were typed in, and the values to the right were extended using the Fill command.

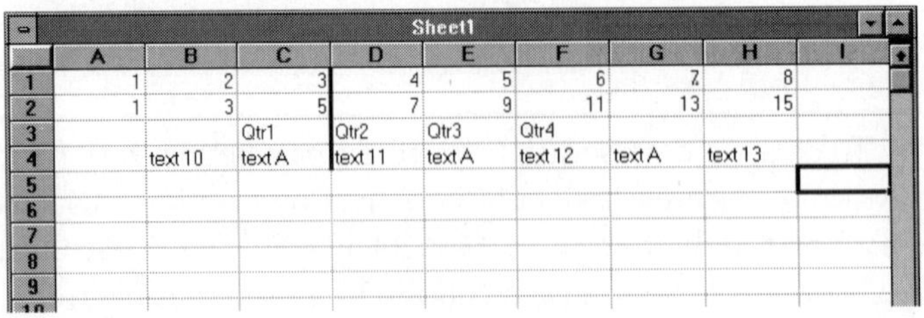

FIGURE 5-39.
We created a different series in each row using the values to the left of the heavy border as examples.

Rows 1 and 2 contain simple series that are created with the regular series command. But rows 3 and 4 show how the AutoFill feature can extrapolate a series even with mixed text and numeric values in cells. If you select cell C3, for example, and try to create a series normally, nothing happens. But when you select the Auto-Fill option, Excel extends the numeric component of the entry in subsequent cells, while simply repeating the text component. Similarly, in row 4, the number in cell B4 is extended in alternate cells, while the text in cell C4 is simply repeated in alternate cells.

Direct cell manipulation

Microsoft Excel Version 4 offers a direct cell manipulation feature that lets you perform many of the most common editing tasks without using commands. Using the mouse in combination with modifier keys, you can cut and paste, copy and paste, clear, delete, and move cells. In addition, you can duplicate much of the functionality of the Fill and Series commands with simple mouse movements.

You turn the direct cell manipulation feature on and off using the Workspace command on the Options menu. You can tell if the feature is turned on by looking at the active selection. A small black square, called the *fill handle*, is visible in the lower right corner of the selection rectangle when direct cell manipulation is turned on, as you can see in Figure 5-40. To activate Excel's direct cell manipulation feature, choose Workspace from the Options menu and select the check box labeled *Cell Drag and Drop*.

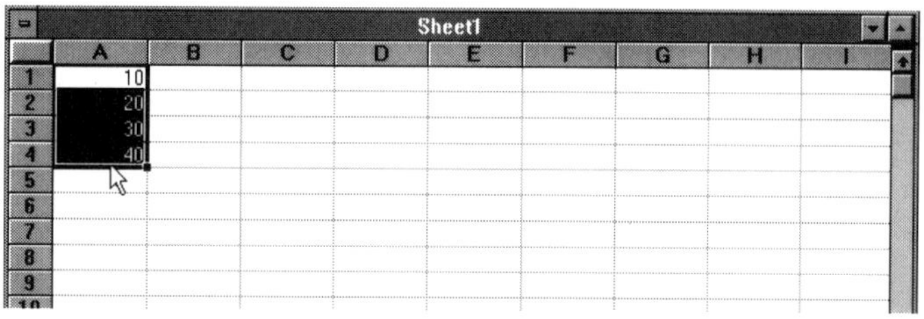

FIGURE 5-40.
When Cell Drag and Drop is activated, the mouse pointer turns into an arrow when you move it over a border of the selection rectangle.

Try moving the mouse pointer around the selection rectangle. When the Cell Drag and Drop option is selected, the mouse pointer changes to an arrow when you position it over a border of the selection rectangle. When you position the mouse pointer over the fill handle, it changes to a bold cross-hair, which indicates a fill, clear, insert, or series procedure.

Excel's formula and reference rules for cutting, pasting, moving, and inserting (discussed earlier in this chapter) also apply to the direct cell manipulation techniques described here.

Moving and copying with the mouse

To quickly cut a cell or range and paste it into a new location, select the cell or range and drag it to where you want it to be. For example, in Figure 5-40, the mouse pointer is positioned over the bottom border of the selection rectangle that encloses cells

A1:A4. When the arrow pointer appears, click the border and drag it to column C. The result is shown in Figure 5-41.

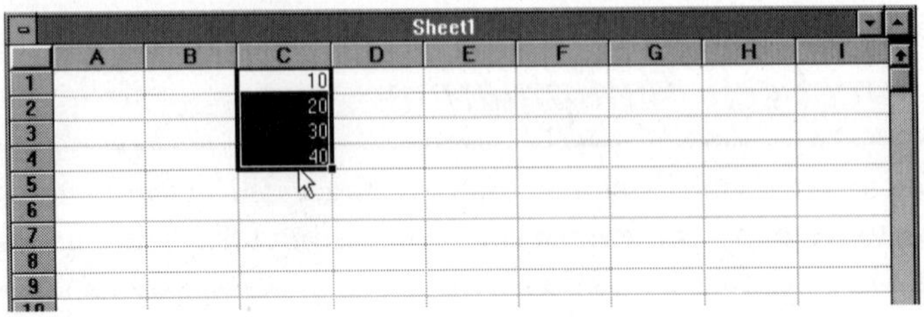

FIGURE 5-41.
Using the mouse, we dragged the selected cells to a new location.

If you want to copy the selection (copy and paste) rather than move it (cut and paste), press Ctrl before you release the border of the selection rectangle. In this case, the mouse pointer appears with a small plus sign next to it, which indicates you are copying rather than moving the selection, as shown in Figure 5-42.

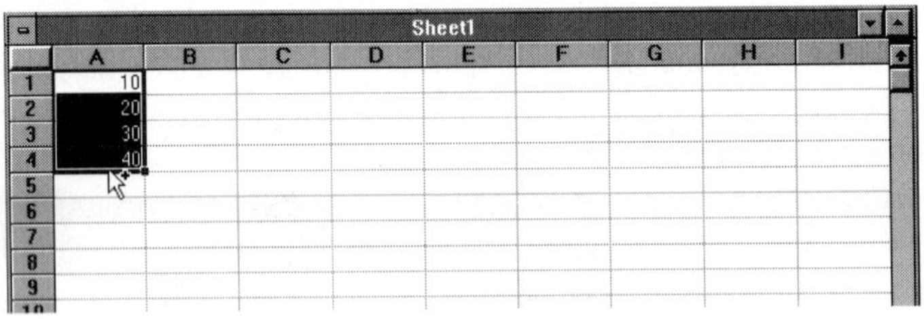

FIGURE 5-42.
Before you finish dragging, press Ctrl to copy the selection. Note the small plus sign next to the arrow pointer.

You can also use the direct cell-manipulation feature to perform Insert Paste operations. For example, in Figure 5-43, we first selected cells A1:A2, then dragged the selection while holding down Shift. As you can see, a gray I-beam indicates where the selected cells will be inserted when you release the mouse button. The I-beam appears wherever the arrow cursor passes over a horizontal or vertical cell border. In this case, the vertical border between cells C1:C2 and D1:D2 is indicated, but we could just as easily insert the cells horizontally, *between* cells C1 and C2. When you release the mouse button, the selected cells move to the new location, as shown in Figure 5-44.

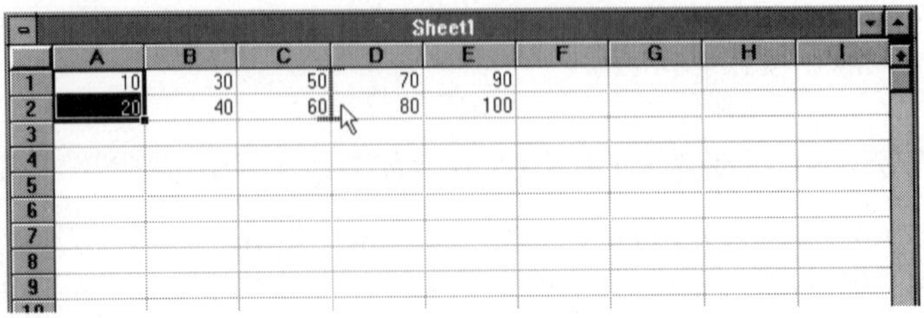

FIGURE 5-43.
When you hold down Shift and drag the selected cells, the gray I-beam indicates where they will be inserted.

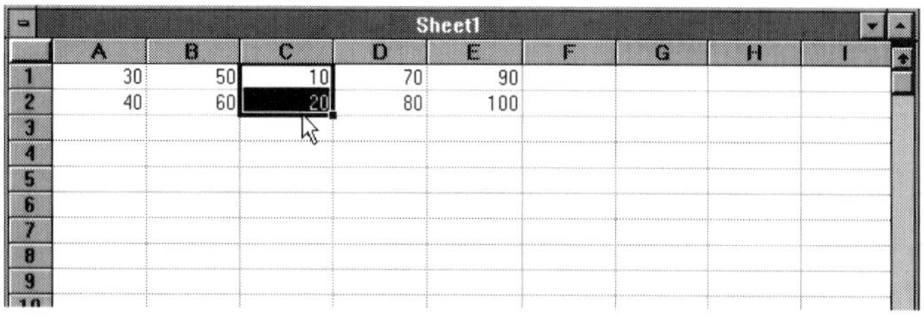

FIGURE 5-44.
The selected cells are inserted in their new location.

	A	B	C	D	E	F	G	H	I
1	30	50	10	70	90				
2	40	60	20	80	100				
3									
4									
5									
6									
7									
8									
9									

If you press Ctrl-Shift while dragging, the selected cells are copied instead of moved to the insertion point. The mouse pointer displays the small plus sign next to the arrow in this case, and inserts a copy of the selected cells in the new location, while leaving the original selected cells intact.

All these techniques work equally well when you select *entire* rows or columns.

Inserting, deleting, and clearing cells with the mouse

To perform the next group of operations, use the fill handle (the small black square in the selection rectangle). If you select a cell or range, the fill handle appears in the lower right corner of the selection rectangle. If you select an entire row or entire rows, the fill handle appears in the lower left corner of the selection, next to the row header. If you select an entire column or entire columns, the fill handle appears in the upper right corner of the selection, near the column header. Using the example worksheet in Figure 5-43, let's say we want to add some numbers between columns A and B. First, we either select cells A1:A2, or the entire column A. Next we click the fill handle and drag one column to the right while holding down Shift. Notice that the mouse pointer becomes a double line with a pair of outward-pointing arrows, indicating that you are inserting cells. The result is shown in Figure 5-45.

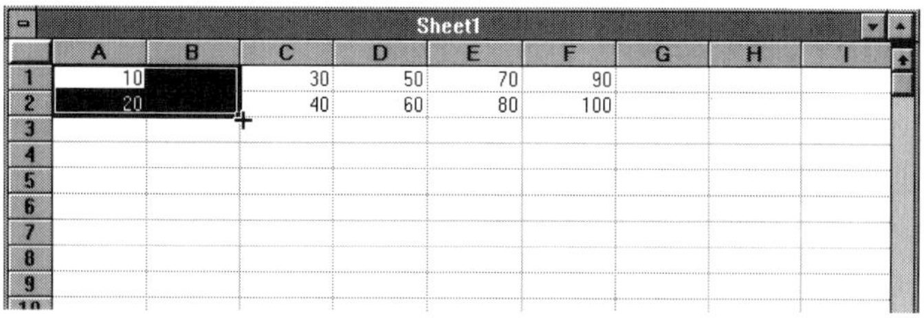

FIGURE 5-45.
We inserted the blank cells in column B by holding down Shift and dragging the fill handle to the right.

	A	B	C	D	E	F	G	H	I
1	10		30	50	70	90			
2	20		40	60	80	100			
3									
4									
5									
6									
7									
8									
9									

You can just as easily delete cells, rows, or columns using the same technique. For example, to delete the cells we just inserted, select cells B1:B2, and then, while holding down Shift, drag the fill handle to the left. When you do this, notice that the selection turns a medium shade of gray, and the mouse pointer changes to a double line with a pair of inward-pointing arrows (as you can see in Figure 5-46), indicating that you are deleting the selection. When you release the mouse button, the selection is deleted as if you had issued the Delete command on the selected cells.

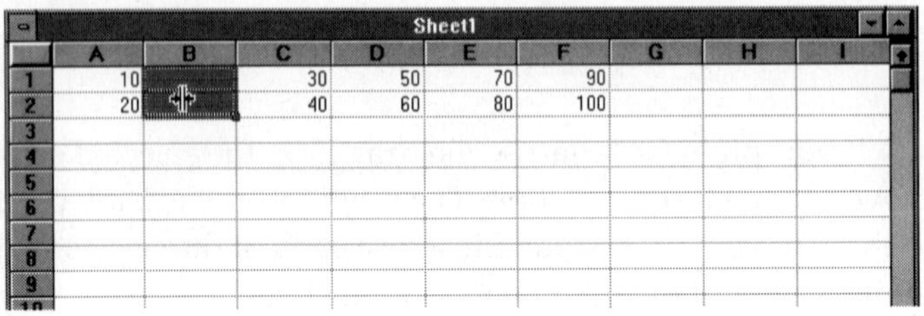

FIGURE 5-46.
Click the fill handle, hold down Shift, and drag back over the selection to delete it. The result looks like the worksheet in Figure 5-43.

If you do not hold Shift down when you drag back over the selected cells, instead of performing a Delete operation, you perform a Clear operation that is equivalent to choosing the Clear command and selecting the Formulas option. (See "The Clear command," earlier in this chapter.) If you hold down Ctrl while dragging back over the selection, it is equivalent to choosing the Clear command and selecting the All option. For example, if you select the range A1:E2 in the worksheet shown in Figure 5-43, and drag the fill handle to the left until the cross-hair pointer is at the beginning of column A, all the selected data is cleared from the cells. This clears formulas only. To clear formulas, formats, and notes, hold down Ctrl while you drag.

Filling and creating series with the mouse

The fill handle lets you perform two other very handy procedures with the mouse: filling cells and creating series. This feature is known as AutoFill.

When you select a single cell, click on the fill handle, and drag in any direction, the contents of that cell are copied into the selected range. When you select a range of cells one of two things occurs. Either the range is copied in the direction you drag the mouse, or the series is extended, depending on the shape of the selection, the direction you drag, and whether or not you are holding down Ctrl. For example, using the worksheet in Figure 5-43, if you select the range A2:E2 and drag the fill handle down, that range is copied in the same way as if you used the Fill Down command, as shown in Figure 5-47.

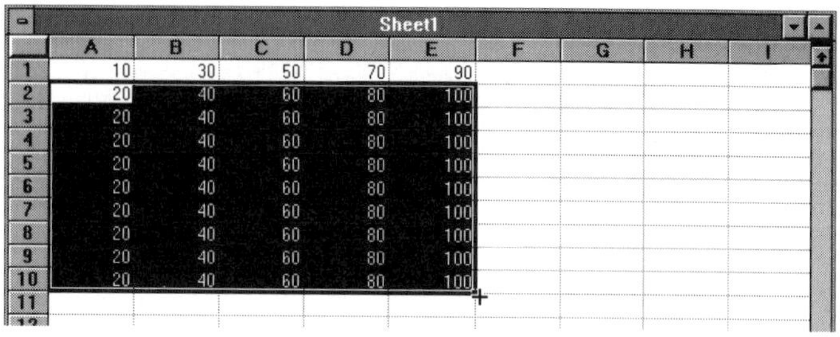

FIGURE 5-47.
You perform a fill operation by selecting the cells to copy and dragging the fill handle.

	A	B	C	D	E	F	G	H	I
1	10	30	50	70	90				
2	20	40	60	80	100				
3	20	40	60	80	100				
4	20	40	60	80	100				
5	20	40	60	80	100				
6	20	40	60	80	100				
7	20	40	60	80	100				
8	20	40	60	80	100				
9	20	40	60	80	100				
10	20	40	60	80	100				
11									

However, if you select cells A1:A2 and drag the fill handle down, you create a series that uses the interval between the two selected values, as shown in column A of Figure 5-48. Alternatively, if you select cells B1:B2 and hold down Ctrl while you drag the fill handle, you copy the selected range down, as shown in column B of Figure 5-48. Note the small plus sign next to the mouse pointer, which indicates a copy operation.

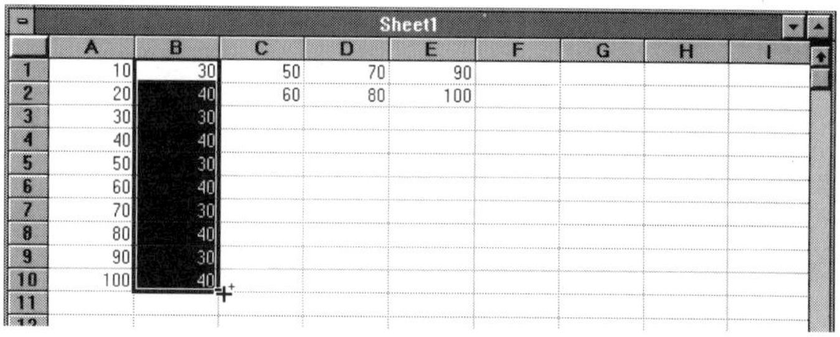

FIGURE 5-48.
We created a series in column A and copied a range in column B.

	A	B	C	D	E	F	G	H	I
1	10	30	50	70	90				
2	20	40	60	80	100				
3	30	30							
4	40	40							
5	50	30							
6	60	40							
7	70	30							
8	80	40							
9	90	30							
10	100	40							
11									

If you select a text value and drag the fill handle, the value is copied into the range you drag into. If, however, the selection contains mixed text and numeric values, the AutoFill feature takes over and extends the numeric component while copying the text component. (See "The Series command," earlier in this chapter for more information about AutoFill.)

You can also extend dates in this way, using a number of different date formats, including *Qtr1*, *Qtr2*, etc. See Chapter 9 for more information.

The Justify and Parse commands

The Justify command on the Format menu lets you split a cell entry and distribute it into two or more adjacent rows of your worksheet. Unlike other formatting commands, Justify affects the contents of your cells, not simply the way in which entries are displayed.

For example, cell A2 in Figure 5-49 contains a long label. Suppose we want to extend this label into cells A3 through A8 to make it more readable. If we select the range A2:A8 and choose Justify from the Format menu, our worksheet looks like the one in Figure 5-50.

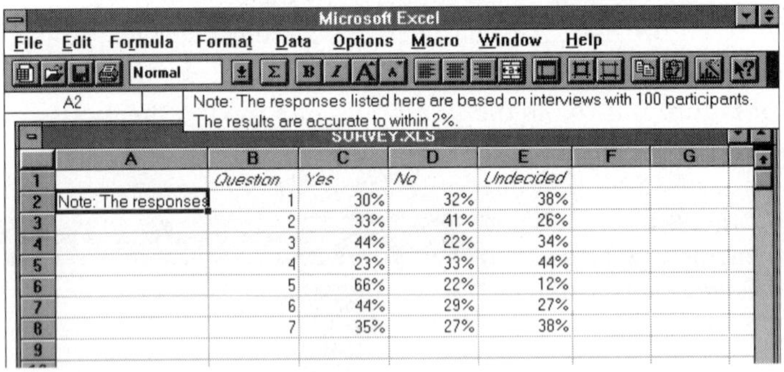

FIGURE 5-49.
Cell A2 contains a long label.

FIGURE 5-50.
We used the Justify command to distribute the label from cell A2 into cells A2:A8.

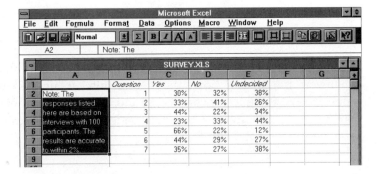

If the selected Justify range isn't large enough to accommodate the long cell entry, Microsoft Excel displays the message *Text will extend below range.* Clicking OK in the alert box extends the length of the selected range to the length required for justification, overwriting the contents of any cells within the extended range in the process. To avoid this, choose Cancel in the alert box, widen the column that contains the range, and repeat the Justify command.

If we later decide to edit the entries in cells A2:A8 or to change the width of the column that contains those labels, we can use the Justify command to redistribute the text. For example, suppose we decide to widen column A in Figure 5-50. We can justify the text in cells A2:A8 again by selecting the range and choosing Justify from the Format menu. Figure 5-51 shows the result.

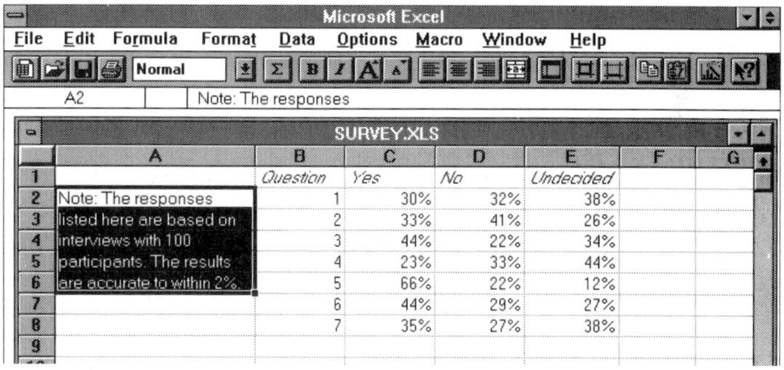

FIGURE 5-51.
*After editing, we used
Justify again to
redistribute the labels.*

If you select a multi-column range when you issue the Justify command, Excel justifies the entries in the leftmost column of the range, using the total width of the range you select as its guideline for determining the length of the justified labels. The cells in adjacent columns are not affected by the command. As a result, you might find that some of your label displays are truncated by the entries in subsequent columns.

Any blank cells in the leftmost column of the justify range serve as "paragraph" separators. That is, Excel groups the labels above and below the blank cells when it justifies text entries.

The Parse command is similar to Justify, except that it distributes cell entries horizontally rather than vertically. For example, if cell A1 contains a long label that you want to distribute into cells A1:E1, you can use Parse to break that label into appropriate portions. Parse is located on the Data menu because you use it most often when you import database information from other programs into Excel. For that reason, we'll save our discussion of the Parse command for Chapter 23.

The Find and Replace commands

Suppose you've built a large worksheet and you now need to find every formula in that worksheet that contains a particular character string or value. The Find command on the Formula menu lets you locate any string of characters, including cell references and range names, in the formulas or values in a worksheet. This command is particularly useful when you want to find linked formulas or error values such as #NAME? — or #REF! What's more, you can use the Replace command to overwrite the strings you locate with new entries.

The Find command

To locate a character string, begin by selecting the range you want to search. If you want to look through the entire worksheet, select a single cell. Microsoft Excel begins its search from that cell, travels through the worksheet, and finishes in the selected cell. If you want to search only a portion of the worksheet, select the appropriate range.

When you issue the Find command, you see a dialog box like the one in Figure 5-52. First specify the Find What string — the group of characters you want to search for. The string can include any letter, number, punctuation mark, or special character.

FIGURE 5-52.
Use the Find dialog box to locate a character string.

The Look by options

The Look by options let you search by row or column. When you select the Rows option, Excel looks through the worksheet horizontally row by row, starting with the currently selected cell. If it finds an occurrence of the Find What string, Excel highlights the cell that contains that occurrence and stops searching. If it doesn't find an occurrence before it reaches the last cell in the active portion of the worksheet, Excel loops back to cell A1 and continues to search through the worksheet until it either finds an occurrence or returns to the originally selected cell. Select the Rows option if you think the string is located below the selected cell.

The Columns option works in almost the same way, except that it searches through the worksheet column by column, beginning with the selected cell. If you think the string you want to search for is to the right of the selected cell, choose the Columns option.

The Look in options

The Look in options tell Excel whether to search in formulas, values, or notes for the Find What string. When you select Formulas, Excel searches for the string in the formulas contained in the worksheet cells. When you select Values, Excel searches for the string in the displayed results of the entries in the worksheet. When you select Notes, Excel examines any text you have attached as a note to a cell. (See "Cell notes," later in this chapter.)

The difference between the Formulas and Values options can be confusing. Remember that the underlying contents of a cell and the displayed value of that cell are often not the same. For example, if a cell contains a formula, the displayed value of the cell is usually the result of that formula — a number like 100 or a character string if the formula involves text. If a cell contains a pure number, the displayed value of the cell might or might not agree with the cell's underlying contents. If the cell has the General format, the displayed value of the cell and the cell's contents usually agree; if the cell contains a number that has another format, however, the contents of the cell and its displayed value are different. The underlying and displayed values of a cell that contains a text entry are usually the same.

Consider the simple worksheet in Figure 5-53. Cells B2 and B3 contain the number 1000. The entry in cell B2 has the General format and the entry in cell B3 has the $#,##0 format. Cell C2, which contains the value 600, has been assigned the name *Test*. Cell C4 contains the formula

    =Test+C3

This formula returns the value 1000. Cell E5 contains the label *Test*.

FIGURE 5-53.
This worksheet demonstrates how you can search for a string in a value or in a formula.

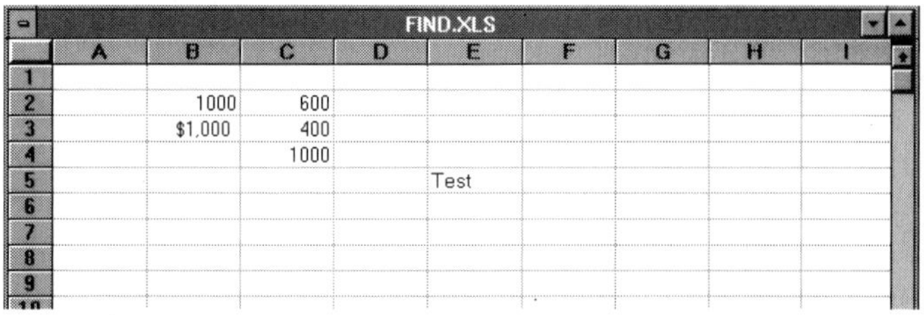

Suppose you select cell A1, choose the Find command (or press Shift-F5), and type *1000* to specify the Find What string. If you select Values as the Look in option, Excel looks at what is displayed in each cell. It first finds the occurrence of the string *1000* in cell B2. If you now press F7 (a keyboard shortcut for repeating the search), it finds the next occurrence of the string in the displayed value of cell C4. Excel ignores the entry in cell B3 when it searches for 1000 using the Look in Values option because the displayed value, $1,000, does not precisely match the Find What string, 1000. Because we're searching through values and not formulas, Excel ignores the fact that the underlying content of the cell is the number 1000.

Now suppose you again select cell A1 and repeat the search, this time selecting the Formulas option. As before, Excel first finds the occurrence of the Find What string in cell B2. If you press F7, Excel next highlights cell B3, which contains the number 1000 formatted as currency. Because you're now searching through the formulas and not the displayed values, the program ignores the format assigned to this cell. Instead, it matches the Find What string to the underlying contents of the cell.

If you press F7 again, Excel once again highlights cell B2. Because this time you're searching through the formulas and not the displayed values of the cells, the search ignores the value in cell C4. Even though this cell displays the value 1000, it actually contains the formula =*Test*+C3, which does not match the Find What string.

Let's look at one more example. If you specify *test* as the Find What string and select the Look in Formulas option, Excel first finds the string *test* in the formula =*Test*+C3 and highlights the cell that contains that formula, C4. (Note that we didn't ask Excel to make the search case-sensitive.) If you press F7, Excel next highlights cell E5, which contains the label *Test*. If you repeat the search but this time select the Look in Values option, Excel finds only the occurrence of the text entry *Test* in cell E5. If you want to find the defined name *Test* in C2, you must use the Goto command on the Formula menu.

The Look at options

The Look at options in the Find dialog box tell Excel whether to find only whole-word occurrences of the string or any occurrence of the string, even when it is a part of another string. For example, suppose a worksheet contains only two entries: the number 998, and the number 99. If you specify 99 as the Find What string and select Whole as the Look at option, Excel finds only the entry 99. But if you select the Part option, Excel finds both the entry 99, which matches the Find What string exactly, and the entry 998, which contains a string that matches the Find What string.

The Part option finds more occurrences of the string than the Whole option. Use the Whole option when you want to narrow the search to precise matches.

The Match Case option

If you select the Match Case check box, Excel distinguishes capital letters from lowercase letters. It finds only those occurrences that match your search string exactly. If you leave this box unselected, Excel disregards the differences between capital and lowercase letters.

Wildcard characters

You can use the wildcard characters * and ? to widen the scope of your searches. Wildcards are helpful when you're searching for a group of similar but not identical entries or when you're searching for an entry you don't quite remember.

The ? character takes the place of any single character in the Find What string. For example, the Find What string *100?* matches the values 1000, 1001, 1002, 1003, and so on up to 1009. (It also matches entries like 100A, 100B, and so on.)

The * character takes the place of one or more characters in a Find What string. For example, the string *1** matches the entries 10, 15, 100, 1111, 10001, 123456789, 123 Maple Street, and 1-800-223-8720.

You can use the wildcard characters anywhere within a Find What string. For example, you can use the string **s* to find all entries in the worksheet that end with s. Or you can use the string **es** to find each cell that contains the string sequence *es* anywhere in its formula or value.

If you want to search for a string that contains ? or *, enter a tilde (~) before the character. For example, to search for the string What?, enter What~ ? as your Find What text.

Repeating the search

After you find the first occurrence of the Find What string, you can press F7 to instruct Excel to search for the next occurrence. If it finds another occurrence, Excel highlights that cell; if not, the highlight remains on the cell with the first occurrence of the string.

You can jump from occurrence to occurrence by repeatedly pressing F7. If you press F7 while the highlight is on the last occurrence of the string, the highlight jumps back to the first occurrence. To search backward through the worksheet, press Shift-F7.

The Replace command

Excel allows you not only to locate characters in your worksheet but also to replace the specified character string with a new string. The Replace command works much like the Find command. When you choose Replace from the Formula menu, you see a dialog box like the one in Figure 5-54. Type the character string you want to search for in the Find What box, and the string you want to substitute in the Replace With box.

FIGURE 5-54.
*Use the Replace
command to replace a
specified string with a
new string.*

For example, suppose you want to replace each occurrence of the name *Joan Smith* with *John Smith*. Type *Joan* in the Find What box and *John* in the Replace With box. Click Find Next to move from one occurrence of the Find What string to the next without changing the contents of the current cell. When you locate an occurrence you want to change, click Replace to substitute the Find What string with the contents of the Replace With box. After replacing the character string in the current cell, Excel automatically moves to the next occurrence.

To replace every occurrence of the Find What string with the contents of the Replace With box, click Replace All. Instead of pausing at each occurrence to allow you to change or skip the current cell, Excel locates all the cells that contain the Find What string and changes them automatically.

You can change the contents of the Replace With box for each occurrence of the Find What string that Excel locates. Use the Find Next button to perform a selective search. Each time you locate an occurrence of the Find What string, enter the appropriate replacement characters in the Replace With box and click Replace.

For example, suppose you want to change the names *Joan Smith* and *John Smith* to *Joan Smythe* and *John Smythe*. Type *Jo?n Smith* in the Find What box, and then click Find Next. When you locate an occurrence of the Find What string, you can type either *Joan Smythe* or *John Smythe* in the Replace With box, and click Replace. When you locate the next occurrence, edit the contents of the Replace With box as needed to provide the correct replacement characters.

NOTE: *Although you can use wildcards in the Find What box to aid in your search, if you enter wildcard characters in the Replace With box, Excel uses a literal * or ? symbol when it replaces each occurrence of your Find What text.*

Checking your spelling

Starting with Excel 4, you no longer have to rely on your own proofreading skills when it comes to correct spelling. The Spelling command on the Options menu lets you check your worksheets for typing errors. You can also use the Check Spelling tool on the Utility toolbar to initiate a spell check. For more information about tools and toolbars, see Appendix A.

You can use the Spelling command to check the entire worksheet or any part of it. If you select a single cell, Excel checks the entire worksheet. If you select more than one cell, Excel checks the selected cells only. If the Formula bar is active, Excel checks its entire contents. If you select characters within the formula bar, Excel checks the selected characters only. If the range you select for spell-checking contains hidden or outlined cells that are not visible, Excel checks these as well. If your worksheet contains graphic objects that contain text such as text boxes, they are also checked if you select a single cell or select those objects. Cells that contain formulas are not checked, however.

When you first issue the Spelling command, you probably will see a dialog box that says: *Custom dictionary CUSTOM.DIC does not exist. Create?* Click OK, and your custom dictionary is created, ready for you to add your own personal set of words.

Figure 5-55 shows how the screen looks after we chose the Spelling command to check a worksheet that contains a couple of typographical errors.

FIGURE 5-55.
The Spelling dialog box not only checks your spelling, but suggests alternatives.

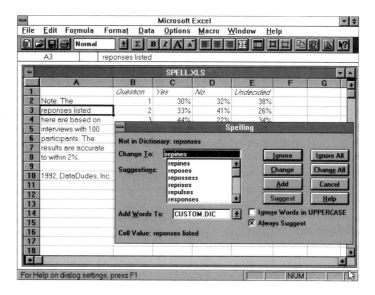

Excel highlights the cell that contains the misspelled word *reponses*, and a dialog box appears that displays a list of suggested alternatives to the word. At this point you can proceed in several ways: You can type the word as you want it spelled into the Change To text box, or select the correct word from the Suggestions list, and then click Change to insert the correctly spelled word. If the word is one that Excel's dictionary does not recognize, but is nonetheless correctly spelled, you can click Ignore or press Enter to leave the selected word alone and continue the spell check. Alternatively, you can click Add to add the word to your custom dictionary, if it is one that crops up often in your worksheets.

In our example, select *responses* from the Suggestions list, and click Change or press Enter. The spell check continues, and the next word selected is DataDudes, the name of "your" company. In this case, you probably want to click Add to include the word in the custom dictionary.

Editing your custom dictionary

Suppose you inadvertently click Add and include a misspelled word in your custom dictionary. Every time you issued the Spelling command, that misspelled word would be checked against the custom dictionary, and Excel would regard it as being spelled correctly. Fortunately, you can edit your custom dictionary. To open the custom dictionary, choose the Open command from the File menu and switch to the WINDOWS\MSAPPS\PROOF directory. Next, choose the All Files (*.*) option from the List Files of Type drop-down list box, select CUSTOM.DIC from the File Name list, then click OK. The file opens to reveal a list, similar to the one shown in Figure 5-56, of all your custom dictionary entries. You can edit this list as you see fit, keeping in mind that the file is text-only, so you cannot format your entries. When you finish, choose the Save As command from the File menu, make sure that *Text* is selected in the Save Files as Type drop-down list box, and click OK.

FIGURE 5-56.
You can open your custom dictionary file for editing.

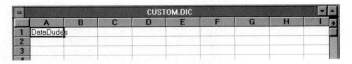

If you choose the Spelling command and Excel finds no incorrectly spelled words, you will see a dialog box that says *Finished spell checking entire sheet*.

Worksheet auditing and documentation

Microsoft Excel has a number of powerful and flexible commands that help you audit and debug your worksheets and document your work. In this section we'll discuss cell notes, the Info window, and the Select Special command.

You can also use text boxes to document worksheets. The use of text boxes is described in Chapter 7.

Cell notes

Excel lets you attach notes to cells to document your work, explain calculations and assumptions, or provide reminders. Select the cell you want to annotate, and then select Note from the Formula menu or press Shift-F2. You see a dialog box like the one shown in Figure 5-57. The reference to the active cell appears in the Cell box at the top of the dialog box. Type your entry in the Text Note text box, and click Add or OK to attach the note to the active cell. When you click OK, Excel closes the dialog box and returns to the worksheet. When you click Add, the dialog box remains open so that you can edit or add additional notes.

Although you can attach only one note to a cell, you can make your note text as long as you like. As you make entries in the Text Note text box, Excel automatically wraps text from one line to the next — don't press Enter to insert line breaks or you'll lock in the note and close the dialog box. If you want to begin a new paragraph in the Text Notes text box, press Ctrl-Enter.

After you add a note to a cell, the cell reference and the first few characters of that note appear in the Notes in Sheet list box on the left side of the dialog box. To edit a note, select it from the list box, activate the Text Note text box, and make your changes. Click Delete to delete the selected note. (You can also use the Notes option in the Clear dialog box to remove notes from a cell or range of cells.)

You can select other cells while the Cell Note dialog box is active to edit their notes or add new notes. First, activate the Cell text box and type a cell reference, or

FIGURE 5-57.
Use the Cell Note dialog box to attach a note to a cell.

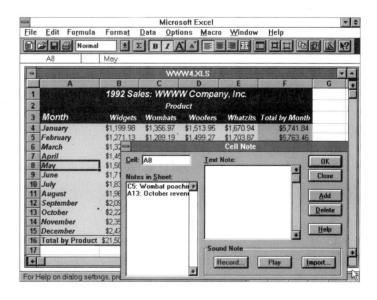

use the mouse or arrow keys to select a cell. (If the dialog box blocks your view of the cell you want to select, you can move it around on the screen by dragging the title bar or by using the Move command on the Cell Note window Control menu.) Next, edit the contents of the Text Note text box just as you edit an entry in the formula bar.

A small dot in the upper right corner of a cell indicates an attached note, as you can see in cell A13 in Figure 5-57. You can suppress the display of this dot with the Options Workspace command.

While you work in the worksheet window, you can review, edit, or delete your notes by double-clicking the cell you want to work with. The Cell Note dialog box reappears and the note for the active cell is displayed.

In addition to clicking OK, you can close the Cell Note dialog box by clicking Close. Close doesn't undo any additions or deletions you've already locked in; it simply cancels any new entries in the Text Note text box and removes the Cell Note dialog box from your screen.

You can print your notes by choosing the Notes option in the Print dialog box, described in Chapter 9, or by printing the contents of the Info window, described in "The Info window," later in this chapter.

Sound notes

Excel also allows you to include audio information in your cell notes. To do this, you must be running Microsoft Windows 3.1 or Windows 3.0 with Windows Multimedia Extensions version 1.0 or later. In addition, you must have recording hardware installed in your computer if you want to record sounds.

To create sounds, use the Record and Play buttons in the Cell Note dialog box. When you click Record, a dialog box appears that contains buttons labeled Record, Stop, Pause, and Play. To record a sound note, click Record and begin your recording. When you are finished, click Stop. You can use the Pause button to interrupt your recording, and the Play button to review the recording you just made. When you are satisfied with your sound note, click Save. Or click Cancel to discard the sound note.

If you click Save, dismissing the Record dialog box, the Record button in the Cell Note dialog box becomes the Erase button, allowing you to remove sound notes from individual cells. After you add a sound note to a cell, an asterisk appears next to the cell address in the Notes in Sheet list of the Cell Note dialog box, indicating that a sound note is attached to that cell.

You can also import a previously recorded sound to use as a sound note. To do this, click Import in the Cell Note dialog box. An Open dialog box named Import Sound appears, with the WAV file type automatically selected in the List Files of Type drop-down list box. You can then switch to the directory that contains your WAV sound files and select the one you want to import.

To play a sound note, click Play in the Cell Note dialog box, or simply double-click the cell on the worksheet.

You can record voice, music, sound effects — anything you like, limited only by the system resources available. The amount of time used by each recording is shown in the scale at the bottom of the Record dialog box. Keep in mind that sound notes take a considerable amount of disk space, so use them judiciously.

The Info window

The Info window offers a great way to monitor the status of the cells in your worksheet. Using this special document window, you can quickly see all the "vital statistics" of the active cell. To open the Info window, select a cell, choose the Workspace command from the Options menu, select the Info Window check box, and then click OK. Figure 5-58 shows the Info window. At the top of the window is the window name, Info, and the name of the currently active worksheet window.

FIGURE 5-58.
The Info window lets you monitor the status of your cells.

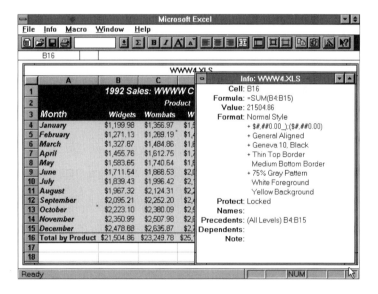

The contents of the application menu bar change when the Info window is active. The Edit, Formula, Format, Data, and Options menus disappear and a new menu called Info takes their place. Initially, you see only three items of information in the Info window: the cell reference, the underlying formula in the cell, and any note attached to the cell. However, you can use the commands on the Info menu to display more information. The Info menu offers nine display options: Cell, Formula, Value, Format, Protection, Names, Precedents (a list of cells the active cell refers to), Dependents (a list of cells that refer to the active cell), and Note. All the commands on the Info menu are toggle commands. A check mark appears beside those currently selected. (Figure 5-58 shows the result of selecting all nine display options.) To deselect a display option, choose that option again.

To switch between the worksheet and the Info window, you can choose one or the other from the list of active documents at the bottom of the Window menu. Alternatively, if you want to keep the Info window in view as you work in your document, resize and reposition the worksheet and Info windows so that they don't overlap. To quickly arrange the windows on your screen, choose the Arrange command from the Window menu to organize your workspace. (We'll cover the Arrange command in Chapter 6.)

To print the contents of the Info window, select the cell or range for which you want to print information (or select a single cell to print the entire worksheet), activate the Info window, and issue the Print command. (For more information about printing, see Chapter 12.)

The Info window remains open until you turn off the option in the Workspace dialog box, so you can quickly obtain information about a number of different cells on your worksheet. Unlike the other Workspace dialog box options, the status of the Info Window option is not preserved after you quit. Each time you start Excel, you must reselect the Info Window option if you want the Info window displayed.

The Select Special command

Select Special is a powerful debugging tool that lets you quickly find cells that meet certain specifications. For example, suppose you find an error in a formula and want to trace all the cells that support that formula, to locate your mistake. You can use the Precedents option in the Select Special dialog box to locate all the cells to which the active cell refers.

When you choose Select Special from the Formula menu, you see a dialog box like the one in Figure 5-59. The options in the Select Special dialog box let you specify certain selection criteria. When you select one of these options and then click OK, Excel highlights the cell or cells that match the criteria you chose. With a few exceptions, if you select a range of cells before you open the Select Special dialog box, Excel searches only the selected range; if the current selection is a single cell or one or more graphic objects, Excel searches the entire worksheet.

FIGURE 5-59.
The Select Special
dialog box is a handy
auditing and
debugging tool.

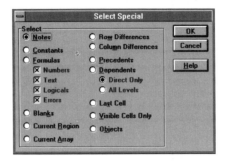

Some of the selections you make with the Select Special options, such as Notes, Precedents, and Dependents, might result in multiple nonadjacent ranges. To navigate through these selections, you can use Enter and Tab to move down or to the right one cell at a time. Shift-Enter and Shift-Tab let you move up or to the left one cell at a time. Ctrl-Tab and Shift-Ctrl-Tab let you jump forward and backward between ranges.

Using Select Special with Show Info

You can also use Select Special in conjunction with the Info window to select a range of cells, and then move through the range to review the relevant data on each cell in the selection. For example, suppose you want to quickly scan all the notes you entered in a specific range of your worksheet. First select the range you're interested in (or a single cell, for the entire worksheet), select Info Window in the Workspace Options dialog box, and then choose the Notes command from the Info menu, if necessary. Arrange the worksheet and Info windows so that they don't overlap — that way you can see the selected cells and the Info window at the same time. Next, issue the Select Special command, select the Notes option, and click OK. Excel highlights all the cells in the selected range that have notes attached to them. Now you can use the Enter and Tab combinations previously described to browse through the annotated cells and view their notes in the Info window.

The Constants, Formulas, and Blanks options locate cells that contain the specified type of entries. When you choose the Constants or Formulas option, Excel activates the Numbers, Text, Logicals, and Errors options in addition to Constants and Formulas. Use these options to narrow your selection criteria.

The Current Region option is handy when you're working in a large, complex worksheet and need to select blocks of cells. (Recall that a region is defined as a continuous rectangular block of cells bounded by blank rows, blank columns, or worksheet borders.) When you choose Current Region, your selection is set to that area of the worksheet.

If the selected cell is part of an array range, you can use the Current Array option to select all the cells in that array. You can also choose this option by pressing Ctrl-/.

The Row Differences and Column Differences options let you compare the entries in a range of cells to spot potential inconsistencies. To use these debugging tools, first select the range of cells you want to compare. The position of the active cell in your selection determines which cell or cells Excel uses to make its comparisons. When searching for row differences, Excel compares the cells in the selection to the cells in the same column as the active cell; when searching for column differences, Excel compares the cells in the selection to the cells in the same row as the active cell.

For example, suppose you've selected the range B10:G20 and cell B10 is the active cell. If you use the Row Differences option, Excel compares the entries in cells C10:G10 to the entry in cell B10, the entries in cells C11:G11 to the entry in cell B11, and so forth. If you choose the Column Differences option, Excel compares the entries in cells B11:B20 to the entry in cell B10, the entries in cells C11:C20 to the entry in cell C10, and so forth.

Among other things, Excel looks for differences in your cell and range references and selects those cells that don't conform to the comparison cell. Suppose cell B10 is your comparison cell and contains the formula

=SUM(B1:B9)

Selecting direct precedent cells with the mouse

A quick and easy way to find all the cells that are directly referred to by a formula is to simply double-click the cell that contains the formula. When you do this, Excel selects the cells directly referenced by the formula, even if they are nonadjacent. This works only if you have not assigned a note to the cell.

This comparison formula refers to the range of cells that begins nine rows above and ends one row above the formula cell. If you select cells B10:G10 and choose the Row Differences option, Excel scans through cells C10:G10 to check for any formulas that don't fit this pattern. For example, cells C10 and D10 should, presumably, contain the formulas

=SUM(C1:C9)

and

=SUM(D1:D9)

If any of the formulas in row 10 don't match this pattern, the Select Special command selects those cells.

Row Differences and Column Differences also check to ensure that all the cells in the selected range contain the same type of entries. For example, if your comparison cell contains a SUM function, Excel flags any cells that contain a function, formula, or value other than SUM. If the comparison cell contains a constant text or numeric value, Excel flags any cells in the selected range that don't exactly match the comparison value.

(To search quickly for row differences, you can select the range you want to search and press Ctrl-\. To search for column differences, select the range you want to search and press Ctrl-Shift-|. These keyboard shortcuts let you bypass the Select Special dialog box.)

The Precedents and Dependents options are perhaps the most powerful options in the Select Special dialog box. They let you trace calculations by locating all the cells that feed into a formula or that depend on the formula in the selected cell. To use these options, begin by selecting the cell whose dependents or precedents you want to trace; issue the Select Special command, and select the Precedents or Dependents option. When you select either of these options, Excel activates the Direct Only and All Levels options. Use these options to set the parameters of your search: Direct Only finds only those cells that are directly dependent on or that directly refer to the active cell; All Levels locates direct precedents and dependents plus those cells that are indirectly linked to the active cell.

The Last Cell option selects the cell at the intersection of the rightmost column and lowest row used by the worksheet. The keyboard shortcut for this selection is Ctrl-End. When you select this option, Excel finds the last cell in the worksheet, not the lower right corner of the current selection.

The Visible Cells option excludes from the current selection any cells in hidden rows or columns. As mentioned in the discussion of outlining in Chapter 2, this option has a mouse shortcut on the toolbar.

The Objects option selects all graphic objects on your worksheet, regardless of the current selection. (For information about working with graphic objects, see Chapter 7.)

The Sort command

You can sort a range of cells by rows vertically or by columns horizontally. Most of the time, sorting is performed vertically using an indicated column as the sort key. A simple example of this is a mailing list. If first names and last names are entered in separate cells of individual rows, you can use the column that contains the last names as the sort key to rearrange the mailing list in alphabetical order. This is a rudimentary illustration of a database. (We explain databases in detail in Chapter 16.) We use the "sort by rows" paradigm for most of this discussion of sorting. In "Column sorts," later in this chapter, we discuss the differences involved in sorting by columns.

To sort a range of cells, first select the range, then choose Sort from the Data menu. Microsoft Excel presents the Sort dialog box shown in Figure 5-60. The entries you make in this dialog box tell Excel which fields to use to sort the range.

FIGURE 5-60.
*Use the Sort dialog
box to rearrange a
selected range of cells.*

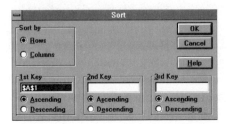

When the Sort dialog box appears, use the 1st Key, 2nd Key, and 3rd Key text boxes to define the columns on which you want to sort and the order of the sort. When you choose the Sort command, Excel always displays the reference of the active cell in the 1st Key text box. To redefine the first sort key, enter a reference to any cell in the column that contains the values on which you want to sort. (The chosen cell need not be in the group of cells you're sorting; but it must be in the same column.)

After you specify the sort key, specify the order of the sort. The default order, Ascending, instructs Excel to arrange the rows so that the row with the lowest value in the sort key column appears at the top of the range and the one with the highest value appears at the bottom. The Descending option tells Excel to arrange the rows so that the one with the highest value in the sort key column appears first and the one with the lowest value appears last.

If you want to sort on more than one column, enter a cell reference in the 2nd Key (and 3rd Key) text box, and again choose the appropriate sort order. When you have defined all the sort keys, click OK. Excel then sorts the database so that the entries in the specified columns are arranged in the selected order.

An example of Sorting

You can use the Sort command to rearrange records in a worksheet like the one shown in Figure 5-61. This worksheet includes two columns: Student and GPA (grade-point average). The rows of data are in an apparently random order. To make this information more useful, you can sort the worksheet so that the record with the highest GPA is at the top, and the record with the lowest GPA is at the bottom.

To sort this worksheet, select the range A2:B16, which includes every row of data in the worksheet. (The sort range does not include the two labels at the top of the rows, or they would be sorted along with the other data.) Next, choose Sort from the Data menu. When the Sort dialog box appears, define the sort keys. Because you want Excel to sort the worksheet on the values in the GPA field, which is located in column B, type a reference to any cell from column B (such as B1) into the 1st Key text box. If you use a mouse, you can enter a cell reference by activating the text box and clicking any cell in column B.

FIGURE 5-61.
This worksheet contains data that is in no particular order.

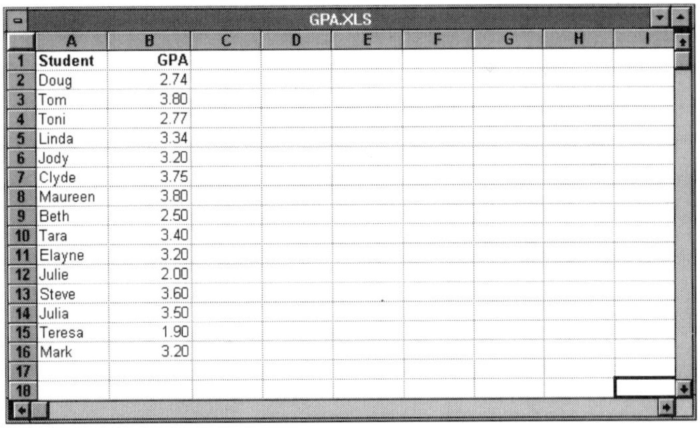

	A	B	C	D	E	F	G	H	I
1	Student	GPA							
2	Doug	2.74							
3	Tom	3.80							
4	Toni	2.77							
5	Linda	3.34							
6	Jody	3.20							
7	Clyde	3.75							
8	Maureen	3.80							
9	Beth	2.50							
10	Tara	3.40							
11	Elayne	3.20							
12	Julie	2.00							
13	Steve	3.60							
14	Julia	3.50							
15	Teresa	1.90							
16	Mark	3.20							
17									
18									

Next specify the order of the sort. In this case, select Descending so that Excel will place the row that contains the highest GPA at the top of the worksheet.

When you're satisfied with the sort settings, click OK. Excel immediately rearranges the worksheet in the order you specified in the Sort dialog box. Thus, Excel places the row that contains the highest GPA at the top of the worksheet, the row that contains the second-highest GPA next, and so forth. Figure 5-62 on the following page shows the result of the sort.

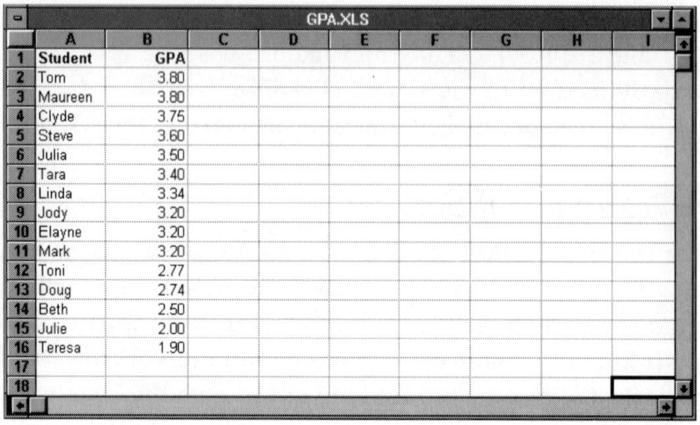

FIGURE 5-62.
We sorted the
worksheet into
descending order
by GPA.

	A	B	C	D	E	F	G	H	I
1	Student	GPA							
2	Tom	3.80							
3	Maureen	3.80							
4	Clyde	3.75							
5	Steve	3.60							
6	Julia	3.50							
7	Tara	3.40							
8	Linda	3.34							
9	Jody	3.20							
10	Elayne	3.20							
11	Mark	3.20							
12	Toni	2.77							
13	Doug	2.74							
14	Beth	2.50							
15	Julie	2.00							
16	Teresa	1.90							
17									
18									

Sort order

Excel sorts the entries in a worksheet column based on the "value" of those entries. If a column contains any numbers or number-producing formulas or functions, an ascending sort puts the smallest numbers at the top of the worksheet and the largest numbers at the bottom. A descending sort on a column that contains numeric entries places the largest numbers first and the smallest numbers last.

When Excel performs an ascending sort on the entries in a column that contains text, it arranges those entries in ascending alphabetic order; that is, entries that begin with A come first and entries that begin with Z come last. For purposes of sorting, Excel does not differentiate between uppercase and lowercase letters; that is, a is the same as A and Z is the same as z. Excel also uses strict alphabetic order. For example, in an ascending sort, AaA comes before AAB.

The entries in any column of a worksheet are usually either numbers or text. In some worksheets, however, one column might contain both number and text entries. If both number and text entries occur, Excel places all number entries before text entries in an ascending sort. If a column contains other entries, such as logical results (TRUE or FALSE) and error messages, Excel performs an ascending sort in this order:

Numbers

Text

Logical values

Error values

Blank cells

Descending sorts arrange the column's non-blank entries in the opposite order.

Undoing a sort

After you sort a worksheet, it is difficult to restore its original order.

You can use the Undo Sort command on the Edit menu to return the rows to their previous order, but the Undo command is ineffective unless you catch your error before you issue another command or make an entry in your worksheet. However, you can take some precautions to ease the task of restoring your worksheet to its original order.

The easiest way to ensure that you can return a worksheet to its original order is to use the Save or Save As command immediately before sorting the worksheet. You can then return the worksheet to its presort order by using the Open command to bring the saved worksheet back into Excel. This technique is useful for restoring a worksheet to its original order immediately after you use the Sort command only. If you make other changes to the worksheet after you sort it, the presort version does not reflect them.

The Sort Tools

You can also use the Sort Ascending and Sort Descending tools, located on the Utility toolbar, to quickly sort your worksheet. To activate the Utility toolbar, click the right mouse button while the pointer is over the Standard toolbar (or any displayed toolbar) and choose Utility from the shortcut menu that appears. If no toolbar is active, choose Toolbars from the Options menu, choose Utility, and click OK.

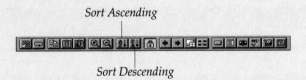

Sort Ascending

Sort Descending

To use the Sort tools, simply select the range you want to sort. Clicking a Sort tool is equivalent to choosing the Sort command and accepting the active cell as the sort key. If you hold down Shift when you click the Sort Ascending tool, it performs a descending sort; vice versa for the Sort Descending tool.

For more information about tools and toolbars, including details on how to customize your own toolbars, see Appendix A.

An alternative technique allows you to restore a worksheet to its original order at any time. Add a new column that contains ascending numbers or text to the unsorted worksheet. Then you can restore the worksheet to its original order whenever you wish by performing an ascending sort on this new column. You can easily delete or hide this column later.

Multiple-column sorts

In most circumstances, you sort a worksheet on only a single column, as we did in Figure 5-62. However, when a worksheet contains many columns and some contain duplicate entries, you'll want to sort on more than one column. Microsoft Excel lets you sort on as many as three columns at a time.

The worksheet in Figure 5-63 includes three columns: Product, Size, and Color. The rows in this worksheet are arranged in a random order. To make this information more meaningful, you can sort the worksheet on the basis of the entries in the Product column. Select cells A2:C16, choose Sort, specify any cell in column A as the sort key, select Ascending, and then click OK. Figure 5-64 shows the result of this single-column sort.

Sorting on more than three columns

Excel allows you to sort a worksheet on only three columns at a time and, in most cases, you won't need more than three columns. However, on those occasions when you want to sort a large worksheet on more than three columns, you can do so by performing successive single-column or multiple-column sorts.

When you perform a three-column sort, you specify the sort columns in order of their importance. You use the least important column as the 3rd Key and the most important column as the 1st Key. Follow this same rule when you sort a worksheet on more than three columns.

Suppose you want to sort a worksheet on the basis of five columns. First decide which column is the primary (first) column and which columns are the second, third, fourth, and fifth. Next perform a two-key sort of the entire range of the worksheet with the fifth most important column as the 2nd Key and the fourth most important column as the 1st Key. Next perform a three-column sort on the rearranged worksheet, with the third column as the 3rd Key, the second as the 2nd Key, and the most important column as the 1st Key. You can use this technique to sort a worksheet on any number of columns.

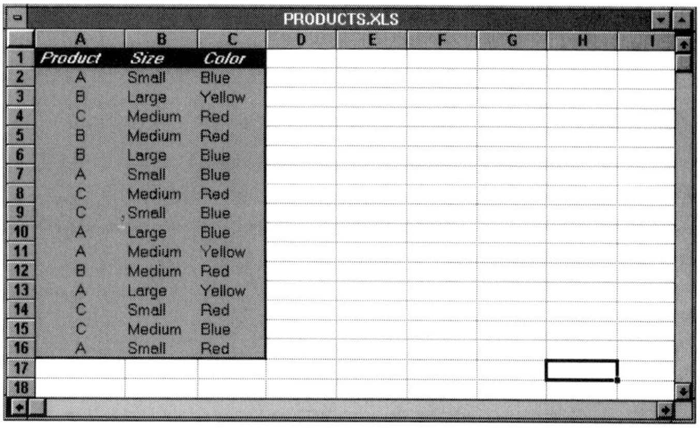

FIGURE 5-63.
The rows in this worksheet are arranged in random order.

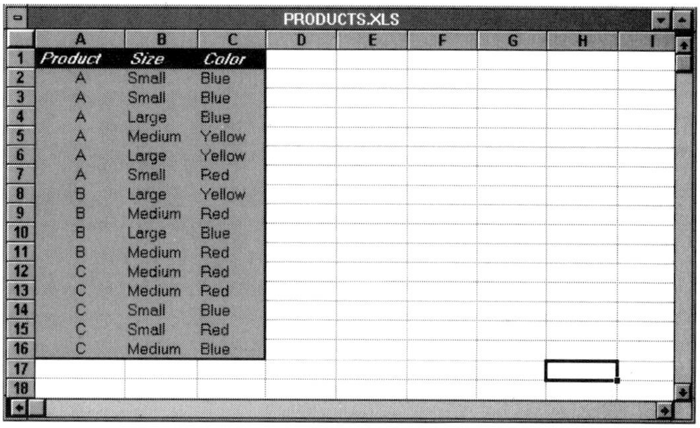

PRODUCTS.XLS

Product	Size	Color
A	Small	Blue
B	Large	Yellow
C	Medium	Red
B	Medium	Red
B	Large	Blue
A	Small	Blue
C	Medium	Red
C	Small	Blue
A	Large	Blue
A	Medium	Yellow
B	Medium	Red
A	Large	Yellow
C	Small	Red
C	Medium	Blue
A	Small	Red

FIGURE 5-64.
We sorted the worksheet into ascending order by product.

PRODUCTS.XLS

Product	Size	Color
A	Small	Blue
A	Small	Blue
A	Large	Blue
A	Medium	Yellow
A	Large	Yellow
A	Small	Red
B	Large	Yellow
B	Medium	Red
B	Large	Blue
B	Medium	Red
C	Medium	Red
C	Medium	Red
C	Small	Blue
C	Small	Red
C	Medium	Blue

Excel rearranged the worksheet in ascending order based on the entries in the Product column. Because this column contains duplicate entries, the sort grouped the rows according to the entries in that column.

Even though the worksheet in Figure 5-64 is better organized than the worksheet in Figure 5-63, the rows within each group of products are still arranged randomly and in the same relative order as they were in the original worksheet. You can use a secondary sort to add some order to the rows within the groups produced by a primary sort.

You can arrange the rows in the Products worksheet into ascending order based on the entries in the Product column (the primary sort), and arrange the rows within each product group in ascending order based on the entries in the Size column (the secondary sort). Select cells A2:C16 and choose Sort from the Data menu to display the Sort dialog box. Then type the reference of any cell in column A into the 1st Key text box and select Ascending. Next type the reference of any cell in column B (the Size column) into the 2nd Key text box, and again select Ascending. Finally, click OK to initiate the sort. Figure 5-65 shows the result of this two-key sort.

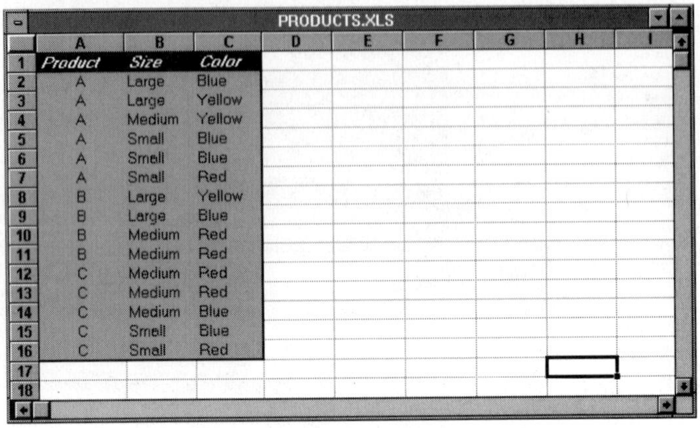

	A	B	C
1	*Product*	*Size*	*Color*
2	A	Large	Blue
3	A	Large	Yellow
4	A	Medium	Yellow
5	A	Small	Blue
6	A	Small	Blue
7	A	Small	Red
8	B	Large	Yellow
9	B	Large	Blue
10	B	Medium	Red
11	B	Medium	Red
12	C	Medium	Red
13	C	Medium	Red
14	C	Medium	Blue
15	C	Small	Blue
16	C	Small	Red

FIGURE 5-65.
The worksheet is arranged in ascending order by product and by size.

Excel grouped all the Product A rows at the top of the worksheet, followed by the Product B rows and then the Product C rows. In this respect, this sort is like the original single-column sort. Looking at column B (the Size column), however, reveals the difference. Instead of being arranged in their original order, the rows within each group are now arranged in order of size. All the Large rows come first within each group, then the Mediums, then the Smalls. Excel can arrange the rows this way not because it knows that Large is bigger than Medium, which is in turn bigger than Small, but because L, the first letter in Large, comes before M, the first letter in Medium, in the alphabet.

Specifying a secondary sort column adds additional organization to the worksheet. You can use a three-column sort to organize the data further. For example, in the Color column, the rows within each size group are still arranged randomly. To organize the rows within each secondary sort group, you can perform a three-column sort.

In this case, sort the worksheet so that the rows within each secondary sort group are arranged in descending order based on the entries in the Color column. To perform this sort, again select cells A2:C16 and choose Sort from the Data menu. Next type the reference of any cell in column A in the 1st Key text box and select Ascending. Then type the reference of any cell in column B in the 2nd Key text box and select Ascending. Finally, type the reference of any cell in column C in the 3rd Key text box and this time select Descending. After you enter these settings, click OK to start the sort. Figure 5-66 shows the results of this three-column sort.

FIGURE 5-66.
*The worksheet is
sorted by product, by
size, and by color.*

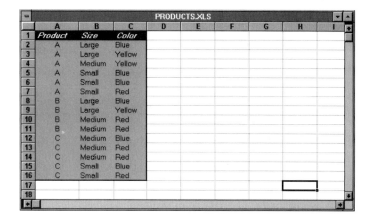

The rows are arranged so that all the Product A entries appear at the top of the worksheet, all the Product B entries appear next, and all the Product C entries appear last. Within each product group, Excel presents the rows in descending order by size (or ascending order alphabetically). Within each size group, the rows are in descending alphabetic order on the basis of the entries in the Color column.

Column sorts

The Sort by field of the Sort dialog box offers two options — Rows and Columns — that let you determine whether Microsoft Excel will sort the selected range by rows or by columns. Usually you use the Rows option when you choose the Sort command. The Rows option tells Excel to treat each row of the selected sort range as an unbreakable unit and, therefore, to sort the worksheet by switching the positions of entire rows.

The Columns option changes the way Excel looks at the sort range by "rotating" it 90 degrees. This option tells Excel to consider the cells in each column in that range to be inseparable. Therefore, Excel sorts the selected range by switching the positions of entire columns, not rows, within the worksheet range.

Although you seldom use the Columns option, it can be useful in some worksheet applications. Suppose you create the simple financial worksheet shown in Figure 5-67 on the following page. This model consists of five columns of financial information, each of which contains Revenues, Expenses, and Profit entries. Columns B, C, D, E, and F contain the information for 1992, 1991, 1990, 1989, and 1988, respectively. To rearrange this worksheet so that the information for 1988 is in column B, the information for 1989 is in column C, and so on, you can perform a "by-column" sort.

FIGURE 5-67.
*A simple financial
worksheet.*

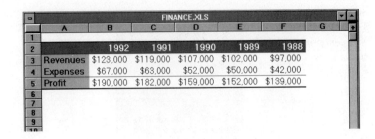

Begin by selecting the sort range — in this case, B2:F5. Next, choose Sort from the Data menu to display the Sort dialog box. Because you want Excel to sort this range on the basis of the entries in row 2 (the year headers), type the reference of any cell in that row (such as cell B2) into the 1st Key text box. You want Excel to place 1988's information in column B and 1992's in column F, so select the Ascending option. Before you sort this range, select the Columns option in the Sort by box. When you click OK, Excel sorts the range into the order shown in Figure 5-68.

FIGURE 5-68.
*We used the Columns
option of the Sort
command to reorder
the years on the
financial worksheet.*

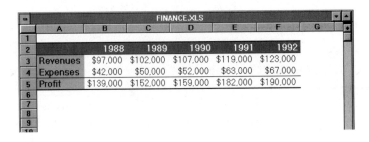

6

Worksheets, Windows, and Workbooks

When you use Microsoft Excel, you're not limited to working with one worksheet at a time. You can keep as many documents open as the memory in your computer — and your taste for complexity — allow. That means, for example, that while preparing a budget worksheet for 1993, you can easily look at an actuals worksheet for 1992. Similarly, you can create a half-dozen charts from a given set of data and quickly move between them to get different visual perspectives on the same set of numbers.

Excel also permits you to open multiple windows on the same document. You'll find this capability beneficial when you want to see two widely separated regions of a worksheet at the same time.

In this chapter, we'll survey the commands and shortcuts for opening, manipulating, navigating, hiding, saving, and closing multiple windows. We'll also look at Excel's powerful *Group Edit* feature, which allows you to format and edit two or more worksheets at once.

We'll examine *workbooks*, a feature that allows you to bind groups of documents together; *named views*, which let you customize combinations of display, workspace, and print settings and save them for easy retrieval; and the Zoom command, with which you can reduce or enlarge the display of your worksheets. We'll also discuss Excel's powerful worksheet linking and consolidation capabilities.

Although most of this chapter focuses on worksheet windows, much of what is said here applies equally to Excel's other two types of document windows — charts and macro sheets. The two exceptions are splitting a single document into multiple windows and consolidating worksheets. You can do both of these with worksheets and macro sheets, but not with charts.

Managing multiple document windows

Each time you start the program, Microsoft Excel ordinarily opens a blank worksheet with the provisional title Sheet1. To open an additional file, simply use the File menu's Open or New command. You can do this as many times as you like until your computer runs out of memory. Each worksheet you open creates its own document window. The new worksheet appears on top of the last active window and becomes the active (or current) window. Each document window is identified by a title bar. The title bar of the *current* document window (the one you are working in at any given moment) is displayed in the same color as the title bar of the Excel application window — the window that houses the program itself and all your document windows.

Note that if you use the File Open command to open a worksheet that you have already brought into Excel, the open copy on your screen is replaced by the version last saved to disk. (An alert box asks you to confirm that you want to revert to the saved version. Click OK if you want to accept.) To work with two or more windows on the same worksheet, use the New Window command on the Window menu. (See "Opening multiple windows on the same document," later in this chapter.)

Navigating between document windows

You can use any of three methods to move from one open document window to another. You can point and click, press Ctrl-F6, or choose a command from the Window menu.

Suppose your three worksheets, EXAMS, EXAMS2, and EXAMS3, overlap one another, as shown in Figure 6-1. In this case, you can change windows by pointing with the mouse and clicking. To move from EXAMS3 to EXAMS2 in Figure 6-1, for example, simply click anywhere in the EXAMS2 worksheet.

If the worksheet to which you want to move is not visible or if you don't have a mouse, you can navigate by pressing Ctrl-F6. Repeatedly pressing this key combination cycles you through all open document windows in the order in which they were opened, from most recent to earliest. Holding down Shift while you press Ctrl-F6 moves you from document to document in the opposite direction.

FIGURE 6-1.
To move to a window that's at least partially visible, simply point and click.

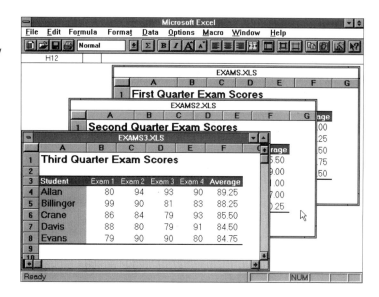

If you have many document windows open, you'll probably find that the Window menu provides the easiest route from one window to another. As shown in Figure 6-2, the bottom section of the Window menu lists the open documents by name. You can move directly to a document by choosing its name from the list.

FIGURE 6-2.
The Window menu is your best navigational tool when you have many documents open at once.

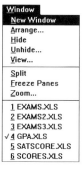

The Window menu can list up to nine documents. If you have more than nine open, the Window menu includes a command called More Windows. When you choose this command, Excel presents a separate list box that contains the names of all open documents — in alphabetic order.

Maximizing document windows

Even when you have several documents open at once, you'll often want to concentrate on a particular one. In that situation, it's helpful to *maximize* the document.

You can do this by clicking the document window's Maximize button. The Maximize button is the upward-pointing arrow at the right edge of the document window's title bar.

A maximized document window expands to fill all the space available within the Excel application window. If you haven't already maximized the application window, you'll want to do that as well by clicking its Maximize button — so that your document window fills as much of the screen as possible.

You'll also notice that the title bar of a maximized document window merges with the title bar of the application window. If you maximize EXAMS, for example, the application window title bar changes to say Microsoft Excel — EXAMS.XLS, and its Control menu icon and Restore button appear at the left and right ends of the Excel menu bar. (See Figure 6-3.)

One other important point to note about maximizing document windows: When you maximize one, you maximize all the others that are open on your screen. If EXAMS, EXAMS2, and EXAMS3 are open at the same time, for example, and you maximize EXAMS, Excel also maximizes EXAMS2 and EXAMS3. You won't see these other windows because they lie behind EXAMS. But you can move to them using either Ctrl-F6 or the Window menu.

FIGURE 6-3.
When a document window is maximized, its title bar merges with the application window title bar.

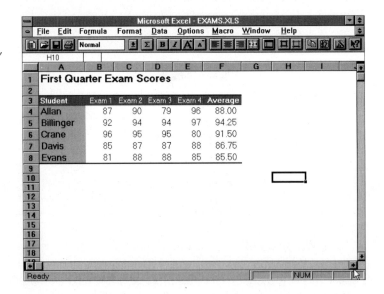

Minimizing document windows

When you have several documents open at once, the screen can sometimes look cluttered and confusing. You can move some of the documents out of the way by *minimizing* them. You can do this by clicking the document window's Minimize button. The document window's Minimize button is the downward-pointing arrow at the right edge of its title bar. A minimized document window collapses to become an icon at the bottom of the document window area, as shown in Figure 6-4.

You can move the icons around the screen, if you want. If you do move them around, you can return them to their default positions at the bottom of the screen by choosing the Arrange Icons command from the Window menu. If any document windows are open that haven't been minimized, the Arrange Icons command becomes the Arrange command and can't be used. (For more information about the Arrange command, see "Arranging document windows," later in this chapter.)

FIGURE 6-4.
Minimized documents become icons at the bottom of the document window area.

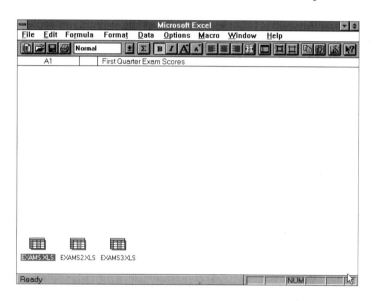

Restoring document windows

To return a document window to the size and position it held before you maximized it, click its Restore button. A document window's Restore button is the two-headed arrow located at the right end of the menu bar. To restore a minimized document window, double-click the icon.

Arranging document windows

When you want to see two or more documents at once, you'll find the Arrange command on the Window menu invaluable. When you choose the Arrange command, you see the dialog box in Figure 6-5 on the following page. This command arranges all open document windows into one of three possible configurations.

You can tile your windows, in which case the screen is divided up equally among the active documents. Alternatively, you can arrange your active documents either *horizontally*, as shown in Figure 6-6, or *vertically*, as shown in Figure 6-7.

FIGURE 6-5.
The Arrange command on the Window menu gives you a choice of several different configurations.

With your documents neatly arranged, you can still "zoom in" on a particular document by clicking its Maximize button. Then when you want the side-by-side view once more, simply restore the document window, and Excel recreates your tiled screen.

The Tiled option in the Arrange Windows dialog box can be handy even when you have only one document open. If that document doesn't fill the available workspace, selecting Tiled makes your document window as large as it can be without being maximized.

The Windows of Active Document options — Sync Horizontal and Sync Vertical, at the bottom of the Arrange Windows dialog box — let you synchronize scrolling of multiple windows containing the same document. (See "Opening multiple windows on the same document," later in this chapter.)

FIGURE 6-6.
These worksheets are arranged horizontally.

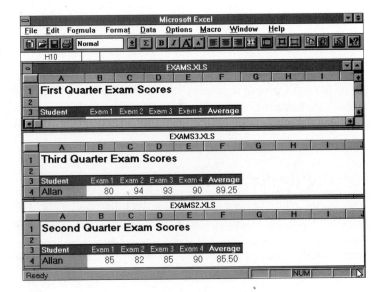

FIGURE 6-7.
*These worksheets are
arranged vertically.*

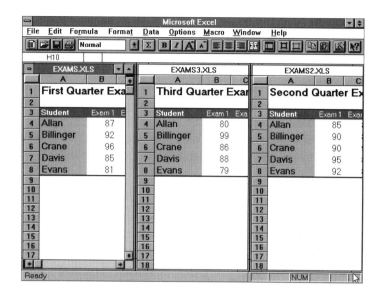

If you choose the Arrange command when minimized window icons are present in the workspace, Excel positions the remaining open documents to leave space at the bottom of the screen. The minimized document icons remain visible even after you choose the Arrange command.

Moving and sizing document windows

You can change the position and size of a document window either by manipulating it with the mouse or by choosing commands from the document window's Control menu.

To move a window with the mouse, position the mouse pointer on the title bar, hold down the mouse button, drag the window to a new position, and release the mouse button. To move a window with the keyboard, press Alt-Hyphen to open its Control menu. Next, choose the Move command and use the arrow keys to relocate the window. When the window is where you want it, press Enter.

To change a window's size with the mouse, position the pointer on one of the window's borders. The pointer changes to a two-headed arrow. Hold down the mouse button while you drag the border inward (to make the window smaller) or outward (to make it larger). To change the window's size with the keyboard, press Alt-Hyphen to open the Control menu and choose the Size command. A four-headed pointer appears in the center of the window. Press one of the four arrow keys to move this pointer to a window border. Next, use the arrow keys to move the border inward or outward. Press Enter when the window has reached the size you want.

Hiding document windows

At times you may need to keep a worksheet or macro sheet open so that you can use the information in that document, but you don't want that macro window to take up room on your screen. For example, you may want to keep a macro sheet open so that you can run macros from it while working in another window. When several open documents clutter your workspace, you can use the Hide command to conceal some of them. Excel can still work with the information in the hidden documents but they won't take up space on your screen.

To hide a window, simply activate the window and choose the Hide command from the Window menu. Excel removes the window display from your workspace, but the document remains open. If you want to bring the hidden window into view, choose the Unhide command from the Window menu. Excel displays a dialog box that lists all hidden windows. Select the window you want to see, and then click OK. The hidden window appears and becomes the active window.

If you've protected the hidden window by choosing the Protect Document command (discussed in Chapter 2), you must enter your password before you can hide or unhide the document window.

If you've hidden all the windows in your workspace, Excel displays an Unhide command on the File menu rather than on the Window menu. When you choose the Unhide command from the File menu, you see a dialog box from which you can select the windows you want to view.

Saving and closing document windows

When you save a document using the Save or Save As commands on the File menu, characteristics such as the window's size, position on the screen, and display settings are also saved in the same file. The next time you open the file, the window will look exactly the same as it did the last time you saved it. (We discussed the Save and Save As commands in Chapter 1. We discuss the Save Workbook command in "The contents page," later in this chapter.)

To close an individual document window, choose the Close command from the File menu. You can also close a window by double-clicking its Control menu icon. (Be sure to double-click the short dash in the upper left corner of the document window, not the longer dash in the upper left corner of the application window. Double-clicking the application window's Control menu icon closes Excel.)

If you've made changes since you last saved your work, a dialog box appears, asking whether you want to save the contents of the window before you close it. If you did not mean to close the window, select the Cancel option.

Opening multiple windows on the same document

Suppose you've created a worksheet called PRODUCTS, like the one shown in Figure 6-8. Currently, only cells A1:I18 are visible. To open a second window on this document, choose the New Window command from the Window menu. Your screen looks like the one in Figure 6-9.

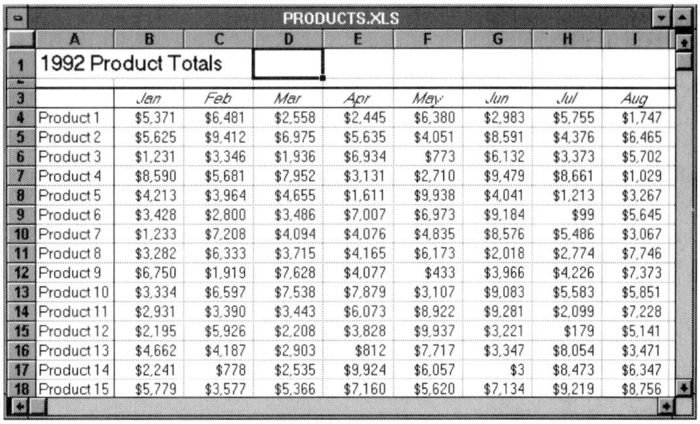

FIGURE 6-8.
Cells A1:I18 are currently visible in this document window.

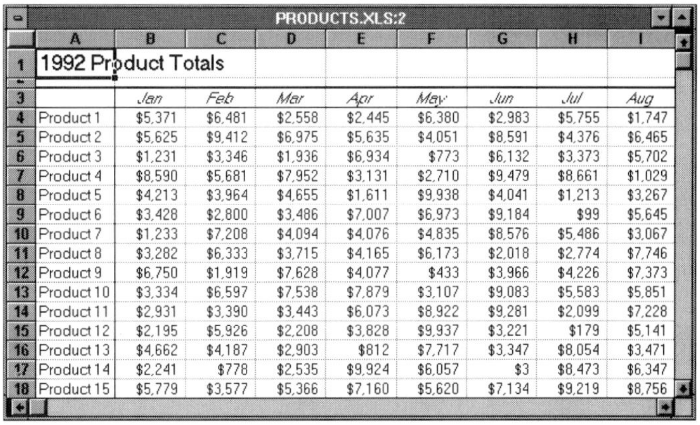

	A	B	C	D	E	F	G	H	I
1	1992 Product Totals								
3		Jan	Feb	Mar	Apr	May	Jun	Jul	Aug
4	Product 1	$5,371	$6,481	$2,558	$2,445	$6,380	$2,983	$5,755	$1,747
5	Product 2	$5,625	$9,412	$6,975	$5,635	$4,051	$8,591	$4,376	$6,465
6	Product 3	$1,231	$3,346	$1,936	$6,934	$773	$6,132	$3,373	$5,702
7	Product 4	$8,590	$5,681	$7,952	$3,131	$2,710	$9,479	$8,661	$1,029
8	Product 5	$4,213	$3,964	$4,655	$1,611	$9,938	$4,041	$1,213	$3,267
9	Product 6	$3,428	$2,800	$3,486	$7,007	$6,973	$9,184	$99	$5,645
10	Product 7	$1,233	$7,208	$4,094	$4,076	$4,835	$8,576	$5,486	$3,067
11	Product 8	$3,282	$6,333	$3,715	$4,165	$6,173	$2,018	$2,774	$7,746
12	Product 9	$6,750	$1,919	$7,628	$4,077	$433	$3,966	$4,226	$7,373
13	Product 10	$3,334	$6,597	$7,538	$7,879	$3,107	$9,083	$5,583	$5,851
14	Product 11	$2,931	$3,390	$3,443	$6,073	$8,922	$9,281	$2,099	$7,228
15	Product 12	$2,195	$5,926	$2,208	$3,828	$9,937	$3,221	$179	$5,141
16	Product 13	$4,662	$4,187	$2,903	$812	$7,717	$3,347	$8,054	$3,471
17	Product 14	$2,241	$778	$2,535	$9,924	$6,057	$3	$8,473	$6,347
18	Product 15	$5,779	$3,577	$5,366	$7,160	$5,620	$7,134	$9,219	$8,756

FIGURE 6-9.
Use the New Window command to open a second window.

	A	B	C	D	E	F	G	H	I
1	1992 Product Totals								
3		Jan	Feb	Mar	Apr	May	Jun	Jul	Aug
4	Product 1	$5,371	$6,481	$2,558	$2,445	$6,380	$2,983	$5,755	$1,747
5	Product 2	$5,625	$9,412	$6,975	$5,635	$4,051	$8,591	$4,376	$6,465
6	Product 3	$1,231	$3,346	$1,936	$6,934	$773	$6,132	$3,373	$5,702
7	Product 4	$8,590	$5,681	$7,952	$3,131	$2,710	$9,479	$8,661	$1,029
8	Product 5	$4,213	$3,964	$4,655	$1,611	$9,938	$4,041	$1,213	$3,267
9	Product 6	$3,428	$2,800	$3,486	$7,007	$6,973	$9,184	$99	$5,645
10	Product 7	$1,233	$7,208	$4,094	$4,076	$4,835	$8,576	$5,486	$3,067
11	Product 8	$3,282	$6,333	$3,715	$4,165	$6,173	$2,018	$2,774	$7,746
12	Product 9	$6,750	$1,919	$7,628	$4,077	$433	$3,966	$4,226	$7,373
13	Product 10	$3,334	$6,597	$7,538	$7,879	$3,107	$9,083	$5,583	$5,851
14	Product 11	$2,931	$3,390	$3,443	$6,073	$8,922	$9,281	$2,099	$7,228
15	Product 12	$2,195	$5,926	$2,208	$3,828	$9,937	$3,221	$179	$5,141
16	Product 13	$4,662	$4,187	$2,903	$812	$7,717	$3,347	$8,054	$3,471
17	Product 14	$2,241	$778	$2,535	$9,924	$6,057	$3	$8,473	$6,347
18	Product 15	$5,779	$3,577	$5,366	$7,160	$5,620	$7,134	$9,219	$8,756

Notice that Microsoft Excel assigns the name PRODUCTS.XLS:2 to the new worksheet window and renames the original worksheet window PRODUCTS.XLS:1. In addition, PRODUCTS.XLS:2 becomes the active window, as indicated by its highlighted title bar, and covers most of PRODUCTS.XLS:1.

It's important to understand the difference between the File menu's New command and the Window menu's New Window command. The File menu's New command creates a new worksheet (or chart or macro sheet), which is displayed in a new window. The worksheet that results from the New command is completely separate from any worksheets that existed before. The New Window command, however, does not create a new worksheet. Instead, this command offers a new porthole through which you can view an open worksheet. If more than one document is open when you issue the New Window command, Excel creates a new window for the active document only.

Any work you do in a window affects the entire document, not only the worksheet as viewed in that window. For instance, when you make an entry into the worksheet in one window, you can view that entry in any of the windows associated with that worksheet. By the same token, if you edit or erase the contents of a cell in one window, you see the change when you look at the same cell, or any cell dependent upon that cell, in another window.

Of course, you can scroll this new window to look at another portion of the worksheet. For example, if you click the down and right scroll arrows in PRODUCTS.XLS:2 a few times, use the scrolling techniques explained in Chapter 2, or use the selection commands from the Formula menu, you can look at cells J19:R36, as shown in Figure 6-10. You can also use the Goto command from the Formula menu to move to a different location.

FIGURE 6-10.
Cells J19:R36 now
appear in the second
window.

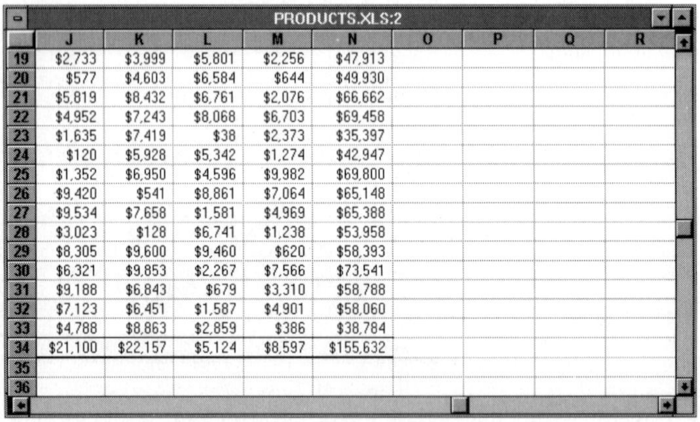

	J	K	L	M	N	O	P	Q	R
19	$2,733	$3,999	$5,801	$2,256	$47,913				
20	$577	$4,603	$6,584	$644	$49,930				
21	$5,819	$8,432	$6,761	$2,076	$66,662				
22	$4,952	$7,243	$8,068	$6,703	$69,458				
23	$1,635	$7,419	$38	$2,373	$35,397				
24	$120	$5,928	$5,342	$1,274	$42,947				
25	$1,352	$6,950	$4,596	$9,982	$69,800				
26	$9,420	$541	$8,861	$7,064	$65,148				
27	$9,534	$7,658	$1,581	$4,969	$65,388				
28	$3,023	$128	$6,741	$1,238	$53,958				
29	$8,305	$9,600	$9,460	$620	$58,393				
30	$6,321	$9,853	$2,267	$7,566	$73,541				
31	$9,188	$6,843	$679	$3,310	$58,788				
32	$7,123	$6,451	$1,587	$4,901	$58,060				
33	$4,788	$8,863	$2,859	$386	$38,784				
34	$21,100	$22,157	$5,124	$8,597	$155,632				
35									
36									

PRODUCTS.XLS:2

Synchronized windows

When you have two or more windows open on the same document, you can use the Arrange command on the Window menu to position the windows on the screen in a way that lets you monitor one area of the worksheet while working in another. (You can also do this with windowpanes within the same window, as we will discuss later in this chapter.)

For example, perhaps you want to watch the effect on the Totals in our PRODUCTS worksheet while entering information into columns B, C, and D. First, scroll PRODUCTS.XLS:2 until cells K1:S18 are the only columns visible. Now, click anywhere in PRODUCT.XLS:1 to make it your active window. Next, choose the Arrange command from the Window menu, and then select the Tiled, Windows of Active Document, and Sync Vertical options. When you press Enter, your screen looks like the one in Figure 6-11.

Now both windows are displayed on the screen side by side, with window 1 at column A, and window 2 at column K. Each window's title bar displays a new indicator: *[VSync]*. This lets you know that the Sync Vertical option is active. If you selected Sync Horizontal, the indicator would read *[HSync]*. If you selected both the Horizontal and Vertical options, it would read *[HVSync]*.

FIGURE 6-11.
Use the Arrange command's Sync Vertical option to lock windows for simultaneous vertical scrolling.

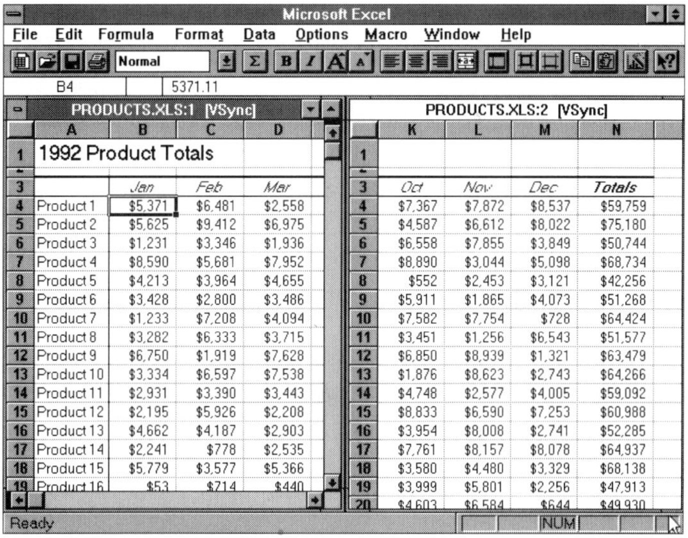

	A	B	C	D
1	1992 Product Totals			
3		Jan	Feb	Mar
4	Product 1	$5,371	$6,481	$2,558
5	Product 2	$5,625	$9,412	$6,975
6	Product 3	$1,231	$3,346	$1,936
7	Product 4	$8,590	$5,681	$7,952
8	Product 5	$4,213	$3,964	$4,655
9	Product 6	$3,428	$2,800	$3,486
10	Product 7	$1,233	$7,208	$4,094
11	Product 8	$3,282	$6,333	$3,715
12	Product 9	$6,750	$1,919	$7,628
13	Product 10	$3,334	$6,597	$7,538
14	Product 11	$2,931	$3,390	$3,443
15	Product 12	$2,195	$5,926	$2,208
16	Product 13	$4,662	$4,187	$2,903
17	Product 14	$2,241	$778	$2,535
18	Product 15	$5,779	$3,577	$5,366
19	Product 16	$53	$714	$440

	K	L	M	N
3	Oct	Nov	Dec	Totals
4	$7,367	$7,872	$8,537	$59,759
5	$4,587	$6,612	$8,022	$75,180
6	$6,558	$7,855	$3,849	$50,744
7	$8,890	$3,044	$5,098	$68,734
8	$552	$2,453	$3,121	$42,256
9	$5,911	$1,865	$4,073	$51,268
10	$7,582	$7,754	$728	$64,424
11	$3,451	$1,256	$6,543	$51,577
12	$6,850	$8,939	$1,321	$63,479
13	$1,876	$8,623	$2,743	$64,266
14	$4,748	$2,577	$4,005	$59,092
15	$8,833	$6,590	$7,253	$60,988
16	$3,954	$8,008	$2,741	$52,285
17	$7,761	$8,157	$8,078	$64,937
18	$3,580	$4,480	$3,329	$68,138
19	$3,999	$5,801	$2,256	$47,913
20	$4,603	$6,584	$644	$49,930

Now, if you scroll down in one window, the other window also scrolls down to the same position. But because you selected only the Sync Vertical option, scrolling to the right in one window does not affect the other. As you might guess, if you select the Sync Horizontal option, scrolling to the right affects both windows, but scrolling up and down affects only the window you are in. If you select both Sync Vertical and Sync Horizontal, the windows keep in step with each other in both directions.

These synchronization options remain in effect until you turn them off in the Arrange dialog box. If you save and close the worksheet, and then reopen it and choose the New Window command, the synchronization option that was in effect when you saved the worksheet will still be in effect. To turn the sync options off, you must deselect them, but leave the Windows of Active Document check box selected when you click OK. If you deselect the Windows of Active Document option, the windows remain synchronized.

Splitting windows into panes

Windowpanes offer another way to view different areas of your worksheet at the same time. Microsoft Excel's windowpane feature lets you split any window on the screen vertically, horizontally, or both vertically and horizontally to create panes of any size.

The windowpane feature, like the Arrange options for multiple windows on the same document, offers synchronized scrolling capability within the same window. Let's use the worksheet in Figure 6-8 as an example. Columns B through M and rows 4 through 33 in this worksheet contain product sales data. Column N and row 34 contain totals. Suppose you want to keep an eye on the totals in column N as you work with the monthly sales figures in columns B through M. You can do this by splitting the window into two panes.

To create a vertical pane using the mouse, point to the black bar on the left side of the horizontal scroll bar (just to the left of the left scroll arrow). This is the *vertical split bar*. When your mouse pointer touches the vertical split bar, it changes to a pair of vertical lines with small horizontal arrows. Now drag the split bar to the right so that it falls on the border between columns G and H. Your worksheet now looks like Figure 6-12. Notice that you have two horizontal scroll bars. Next, move your pointer to the horizontal scroll bar beneath the right pane and scroll column N into view. Your worksheet looks like the one in Figure 6-13.

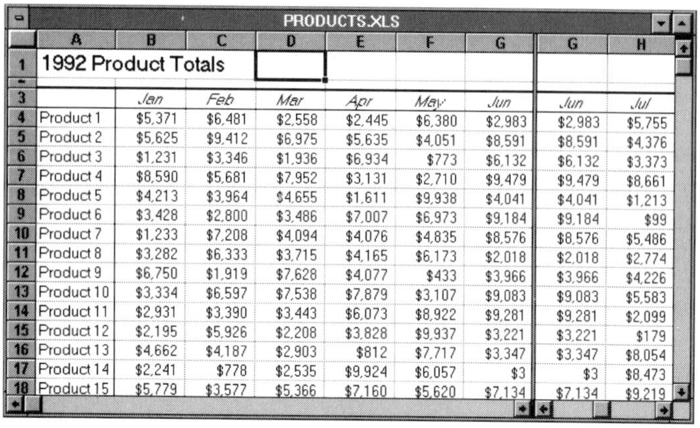

FIGURE 6-12.
We split the window into two vertical panes.

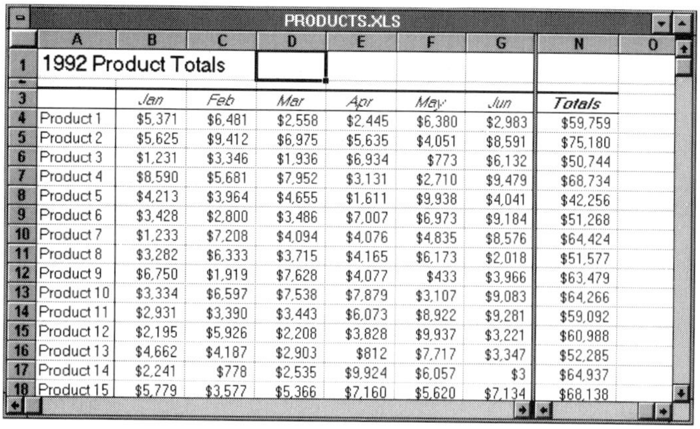

	A	B	C	D	E	F	G	G	H
1	1992 Product Totals								
3		Jan	Feb	Mar	Apr	May	Jun	Jun	Jul
4	Product 1	$5,371	$6,481	$2,558	$2,445	$6,380	$2,983	$2,983	$5,755
5	Product 2	$5,625	$9,412	$6,975	$5,635	$4,051	$8,591	$8,591	$4,376
6	Product 3	$1,231	$3,346	$1,936	$6,934	$773	$6,132	$6,132	$3,373
7	Product 4	$8,590	$5,681	$7,952	$3,131	$2,710	$9,479	$9,479	$8,661
8	Product 5	$4,213	$3,964	$4,655	$1,611	$9,938	$4,041	$4,041	$1,213
9	Product 6	$3,428	$2,800	$3,486	$7,007	$6,973	$9,184	$9,184	$99
10	Product 7	$1,233	$7,208	$4,094	$4,076	$4,835	$8,576	$8,576	$5,486
11	Product 8	$3,282	$6,333	$3,715	$4,165	$6,173	$2,018	$2,018	$2,774
12	Product 9	$6,750	$1,919	$7,628	$4,077	$433	$3,966	$3,966	$4,226
13	Product 10	$3,334	$6,597	$7,538	$7,879	$3,107	$9,083	$9,083	$5,583
14	Product 11	$2,931	$3,390	$3,443	$6,073	$8,922	$9,281	$9,281	$2,099
15	Product 12	$2,195	$5,926	$2,208	$3,828	$9,937	$3,221	$3,221	$179
16	Product 13	$4,662	$4,187	$2,903	$812	$7,717	$3,347	$3,347	$8,054
17	Product 14	$2,241	$778	$2,535	$9,924	$6,057	$3	$3	$8,473
18	Product 15	$5,779	$3,577	$5,366	$7,160	$5,620	$7,134	$7,134	$9,219

FIGURE 6-13.
We scrolled column N into view in the right pane.

	A	B	C	D	E	F	G	N	O
1	1992 Product Totals								
3		Jan	Feb	Mar	Apr	May	Jun	Totals	
4	Product 1	$5,371	$6,481	$2,558	$2,445	$6,380	$2,983	$59,759	
5	Product 2	$5,625	$9,412	$6,975	$5,635	$4,051	$8,591	$75,180	
6	Product 3	$1,231	$3,346	$1,936	$6,934	$773	$6,132	$50,744	
7	Product 4	$8,590	$5,681	$7,952	$3,131	$2,710	$9,479	$68,734	
8	Product 5	$4,213	$3,964	$4,655	$1,611	$9,938	$4,041	$42,256	
9	Product 6	$3,428	$2,800	$3,486	$7,007	$6,973	$9,184	$51,268	
10	Product 7	$1,233	$7,208	$4,094	$4,076	$4,835	$8,576	$64,424	
11	Product 8	$3,282	$6,333	$3,715	$4,165	$6,173	$2,018	$51,577	
12	Product 9	$6,750	$1,919	$7,628	$4,077	$433	$3,966	$63,479	
13	Product 10	$3,334	$6,597	$7,538	$7,879	$3,107	$9,083	$64,266	
14	Product 11	$2,931	$3,390	$3,443	$6,073	$8,922	$9,281	$59,092	
15	Product 12	$2,195	$5,926	$2,208	$3,828	$9,937	$3,221	$60,988	
16	Product 13	$4,662	$4,187	$2,903	$812	$7,717	$3,347	$52,285	
17	Product 14	$2,241	$778	$2,535	$9,924	$6,057	$3	$64,937	
18	Product 15	$5,779	$3,577	$5,366	$7,160	$5,620	$7,134	$68,138	

Now you can use the scroll bars in the large pane, the scrolling techniques discussed in Chapter 2, or the selection commands on the Formula menu to scroll between columns A and M without losing sight of the totals in column N. In addition, when you scroll between rows 1 and 34, you'll always see the corresponding totals in column N. For example, if you scroll down until rows 18 through 34 are in view in the large pane, those same rows will be visible in the smaller pane.

If you also want to keep an eye on the monthly totals in row 34, you can create a horizontal pane. Before you split the window, scroll the worksheet so that row 35 appears at the bottom of the window. (The new window will scroll up one row — that's why you have to include row 35.) Next, drag the *horizontal split bar* (the black bar at the top of the vertical scroll bar) toward the bottom of the window so that only two rows appear in the bottom two panes. Click the down arrow in the lower pane's scroll bar once to reposition row 34. Figure 6-14 shows the result.

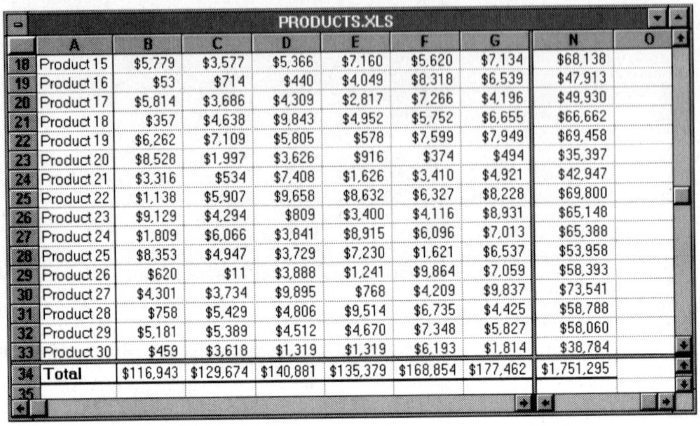

FIGURE 6-14.
We created a horizontal pane so that we can keep an eye on our totals in row 34.

	A	B	C	D	E	F	G	N	O
18	Product 15	$5,779	$3,577	$5,366	$7,160	$5,620	$7,134	$68,138	
19	Product 16	$53	$714	$440	$4,049	$8,318	$6,539	$47,913	
20	Product 17	$5,814	$3,686	$4,309	$2,817	$7,266	$4,196	$49,930	
21	Product 18	$357	$4,638	$9,843	$4,952	$5,752	$6,655	$66,662	
22	Product 19	$6,262	$7,109	$5,805	$578	$7,599	$7,949	$69,458	
23	Product 20	$8,528	$1,997	$3,626	$916	$374	$494	$35,397	
24	Product 21	$3,316	$534	$7,408	$1,626	$3,410	$4,921	$42,947	
25	Product 22	$1,138	$5,907	$9,658	$8,632	$6,327	$8,228	$69,800	
26	Product 23	$9,129	$4,294	$809	$3,400	$4,116	$8,931	$65,148	
27	Product 24	$1,809	$6,066	$3,841	$8,915	$6,096	$7,013	$65,388	
28	Product 25	$8,353	$4,947	$3,729	$7,230	$1,621	$6,537	$53,958	
29	Product 26	$620	$11	$3,888	$1,241	$9,864	$7,059	$58,393	
30	Product 27	$4,301	$3,734	$9,895	$768	$4,209	$9,837	$73,541	
31	Product 28	$758	$5,429	$4,806	$9,514	$6,735	$4,425	$58,788	
32	Product 29	$5,181	$5,389	$4,512	$4,670	$7,348	$5,827	$58,060	
33	Product 30	$459	$3,618	$1,319	$1,319	$6,193	$1,814	$38,784	
34	Total	$116,943	$129,674	$140,881	$135,379	$168,854	$177,462	$1,751,295	
35									

You can quickly create both horizontal and vertical windowpanes by choosing the Split command from the Window menu. The Split command divides your window into four equal panes, with the split bars positioned in the middle of the window. You can then reposition the split bars as you like. After you split a window, the Split command changes to the Remove Split command, which removes one or both sets of split bars from the active window.

To activate a pane, click that pane with the mouse.

You can change the size of your windowpanes at any time by dragging the split bars or choosing the Split command from the Control menu and pressing the arrow keys. To remove a pane, choose the Remove Split command from the Window menu, or use techniques described earlier in this section to move the split bar to the window border.

Freezing panes

After you've split a window into panes, you can freeze the top panes, the left panes, or both by choosing the Freeze Panes command from the Window menu. If you've split a window vertically, Freeze Panes "locks in" the columns that are in view in the left pane so that you can scroll through the worksheet without losing sight of these columns. Similarly, if you've split a window horizontally, Freeze Panes locks in the rows that are in view in the top pane. If you've split a window both vertically and horizontally, both the rows in the top pane and the columns in the left pane are frozen.

In Figure 6-15, we split the window vertically and horizontally to display the code entries in column A and the month entries in row 3. To keep this information in view as we enter and edit data in the worksheet, we can issue the Freeze Panes command. Figure 6-16 shows the result of scrolling the window after freezing the panes.

Notice that the double-line pane dividers have changed to single-line pane dividers. Now we can scroll through the remainder of the worksheet without losing sight of the entries in column A and row 3.

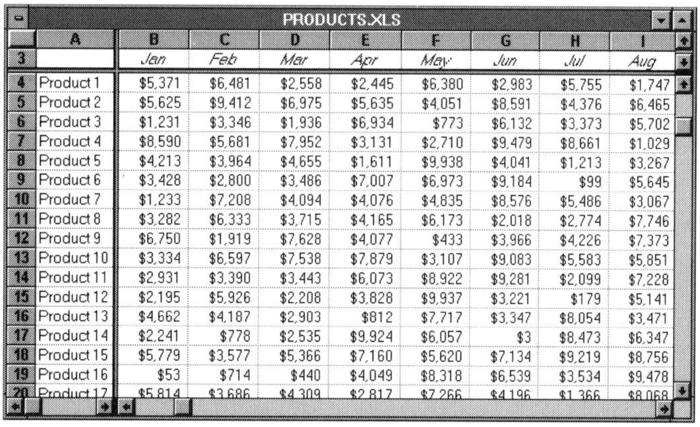

FIGURE 6-15.
Column A and row 3 are displayed in separate windowpanes.

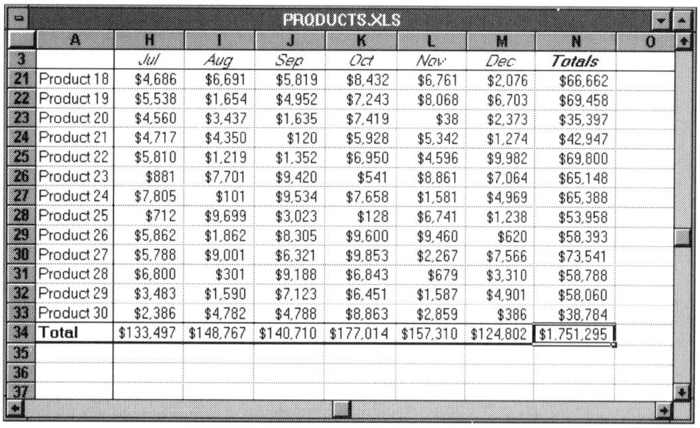

	A	B	C	D	E	F	G	H	I
3		Jan	Feb	Mar	Apr	May	Jun	Jul	Aug
4	Product 1	$5,371	$6,481	$2,558	$2,445	$6,380	$2,983	$5,755	$1,747
5	Product 2	$5,625	$9,412	$6,975	$5,635	$4,051	$8,591	$4,376	$6,465
6	Product 3	$1,231	$3,346	$1,936	$6,934	$773	$6,132	$3,373	$5,702
7	Product 4	$8,590	$5,681	$7,952	$3,131	$2,710	$9,479	$8,661	$1,029
8	Product 5	$4,213	$3,964	$4,655	$1,611	$9,938	$4,041	$1,213	$3,267
9	Product 6	$3,428	$2,800	$3,486	$7,007	$6,973	$9,184	$99	$5,645
10	Product 7	$1,233	$7,208	$4,094	$4,076	$4,835	$8,576	$5,486	$3,067
11	Product 8	$3,282	$6,333	$3,715	$4,165	$6,173	$2,018	$2,774	$7,746
12	Product 9	$6,750	$1,919	$7,628	$4,077	$433	$3,966	$4,226	$7,373
13	Product 10	$3,334	$6,597	$7,538	$7,879	$3,107	$9,083	$5,583	$5,851
14	Product 11	$2,931	$3,390	$3,443	$6,073	$8,922	$9,281	$2,099	$7,228
15	Product 12	$2,195	$5,926	$2,208	$3,828	$9,937	$3,221	$179	$5,141
16	Product 13	$4,662	$4,187	$2,903	$812	$7,717	$3,347	$8,054	$3,471
17	Product 14	$2,241	$778	$2,535	$9,924	$6,057	$3	$8,473	$6,347
18	Product 15	$5,779	$3,577	$5,366	$7,160	$5,620	$7,134	$9,219	$8,756
19	Product 16	$53	$714	$440	$4,049	$8,318	$6,539	$3,534	$9,478
20	Product 17	$5,814	$3,686	$4,309	$2,817	$7,266	$4,196	$1,366	$8,068

FIGURE 6-16.
The Freeze Panes command locks in the data in the top and left panes.

	A	H	I	J	K	L	M	N	O
3		Jul	Aug	Sep	Oct	Nov	Dec	Totals	
21	Product 18	$4,686	$6,691	$5,819	$8,432	$6,761	$2,076	$66,662	
22	Product 19	$5,538	$1,654	$4,952	$7,243	$8,068	$6,703	$69,458	
23	Product 20	$4,560	$3,437	$1,635	$7,419	$38	$2,373	$35,397	
24	Product 21	$4,717	$4,350	$120	$5,928	$5,342	$1,274	$42,947	
25	Product 22	$5,810	$1,219	$1,352	$6,950	$4,596	$9,982	$69,800	
26	Product 23	$881	$7,701	$9,420	$541	$8,861	$7,064	$65,148	
27	Product 24	$7,805	$101	$9,534	$7,658	$1,581	$4,969	$65,388	
28	Product 25	$712	$9,699	$3,023	$128	$6,741	$1,238	$53,958	
29	Product 26	$5,862	$1,862	$8,305	$9,600	$9,460	$620	$58,393	
30	Product 27	$5,788	$9,001	$6,321	$9,853	$2,267	$7,566	$73,541	
31	Product 28	$6,800	$301	$9,188	$6,843	$679	$3,310	$58,788	
32	Product 29	$3,483	$1,590	$7,123	$6,451	$1,587	$4,901	$58,060	
33	Product 30	$2,386	$4,782	$4,788	$8,863	$2,859	$386	$38,784	
34	Total	$133,497	$148,767	$140,710	$177,014	$157,310	$124,802	$1,751,295	
35									
36									
37									

You can also use the Freeze Panes command directly, without first displaying the split bars. For example, if you select cell B4 in PRODUCTS.XLS and choose the Freeze Panes command, Excel simultaneously splits the window and freezes the panes above and to the left of the active cell. After you do this, rows 1 through 3 and column A are frozen, so that you can scroll through the detail data in the range B4:N34 while the labels stay in place. If you use this method, subsequently choosing the Unfreeze Panes command both unfreezes the panes and removes the split bars.

If you've created two or more windows to view the same document, you can split each window into panes and use the Freeze Panes command to freeze different areas in each window. To unfreeze the panes in the active window, choose Unfreeze Panes from the Window menu.

Zooming windows

The Zoom command on the Window menu lets you change the size of your worksheet display. If, for example, you want to see the entire active worksheet area to check its overall appearance, you can use the Zoom command to reduce the on-screen display to the necessary size. When you choose the Zoom command, the dialog box in Figure 6-17 appears.

The zoom tools

You can also use the Zoom In and Zoom Out tools, located on the Utility toolbar, to quickly change the size of your display. To activate the Utility toolbar, click the right mouse button while the pointer is over the Standard toolbar (or any displayed toolbar), and choose Utility from the shortcut menu that appears. If no toolbar is active, choose Toolbars from the Options menu, select Utility, and click OK.

Zoom In

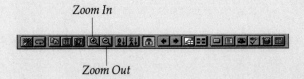

Zoom Out

When you click one of the zoom tools, the display changes to the next default reduction or enlargement option in that direction. For example, if you click the Zoom Out tool when the worksheet is at 100%, the display changes to 75% reduction. If you want to use the Fit Selection or Custom options, use the Zoom command. For more information about tools and toolbars, including details on customizing toolbars, see Appendix A.

FIGURE 6-17.

*The Zoom command
gives you control over
the size of your
on-screen display.*

The dialog box gives you three reduction options; one enlargement option; a Fit Selection option that determines the necessary reduction or enlargement for you, based on the shape of your cell selection and the size of your window; and a Custom edit box, where you can specify reduction as low as 10 percent or enlargement as high as 400 percent.

For example, using the PRODUCTS.XLS worksheet from Figure 6-8, we'll select the entire active area of the worksheet by selecting cell A1 and pressing Ctrl-Shift-End. (If the Alternate Navigation Keys option is active, press Ctrl-Shift-End, followed by End, and then the Down arrow key until the last active cell is selected.) Next, choose Zoom from the Window menu, select the Fit Selection option, and click OK. The window changes to look like Figure 6-18.

Now the entire worksheet is displayed on the screen. Of course, reading the numbers is a problem at this size, but you can select another reduction or enlargement size for that purpose. Choose the Zoom command again, and notice that the

FIGURE 6-18.

*Using the Zoom
command, you can fit
the whole worksheet
on the screen at once.*

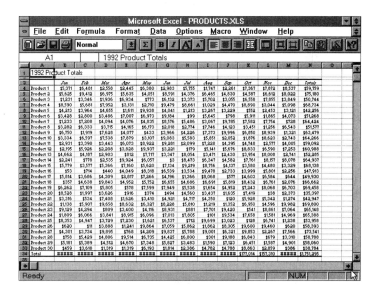

Custom option (not the Fit Selection option) is activated, with 60% entered in the text box. When you select the Fit Selection option, Microsoft Excel determines the proper reduction and displays it here. The next time you want to display the entire worksheet, you can type this number into the Custom box instead of selecting the entire worksheet.

With the Zoom dialog box still open, select the 200% option and click OK. The worksheet changes to look like Figure 6-19.

The zoom option that is in effect when you save the worksheet is active again when you reopen it.

FIGURE 6-19.
You can enlarge your worksheets for easier viewing or presentation purposes.

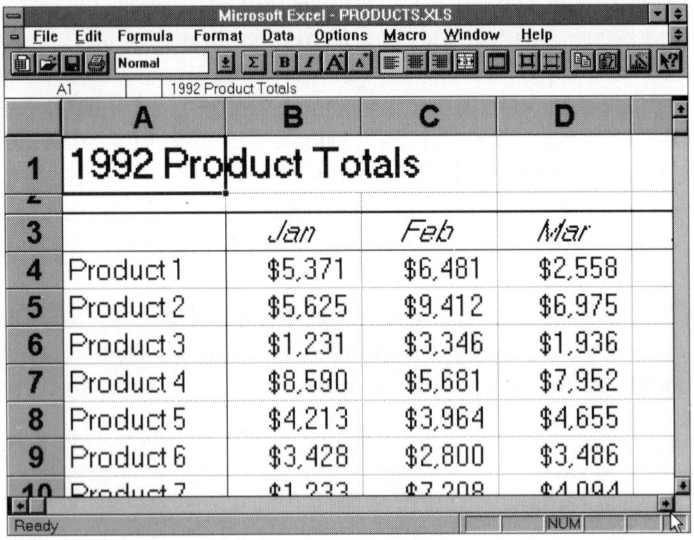

	A	B	C	D
1	1992 Product Totals			
2				
3		*Jan*	*Feb*	*Mar*
4	Product 1	$5,371	$6,481	$2,558
5	Product 2	$5,625	$9,412	$6,975
6	Product 3	$1,231	$3,346	$1,936
7	Product 4	$8,590	$5,681	$7,952
8	Product 5	$4,213	$3,964	$4,655
9	Product 6	$3,428	$2,800	$3,486
10	Product 7	$1,233	$7,208	$4,094

Named views

Suppose you determine the display characteristics and print settings you want your worksheet to have for a particular purpose, such as editing, but you want to set it up differently, perhaps for an onscreen presentation. Using the View command on the Window menu, you can assign names to different sets of options. You can then save these sets of options and select one by name when you need it, rather than implementing the changes in your worksheet manually.

Using the Views dialog box, shown in Figure 6-20, the View command gives you instant access to the sets of options, known as *named views,* that you define.

FIGURE 6-20.
*The View command
lets you store different
sets of display and
print settings with
your worksheet.*

NOTE: *The View feature is a Microsoft Excel add-in. If the View command does not appear
on your Window menu, you need to install the VIEWS.XLA add-in. You can run the Excel
setup program again to specify a custom installation that includes this add-in, or see Chapter
21 for more information about add-ins.*

The settings that are stored in named views include row heights, column
widths, display dialog box options, window size and position on the screen, windowpane settings, the cells that are selected at the time the definition is created, and
the print settings. (Printing and print settings are covered in Chapter 12.)

When you first choose the View command, the Views dialog box is empty. To
define a named view, choose the View command and click Add. You will see a dialog
box like the one in Figure 6-21.

FIGURE 6-21.
*You define a name for
the current set of
display and print
settings with the Add
View dialog box.*

Simply type a name in the Name edit box, select the options you want, and click
OK. The next time you choose the View command, the name you entered in the Add
View dialog box appears in the Views list. The Print Settings and Hidden Rows and
Columns options let you choose to include the corresponding settings in your view
definition.

Linking worksheets

One of Microsoft Excel's most often used features is its ability to create dynamic
links between worksheets. You'll find a number of advantages to linking worksheets.
First, you can break large, complex worksheet models into more manageable

portions. For example, instead of placing all your company's budget data in one worksheet, you can create several departmental budgets. You can then create a master budget worksheet to draw relevant data from the individual departmental models, which are called *supporting* worksheets. Linked worksheets also give you the flexibility to extract any number of reports and analyses from a group of supporting worksheets.

Besides creating more manageable and flexible models, linked worksheets can save recalculation time and memory. You must keep only the data you need open in your workspace at any given time. Excel reads the relevant data from disk to ensure that your linked references are always up to date.

In addition to linking Excel worksheets to one another, you can link Excel worksheets to worksheets created in any version of Lotus 1-2-3, including 1-2-3 for Windows. All the procedures described in this section for linking XLS files to XLS files also apply to links between XLS files and WKS, WK1, or WK3 files. (For more information about working with Lotus 1-2-3 files in Excel, see Chapter 23.)

You can establish links between worksheets in two basic ways. You can either build an external-reference formula yourself (by typing, pointing with the mouse, or using the File menu's Paste Link command), or you can use Excel's automatic consolidation feature. The consolidation feature is particularly useful for linking two or more worksheets that store the same kind of information and have a similar structure. The next section describes the procedures for creating and working with external-reference formulas. (For information about the automatic consolidation feature, see "Consolidating worksheets," later in this chapter.)

Creating external-reference formulas

Creating a formula that links two worksheets is like building any other formula. The only difference between a linked formula and a regular formula is that in a linked formula, you must include the name of the external worksheet, followed by an exclamation mark.

For example, consider the two worksheets shown in Figure 6-22. You can link cell A1 in the worksheet named LINK2 to cell A8 in the worksheet named LINK1. To do this, select cell A1 in LINK2 and enter the formula

=LINK1.XLS!$A$8

Cell A1 in LINK2 assumes the value of cell A8 in LINK1. In this example, LINK2 is the *dependent worksheet* and LINK1 is the *supporting worksheet*. Analogously, cell A1 in LINK2 is referred to as the *dependent formula* and A8 in LINK1 is the *supporting formula*.

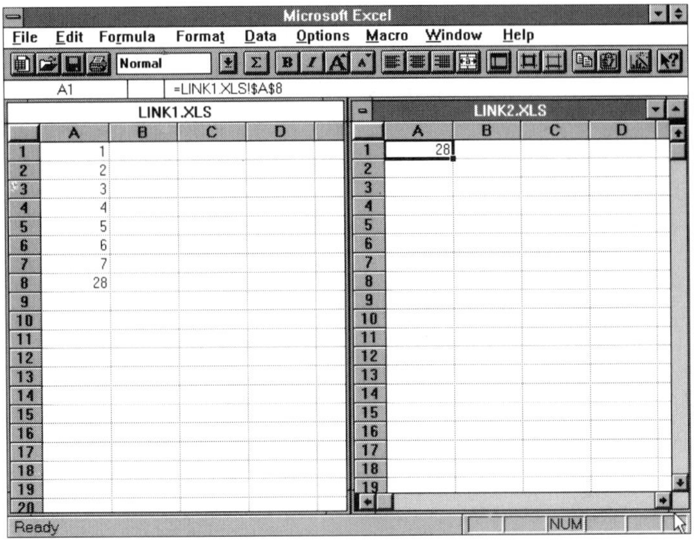

FIGURE 6-22.
Cell A1 in the dependent worksheet, LINK2, is linked to cell A8 in the supporting worksheet, LINK1.

Pasting linked references into a formula is similar to pasting standard cell references. For example, to enter the same formula in cell A1 of LINK2, select the cell, type an equal sign, and then activate the LINK1 worksheet and select cell A8. Alternatively, you can paste the linked reference by first activating cell A8 of LINK1, choosing the Copy command, and then activating cell A1 of LINK2 and choosing the Paste Link command from the Edit menu.

You can use names instead of cell references in dependent formulas. For example, if cell A8 in LINK1 is named *Test*, then the formula

=LINK1.XLS!Test

is identical to the formula

=LINK1.XLS!$A$8

You can also create formulas that refer to ranges in the supporting worksheet. Suppose you want to enter a formula in cell A2 of LINK2 that averages the values in cells A1:A7 of LINK1. To do this, select cell A2 of LINK2, type

=AVERAGE(

activate LINK1, drag through cells A1:A7 to paste your linked range reference into the formula bar, and type a close parenthesis to complete the formula. The result looks like this:

=AVERAGE(LINK1.XLS!$A$1:$A$7)

You can't use the Paste Link command to create the reference to the range A1:A7 in this formula. However, you can use Paste Link to create linked array references. For example, you can create a linked array formula that refers to cells A1:A7 of LINK1. To do this, select cells A1:A7 in LINK1, issue the Copy command, activate LINK2, select the cell you want to use as the first cell for your linked array formula, and choose Paste Link. Excel automatically selects an array range the same size and shape as the copy range and enters the dependent array formula

{=LINK1.XLS!$A$1:$A$7}

in each cell of that range.

Linking multiple worksheets

Excel also lets you build formulas that link several worksheets at once. For example, suppose you've created three worksheets — JAN, FEB, and MAR. You want to build a formula in cell A1 of MAR that totals the values in cell A1 of JAN and cell A1 of FEB. You can do this by entering the dependent formula

=JAN.XLS!A1+FEB.XLS!A1

into cell A1 of MAR. In this example, MAR is directly dependent on both FEB and JAN.

Saving linked worksheets

As mentioned in Chapter 1, you use the Save As command from the File menu to give your worksheets descriptive names when you save them. For example, suppose you're modeling your company's 1992 budget in a worksheet called Sheet1. Later when you save the worksheet, you can use the Save As command to give the worksheet a name such as BUDGET92.

Now suppose that another active worksheet, called ACTUAL, contains links to your budget worksheet and, therefore, is dependent on the budget worksheet for some of its information. These links identify the budget worksheet as Sheet1. If you use Save As to save Sheet1 as BUDGET92 *while* ACTUAL is still open, all the references to Sheet1 in the ACTUAL worksheet will change to BUDGET92. Thus, if ACTUAL contains the reference

=Sheet1!A1

it changes to

=BUDGET92.XLS!A1

If, on the other hand, you try to close the dependent worksheet, ACTUAL, before you save the supporting worksheet, Sheet1, you see the warning *Save ACTUAL.XLS with references to unsaved documents?* If you click OK, Excel saves ACTUAL. However, if you then use the Save As command to save Sheet1 as BUDGET92, the references to Sheet1 in ACTUAL are not updated. The dependent formulas in ACTUAL continue to assume that the name of the budget worksheet is Sheet1. Thus, when you reopen ACTUAL, Excel will be unable to find the worksheet Sheet1 and will display the dialog box in Figure 6-23. When you see this dialog box, you simply select the name of the file or directory that contains the file Excel is searching for. However, if you cannot remember the name of your supporting worksheet, you can click Cancel. When you remember the name, you will have to use the Links command to redirect the links. (The Links command is described in "Opening supporting worksheets," later in this chapter.)

FIGURE 6-23.
The File Not Found dialog box appears if Excel can't locate the supporting worksheet.

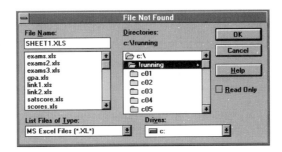

Opening a dependent worksheet

When you save a worksheet that contains dependent formulas, Excel stores the most recent results of those formulas. If you open and use the supporting worksheet after you close the dependent worksheet, the values of some of the cells in the supporting worksheet might be changed. When you open the dependent worksheet, Excel retains the saved values of the external references in the dependent formulas, but it displays an alert box with the message *Update references to unopened documents?* This alert box lets you tell Excel whether to read the current values from the closed worksheets on the disk.

If you click No, Excel opens the dependent worksheet without updating any references to the supporting worksheets. All the dependent formulas in the worksheet retain their last saved values.

If you click Yes, Excel searches for the supporting worksheets. If it finds them, it reads the values from the supporting files and updates the dependent formulas in the dependent worksheet. Excel does not open the supporting worksheets; it merely reads the appropriate values from those worksheets.

If Excel can't find one or more of the supporting files, it displays a dialog box like the one in Figure 6-23. In this dialog box, you can choose to cancel the update process, change the current directory, or identify the file.

Opening supporting worksheets

In addition to the File Open command, Excel provides two ways to open supporting worksheets: by double-clicking external-reference cells and by using the File Links command.

Whenever you double-click a cell that contains an external-reference formula but does not contain a note, Excel activates the supporting worksheet and selects the referenced cell or range. (See Chapter 5 for a full discussion of cell notes.) If the supporting worksheet is not open, Excel retrieves it from disk. (If the external-reference formula references more than one worksheet, Excel activates only the one named first.)

The Links command on the File menu is a convenient way to open in one step all the worksheets on which another worksheet depends. The main difference between the Links and Open commands is that Open presents a list of all the files in the current directory, whereas Links lists only those files that support the active worksheet. (Using Links is a handy way to look up the names of all the supporting worksheets of a dependent worksheet.)

For example, suppose you're building a spreadsheet, TOTALS, that depends on two other spreadsheets, GROUP1 and GROUP2. GROUP1 and GROUP2 are currently closed. To open both worksheets at once, simply choose the Links command. You'll see a dialog box like the one shown in Figure 6-24. Notice that the file list includes only the two files that support TOTALS. Now select both names, GROUP1 and GROUP2. You can select several names at one time with the mouse by holding down Shift and dragging through or clicking the desired names. Finally, click Open. Excel opens both of the worksheets on which TOTALS depends.

FIGURE 6-24.
Use the Links dialog box to quickly locate all your supporting worksheets.

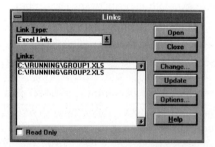

Although you'll usually open all the supporting worksheets at once, you can use Links to open them one at a time. To do this, you must issue a separate Links command for every worksheet you want to open. Be careful — the order in which you open the files is important. For example, suppose you select the name GROUP1 in the Links dialog box and then click Open. GROUP1 now appears as the active document. However, if you try to use the Links command to open GROUP2, you'll get surprising results. Because GROUP1 is now the active worksheet, when you choose the Links command again to open GROUP2, Excel displays a list of any worksheets that support GROUP1 instead of those that support TOTALS. To see a list of the worksheets that support TOTALS, you must activate that worksheet before you repeat the Links command.

Updating links without opening supporting documents

You can also use the File Links command to update external-reference formulas without opening the supporting documents. This is useful if you use Excel on a network and one of your colleagues is working with a supporting document. Suppose you have a worksheet named BUDGET92 with formulas that reference values in another worksheet named ACTUAL91. Suppose that another member of your work group is making last-minute changes to ACTUAL91.

If you open BUDGET92, Excel asks if you want to update references to un-opened documents (in this case, to ACTUAL91.XLS). You answer Yes, because you want your worksheet to reflect the latest values in the supporting document. After a period of time, you want to update your BUDGET92 worksheet again because ACTUAL91 underwent further changes. You can choose the File Links command, select ACTUAL91.XLS in the Links list box, and then click Update. Excel gets the relevant values from the last version of ACTUAL91.XLS that was saved on disk.

Redirecting links

Excel can access documents stored in different directories. As long as you use the Save As command to save all supporting worksheets before you close the dependent worksheet, Excel remembers the location of all supporting files. If you rename a supporting worksheet or move it to another directory, you must redirect your worksheet links before Excel can update your external references.

To redirect your worksheet links, select the original name of the supporting file or files in the Links list box and then choose Change. Figure 6-25 on the following page shows the resulting dialog box. In this dialog box, select the name of the new file or renamed file for your dependent formulas. If necessary, you can choose a new directory from the list box on the right. Alternatively, you can type a new pathname in the File Name text box. When you click OK, Excel changes all references to the supporting worksheet to the new filename.

FIGURE 6-25.
When you use the
Change button to
redirect your
worksheet links, you
see a dialog box like
this one.

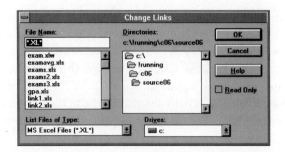

Copying, cutting, and pasting in linked worksheets

You can use absolute or relative references to cells in other worksheets the same way you use absolute or relative references within a single worksheet. Absolute and relative references to cells in supporting worksheets respond to the Copy, Cut, and Paste commands in much the same way as references to cells in the same worksheet.

For example, suppose you create the formula

=FORM2.XLS!Z1

in cell A1 of FORM1 and use the Copy and Paste commands to copy this formula into cell B1. The formula in cell B1 becomes

=FORM2.XLS!AA1

The original formula changed when it was copied to cell B1 because the reference to cell Z1 in FORM2 is relative. However, if the formula in cell A1 of FORM1 contains an absolute reference to cell Z1 in FORM2, as in

=FORM2.XLS!$Z$1

the result of copying and pasting the formula in cell B1 would still be

=FORM2.XLS!$Z$1

Copying and pasting between worksheets

When you copy from one worksheet to another a dependent formula that includes a relative reference to a third worksheet, that reference is adjusted to reflect the new position of the formula. Suppose cell A1 in FORM1 contains the formula

=FORM2.XLS!A1

If you copy and paste that formula from cell A1 in FORM1 into cell B5 in FORM3, the result is the formula

=FORM2.XLS!B5

The formula is adjusted to reflect its new relative position.

If you copy a formula that contains an absolute reference to another worksheet, that formula remains the same. Suppose cell A1 in FORM1 contains the formula

=FORM2.XLS!$A$1

If you copy and paste that formula into cell B5 in FORM3, the resulting formula remains

=FORM2.XLS!$A$1

Even if you copy a dependent formula into the worksheet to which the formula refers, it is still a dependent formula. For example, if you copy the formula

=FORM2.XLS!A3

from cell A1 of FORM1 into cell A1 of FORM2, the result is still

=FORM2.XLS!A3

The reference to the worksheet named FORM2 remains, even though it now exists in the same worksheet.

Cutting and pasting between worksheets

You can also cut a dependent formula and paste it into another worksheet. Cutting and pasting dependent formulas is the same as cutting and pasting regular formulas.

Excel does not adjust the relative references in a formula when you cut it from one worksheet and paste it into another, as it does when you copy a formula. For example, suppose cell A1 in FORM1 contains the formula

=FORM2.XLS!A1

If you cut that formula and paste it in cell B5 of FORM3, the result is still the formula

=FORM2.XLS!A1

Cutting and pasting cells referred to by dependent formulas

As stated in Chapter 5, when you cut and paste cells, Microsoft Excel adjusts any references to those cells in the formulas of the worksheet. Dependent formulas follow the same rules. When you cut and paste a cell referred to by a dependent formula in a closed worksheet, that formula is also adjusted to reflect the change.

Suppose you create the formula

=FORM2.XLS!A10

in cell A1 in FORM1. If you close FORM1 and use the Cut and Paste commands to move the entry in cell A10 of FORM2 to cell B10 of FORM2, the formula in cell A1 of FORM1 automatically changes to

=FORM2.XLS!B10

You might expect the link to be broken, because the sheet containing the formula was closed when you modified the referenced cell. Excel nonetheless manages to keep track of things.

Note that this clever feature works in Excel 4, but not in previous versions of Excel. If you are using Excel 3, for example, you can use a name in the dependent formula to achieve the same effect. Suppose you name cell A10 in FORM2 Test and then enter the formula

    =FORM2.XLS!Test

in cell A1 of FORM1. If you use Cut and Paste to move the entry in cell A10 of FORM2 to cell B10 of FORM2, Excel moves the name Test to cell B10 as well, and the link is preserved, regardless of which version of Excel you are using.

Severing links between worksheets

If you want to cut the links between worksheets, you can use the Paste Special command from the Edit menu to change all the external references in your dependent formula to constant values. Of course, you won't be able to update the references, because all ties to the supporting worksheets are removed.

First select the linked cell or cells, and choose the Copy command from the Edit menu. Then choose the Paste Special command. When the Paste Special dialog box appears, select the Values option and click OK. As a precaution, use the Find command from the Formula menu to look for any dependent formulas you might have missed. Enter the exclamation mark required in all dependent formulas in the Find What box, and then select the Formulas option. When you click OK, Excel searches your worksheet for any references to supporting worksheets.

When a cell contains both an external reference and a formula, you can preserve the formula while eliminating the external reference. To do this, select the cell and then, in the formula bar, select the portion of the cell that contains the external reference. Click the Calculate Now tool on the Utilities toolbar, or press F9. Excel changes the external reference to a value without changing the rest of the formula.

Editing groups of documents simultaneously

Microsoft Excel's Group Edit command on the Options menu lets you add, edit, or format data in two or more worksheets at the same time. You'll find this feature particularly handy when you're creating or modifying a set of worksheets that are similar in purpose and structure — a set of monthly reports or departmental budgets, for example.

To see how the Group Edit feature works, imagine that you have the worksheets EXAMS, EXAMS2, and EXAMS3 displayed as shown in Figure 6-26. You want

FIGURE 6-26.
We'll use these worksheets as an example for group editing.

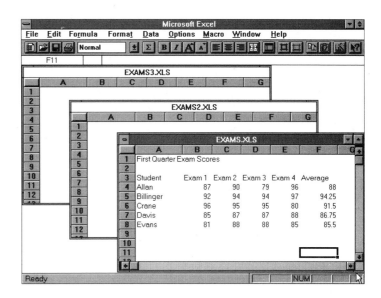

to add the same set of formatting options to each worksheet. You can enter these formats in one worksheet and then use the Copy command to recreate them in the other two. But a simpler approach is to define all three worksheets as a group, and then format all members of the group at the same time.

To define these three worksheets as a group, start by selecting any one of them. Next, pull down the Options menu and choose Group Edit. Excel presents the dialog box shown in Figure 6-27.

FIGURE 6-27.
The Group Edit dialog box lists all open (and unhidden) worksheets and macro sheets.

The dialog box lists all open and unhidden worksheets and macro sheets. (Charts cannot be included in a group.) Excel assumes that you want to include all the worksheets but none of the macro sheets, so it highlights the name of each worksheet file but none of the macro sheets. To alter this default selection, hold down Ctrl and click the name of any file you want to add or remove. To create the group, click OK. As Figure 6-28 on the following page shows, Excel responds by adding the designation *[Group]* to the title bar of each window in the group.

Now that you've created a group that consists of EXAMS, EXAMS2, and EXAMS3, you can add formatting, formulas, or any other data to the current worksheet, and all three member worksheets will be modified at the same time.

FIGURE 6-28.
Excel indicates a group by modifying the title bar of each member document.

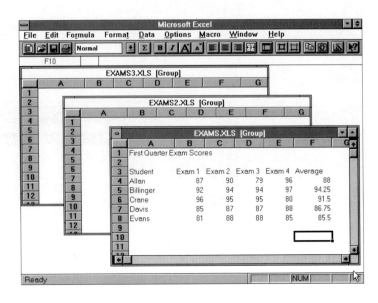

(However, when you change to another worksheet — even another worksheet in the workgroup — "Group mode" is cancelled.) For example, we applied formatting to the EXAMS worksheet using the AutoFormat command and adjusted some of the font sizes and column widths to arrive at the worksheet in Figure 6-29. Notice that EXAMS2 and EXAMS3 now contain the same formats applied to EXAMS.

FIGURE 6-29.
The work you do to the active worksheet in a group is applied to all group members at the same time.

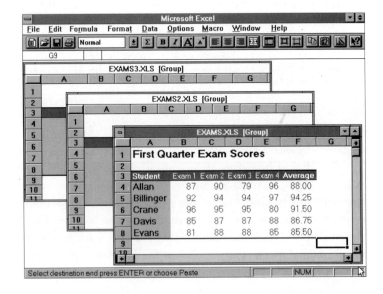

What you can do with group editing

In addition to facilitating data entry, the Group Edit feature lets you carry out a number of other actions on the same cells of all member documents at the same time.

Text entry

The most obvious use for the Group Edit feature is entering labels. Whatever you type in one window is duplicated in all windows belonging to the group.

Formatting

Any formatting change you make with the Number, Alignment, Font, Border, Patterns, Protection, AutoFormat, Column Width, or Row Height command is carried out on all group members at the same time. For example, if you assign the 0.00 format to cells A1:A10 in one document, that format is also applied to A1:A10 in the other group documents, overriding any formatting you previously applied.

Assigning styles

If you assign a style to a range of cells in one document, that style is assigned to the same range in the other documents — provided the style exists in each document. For example, if, prior to creating the group, you defined a style called Students in EXAMS but didn't define that style in EXAMS2 or EXAMS3, then you will not be able to apply STUDENTS to all three worksheets at once, even if the three constitute a group. You can, however, *define* a style during a group editing session, and that style is defined for all group members as well. When a style is defined, you can apply it at your whim.

Saving and closing files

When Group mode is in effect, the Close, Save, and Save Workbook commands on the File menu are applied to all members of the group. You'll find the Save Workbook command particularly handy if you have a number of open documents and you want to create a workbook file for some of them only. (We'll discuss workbooks later in this chapter.)

Note that while Group mode is in effect, the File menu's New, Open, and Delete commands are dimmed. To create a new file, retrieve one from disk, or delete a disk file, you need to end the group editing session first. (See "Ending a group editing session," later in this chapter.)

Printing files

When Group mode is in effect, all printing commands on the File menu are applied to every document in your group at the same time.

Commands on the Edit menu

All commands on the Edit menu are applied to every group document at the same time. In addition, during a group editing session, the Edit menu changes to make a Fill Group command available. This command lets you duplicate existing material in the current worksheet in all other group documents. It is like performing a Copy and Paste in each worksheet, only a lot quicker.

To use the Fill Group command, select the cell or range you want to copy, and then open the Edit menu and choose Fill Group. Excel presents the dialog box shown in Figure 6-30. As you can see, this command gives you some of the same flexibility as the Paste Special command (described in Chapter 5). You can copy all the attributes of the selection, only the formulas, or only the formats to all the worksheets in the group.

FIGURE 6-30.
Choose the Fill Group command to duplicate a selection in all member documents.

Commands on the Formula menu

When Group mode is in effect, you can use the Formula menu's Paste Function command to help build a formula that you will use in all member documents. The Goto, Show Active Cell, and Select Special commands are also available.

The Data Series command

You can use the Data Series command (discussed in Chapter 5) to create a linear or growth series in all group documents at once. Note that this command uses the value of the active cell as the starting value for the series. That starting value doesn't have to be the same in each member worksheet.

Options Menu commands

With Group mode in effect, you can use the Workspace command to apply Workspace options to all member documents at the same time. Thus, for example, you can take advantage of the Fixed Decimal feature in the Workspace dialog box to simplify the entry of dollars-and-cents values in several worksheets simultaneously.

Arranging the group

When Group mode is in effect, you can use the Window menu's Arrange command to adjust the position of the group on screen, using the same options discussed in "Arranging document windows," earlier in this chapter.

Adding documents to or removing documents from the group

Although you can't create new documents or retrieve files from disk when a group is in effect, you can add already open worksheets to your group. For example, if you have EXAMS, EXAMS2, EXAMS3, and EXAMS4 open in Excel, and you created a group that consists of EXAMS, EXAMS2, and EXAMS3, you can add EXAMS4 to the group at any time. To do this, choose the Group Edit command again, and hold down Ctrl while you select EXAMS4.XLS.

You can also remove documents from a group without ending the group session. Simply choose the Group Edit command, and then hold down Ctrl while you click the name of a document you want to remove.

Ending a group editing session

Excel remains in Group mode only as long as you remain in the worksheet that was active when you created the group. To end the group editing session, simply activate another worksheet by clicking it or using the keyboard equivalent.

Consolidating worksheets

The Consolidate command on the Data menu can assemble information from up to 255 supporting worksheets into a single "roll-up" worksheet. If you have financial information for each of your company's divisions in separate divisional worksheets, you can use the Consolidate command to create a master sheet that adds up the corresponding items in each divisional sheet.

You can use the Consolidate command in a number of ways. You can link the consolidated data to the supporting data so that subsequent changes in the supporting worksheets are reflected in the consolidation worksheet. Or you can simply consolidate the supporting data, without creating a link.

You can consolidate *by position* or *by category*. If you consolidate by position, Microsoft Excel gathers information from the same cell location in each supporting worksheet. If you consolidate by category, Excel uses column or row headings as the basis for associating worksheets. Consolidating by category gives you more flexibility in the way you set up your supporting worksheets. If your January column is column B in one worksheet and column D in another, for example, you can still roll up the January numbers if you consolidate by category.

You can perform the consolidation using a variety of functions. The default function is SUM, which adds the data items from each supporting worksheet and places their totals in the consolidation worksheet. But you can also use any of the following functions: AVERAGE, COUNT, COUNTA, MAX, MIN, PRODUCT, STDEV, STDEVP, VAR, and VARP. (See Chapter 8 for details about these functions.)

You can consolidate worksheets that are currently open, or you can consolidate worksheets that are in disk files. The worksheet that receives the consolidated data must be open, but supporting worksheets can be inactive — provided you give Excel the correct path information so that it can find each file. All supporting worksheets must be saved before you begin consolidation.

You can consolidate data from Lotus 1-2-3 worksheets as well as from Excel worksheets.

We will now discuss three examples — a consolidation by position, a consolidation by category, and a consolidation by category with links created to the source data.

Using templates or the Group Edit command to simplify consolidation

The more similar your supporting worksheets are, the easier it is to set up and perform a consolidation. If you're creating subsidiary worksheets from scratch, you can achieve consistency by defining all your subsidiary worksheets as a group using the Group Edit command on the Options menu before you begin to create row and column headings. All worksheets in the group will then have the same headings in the same positions.

You can also achieve consistency by building all supporting worksheets from a common template (XLT) file. You'll find the template approach more effective if you can't create all your supporting worksheets at the same time — for example, if there are too many to fit in memory all at once. (Templates are described in Chapter 4.)

Consolidating by position

When you consolidate by position, Excel applies the consolidation function (SUM, AVERAGE, or whatever else you choose) to the same cell coordinates in each supporting worksheet. This is the simplest way to consolidate, but it requires that your supporting worksheets be identically laid out.

Figure 6-31 shows a simple example of three supporting worksheets — EXAMS, EXAMS2, and EXAMS3 — that can be consolidated by position. Each worksheet has five columns and five rows of identically structured data. We will consolidate them into the worksheet named EXAMAVG.

The first step is to activate the consolidation worksheet and select the *destination area* — the block of cells that will receive the consolidated data. In Figure 6-31, the destination area is the range B4:F8 of EXAMAVG. Next choose the Consolidate command from the Data menu. Excel displays the dialog box shown in Figure 6-32.

FIGURE 6-31.
We'll use the Consolidate command on the Data menu to consolidate information from EXAMS, EXAMS2, and EXAMS3 into EXAMAVG.

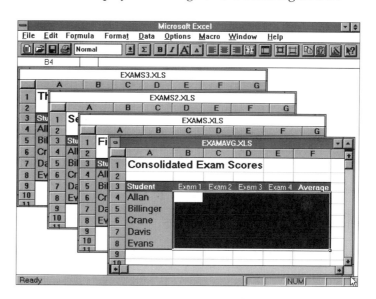

FIGURE 6-32.
In the Consolidate dialog box, you choose a consolidation function, specify source ranges, and select consolidation options.

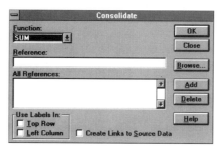

For a consolidation by position, leave the two Use Labels In check boxes unselected. Because you're not going to create a link with the source worksheets, leave the Create Links to Source Data check box unselected as well. Because you will be averaging values from each of the source worksheets, you need to select the AVERAGE function from the Function drop-down list box.

The final step is to tell Excel which source ranges to consolidate. You can type a reference for each source range in the Reference text box. Or you can point to each range with the mouse. Pointing is simpler, but you need to type any references to source worksheets that are not open in memory.

If you use the mouse to select your source ranges, remember that you can drag the dialog box out of your way by pointing to the dialog box's title bar and moving it off to the side. If a source worksheet is covered by other worksheets, you can get to it by choosing the appropriate command from the Window menu. And if you can't see the source range in a worksheet, maximize that worksheet so you can see more of it. You can do all these window maneuvers while you make your selection; the dialog box remains active until you close it.

If you type a reference, it must have the following form:

FILENAME.XLS!##:##

If the source range has been assigned a name, you can use the name in place of ##:##.

After entering each source reference, click Add. Excel then transfers the reference from the Reference text box to the All References list box. Figure 6-33 shows the dialog box filled out for our consolidate-by-position example. Note that we chose the AVERAGE function for this particular consolidation.

FIGURE 6-33.
The Consolidate command will use the references in the All References list to create our consolidated averages.

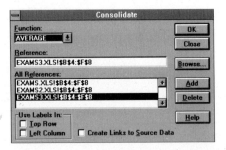

Notice that we selected B4:F8 in each of our source worksheets. Because we're consolidating by position and our consolidation worksheet has the appropriate column and row headings, our source references should include only the actual values we want to consolidate.

With the dialog box filled out, you can click OK. Excel rolls the source numbers up into the destination area, as shown in Figure 6-34.

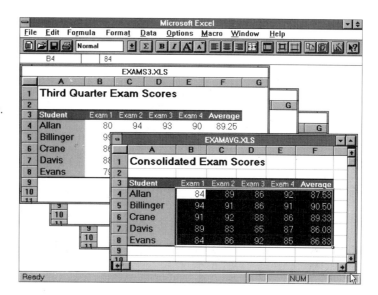

FIGURE 6-34.
*Range B4:F8 in
EXAMAVG now
contains the averages
of the corresponding
cells in the three
supporting worksheets.*

Consolidating by category

Now let's look at a more complex example. We'll roll up averages from worksheets similar to our previous examples, except this time each worksheet includes some different students, and different numbers of students. (See Figure 6-35 on the following page.)

The consolidation worksheet has column headings for Exam 1 through Exam 4 — each worksheet is the same in this respect. But the consolidation worksheet has no row headings. We need to omit the row headings because they are not consistently arranged in our source worksheets. As we'll see, the Consolidate command will enter the row headings for us.

As before, we first select the destination area. This time the destination area must include column A — so that Excel will have somewhere to enter the consolidated row headings. But how many rows should the destination area include? To answer that, we can look at each source worksheet and determine how many unique line items we have. But there's an easier way. Simply select cell A4 as the destination area. When you specify a single cell as your destination area, the Consolidate command fills out the area below and to the right of that cell as needed. In our example, we inserted more than enough rows to accommodate the data in order to preserve our formatting.

Next, we use the Data Consolidate command and fill out the dialog box. This time we want to consolidate by row categories, so we select the Left Column check box.

The consolidation worksheet already has column headings, so we can omit them from the source worksheet references. But our source references must include

FIGURE 6-35.
*We'll use the
categories (students)
in the left column of
each source worksheet
as the basis for
consolidation.*

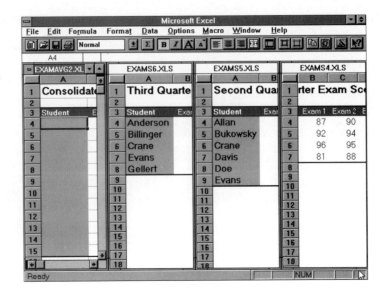

each row heading and extend from column A to column F (from the row headings column to the Average column). So we enter the following source references:

=EXAMS4.XLS!$A$4:$F$7

=EXAMS5.XLS!$A$4:$F$9

=EXAMS6.XLS!$A$4:$F$8

When we click OK, Excel fills out EXAMAVG2.XLS as shown in Figure 6-36. (We've enlarged the worksheet to give you a better view of the results.)

FIGURE 6-36.
*The Consolidate
command created a
separate line item in
the consolidation
worksheet for each
unique item in the
source worksheets.*

	Microsoft Excel - EXAMAVG2.XLS							
File Edit Formula Format Data Options Macro Window Help								
H16								
	A	B	C	D	E	F	G	H	I
1	**Consolidated Exam Scores**							
2								
3	Student	Exam 1	Exam 2	Exam 3	Exam 4	Average		
4	Allan	86	86	82	93	86.75		
5	Anderson	80	94	93	90	89.25		
6	Billinger	96	92	88	90	91.25		
7	Connors	96	95	95	80	91.50		
8	Green	81	88	88	85	85.50		
9	Bukowsky	90	88	84	94	89.00		
10	Crane	88	91	85	89	88.25		
11	Davis	95	82	89	82	87.00		
12	Doe	89	91	87	99	91.50		
13	Evans	90	80	89	91	87.38		
14	Gellert	79	90	90	80	84.75		
15								
16								
17								

Ready   NUM

The consolidation worksheet now includes a line item that corresponds to each unique line item in the source worksheets. Where two or more worksheets have the same line item, the consolidation worksheet performs the selected mathematical operation on the corresponding figures for each column position.

Creating links to the source worksheets

In the previous examples, we simply rolled numbers together with the AVERAGE function. The result was a series of constants in the consolidation worksheet. Subsequent changes to the source worksheets will not affect the consolidation worksheet unless we repeat the consolidation.

You can also use the Consolidate command to forge a permanent link between consolidation and source worksheets. To do this, select the Create Links to Source Data check box, and then carry out the consolidation the same way you would without the links.

When you consolidate with the linked option, Excel creates an outline in the consolidation worksheet, as shown in Figure 6-37. (See Chapter 2 for a complete explanation of outlines.) Each source line item is linked separately to the consolidation worksheet, and Excel automatically creates the appropriate summary items. You might have to adjust your formatting after you perform a linking consolidation, because additional rows and columns are created. In Figure 6-37, we copied the shading from column A into column B, which was inserted in the process of consolidation.

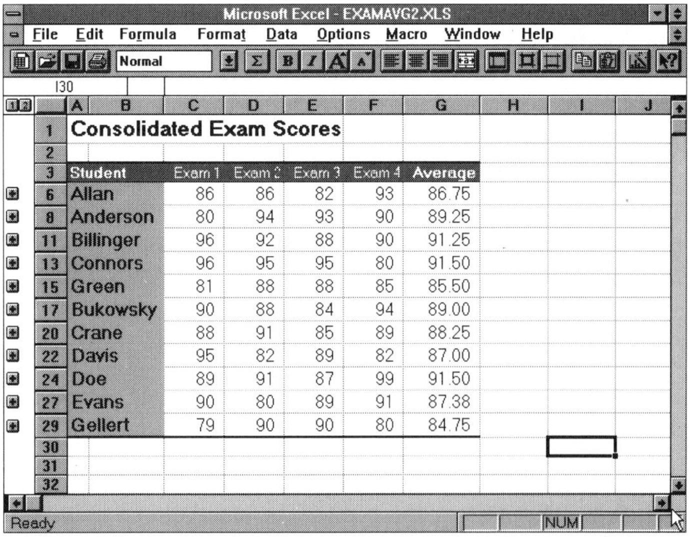

FIGURE 6-37.

When you create links to the source worksheets, your consolidation worksheet is automatically outlined with linking formulas hidden in subordinate outline levels.

Student	Exam 1	Exam 2	Exam 3	Exam 4	Average
Allan	86	86	82	93	86.75
Anderson	80	94	93	90	89.25
Billinger	96	92	88	90	91.25
Connors	96	95	95	80	91.50
Green	81	88	88	85	85.50
Bukowsky	90	88	84	94	89.00
Crane	88	91	85	89	88.25
Davis	95	82	89	82	87.00
Doe	89	91	87	99	91.50
Evans	90	80	89	91	87.38
Gellert	79	90	90	80	84.75

Consolidated Exam Scores

Working with workbooks

As you've seen, you can create temporary relationships between documents using the Group Edit and consolidation features. If you want to connect documents more permanently, then *workbooks* are the answer. With workbooks, you can

- Keep groups of related documents together in one master document
- Create "workgroup" documents that control a number of other individual documents
- Combine the above options

Like named views, workbooks preserve window placement and display settings for each of their member documents. You can add password protection to a collection of documents saved as a workbook, rather than assigning passwords to each individual document. And you can include worksheets, charts, and macro sheets together in a single workbook. You can also place workbooks in the XLSTART directory so that they are opened automatically each time you start Microsoft Excel.

A document is said to be *bound* into a workbook when it is contained in the workbook file. When you do this, the bound document no longer appears on disk as a separate file, but "disappears" into the workbook file. Similarly, a document is said to be *unbound* when it remains as a separate disk file. In this case, the workbook stores information about the document, and when you open the workbook file, the unbound document is also opened.

Workbooks are a great organizational tool. For example, you can bind together all the documents that relate to a particular project or all documents maintained by a particular individual. This can eliminate a considerable amount of clutter on your hard drive, as well as reduce the number of steps necessary simply to get your workspace set up each day. The more documents you have to manage, the more valuable the workbook can be.

You can also use workbooks as a multi-user management tool. For example, you can bind groups of documents together into discrete groups for individual tasks or individual users and include unbound documents such as macro sheets that are used by all.

The contents page

We created a workbook that contains our latest EXAMS worksheets, the *contents page* of which is shown in Figure 6-38. The contents page is a document that lists all the documents included in the workbook. To create this workbook, we simply chose the Save Workbook command from the File menu while all four documents were open, and supplied the name EXAM.

The three buttons in the lower left corner let you add, remove, bind, unbind, or even rename your workbook documents. When you click Add, a dialog box appears

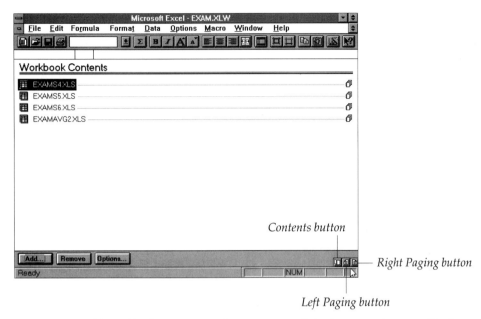

Contents button

Right Paging button

Left Paging button

FIGURE 6-38. *This workbook contents page lets us manage all the documents in our workbook.*

appears that lists all the active documents that are not already included in the workbook, as shown in Figure 6-39. If you want to add a document that is not open, click Open to display the Open dialog box. Similarly, you can click New to display the New dialog box.

FIGURE 6-39.
You can add open,
unopened, or new
documents to your
workbook.

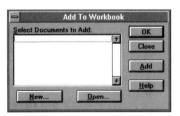

The Remove button removes the selected document from the workbook, but leaves it open in the workspace. To verify this, select the EXAMAVG2.XLS file, click the Remove button, and then display the Window menu. The list of open files at the bottom of the menu now reads as follows:

1 [EXAM.XLW]EXAMS4.XLS

2 [EXAM.XLW]EXAMS5.XLS

3 [EXAM.XLW]EXAMS6.XLS

4 EXAM.XLW

5 EXAMAVG2.XLS

Notice that the three documents that remain in the workbook appear preceded by the *[EXAM.XLW]* designation, which is the name we gave our workbook. The EXAM.XLW contents page itself is listed as a separate document, and the EXAMAVG2.XLS file we just removed appears on the list as a normal worksheet document.

Another way to remove documents from the workbook is to click a worksheet name in the list on the contents page, drag it beyond the contents page window, and release the mouse button. (You cannot maximize the contents page window when you do this.) You can also use the Clear command to remove documents from the contents page. The Clear command and the Remove button don't delete or close the document; they merely remove it from the active workbook. The worksheets remain open in memory.

Let's put the EXAMAVG2.XLS file back into the workbook. Click Add, select the filename in the list box, click Add, then click Close. Now click Options. You'll see a dialog box like the one in Figure 6-40.

FIGURE 6-40.
You can use the
Document Options
dialog box to bind,
unbind, or rename
workbook documents.

As you can see, this dialog box provides one way of specifying whether a document is included as a bound or unbound component of the workbook. When you first choose the Save Workbook command, all open documents appear on the contents page as bound documents. To unbind the selected document, select the Separate file option and click OK. Notice that the small icon to the right of the selected file changes, as shown in Figure 6-41. You can also change a document from bound to unbound by clicking on the small icons at the right side of the contents page.

FIGURE 6-41.
The icons to the right
of the filenames
indicate whether they
are bound or unbound.

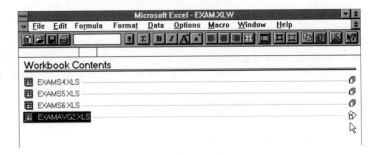

Reordering workbook contents

If the sheets in your workbook are inappropriately organized, you can easily reorganize them by dragging them into a different order on your workbook contents page. For example, suppose your workbook has 13 separate worksheets — one for each month, plus a summary page. If the sheets are arranged alphabetically, you might want to reorganize them chronologically. Simply click on the name of a sheet you want to move, drag it to the new location, and release the mouse button.

Using long filenames

The Document Options dialog box lets you set parameters for the selected document. If you choose to bind the document into the workbook file, you have a special opportunity to rename the file with a filename of up to 32 characters. You can use more descriptive and easily understood filenames for your documents by binding them together into workbook files. Rather than the typical lists of names like EXAMS3, EXAMS4, and so on, you can have just one workbook called EXAM, and use names for your bound documents such as *Exam Averages for 1992*, as demonstrated in Figure 6-42.

FIGURE 6-42.
You can use up to 32-character filenames in your bound workbook documents.

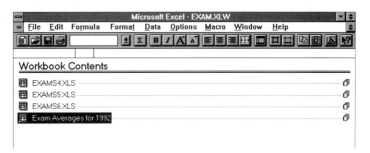

Note, however, that if you want to unbind a document with a long filename, you must rename it using an eight-character name so it conforms to MS-DOS again.

Navigating and managing workbook documents

The three small buttons in the lower right corner of the workbook contents page, as shown in Figure 6-38, help you navigate through the documents in your workbook. These buttons also appear in the scroll bar of each document associated with your workbook (unless the Scroll Bars option in the Workspace dialog box is turned off). The Contents Page button returns you to the workbook contents page from any other document. The Right Paging button moves you to the next worksheet, and the Left Paging button moves you to the previous worksheet. You can also double-click any worksheet name listed on the contents page to switch to that worksheet.

You can protect workbook documents the same way you do any other type of document. When you do so, all bound documents are protected; you do not need to protect them individually. You must apply protection to individual unbound documents, however. The Protect Document command on the Options menu and the Cell Protection command on the Format menu are discussed in Chapter 2.

When you save existing files in a workbook as bound documents, Excel saves them along with the workbook. If you do this, check your disk, and you'll notice that the original files are still there. The workbook does not need the original files. You can choose to keep them, move them, or delete them as you see fit. Any changes you make to the workbook documents will be saved with the workbook and will not update the original files on disk. In the interests of better file management, you should remove the originals and make your backups of the actual working files — the workbook files.

Bound windows

So far, our workbook example has dealt with a group of discrete documents that we bound into a workbook. Each document still resides in its own window, and the documents in their separate windows comprise the workbook. But you can close the individual windows of documents that are bound into a workbook — yet they remain available through the contents page as *bound windows*.

For example, close each of the EXAMS worksheet windows, but leave the contents page open. Now click the Right Paging button. You'll see the EXAMS4 worksheet (or whichever worksheet you placed first on the contents page). We closed the window, but the worksheet still appears! This is a characteristic of a bound worksheet. Bound sheets are not only contained within the same file on disk, they are actually available in the workbook window, even if a separate window is not currently open for that worksheet. If you drag the window to one side, you'll see that no other windows are hiding behind it. You just switched from one "window" to another without actually leaving the window!

Each time you click one of the paging buttons, another bound sheet appears in the same window, and in the same location. To see the current status of windows, open the Window menu and check the list at the bottom. Currently, only one window is listed here. But separate windows would be listed here as well, along with the name of the workbook. You will notice, however, that the name of the current window changes as you page through the bound windows in a workbook, and the name at the bottom of the Window menu also changes to reflect the name of the visible worksheet.

Bound windows are handy for keeping your workspace uncluttered, especially if you are working with more than one workbook at a time. But you might still want to see certain sheets in their own windows. For example, suppose you want the Exam Averages worksheet to be in its own window, but you want to leave the other windows bound together. To open a bound worksheet as a separate window, hold down Ctrl and double-click the worksheet name in the contents page. When you do this, Excel creates a separate window for that document. The combination of bound windows and separate windows that exists when you choose the Save Workspace command on the File menu will be active the next time you open your workbook.

Managing multiple workbooks

You can have more than one workbook open at the same time. You can also move and copy documents between workbooks. To move documents from one workbook to another, select the name or names you want to move in the contents page, and then use the Cut and Paste commands, or drag the selection to the new workbook. If the workbook is minimized to an icon at the bottom of the screen, you can drag the selected document names to the icon and release the mouse button.

To copy documents from one workbook to another, use the Copy and Paste commands, or hold down Ctrl and drag the selection to the new workbook.

Workbook linking formulas

In addition to the file-linking capabilities described earlier in this chapter, you can create specialized linking formulas that let you specify a range of workbook documents in much the same way as you specify cell ranges. For example, the formula

        =AVERAGE([BOOK1.XLW]AAA.XLS:CCC.XLS!A5)

returns the average of the values contained in cell A5 on all the worksheets within the range AAA.XLS:CCC.XLS. The range of bound workbook documents you specify is determined by the order of documents as shown in the contents page of the workbook. For example, if the worksheets contained in BOOK1.XLS are in the order AAA.XLS, BBB.XLS, CCC.XLS, then the average uses the contents of cell A5 in all three sheets. If, on the other hand, the sheets are in the order AAA.XLS, CCC.XLS, BBB.XLS, only the first two sheets will be used in the formula.

Once you have created a workbook linking formula you can, however, re-arrange the referenced worksheets on the contents page, and the formula adjusts accordingly. For example, if we create the above formula and then change the order of the documents on the contents page, the formula changes to read

        =AVERAGE([BOOK1.XLW]AAA.XLS!A5,[BOOK1.XLW]BBB.XLS!A5,
            [BOOK1.XLW]CCC.XLS!A5)

which allows the worksheets to be rearranged in any manner.

You can use only bound workbook documents in workbook-linking formulas. But after you've created a linking formula, you can unbind documents in the referenced range, and the formula will adjust accordingly.

Opening 3-D Lotus 1-2-3 files and Microsoft Excel 3.0 workspace files

Excel opens Lotus 1-2-3 WK3 files that contain multiple worksheets as workbooks. The individual worksheets are opened as bound workbook documents, which you can unbind if you choose. Three-dimensional formulas are converted into the corresponding Excel linking formulas.

Similarly, workspace files created with Excel 3.0 are also converted into workbooks. However, the individual worksheets in the workspace are opened as unbound documents in the workbook and remain as separate files on disk unless you decide to bind them together.

7

Worksheet Graphics

*W*ith Microsoft Excel 4, you can create a wide variety of graphic objects, such as boxes, lines, circles, ovals, arcs, freehand polygons, text boxes, and buttons. You can specify font, pattern, color, and line formats, and you can position graphics in relation to the worksheet or to other objects. You can protect objects, and you can assign macros to run when an object is selected, so that the object operates like a button in a dialog box.

When you see how easily you can incorporate graphics into your worksheets, you'll soon find all sorts of ways to use them. Bear in mind that the techniques for working with graphics described in this chapter apply to both worksheets and macro sheets.

Creating graphic objects

Before we get started, you might want to display the Drawing and Utility toolbars, which contain the tools we describe in this chapter. Also, hiding the Standard toolbar and maximizing the document window will help in freeing up as much screen space as possible. The easiest way to change toolbars is to click the Standard toolbar with the right mouse button and then choose Drawing from the shortcut menu. Repeat the same procedure to choose Utility from the shortcut menu. Finally, repeat the procedure once more, but this time choose Standard from the menu to dismiss the Standard toolbar.

If you have ever used a drawing program such as CorelDraw or Aldus Free-hand, you already know the basics of how to create lines, boxes, ovals, and arcs. In Microsoft Excel, you simply click the drawing tool you want on the Drawing or Utility toolbar, and then drag the pointer to create the object. Figure 7-1 identifies the drawing tools.

FIGURE 7-1.
The Drawing and Utility toolbars.

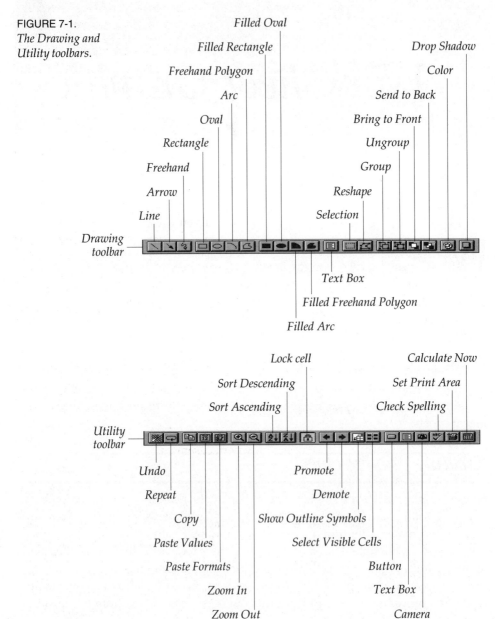

For example, to create a box, select the Filled Rectangle tool, and then drag the crosshair pointer anywhere on the worksheet to draw a simple box shape. The result looks something like Figure 7-2. Notice that Excel displays Rectangle 1 at the left end of the formula bar.

FIGURE 7-2.
You have created a
simple box using the
Filled Rectangle tool.

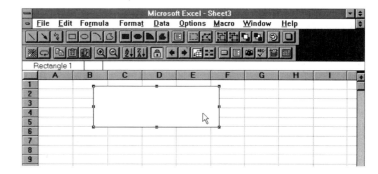

When you finish drawing the box, the mouse pointer resumes its usual cross shape, indicating that you are no longer in drawing mode. Excel leaves drawing mode each time you finish drawing an object. If you want to draw several boxes, you can select the Filled Rectangle tool each time you want to start a new box, or you can double-click the tool when you first select it to lock Excel into drawing mode. The tool you double-click then remains active until you cancel the drawing session or select another tool. To cancel the drawing session, you simply click the tool again. You can also cancel drawing mode by clicking anywhere in the worksheet without dragging. You can hold down Shift while creating objects to achieve the following effects:

- The Line and Arrow tools draw horizontal, vertical, or diagonal lines.
- The Freehand tool fills the interior of the objects you draw.
- The Rectangle and Filled Rectangle tools draw perfect squares.
- The Oval and Filled Oval tools draw perfect circles.
- The Arc and Filled Arc tools draw perfect semicircles.

Figure 7-3 on the following page shows objects drawn with and without the Shift key.

If you hold down Alt while you create an object, the edges of your objects are forced to follow the gridlines, so you can use the gridlines on the worksheet as a drawing grid. Interestingly, pressing Shift and Alt together to draw a circle or square aligned to the grid causes a dilemma. Excel tries to keep the proportions correct while sticking to the grid. But Alt takes precedence over Shift, and the grid wins out. You will have to either draw a shifted object or force alignment to the grid; trying to do both at once usually produces an object that is slightly out of proportion.

Any objects you create appear to "float" over the worksheet, on a separate layer. Objects are separate from the worksheet and can be grouped and formatted as

FIGURE 7-3.
*When you create
objects, hold down
Shift to constrain
them along horizontal,
vertical, or diagonal
lines. (The labels at
the right of the
worksheet are text
boxes created with the
Text Box tool.)*

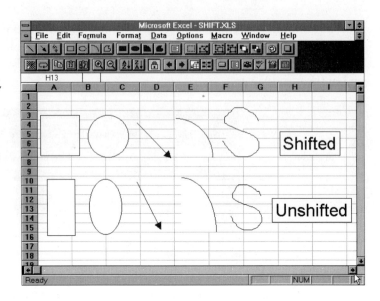

discrete items. You can also use the Object Properties command, discussed in "Positioning objects," later in this chapter, to adjust the relationship of objects to the worksheet.

After you create a graphic, you can manipulate it in a variety of ways. When you move the mouse pointer inside the perimeter of an object, it changes shape to the standard Windows arrow. This means you can select the object or move it elsewhere by dragging. If you select the object and point to one of the handles that appears on its perimeter, the pointer turns into a double-headed arrow with which you can stretch and resize the object. If you drag a center handle, you can change its height or change its width. If you hold down Shift while dragging a corner handle, you can resize the object both vertically and horizontally simultaneously, so that the object retains its shape while you resize it.

Drawing freehand lines and freehand polygons

The Freehand tool lets you use your mouse to draw unconstrained lines. If you hold down Shift while drawing with this tool, Excel fills the inside of the object you create. If you hold down Alt, your lines are constrained to the gridlines. You can also create a freehand-tool-type line with the Freehand Polygon tools. The difference between using the Freehand tool and the Freehand Polygon tools in this instance is that releasing the mouse button does not end the drawing. You must click the beginning point or double-click where you wish to stop drawing to complete the freehand polygon shape and release the Freehand Polygon tool from drawing mode.

For example, if you click the Freehand Polygon tool, and then click anywhere on the worksheet to begin drawing, the line remains anchored to that point. If you release the mouse button, the line stretches from that point to the crosshair mouse pointer like a rubber band. If you stretch the line out and click again, you create a straight line between the two anchor points where you clicked the mouse. You can continue this as long as you want, creating lines between each mouse click. (This is how we created the "starburst" image in Figure 7-10.) You can also hold down the mouse button while you draw a freehand polygon to add a freehand line. This lets you create a hybrid object with both straight and curved lines. Your freehand polygon will not be complete until you close the freehand polygon shape by clicking the point where you began to draw or double-click where you wish to stop drawing.

The Reshape tool

Drawing an attractive freehand line or freehand polygon shape can be challenging with a mouse. With this in mind, Excel includes a Reshape tool that changes the frame of a freehand line or a freehand polygon to a series of points, which you can drag to reshape the image.

When you select a freehand polygon, eight handles appear around it, just as with objects drawn with the Rectangle, Arc, or Oval tools. Eight handles also appear around objects drawn with the Freehand tool, but only two endpoint handles appear for straight lines. If you want to adjust the shape of a freehand polygon or freehand line, select it and then click the Reshape tool. A new set of handles appears, following the curves and corners of the image. Now you can drag any or all of these handles to new positions, as necessary.

For example, in Figure 7-4 on the following page, the shape on the left looks as it did when originally created using the Freehand Polygon tool. The shape on the right is the same freehand polygon after first selecting it and then clicking the Reshape tool.

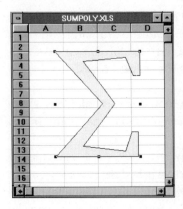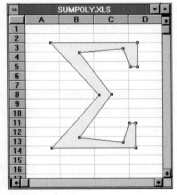

FIGURE 7-4. *When you click the Reshape tool, handles appear at each corner, as in the image on the right.*

Using the text box and button tools

Using the Text Box tool, you can add comments, headings, legends, and other text to your worksheets, to give them more impact or to clarify them. You can use different fonts and font formats in the same text box, but all the text in a cell must have the same font, size, and format. You can add patterns and colors to the text box background, and you can rotate the text inside the box to orient it vertically. When you select the Text Box tool and draw a box, a blinking insertion point appears in the box, indicating you can begin typing. Text is left-aligned by default, but you can use the alignment tools on the Standard toolbar or the Alignment command on the Format menu to realign the text. And like any other object, you can use the Assign to Object command to assign a macro to run when the text box is selected, as we discuss in "Assigning macros to objects," later in this chapter. (We discuss macros in detail in Chapters 19, 20, and 21.)

Excel also has a Button tool, which is similar to the Text Box tool, with a few notable differences. When you use the Button tool to draw a button, Excel gives the button a title, such as Button 1, draws a rounded-corner box with three-dimensional shading, and centers the text both vertically and horizontally. As soon as you finish drawing the button, the Assign To Object dialog box appears so you can immediately assign a macro to the button. If you have a macro sheet open, the names of the macros appear in the Assign To Object dialog box. If no macros are available yet, you can click Cancel. After the dialog box closes, Excel selects the new button. When you move the pointer near the text (Button 1) in the button, the pointer changes into an I-beam so you can edit and format the text inside the button. You can change the text format of the Button tool, but you cannot format a button with patterns or colors.

After you assign a macro to a button (or to any other object), clicking it causes Excel not to select the button but to run the macro assigned to it instead. What do you do if you want to edit the text again? You must either use the selection tool or hold down Ctrl and click the button to select it.

Figure 7-5 shows a worksheet with two buttons at the bottom of the screen. The right button is being "pressed" with the mouse pointer. Notice that the button image changes to simulate how a pressed button looks. Also notice that the mouse pointer becomes a pointing hand when it passes over a button or any other graphic object to which a macro is assigned. This is a helpful visual clue, especially if you assign a macro to an object other than a button.

The Text command replaces the Alignment command on the Format menu when you select a text box or button object. Figure 7-6 shows the Text dialog box as it appears when you choose Text while a text box is selected. The Text dialog box that appears when a button is selected is almost identical; however, the Patterns button is missing. Because you can rotate the text in a text box, the Text command offers both Horizontal and Vertical alignment options, similar to the ones available in the Alignment dialog box for cells.

FIGURE 7-5.
The Click Here buttons were created with the Button tool.

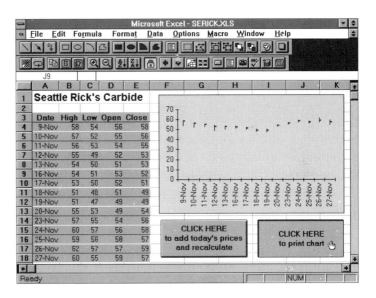

FIGURE 7-6.
The Text command provides formatting options for objects drawn with the Text Box and Button tools.

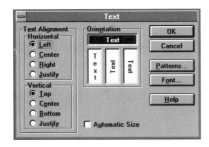

In Figure 7-7, you can see the effects of the various alignment and orientation options on text in buttons and text boxes. (We used text boxes in the figure.) We formatted the text boxes with the "Center center" label with the Automatic Size option turned on, which adjusts the size of the text box or button to fit the text it contains. The Patterns and Font buttons in the Text dialog box are conveniences that let you switch to the corresponding dialog box to apply additional formatting without having to close the Text dialog box.

FIGURE 7-7.
This figure illustrates some of the different alignment and orientation options available in the Text dialog box. The Center center boxes have the Automatic Size option turned on.

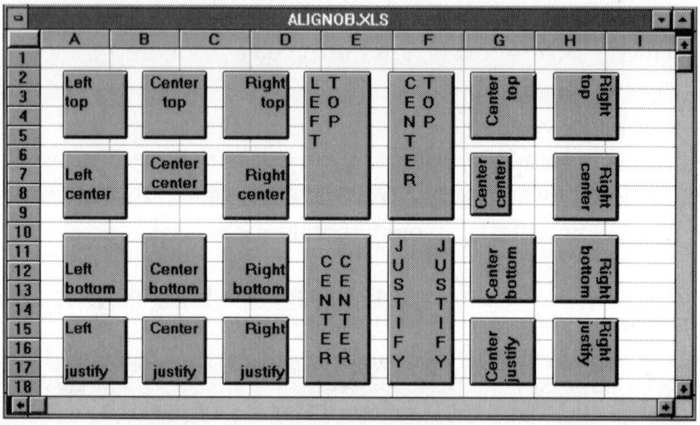

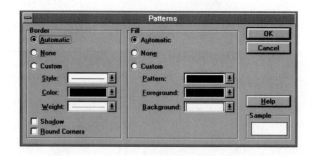

Applying patterns and colors to objects

In Chapter 4, we discussed using the Patterns command on the Format menu to add patterns, colors, and shading to cells. You can apply the same patterns to objects. Figure 7-8 shows the dialog box that appears when you select an object and choose the Patterns command. You can also invoke the Patterns dialog box by double-clicking an object.

FIGURE 7-8.
This Patterns dialog box appears when you select an object and choose the Patterns command.

Notice that when you choose Patterns while an object is selected, the dialog box differs from the one that appears when you choose the same command with a worksheet cell selected. The object Patterns dialog box gives you control over border style, color, and weight, as well as over fill pattern and color.

The dialog box in Figure 7-8 appears if a rectangle, worksheet chart, or text box is selected. If an oval, circle, freehand polygon, freehand line, or worksheet picture is selected, the dialog box is the same, except that the Round Corners check box is not available. Similarly, if an arc is selected, the same dialog box is used, except that both the Round Corners and Shadow check boxes are not available. (Worksheet charts are discussed in Chapter 13. Worksheet pictures are discussed in "Taking pictures of your worksheets," later in this chapter.)

The Border options include Style, Color, and Weight, along with the Shadow and Round Corners check boxes. When you choose the Automatic border style, the result is a thin solid black line. You can select from eight different style options, including four different types of dotted lines and three shades of gray. The Color options include the 16 colors that appear in the Color Palette dialog box (discussed in "Using the Color Palette command," later in this chapter). The available border weights are hairline, thin, medium, and thick; the dotted line that appears in the drop-down list indicates the hairline option. If you click the Shadow check box, the object is displayed with a black drop shadow behind it. The Round Corners option applies rounded corners to the selected object.

With a color monitor, you can take full advantage of the Foreground and Background options in the Fill options area. When you select a pattern, the foreground color is assigned to the black areas in the pattern, and the background color is assigned to the white areas. For example, if you select the default pattern — solid black — and dark green as your foreground color, the object is a solid dark green. Any background color you select has no effect because the pattern has no white areas. If you select a pattern made up of both black and white areas, you can combine foreground and background colors. If you have a monochrome monitor, you are limited to combinations of blacks, whites, and resulting grays, but you can still create interesting patterns for objects.

You can see the effects of any combination of Border and Fill options by looking at the Sample box in the lower right corner of the dialog box. Samples of the available colors also appear in the Foreground and Background drop-down list boxes. On a monochrome monitor, colors are indicated by varying shades of gray in the Sample box when you select the solid pattern. Other patterns are displayed in black and white. You can see only the names of the colors in the list boxes. Any color formats you apply are retained, however, for later color display or printing.

If you select a line or an arrow and then choose the Patterns command, you see the dialog box shown in Figure 7-9 on the following page. In addition to the Style, Color, and Weight options, this dialog box lets you attach an arrowhead to the line or remove one from it. If you draw a line to which you want to add an arrowhead, remember that the arrowhead will appear at the end of the line — that is, the place where you release the mouse button.

FIGURE 7-9.
When a line is selected, the Patterns dialog box lets you turn lines into arrows, and vice versa.

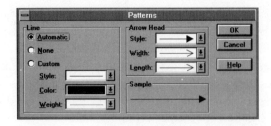

When you select a line, the Line options available in the Patterns dialog box are exactly the same as those available when you select an arc. The Arrow Head options let you tailor the arrows to your liking. The styles available are no arrow, open head, and closed head. The Width option lets you create narrow, medium, or wide arrowheads, and the Length option lets you create short, medium, or long arrowheads.

The Color and Drop Shadow tools

You can use the Color tool on the Drawing toolbar as an easy way to apply colors without using the Patterns dialog box. If you select an object and click the Color tool, it applies the next color in the Patterns dialog box. If you have selected a line or arrow, the Color tool cycles through the options in the Color drop-down list. If you have selected a solid or freehand object, the Color tool cycles through the colors as if you had chosen the same color in both the Foreground and Background drop-down lists. Each time you click the Color tool, the next color is applied. To select the previous color, hold down Shift as you click.

You use the Drop Shadow tool to add depth to any graphic object, except for lines, arrows, and arcs. For example, in Figure 7-10 we created a box using the

FIGURE 7-10.
The Patterns command and the Color, Text Box, Arrow, and Drop Shadow tools were used to create these graphic objects in less than a minute.

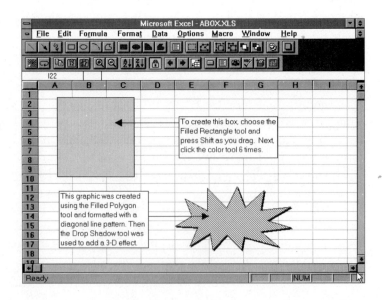

Rectangle tool and formatted it using the Color and Drop Shadow tools. We created the second graphic with the Filled Freehand Polygon tool and formatted it using the Patterns command and Drop Shadow tool. We then drew the text boxes and entered the text without applying additional formatting. We created the arrows by holding down Shift while dragging to create straight lines.

Using the Color Palette command

The Color Palette command on the Options menu determines the colors that are available in the Patterns, Font, and Borders dialog boxes. On a color monitor, these color options appear in color; on a monochrome monitor, Excel indicates them by name.

If you have a color monitor, you can edit the colors using the Edit option. If you define a color palette for use in one worksheet, you can copy that palette into the current worksheet using the Copy Colors From list box at the bottom of the Color Palette dialog box. You can also use one of Excel's 12 predefined color palettes with the Custom Palettes add-in command. You can also modify one of the two User palettes, available with the Custom Palettes command, to include your own color scheme. All these procedures are described in Chapter 4.

If you copy an object that has been formatted with a custom color to a document in which that color has not been defined, the custom color is copied along with the object. The copied color does not, however, replace any color in the palette, nor do any changes you subsequently make to the colors in the palette have any effect upon the copied color.

Selecting and grouping objects

Sometimes you will find it convenient to move, resize, or even reformat more than one object at a time. You might want to move several objects at once while preserving their positions relative to one another. For these purposes, Excel includes two helpful features: the Selection tool on the Drawing toolbar and the Group command on the Format menu.

The Selection tool lets you select a group of objects by dragging a selection rectangle around them, as shown in Figure 7-11 on the following page. Alternatively, you can click each of the objects you want to group together while holding down Shift. You can also select all objects on the current worksheet by choosing the Select Special command from the Formula menu and selecting the Objects option.

When you select the group of objects, you can lock them together using the Group command on the Format menu, or the Group tool on the Drawing toolbar. The sets of handles around each selected object are replaced by a single set of handles for the entire group, as shown in Figure 7-12 on the following page.

After you group a set of objects, you can manipulate them as a single object. You can resize them together by dragging the group selection handles, you can

FIGURE 7-11.
*You use the Selection
tool to drag a rect-
angle around the
objects you want
to select.*

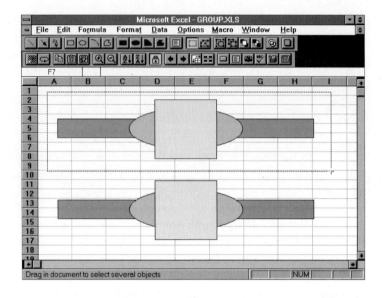

FIGURE 7-12.
*The objects at the
bottom were selected
individually, and
the objects at the top
were grouped.*

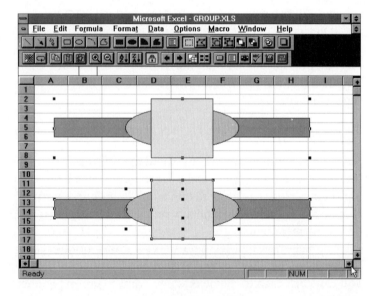

move them as one object, and you can apply formatting to them as a group. When
you apply formatting, however, the separate objects might behave differently, especially if you have grouped different kinds of objects with different formats. It is
best to apply formatting before grouping, unless you have a group of similar objects.

To ungroup a set of objects, first select the group. When you select a grouped object, the Group command on the Format menu changes to the Ungroup command, which you can choose to ungroup the selected group. Alternatively, you can click the Ungroup tool on the Drawing toolbar.

Positioning objects

You can adjust the position of objects in relation to each other using the Bring to Front and Send to Back commands on the Format menu. Alternatively, you can use the Bring to Front and Send to Back tools on the Drawing toolbar. Figure 7-13 shows two identical sets of ungrouped objects. Think of the objects on a worksheet as being stacked on top of each other. In the set at the bottom, we brought the rectangle to the front of the stack, and we sent the square to the back of the stack.

You can change the way objects are attached to a worksheet or macro sheet using the Object Properties command on the Format menu. The Object Properties dialog box is shown in Figure 7-14.

FIGURE 7-13.
You can reposition objects in relation to each other with the Bring to Front and Send to Back tools on the Drawing toolbar with the corresponding Format menu commands.

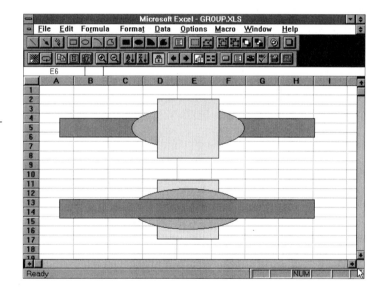

FIGURE 7-14.
You can control how cell changes affect graphics.

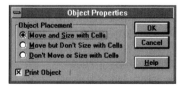

The default placement option is Move and Size with Cells, meaning that if you do anything to change the size or shape of the underlying cells, the object adjusts accordingly. For example, Figure 7-15 shows how the size and shape of three objects, which were originally identical, change as the width and height of underlying cells change.

An *underlying cell* is any cell whose right and bottom border is between the upper left corner and the lower right corner of the object. In Figure 7-15, notice that the object at the upper left is just touching the top border of cell A5, which is not an underlying cell, whereas the top of the object breaks across the crucial bottom border of cell A1, which therefore qualifies as an underlying cell. Similarly, none of the cells in column B are underlying cells because their right borders are not covered by the object.

If you insert rows or columns before you format an object with the Move and Size with Cells option, the object moves accordingly. If you insert rows or columns between the first and last underlying cells, the object stretches to accommodate the insertion.

If you select the Move but Don't Size with Cells option in the Object Placement dialog box, the object retains its shape and proportion, but moves when you insert or delete rows and columns. If you select the Don't Move or Size with Cells option, the object is not affected by any changes you make to the underlying cells and floats above the worksheet.

The Print Object check box at the bottom of the Object Properties dialog box is normally turned on. If you turn this option off, the selected object is not printed when you print the worksheet. For more information about printing, see Chapter 12.

FIGURE 7-15.
When you select the Move and Size with Cells option of the Object Properties command, the object responds to any changes made to the underlying cells.

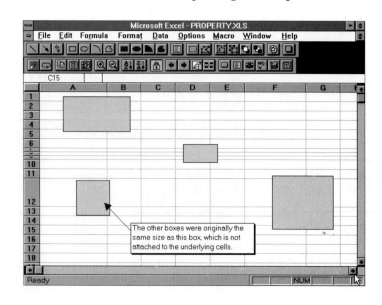

Controlling the display of objects

If you want to speed up the scrolling of your worksheet, you can use the Objects option of the Display command on the Options menu. Normally, the Show All option is active, but if you want to speed things up a bit, you can choose the Show Place-holders option. When you do this, your objects are reduced to simple patterns, indicating their locations on the worksheet. You can still add, delete, move, size, format, group, and ungroup objects when you choose this option, but you must reinstate the Show All option when you print.

The other available option is Hide All, which, as you might guess, suppresses the display of objects entirely, speeding screen redraw time even more. Although you cannot modify objects when Hide All is activated, you can still effect changes. If an object's Object Properties setting is *not* Don't Move or Size with Cells, it will still respond to adjustments made to the row height or column width of under-lying cells.

Protecting objects

The Object Protection command on the Format menu lets you lock objects to prevent them from being selected, moved, formatted, or sized. You can also use the Lock Text check box, which is visible only when a text box is selected, to protect the text contents of a text box. Newly drawn objects are automatically assigned the Locked format. However, you must choose the Protect Document command from the Options menu to turn on worksheet security and activate object protection. For more information about the Protect Document command, see Chapter 2.

Assigning macros to objects

If you create worksheets for less experienced users or for interactive training or demonstrations, you will find Microsoft Excel's Assign Macro To Object command very useful. For example, you can create a worksheet template with a button that starts an elaborate macro to demonstrate how to use that particular template. You might also want to create buttons that run macros you use often.

The ability to run a macro by selecting an object is extremely powerful, but it is actually very simple to implement. First, create the macro by writing it in a macro sheet or recording it. (For detailed information about macros, see Chapters 19, 20, and 21.) Next, simply select the object to which you want to assign the macro, choose the Assign Macro To Object command from the Macro menu, and select the macro you want from the list. Every macro in open macro sheets appears in the Assign Macro list box. Figure 7-16 on the following page shows the Assign To Object dialog box.

FIGURE 7-16.
You use the Assign
To Object command
to link a macro with
an object.

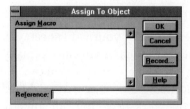

When you select a macro from the list, the reference appears in the Reference text box at the bottom of the dialog box. Optionally, you can type the reference into the Reference text box yourself. When you click OK, Excel assigns the macro to the selected object. The next time you click the object, it flashes — or if the object is a button, it appears "depressed" — and Excel runs the assigned macro. The macro sheet must be open for the macro to run when you click the object; if the macro sheet is not open, Excel opens it for you automatically. After you assign a macro to an object, selection handles no longer appear when you click the object. If you want to edit the object, you must hold down Ctrl while you click the object. The selection handles then appear, and you can edit the object normally.

You can use the Record button in the Assign To Object dialog box to immediately begin recording a new macro for the object. We will discuss the recording of macros in Chapter 19.

Taking pictures of your worksheets

Microsoft Excel has two ways to take "pictures" of your worksheets and macro sheets: the Camera tool on the Utility toolbar and the Copy Picture command (which appears on the Edit menu when you press Shift).

The Camera tool provides an image that is linked to the source document. This image is like another window on that document, and it changes whenever a change is made to the range of cells that you originally copied. The Copy Picture command on the Edit menu copies an image of the selected area of the screen to the Clipboard, whether the image is a chart or a range of cells. The image created by the Copy Picture command is a snapshot of the worksheet, macro sheet, or chart at a particular moment. But when it is pasted back into your worksheet, it is not in any way linked to the source document, and it does not change if the source document changes. However, some other applications, such as Word for Windows, can use the image to create a link to the source worksheet.

Using the Camera tool

With the Camera tool, you can copy an image of a range of cells and paste the image anywhere in the same worksheet or in another worksheet. Copying an image is not the same as copying the same range of cells with the Copy command on the Edit menu: When you copy an image, you copy a linked image of the cell, not its contents. As a result, the image changes dynamically as the contents of the original cells change.

For example, Figure 7-17 shows two worksheets side by side. If you select the range A1:C7 in PICTURE1 and click the Worksheet picture tool, the pointer changes from the shaded cross to a crosshair pointer. Click anywhere in PICTURE2 to select it, and click where you want the upper left corner of the picture to appear. Excel inserts the resulting embedded picture shown on the right in Figure 7-17. Any graphic objects within or overlapping the range are also copied. You cannot create a frame in which to paste the picture as you can with worksheet charts. The pasted picture is always exactly the same size as the original selection.

After you paste the picture, you can change its size and proportions by dragging its selection handles. You can treat an object created by the Camera tool like any other graphic object. Keep in mind, though, that changing the size of the embedded picture distorts the image, as shown in Figure 7-18 on the following page. Changes in shape, size, or formatting do not affect the dynamic updating of the data displayed in the picture, however.

Notice that the formula bar in Figure 7-18 indicates that the selected object is called Picture 3 and that a formula is associated with it, much like any other cell-linking formula. (For more about cell links, see Chapter 3.) After you create the worksheet picture, you can change the formula in the formula bar, and the picture will change accordingly. For example, the formula shown for the object created by the Camera tool is

=PICTURE1.XLS!$A$1:$C$7

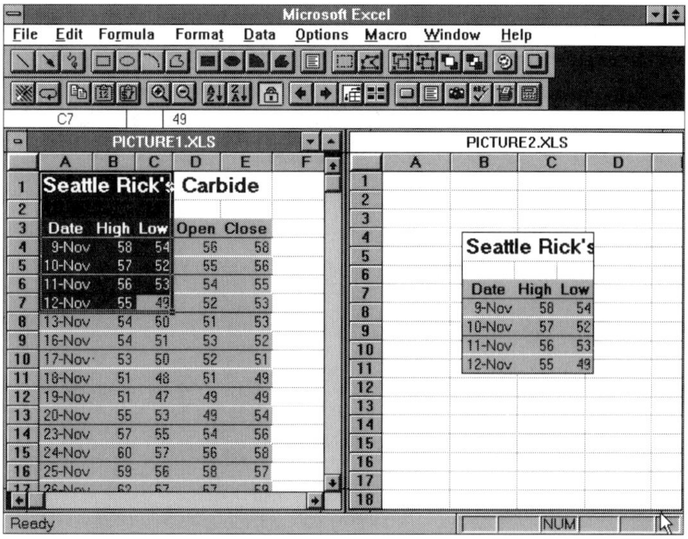

FIGURE 7-17.
The Camera tool creates a linked image of a selected cell range.

FIGURE 7-18.
*A linked picture
created with the
Camera tool can be
manipulated like any
other graphic object.*

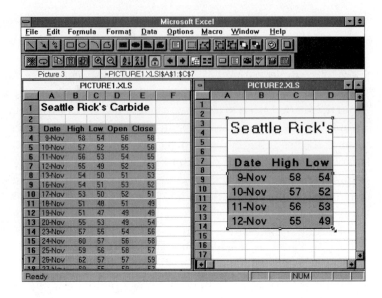

If you change the formula to

=PICTURE1.XLS!$A$1:$C$9

the picture adjusts to include the extra rows, as shown in Figure 7-19. You can even change the reference formula to link a completely different worksheet. Notice that the picture does not change in size, but the image in the frame compresses to make room for the extra rows.

FIGURE 7-19.
*If you change the
cell references for a
Camera tool picture,
the picture changes
accordingly.*

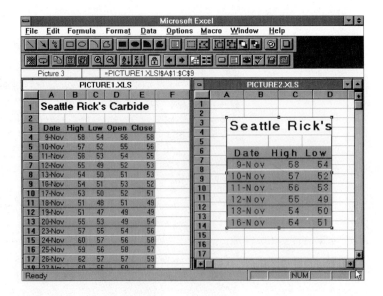

The link that exists between the source and destination document exhibits another distinctive and useful characteristic. Suppose you close the PICTURE1 worksheet in Figure 7-18. If you then double-click the pasted-in image in PICTURE2, PICTURE1 opens automatically. This is an example of Object Linking and Embedding (OLE), which will be explained more fully in Chapter 22.

Using the Copy Picture command

Like the Camera tool, the Copy Picture command creates an image — with one important difference. The copied picture is static, with no links to any worksheet. Static pictures are useful when you don't need to update or when the speed with which Excel recalculates the worksheet is more important than updating. You can add images of charts, worksheets, and macro sheets to reports or other documents via the Clipboard. After you take a picture using the Copy Picture command, you can even paste it into other applications that accept Windows Clipboard-format images.

To use the Copy Picture command, first select the cells (or the object or chart) you want to copy, hold down Shift, and choose the Copy Picture command from the Edit menu. Excel displays the dialog box shown in Figure 7-20.

FIGURE 7-20.
The Copy Picture
dialog box lets you
control the appearance
of the picture.

The default option, As Shown on Screen, reproduces the selection at the moment you take the picture, including row and column headings, gridlines, and borders. Row and Column headings are always included when the As Shown on Screen option is selected no matter where in the worksheet or macro sheet the selection is, unless you turn them off with the Display command. The As Shown when Printed option reflects the settings in the Page Setup dialog box that control the printing of gridlines and row and column headings. For example, the worksheet in Figure 7-21 on the following page contains two pictures of the same area. We created the top one with the As Shown on Screen option selected and the bottom one with the As Shown when Printed option selected. (The Page Setup option for printing row and column headings is off, and the option for printing gridlines is on.) Notice the difference in the way screen gridlines and printed gridlines look.

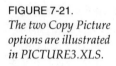

FIGURE 7-21.
The two Copy Picture
options are illustrated
in PICTURE3.XLS.

The Format options in the Copy Picture dialog box, Picture and Bitmap, give you a choice between the two principal types of graphic images: drawn and painted. If you select the Picture option, you get a drawn image made up of lines and curves, which you can scale proportionately. If you select the Bitmap option, you get a painted image made up of individual pixels, which might not scale or print as well.

To use the Copy Picture command, hold down Shift while clicking the Edit menu. The Copy command becomes the Copy Picture command, the Paste command becomes the Paste Picture command, and the Link command becomes the Paste Picture Link command. For example, if you select the range A1:C6 and choose Copy Picture from the Edit menu while holding down Shift, an image of the selection is copied to the Clipboard. You can then paste the image anywhere you want — in another location on the worksheet, in another worksheet, or even in a document from another application. You can paste the image into an Excel document with the Paste command or the Paste Picture command with the same result. If you simply use the Copy command and then use the Paste Picture Link command, you create a dynamic image that changes along with the copied area, which is essentially the same as using the Camera tool.

Exchanging graphics with other programs

You can import graphics into Microsoft Excel from other programs that produce files compatible with the Windows Clipboard, such as Windows Paintbrush. You can also copy a picture created from an Excel chart or worksheet and paste it into another application, such as Microsoft Word for Windows.

If the application used to create the graphic you want to import into Excel supports Dynamic Data Exchange (DDE) or Object Linking and Embedding (OLE), you might be able to establish a link between the source file and the graphic. After you import the graphic into Excel, the link allows the graphic to be updated automatically if the source document changes. See Chapter 22 for more information on DDE and OLE.

To import a graphic from another application, begin by opening the file that contains the graphic in the parent application, and copy the image you want to the Clipboard (usually using the Copy command). Next, start Excel, open the worksheet or macro sheet into which you want to paste the graphic, and then choose the Paste or Paste Link command. Figure 7-22 shows a graphic image created in Windows Paintbrush, which has been pasted twice into an Excel worksheet. The image on the left shows the graphic when you first paste it into Excel — the border is added automatically. On the right, the image has been pasted over an Excel text box to create a logo. We added the drop shadow with the Drop Shadow tool. Note the different fonts and sizes used in the text box.

FIGURE 7-22.
You can incorporate graphics from other applications into your Excel documents.

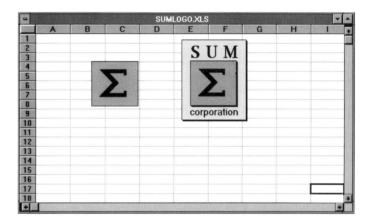

As with other graphic objects, you can resize, position, protect, and assign macros to pasted-in images. You can add borders with the Patterns command, but if you try to use a fill pattern, Excel ignores it.

You can also copy images of Excel worksheets and charts using the Copy Picture command and paste them, via the Clipboard, into other applications that support the Clipboard format. Follow the procedure described earlier for the Copy Picture command, and then use the Paste command to paste the image in the destination document as you would any other graphic. As already mentioned, you can establish links to Excel from the destination document. For more information on exporting images and using DDE and OLE, see Chapter 22.

The Insert Object command

The Insert Object command on the Edit menu gives you direct access to other applications you use to create an object, or edit an existing object that you will subsequently insert into your worksheet. When you choose the Insert Object command, a dialog box appears that lists the applications that are available for you to create Excel objects. This list will vary, depending on the configuration of your system. But it is likely that the Picture or Paintbrush Picture object type will be available.

When you choose an item from the Object Type list, a small frame is inserted in the worksheet at the location of the active cell, and the application needed to create or edit that object type is automatically loaded. When you are finished, you usually will see that the Exit command is replaced by the Exit and Return to *[filename]* command. When you choose this command, the Excel application window reappears, and the object you just created is inserted at the location of the active cell. (For more information about the Insert Object command, see Chapter 23.)

8

Built-in Functions

Worksheet functions are special tools that let you perform complex calculations quickly and easily. You can use some functions, such as SUM, AVERAGE, and NPV, instead of mathematical formulas. Other functions, such as IF and VLOOKUP, cannot be duplicated by formulas.

Worksheet functions are like the special function keys on sophisticated calculators. Just as many calculators have buttons that compute square roots, logarithms, and present values, Microsoft Excel has 310 built-in functions that perform these calculations — and many more.

Getting more help with worksheet functions

Because of the number of Microsoft Excel's worksheet functions (not to mention the additional macro functions), we made some judgments about which functions to focus on and which to mention only briefly. Fortunately, two very good alternate resources are available: Excel's documentation and on-line Help. The on-line Help system supplements Excel's excellent documentation and includes a detailed explanation of each worksheet function.

The easiest way to get more information about a function is to choose the Search command from the Help menu, type the name of the function you want, and press Enter twice. If you want to browse through a number of function help topics, choose the Contents command from the Help menu (or the Contents button at the top of the Help window), and click Worksheet Functions in the Reference list. You can then click the category of function you want to browse through, or click All to look at the entire list.

The power of functions

Let's look at an example that demonstrates the power of Microsoft Excel's functions. The worksheet in Figure 8-1 shows monthly pet sales for a 12-month period. To find the total yak sales for the year, you could enter the formula

=B4+B5+B6+B7+B8+B9+B10+B11+B12+B13+B14+B15

in cell B16, but this formula is bulky and takes too long to enter. Consider the shorthand formula

=SUM(B4:B15)

which also tells Excel to add the numbers stored in the range B4 through B15. The results of this formula and the longer version are identical: $8,094.

The more complex the formula you need to build, the more time you will save by using functions. Suppose you're considering a real-estate purchase and you want to calculate the net present value of the purchase price to determine whether the investment is worthwhile. To do this calculation without functions, you would have to build a formula similar to this:

=(A1/(1+.15))+(B1/(1+.15)^2)+(C1/(1+.15)^3)+(D1/(1+.15)^4)

The NPV function performs the same calculation with only 15 keystrokes:

=NPV(.15,A1:D1)

FIGURE 8-1.
In this example, the SUM function calculates yak sales for a 12-month period.

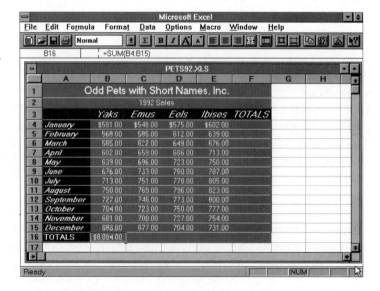

The form of functions

Worksheet functions have two elements: the function name and the argument (or arguments). Function names are descriptive terms, such as SUM and AVERAGE, that identify the operation you want to perform. Arguments tell Microsoft Excel which values or cells you want the function to act on. For example, in the function

=SUM(C3:C5)

SUM is the function name and C3:C5 is the argument. This function sums, or totals, the numbers in cells C3, C4, and C5.

The equal sign at the beginning of this statement indicates that the entry is a formula, not a text entry. If you leave out the equal sign, Excel interprets this entry as the text *SUM(C3:C5)*.

Notice that the argument is surrounded by parentheses. The left parenthesis marks the beginning of the function's argument. This delimiter must appear immediately after the function name, with no spaces. If you enter a space or some other character between the function name and the left parenthesis, you'll see the alert message *Error in formula*.

Using arguments

You often use more than one argument in a function; arguments are separated by commas. For example, the function

=SUM(C1,C2,C5)

tells Excel to total the numbers in cells C1, C2, and C5.

You can include as many as 30 arguments in a function (but don't exceed the 1024-character limit for cell entries). However, a single argument can refer to any number of cells in your worksheet. For example, the function

=SUM(A1:A5,C2:C10,D3:D17)

has three arguments but totals the numbers in 29 cells. These cells can contain numbers or formulas that refer to more ranges or cells. You can create a powerful hierarchy of calculations to perform complex worksheet operations.

Different types of arguments

In the examples presented so far, all the arguments have been cell references. You can also use literal numbers, text, range names, other functions, arrays, logical values, error values, and other types of entries as the arguments in functions.

Numbers

The arguments in a function can be literal numbers. For example, the function

=SUM(327,209,176)

totals the numbers 327, 209, and 176. Usually you enter the numbers you want to use in cells of the worksheet and then refer to those cells as the arguments in your functions. By using cell references, you make your functions easier to understand and modify.

Range names

You can also use range names as the arguments of functions. For example, if you use the Define Name command from the Formula menu to assign the name *Test* to the range C3:C5, you can use the formula

    =SUM(Test)

to compute the sum of the numbers in cells C3, C4, and C5.

Other functions

You can use other functions as arguments, using a technique called nesting. For example, in the function

    =SUM(SIN(A1),COS(A2))

the SIN(A1) and COS(A2) functions are arguments of the SUM function.

Arrays

You can use arrays as arguments in functions. Some functions, such as TREND and TRANSPOSE, require the use of array arguments; other functions can accept array arguments even though they do not require them. (For more information on arrays, see Chapter 3.)

Mixed argument types

You can mix argument types within a function. For example, the formula

    =AVERAGE(Group1,A3,5*3)

uses a named range, a single-cell reference, and an embedded formula to arrive at a single value. All three arguments are acceptable to Excel.

Functions without arguments

A few functions, such as PI and TRUE, have no arguments. These functions are generally embedded, or nested, in other formulas or functions.

Optional arguments

A number of functions don't require that you use all their arguments every time. For example, the PV function requires only three of its five arguments; the other two arguments are referred to as *optional*.

If you omit an optional argument that occurs in the middle of the function, you must still enter a comma as a delimiter for that argument. For example,

=PV(10%,5, , 5000)

If the optional argument is at the end of the function, you can simply omit it.

Other types of arguments

Excel accepts two other types of arguments: conditional tests, which involve using logical values and error values as arguments, and text strings. The uses of conditional tests are discussed in "Logical functions," and text strings are discussed in "Text functions," later in this chapter.

Entering functions

You can enter functions in your worksheet in two different ways: You can type the function from the keyboard, or you can choose the Paste Function command from the Formula menu. If you type the function name, use lowercase letters. Because Excel translates all function names to capital letters, any function name you misspell will remain in lowercase letters. This trick makes it easy to spot any typing mistakes you make.

Using the Paste Function command

When you select a cell and choose the Paste Function command, Excel provides you with lists of function categories and function names. Figure 8-2 shows part of these lists. To select a function, first select a category from the Function Category list (or select the All category). Then scroll through the alphabetic Paste Function list and choose the function you want to use, or type the first letter of the function until the name appears in the box. When you click OK or press Enter, Excel enters the equal sign (if you're inserting the function at the beginning of a formula), the function name, and a set of parentheses in the formula. The insertion point appears between the parentheses. All you have to do is enter the arguments and separators.

FIGURE 8-2.
Use the Paste Function dialog box to enter functions into the formula bar.

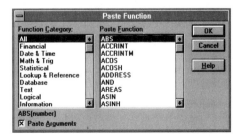

Pasting arguments

The Paste Arguments option is selected by default. If you leave it selected, Excel pastes both the function name and the names of its arguments into the formula bar. You can then select and replace each argument name.

Suppose you want to use the PMT function in your worksheet but can't remember the proper order of the arguments. If you choose the Paste Arguments option, this entry appears in the formula bar:

=PMT(*rate,nper,pv,fv,type*)

The argument *rate* is already selected, so type the appropriate value or indicate the cell that contains the value you want to use. Replace the remaining four arguments with the appropriate entries.

Some functions, such as INDEX, have more than one form. If this is the case, Excel presents you with a second Paste Function dialog box from which you select the form you want to use. (See Figure 8-3.)

FIGURE 8-3.
If a function has more than one form, Excel displays the second Paste Function dialog box.

Pasting cell references and range names

As with any other formula, you can paste cell references and range names into your functions. Suppose you want to enter in cell C11 a function that averages the cells in the range C2:C10. Select cell C11 and either type *=AVERAGE(* or use the Paste Function command to select the function. Next, select the range C2:C10. A marquee appears around the selected cells. (If you type the function name, rather than using the Paste Function command, you must add the closing right parenthesis only if

---

Pasting arguments with the keyboard

Starting with version 4 of Excel, you can use a keyboard shortcut to paste arguments in functions, provided you know the name of the function you want. After you type the function name in the formula bar, press Ctrl-A. Excel adds the parentheses and the required arguments. This is particularly useful for easy-to-remember function names that have long strings of arguments.

you nest the function within a formula. Usually, Excel will be able to supply the right parenthesis for you.) When you press Enter to lock in the formula, the marquee disappears, and a reference to your selected range appears in the formula bar.

If you define range names in your worksheets, you can also paste them into your formulas. To paste a range name, choose Paste Name from the Formula menu and select the range name from the list in the Paste Name dialog box. When you click OK, the range name appears in the formula bar at the insertion point.

The following sections discuss Excel's statistical, arithmetic, logarithmic, trigonometric, financial, text, logical, array, and miscellaneous functions.

Tools for pasting functions and range names

Excel provides tools on the Macro toolbar that are equivalent to choosing the Paste Function and Paste Name commands. Even though these tools are on the Macro toolbar, you can use them on worksheets — you might want to include them on a custom toolbar. When you click the Paste Function tool, the Paste Function dialog box appears. Similarly, when you click the Paste Name tool, the Paste Name dialog box appears. For more information about tools and toolbars, including how to customize your own toolbars, see Appendix A.

Statistical functions

Microsoft Excel's statistical functions let you analyze groups of numbers. In this section we limit the discussion to the 14 most commonly used statistical functions. Excel also offers the advanced statistical functions LINEST, LOGEST, TREND, and GROWTH. These advanced functions operate on arrays and are discussed in "Array functions," later in this chapter. Excel provides a number of other advanced statistical functions in the Analysis ToolPak add-in, which is discussed in Chapter 10.

Excel 4 includes many statistical functions that are likely to be used only by those with a background in statistical analysis. Space limitations prevent us from covering these functions here. Instead, we have chosen to concentrate on the functions that we consider most widely applicable to business users. You can find information about any of Excel's functions in the Excel on-line Help system.

The SUM function

The SUM function computes the total of a series of numbers and has the form

=SUM(*numbers*)

The *numbers* argument can contain as many as 30 entries that consist of any number, formula, range name, or cell reference that results in a number. SUM ignores any argument that refers to a text string, logical value, or blank cell.

Entering the SUM function from the Standard toolbar

Because SUM is such a commonly used function, Excel provides a toolbar shortcut
for entering this function. If you click the AutoSum tool (Σ on the Standard toolbar),
Excel creates an =SUM( ) formula for you, making its best guess about which numbers you want to add up. For example, if you make cell C16 in Figure 8-4 the active
cell and then click the AutoSum tool, Excel proposes the formula shown in the
formula bar — =SUM(C4:C15).

If the SUM formula has the correct argument, click the AutoSum tool a second
time or press Enter. If the argument proposed is not correct, you can edit it. One
easy way to edit the proposed argument is to drag the mouse across the range of
cells you want to add; Excel then replaces its proposed argument with your
selection.

You can even use the AutoSum tool to enter several SUM formulas at once. In
Figure 8-4, for example, if we had first selected cells C16:E16 and then clicked the
AutoSum tool, Excel would have proposed the appropriate SUM formula in C16.
When we clicked the AutoSum tool a second time to accept that formula, Excel
would have locked the formula into C16 and replicated it across the row into D16
through E16. (You can use the same technique to replicate a SUM formula up or
down a column.)

Expanding the argument of a SUM formula

Expanding a SUM range to include a new value is much easier than expanding a
range totaled with ordinary addition operators. Suppose cell F4 in Figure 8-5 contains the formula

    =B4+C4+D4+E4

FIGURE 8-4.
*When you click the
AutoSum tool, Excel
proposes the formula
=SUM(C4:C15).*

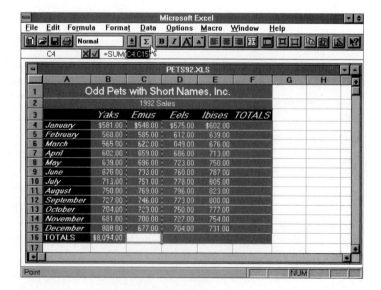

FIGURE 8-5.
The formula =B4+C4+D4+E4 calculates total sales for January.

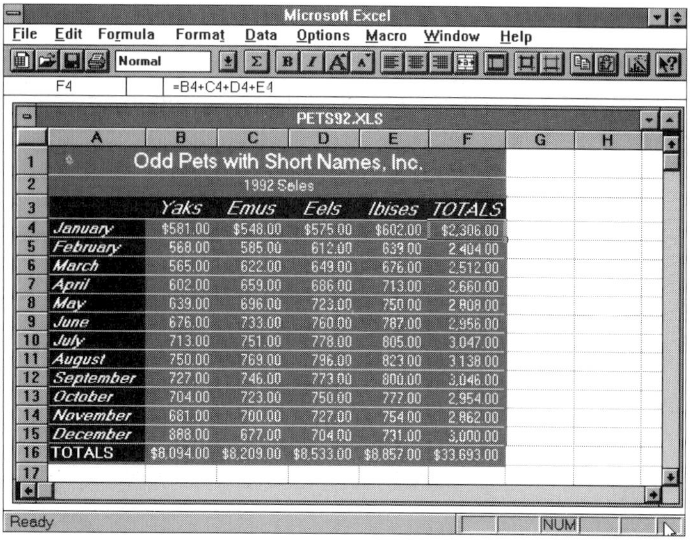

	Yaks	Emus	Eels	Ibises	TOTALS
January	$581.00	$548.00	$575.00	$602.00	$2,306.00
February	568.00	585.00	612.00	639.00	2,404.00
March	565.00	622.00	649.00	676.00	2,512.00
April	602.00	659.00	686.00	713.00	2,660.00
May	639.00	696.00	723.00	750.00	2,808.00
June	676.00	733.00	760.00	787.00	2,956.00
July	713.00	751.00	778.00	805.00	3,047.00
August	750.00	769.00	796.00	823.00	3,138.00
September	727.00	746.00	773.00	800.00	3,046.00
October	704.00	723.00	750.00	777.00	2,954.00
November	681.00	700.00	727.00	754.00	2,862.00
December	888.00	677.00	704.00	731.00	3,000.00
TOTALS	$8,094.00	$8,209.00	$8,533.00	$8,857.00	$33,693.00

If after you enter this formula you discover that you omitted the category *Bats*, you can select column C and then choose the Insert command from the Edit menu to add a column of cells for the new category. Excel adjusts the totals formulas, which now appear in column G, to account for your insertion, but it won't add the new category to those totals. For example, in Figure 8-6, the formula in cell G4 now reads

=B4+D4+E4+F4

FIGURE 8-6.
Although a new category was added, the totals do not change because the formula referenced the individual cells.

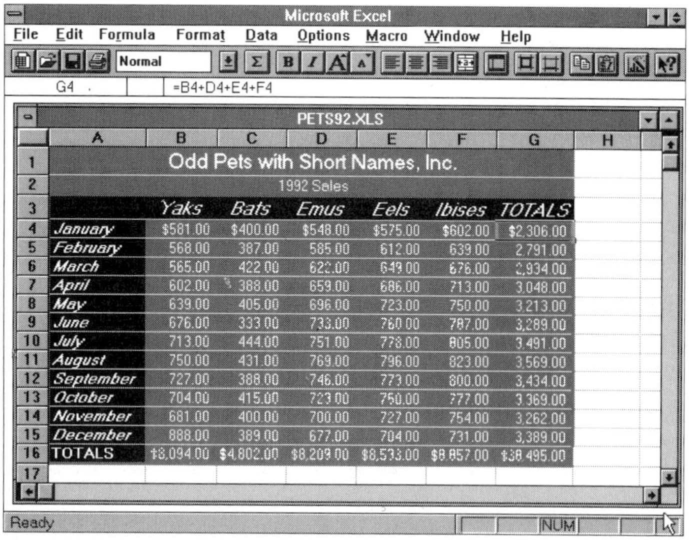

	Yaks	Bats	Emus	Eels	Ibises	TOTALS
January	$581.00	$400.00	$548.00	$575.00	$602.00	$2,306.00
February	568.00	387.00	585.00	612.00	639.00	2,791.00
March	565.00	422.00	622.00	649.00	676.00	2,934.00
April	602.00	388.00	659.00	686.00	713.00	3,048.00
May	639.00	405.00	696.00	723.00	750.00	3,213.00
June	676.00	333.00	733.00	760.00	787.00	3,289.00
July	713.00	444.00	751.00	778.00	805.00	3,491.00
August	750.00	431.00	769.00	796.00	823.00	3,569.00
September	727.00	388.00	746.00	773.00	800.00	3,434.00
October	704.00	415.00	723.00	750.00	777.00	3,369.00
November	681.00	400.00	700.00	727.00	754.00	3,262.00
December	888.00	389.00	677.00	704.00	731.00	3,389.00
TOTALS	$8,094.00	$4,802.00	$8,209.00	$8,533.00	$8,857.00	$38,495.00

If instead you use the SUM function to create the formula

=SUM(B4:E4)

in cell F4 of Figure 8-5, Excel expands the range referred to in the *numbers* argument to make it include your new column. Because Excel always adjusts cell ranges when you insert or delete rows and columns within the range, the formula is updated automatically to read

=SUM(B4:F4)

Keep in mind that the *numbers* argument of a SUM function does not have to refer to an adjacent range. Suppose you want to add a set of numbers located in cells A3, B12, and G13 through H15 of your worksheet. You can enter each of these cell references as a separate argument:

=SUM(A3,B12,G13:H15)

Using extra cells in your ranges

Although formulas that use the SUM function are more adaptable than those that use the addition operator (+), you will still run into problems if you add a cell to the beginning or end of a range. As an example, take a look at this worksheet:

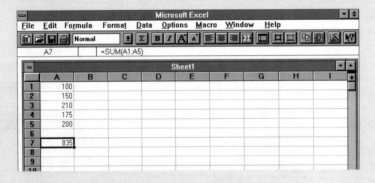

Cell A7 contains the formula

=SUM(A1:A5)

Suppose you decide to insert a row in the worksheet below row 5. You select cell A6 and choose the Insert command from the Edit menu. Next, you enter the number 100 in cell A6.

You can also assign a range name to this set of cells and use that name as the *numbers* argument. To assign a name to the cells in the previous formula, simply click cell A3, hold down Ctrl, and click cell B12. Then, without releasing Ctrl, select cells G13 through H15. (From the keyboard, use Add mode.) After you select the eight cells in this range, use the Define Name command to assign a range name, such as *Group1*, to this collection of cells, and enter the formula

=SUM(Group1)

The AVERAGE function

The AVERAGE function computes the arithmetic mean, or average, of the numbers in a range. The form of this function is

=AVERAGE(*numbers*)

Because the formula, which is now in cell A8, refers only to the range A1:A5, the formula didn't change when you inserted the new row. Obviously, the new number in cell A6 is not included in the total.

You can use the fact that Excel ignores text entries and blank cells when it performs the SUM function to overcome this problem. Suppose the original SUM function in cell A7 is

=SUM(A1:A6)

Because the SUM function ignores arguments that refer to blank cells, this function returns the same result as the previous version. However, when you insert the new row below row 5, the new version of the formula changes to

=SUM(A1:A7)

As you can see, this function includes the new entry in cell A6.

This tip applies to all the mathematical functions discussed in this section. Because you use these functions so often, including blank cells in an argument can save a lot of time and frustration. We suggest that you get into the habit of including an extra row or column in the arguments of these functions whenever you can.

AVERAGE computes the average the same way you do: It sums a series of numeric values and then divides the result by the number of values in the argument. AVERAGE can include as many as 30 arguments. Like SUM, AVERAGE ignores blank, logical, and text cells.

Also like SUM, the AVERAGE function can be used instead of long formulas. For example, to calculate the average sales in cells B4 through B15 of Figure 8-5, you might use the formula

=(B4+B5+B6+B7+B8+B9+B10+B11+B12+B13+B14+B15)/12

to arrive at the number $674.50. This method has the same drawbacks as using the + operator instead of the SUM function: You have to edit the cell references and the divisor each time you change the range you want to average.

The AVERAGE function calculates the sum and number of values for you. For example, you can use the formula

=AVERAGE(B4:B15)

to arrive at the arithmetic mean: $674.50.

The MEDIAN function

The MEDIAN function computes the median of a set of numbers. The form of this function is

=MEDIAN(*numbers*)

The median is the number in the middle of the set. An equal number of values lie above and below the median. For example, the formula

=MEDIAN(1,3,5,6,7)

returns 5. Two numbers (6 and 7) lie above 5 and two (1 and 3) lie below. If the argument for the MEDIAN function includes an even number of values, the value returned is the average of the two that lie in the middle. Thus, the formula

=MEDIAN(0,4,6,11,16,18)

returns 8.5, because 8.5 is the average of 6 and 11, the two numbers that lie in the middle of the set.

Like SUM, AVERAGE, and most other statistical functions, MEDIAN can accept as many as 30 arguments. Because each argument can be a range, however, the function can operate on a practically unlimited number of values. Any text values within a range argument for MEDIAN are ignored.

The MODE function

The MODE function determines the one value that occurs most frequently in a range. The form of this function is

=MODE(*numbers*)

The mode is the most frequently occurring number in the range. The range can also contain blank cells, or logical values. For example, the formula

=MODE(1,3,3,6,7)

returns 3. If the number of values in the range is zero, MODE returns #N/A! If no number occurs more than once, MODE returns #NUM!

WARNING: *If two or more values in the* numbers *argument are tied as the most frequent value, the* MODE *function returns only the tied value that appears first in* numbers.

The MAX function

Excel's MAX function returns the largest value in a range. The form of this function is

=MAX(*numbers*)

As with SUM and AVERAGE, the argument of MAX is usually a range. For example, you can use the formula

=MAX(B4:B15)

in the worksheet in Figure 8-5 to determine the amount of the largest monthly sales of yaks: $888.

MAX can include as many as 30 arguments. If you assign a name to the range you want to analyze, you can use that name as the argument of this function. Like SUM, MAX ignores cells in the argument range that are blank or that contain text or logical values. If there are no numbers in the arguments, MAX returns 0.

The MIN function

The MIN function returns the smallest value in a range. The form of the MIN function is

=MIN(*numbers*)

As with MAX, the argument of MIN is usually a range. For example, in the worksheet in Figure 8-5, you can use the formula

=MIN(B4:B15)

to determine the smallest monthly yak sales: $565.

MIN can include as many as 30 arguments. If you assign a name to the range you want to analyze, you can use that name as the argument of this function. Also like MAX, MIN ignores cells in the argument range that are blank or that contain text or logical values. If there are no numbers in the arguments, MIN returns 0.

The COUNT and COUNTA functions

The COUNT function tells you how many cells in a given range contain numbers, including dates and formulas that evaluate to numbers. The form of the COUNT function is

=COUNT(*range*)

For example, in the worksheet in Figure 8-7, you can use the formula

=COUNT(B4:B15)

to determine the number of cells in the range B4:B15 that contain numbers. This formula returns the answer 8.

COUNT can contain as many as 30 arguments, and it ignores blank cells and cells that contain text, logical, and error values.

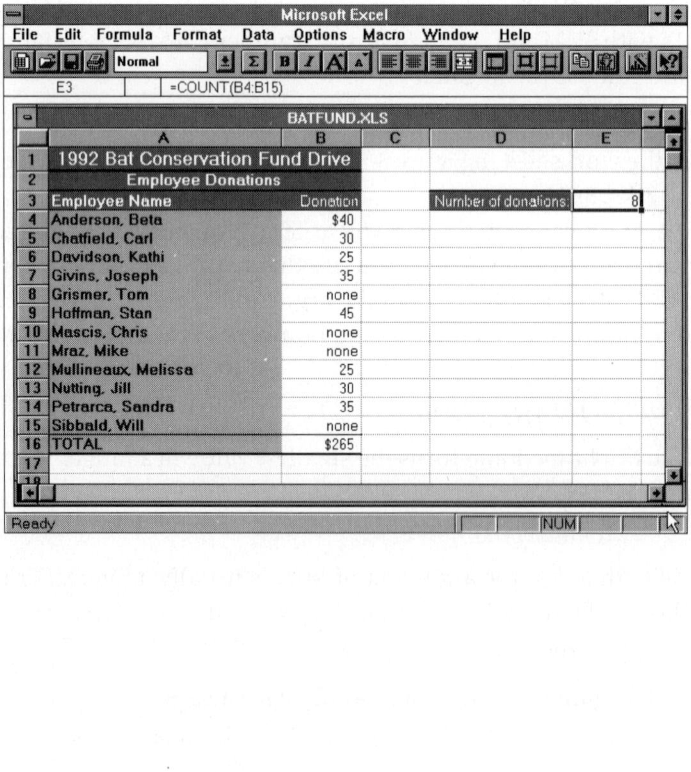

FIGURE 8-7.
*The COUNT function
ignores cells without
numbers.*

The COUNT function counts only the numbers in a range. To count all non-blank cells, use COUNTA. The form of the COUNTA function is

=COUNTA(*range*)

Using the worksheet in Figure 8-7, the formula

=COUNTA(B4:B15)

returns the value 12, because the range B4:B15 contains 8 numbers and 4 labels.

COUNTA can contain as many as 30 arguments, and it ignores blank cells.

The SUMPRODUCT and SUMSQ functions

The SUMPRODUCT function multiplies the corresponding members of each of two or more sets of numbers and returns the sum of the products. The form of this function is

=SUMPRODUCT(*array1,array2,...*)

Figure 8-8 shows a worksheet that uses SUMPRODUCT.

FIGURE 8-8.
This worksheet uses SUMPRODUCT to calculate how many sprockets are needed to produce the desired numbers of all six types of widget.

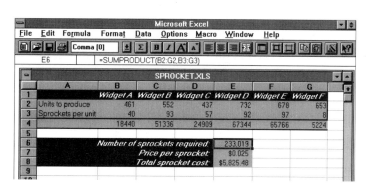

The formula in E6,

=SUMPRODUCT(B2:G2,B3:G3)

determines the total number of sprockets that are required to produce the desired number of all six widget types. It does this by multiplying B2*B3, C2*C3, and so on through G2*G3 and then totaling the six products.

SUMPRODUCT can accept as many as 30 range arguments. Each argument must have the same number of cells.

The SUMSQ function is similar to the SUMPRODUCT function, except that it squares the members of one set of numbers and returns the sum of the squares, rather than the products. The form of this function is

=SUMSQ(*number1,number2,...*)

where the arguments can be up to 30 numbers or a reference to a single array in the worksheet. For example, the formula

=SUMSQ(5,6)

returns 61, or (25+36).

Calculating variance and standard deviation

Four statistical functions — VAR, VARP, STDEV, and STDEVP — compute the variance and standard deviation of the numbers in a range.

Variance and standard deviation are both statistics that measure the dispersion of a group of numbers. As a rule, about 68 percent of a normally distributed population falls within one standard deviation of the mean and about 95 percent of the population falls within two standard deviations. A large standard deviation indicates that the population is widely dispersed from the mean; a small standard deviation indicates that the population is tightly packed around the mean.

Before you calculate the variance and standard deviation of a group of values, you must determine whether those values represent the total population or only a representative sample of that population. The VAR and STDEV functions assume that the values you are working with represent only a sample of your total test population; the VARP and STDEVP functions let you treat the set of values you're analyzing as a total population.

You can use as many as 30 arguments in each of the four functions. Each of these functions ignores cells that are blanks, or cells that contain logical values or text.

Calculating sample statistics: VAR and STDEV

The VAR and STDEV functions take the forms

=VAR(*numbers*)

and

=STDEV(*numbers*)

The worksheet in Figure 8-9 shows exam scores for five students and assumes that the test scores in cells B4 through E8 represent only a part of the total population.

Cell C11 contains the formula

=AVERAGE(B4:E8)

FIGURE 8-9.
The VAR and STDEV functions measure the dispersion of sample exam scores.

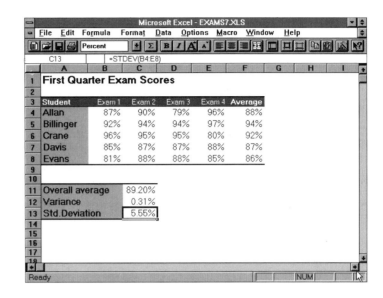

which returns the average of the exam scores: 89.20%. Cells C12 and C13 use the VAR and STDEV functions to calculate the variance and the standard deviation for this sample group of test scores with the formulas

=VAR(B4:E8)

and

=STDEV(B4:E8)

The VAR function returns 0.31%, and the STDEV function returns 5.55%. Assuming that the test scores in our example are normally distributed, we can deduce that about 68 percent of the students scored between 83.65 percent (89.20−5.55) and 94.75 percent (89.20 + 5.55).

Calculating total population statistics: VARP and STDEVP

If the numbers you're analyzing represent the entire population rather than only a sample, you should use the VARP and STDEVP functions to calculate variance and standard deviation. Use the formula

=VARP(*numbers*)

to compute the population variance. To find the standard deviation for the total population, use the formula

=STDEVP(*numbers*)

If we assume that cells A4 through D18 in the worksheet in Figure 8-9 represent the total population, we can calculate the variance and standard deviation with the formulas

=VARP(A4:D18)

and

=STDEVP(A4:D18)

The VARP function returns 0.29%, and the STDEVP function returns 5.41%.

Arithmetic functions

The 27 arithmetic functions let you perform specialized arithmetic calculations quickly and easily. Other arithmetic functions are available in the Analysis ToolPak add-in, which is discussed in Chapter 10.

The ABS function

The ABS function returns the absolute value of a number or formula. The form of this function is

=ABS(*number*)

where *number* is a number, a reference to a cell that contains a value, or a formula that results in a number. For example, if cell A1 contains the number –75, the formula

=ABS(A1)

returns 75. If the number referred to by the argument is positive, ABS returns that number unchanged.

The SIGN function

You can use the SIGN function to determine whether an argument results in a negative, positive, or zero value. The form of this function is

=SIGN(*number*)

The *number* argument can be a number, a reference to a cell that contains a number, or a formula that results in a number. If *number* is positive, the SIGN function returns the value 1; if *number* is negative, it returns the value –1; if *number* is 0, it returns 0.

For example, suppose cells A1 through A3 contain the numbers 10, –20, and –5. The formula

=SIGN(SUM(A1:A3))

adds the numbers 10, –20, and –5 (resulting in the value –15) and determines whether the resulting value is positive or negative. Because the embedded SUM formula results in a negative value, the SIGN function returns the value –1.

The ROUND and MROUND functions

The ROUND function lets you eliminate unwanted decimal places from numbers. ROUND rounds the number referred to by its argument to a specified number of decimal places. The form of the ROUND function is

=ROUND(*number, decimal places*)

The *decimal places* argument can be any positive or negative integer. Specifying a negative *decimal places* argument rounds to the left of the decimal. Microsoft Excel rounds down digits less than 5 and rounds up digits greater than or equal to 5. The following table shows several examples of the ROUND function:

Entry	Display
=ROUND(123.4567,−1)	120
=ROUND(123.4567,−2)	100
=ROUND(123.4567,0)	123
=ROUND(123.4567,1)	123.5
=ROUND(123.4567,2)	123.46
=ROUND(123.4567,3)	123.457

The MROUND function gives you the added ability to round to the nearest multiple that you specify. This function is available when you load the Analysis ToolPak add-in. The form of this function is

=MROUND(*number, multiple*)

where *multiple* is any number you want to use as a rounding unit. The following examples give you an idea of how the MROUND function operates:

Entry	Display
=MROUND(6,10)	10
=MROUND(123,25)	125
=MROUND(5.7,0.2)	5.8
=MROUND(1,0.5)	1

Rounding with the EVEN and ODD functions

The pair of statistical functions EVEN and ODD also perform rounding operations. The EVEN function rounds a number upward to the nearest even integer. The ODD function rounds a number upward to the nearest odd integer. Negative numbers are rounded downward. The forms of these functions are

=EVEN(*number*)

and

=ODD(*number*)

The following table shows some examples of these functions in action:

Entry	Display
=EVEN(23.4)	24
=EVEN(2)	2
=EVEN(3)	4
=EVEN(−3)	−4
=ODD(23.4)	25
=ODD(3)	3
=ODD(4)	5
=ODD(−4)	−5

Rounding with the FLOOR and CEILING functions

The FLOOR and CEILING functions also perform rounding operations. The FLOOR function rounds a number downward to the nearest given multiple. The CEILING function rounds a number upward to the nearest given multiple. These functions take the forms

=FLOOR(*number,multiple*)

and

=CEILING(*number,multiple*)

In both cases, the value of *multiple* must be positive. If *multiple* is negative, Excel returns #NUM! The following table shows some examples of these functions in action:

Entry	Display
=FLOOR(23.4,0.5)	23
=FLOOR(5,3)	3
=FLOOR(5,−1)	#NUM!
=FLOOR(5,1.5)	4.5
=CEILING(23.4,5)	25
=CEILING(5,3)	6
=CEILING(5,−1)	#NUM!
=CEILING(5,1.5)	6

The INT function

The INT function rounds numbers *down* to the nearest whole number. The form of this function is

=INT(*number*)

For example, the formula

=INT(100.01)

returns the value 100, as does the formula

=INT(100.99999999)

even though the number 100.99999999 is essentially equal to 101.

When *number* is negative, INT still rounds that number down to the nearest integer. For example, the formula

=INT(–100.99999999)

results in the value –101.

The TRUNC function

The TRUNC function truncates everything to the right of the decimal point, which results in an integer with no decimal places. The form of the TRUNC function is

=TRUNC(*number*)

For example, the function

=TRUNC(13.978)

returns the number 13.

Although ROUND, INT, and TRUNC can all be used to eliminate unwanted decimals, the three functions work differently. ROUND rounds up or down to the number of decimal places you specify and INT rounds down to the nearest whole number. The primary difference between INT and TRUNC is in the treatment of negative values. If you use the value –100.99999999 as your *number* argument in an INT function, you get the result –101. However, the TRUNC function

=TRUNC(–100.99999999)

eliminates the decimal portion of the *number* argument and returns the number –100.

The RAND and RANDBETWEEN functions

The RAND function generates a random number between 0 and 1. The form of the function is

=RAND()

RAND is one of the few Excel functions that doesn't take an argument. As with all functions that take no arguments, you must still enter the parentheses after the function name.

The result of a RAND function changes each time you recalculate your worksheet. If you use automatic recalculation, this means that the value of the RAND function changes each time you make a worksheet entry.

The RAND function returns real numbers between 0 and 1. To get random integers between any other end points, you can use the RANDBETWEEN function. The form of this function is

=RANDBETWEEN(*bottom,top*)

where *bottom* represents the smallest and *top* represents the largest integers you want to use.

The RANDBETWEEN function is included in the add-in macro sheet called ADDINFNS.XLA. To open this macro sheet, choose Add-ins from the Options menu, click the Add button, switch to the EXCEL\LIBRARY subdirectory, select ADDINFNS.XLA, and click OK.

The FACT function

The FACT function calculates the factorial value of any number. (The *factorial* of a number is the product of all the positive integers from 1 to the specified number. For example, 3 factorial, or 3!, is the product $1 \times 2 \times 3 = 6$.) The FACT function takes the form

=FACT(*number*)

The *number* argument must be a positive integer. For example, FACT(1) equals 1, but FACT(–1) equals #NUM! If *number* is not an integer, FACT truncates it.

To solve for 10!, use the formula

=FACT(10)

This formula returns the factorial value 3628800.

Using Paste Special with RAND

The Paste Special command lets you lock in a series of random numbers so that you can recreate a set of calculations later. To lock in the results of your RAND function, select the cell or range that contains the function and choose the Copy command from the Edit menu. Next, choose Paste Special from the Edit menu. Select the Values option from the Paste Special dialog box and check to be sure the Operation option is set to None. Click OK to overwrite the RAND formulas with the displayed values.

The PRODUCT function

The PRODUCT function multiplies all the numbers included as arguments. The function takes the form

=PRODUCT(*numbers*)

The PRODUCT function can multiply as many as 30 arguments. If you include text, logical values, or blank cells in an argument, Excel ignores them.

The MOD function

The MOD function computes the remainder from a division operation. The form of the function is

=MOD(*dividend,divisor*)

The result of the function is the remainder that results from dividing *dividend* by *divisor*. For example, the function

=MOD(9,4)

returns 1, the remainder that results from dividing 9 by 4.

If the dividend is smaller than the divisor, the result of the function equals the dividend. For example, the function

=MOD(5,11)

returns 5. If the dividend is exactly divisible by the divisor, the result of the function is 0. If the divisor is 0, MOD returns a #DIV/0! error value.

The PI function

The PI function returns the value of the constant π, accurate to 14 decimal places: 3.14159265358979. The form of the function is

=PI()

As with RAND, even though PI has no arguments, you must still enter empty parentheses after the function name.

You'll probably use PI in conjunction with another formula or function. For example, to calculate the area of a circle, you multiply PI by the square of the circle's radius. The formula

=PI()*(5^2)

computes the area of a circle with a radius of 5. The result of this formula is 78.54.

The SQRT function

The SQRT function returns the positive square root of a number. The form is

=SQRT(*number*)

The *number* argument must be a positive value or a reference to a cell that contains a positive value. The result of the function is the square root of the *number* argument. For example, the function

=SQRT(4)

returns the value 2.

If you enter a negative number, SQRT returns a #NUM! error value.

The COMBIN function

The COMBIN function determines the number of possible combinations or groups of items available, given a total number of items available and the number you want in each group. This function takes the form

=COMBIN(*total, number chosen*)

where *total* is the total number of items available and *number chosen* is the number of items you want to group in each combination. For example, to determine how many different combinations of 12-player football teams is possible, given a total number of 17 players, use the formula

=COMBIN(17,12)

which produces a result of 6188.

Logarithmic functions

Microsoft Excel offers four logarithmic functions: LOG10, LOG, LN, and EXP. Excel also provides several other advanced logarithmic functions in the Analysis ToolPak add-in, which is discussed in Chapter 10.

The LOG10 function

The LOG10 function returns the base 10 logarithm for the number or cell reference in the argument. The form of this function is

=LOG10(*number*)

The *number* argument must be a positive value or a reference to a cell that contains a positive value. If the *number* argument is negative, the function returns the error value #NUM!

For example, the formula

=LOG10(100)

returns the value 2.

The LOG function

The LOG function returns the logarithm of a positive number using a specified base. The form of the function is

=LOG(*number,base*)

For example, the formula

=LOG(5,2)

returns the value 2.321928.

If you don't include *base* in the argument, Excel assumes the base is 10.

The LN function

The LN function returns the natural (base *e*) logarithm of the positive number referred to by its argument. The form of the function is

=LN(*number*)

For example, the formula

=LN(2)

returns the value 0.693147.

The EXP function

EXP computes the value of the constant *e* (which equals 2.71828182845905) raised to the power specified by the function's argument. The form of the function is

=EXP(*number*)

For example,

=EXP(2)

equals 7.3890561, or 2.7182818 times 2.7182818.

EXP is the inverse of the LN function. For example, if cell A1 contains the formula

=LN(8)

then, because EXP is the inverse of the LN function, the formula

=EXP(A1)

returns 8.

Trigonometric functions

For its trigonometric functions, Microsoft Excel measures angles in *radians* rather than degrees. Radians measure the size of an angle based on the constant π (approximately 3.14). Although you can construct your own formulas to convert radians to degrees and vice versa, Excel provides two add-in functions, RADIANS and DEGREES, that make trigonometric life easier for you.

The RADIANS and DEGREES functions

Both the RADIANS and DEGREES functions are included in the ADDINFNS.XLA add-in macro sheet. To open this macro sheet, choose the Add-ins command from the Options menu, click Add, switch to the EXCEL\LIBRARY subdirectory, select ADDINFNS.XLA, and click OK.

You can convert radians to degrees using the DEGREES function. The form of this function is

DEGREES(*angle in radians*)

You can convert degrees to radians using the RADIANS function. The form of this function is

RADIANS(*angle in degrees*)

For example, the formula

=RADIANS(180)

returns 3.141593, while the formula

=DEGREES(3.141593)

returns 180.

The SIN function

The SIN function returns the sine of an angle. This function takes the form

=SIN(*angle in radians*)

For example, the formula

=SIN(1.5)

returns the value 0.997495.

The COS function

COS, the complement of SIN, calculates the cosine of an angle. This function takes the form

=COS(*angle in radians*)

For example, the formula

=COS(1.5)

returns the value 0.070737.

The TAN function

The TAN function computes the tangent of an angle. TAN has the form

=TAN(*angle in radians*)

For example, the formula

=TAN(1.5)

returns the tangent of an angle of 1.5 radians: 14.10142.

The ASIN and ACOS functions

The ASIN and ACOS functions compute the arcsine and arccosine of a value. These functions return a value that represents the radian measure of an angle. The forms of these functions are

=ASIN(*sine of angle*)

and

=ACOS(*cosine of angle*)

You can remember the purpose of these functions with the phrase "the angle whose." For example, the function

=ASIN(0)

returns the value 0, or the radian measure of "the angle whose" sine is 0. The function

=ACOS(0)

returns the value 1.570796, or the radian measure of "the angle whose" cosine is 0.

The argument for the ACOS and ASIN functions must be in the range –1 through 1. Any value outside this range results in a #NUM! error value. ASIN always returns a value between –1.57 and 1.57 radians. ACOS always returns a value between 0 and 3.14 radians.

The ATAN and ATAN2 functions

The ATAN function computes the arctangent of a tangent value. Its form is

=ATAN(*tangent of angle*)

For example, the function

=ATAN(2)

returns the measure, in radians, of the angle whose tangent is 2: 1.107149.

ATAN always returns a value between −1.57 and 1.57 radians.

ATAN2 returns the four-quadrant arctangent of the tangent described in the argument. ATAN2 requires two arguments and has the form

=ATAN2(*x-number,y-number*)

where *x-number* and *y-number* are the x-axis and y-axis coordinates of a point. The result of the function is the measure of the angle from the x-axis to the specified point. The result of ATAN2 always falls in the range −3.1416 through 3.1416. Either *x-number* or *y-number* can be 0; if both values are 0, however, the function returns the error value #DIV/0!

The SINH function

The SINH function returns the hyperbolic sine of a number. Its form is

=SINH(*number*)

For example, the function

=SINH(A1)

returns 3.62686 if cell A1 has the value 2.

The COSH function

The COSH function returns the hyperbolic cosine of a number. Its form is

=COSH(*number*)

For example, the function

=COSH(1.5)

returns 2.35241.

The TANH function

The TANH function returns the hyperbolic tangent of a number. Its form is

=TANH(*number*)

For example, the function

=TANH(1)

returns 0.761594.

The ASINH, ACOSH, and ATANH functions

The ASINH, ACOSH, and ATANH functions are the inverse of the SINH, COSH, and TANH functions. For example, the ASINH function returns (in radians) the angle whose hyperbolic sine is specified in the ASINH function's argument. Each function takes a single numeric argument.

Financial functions

Microsoft Excel's 50 financial functions let you perform common business calculations, such as net present value and future value, without building long and complex formulas.

Many of the following functions are supplied with the Analysis ToolPak add-in. If you are unable to find any of these functions, you probably need to open the Analysis ToolPak. To do so, choose the Add-ins command from the Options menu, click the Add button, switch to the EXCEL\LIBRARY\ANALYSIS subdirectory, select ANALYSF.XLA, and click OK. The Analysis ToolPak also includes a number of statistical and engineering functions, some of which are discussed in Chapter 10. (For more information about add-ins, see Chapter 21.)

Financial arguments

Most of the financial functions accept similar arguments. To streamline this section, we will define the common arguments here and explain differences in usage where appropriate. Another list accompanies the section on depreciation.

Argument	Description
future value	Value of investment at end of term
inflow 1, inflow 2, ..., inflow n	Payments when the individual amounts differ
number of periods	Term of the investment
payment	Periodic payment
type	When the payment is received; 0 = at end of period (default), 1 = at beginning of period
period	Number of individual periodic payments
present value	Value of investment today
rate	Discount rate or interest rate

The PV function

Present value is one of the most common methods for measuring the attractiveness of an investment. Simply put, the present value of an investment is today's value of a long-term investment. The present value is determined by discounting the inflows of the investment back to the present time. If the present value of the inflows is greater than the cost of the investment, the investment is a good one.

Excel's PV function computes the present value of a series of equal periodic payments or of a lump-sum payment. (A stream of constant payments is often called an ordinary annuity.) The PV function has the form

=PV(*rate,number of periods,payment,future value,type*)

where the *future value* and *type* arguments are optional. You use the optional *future value* argument in place of *payment* to compute the present value of a lump-sum payment.

Suppose you are presented with an investment opportunity that returns $1,000 a year over the next five years. To receive this annuity, you have to invest $3,000. Are you willing to pay $3,000 today to earn $5,000 over the next five years? To decide whether this investment is acceptable, you need to determine the present value of the stream of $1,000 payments you will receive.

We'll assume you can also invest your money in a money-market account at 10 percent, so we'll use 10 percent as the discount rate of the investment. (Because this discount rate is a sort of "hurdle" over which an investment must leap before it becomes attractive to you, it is often called the *hurdle rate*.)

To determine the present value of this investment, you can use the formula

=PV(10%,5,1000)

This formula returns the value –3790.79, meaning that you should be willing to spend $3,790.79 now to receive $5,000 over the next five years. Because your investment is only $3,000, you decide that this is an acceptable investment.

The future value argument

Suppose that you're offered $5,000 at the end of five years, rather than $1,000 for each of the next five years. Is the investment still as attractive? To find out, you can use the formula

=PV(10%,5,,5000)

(You must include a comma as a placeholder for the unused *payment* argument, so Excel will know that 5000 is a *future value* argument.) This formula returns the present value –3104.61, which means that, at a hurdle rate of 10 percent, you should be willing to spend $3,104.61 to receive $5,000 in five years. Although the proposal is not as attractive under these terms, it is still acceptable because your investment is only $3,000.

The type *argument*

The *type* argument lets you determine whether payments are made at the beginning or end of each period. A *type* argument of 1 means the payments are made at the beginning of each period; a *type* argument of 0 means the payments occur at the end of each period. If you don't enter a value for *type*, Excel uses the default value 0.

The NPV function

Net present value, another common formula, is used to determine the profitability of an investment. In general, any investment that yields a net present value greater than zero is considered profitable. The form of this function is

=NPV(*rate,inflow 1,inflow 2,...,inflow n*)

NPV differs from PV in one important respect. Whereas PV assumes a constant stream of inflows, NPV allows an uneven stream. Furthermore, the inflows can include as many as 29 values as arguments or any number of values if you use an array as the argument. For example, suppose you are contemplating an investment on which you expect to incur a loss of $55,000 at the end of the first year, followed by gains of $95,000, $140,000, and $185,000 at the ends of the second, third, and fourth years. You will invest $250,000 up front, and the hurdle rate is 12 percent. To evaluate this investment, you can use the formula

=NPV(12%,-55000,95000,140000,185000)-250000

The result, -6153.65, tells you not to expect a net profit from this investment. (To determine what initial cost or interest rate would justify the investment, you can use Excel's Goal Seek command, which is described in Chapter 11.)

Note that this formula does not include the up-front cost of the investment as an argument for the NPV function. You could include it, making the formula read

=NPV(12%,-250000,-55000,95000,140000,185000)

but the result would be valid only if you make the initial $250,000 payment at the end of the first year. The NPV function assumes that all payments and receipts occur at the ends of periods, rather than the beginnings.

The FV function

The FV function computes the future value of an investment. The investment can occur as a lump sum or as a stream of payments. Future value is essentially the opposite of present value. The FV function calculates the value at some future date of a constant stream of payments made over a period of time.

FV takes the form

=FV(*rate,number of periods,payment,present value,type*)

where the *present value* and *type* arguments are optional. You use *present value* instead of *payment* to compute the future value of a lump-sum investment. Suppose you're thinking about starting an IRA account. You plan to deposit $2,000 at the beginning of each year, and you expect the average rate of return on the IRA to be 11 percent per year for the entire term. Assuming you're now 30 years old, how much money will your account accumulate by the time you're 65? You can use the formula

=FV(11%,35,–2000,,1)

to learn that your IRA will accumulate $758,328.81 at the end of 35 years.

Now assume that you started an IRA account three years ago and have already accumulated $7,500 in your account. You can use the formula

=FV(11%,35,–2000,–7500,1)

to learn that your IRA will grow to $1,047,640.19 at the end of 35 years.

The *type* argument — 1 if payments occur at the beginning of the period or 0 if they occur at the end — is particularly important in financial calculations that span many years. For example, if you use the default value 0 for the *type* argument in the formula above, Excel would return the value $972,490.49 — a difference of more than $75,000!

The PMT function

The PMT function computes the periodic payment required to amortize a loan across a specified number of periods. The form of this function is

=PMT(*rate,number of periods,present value,future value,type*)

where the *future value* and *type* arguments are optional; if you omit them, Excel uses 0.

Suppose you want to take out a 25-year mortgage for $100,000. Assuming an interest rate of 11 percent, what will your monthly payments be?

First, divide the 11-percent interest rate by 12 to arrive at a monthly rate (approximately 0.92 percent). Second, convert the number of periods into months by multiplying 25 by 12 (300). Now plug the monthly rate, number of periods, and loan amount into the PMT formula

=PMT(0.92%,300,100000)

to compute the monthly mortgage payment, which turns out to be –$983. (Remember, when you make a payment, the amount is a negative number; when you receive a payment, the amount is a positive number.)

Because 0.92 percent is an approximation, you could use the formula

=PMT((11/12)%,300,100000)

for a more accurate result. This formula returns –$980.11.

The IPMT function

The IPMT function computes the interest component of the payment required to repay an amount over a specified time period, with constant periodic payments and a constant interest rate. The IPMT function has the form

=IPMT(*rate,period,number of periods,present value,future value,type*)

where *future value* and *type* arguments are optional; if you omit them, Excel assumes they are 0.

As in the previous example, suppose you borrow $100,000 for 25 years at 11 percent interest. The formula

=IPMT((11/12)%,1,300,100000)

tells you that the interest component of the payment due for the first month is –$916.67. The formula

=IPMT((11/12)%,300,300,100000)

tells you that the interest component of the final payment of the same loan is –$8.90.

The PPMT function

The PPMT function computes the principal component of the payment that is required to repay an amount over a specified time period, with constant periodic payments and a constant interest rate. If you compute both IPMT and PPMT for the same period, you can add the results to obtain the total payment.

The PPMT function has the form

=PPMT(*rate,period,number of periods,present value,future value,type*)

where the *future value* and *type* arguments are optional; if you omit them, Excel assumes they are 0.

Again suppose you borrow $100,000 for 25 years at 11 percent interest. The formula

=PPMT((11/12)%,1,300,100000)

tells you that the principal component of the payment for the first month of the loan is –$63.45. The formula

=PPMT((11/12)%,300,300,100000)

tells you that the principal component of the final payment of the same loan is –$971.21.

The NPER function

NPER computes the number of periods required to amortize a loan, given a specified periodic payment. The form of this function is

=NPER(*rate,payment,present value,future value,type*)

where the *future value* and *type* arguments are optional; if you omit them, Excel assumes they are 0.

Suppose you can afford mortgage payments of $1,200 per month and you want to know how long it will take to pay off the $100,000 loan at 11 percent interest. The formula

=NPER((11/12)%,−1200,100000)

tells you that your mortgage payments will extend over 158.19 months.

If the payment argument is too small to amortize the loan at the indicated rate of interest, the function returns an error value. The monthly payment must always at least equal the period interest rate times the principal amount; otherwise the loan will never be amortized. For example, the formula

=NPER((11/12)%,−750,100000)

returns the error value #NUM! In this case, the monthly payment must be at least $916.67, or $100,000 times (11/12)%.

Functions for calculating the rate of return

The RATE, IRR, XIRR, and MIRR functions compute the continuously paid rates of return on investments. RATE computes the rate of return on an investment that generates constant periodic payments, IRR computes the internal rate of return on investments that have fluctuating payments, and MIRR computes the modified internal rate of return.

The RATE function

RATE lets you determine the rate of return of an investment that generates a series of equal periodic payments or a single lump-sum payment. The RATE function has the form

=RATE(*number of periods,payment,present value,future value,type,guess*)

The *future value, type,* and *guess* arguments are optional. You can use *future value* in place of *payment* to compute the rate of a lump-sum payment. The *guess* argument gives Excel a starting place for calculating the rate. If you omit the *future value* and *type* arguments, Excel assumes they are 0.

Suppose you're considering an investment that will pay you five annual $1,000 payments. The investment costs $3,000. To determine the actual annual rate of return on your investment, you can use the formula

=RATE(5,1000,−3000)

This formula returns 0.1986 (19.86 percent), the rate of return on this investment.

The RATE function uses an iterative process to compute the rate of return. The function begins by computing the net present value of the investment at the *guess* rate. If that first net present value is greater than zero, the function selects a higher rate and repeats the net present value calculation; if the first net present value is less than zero, a lower rate is selected for the second iteration. RATE continues this process until it arrives at the correct rate of return or until it has gone through 20 iterations.

If you omit the *guess* argument, Excel begins with a guess of 0.1 (10 percent). If you receive the error value #NUM! when you enter the RATE function, the program is probably trying to tell you that it could not calculate the rate within 20 iterations. If this occurs, try entering a different *guess* rate to give the function a running start. A rate between 10 percent and 100 percent usually works.

The IRR function

The internal rate of return of an investment is the rate that causes the net present value of the investment to equal zero. In other words, the internal rate of return is the rate that causes the present value of the inflows from an investment to exactly equal the cost of the investment.

Internal rate of return, like net present value, is used to compare one investment opportunity with another. An attractive investment is one whose net present value, discounted at the appropriate hurdle rate, is greater than zero. Turn that equation around and you can see that the discount rate required to generate a net present value of zero must be greater than the hurdle rate. Thus, an attractive investment is one where the discount rate required to yield a net present value of zero — that is, the internal rate of return — is greater than the hurdle rate.

Excel's IRR function is closely related to the RATE function. The difference between RATE and IRR is similar to the difference between the PV and NPV functions. Like NPV, IRR accounts for investment costs and unequal payments.

The form of the IRR function is

=IRR(*values,guess*)

where *values* is an array or a reference to a range of cells that contains numbers. You must include at least one positive and one negative value in the *values* array or range. IRR ignores blanks, logical values, and text. IRR assumes that transactions occur at the end of a period and returns the equivalent interest rate for that period's length.

Suppose you agree to pay $120,000 to buy a condominium. Over the next five years, you expect to receive $25,000; $27,000; $35,000; $38,000; and $40,000 in net rental income. You can set up a simple worksheet that contains your investment and income information. Enter these six values into cells A1:A6 of the worksheet (making sure to enter the initial $120,000 investment as a negative value). Then you can use the formula

=IRR(A1:A6)

to compute the internal rate of return of 10.63 percent. If the hurdle rate is 10 percent, this condominium purchase can be considered a good investment.

As with RATE, the *guess* argument is optional. If you receive a #NUM! error value when you enter an IRR function, you can include a *guess* argument in the function to help Excel reach the answer.

The MIRR function

The MIRR function is similar to IRR in that it also calculates the rate of return of an investment. The difference is that MIRR takes into account the cost of the money you borrow to finance the investment and the fact that you will probably reinvest the cash generated by it. MIRR assumes that transactions occur at the end of a period and returns the equivalent interest rate for that period's length.

MIRR takes the form

=MIRR(*values,cost of funds,reinvestment*)

The *values* argument must be either an array or a reference to a range of cells that contains numbers. You must include at least one positive and one negative value in the *values* array or range. The *cost of funds* argument is the rate at which you borrow the money you need to make the investment. The *reinvestment* argument is the rate at which you invest the cash flow.

To continue with the previous example, you can use the formula

=MIRR(A1:A6,10%,12%)

to calculate a modified internal rate of return of 11.17 percent, assuming a cost of funds rate of 10 percent and a reinvestment rate of 12 percent.

Functions for calculating depreciation

Excel has five functions to help you determine the depreciation of an asset for a specific period. The following table lists the commonly used arguments for these functions.

Argument	Description
cost	Initial cost of asset
life	Length of time asset will be depreciated
salvage	Asset value at end of *life*
period	Individual time period to be computed

The SLN function

SLN lets you determine the straight-line depreciation for an asset for a single period. The straight-line depreciation method assumes that depreciation is uniform throughout the useful life of the asset. The cost or basis of the asset, less its estimated salvage value, is deductible in equal amounts over the life of the asset. The SLN function has the form

=SLN(*cost,salvage,life*)

Suppose you want to depreciate a machine that costs $8,000 new and has a lifetime of 10 years and a salvage value of $500. The formula

=SLN(8000,500,10)

tells you that the straight-line depreciation would be $750 each year.

The DDB and DB functions

DDB computes an asset's depreciation with the double-declining balance method, which returns depreciation at an accelerated rate — more in the early periods and less later. Using this method, depreciation is computed as a percentage of the net book value of the asset (the cost of the asset less any prior years' depreciation).

The first three arguments for the DDB function are the same as the arguments for SLN. However, because the double-declining depreciation method produces a different depreciation expense for each period during the life of the asset, DDB requires an extra argument. The function has the form

=DDB(*cost,salvage,life,period,factor*)

where all DDB arguments must be positive numbers and you must use the same time units for *life* and *period;* that is, if you express *life* in months, *period* must also be in months. The *factor* argument is optional, with a default value of 2, which indicates the normal double-declining balance method. Using 3 for factor would indicate the triple-declining balance method.

Suppose you want to depreciate a machine that costs $5,000 new and has a lifetime of five years (60 months) and a salvage value of $100. The formula

=DDB(5000,100,60,1)

tells you that the double-declining balance depreciation for the first month would be $166.67. The formula

=DDB(5000,100,5,1)

tells you that the double-declining balance depreciation for the first year would be $2,000.00. The formula

=DDB(5000,100,5,5)

tells you that the double-declining balance depreciation for the last year would be $259.20.

The DB function adheres to the same rules used for the DDB function, except that it uses the fixed-declining balance method, and lets you calculate the depreciation when the asset is not owned for a full 12 months during the first year. The form of this function is

=DB(*cost,salvage,life,period,month*)

where *month* is the number of months in the first year. If omitted, Excel assumes *month* to be 12, indicating the depreciation for the entire year. For example, to calculate the first six months of depreciation on a $5,000 item with a salvage value of $100 and a life of five years, use the formula

=DB(5000,100,5,1,6)

which returns a six-month depreciation total of $1,358.

The VDB function

VDB computes the depreciation of an asset for any complete or partial period, using either the double-declining balance or another accelerated-depreciation factor that you specify. The function's form is

=VDB(*cost,salvage,life,start,end,factor,no_switch*)

where *start* is the period prior to the starting period, and *end* is the ending period. *Start* and *end* let you determine the depreciation for any period during the life of the asset.

The last two arguments are optional. If you don't specify *factor*, Excel assumes that argument is 2 and uses the double-declining balance method. If you omit *no_switch*, Excel automatically switches to straight-line depreciation when the straight-line method produces a larger depreciation than the factor you specify. To prevent Excel from making this switch, specify a *no_switch* value of 1 (TRUE).

Assume you have purchased a $15,000 asset at the end of the first quarter of the current year and that this asset will have a salvage value of $2,000 after five years. To determine the depreciation of this asset next year (the fourth to seventh quarters of its use), you can use the following formula:

=VDB(15000,2000,20,3,7)

This formula does not include a *factor* argument, so Excel calculates the depreciation using the double-declining balance method. To determine the depreciation for the same period using a factor of 1.5, you write the formula

=VDB(15000,2000,20,3,7,1.5)

The SYD function

SYD computes an asset's depreciation for a specific time period with the sum-of-the-years'-digits method. Using the sum-of-the-years'-digits method, depreciation is calculated on the cost of the item less its salvage value. Like the double-declining balance method, the sum-of-the-years'-digits method is an accelerated depreciation method. The SYD function has the form

=SYD(*cost,salvage,life,period*)

As with DDB, you must use the same time units for life and period.

Suppose you want to depreciate a machine that costs $15,000 and has a lifetime of three years and a salvage value of $1,250. The formula

=SYD(15000,1250,3,1)

tells you that the sum-of-the-years'-digits depreciation for the first year would be $6,875. The formula

=SYD(15000,1250,3,3)

tells you that the sum-of-the-years'-digits depreciation for the third year would be $2,291.67.

Text functions

Microsoft Excel's text functions convert numeric text entries into numbers, number entries into text strings, and let you manipulate the text strings themselves.

The VALUE function

If you enter numbers in your worksheet in text format (enclosed in quotation marks), you can use the VALUE function to convert that text into a numeric value. The VALUE function has the form

=VALUE(*text*)

The *text* argument can be a literal string enclosed in quotation marks or a reference to a cell that contains text. The text string to be converted can be in any recognized format, including user-created custom formats. (See Chapter 4 for more information on Excel's formats.)

For example, the formula

=VALUE("40205")

returns the numeric value 40205. If cell A10 contains the text entry "40205", the formula

=VALUE(A10)

also returns the number 40205.

VALUE can convert text entries in the form of dates into numeric date values. For example, the formula

=VALUE("1/1/87")

returns the serial date value 31778. (Excel's handling of dates is discussed in Chapter 9.)

Because Excel converts numeric text into numbers for calculations, you generally don't have to use VALUE before using a number entered as text in a formula.

The TEXT function

The TEXT function converts a number into a text string with a specified format. TEXT has the form

=TEXT(*number,format*)

The *number* argument can be a number, a formula, or a cell reference. The *format* argument designates how the resulting string is displayed. You can use any of Excel's formatting symbols ($, #, 0, and so on) except the asterisk to specify the format you want; you cannot use the General format. For example, the formula

=TEXT(98/4,"0.00")

returns the text string 24.50.

The DOLLAR function

Like the TEXT function, the DOLLAR function converts a number into a string. However, DOLLAR formats the resulting string as currency with the number of decimal places you specify. The DOLLAR function has the form

=DOLLAR(*number,number of decimals*)

For example, the formula

=DOLLAR(45.899,2)

returns the text string $45.90, and the formula

=DOLLAR(45.899,0)

returns the text string $46. Notice that Excel rounds the number when necessary. If you omit a *number of decimals* argument for the DOLLAR function, Excel uses two decimal places. If you use a negative number for the *number of decimals* argument, Excel rounds to the left of the decimal point.

The FIXED function

The FIXED function rounds a number to the specified number of decimal places and displays the result as text. The form of this function is

=FIXED(*number,number of decimals*)

For example, the formula

=FIXED(98.786,2)

returns the text string 98.79.

If you don't include a *number of decimals* argument for the FIXED function, Excel uses two decimal places. If you use a negative number for *number of decimals,* Excel rounds to the left of the decimal point. For example, the formula

=FIXED(98.786,−1)

returns the text string 100.

The REPT function

The REPT function lets you create a string made up of one or more characters repeated a specified number of times. The form of REPT is

=REPT(*text,repeat number*)

The *text* argument specifies the text string to be repeated. This argument must be enclosed in quotation marks. The *repeat number* argument specifies how many times to repeat the text string and can be any integer from 0 through 255. If you enter 0 for the *repeat number* argument, REPT leaves the cell blank; if *repeat number* is not an integer, REPT ignores the decimal portion of the number.

Suppose you want to create a row of asterisks 150 characters wide. Enter the formula

=REPT("*",150)

The result is a string of 150 asterisks.

The *text* argument can be more than one character. For example, the formula

=REPT("-*",75)

results in a row of asterisks and hyphens 150 characters long. The *repeat number* argument specifies the number of times you want the *text* argument to be repeated, not the total number of characters you want to create. If the text string is two characters long, the length of the resulting label is twice the *repeat number* argument.

The LEN function

The LEN function returns the number of characters in an entry. The form of the function is

=LEN(*text*)

The text argument can be a literal number, a literal string in quotes, or a reference to a cell. For example, the formula

=LEN("Test")

returns 4. If cell A1 contains the label *Test*, then the formula

=LEN(A1)

also returns 4.

The LEN function returns the length of the displayed text or value, not the length of the underlying cell contents. For example, if cell A10 contains the formula

=A1+A2+A3+A4+A5+A6+A7+A8

the result of this formula is 25. The formula

=LEN(A10)

returns 2, the length of the result of the formula at A10.

The cell referred to by the argument of the LEN function can be a cell that contains another string function. For example, if cell A1 contains the REPT function

=REPT("-*",75)

the formula

=LEN(A1)

returns the value 150.

The MID function

You can use the MID function to extract a series of characters (a substring) from a text string. The form of the function is

=MID(*text,starting position,number of characters*)

where *text* is the string from which you want to extract the substring, *starting position* is the place in the string where the substring begins (relative to the left end of the string), and *number of characters* is the number of characters you want to extract. The *text* argument can be a literal string enclosed in quotation marks, but it is usually a reference to a cell that contains text.

For example, suppose cell A1 contains the label *This is a long label entry*. You can use the formula

=MID(A1,11,10)

to extract the characters *long label* from the entry in cell A1.

The ASCII functions: CHAR and CODE

Every computer uses numeric codes to represent characters. The most prevalent system of numeric codes is called ASCII, or American Standard Code for Information Interchange. ASCII uses a code of one to three digits to represent each number, letter, and symbol.

The CHAR and CODE functions deal with these ASCII codes. The CHAR function returns the ASCII character that corresponds to a code number, and the CODE function returns the ASCII code number for the first character specified. The forms of these two functions are

   =CHAR(*number*)

and

   =CODE(*text*)

For example, the formula

   =CHAR(83)

returns *S*, and the formula

   =CODE("S")

returns 83.

The removal functions: TRIM and CLEAN

Excel offers two removal functions: the TRIM function, which eliminates leading, trailing, and extra blank characters from a string, leaving only a single space between words; and the CLEAN function, which eliminates all nonprintable characters from a string.

Often leading and trailing blank characters prevent you from correctly sorting entries in your worksheet or database. Also, if you use string functions to manipulate labels in your worksheet, these extra spaces can prevent your formulas from working correctly. The TRIM function, which has the form

   =TRIM(*text*)

removes all spaces in text except for one space between words. For example, if cell A1 of your worksheet contains the string *Fuzzy   Wuzzy   was   a   bear*, the formula

   =TRIM(A1)

returns *Fuzzy Wuzzy was a bear.*

The CLEAN function is similar to TRIM, except that it operates only on nonprintable characters. CLEAN is especially useful if you import data from another program and some entries contain nonprintable characters, such as tab markers and other program-specific codes. (These characters are displayed in your worksheet as bold vertical bars or small boxes.) You can use CLEAN to remove these characters from your text. The CLEAN function has the form

=CLEAN(*text*)

The REPLACE function

The REPLACE function replaces one string of characters with another string of characters. The REPLACE function has the form

=REPLACE(*old text,start num,num chars,new text*)

The *old text* argument is the text string in which you want to replace some characters. The next two arguments, *start num* and *num chars,* indicate which characters you want to replace (relative to the left end of the string). The *new text* argument is the text string you want to insert. The *old text* and *new text* arguments must be literal strings surrounded by quotation marks, or formulas or references that result in strings. If the new text makes the label longer than 255 characters, REPLACE returns an #N/A! error value.

Suppose cell A3 in your worksheet contains the label *Millie Potter, Psychic.* You want to place this label in cell A6, replacing the first six characters with the string *Mildred.* To do this, use the formula

=REPLACE(A3,1,6,"Mildred")

The new label is *Mildred Potter, Psychic.* Note that the label in A3 remains unchanged — the new label is displayed only in cell A6, where you entered the formula.

The SUBSTITUTE function

The SUBSTITUTE function substitutes new text for old text, just as REPLACE does. However, with SUBSTITUTE you don't specify the start number and number of characters to replace. Instead, you specify the exact text you want replaced.

The SUBSTITUTE function takes the form

=SUBSTITUTE(*text,old text,new text,instance number*)

For example, if cell A4 in your worksheet contains the label *candy* and you want to place it in cell D6 and change it to *dandy,* use the formula

=SUBSTITUTE(A4,"c","d")

When you enter this formula in cell D6, the label in cell A4 doesn't change — the new label is displayed only in cell D6.

The *instance number* argument is optional. It tells Excel to replace only the specified occurrence of *old text*. For example, suppose cell A1 contains the label *through the hoop* and you want to create a similar label that substitutes the word *loop* for *hoop*. You can do this with the formula

=SUBSTITUTE(A1,"h","l",4)

In this formula, the 4 tells Excel to substitute an *l* for the fourth *h* in the label in cell A1. If you don't include *instance number*, Excel changes all occurrences of *old text* to *new text*.

The EXACT function

The EXACT function lets you determine whether two strings match exactly, including uppercase and lowercase letters. The EXACT function takes the form

=EXACT(*text1*,*text2*)

If *text1* and *text2* are identical, including capitalization, EXACT returns TRUE; if *text1* and *text2* are not identical, EXACT returns FALSE. Thus, EXACT is a conditional-testing function that operates on strings. The *text1* and *text2* arguments must be either literal strings enclosed in quotation marks or references to cells that contain text.

For example, if cell A5 and cell A6 of your worksheet both contain the label *Totals*, the formula

=EXACT(A5,A6)

returns a TRUE value.

If you want to compare two strings for which differences in capitalization don't matter, use the equal sign (=) as described in "Conditional tests," later in this chapter.

The substring functions

Excel provides four functions to locate and report portions of a text string: FIND, SEARCH, RIGHT, and LEFT.

The FIND and SEARCH functions

The FIND and SEARCH functions let you locate the position of a substring within a string. Both functions return the number of the character where Excel first finds the text. (Excel counts blank spaces and punctuation marks as characters.)

These two functions work the same way, except that FIND is case-sensitive and SEARCH allows wildcards. The functions follow the forms

=FIND(*find text,within text,start at num*)

and

=SEARCH(*find text,within text,start at num*)

The *find text* argument identifies the text sought and the *within text* argument indicates where to look for it. You can use either literal text enclosed in quotation marks or a cell reference for either of these arguments. The optional *start at num* argument specifies the character position in *within text* where you want to begin your search. This argument is helpful when there is more than one occurrence of *find text* in *within text*. If you omit *start at num*, Excel reports the first match located.

You get a #VALUE! error if *find text* isn't contained in *within text*, if *start at num* isn't greater than zero, or if *start at num* is greater than the number of characters in *within text* or greater than the position of the last occurrence of *find text*.

To locate the *p* in the string *A Night at the Opera*, use the formula

=FIND("p","A Night at the Opera")

This formula returns 17, because the *p* is the seventeenth character in the string.

If you're not sure of the character sequence you're searching for, you can use the SEARCH function and include wildcards in your *find text* string. To search for a single character that occupies a specific position, use a question-mark character (?); to search for any sequence of characters that occupies a specific position, use an asterisk (*). (We discuss wildcards further in Chapters 5 and 17.)

Suppose you've used the names *Smith* and *Smyth* in your worksheet. To ensure that either name is found when cell A1 is checked, use the formula

=SEARCH("Sm?th",A1)

If cell A1 contains the name *John Smith* or the name *John Smyth*, the SEARCH function returns the value 6 — the starting point for the string *Sm?th*. If you're not sure of the number of characters, use the * wildcard. For example, to find the position of the name *Allan* or *Alan* in cell A1, use the formula

=SEARCH("A*an",A1)

The RIGHT and LEFT functions

The RIGHT function returns the rightmost series of characters from a string argument; the LEFT function returns the leftmost series of characters from a string argument. These functions have the forms

=RIGHT(*text,number of characters*)

and

=LEFT(*text,number of characters*)

The *number of characters* argument indicates the number of characters to extract from the *text* argument. These functions count blank spaces in the *text* argument as characters; if there are leading or trailing characters, you might want to use a TRIM function within the RIGHT or LEFT functions to ensure the expected result.

The *number of characters* argument must be greater than zero. If you omit *number of characters*, Excel assumes it is 1. If *number of characters* is greater than the number of characters in *text*, RIGHT and LEFT return the entire *text* argument.

Suppose you enter the label *This is a test* in cell A1 of your worksheet. The formula

=RIGHT(A1,4)

returns the label *test*.

The case functions: UPPER, LOWER, and PROPER

Excel provides three functions for manipulating case in text strings. The UPPER and LOWER functions convert a text string to all uppercase and all lowercase letters. The PROPER function lets you capitalize the first letter in each word of a text string and any other letters in the text that do not follow another letter; all other letters are converted to lowercase. These functions take these forms:

=UPPER(*text*)

=LOWER(*text*)

=PROPER(*text*)

Suppose you enter a series of names in your worksheet and you want all these entries to appear in capital letters. Cell A1 might contain the label *john Johnson*. You can use the formula

=UPPER(A1)

to return *JOHN JOHNSON*. Similarly, the formulas

=LOWER(A1)

and

=PROPER(A1)

return the labels *john johnson* and *John Johnson*.

Logical functions

Microsoft Excel has a rich set of logical functions, including some that are available when you load the Analysis ToolPak add-in. Most logical functions use conditional tests to determine whether a specified condition is true or false.

Conditional tests

A conditional test is an equation that compares two numbers, functions, formulas, or labels. For example, each of these formulas is a conditional test:

=A1>A2

=5–35>5*2

=AVERAGE(B1:B6)=SUM(6,7,8)

=C2="Female"

=COUNT(A1:A10)=COUNT(B1:B10)

=LEN(A1)<10

Every conditional test must include at least one logical operator. Logical operators define the test relationship between elements of the conditional test. For example, in the conditional test A1>A2, the greater-than symbol (>) is the logical operator used to compare the test values stored in cells A1 and A2. Excel offers these six logical operators:

Operator	Definition
=	Equal to
>	Greater than
<	Less than
>=	Greater than or equal to
<=	Less than or equal to
<>	Not equal to

Every conditional test must be either true or false. For example, the conditional test

=Z1=10

is true if the value in Z1 is equal to 10 and false if Z1 contains any other value.

The IF function

The conditional function IF has the form

=IF(*conditional test, true value, false value*)

This function can be read: *If the conditional test is true, then return the true value; otherwise, return the false value.*

For example, the formula

=IF(Z100<22, 5,10)

returns 5 if the value in cell Z100 is less than 22; otherwise, it returns 10.

You can use other functions as the arguments within an IF function. For example, the formula

=IF(SUM(A1:A10)>0,SUM(A1:A10),0)

returns the result of SUM(A1:A10) if SUM(A1:A10) is greater than 0; otherwise, the function returns the value 0.

Using text in IF

You can also use arguments in IF functions. For example, the worksheet in Figure 8-10 lists exam scores for a group of students. The formula

=IF(E4>80%,"Pass","Fail")

entered in cell G4 tells Excel to use the average of the test scores contained in cell E4. If the average is greater than 80%, the function returns the true value *Pass;* if the average is less than or equal to 80%, the function returns the false value *Fail.*

FIGURE 8-10.
You can use the IF function to return a text string.

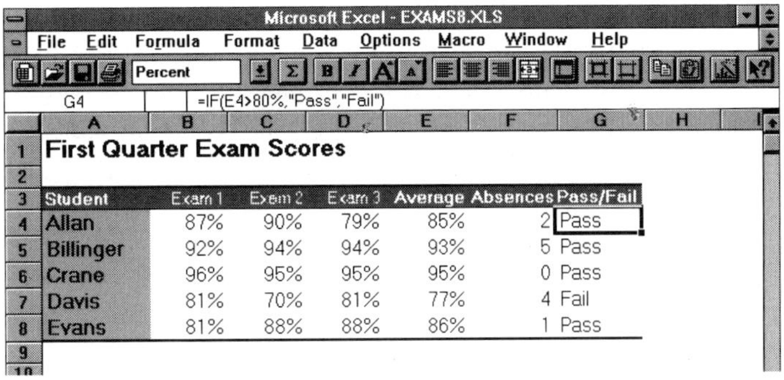
Microsoft Excel - EXAMS8.XLS
File Edit Formula Format Data Options Macro Window Help
Percent
G4
=IF(E4>80%,"Pass","Fail")
First Quarter Exam Scores
Student Exam 1 Exam 2 Exam 3 Average Absences Pass/Fail
Allan 87% 90% 79% 85% 2 Pass
Billinger 92% 94% 94% 93% 5 Pass
Crane 96% 95% 95% 95% 0 Pass
Davis 81% 70% 81% 77% 4 Fail
Evans 81% 88% 88% 86% 1 Pass

You can take advantage of Excel's ability to use text arguments in IF functions to return nothing, instead of a 0, if the result of a test is false. For example, the formula

=IF(SUM(A1:A10)>0,SUM(A1:A10),"")

returns nothing if the conditional test is false.

The *conditional test* argument of an IF function can also consist of text. For example, the formula

=IF(A1="Test",100,200)

returns the value 100 if cell A1 contains the text *Test* and 200 if it contains any other entry. The match between the two text entries must be exact in all respects except capitalization.

You must always enclose text strings in quotation marks when you use them in the IF function (or in any other function, for that matter). If you neglect to enclose the strings in quotation marks, Excel assumes they are range names.

The TRUE and FALSE functions

The TRUE and FALSE functions offer alternative ways to represent the logical conditions TRUE and FALSE. Neither of these accepts arguments; these functions take the forms

=TRUE()

and

=FALSE()

For example, suppose cell B5 contains a logical test formula. If you enter the formula

=IF(B5=FALSE(),"Warning!","OK")

in another cell, the new formula returns *Warning!* if the result of the logical formula in B5 is FALSE or *OK* if the result of B5 is TRUE.

Complex operators

Excel offers three additional functions that let you develop compound conditional tests: AND, OR, and NOT. These functions work in conjunction with the simple logical operators =, >,< , >=,<= and<>. AND and OR can take up to 30 logical arguments each, in the forms

=AND(*logical 1,logical 2,...,logical 30*)

and

=OR(*logical 1,logical 2,...,logical 30*)

NOT takes only one argument, in the form

=NOT(*logical*)

Arguments for AND, OR, and NOT can be conditional tests or they can be arrays or references to cells that contain logical values.

To illustrate the power of these operators, let's expand on the formula in Figure 8-10. Suppose you want Excel to return the text string *PASS* only if the student has an average score above 80 and fewer than five unexcused absences. You can accomplish this with the formula

=IF(AND(E4>80%,F4<5),"PASS","FAIL")

Although the OR function takes the same arguments as AND, the results are radically different. For example, if you enter the formula

=IF(OR(E4>80%,F4<5),"PASS","FAIL")

you're instructing Excel to return *PASS* if the student's average test score is greater than 80 *or* if the student has fewer than five absences. In other words, OR returns the true value if any *one* of the conditional tests is true, but AND returns the true value only if *all* the conditional tests are true.

The NOT function is used to negate a condition. NOT instructs Excel to return *true value* if the argument is false and *false value* if the argument is true. NOT might be better described as the "unless" function. For example, the formula

=IF(NOT(A1=2),"Go","NoGo")

tells Excel to return the text string *Go* "unless" the value of cell A1 is 2.

The ISBLANK function

You can use the ISBLANK function to determine whether a referenced cell is blank. ISBLANK has the form

=ISBLANK(*value*)

where *value* is a reference to a cell or range. If *value* refers to a blank cell or range, the function returns the value TRUE; otherwise, it returns FALSE.

Trapping errors: ISERR, ISERROR, and ISNA

If a formula in your worksheet refers to a cell that returns an error, that formula also returns an error. For example, if cell A1 returns an error, the formula

=A1/10

also returns an error. The same thing happens if the formula refers to a cell that returns an #N/A error value.

Three specialized logical functions ISERR, ISERROR, and ISNA let you test the value of an argument or cell to determine whether it contains either an error value or the value #N/A. ISERR tests for all error values except #N/A; ISERROR tests for all error values, including #N/A; and ISNA tests for #N/A values only. These functions let you selectively "trap" errors and #N/A values, preventing them from filtering through the worksheet. These functions take the forms

=ISERR(*value*)

and

=ISERROR(*value*)

and

=ISNA(*value*)

Although *value* can be a number, a formula, or literal text, it is usually a reference to a cell or range. Only one cell within a range need contain an applicable error for the function to return a TRUE value.

Typically, ISERR, ISERROR, and ISNA are used as conditional tests in IF functions. For example, the formula

=IF(ISERROR(A1/A2),0,A1/A2)

tests the formula A1/A2. If A1/A2 returns an error (as it will if A2 is blank or contains the value 0), then the ISERROR function is true and the IF function returns the value 0. If A1/A2 does not return an error, the function returns the result of A1/A2. Similarly, the formula

=IF(ISNA(A1),0,A1*10)

tests the value in cell A1. If that value is #N/A, the IF function returns 0; otherwise, it returns the product of A1 times 10.

The ERROR.TYPE function

An alternative to the ISERR, ISERROR, or ISNA functions is the ERROR.TYPE function, which is actually a macro function, but can also be used on worksheets. The ERROR.TYPE function can be more useful, because instead of trapping specific errors, it traps any error and returns a code value that indicates the type of error detected. ERROR.TYPE can also be used in an IF formula to detect a specific error type. This function has the form

=ERROR.TYPE(*error value*)

where *error value* corresponds to one of the following codes:

Error value	Code
#NULL!	1
#DIV/0!	2
#VALUE!	3
#REF!	4
#NAME?	5
#NUM!	6
#N/A	7
Anything else	#N/A

For example, you can construct a formula that checks cell A5 for any error value, and returns the code associated with that particular error value. If cell A5 contains the #REF! error, the formula

=ERROR.TYPE(A5)

returns the code 4.

The ISREF function

The ISREF function works like ISERROR and ISNA, except that ISREF tests to see what kind of entry the cell contains.

ISREF takes the form

=ISREF(*value*)

It returns the logical value TRUE if the *value* argument is a cell reference; argument is any other kind of entry, it returns the value FALSE.

ISREF is generally used in macros.

The ISNUMBER function

You use the ISNUMBER function to determine whether an entry is a number. ISNUMBER takes the form

=ISNUMBER(*value*)

Suppose you want to know if the entry in cell A5 is a number. The formula

=ISNUMBER(A5)

returns TRUE if cell A5 contains a number or a formula that results in a number; otherwise, it returns FALSE.

The ISTEXT and ISNONTEXT functions

The ISTEXT and ISNONTEXT functions let you test whether an entry is text. These functions take the forms

=ISTEXT(*value*)

and

=ISNONTEXT(*value*)

Suppose you want to determine whether or not the entry in cell C35 is text. If you use the formula

=ISTEXT(C35)

and the entry in C35 is text or a formula that returns text, Excel returns TRUE. If you test the same cell using the formula

=ISNONTEXT(C35)

Excel returns FALSE.

The ISLOGICAL function

You can use the ISLOGICAL function to determine whether a cell contains a logical value. ISLOGICAL follows the form

=ISLOGICAL(*value*)

If the cell contains a logical value, Excel returns TRUE; otherwise, it returns FALSE.

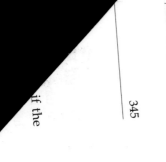

345

if the

a logical problem even with complex operators like
e cases, Excel lets you nest IF functions to create a
e, the formula

ND(A1<100,A1>=80),"Usually",
)),"Sometimes","Who cares?")))

. The formula can be read: *If the value in cell A1 equals
rs; otherwise, if the value in cell A1 falls between 80 and
...., oo ...rough 99), return the text string* Usually; *otherwise, if the value in cell
A1 falls between 60 and 80 (60 through 79), return the text string* Sometimes; *and, finally,
if none of these conditions is true, return the text string* Who cares?

You can string together as many as seven nested IF arguments, as long as you
don't exceed the 1024-character limit on single-cell entries.

Other uses for conditional functions

All of the conditional functions described here can be used as stand-alone formulas
in your worksheet. Although you usually use functions like AND, OR, NOT,
ISERROR, ISNA, and ISREF within an IF function, you can also use formulas like

=AND(A1>A2,A2<A3)

to perform simple conditional tests. This formula returns the value TRUE if the value
in A1 is greater than the value in A2 and the value in A2 is less than the value in A3.
You might use this type of formula to assign TRUE and FALSE values to a range of
numeric database cells, and then use the TRUE and FALSE conditions as selection
criteria for printing a specialized report.

Lookup functions

The logical functions we just discussed return one of two values based upon a test.
There are times, however, when you need more flexibility. Microsoft Excel offers
several functions that let you "look up" information stored in a list or a table.

The CHOOSE function

The CHOOSE function lets you retrieve items from a list of values, labels, or cell
references in a cell by using an index number. CHOOSE has the form

=CHOOSE(*index,value 1,value 2,...value n*)

where *index* is the number of the item that you want to look up and *value 1, value 2,*
and so on are the elements of the list. The *index* value must always be positive and

cannot exceed the number of elements in the list. If you use an index value less than 1 or greater than the number of values in the list, Excel returns a #VALUE! error.

The CHOOSE function returns the value of the element of the list that occupies the position indicated by *index*. For example, the function

=CHOOSE(2,6,1,8,9,3)

returns the value 1, because 1 is the second item in the list. (The *index* value itself is not part of the list.)

The arguments of CHOOSE can be cell references. If you use a cell reference for *index*, Excel selects an item from the list according to the value stored in that cell. Suppose cell A11 contains the formula

=CHOOSE(A10,0.15,0.22,0.21,0.21,0.26)

If cell A10 contains the value 5, the CHOOSE function returns the value 0.26; if cell A10 contains the value 1, the function returns the value 0.15. Similarly, if cell C1 contains the value 0.15, C2 the value 0.22, and C3, C4, and C5 the value 0.21, then the formula

=CHOOSE(A10,C1,C2,C3,C4,C5)

returns 0.15 if cell A10 contains the value 1 and returns 0.21 if cell A10 contains the value 3, 4, or 5.

The list of values cannot be a range. You might be tempted to create a function like

=CHOOSE(A10,C1:C5)

to take the place of the longer function in the previous example. If you do, however, all you will get back is a #VALUE! error.

The elements in the list can be text strings. For example, the function

=CHOOSE(3,"First","Second","Third")

selects the third item from the list and returns the text string *Third*.

The MATCH function

The MATCH function is closely related to the CHOOSE function. However, where CHOOSE returns the item that occupies the position in a list specified by the *index* argument, MATCH returns the position of the item in the list that most closely matches a lookup value. The form of this function is

=MATCH(*lookup value,lookup range,type*)

where *lookup value* is the value or string to look up and *lookup range* is the range that contains the values with which to compare *lookup value*. The *lookup value* argument can be a value, a cell reference, or text enclosed in quotation marks; *lookup range* must be a reference to a range or a range name.

Consider the worksheet in Figure 8-11. If you enter the formula

=MATCH(10,A1:D1,0)

in cell E1, the result is 1, because the cell in the first position of the *lookup range* argument contains a value that matches *lookup value.*

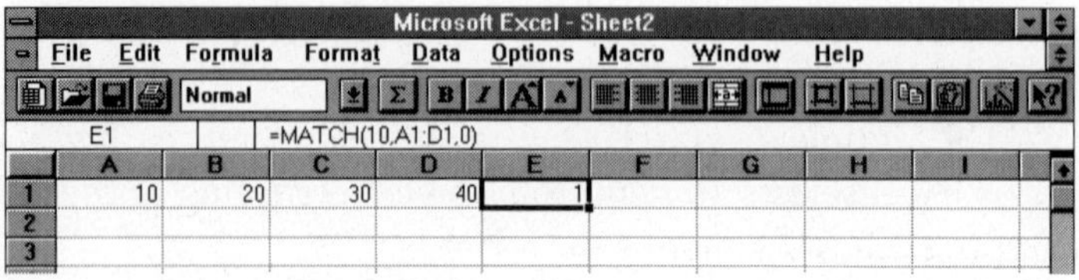

FIGURE 8-11.
*The MATCH
function locates the
position of a value
in a list.*

The *type* argument defines the rules for the search. This optional argument must be 1, 0, or –1. If the *type* argument is 1 or is omitted altogether, the MATCH function looks for the largest value in the range that is less than or equal to *lookup value.* For example, in the worksheet shown in Figure 8-11, the formula

=MATCH(19,A1:D1,1)

would return the value 1, because 10, the first item in the range, is the largest value in the range that doesn't exceed *lookup value,* 19. If no items in the range are less than or equal to *lookup value,* the function returns the error value #N/A.

If *type* is 0, the MATCH function looks for an exact match between *lookup value* and the values in the range. If no items in the range exactly match *lookup value,* the function returns the error value #N/A. In addition, the lookup range need not be sorted if the *type* argument is 0.

If *type* is 0 and *lookup value* is text, you can use the wildcards * and ? in the *lookup value* argument.

If *type* is 1, the elements in *lookup range* must be sorted in ascending order for the function to work properly. If you rearrange the items in the range A1:D1 to look like Figure 8-12, the formula

=MATCH(20,A1:D1,1)

returns the value 1, instead of the value you probably expected: 4.

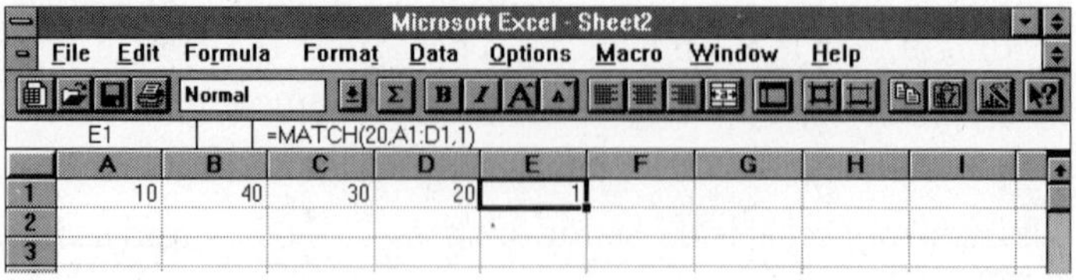

FIGURE 8-12.
*MATCH does not
work properly with a
type argument of 1 if
the lookup range is
not in ascending order.*

If *type* is –1, MATCH looks for the smallest value in the range that is greater than or equal to *lookup value*. When type is –1, the items in the list must be in descending order. If no items in the range are greater than or equal to *lookup value*, the function returns the error value #N/A.

Lookup value and the items in the range can also be text strings. For example, if cells A1:D1 contain the text entries shown in Figure 8-13, the formula

=MATCH("Twenty",A1:D1,0)

returns the value 2. When you use MATCH to locate text strings, you usually specify a *type* argument of 0 (an exact match).

FIGURE 8-13.
MATCH locates the position of a text string.

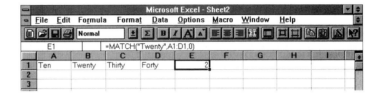

The VLOOKUP and HLOOKUP functions

HLOOKUP and VLOOKUP are nearly identical functions that let you look up information stored in tables you've constructed. The forms of these lookup functions are

=VLOOKUP(*lookup value,lookup range,index number*)

and

=HLOOKUP(*lookup value,lookup range,index number*)

where *lookup value* is the value to look up in the table, *lookup range* is the range that contains the lookup table, and *index number* designates the column or row of the table from which to select the result.

The HLOOKUP and VLOOKUP functions work by comparing *lookup value* to a list of comparison values in a *lookup table*. This table is defined by the *lookup range* argument. The only difference between HLOOKUP and VLOOKUP is the type of table each function uses: HLOOKUP works with horizontal tables (tables arranged in rows); VLOOKUP works with vertical tables (tables arranged in columns).

When we say that a table is horizontal or vertical, we are telling Excel where the comparison values are located. If the values are in the leftmost column of the table, the table is vertical; if the values are in the first row of the table, the table is horizontal. (We also use the term *comparison range* to denote the row or column that contains the comparison values.)

The comparison values in a lookup table can be numbers or text. In either case, they must be arranged in ascending order if HLOOKUP and VLOOKUP are to function properly. In addition, no comparison value should be used more than once in a table.

The *index number* argument (sometimes called the *offset*) tells the lookup function which column or row of the table to look in for the function's result. The first row or column in the table has an index number of 1, so if the index number in a lookup function is 1, the result of the function is one of the comparison values.

The *index number* argument must be greater than or equal to 1 and must never be greater than the number of rows or columns in the table; that is, if a vertical table is three columns wide, the index number cannot be greater than 3. If any value does not meet these rules, the function returns an error value.

The VLOOKUP function

You can use the VLOOKUP function to access the table in Figure 8-14. The formula

=VLOOKUP(8,B2:E6,3)

returns the value 21.

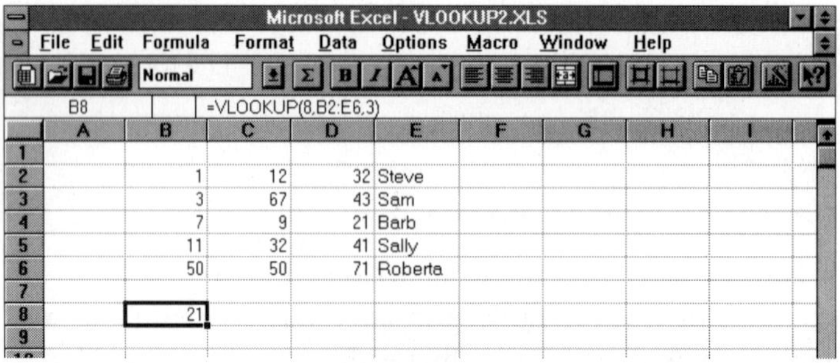

FIGURE 8-14.
*You can use the
VLOOKUP function
to retrieve information
from a table like
this one.*

The function locates first the table range and then the column that contains the comparison values — in this case, column B. Next, it scans the comparison values in column B to find the largest value less than or equal to the lookup value in the formula. In the example, because the third comparison value, 7, is less than the lookup value and because the fourth comparison value, 11, is greater than the lookup value, the function knows that its result is somewhere in row 4 (row 3 of the table).

The function then uses the index number to determine which column in the lookup table to probe for the data. In this example, the index number is 3, so column

D contains the data you want. (The column that contains the comparison values has an index number of 1.) The function, therefore, returns the number from row 4, column D:21.

The *lookup value* argument in a lookup function can be a value, a cell reference, or text enclosed in quotation marks. The *lookup range* can be indicated by cell references or a range name. If we assign the name *Table* to the range B2:E6 in Figure 8-14 and enter the number 8 in cell A1, the formula

=VLOOKUP(A1,Table,3)

returns the same result as the previous example.

Remember that these lookup functions search for the greatest comparison value that is less than or equal to the lookup value, not for an exact match between the comparison value and the lookup value. If all the comparison values in the first row or column of the table range are greater than the lookup value, the function returns the error value #N/A. If, however, all the comparison values are less than the lookup value, the function returns the data value that corresponds to the last (largest) comparison value in the table.

You can also use the lookup functions to look up text. For example, the formula

=VLOOKUP(8,B2:E6,4)

returns the text string *Barb* from the table in Figure 8-14.

The comparison values in a table can also be text strings. Figure 8-15 shows a vertical lookup table that uses text comparison values. For example, the formula

=VLOOKUP("Doug",B2:C6,2)

returns the value 46000. (If you use a text string as the lookup value in your lookup table, you must enclose the string in quotation marks.)

FIGURE 8-15.
*You can use
VLOOKUP with text
comparison values.*

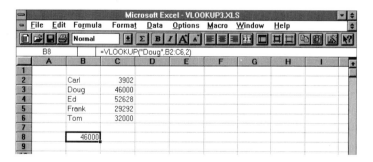

The usefulness of text comparison values is limited in Excel because the comparison values must be arranged in alphabetic order if the function is to work properly. In addition, Excel uses the same "greatest value that is not greater than the lookup value" method it uses with numeric values, rather than an absolute match method, for selecting the correct comparison value. Thus, the formula

=VLOOKUP("Steve",B2:C6,2)

returns the value 29292, the number that corresponds to the comparison value *Frank*, which is the "greatest" comparison value that is "less than" the lookup value *Steve*. Although this method is consistent, it does not yield the expected results.

You can combine numbers, text, and logical entries in the comparison range, but you still must arrange the elements in the range in ascending order according to Excel's sorting rules: first numbers, then text, and then logical values.

The vertical lookup function for the table in Figure 8-16 fails because the comparison values in column B are not in ascending order. The formula

=VLOOKUP(4,B2:C6,2)

returns the value 100 instead of 500. This occurs because the VLOOKUP function searches the comparison value list only until it comes to a number greater than the lookup value. When it finds such a value — in this case, 5 — it stops the search, backs up to the previous comparison value, and uses that row to obtain the result. Any comparison values below the first value that are not greater than the lookup value are ignored.

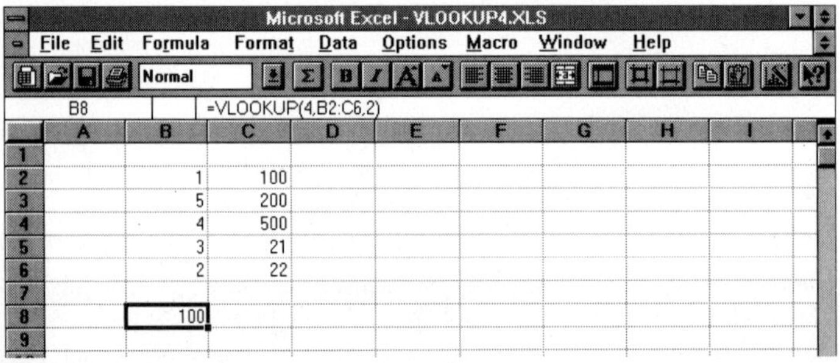

FIGURE 8-16.
*The VLOOKUP
function does not
work properly unless
the comparison values
are in ascending order.*

The HLOOKUP function

The horizontal lookup function, HLOOKUP, is similar to the vertical lookup function, except that it reads information from horizontal tables. All the rules that apply to VLOOKUP apply to HLOOKUP.

The worksheet in Figure 8-17 shows an example of a horizontal lookup table. The formula

=HLOOKUP(6,B2:E7,3)

returns the value 101 from this table because the lookup value, 6, equals the comparison value in column C, and the index number, 3, tells the function to look in the third row of the table for the correct item.

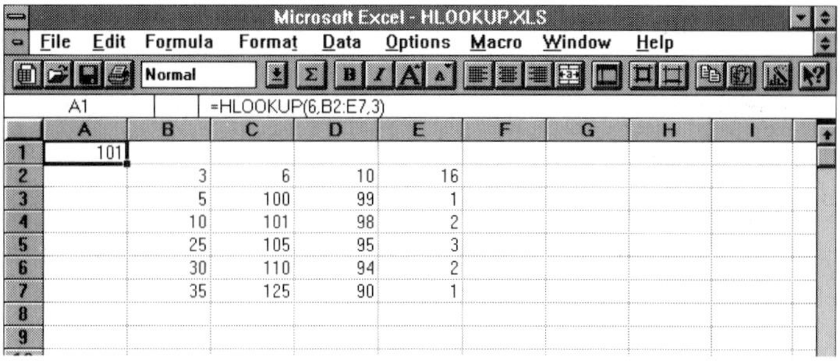

FIGURE 8-17.
*The HLOOKUP
function retrieves
information from a
horizontal table.*

The LOOKUP function

The LOOKUP function has two forms. In both forms, it is similar to VLOOKUP and HLOOKUP.

The first form

The first form of LOOKUP is

=LOOKUP(*lookup value,lookup range,result range*)

where *lookup value* is the value to look up in the lookup range, *lookup range* is the range that contains the comparison values, and *result range* is the range that contains the possible results. (The Excel manual uses the terms *lookup vector* and *result vector* to describe the lookup range and the result range.)

Like HLOOKUP and VLOOKUP, LOOKUP searches *lookup range* for the largest comparison value that is not greater than *lookup value*. It then selects the matching result from *result range*. For example, consider the worksheet in Figure 8-18. The formula

=LOOKUP(3,B3:B7,E3:E7)

compares the lookup value, 3, with the values in the lookup range, B3:B7. After determining that the entry in cell B5, the third cell of the lookup range, is the largest entry in the range that is not greater than the lookup value, the function then looks to the third cell of the result range, E5, for the result of the formula: 300.

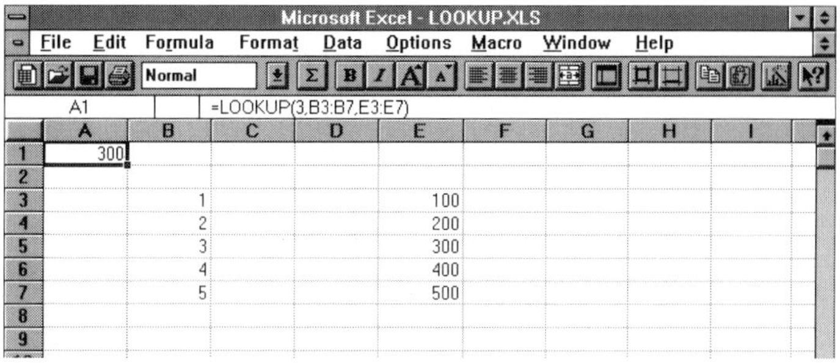

FIGURE 8-18.
*The LOOKUP
function also retrieves
information from
a range.*

Although the lookup range and the result range are often parallel in the worksheet, they don't have to be. One range can be horizontal and the other vertical. The result range must have exactly the same number of elements as the lookup range, however. For example, in Figure 8-19, the formula

=LOOKUP(3,A1:A5,D6:H6)

returns 300. Both the lookup range, A1:A5, and the result range, D6:H6, have five elements. The lookup value, 3, matches the entry in the third cell of the lookup range. The result of the formula is the entry in the third cell of the result range: 300.

All the rules that apply to VLOOKUP and HLOOKUP apply to the first form of LOOKUP.

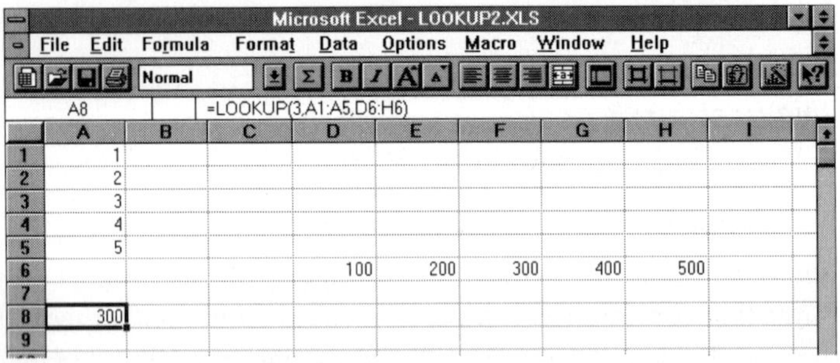

FIGURE 8-19.
The LOOKUP
function can retrieve
information from a
nonparallel cell range.

The second form

The second form of LOOKUP is

=LOOKUP(*lookup value,lookup range*)

where *lookup value* is the value to look up in the table, and *lookup range* is the range that contains the lookup table. This form of the LOOKUP function has no index number argument or result range. The result is always taken from the last row or the last column of the lookup range.

You can use this form of LOOKUP to read from either a horizontal or a vertical table. LOOKUP uses the dimensions of the table to figure out where the comparison values are. If the table is taller than it is wide or if the table is square, the function assumes that the comparison values are in the leftmost column of the table. If the table is wider than it is tall, the function views the table as horizontal and assumes the comparison values are in the first row of the table.

In every other way, the second form of the LOOKUP function is identical to HLOOKUP and VLOOKUP.

For the most part, you'll find HLOOKUP and VLOOKUP preferable to the second form of LOOKUP because they are more predictable and controllable. LOOKUP is important only if you import Multiplan models into Excel.

The INDEX function

Like CHOOSE and LOOKUP, INDEX is a lookup function. Its form is

=INDEX(*index range,row,column,area*)

where *index range* is the range or ranges that contain the index table, and *row* and *column* describe the row and column coordinates of the particular cell being referenced. The *area* argument is used only when *index range* contains more than one range.

The INDEX function requires that you create an index table — a rectangular range that includes at least four cells. The cells in the table can contain numbers, text, or formulas. Figure 8-20 shows an example of an index table. The formula in cell A1

=INDEX(C3:E6,A2,A3)

uses the row coordinate in cell A2 and the column coordinate in cell A3 to extract a value from the table. Because cell A2 contains the number 3 and cell A3 contains the number 2, the function returns the address of the cell in the third row and the second column of the table: D5.

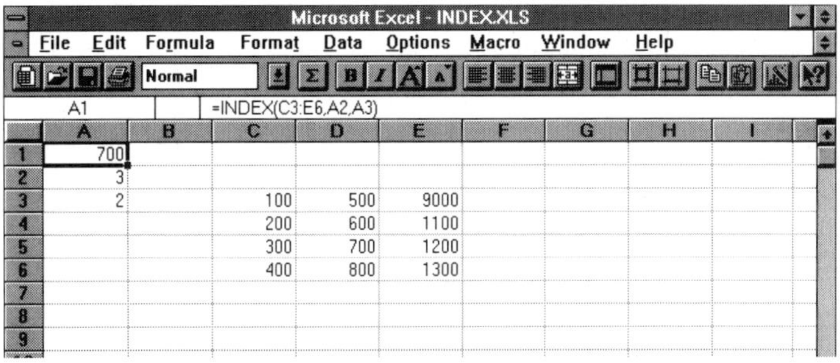

FIGURE 8-20.
Use the INDEX function to retrieve the address of the cell where information is located.

The INDEX function returns the address of the cell at the indicated position in the table, not the entry stored in that cell. However, Excel displays the contents of the cell, not the cell address. Thus, even though the actual result of the previous INDEX function is D5, the apparent result is the number 700 — the contents of that cell.

The *row* and *column* arguments must be positive. If *row* or *column* is less than or equal to 0, the function displays the error value #VALUE! However, because the INDEX function returns the cell address of the indicated position in the table, a *row* or *column* argument of 0 actually returns a reference to the entire column or row indicated. Using the worksheet in Figure 8-20, the formula

=INDEX(C3:E6,0,2)

displays the result #VALUE! However, the formula

=SUM(INDEX(C3:E6,0,2))

sums the values in the second column, D, and returns the result 2600.

If the *row* argument is greater than the number of rows in the table or if the *column* argument is greater than the number of columns, the function returns the error value #REF!

If the index table is only one row deep or one column wide, you can use only one index to select a value. For example, the formula

=INDEX(C3:C6,2)

returns the value 200 from the table in Figure 8-20. Similarly, the formula

=INDEX(C3:E3,2)

returns the value 500. The INDEX function is similar to the CHOOSE function when used with a one-dimensional table.

The *area* argument is important only when *index range* contains several areas. In this case, you must include the *area* argument to tell the INDEX function which area to use. For example, in the formula

=INDEX((A1:C5,D6:F10),1,1,2)

the index range comprises two areas: A1:C5 and D6:F10. The *area* argument, 2, tells INDEX to work on the second of these areas.

The *area* argument must always be a positive integer. If *area* is less than 1, the function returns the error value #REF!

We'll cover the array form of INDEX in "The INDEX function (array form)," later in this chapter.

Information functions

This section discusses Microsoft Excel's Information functions. In the Excel documentation, the IS functions (ISBLANK, ISTEXT, and so on) are also considered Information functions, but we include them with the Logical functions, discussed earlier in this chapter.

The CELL function

You can use the CELL function to obtain information about the formatting, location, or contents of a cell. Usually, you'll use the CELL function to learn about a single cell, but you can use it for a range also. When you do this, Excel furnishes information about the upper left cell in the selection.

CELL takes the form

=CELL(*type of info,reference*)

The result of the function depends on the type of entry in the referenced cell. The following table shows the 12 available *type of info* arguments and the information that each returns. These arguments must be inside quotation marks.

Argument	Returns
"width"	Width of specified cell, rounded to nearest whole number
"row"	Row number of specified cell; same as ROW(reference)
"col"	Column number of specified cell; same as COLUMN(*reference*)
"protect"	Protection status of specified cell: 0 if cell not locked, 1 if cell locked
"address"	Absolute address of specified cell
"contents"	Contents of specified cell
"format"	Format of specified cell, represented as a code (see table of format codes, which follows)
"prefix"	Label prefix of specified cell: ' if left or General alignment " if right alignment ^ if centered alignment \ if fill alignment nothing, if anything else
"type"	Type of entry in specified cell: b if cell is blank l (lowercase L) if cell contains a text constant v if cell contains anything else
"color"	Color for negative values: 0 if negative in normal color 1 if negative in different color
"parenthesis"	Parenthesis for positive values: 0 if no parenthesis, 1 if parenthesis
"filename"	The name of the file that contains the cell

The following table shows the codes for Excel's formats. (If you format *reference* with a customized format, Excel returns the format closest to the custom format.)

Format	Code	Format	Code
General	G	0%	P0
0	F0	0.00%	P2
(0)	F0()	0.00E+00	S2
#,##0	,0	d-mmm-yy	D1
(#,##0)	,0()	d-mmm	D2
0.00	F2	mmm-yy	D3
#,##0.00	,2	m/d/yy or m/d/yy h:mm	D4
$#,##0_); ($#,##0)	C0	h:mm:ss AM/PM	D6
$#,##0_);[Red]($#,##0)	C0–	h:mm AM/PM	D7
$#,##0.00_); ($#,##0.00)	C2	h:mm:ss	D8
$#,##0.00_);[Red]($#,##0.00)	C2–	h:mm	D9

The INFO function

You can use the INFO function to obtain information about the current state of the operating environment.

INFO takes the form

=INFO(*type*)

The type argument tells Excel what kind of information you are looking for. It must be one of the text strings listed in the left column of the following table (and it must be enclosed in quotation marks).

Argument	Returns
"directory"	Pathname of the current directory
"memavail"	Amount of memory available (in bytes)
"memused"	Amount of memory currently being used for data
"numfile"	Number of open worksheets
"origin"	Absolute cell reference of cell in upper left corner of screen preceded by "$A:"
"osversion"	Name and version of the operating system in use
"recalc"	Recalculation mode in effect (either "Automatic" or "Manual")
"release"	Version of Microsoft Excel in use
"system"	Name of the operating environment ("pcdos" for Windows, "pcos2" for OS/2, "Mac" for Macintosh)
"totmem"	Total amount of memory available, including amount already in use

The translation functions: N and T

The N function translates values into numbers; the T function translates values into text. With most Excel functions, when you enter an argument that doesn't generate the correct type of data, the program automatically translates it, so you don't generally need to use N or T in formulas. Excel includes them for compatibility with other worksheet programs.

The translation functions have the forms

=N(*value*)

and

=T(*value*)

With the N function, if you enter a number or a reference to a cell that contains a number, N returns that number. If you enter the logical value TRUE or a reference to a cell that evaluates to TRUE, N returns 1. If you enter a date with one of Excel's date formats, N returns that date's serial number. If you enter anything else, it returns 0.

If the *value* argument of a T function is text, the function returns that text. If the argument is anything else, the T function returns a null text string (" ").

The INDIRECT function

You can use the INDIRECT function to find out the contents of a cell from its reference. INDIRECT takes the form

=INDIRECT(*reference,type of ref*)

where *reference* is an A1 reference, an R1C1 reference, or a cell name, and *type of ref* is a logical value that indicates which of these types of reference you're using. If *type of ref* is FALSE, Excel interprets *reference* as the R1C1 format; if *type of ref* is TRUE or is omitted, Excel interprets *reference* as the A1 format. If your entry for *reference* isn't valid, INDIRECT returns #REF!

For example, if cell C6 contains the text value B3 and cell B3 contains the value 2.888, the formula

=INDIRECT(C6)

returns the value 2.888. If cell C6 contains the text value R3C2, you use the formula

=INDIRECT(R6C3,FALSE)

to obtain this value.

You must select the R1C1 option with the Workspace command on the Options menu before you can use the R1C1 form of INDIRECT.

The OFFSET function

The OFFSET function returns a reference located at a specified position relative to another reference. The function takes the form

=OFFSET(*reference,rows,cols,height,width*)

where *reference* specifies the position from which the offset is calculated, *rows* and *cols* specify the vertical and horizontal distances between *reference* and the reference returned by the function, and *height* and *width* specify the shape of the reference returned by the function. Positive values for *rows* and *cols* specify offsets below and to the right of *reference*, respectively. Negative values specify offsets above and to the left of *reference*. The *height* and *width* arguments are optional. If they're omitted, the function returns a reference of the same dimensions as *reference*. If included, *height* and *width* must be positive.

    The OFFSET function is most commonly used in macros, as an argument of FORMULA, SELECT, or SELECTION. (See the description of those functions in Chapter 20.) But you can also use it in worksheets.

The TYPE function

You can use the TYPE function to determine whether a cell contains text, a number, a logical value, an array, or an error value. TYPE takes the form

=TYPE(*cell reference*)

The result of the TYPE function is a code for the type of entry in the referenced cell: 1 for a number, 2 for text, 4 for a logical value (TRUE or FALSE), 8 for a formula, 16 for an error value, and 64 for an array.

    If cell A1 contains the number 100, the formula

=TYPE(A1)

returns 1. If A1 contains the text entry *Microsoft Excel*, the formula returns 2.

The AREAS function

An area is a single cell or a rectangular block of cells. Use the AREAS function to determine the number of areas in a range. The function has the form

=AREAS(*reference*)

The result of the function is the number of areas referred to by the argument.

    Suppose you assign the name *Test* to the range A1:C5,D6,E7:G10. The function

=AREAS(Test)

returns the number 3, the number of areas in the range *Test*.

The ROW and COLUMN functions

Although the names of the ROW and COLUMN functions are nearly the same as the names of two array functions, ROWS and COLUMNS, the functions are quite different. (See "The Rows and Columns function," later in this chapter.)

The forms of the ROW and COLUMN functions are

=ROW(*cell reference*)

and

=COLUMN(*cell reference*)

The result of these functions is the row or column number of the cell referred to by the function's argument. For example, the formula

=ROW(H5)

returns the result 5.

If the argument is omitted, the result is the row or column number of the cell that contains the function.

If the argument of the ROW or COLUMN function is a range or a range name, the result of the function is an array that consists of the row or column numbers of each of the rows or columns in the range. For example, the formula

=ROW(A1:A10)

returns the array {1;2;3;4;5;6;7;8;9;10}.

The NA function

NA is a placeholder function. Unlike most functions, NA takes no arguments. The form of the function is

=NA()

When you enter the NA function in a cell, that cell and all formulas that refer to that cell return the result #N/A. Some functions return the #N/A function as a type of error value.

Suppose several formulas in your worksheet depend on the value in a cell, but you aren't certain of the value the cell should contain. Instead of entering a guess, you can enter the NA function in the cell as a placeholder. Until you replace the NA function with the correct value, any formula in the worksheet that refers to that cell displays the result #N/A.

You'll use N/A primarily for marking blank cells to help you avoid including those cells in calculations.

Array functions

As shown in Chapter 3, you can use arrays as arguments in almost any type of formula. Although most Microsoft Excel functions can accept array arguments, a few *require* arrays as arguments. We'll look at these functions now.

The ROWS and COLUMNS functions

The ROWS function returns the number of rows in a reference or an array. The form of the ROWS function is

=ROWS(*array*)

The *array* argument can be an array constant, a range reference, or a range name. The result of the function is the number of rows in the array. For example, the result of the formula

=ROWS({100,200,300;1000,2000,3000})

is 2, because the array-constant argument contains two "rows." Similarly, the formula

=ROWS(A1:A10)

returns 10, because the range A1:A10 contains 10 rows.

The COLUMNS function is identical to the ROWS function, except that it returns the number of columns in the *array* argument. For example, the formula

=COLUMNS(A1:C10)

returns 3, because the range A1:C10 contains three columns.

The ROWS and COLUMNS functions are analogous to the COUNT and COUNTA functions. However, unlike these functions, which return the number of cells in a range that contain numbers (or the number of cells that contain any type of entry, in the case of COUNTA), ROWS and COLUMNS return the number of rows or columns in the range. Because of this difference, you can use these functions in combination with COUNT or COUNTA to determine the ratio between the cells in a range that contain values and the total number of cells in the range.

For example, in Figure 8-7 earlier in this chapter we used the COUNT function to determine the number of employees who had contributed to the Bat Conservation Fund. We can combine the COUNT and ROWS functions to determine the percentage of employees who made a contribution, using a formula in the form

=COUNT(##:##)/ROWS(##:##)

where ##:## is the range of cells that contains the donations.

The TRANSPOSE function

The TRANSPOSE function exchanges the rows and columns of a range or an array. The form of this function is

=TRANSPOSE(*array*)

If the array is vertical, the resulting array is horizontal. If the array is horizontal, the resulting array is vertical. For example, the result of the formula

={=TRANSPOSE({5,4,3,2,1})}

is the array {5;4;3;2;1}, and the result of the formula

={=TRANSPOSE({1;2;3;4;5})}

is the array {1,2,3,4,5}.

Suppose you want to transpose the entries in cells A1:C7 in the worksheet shown in Figure 8-21 so that they fill cells A9:G11. Select the range A9:G11, type

=TRANSPOSE(A1:C7)

and then press Shift-Ctrl-Enter. Figure 8-21 shows the results. Each cell in this range contains the array formula

={=TRANSPOSE(A1:C7)}

FIGURE 8-21.
We used the TRANSPOSE function to transpose the entries from cells A1:C7 into cells A9:G11.

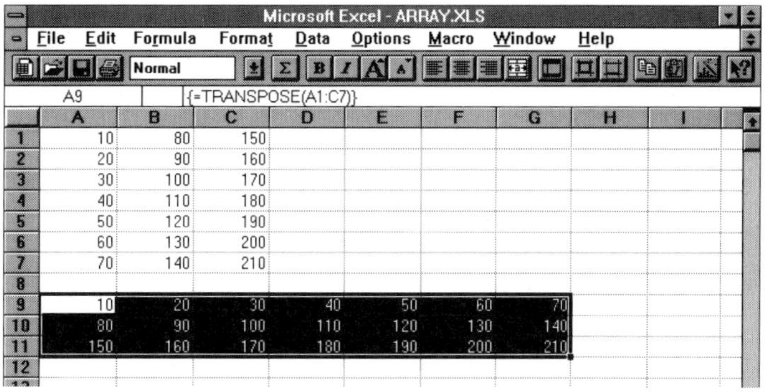

The SUMX2PY2, SUMX2MY2, and SUMXMY2 functions

These three functions let you perform three variations on sum-of-the-sum-of-the-squares operations, which are commonly used in many statistical calculations.

The SUMX2PY2 function calculates the sum of the sum of the squares of the corresponding values in X and Y, where X and Y are arrays that contain the same number of elements. The SUMX2MY2 function calculates the sum of the differences of the squares of the corresponding values in X and Y. And finally, the SUMXMY2 function calculates the sum of the squares of the differences of the corresponding values in X and Y. The forms of these functions are identical:

=SUMX2PY2(*arrayX,arrayY*)

=SUMX2MY2(*arrayX,arrayY*)

=SUMXMY2(*arrayX,arrayY*)

For example, if we use the same two arrays for all three functions, we can build the following formulas:

=SUMX2PY2({1,2,3,4},{2,4,6,8})

which returns 150;

=SUMX2MY2({1,2,3,4},{2,4,6,8})

which returns –90; and

=SUMXMY2({1,2,3,4},{2,4,6,8})

which returns 30.

The INDEX function (array form)

The first form of the INDEX function is described earlier in this chapter. The second form is used only with arrays. It has the syntax

=INDEX(*array,row,column*)

The result is the value at the position in the *array* argument indicated by the *row* and *column* arguments.

For example, the formula

=INDEX({10,20,30;40,50,60},1,2)

returns the value 20, because 20 is the item in the second column of the first row of the array.

As with the first form of INDEX, you need supply only the *column* argument if the array is only one row deep, or only the *row* argument if the array is only one column wide. Also like the first form, the *row* and *column* arguments must be positive integers. In addition, if the *row* or *column* argument exceeds the number of rows or columns in the array, the function returns the error message #REF!

The LINEST, TREND, FORECAST, SLOPE, STEYX, LOGEST, and GROWTH functions

Excel includes several array functions for performing linear or exponential regression. Each of these functions is entered as an array formula and produces an array result. You can use each of these functions with one or several independent variables.

The LINEST, TREND, FORECAST, SLOPE, and STEYX functions are used for linear regression. The array returned by LINEST provides a mathematical description of the straight line that best fits a set of known data. You can include an optional argument to return standard statistical measures of the validity of the regression line. TREND calculates points along the regression line, letting you plot a "trend" line and to extrapolate from your known data. The FORECAST function calculates the predicted value for a particular point along a linear regression line. The SLOPE function returns a value that indicates the slope of a regression line, based on vertical distance divided by horizontal distance between any two points. The STEYX function calculates the standard error produced by the regression.

The LOGEST and GROWTH functions are used for exponential regression (curve fitting). LOGEST returns an array that mathematically describes the exponential curve that best fits a set of known data. You can include an optional argument to return validity statistics. GROWTH calculates points along the regression curve, letting you plot the curve and extrapolate from it.

Calculating linear regression statistics

The following equation algebraically describes a straight line:

$$y = mx + b$$

where x is the independent variable, y is the dependent variable, m represents the slope of your line, and b represents the *y-intercept* — the point at which the line crosses the y-axis in an XY plot.

When a line represents the consolidation of a number of independent variables, the formula can be expanded to

$$y = m_1x_1 + m_2x_2 + ... + m_nx_n + b$$

where y is the dependent variable, x_1 through x_n are n independent variables, m_1 through m_n are the coefficients of each independent variable, and b is a constant.

The LINEST function uses this more general formula to return the values of m_1 through m_n and the value of b, given a known set of values for y and a known set of values for each independent variable. The syntax of the function is

=LINEST(*known_y's,known_x's,const,stats*)

The *const* and *stats* arguments are optional. If either is included, it must be a logical constant — either TRUE or FALSE. (You can substitute 1 for TRUE and 0 for FALSE if you want.) The default settings for *const* and *stats* are TRUE and FALSE, respectively. If you set *const* to FALSE, Excel forces *b* (the last term in the straight-line equation) to be 0. If you set *stats* to TRUE, the array returned by LINEST includes the following validation statistics:

se_1 through se_n	Standard error values for each coefficient
se_b	Standard error value for b
r^2	Coefficient of determination
se(y)	Standard error value for y
F	F statistic
df	Degrees of freedom
SS_{reg}	Regression sum of squares
SS_{resid}	Residual sum of squares

We will show you one application of these statistics in "Linear and multiple regression," later in this chapter.

The *known_y's* argument can be a single column, a single row, or a rectangular range of cells. If it's a single column, then each column in the *known_x's* argument is considered to be a separate independent variable. Similarly, if *known_y's* is a single row, then each row in the *known_x's* argument is considered to be a separate independent variable. If *known_y's* is a rectangular range, then you can use only one independent variable; *known_x's* in this case should be a rectangular range of the same size and shape as *known_y's*.

If you omit the *known_x's* argument, Excel uses the sequence 1, 2, 3, 4, and so on.

Before writing a formula using LINEST, you need to select a range large enough to hold the result array returned by the function. Next, type the function and press Shift-Ctrl-Enter to lock it in.

If you omit the *stats* argument (or set it explicitly to FALSE), the result array encompasses one cell for each of your independent variables, plus one cell for b. If you include the validation statistics, the result array looks like this:

m_n	m_{n-1}	...	m_2	m_1	b
se_n	se_{n-1}	...	se_2	se_1	se_b
r^2	se_y				
F	df				
SS_{reg}	SS_{resid}				

With or without validation statistics, note that the coefficients and standard error values for your independent variables are returned in the opposite order from your input data. If you have four independent variables organized in four columns, LINEST evaluates the leftmost column as x_1, but it returns m_1 in the fourth column of the result array.

Figure 8-22 presents a simple example of the use of LINEST, which involves one independent variable. The entries in column B of this worksheet represent a year's monthly sales figures for a small business. The numbers in column A represent the months of the year. Suppose you want to compute the slope and y-intercept of the regression line that best describes the relationship between the sales figures and the months of the year. In other words, you want to describe the trend of the data. To do this, select the range F5:G5, type the formula

=LINEST(B3:B14,A3:A14)

and press Shift-Ctrl-Enter. The resulting number in cell F5, 366.6958, is the slope of the regression line; the number in cell G5, 11001.73, is the y-intercept of the line.

Finding points on the linear regression (trend) line

The LINEST function returns a mathematical description of the straight line that best fits known data. The TREND function, in contrast, returns points along that best-fit line. You can use the array of numbers returned by TREND to plot a trend

FIGURE 8-22.
We used the LINEST function to compute the slope and y-intercept of a regression line.

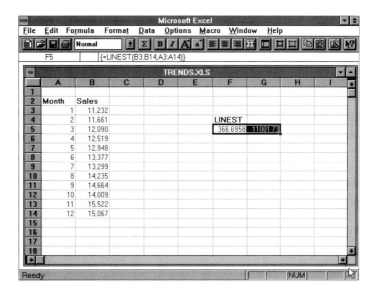

line — a straight line that helps make sense of actual data. You can also use TREND to extrapolate — that is, to make intelligent guesses about future data, based on the tendencies exhibited by known data. (Be careful. Although TREND can be used to

Linear and multiple regression

You can use the LINEST function to perform multiple-regression calculations, with the help of the *constant* and *statistics* arguments. The term *regression*, as it's used here, might be confusing to some people, because regression is commonly used to mean a *movement backward*, whereas in the world of finance, regression is often used to predict the future. To better understand the concept, keep in mind the following definition: *Regression is a statistical technique that lets you summarize in the form of an equation a set of data that can otherwise be presented by a graph.*

Often, businesses try to predict the future by using sales and percent-of-sales projections based on past history. A simple percent-of-sales technique identifies the assets and liabilities that vary along with sales, determines the proportion of each, and assigns them appropriate percentages. Although using simple percent-of-sales forecasting is often sufficient for slow or steady short-term growth patterns, the technique rapidly loses accuracy as growth accelerates.

Regression analysis uses more sophisticated equations to analyze larger sets of data and translate them into coordinates on a line or curve. In the past, regression analysis was not widely used because of the sheer complexity of the equations involved. Since spreadsheet programs such as Microsoft Excel began offering built-in regression functions, the use of regression analysis has become much more widespread.

Linear regression is the analysis of a single set of data and produces the slope of the line and the y-intercept for the point you want to project. Based on a year's worth of sales figures, linear regression can tell you the projected sales for March of the following year by giving you the slope and y-intercept of the line that represents projected sales.

Multiple regression is the analysis of more than one set of data, which often produces a more realistic projection. For example, suppose you want to project the appropriate price for a house in your area based on square footage, number of bathrooms, lot size, and age. Using a multiple-regression formula, you can estimate a price, based on a matrix of information gathered from existing houses.

plot the straight line best fitted to known data, it can't tell you whether that line is a good predictor of the future. The validation statistics returned by LINEST can help you make that assessment.)

The TREND function accepts four arguments:

=TREND(*known_y's,known_x's,new_x's,const*)

The first two arguments represent the known values of your dependent and independent variables, respectively. As in LINEST, the *known_y's* argument is a single column, a single row, or a rectangular range. The *known_x's* argument also is laid out exactly as described for LINEST.

The third and fourth arguments are optional. If you omit *new_x's*, TREND considers *new_x's* to be identical to *known_x's*. If you include *const*, the value of that argument must be TRUE or FALSE (or 1 or 0). If *const* is TRUE, TREND forces *b* to be 0.

To calculate the trend-line data points that best fit your known data, simply omit the third and fourth arguments from the function. Your result array will be the same size as your *known_x's* range. In Figure 8-23, we used TREND to find the value of each point on the regression line that describes the data set from the example in Figure 8-22. To create these values, we selected the range C3:C14, typed the formula

=TREND(B3:B14,A3:A14)

and then pressed Shift-Ctrl-Enter.

To extrapolate from existing data, supply a range for *new x's*. You can supply as many or as few cells for *new x's* as you want. Your result array will be the same size as your *new x's* range. In Figure 8-24 on the following page, we used TREND to

FIGURE 8-23.
We used the TREND function to create a data series that can be plotted as a line on a chart.

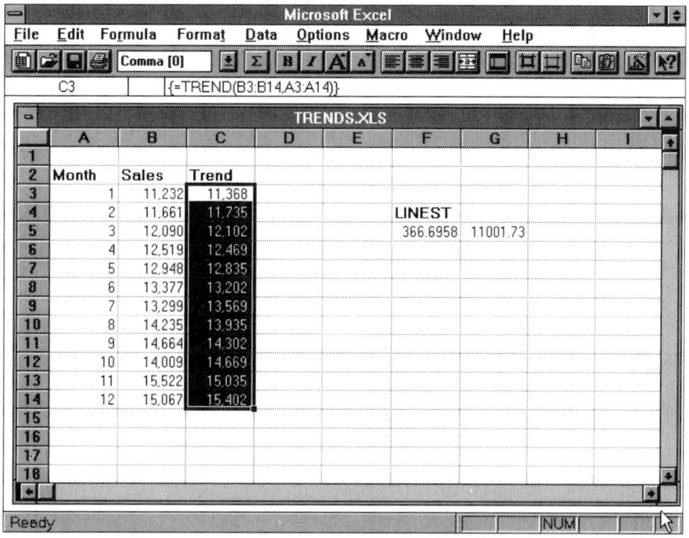

FIGURE 8-24.
*We used TREND
to predict the sales
figures for months
13, 14, and 15.*

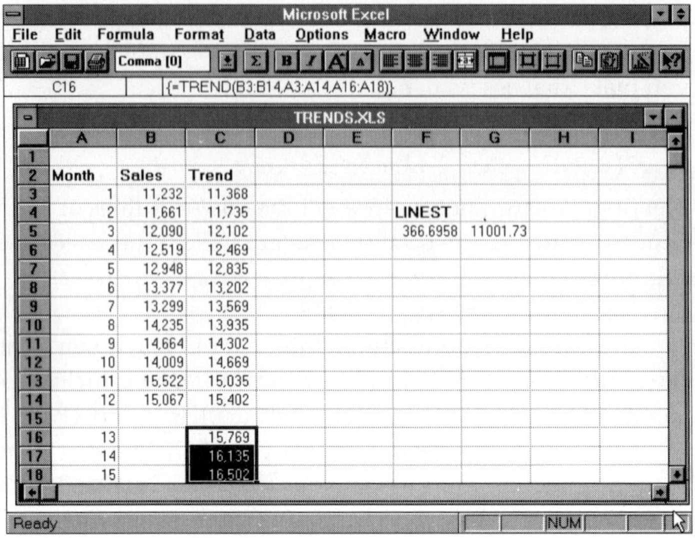

calculate predicted sales values for the 13th, 14th, and 15th months. To arrive at these values, we entered the numbers 13 through 15 in A16:A18, selected C13:C15, typed the formula

=TREND(B3:B14,A3:A14,A16:A18)

and then pressed Shift-Ctrl-Enter.

The FORECAST function is similar to TREND, except that rather than returning an array that defines a line, FORECAST returns a single point along that line. The FORECAST function has the form

=FORECAST(*x,known_y's,known_x's*)

where *x* is the data point for which you want to extrapolate a value. For example, if we use the FORECAST function to extrapolate the value in cell C18 in Figure 8-24, we will arrive at the same number using the formula

=FORECAST(15,B3:B14,A3:A14)

where the *x* argument refers to the 15th data point on the regression line. We can use this function to calculate any point into the future.

The SLOPE function returns a number that represents the slope of the linear regression line. This is the same as the first number in the array that is returned by the LINEST function. Thus SLOPE calculates the trajectory of the same line along which we used the FORECAST and TREND functions to calculate the values of data points. The *slope* is defined as the vertical distance divided by the horizontal distance between any two points on the regression line. The function takes the form

=SLOPE(*known_y's,known_x's*)

Again using our example, our slope formula is

=SLOPE(B3:B14,A3:A14)

which returns a value of 366.698.

The STEYX function lets you calculate the standard error of a regression, a measure of the amount of error accrued in predicting a y for each given x. The form of the function is familiar:

=STEYX(*known_y's,known_x's*)

If we apply this function to our model, the formula is

=STEYX(B3:B14,A3:A14)

which returns a standard error value of 338.82.

Calculating exponential regression statistics

The LOGEST function works just like the LINEST function, except that you use it to analyze data that is nonlinear. The equation that describes an exponential curve is

$$y = b * m_1 x_1 * m_2 x_2 * ... * m_n x_n$$

If you have only one independent variable, the equation is

$$y = b * m_x$$

LOGEST returns coefficient values for each independent variable plus a value for the constant b. If you set the optional *stats* to TRUE, the function also returns validation statistics.

LOGEST accepts the same four arguments as LINEST and returns a result array in the same fashion. (See the preceding discussion of LINEST.)

Finding points on the exponential regression curve

The LOGEST function returns a mathematical description of the exponential curve best fitted to a set of observed data. The GROWTH function lets you find points that lie along that curve.

The GROWTH function works exactly like its linear counterpart, TREND. (See the preceding discussion of TREND.)

Other functions

Excel offers two other groups of functions not discussed here: date and time functions and database statistical functions. Both of these types of functions require more knowledge about how Excel works, so we discuss them separately. We explain date functions in Chapter 9 and database statistical functions in Chapter 16.

In addition to all these built-in functions, Excel lets you create your own functions. You'll learn to do this in the section on building macro functions in Chapter 19.

9

Date and Time

Microsoft Excel lets you enter date values and time values in your worksheet to "date stamp" documents, for example, or to perform date and time arithmetic. This chapter explains how you work with dates and times in your Excel worksheets.

Excel's date and time capabilities make creating a production schedule or a monthly billing system relatively simple. For example, the Series command on the Data menu lets you enter a long series of row or column headers in your worksheet in date format; thus, you can enter a month or even a year of dates in seconds. The date and time functions let you perform worksheet calculations quickly and accurately. For example, if you use your worksheet to calculate your company's monthly payroll, you might use the HOUR function to determine the number of hours worked each day, and the WEEKDAY function to determine whether employees should be paid at the standard rate (for Monday through Friday) or at the overtime rate (for Saturdays and Sundays). Each of these topics is discussed in this chapter.

How Microsoft Excel remembers dates and times

The basic unit of time in Microsoft Excel is the day. Each day is represented by an integer from 1 through 65380. The base date, represented by the integer 1, is Sunday, January 1, 1900. The maximum day value, 65380, represents December 31, 2078. Each day value you enter in your worksheet represents the number of days that have elapsed between the base date and the specified date. Thus, the date January 1, 1992, is represented by the integer 33604, because 33603 days have elapsed between the base date and January 1, 1992.

The time of day is a decimal value that represents the portion of a day that has elapsed between the beginning of the day — 12:00 midnight — and the specified time. The time 12:00 noon, for example, is represented by the value 0.5, because the difference between midnight and noon is exactly half a day. The time/date combination 2:09:03 PM, October 25, 1992, is represented by the number 33902.5896180556.

By assigning serial values to days, hours, minutes, and seconds, Excel lets you perform sophisticated date and time arithmetic. You can manipulate dates and times in your worksheet formulas just as you do other types of values.

The 1904 Date System

Excel's 1904 Date System option lets you change Excel's base date (the date that corresponds to the serial number 1) from January 1, 1900 to January 2, 1904 — the base date used by Microsoft Excel for the Macintosh. To do this, simply choose Calculation from the Options menu, and turn on the 1904 Date System option. Underlying date values remain the same, but the display of all dates in the worksheet changes. When you turn on the 1904 Date System option, any serial date you enter in your Excel for Windows worksheet matches the corresponding serial date from the Excel for the Macintosh worksheet. If you transfer information into Excel for Windows from a worksheet created in Excel for the Macintosh, this option ensures that the serial dates in the worksheet are evaluated correctly. In this book, we use the 1900 Date System, which is the standard for Windows and MS-DOS programs.

If you transfer documents between Excel for the Macintosh and Excel for Windows, the proper date system for the worksheet is automatically set for you. When the date system changes, existing date values display different dates, but the underlying values do not change. Therefore, if you change date systems after you have begun entering dates into a worksheet, all your dates will be off by four years.

Functions and formats

The serial values that represent dates and times don't look like dates and times, so they're nearly impossible to understand. Fortunately, Microsoft Excel offers two sets of tools that make it easy to work with these serial values: functions, which allow you to use dates and times in formulas; and formats, which convert serial values into an understandable form.

Entering a date or a time in the Excel worksheet is usually a two-step process. First, you use a function to calculate the date or time in a cell; the result of this function is the serial value of the specified date or time. Second, you use a date or time format to display the result in recognizable form. (You can often combine these two steps by entering your date and time values "in format." This process is described in the sections "An easier way to enter date numbers," and "An easier way to enter time numbers," later in this chapter.)

The DATE function

The basic date function in Excel is DATE, which lets you enter a date in a cell of the worksheet. The form of this function is

$$=DATE(yy,mm,dd)$$

where yy is the year, mm is the month, and dd is the day. The arguments in the DATE function must appear in descending order of magnitude: years, months, days.

The result of DATE is a serial value that represents the number of days that have elapsed between the base date and the indicated date. For example, if you use the formula

$$=DATE(92,12,25)$$

to enter the date December 25, 1992, the result in the worksheet is the serial value 33963, which Excel displays as 12/25/92.

Excel interprets DATE function arguments liberally. When you enter a DATE function, your day argument can be much higher than the last day of the month; the program will simply count forward into the next month. For example, if you enter the formula

$$=DATE(92,7,50)$$

the program stores the serial date value for August 19, 1992. This comes in handy when performing date arithmetic.

Your day argument can be as high as you want, as long as it does not exceed the maximum serial date value of 65380. Similarly, your month argument can be higher than 12. Excel simply counts forward into subsequent years to interpret a DATE function whose month argument is 13 or higher.

If you use 0 as the day argument in a DATE function, Excel interprets the value as the last day of the previous month. Thus, if you enter

=DATE(92,3,0)

the program stores the serial date value for February 29, 1992. Similarly, if you enter 0 for the month, December of the previous year is displayed. When you enter DATE(93,0,0), Excel moves back both the month and the day, to store the serial value for November 30, 1992.

Also, you can use a negative number in the day argument to "count backward" in the previous month. If you enter the formula

=DATE(92,8,–6)

Excel stores the serial value for the date July 25, 1992.

The year 2000 and beyond

Most of the date values you enter will fall in the 1900s. As the preceding example shows, when you enter a date value that falls within this range, you need enter only the last two digits of the year value. If you want to enter a year value from 2000 through 2078, however, you must use either the values 100 through 178 or the full year value.

For example, to enter the date January 1, 2010, you can use either

=DATE(110,1,1)

or

=DATE(2010,1,1)

The TODAY function

The TODAY function is a special form of the DATE function. Although the DATE function can return the serial value of any date, TODAY always returns the serial value of the current date. The form of this function is

=TODAY( )

The TODAY function does not take an argument.

Use this function when you want a date on your worksheet always to reflect the current date.

Formatting dates

After you use the DATE function to enter a date in the worksheet, you can use the Number command on the Format menu to present that date in recognizable form. Excel offers five date formats: m/d/yy, d-mmm-yy, d-mmm, mmm-yy, and m/d/yy h:mm. The results of the function DATE(92,12,25) — serial value 33963 — using these formats are

Format	Display
m/d/yy	12/25/92
d-mmm-yy	25-Dec-92
d-mmm	25-Dec
mmm-yy	Dec-92
m/d/yy h:mm	12/25/92 00:00

To assign a date format to a cell, select that cell, choose Number from the Format menu, select the date format you want, and click OK.

An easier way to enter date numbers

In Chapter 4, you learned that you can enter a number in a cell and format that number in one step by typing the number in format. You can use this same technique to enter dates in the worksheet. For example, to enter the date December 25, 1992, in a cell, you select that cell and type *12/25/92* or *12-25-92*. (You can use either slashes or hyphens as separators.) When you use this technique, Excel does not display the date's serial value in the formula bar; instead, it assigns the m/d/yy format to the

---

Using the VALUE function
to determine a date's serial value

When you type a date value in your worksheet instead of using the DATE function, you won't see the underlying serial date value for that date. You can determine the serial value by using Excel's VALUE function. For example, if cell A1 of your worksheet contains the date entry 5/1/92, you can use the formula

=VALUE(A1)

to determine that the serial date value for this entry is 33725.

cell (if the cell isn't already formatted), and displays 12/25/1992 in the formula bar. (For the years 2000 through 2078, you must type the complete year value; the program doesn't accept a year value of 100 or above for in-format date entries.)

You can use any built-in format to enter dates in this way. If your entry doesn't exactly match a built-in format, Excel attempts to match a format to your entry. For example, when you type *1 Dec* in a cell, you'll see the formatted entry 1-Dec. The entry in the formula bar still appears in mm/dd/yyyy format (12/1/1992, if the current year is 1992), so you can edit the date value more easily. You can also create your own date formats. (See "Creating your own date and time formats," later in this chapter.)

Using date arithmetic

After you've entered a date in a worksheet, you can use it in formulas and functions as you would any other value. Suppose you want to calculate the date 200 days after December 25, 1992. If cell A1 contains the formula

=DATE(92,12,25)

you can use the formula

A1+200

to compute the serial value of the date 200 days later, which is 34163.

You can also find the number of weeks between December 25, 1992 and May 13, 1993. Use the formula

=(DATE(93,5,13)−DATE(92,12,25))/7

to find the answer, which is 19.9 weeks.

If you enter a date value in format, you can still perform mathematical calculations on that date, even though the serial date value doesn't appear in the cell or formula bar.

Calculating date intervals based on a 360-day year

Certain date calculations routinely used in the securities industry are based on an artificial 360-day year, which contains twelve 30-day months. If you need to make such calculations, use Excel's DAYS360 function instead of simply subtracting one date from another. The syntax of this function is

=DAYS360(*Start date,End date*)

So, for example, to determine the number of days between July 1, 1992 and December 15, 1992, based on the 360-day year, use the formula

=DAYS360("7-1-92","12-15-92")

You can also reference cells that contain the start and end dates. For example, if cell A1 holds the formula

=DATE(92,7,1)

and cell A2 holds the formula

=DATE(92,12,15)

you can calculate the interval between these dates by writing the formula

=DAYS360(A1,A2)

Creating date series

Although you can create an evenly spaced series of dates in a row or column of a worksheet in several ways, Excel offers a special tool that makes the job easy: the Series command on the Data menu. This command lets you build a series of dates that are days, weeks, months, or years apart.

Creating an end-of-month series

To create a series using the last day of each month, begin with a day in a month that has 31 days, such as March 31, 1991. Here are the results of entering this date in cell A1 and then creating the series.

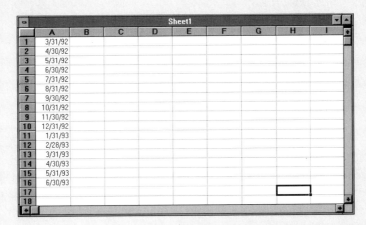

The dates now indicate the last day of each month.

Suppose you want to create a series of dates in cells A1 through A16 in a worksheet. The series begins with March 1, 1992, and the dates in the series must be exactly one month apart. First, enter the formula

=DATE(92,3,1)

in cell A1. Next, select the range A1:A16, and then choose Series from the Data menu. Figure 9-1 shows the Series dialog box. From this box, choose Columns to create a columnar series, and then choose Date to create a date series. Finally, choose Month to specify the interval, be sure the Step Value is 1, and then click OK.

FIGURE 9-1.
Use the Series dialog box to create a date series.

Figure 9-2 shows the result of this command. The range A1:A16 contains a series of dates exactly one month apart.

FIGURE 9-2.
Using the DATE function and the Series command, we created a series of dates one month apart.

	A	B	C	D	E	F	G	H	I
1	3/1/92								
2	4/1/92								
3	5/1/92								
4	6/1/92								
5	7/1/92								
6	8/1/92								
7	9/1/92								
8	10/1/92								
9	11/1/92								
10	12/1/92								
11	1/1/93								
12	2/1/93								
13	3/1/93								
14	4/1/93								
15	5/1/93								
16	6/1/93								
17									
18									

The other choices in the Date Unit box of the Series dialog box let you specify different intervals for your date series. The Day option builds a series of dates one or more days apart (depending on the step value); the Weekday option creates a series of dates using only the five working days of the week. The Year option builds an annual date series.

Excel provides further flexibility with the Step Value and Stop Value options. The Step Value option lets you specify the increase for each successive cell. For example, by typing 2 in the Step Value text box and selecting Date in the Type box and Month in the Date Unit box, you can create a series of dates for every other month. By typing a negative number in the Step Value box, you can create a descending (decreasing) series.

You can also enter a formatted date value in the Stop Value text box. For example, suppose you want to enter a series of dates that extends from 1/1/91 through 12/31/95 in your worksheet and you don't know the serial date value for December 31, 1995. You can simply type the formatted date value 12/31/95 in the Stop Value text box; Excel interprets the entry as 35064.

Creating date series using the AutoFill feature

In Chapter 5, we introduced you to the AutoFill feature. The AutoFill feature lets you create data series with the mouse, without using the Series command. This feature also lets you create date series quickly and easily. You do this *by example*. To illustrate, suppose that to create the one-month date series in Figure 9-2, we entered the date 3/1/92 in cell A1, and the date 4/1/92 in cell A2. Note that Excel accepts these as dates entered in format. Now, with the mouse, select cells A1:A2. Next, move the mouse pointer over the small black fill handle at the lower right of the selection. (If the fill handle is not visible, choose Workspace from the Options menu, and activate the Cell Drag and Drop option.) The shaded-cross mouse pointer changes to a narrow crosshair when it is over the fill handle. Now drag the fill handle until cells A1:A16 are selected. When you release the mouse button, the AutoFill feature creates the same data series shown in Figure 9-2.

Excel's AutoFill feature uses the selected cells to determine the type of series you intend to create with the fill handle. As described in Chapter 4, text and nonsequential values are copied when the fill handle is used to extend a selection, and sequential numeric values are incremented automatically. Similarly, date values are extended sequentially, as shown in Figure 9-3.

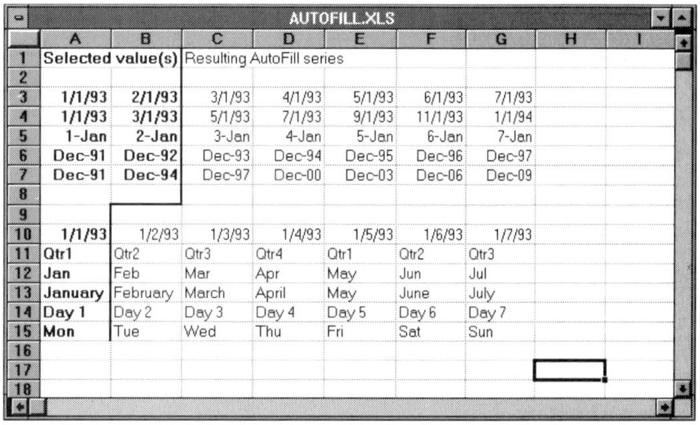
AUTOFILL.XLS

	A	B	C	D	E	F	G	H	I
1	Selected value(s)		Resulting AutoFill series						
2									
3	1/1/93	2/1/93	3/1/93	4/1/93	5/1/93	6/1/93	7/1/93		
4	1/1/93	3/1/93	5/1/93	7/1/93	9/1/93	11/1/93	1/1/94		
5	1-Jan	2-Jan	3-Jan	4-Jan	5-Jan	6-Jan	7-Jan		
6	Dec-91	Dec-92	Dec-93	Dec-94	Dec-95	Dec-96	Dec-97		
7	Dec-91	Dec-94	Dec-97	Dec-00	Dec-03	Dec-06	Dec-09		
8									
9									
10	1/1/93	1/2/93	1/3/93	1/4/93	1/5/93	1/6/93	1/7/93		
11	Qtr1	Qtr2	Qtr3	Qtr4	Qtr1	Qtr2	Qtr3		
12	Jan	Feb	Mar	Apr	May	Jun	Jul		
13	January	February	March	April	May	June	July		
14	Day 1	Day 2	Day 3	Day 4	Day 5	Day 6	Day 7		
15	Mon	Tue	Wed	Thu	Fri	Sat	Sun		
16									
17									
18									

FIGURE 9-3.
Using the AutoFill feature we started with the values shown in bold and created the values to the right.

In row 3, a common monthly increment is extended as expected, while row 4 contains a bimonthly series created using 1/1/93 and 3/1/93 as starting values. Rows 5 and 6 illustrate different formats and increments, while row 7 contains a three-year series. The second group in Figure 9-3 shows how even a single cell can provide enough for Excel to use in determining a series. When you use the fill handle on single-cell values like the ones in rows 10 through 15, Excel assumes you want to increment the numeric value in each cell. (If instead you want to copy the cell by dragging, hold down Ctrl while dragging the fill handle.) Notice, however, that the entries in rows 11 through 15 contain text values. The AutoFill feature recognizes text entries for days and months, and extends them as if they were numeric values. In addition, whenever a cell contains a mixed text and numeric entry, the AutoFill feature automatically copies the text portion (if it is not the name of a month or day), and increments the numeric portion, as shown in rows 11 and 14 of Figure 9-3.

The TIME function

Making time entries is similar to making date entries. First use a function to enter the appropriate time in a cell, and then use one of Excel's four built-in time formats to make the result look understandable.

The primary time function is TIME. The form of this function is

=TIME(*hh,mm,ss*)

where *hh* is the hours, *mm* the minutes, and *ss* the seconds. The *ss* argument is optional. If you omit it, however, you must include a comma after the *mm* argument, like this

=TIME(*hh,mm,*)

The result of the TIME function is a decimal value that represents how much of the day has elapsed between midnight and the specified time.

The TIME function uses the 24-hour, or military, time convention. On the 24-hour clock, 3:00 AM is 3 o'clock, 2:00 PM is 14 o'clock, and 11:00 PM is 23 o'clock. Thus, 2:15 PM is represented by the formula

=TIME(14,15,)

which returns the decimal value 0.59375, or 2:15 PM. For times between 12:00 midnight and 1:00 AM, the *hh* argument is always 0.

As with the DATE function, you can use large numbers and negative numbers as arguments in TIME. For example, if you want to know the time 35 seconds before 5:00:14, you can use the formula

=TIME(5,0,14−35)

Excel returns 0.208090277778, or 4:59:39 AM. Similarly, the formula

=TIME(12,60,)

refers to 1:00 PM. Normally the maximum value for the *mm* argument is 59, so when Excel encounters the minute value 60, it carries the extra minute to the next hour.

Formatting times

Excel offers five built-in time formats: h:mm AM/PM, h:mm:ss AM/PM, h:mm, h:mm:ss, and m/d/yy h:mm (a crossover format that appears in both the Date and Time format categories). Here is the result of the function TIME(13,52,32) — serial value 0.578148148 — using each of these formats:

Format	Display
h:mm AM/PM	1:52 PM
h:mm:ss AM/PM	1:52:32 PM
h:mm	13:52
h:mm:ss	13:52:32
m/d/yy h:mm	1/0/00 13:52

Notice that the first two formats display the time in traditional 12-hour clock form, and the last three formats use the 24-hour convention. In addition, the last format displays the date as 1/0/00, because no date was given in the formula.

To assign a time format to a cell, select that cell, choose Number from the Format menu, select the time format you want to use, and then click OK.

An easier way to enter time numbers

You can bypass the standard two-step method of entering times by entering the time in format. Simply select the cell in which you want to make the entry and type the time in one of the following forms: hh:mm:ss, hh:mm, hh:mm:ss AM/PM, hh:mm AM/PM, or m/d/yy hh:mm. Notice that the parts of the time entries must be separated by colons.

To enter the time *2:15 PM* in a cell, select the cell and type *2:15 PM* or *14:15*. Either way, Excel enters the serial time value 0.59375 in the cell and assigns a time format to that value. (If you don't include the AM/PM or am/pm notation in the time, Excel uses the 24-hour-clock convention.)

Using time arithmetic

You can use time values in formulas and functions, just as you can use date values. However, the results of time arithmetic are not as easy to understand as the results of date arithmetic.

If you want to know how much time has elapsed between 8:22 AM and 10:45 PM, you can determine this with the formula

=TIME(22,45,)–TIME(8,22,)

The result of the formula is 2:23 PM. This tells you that there are 14 hours and 23 minutes between the two times.

Suppose you want to determine the time that is 2 hours, 23 minutes, and 17 seconds after 12:35:23 PM. The formula

=TIME(12,35,23)+TIME(2,23,17)

returns the correct answer: 2:58 PM. Note that Excel's default answer doesn't display the seconds, but the cell still maintains the value 0.624074074. In this formula, the arguments 2, 23, and 17 represent not an absolute time (2:23:17 AM) but an interval of time (2 hours, 23 minutes, 17 seconds). This format is perfectly acceptable to Excel.

Combining date and time formats

In addition to the built-in formats that display dates and times, Microsoft Excel offers a combined format — m/d/yy h:mm — that displays the date and time in one cell. For example, if a cell in your worksheet contains the serial value 35261.125 and you apply the m/d/yy h:mm format to that entry, you'll see the date and time displayed as 7/15/96 3:00. When you enter both date and time in format, you can type either *6/21/91 16:30* or *4:30 PM 6-21-91*.

The NOW function

You can use the NOW function to enter the current date and time in a cell. The form of this function is simply

=NOW()

NOW does not take an argument. The result of the function is a date/time value that includes an integer (the date) and a decimal value (the time). For example, if today is July 21, 1992, and the time is 11:45 AM, the NOW function returns the value 33806.4895833333.

Excel doesn't update the value of NOW continuously. The function is updated each time you calculate the worksheet (by making an entry, by choosing Calculate Now from the Options menu, or by pressing F9 or Ctrl-=). If you notice that the value of a cell that contains the NOW function is not up to date, you can correct the problem by recalculating the worksheet.

NOW is an example of a *volatile* function, that is, one whose calculated value is subject to change. If you open a worksheet that contains one or more NOW functions, and then immediately close the worksheet, Excel prompts you to save your changes even though you haven't made any. This happens because the current value of NOW has changed since the last time you used the worksheet. (Another example of a volatile function is RAND.)

Creating your own date and time formats

To supplement the four standard date and time formats, Microsoft Excel lets you create your own custom formats. The technique is essentially the same as the technique for creating custom numeric formats.

The following table shows the formatting symbols you can use to create special date and time formats. Keep in mind two points about these symbols. First, when you use the symbol *m* immediately after an *h* or the symbol *mm* immediately after an *hh*, Excel displays minutes instead of months; otherwise, Excel assumes that *m* means months. Second, if you include one of the symbols AM/PM, am/pm, A/P, or a/p in a time format, Excel displays the time in conventional 12-hour clock form; if you omit these symbols, the time appears in 24-hour form.

Symbol	Display
General	Number in General format
d	Day number without leading 0 (1–31)
dd	Day number with leading 0 (01–31)
ddd	Day-of-week abbreviation (Sun–Sat)
dddd	Day-of-week name (Sunday–Saturday)
m	Month number without leading 0 (1–12)
mm	Month number with leading 0 (01–12)
mmm	Month name abbreviation (Jan–Dec)
mmmm	Complete month name (January–December)
yy	Last two digits of year number (00–99)
yyyy	Entire year number (1900–2078)
h	Hour without leading 0 (0–23)
hh	Hour with leading 0 (00–23)
m	Minute without leading 0 (0–59)
mm	Minute with leading 0 (00–59)
s	Second without leading 0 (0–59)
ss	Second with leading 0 (00–59)
AM/PM	Time in AM/PM notation
am/pm	Time in am/pm notation
A/P	Time in A/P notation
a/p	Time in a/p notation

Suppose you want to create a format that displays a date in the fullest possible form, so that, for example, the date entry 12/25/92 appears as December 25, 1992. Select the cell that contains the entry you want to format, choose Number from the Format menu, and type

mmmm d, yyyy

in the Format text box. When you click OK, Excel stores the new format in the list of formats and displays the date in the selected cell in full.

To create a format that displays the day of the week in addition to the date, use the format

dddd, mmmm d, yyyy

If you use this format with the formula

=DATE(92,12,25)

the date appears as Friday, December 25, 1992.

You can use the same techniques to display only a portion of a date or time. For example, the format

mmmm

displays the date December 25, 1992 as the word *December.*

After you add a custom format to the Number dialog box, you only have to select the cells you want to format, choose the Number command from the Format menu, select the custom format from the dialog box, and then click OK or press Enter.

Secondary date and time functions

In addition to the primary date and time functions, DATE, TODAY, TIME, and NOW, Microsoft Excel offers a convenient set of secondary functions: WEEKDAY, YEAR, MONTH, DAY, HOUR, MINUTE, and SECOND. These functions let you extract information about the date and time values in your worksheet. Two other secondary functions, DATEVALUE and TIMEVALUE, are helpful when you need to perform date and time calculations.

The WEEKDAY function

The WEEKDAY function returns the day of the week for a specific date. The form of this function is

=WEEKDAY(*date*)

The *date* argument can be a serial value, a reference to a cell that contains either a date function or a serial date value, or text, such as 1/27/93 or January 27, 1993. If you use text, be sure to enclose it in quotation marks.

The result of the WEEKDAY function is a number from 1 through 7 that matches the day of the week for the date. For example, if the date is a Sunday, the function returns the number 1.

TIP: Format a cell containing Weekday function in one of the day-of-week formats. This formatting lets you use the weekday value in other functions and still have a meaningful display on the screen.

The YEAR, MONTH, and DAY functions

The YEAR, MONTH, and DAY functions return the value of the year, month, and day terms of a serial date/time number. The forms of these three functions are nearly identical:

=YEAR(*date*)

=MONTH(*date*)

=DAY(*date*)

The *date* argument can be a serial date value, a reference to a cell that contains either a date function or a serial date value, or a text date enclosed in quotation marks.

The result of these functions is the value of the specified term of the *date* argument. For example, if cell A1 contains the formula

=DATE(92,12,25)

the formula

=YEAR(A1)

returns the value 1992, the formula

=MONTH(A1)

returns the value 12, and the formula

=DAY(A1)

returns the value 25.

The HOUR, MINUTE, and SECOND functions

Just as the YEAR, MONTH, and DAY functions let you extract the year, month, and day terms of a serial date/time number, the HOUR, MINUTE, and SECOND functions extract the hour, minute, and second portions of a serial date/time number. The forms of these three functions are similar:

=HOUR(*time*)

=MINUTE(*time*)

=SECOND(*time*)

The result of these functions is the value of the specified term of the *time* argument. For example, if cell B1 contains the formula

=TIME(12,15,35)

then the formula

=HOUR(B1)

returns the value 12, the formula

=MINUTE(B1)

returns the value 15, and the formula

=SECOND(B1)

returns the value 35.

The DATEVALUE and TIMEVALUE functions

DATEVALUE translates a date into a serial number. It is similar to the DATE function, except that you must enter a text argument. The form of this function is

=DATEVALUE(*date text*)

where *date text* represents any date between January 1, 1900 and December 31, 2078, in any of Excel's built-in date formats. (Remember the quotation marks around the text.) For example, the formula

=DATEVALUE("1/1/93")

returns the serial number 33970. If you enter *date text* without a year, Excel uses the current year from your computer's internal clock.

The function TIMEVALUE translates a time into a decimal value. It is similar to the TIME function, except that you must enter a text argument. The form of this function is

=TIMEVALUE(*time text*)

where *time text* represents a time in any of Excel's built-in time formats. (Remember the quotation marks around the text.) For example, if you enter

=TIMEVALUE("4:30 PM")

the function returns the decimal value 0.6875.

Specialized date functions

Microsoft Excel also includes a set of date functions that performs specialized operations such as calculations for the maturity dates of securities, payroll, and work schedules. The functions described in this section are available only when you install the Analysis Toolpak add-in. For more information about add-ins, see Chapter 21.

The EDATE and EOMONTH functions

The EDATE function lets you calculate the exact date that falls an indicated number of months before or after a given date. The form of this function is

=EDATE(*start date,months*)

where *start date* is the date you want to measure from, and *months* is an integer value that indicates the number of months from the start date you want the function to calculate. If the month argument is positive, the function returns a date after the start date; if the month argument is negative, the function returns a date previous to the start date.

For example, to find the date that falls exactly 23 months after June 12, 1992, enter the formula

=EDATE(33767,23)

which returns the value 34466, or May 12, 1994.

The EOMONTH function returns a date that is an indicated number of months before or after a given date. EOMONTH is similar to the EDATE function, except that the value returned is always the last day of the month. The function has the form

=EOMONTH(*start date,months*)

For example, to calculate the serial date that is the last day of the month that is 23 months after June 12, 1992, enter the formula

=EOMONTH(33767,23)

which returns 34485, or May 31, 1994.

The YEARFRAC function

The YEARFRAC function calculates a decimal number that represents the portion of a year that falls between two given dates. The form of this function is

=YEARFRAC(*start date,end date,basis*)

where *start date* and *end date* specify the period of time you want to convert to a fractional year, and *basis* is the type of day count you want to use. A basis of 0 (or omitted) indicates 30/360, a basis of 1 indicates actual/actual, a basis of 2 indicates actual/360, and a basis of 3 indicates actual/365.

For example, to determine the fraction of a year that falls between 4/12/92 and 12/15/92, enter the formula

=YEARFRAC(33706,33953)

which returns 0.678, based on the default 30-day month and 360-day year.

The WORKDAY and NETWORKDAYS functions

The WORKDAY and NETWORKDAYS functions provide an invaluable service to anyone who needs to make payroll or benefits calculations, or determine work schedules. Both of these functions return values that are based on working days only, excluding weekend days. In addition, you can choose whether you want to include holidays in the calculation, and specify the exact holiday dates to include.

The WORKDAY function returns the date that is exactly the indicated number of working days before or after a given date. The form of this function is

=WORKDAY(*start date,days,holidays*)

where *start date* is the date you want the function to count from, and *days* is the number of workdays before or after the start date, excluding weekends and holidays. Use a positive value for *days* to count forward from the start date; use a negative value to count backward. The optional *holidays* argument can be an array or a reference to a cell range that contains the dates you want to exclude from the calculations. Add any dates that you want to exclude to this array or range. If you leave *holidays* blank, the function counts all weekdays from the start date. For example, to determine the date that is 100 working days from the current date, use the formula

=WORKDAY(NOW(),100)

To exclude holidays for 1992, the following formula uses the serial date values for February 17, May 25, September 7, October 12, November 26, and December 25 as the *holidays* argument, entered in array style:

=WORKDAY(NOW(),100,{33651,33749,33854,33889,33934,33963})

Similarly, the NETWORKDAYS function calculates the number of working days between two given dates. This function takes the form

=NETWORKDAYS(*start date,end date,holidays*)

where *end date* is the last date you want to include in the range. Again, you can choose to exclude holidays, if you want. For example, to determine the number of working days (holidays included) between January 15, 1993 and June 30, 1993, use the formula

=NETWORKDAYS(33984,34150)

which results in a value of 118.

10

The Analysis ToolPak

*A*s its name suggests, the Analysis ToolPak is a collection of tools that augments Microsoft Excel's built-in analytic capability. The ToolPak lets you create histograms, generate random-number sets that are not uniformly distributed, produce rank-and-percentile tables, apply Fourier and other transformations to your data, extract random or periodic samples from a data set, perform regression analysis, return various statistical measures of a data sample, and more.

The capabilities of the Analysis ToolPak are broad enough to warrant a book of their own. In this chapter we'll focus on a few of those capabilities. For details about specific commands and functions that are not covered here, we recommend Excel's excellent on-line Help system.

Accessing the Analysis ToolPak

The Analysis ToolPak is an add-in module that provides 90 new functions and 19 new commands. If you performed a complete installation of Excel, the add-in is available each time you start an Excel session. You can use the ToolPak functions just as you would other Excel functions, and you can access the ToolPak commands by pulling down the Options menu and choosing Analysis Tools. The first time you do this, you'll have to wait a moment while Excel reads a file from disk. Then you'll see the dialog box shown in Figure 10-1. To use an analysis tool, select its name from the list box and fill out any dialog boxes that appear. In most cases, completing the dialog box means pointing out the data you want to analyze (your input range), telling Excel where you want it to write its analysis (the output range), and choosing the options you want.

FIGURE 10-1.
After attaching itself to Excel, the Analysis ToolPak presents a list of its tools.

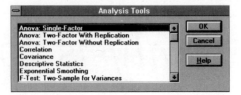

If the Analysis Tools command does not appear on your Options menu, or if a formula that uses a ToolPak function returns a #NAME? error, you must attach the ToolPak add-in by rerunning the Setup program. Put disk 1 of your Excel distribution disks in a floppy drive, use Program Manager's File Run command to run A:SETUP (or B:SETUP, as the case may be), choose Custom Installation, and select Analysis ToolPak from the options presented.

Analyzing distribution and generating histograms

A distribution analysis reports the number of items in a data range that fall between specified boundaries. A histogram is a chart (usually a simple column chart) that plots a distribution analysis.

To see how Microsoft Excel's distribution-analysis commands work, let's suppose we have the table of SAT scores shown in Figure 10-2. We'd like to see a breakdown of the total scores at 50-point intervals. Our table consists of 1000 scores, all of which fall within the range 900 to 1400, so we'll start by setting up the distribution "bins" shown in column F of Figure 10-3.

The bins don't have to be equally spaced, as these are, but they must be in ascending order. (If they are equally spaced, you can create the bins easily by using the Fill Down or Data Series command.) The input range must contain numeric data only.

FIGURE 10-2.
*We'll use the
Histogram command
to analyze and chart
these test scores.*

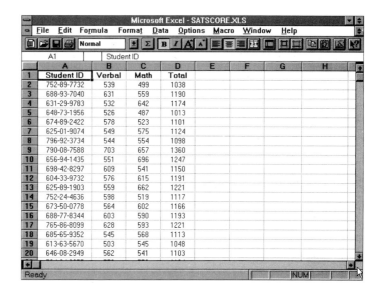

FIGURE 10-3.
*First create
distribution bins.
The bins must be
in ascending order,
but they don't have to
be equally spaced.*

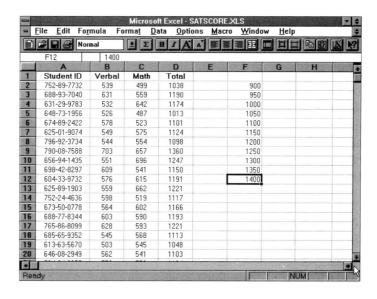

Next, we'll choose Analysis Tools from the Options menu and select the Histogram command from the ToolPak's main list box. The Histogram dialog box appears, as shown in Figure 10-4.

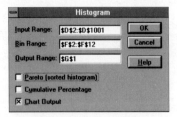

The Histogram command requires three items of information — the range that contains the data we want to analyze, the location of our distribution bins, and the upper left cell of the range where we want the analysis to appear. Optionally, it can also create a *pareto* (sorted) analysis, include cumulative percentages, and generate a chart. For now, we'll accept the chart and skip the other options. (We'll come back to them later.) When we click OK, Excel creates a chart and writes its analysis in columns G and H. The analysis is shown in Figure 10-5.

Next to each bin value in the output range, the Histogram command reports the number of input values that are equal to or greater than the bin value but less than the next bin value. The last value in the table (0 in Figure 10-5) reports the number of input values equal to or greater than the last bin value.

Note that the command duplicates your column of bin values as the leftmost column of its output range. This duplication is convenient if you want to put the output in some other corner of your worksheet (or on another worksheet), but not

FIGURE 10-5.

*The analysis tells us
that 5 scores were at
least 900 but less than
950, 13 were at least
950 but less than
1000, and so on.*

Microsoft Excel - SATSCORE.XLS

File   Edit   Formula   Format   Data   Options   Macro   Window   Help

Normal

	A	B	C	D	E	F	G	H
1	Student ID	Verbal	Math	Total			Bin	Frequency
2	752-89-7732	539	499	1038		900	900	5
3	688-93-7040	631	559	1190		950	950	13
4	631-29-9783	532	642	1174		1000	1000	56
5	648-73-1956	526	487	1013		1050	1050	157
6	674-89-2422	578	523	1101		1100	1100	272
7	625-01-9074	549	575	1124		1150	1150	240
8	796-92-3734	544	554	1098		1200	1200	173
9	790-08-7588	703	657	1360		1250	1250	64
10	656-94-1435	551	696	1247		1300	1300	17
11	698-42-8297	609	541	1150		1350	1350	3
12	604-33-9732	576	615	1191		1400	1400	0
13	625-89-1903	559	662	1221				
14	752-24-4636	598	519	1117				
15	673-50-0778	564	602	1166				
16	688-77-8344	603	590	1193				
17	765-86-8099	628	593	1221				
18	685-65-9352	545	568	1113				
19	613-63-5670	503	545	1048				
20	646-08-2949	562	541	1103				

Ready   NUM if you want it to go right next to the bin values. Unfortunately, you'll get an error message if you try to write the output over the bin-value range, so if you're planting the output right next to the bins as we did in Figure 10-5, you might want to drag the output range (after the command has finished!) and move it one column to the left. You can do this easily with Excel's direct cell manipulation feature.

Also note that, because the Histogram command copies your bin-value range, it's best to use constants, rather than formulas, for the numbers in that range. If you do use formulas, be sure they don't include relative references; otherwise, when the Histogram copies the range, the formulas might produce unwanted results.

Charting the distribution analysis

If you want the ToolPak to generate a chart at the same time it performs its analysis, select Chart Output from the Histogram dialog box. The chart created from the data set in Figure 10-2 is shown in Figure 10-6.

This is a standard Excel column chart, displayed in a separate window. For details about formatting, saving, embedding, printing, and editing Excel charts, see Chapters 13 through 15.

FIGURE 10-6.
The Histogram can automatically create a column chart like this one.

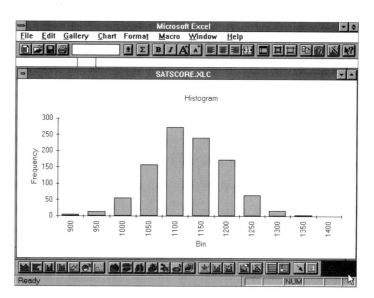

The Pareto and Cumulative Percentage options

The other two options offered by the Histogram command let you sort the output (in descending order) and create a table that lists the cumulative percentages of each bin level. By choosing to create a table of cumulative percentages with the data in Figure 10-2, for example, you learn that 50.3 percent of the student population scored below 1150.

Omitting the bin range

If you want, you can leave the Bin Range line blank when you fill out the Histogram dialog box. Excel then chooses evenly distributed bin intervals, using the minimum and maximum values in the input range as end points. The number of intervals is equal to the square root of the number of input values.

Analyzing distribution with the FREQUENCY function

The Histogram command generates a set of constants. If you'd rather create formulas linked to the input values, you can use the ToolPak's FREQUENCY function. This is an array function that uses the syntax

=FREQUENCY(*data_array,bins_array*)

To use the FREQUENCY function, start by setting up a column of bin values, just as you would with the Histogram command. Next, select the entire area where you want the output to appear. This must also be a column of cells; the FREQUENCY command won't write to a row or multi-column range. Enter the formula, specifying the input range as your first argument and the bin range as your second. Finally, terminate the formula by pressing Ctrl-Shift-Enter. Figure 10-7 shows the FREQUENCY function applied to the data in Figure 10-2.

WARNING: *The FREQUENCY function does not interpret the bin-value range the same way the Histogram command does. With the Histogram command, each value in the output range represents the number of input values that are greater than or equal to the current (adjacent) bin value and less than the following bin value. With the FREQUENCY function, each output represents the number of inputs that are greater than the previous bin value and*

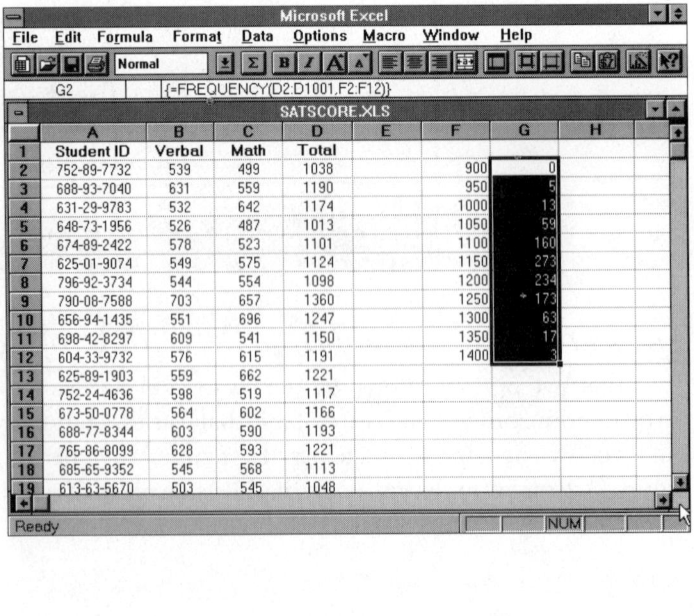
Microsoft Excel
File Edit Formula Format Data Options Macro Window Help
Normal
G2
{=FREQUENCY(D2:D1001,F2:F12)}
SATSCORE.XLS
A B C D E F G H
1 Student ID Verbal Math Total
2 752-89-7732 539 499 1038 900 0
3 688-93-7040 631 559 1190 950 5
4 631-29-9783 532 642 1174 1000 13
5 648-73-1956 526 487 1013 1050 59
6 674-89-2422 578 523 1101 1100 160
7 625-01-9074 549 575 1124 1150 273
8 796-92-3734 544 554 1098 1200 234
9 790-08-7588 703 657 1360 1250 173
10 656-94-1435 551 696 1247 1300 63
11 698-42-8297 609 541 1150 1350 17
12 604-33-9732 576 615 1191 1400 3
13 625-89-1903 559 662 1221
14 752-24-4636 598 519 1117
15 673-50-0778 564 602 1166
16 688-77-8344 603 590 1193
17 765-86-8099 628 593 1221
18 685-65-9352 545 568 1113
19 613-63-5670 503 545 1048
Ready
NUM

FIGURE 10-7.
To link the distribution analysis to the input data (so that if the data change, the analysis stays current), use the FREQUENCY function.

less than or equal to the current bin value. If you're used to using Lotus 1-2-3's /Data Distribution command, you'll probably want to stick with the FREQUENCY function and avoid the Histogram command. The FREQUENCY function returns exactly the same results as would be returned by /DD in 1-2-3.

Generating a rank and percentile report

Suppose you want to rank the scores shown in Figure 10-2. Clearly you can do this by sorting the data. (Microsoft Excel's sorting procedures are described in Chapter 5.) If you sort in descending order, the best score appears at the top and the worst score appears at the bottom of the column. To find the rank of any score, you might want to create an ascending series of numbers alongside the sorted scores, with 1 beside the best score and 1000 beside the worst.

The Analysis ToolPak includes a Rank and Percentile command that not only does these tasks for you, but also creates percentile figures for each value in your input range. To use this command, choose the Options menu's Analysis Tools command and select Rank and Percentile. The dialog box that appears asks for input and output ranges; as with the Histogram command, the input range must contain numeric data only.

Columns E through H in Figure 10-8 show the result of the Rank and Percentile command as applied to column D of the test-score data in Figure 10-2. The first row of this report tells us that the 812th item in the input range was a score of 1387 and that this score ranked first and was better than 100 percent of the other scores. Row 2 says that the second-best score was 1360, was the eighth item in the input range, and was better than 99 percent of the competition — and so on.

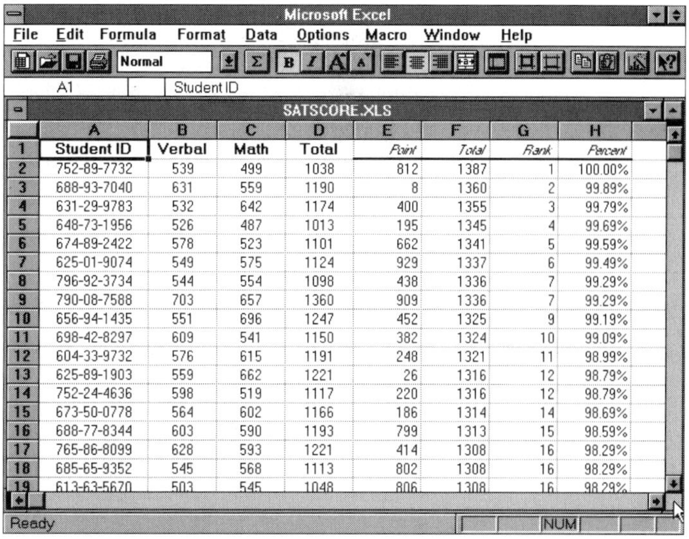

FIGURE 10-8.
We used the Rank and Percentile command to analyze the totals listed in column D. The command produced the report in columns E through H.

	A	B	C	D	E	F	G	H
1	Student ID	Verbal	Math	Total	*Point*	*Total*	*Rank*	*Percent*
2	752-89-7732	539	499	1038	812	1387	1	100.00%
3	688-93-7040	631	559	1190	8	1360	2	99.89%
4	631-29-9783	532	642	1174	400	1355	3	99.79%
5	648-73-1956	526	487	1013	195	1345	4	99.69%
6	674-89-2422	578	523	1101	662	1341	5	99.59%
7	625-01-9074	549	575	1124	929	1337	6	99.49%
8	796-92-3734	544	554	1098	438	1336	7	99.29%
9	790-08-7588	703	657	1360	909	1336	7	99.29%
10	656-94-1435	551	696	1247	452	1325	9	99.19%
11	698-42-8297	609	541	1150	382	1324	10	99.09%
12	604-33-9732	576	615	1191	248	1321	11	98.99%
13	625-89-1903	559	662	1221	26	1316	12	98.79%
14	752-24-4636	598	519	1117	220	1316	12	98.79%
15	673-50-0778	564	602	1166	186	1314	14	98.69%
16	688-77-8344	603	590	1193	799	1313	15	98.59%
17	765-86-8099	628	593	1221	414	1308	16	98.29%
18	685-65-9352	545	568	1113	802	1308	16	98.29%
19	613-63-5670	503	545	1048	806	1308	16	98.29%

On looking at this output table, you presumably would want to know the student ID number of the person whose score was the 812th item in the input range, the ID for the student whose score was the 8th item, and so on. One easy way to make this information available is to insert a new column next to the rank column. Add the heading *Student ID,* and then use the INDEX function to get the ID numbers. Figure 10-9 shows the result. (For details about the INDEX function, see Chapter 8.)

In our example, we applied the Rank and Percentile command to a single column of data. We could also use it to analyze all three scores — verbal, math, and total. In that case, we would specify the entire block of B1:D1001 as our input range, and the command would generate 12 columns of output — 4 for each input column.

NOTE: *Be sure that the data you analyze consists only of numeric constants or formulas that use absolute references. If the input cells contain formulas with relative references, these references might become scrambled in the output range when they're sorted.*

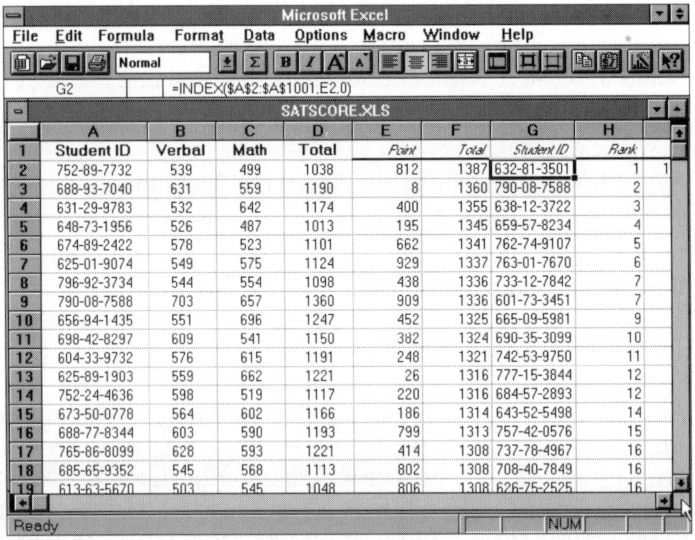

	A	B	C	D	E	F	G	H	
1	Student ID	Verbal	Math	Total	*Point*	*Total*	*Student ID*	*Rank*	
2	752-89-7732	539	499	1038	812	1387	632-81-3501	1	1
3	688-93-7040	631	559	1190	8	1360	790-08-7588	2	
4	631-29-9783	532	642	1174	400	1355	638-12-3722	3	
5	648-73-1956	526	487	1013	195	1345	659-57-8234	4	
6	674-89-2422	578	523	1101	662	1341	762-74-9107	5	
7	625-01-9074	549	575	1124	929	1337	763-01-7670	6	
8	796-92-3734	544	554	1098	438	1336	733-12-7842	7	
9	790-08-7588	703	657	1360	909	1336	601-73-3451	7	
10	656-94-1435	551	696	1247	452	1325	665-09-5981	9	
11	698-42-8297	609	541	1150	382	1324	690-35-3099	10	
12	604-33-9732	576	615	1191	248	1321	742-53-9750	11	
13	625-89-1903	559	662	1221	26	1316	777-15-3844	12	
14	752-24-4636	598	519	1117	220	1316	684-57-2893	12	
15	673-50-0778	564	602	1166	186	1314	643-52-5498	14	
16	688-77-8344	603	590	1193	799	1313	757-42-0576	15	
17	765-86-8099	628	593	1221	414	1308	737-78-4967	16	
18	685-65-9352	545	568	1113	802	1308	708-40-7849	16	
19	613-63-5670	503	545	1048	806	1308	626-75-2525	16	

FIGURE 10-9.
We used the INDEX function to match student ID numbers with the ranked scores.

Using functions to analyze rank and percentile

The Analysis ToolPak includes several worksheet functions that extract rank-and-percentile information from a set of input values. These functions are PERCENTRANK, PERCENTILE, QUARTILE, SMALL, LARGE, and RANK.

PERCENTRANK

The PERCENTRANK function returns a percentile ranking for any member of a data set. You can use this function to create a percentile table that's linked to the input range so that if the input values change, the percentile figures remain up-to-date. We used this function to create the percentile ranking in column E of Figure 10-10.

FIGURE 10-10.

If you want percentile figures to be linked to input values, or if you want more than two digits' precision, use the PERCENTRANK function.

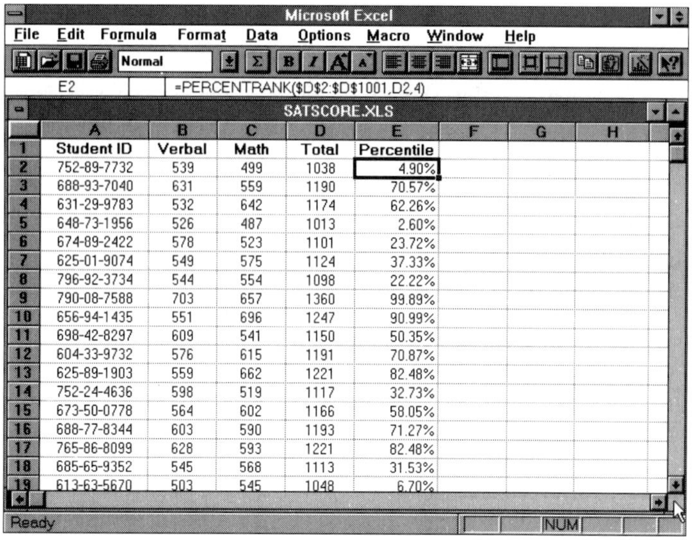

The PERCENTRANK function takes three arguments. The first argument specifies the input range (D2:D1001, in our example), and the second specifies the value whose rank you want to obtain. The third argument is optional and indicates the number of digits of precision you want. If the third argument is omitted, Excel assumes precision to be three digits.

PERCENTILE and QUARTILE

The PERCENTILE function lets you determine which member of an input range stands at a specified percentile ranking. For example, to find out which score in Figure 10-10 represents the 87th percentile, we can use the formula

=PERCENTILE(D2:D1001,.87)

Note that you must express the percentile as a decimal fraction greater than 0 and less than or equal to 1.

The QUARTILE function works much like the PERCENTILE function, except that it can return only the lowest, 25th percentile, median, 75th percentile, or highest value in the input set. The first of the function's arguments specifies the input range. The second argument must be 0, 1, 2, 3, or 4 and has the following significance:

Argument	Returns
0	Lowest value
1	25th percentile value
2	Median (50th percentile) value
3	75th percentile value
4	Highest value

Note that you can use the MIN, MEDIAN, and MAX functions instead of QUAR-TILE(*range*,0), QUARTILE(*range*,2), and QUARTILE(*range*,4), respectively. These functions are noticeably faster than QUARTILE, particularly with large data sets.

SMALL and LARGE

The SMALL and LARGE functions return the *k*th smallest and *k*th largest values in an input range. For example, to find the 15th highest score in Figure 10-10, you can write the formula

=LARGE(D2:D1001,15)

RANK

The RANK function returns the ranked position of a particular number within a set of numbers. For example, to find out what ranking the score 1200 has in the data set in Figure 10-10, you can write the formula

=RANK(1200,D2:D1001)

By default, the highest value is ranked 1, the second highest is ranked 2, and so on. If you want the values ranked from the bottom instead of the top, add a third argument to the function. Use any value other than 0 as the third argument.

Note that if there is no exact match between the RANK function's first argument and the input values, the function returns #N/A!

Generating random numbers

Microsoft Excel's standard random-number function, RAND, generates a uniform distribution of random real numbers between 0 and 1. That is, from a set of formulas based on the RAND function, all values between 0 and 1 are equally likely to be returned. Figure 10-11 illustrates the distribution of one particular trial of 5000 RAND formulas. Note that because the sample is relatively small, the distribution is by no means perfectly level. Nevertheless, repeated tests of this kind would demonstrate that the RAND function does not favor any position within its distribution spectrum.

The random-number component of the Analysis ToolPak lets you create sets of random numbers that are not uniformly distributed. Such random-number sets might be useful for such things as Monte Carlo decision analysis and other kinds of simulations. Six distribution types are offered: Uniform, Normal, Bernoulli, Binomial, Poisson, and Discrete (user-defined). In addition, the Patterned option lets

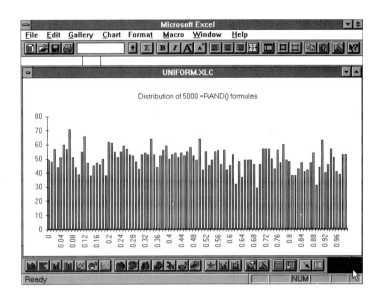

FIGURE 10-11.
Excel's RAND function returns uniformly distributed real numbers between 0 and 1.

you create non-random numbers at specified intervals. (The Patterned option can serve as an alternative to Excel's Data Series command; refer to the "The Patterned option," later in this chapter.)

Specifying a seed value

With any of the Random Number command's distribution types, you can choose to specify a seed value. Each time you generate a random-number set in a particular distribution using a particular seed, you will get exactly the same sequence of numbers. Therefore, you should use this option only if you need to reproduce a random-number sequence for some reason.

Other random-number parameters

When you choose the Random Number command, you'll see a dialog box similar to the one shown in Figure 10-12 on the following page. For all distribution types, you specify an output range and how many numbers you want. Leave the Random Seed line blank unless you want the same numbers to appear each time you use the command. The Parameters section of this dialog box changes, depending on which kind of distribution you select. As the figure shows, when you choose uniform distribution, you can specify the end points of the distribution.

FIGURE 10-12.
*The Parameters
section of this dialog
box changes,
depending on the
distribution type
you choose.*

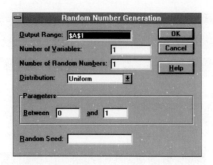

Use the Output Range text box to tell Excel where you want your random numbers to go. If the range you specify already has data in it, you'll see a warning message before the data is overwritten. The Number of Variables and Number of Random Numbers text boxes let you tell the program how many columns of numbers you want and how many numbers you want in each. If you want 10 columns of 100 numbers each, for example, put 10 on the Number of Variables line and 100 on the Number of Random Numbers line.

The Uniform Distribution option

The Random Number command's Uniform Distribution option works the same way as the RAND function, generating an evenly distributed set of real numbers between specified end points. You can use this option as a more convenient alternative to RAND when you want end points other than 0 and 1 or when you want sets of numbers to be based on the same seed.

If you want to generate random integers between specified end points, use the RANDBETWEEN function (discussed in Chapter 8).

The normal distribution

The normal distribution is characterized by the following:

- One particular value, the mean, is more likely to be returned than any other value.

- Values above the mean are as likely to occur as values below the mean.

- Values close to the mean are more likely to occur than values distant from the mean.

To generate normally distributed random numbers, you specify two parameters, the mean and the standard deviation. The standard deviation is the average absolute difference between the random numbers and the mean. Approximately 68 percent of the values in a normal distribution will fall within one standard deviation of the mean.

Note that you can use the Analysis ToolPak's Descriptive Statistics command, described later in this chapter, to verify the "normalcy" of a normally distributed set of random numbers. Figure 10-13, for example, shows a distribution curve and a table of descriptive statistics for a set of 1000 random numbers generated with the Normal Distribution option, using a mean of 100 and a standard deviation of 2. Again, you should note that, because the sample is small, the output of the Random Number command does not accord perfectly with statistical theory!

FIGURE 10-13.
We generated 1000 normally distributed random numbers, using 100 as the mean and 2 as the standard deviation.

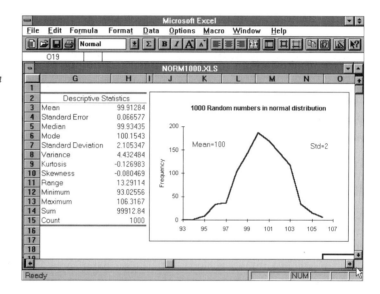

The Bernoulli distribution

The Bernoulli distribution simulates the probability of success of a number of trials, given that all trials have an equal probability of succeeding and that the success of one trial has no impact on the success of the remaining trials. All values in the Bernoulli distribution's output are either 0 or 1. The probability that each cell will return a 1 is given by the distribution's sole parameter, p. So, for example, if you want 1000 random Bernoulli values whose most likely sum is 270, you would define a 1000-cell output range and specify a p of 0.27. The value of p must be between 0 and 1.

The binomial distribution

The binomial distribution simulates the number of successes in a fixed number of trials, given a specified probability rate. As with the Bernoulli distribution, the trials are assumed to be independent — the outcome of one has no effect on any other.

To generate binomially distributed numbers, you specify two parameters: p (the probability that any trial will succeed) and the number of trials. Note that "succeed" in this context has no value implication. You can use this distribution to simulate failure as readily as success.

Suppose, for example, you manufacture a product in lots of 1000 and that your historical defective-part rate is 1 in 65. To simulate the number of defective units that are likely to occur in each lot, you would specify .015385 ($\frac{1}{65}$) as p and 1000 as the number of trials. (Note that you must provide a decimal fraction between 0 and 1 as the p parameter. The dialog box won't accept a formula.)

The Poisson distribution

The Poisson distribution lets you simulate the number of times an event occurs within a particular time span, given a certain probability of occurrence. The occurrences are assumed to be independent; that is, each occurrence has no effect on the likelihood of others.

The Poisson distribution takes a single parameter, *lambda*, which represents the probability of an individual occurrence. The value of *lambda* must be between 0 and 1.

The Discrete option

The Discrete option lets you create your own distribution pattern by specifying a table of possible outcomes along with the probability associated with each outcome. The probability values must be between 0 and 1, and the total of the probabilities must be exactly 1. The Random Number command asks you to specify the possible outcomes and their probabilities as a two-column range. This range is the only parameter used by the Discrete option.

In Figure 10-14, we used the Discrete option with a table of probabilities to create a "triangular" distribution. The table of outcomes and probabilities occupies the range A2:B20. The theoretical distribution is shown in the chart in the upper right corner of the worksheet. The chart in the lower right corner shows the actual distribution of the set of 1000 random numbers generated by the Random Number command.

Outcome	Probability	Results
500	0.01	1600
600	0.02	800
700	0.03	800
800	0.04	600
900	0.05	1000
1000	0.06	1500
1100	0.07	1600
1200	0.08	2100
1300	0.09	1100
1400	0.1	600
1500	0.09	1400
1600	0.08	2300
1700	0.07	2000
1800	0.06	1000
1900	0.05	1400
2000	0.04	1800
2100	0.03	1300
2200	0.02	1500
2300	0.01	1700

FIGURE 10-14.
We used the Discrete option to generate a set of random numbers with a triangular distribution.

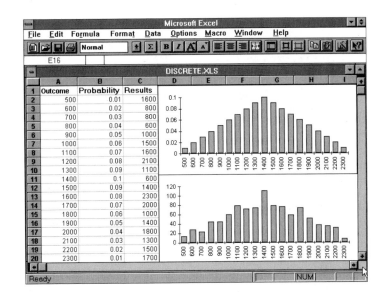

The Patterned option

The Random Number command includes a Patterned option that actually generates nonrandom numbers. After you select the Patterned option, the dialog box shown in Figure 10-15 appears.

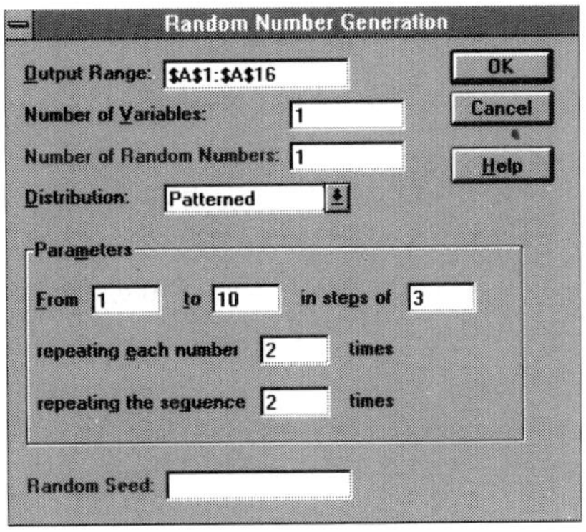

FIGURE 10-15.
The Patterned option lets you create an arithmetic series with optional repetitions.

You can think of the Patterned option as a kind of fancy Data Series command. It lets you create one or more arithmetic series with optional internal repetitions. For example, to create the series 1, 1, 4, 4, 7, 7, 10, 10, 1, 1, 4, 4, 7, 7, 10, 10, you would fill out the dialog box as shown in Figure 10-15, asking for two sequences of 1 to 10, using skip values of 3, and repeating each number twice within each cycle.

If skipping at the skip interval would take the series over the specified upper value, the command includes the upper value by truncating the last interval. For example, if you asked for a skip value of 4 in the range 1 to 10, you would get 1, 5, 9, and 10.

Sampling a population of numbers

The Analysis ToolPak's Sampling command lets you extract a subset of a set of numbers. From an input population, you can select either a specified number of values at random or every nth value. The command copies the extracted numbers to a specified output range. Figure 10-16 shows the dialog box that appears when you use the Sampling command.

FIGURE 10-16.
The Sampling command lets you extract a random or periodic subset of a numeric population.

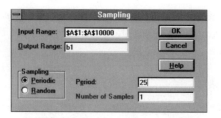

The values in your input range must be numeric. If you want to extract items from a range of text values, you can set up a series of ascending integers beginning at 1 in a column alongside the text values. Next, use the Sampling command to extract numbers from this series. Finally, extract your text values by using the resulting numbers as arguments for the INDEX function. (For an example of the use of the INDEX function, see Figure 10-9, earlier in this chapter.)

Your input range can include blank values or dates, assuming the dates were entered as numbers, not as text strings. Thus, for example, if you want to simplify a chart of daily commodity prices, you can use the Sampling command to extract every nth data point and then create a new plot from the extracted data.

Calculating moving averages

A moving average is a forecasting technique that simplifies trend analysis by "dampening" historical fluctuations. For example, suppose you have the three-year demand curve shown in Figure 10-17. To generate a less "noisy" trend line from this data, you can plot a three-month moving average. The first point in the moving average line would be the average of the first three monthly figures (January through March, 1989). The next point would average the second-through-fourth monthly figures (February through April, 1989), and so on. You can use the Moving Average command to perform this analysis for you.

The Moving Average command requires three pieces of information: an input range (the range that contains the data you want to analyze), an output range (where you want the averaged data to appear), and the averaging interval. For a three-month moving average, for example, you would specify an interval of 3.

Figure 10-18 on the following page shows our original demand curve superimposed by a three-month moving average. The Moving Average command produced the data in column C, which were used to create the thick plot line in the chart. Note that the first two cells in the command's output range contain #N/A! values. Where the interval is n, you will always have $n-1$ #N/A!'s at the beginning of your output. But including those values in a chart presents no problem because Excel simply leaves the first area of the plot line blank.

FIGURE 10-17.
We charted three
years of historic data.

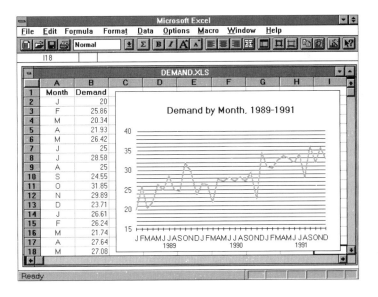

FIGURE 10-18.
The Moving Average command gives us a better perspective of the overall trend.

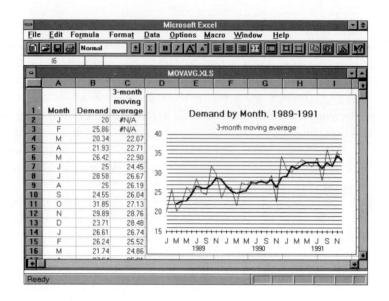

Descriptive statistics

The last Analysis ToolPak command we'll discuss in this chapter provides a table of descriptive statistics for one or more sets of input values. For each variable in your input range, the output table includes the following information: the mean, standard error, median, mode, standard deviation, variance, kurtosis, skewness, range, minimum, maximum, sum, count, kth largest and smallest (for any value of k you want to specify), and the confidence level for the mean. The dialog box for the Descriptive Statistics command is shown in Figure 10-19.

FIGURE 10-19.
Use the Descriptive Statistics command to create a table of descriptive statistics.

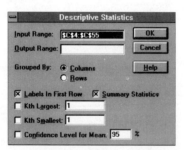

To use the Descriptive Statistics command, specify an input range that consists of one or more variables, an output range, and whether your variables are arranged by column or by row. If you include a row of labels, be sure to select the Labels in First Row option. Excel will then use these labels to identify the variables in its output table. Choose the Summary Statistics option if you want a detailed output table. If you want only a few items in the output report (such as the *k*th largest or smallest value), leave this check box empty and use the remaining check boxes to tell Excel which information you want.

Like the other commands in the Analysis ToolPak, Descriptive Statistics creates a table of constants. If a table of constants doesn't suit your needs, you can get most of the same statistical data from other ToolPak or Excel functions. These functions, and their syntax, are listed in the following table:

To obtain this statistic	Use this formula
Mean	=AVERAGE(*range*)
Median	=MEDIAN(*range*)
Mode	=MODE(*range*)
Standard deviation (sample)	=STDEV(*range*)
Standard deviation (population)	=STDEVP(*range*)
Variance (sample)	=VAR(*range*)
Variance (population)	=VARP(*range*)
Kurtosis	=KURT(*range*)
Skewness	=SKEW(*range*)
Range	=MAX(*range*)–MIN(*range*)
Minimum	=MIN(*range*)
Maximum	=MAX(*range*)
Sum	=SUM(*count*)
Count	=COUNT(*range*)
*k*th largest	=LARGE(*range,k*)
*k*th smallest	=SMALL(*range,k*)

11

What-If Analysis

*O*ne of the most important benefits of spreadsheet software is that it lets you perform *what-if analysis* quickly and easily. You can change key variables and instantly see the effect of those changes on other cells in your worksheet. For example, if you're using Microsoft Excel to help decide whether to lease or purchase a car, you can test your financial model with different assumptions about interest rate and down payment, and you can see the effects of varying rates on "bottom line" measures, such as your total interest paid.

The automatic recalculation feature common to all spreadsheet programs provides some degree of what-if capability. If you change the value of a particular cell in any spreadsheet program and your model is set to recalculate automatically, all the cells whose values depend on the value of the cell you changed are immediately recalculated.

Excel 4 augments this basic capability with these advanced what-if features:

- The Data Table command, which creates *sensitivity* tables by varying the value of one or two input cells

- The Scenario Manager, which lets you name various combinations of assumptions and create a summary table of their impacts

- The Goal Seek command, which automatically finds the value of an input cell that will produce a desired result at a given output cell

- The Solver, an add-in that takes the trial and error out of optimization problems by using advanced mathematics and iterative recalculation to find which combination of adjustable values produces a desired effect — such as maximizing profit or minimizing expenses — while meeting specified constraints

We discuss all of these features in this chapter.

Sensitivity tables

A sensitivity table summarizes the impact of one or two variables on formulas that use those variables. Microsoft Excel's Data Table command lets you create two kinds of tables. You can supply a single input variable and test the variable's impact on more than one formula, or you can supply two input variables and test their effects on a single output formula.

Sensitivity tables based on one input

Suppose you're considering buying a house that would require you to take a 30-year, $200,000 mortgage, and you need to calculate your monthly payments on that loan. You would like to see the outcome for several interest rates. A one-variable sensitivity table will give you the information you need.

To create this table, we'll start by entering the various interest rates we want to test — 9, 9.5, 10, 10.5, 11, and 11.5 percent — in cells B3:B8 in a fresh worksheet. We'll call this range the *input range,* because it contains the inputs we want to test. Next, we enter the *table formula*

=PMT(A2/12,360,200000)

in cell C2. In this formula, A2/12 is the monthly interest rate, 360 is the term of the loan in months, and 200000 is the loan principal. Notice that this formula refers to cell A2, which is currently blank. (Excel assigns a value of 0 to a function argument when the argument refers to a blank cell.) As you can see in Figure 11-1, because A2 is blank, the function returns a spurious result: the payment required to amortize the loan at an interest rate of 0 percent. Actually, cell A2 is merely a placeholder through which Excel will feed the individual variables in the input range. This placeholder can be any cell in the worksheet outside the table range. You'll see in a moment why this formula refers to cell A2.

FIGURE 11-1.

We begin building our sensitivity table by entering the interest rates and the PMT function into the worksheet.

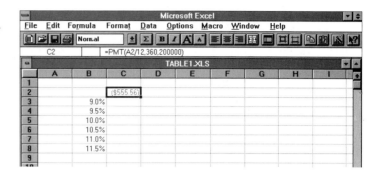

Next, define the *data-table range* by selecting it. In Excel, the data-table range is always the smallest rectangular range that includes the table formula and all the values in the input range. In this case, you select the range B2:C8.

Now choose Table from the Data menu. When you do this, you see the dialog box shown in Figure 11-2. The Row Input Cell and Column Input Cell options define the location of what we call the *input cell*. The input cell is the placeholder cell referred to, at least indirectly, by the table formula. In this example, A2 is the input cell. For the table to work properly, you must enter the input-cell reference in the correct section of the dialog box. If the values in the input range are arranged in a column, you should enter the input-cell reference in the Column Input Cell text box. If the input values are arranged in a row, you should enter the input-cell reference in the Row Input Cell text box. Because the input values in this example are arranged in a column, enter the input-cell reference in the Column Input Cell text box by selecting it and either typing the absolute reference of the input cell, $A$2, or pointing to that cell and clicking.

FIGURE 11-2.

Use the Table dialog box to specify your input cell.

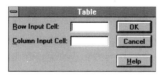

When you lock in your dialog-box settings, Excel enters the six results of the table formula (one result for each input value) into the range C3:C8, as shown in Figure 11-3 on the following page.

FIGURE 11-3.
The monthly loan payments for each interest rate now appear in the sensitivity table.

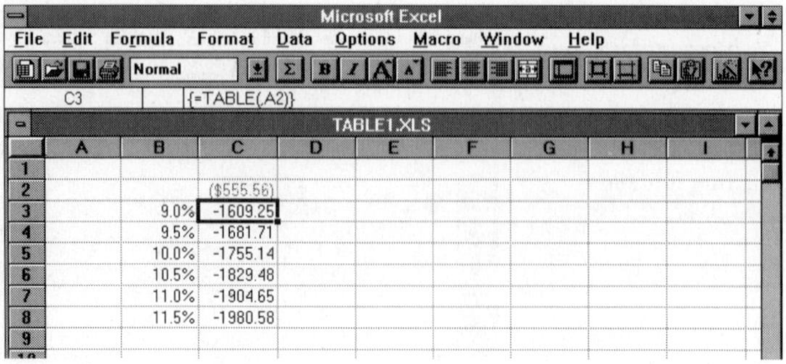

When you create this sensitivity table, Excel enters the formula

{=TABLE(,A2)}

into each cell in the range C3:C8 (the results range). Notice that the formula is enclosed in braces to show that the cell is part of an array. The TABLE formula takes the form

=TABLE(*row input cell,column input cell*)

Because the one-input table in our example is arranged in a columnar format, Excel places the column input reference, A2, as the second argument in the formula. We're not using a row input cell in this table, so that argument is left blank. Notice, however, that the comma is used to tell Excel that an argument has been omitted.

In our sample table, the TABLE formula computes the results of the PMT function using each of the interest rates in column B. For example, the formula in cell C5 computes the payment at a rate of 10.0 percent.

After you've built the table, you can change the table formula or any of the variables in the list to create a different set of results. For example, suppose you decide to borrow only $185,000 to buy your house. If you change the formula in cell C2 to

=PMT(A2/12,360,185000)

the values in the table also change, as shown in Figure 11-4.

FIGURE 11-4.
When we changed the loan amount, Excel recalculated the table.

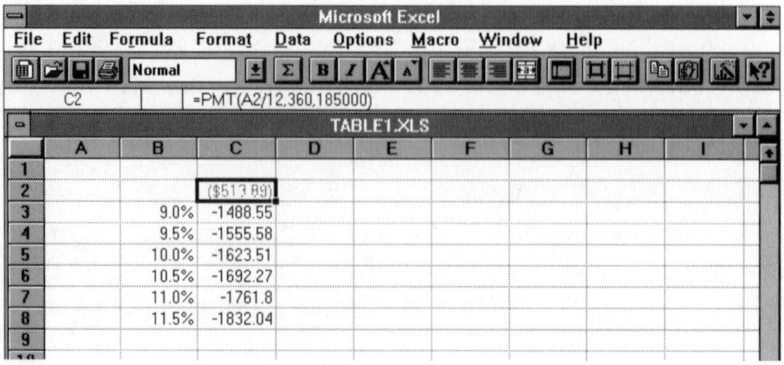

Single-variable tables with more than one output formula

You can include as many output formulas as you want in a one-variable sensitivity table. If your input range is in a column, enter the second output formula directly to the right of the first one, the third to the right of the second, and so on.

You can expand the table in Figure 11-3 to include two formulas. Suppose you're also thinking about buying a house that would require you to take out a $180,000 mortgage. You want to know what your monthly payments would be on that mortgage at each of the interest rates in the input range, and you want to be able to compare these payments with those for the $200,000 mortgage.

To create this new table, enter the formula

=PMT(A2/12,360,180000)

in cell D2. Notice that, like the first formula, this formula refers to cell A2, the input cell. Next select the table range B2:D8, choose the Table command, and enter the input-cell reference in the Column Input Cell text box. Figure 11-5 shows the result. As before, each cell in the range C3:D8 contains the formula

{=TABLE(,A2)}

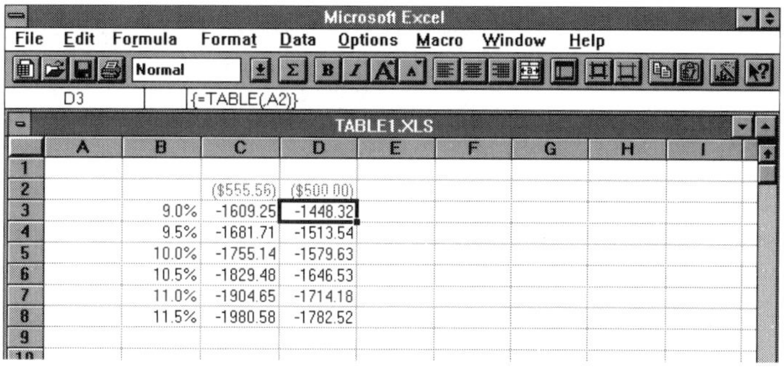

FIGURE 11-5.
This table computes the monthly payments on two loan amounts at various interest rates.

These formulas compute the results of the formulas in cells C2 and D2 at each interest rate in the input range. For example, the formula in cell D4 computes the result of the formula in cell D2 at the rate in cell B4, 9.5 percent.

Sensitivity tables based on two inputs

The sensitivity tables considered so far compute the effect of a single variable on one or more formulas. Excel also lets you create tables that compute the results of a formula as two variables change.

Suppose you want to build a sensitivity table that computes the monthly payment on a $200,000 mortgage, but this time you want to vary not only the interest rate but also the term of the loan. You want to know what effect changing the term to 30, 25, 20, or 15 years (360, 300, 240, or 180 months) will have on your monthly payment.

To create this table, first enter the six interest rates you want to test in the range B3:B8. Next enter the different monthly terms in cells C2:F2.

Now you can create the table formula. Because this is a two-variable table, the formula must be entered in the cell at the intersection of the row and column that contain the two sets of input values — cell B2 in this example. Although you can include as many formulas as you want in a one-input sensitivity table, you can include only one output formula in a two-input table. The formula for this table is

=PMT(A1/12,B1,200000)

Figure 11-6 shows the formula with two blank cells: A1 and B1. Because both these cells are blank, the table formula returns the error value #DIV/0! This spurious result does not affect the performance of the table.

FIGURE 11-6.
Cell B2 contains the
formula for the
two-input table.

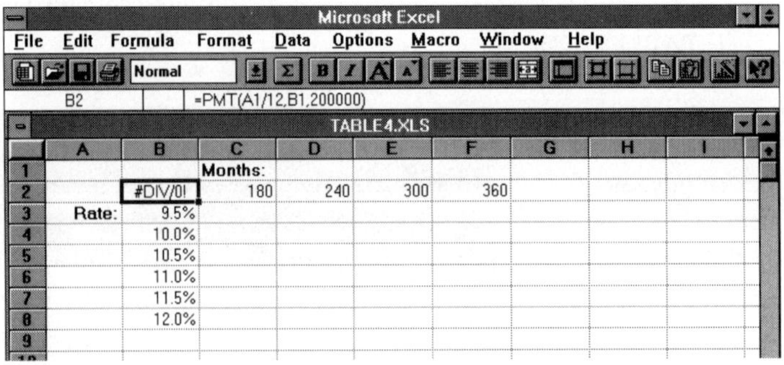

Next, select the table range. As with the one-input table, the table range for a two-input table is the smallest rectangular block that includes all the input values and the table formula. In this example, the table range is B2:F8.

After you select the table range, use the Table command to define the input cells. Because this is a two-input table, you must define two input cells: one for the input values stored in column B and one for the input values stored in row 2. Enter the reference for the first input cell, $A$1, in the Column Input Cell text box, and enter the reference for the second input cell, $B$1, in the Row Input Cell text box. After you enter data in the input cells, press Enter or click OK to compute the table. Figure 11-7 shows the result.

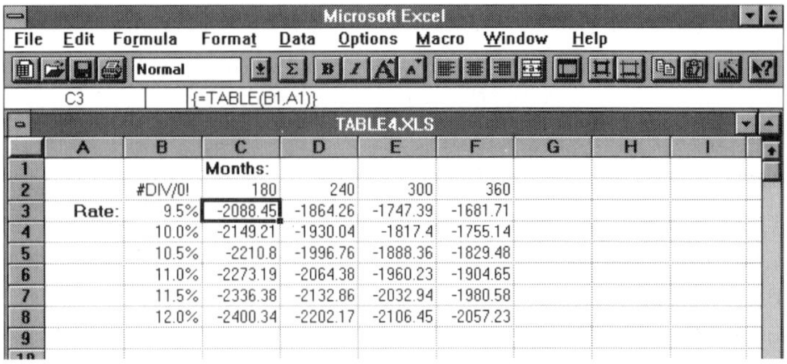

FIGURE 11-7.
This table calculates the monthly payments using various interest rates and terms.

	A	B	C	D	E	F	G	H	I
1			Months:						
2		#DIV/0!	180	240	300	360			
3	Rate:	9.5%	-2088.45	-1864.26	-1747.39	-1681.71			
4		10.0%	-2149.21	-1930.04	-1817.4	-1755.14			
5		10.5%	-2210.8	-1996.76	-1888.36	-1829.48			
6		11.0%	-2273.19	-2064.38	-1960.23	-1904.65			
7		11.5%	-2336.38	-2132.86	-2032.94	-1980.58			
8		12.0%	-2400.34	-2202.17	-2106.45	-2057.23			
9									

As in the previous examples, Excel enters a TABLE array formula in the output range, C3:F8. Because this table has two sets of variables, the TABLE formula includes two references:

{=TABLE(B1,A1)}

The values in the results range are the monthly payments required to amortize the mortgage at each combination of interest rates and terms. For example, the number in cell D6, −2064.38, is the payment required to amortize a $200,000 mortgage over 240 months at an interest rate of 11.0 percent.

Be careful not to reverse the input cells in a two-variable table. If you do, Excel uses the input values in the wrong place in the table formula, which creates a set of meaningless results. For example, if you reverse the input cells in this example, Excel would have used the numbers in the range C2:F2 as interest rates and the numbers in the range B3:B8 as terms.

Editing tables

Although you can edit the input values or formula in the left column or top row of a table, you can't edit the results in the individual cells. For example, if you try to edit cell D7 in Figure 11-7, Excel displays the alert message *Cannot change part of a table*. Thus, if you make a mistake when you set up a data table — for example, you enter an incorrect reference as the input cell — you can't clear an individual cell. Instead, you must select all the results, use the Clear command, and then recompute the table.

You can copy the table results to a different part of the worksheet. You might want to do this to save the table's current results before you make a change to the table formula or to the variables. To copy the results of the sample table in Figure 11-7 from the range C3:F8 to the range C10:F15, select cells C3:F8, choose the Copy command from the Edit menu, select cell C10, and then choose the Paste command. (You can also use direct cell manipulation to copy it, as described in Chapter 5.) As Figure 11-8 shows, the numbers in C10:F15 are constants, not array formulas. Excel changes the results of the table from a set of array formulas to their numeric values when you copy the results out of the table range.

You can delete a table if you no longer need it, or if you have made so many mistakes in it that you want to start over. Select all cells that contain the table — input values, formulas, and results — and choose the Clear command from the Edit menu.

FIGURE 11-8.
Copying the results range to another part of the worksheet transfers the numeric values, not the formulas.

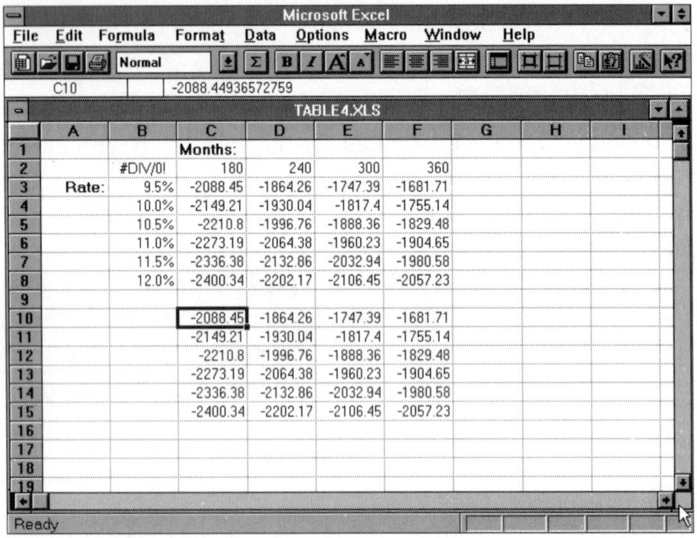

The Scenario Manager

Sensitivity tables are fine for relatively simple situations that involve only one or two variables. But real-world decisions usually involve many more unknowns than that. To help you model more complicated problems that involve up to nine variables at once, Microsoft Excel 4 provides an add-in called the Scenario Manager. If you did a complete installation of Excel 4, the Scenario Manager command will appear on your Formula menu. If the Scenario Manager does not appear, you can install it by rerunning the Excel Setup program and choosing Custom Installation.

A *scenario* is a named combination of values assigned to one or more variable cells. The Scenario Manager lets you create as many scenarios as you like for a set of variables. In addition, the Scenario Manager works hand-in-hand with the Report Manager add-in, which is described in Chapter 12. After you create scenarios with the Scenario Manager, you can use the Report Manager dialog box to select the scenarios you want to print.

To see how the Scenario Manager works, imagine that you manage a grocery store whose profit picture is modeled by the worksheet shown in Figure 11-9. The numbers in D5:D6, D8, and E11:E16 are recent historical averages. You're interested in testing the impact of changes in these cells on the bottom line, shown in cell E18. Nine variables are far too many for the Data Table command, but the Scenario Manager can help.

FIGURE 11-9.
We'll use the Scenario Manager to model the effects of changing values at D5:D6, D8, and E11:E16 of this worksheet.

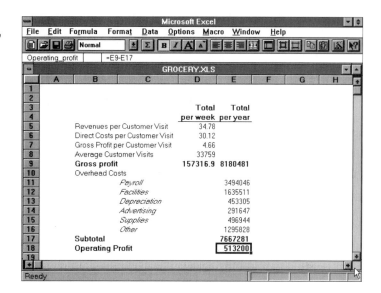

Defining scenarios

Before you begin using the Scenario Manager, it's a good idea to name the cells you plan to use as variables, as well as any cells whose values are dependent on your variable cells. This step is not required, but it makes the add-in's summary report, as well as some of its dialog boxes, more intelligible.

When you choose the Formula menu's Scenario Manager command, the dialog box shown in Figure 11-10 on the following page appears. First, indicate which cells you plan to vary by filling out the Changing Cells text box. By default, this text box displays the address of the cell or range that was selected when you chose the Scenario Manager command, but you can change it.

FIGURE 11-10.
The Scenario Mana-
ger first asks you to
specify the names or
addresses of each cell
you plan to vary.

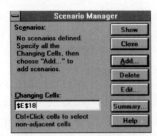

To specify your variable cells, either type their names or addresses or select each cell with the mouse. If you want to point to cells and the dialog box is in your way, click its title bar and drag it to the side. To specify a range of adjacent cells, you can drag the mouse over the range, or you can type a range reference (for example, D5:D6). As you fill out this part of the dialog box, a marquee appears around each cell you specify, as shown in Figure 11-11.

After you specify your variable cells, click Add to create your first scenario. When you click Add, a new dialog box appears, prompting you for a scenario name and suggesting a set of variable values. As Figure 11-12 shows, the default values for your variables are the values currently in the worksheet.

FIGURE 11-11.
The Scenario
Manager highlights
the variable cells with
marquees.

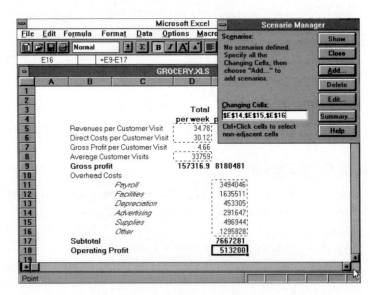

FIGURE 11-12.
To create a scenario,
click the Add button,
supply a scenario
name, and then enter
values for your
variable cells.

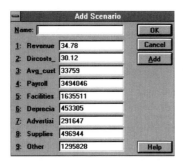

To complete the scenario, simply supply a name and edit the variable values. In each variable text box, you can enter either a constant or a formula. For example, if you want to increase the value of the first variable in Figure 11-12 (from cell D5), you can click the left side of the first variable's text box, and type *=1.1** to create a formula that multiplies the current value by 1.1.

After naming your scenario and filling out the variables, you can either click OK to return to your worksheet or click Add to create another scenario. You can create as many scenarios as you want at this time, and you can return to the Scenario Manager at a later time to create more scenarios or edit existing ones.

Using the Show button to view scenarios

After you've created a few scenarios, you might want to start testing their effects on your worksheet. You do this by invoking the Scenario Manager if necessary, selecting a scenario name in the Scenario Manager dialog box, and clicking Show. The Scenario Manager replaces the variable values currently in the worksheet with the values you specified when you created the selected scenario. Figure 11-13 on the following page shows how your worksheet might appear if you used the Show button with a scenario that increased average customer visits by 5 percent and reduced revenues per customer visit by the same amount.

The Scenario Manager dialog box remains on screen when you use the Show button so you can look at the results of other scenarios without returning to the worksheet. When you click Close or press Esc to close the Scenario Manager dialog box, the last scenario you looked at remains on the worksheet. You can reverse the effect of the last shown scenario by choosing the Edit menu's Undo command. But, as usual, you must use the Undo command before you make any other changes to the worksheet.

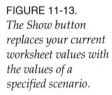

FIGURE 11-13.
*The Show button
replaces your current
worksheet values with
the values of a
specified scenario.*

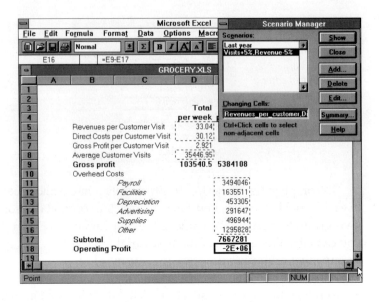

CAUTION: *The Scenario Manager's Show button replaces your worksheet's current
values with the values of the selected scenario. You can use the Edit menu's Undo command
to reverse this action when you return to the worksheet. But if you looked at two or more
scenarios, the Undo command reverses the effect of only the most recently shown scenario.
Therefore, you should always save your worksheet before experimenting with the Scenario
Manager's Show button.*

Turning scenarios into workbook pages

You can preserve the effects of alternative scenarios, as well as the values currently
on your worksheet, by saving each scenario as a separate worksheet and then binding the worksheets into a workbook file. (For more about Excel's workbook feature,
see Chapter 6.) Here's one way to create such a workbook:

1. After you define your scenarios, save your worksheet with its current
    values.

2. Choose the Scenario Manager command, select your first scenario, and click
    Show.

3. Click Close or press Esc to return to the worksheet. Use the File Save As
    command to save this worksheet under a new name. Choose a name that's
    clearly related to the name of your first scenario.

4. Without closing the current (renamed) file, reopen your file under its
    original name. (You'll find it in the first position in the recent file list at the
    bottom of the File menu.)

5. Repeat steps 2 through 4 for each scenario in turn.

6. Use the File Save Workbook command to bind all your scenarios into a common XLW file.

This sequence of steps copies your original worksheet several times and assigns the values from a different scenario to each copy.

Creating a summary worksheet

The Summary button in the Scenario Manager dialog box creates a table that shows the values each scenario assigns to each variable. Optionally, this summary table also shows the impact of each scenario on one or more result cells. Figure 11-14 shows the dialog box that appears if we click the Summary button in our grocery worksheet.

In the top part of this dialog box, the Scenario Manager lists your variable cells. You can't change these here, but you can change the optional result cell that appears in the bottom of the dialog box. As a default result cell, the Scenario Manager proposes the cell that happens to be the final dependent of your variable cells — in this case, the Operating Profit figure in cell E18. If you want additional result cells, a different result cell, or no result cells in your summary, modify the add-in's default by pointing with the mouse or typing a new reference.

When you click OK, the Scenario Manager creates its summary table on a new worksheet, as shown in Figure 11-15 on the following page. Note that the summary table lists your variable cells and one or more result cells by name if you have supplied names for them. The names of the scenarios, however, appear as column

FIGURE 11-14.
Clicking the Summary button creates a table that summarizes the impact of each scenario on one or more "bottom-line" cells.

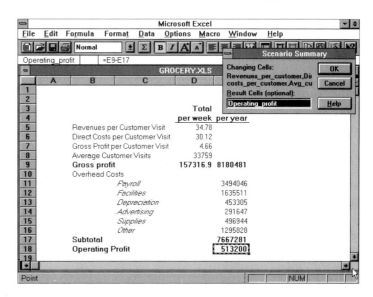

FIGURE 11-15.
*The Scenario
Manager creates
its summary table
on a new worksheet.
Variable and result
cells are listed by
name if you have
named them, and
scenarios are pre-
sented in the order
in which they were
defined.*

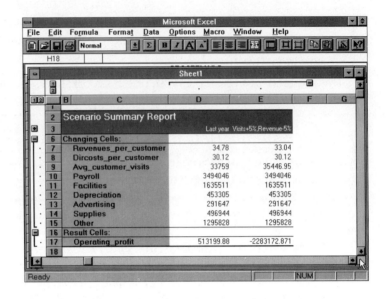

headings, and the columns appear in the order in which the scenarios were defined. You might want to use Excel's Data Sort command (described in Chapter 5) to sort the columns according to the value of one of your result cells. You might also want to add more descriptive text to each column's scenario. You can do that by inserting new rows below the column headings, by creating text boxes, or by using Excel's Formula Note command.

If you're saving individual scenarios as workbook pages, as suggested earlier in this section, you'll probably want to name the new summary worksheet and bind it into your workbook.

Adding, editing, and deleting scenarios

Scenarios are saved with all other worksheet data when you use Excel's File Save command. This means that each time you load a worksheet, any scenarios associated with that document are still available for you to work with. You can add new scenarios as you go by choosing the Scenario Manager command and clicking Add. You can also edit an existing scenario by selecting its name in the Scenario Manager dialog box and clicking Edit. As time goes by, you'll probably also want to prune your scenario list, getting rid of scenarios that are no longer useful. As you would expect, you can do that by selecting a scenario name and clicking Delete.

You can also use the Scenario Manager dialog box to modify your variable cells. You can add variable cells, remove existing variable cells, or specify a completely different set of variables. The Scenario Manager can manage only one set of variables at a time, however, so if you specify an entirely new set of variables, all your previous scenarios will be deleted. You will see a warning message to that effect if you specify a new set of variable cells.

The Goal Seek command

Every spreadsheet program lets you change the value of input cells and see what effect that has on dependent cells. Microsoft Excel also lets you reverse this what-if process. With the Formula menu's Goal Seek command, you can compute the value that produces the result you're aiming for.

Suppose you want to know what size 30-year mortgage you can afford if the interest rate is 9.5 percent and you must limit your monthly payments to $4,000. Figure 11-16 shows how you can set up this problem.

FIGURE 11-16.
Excel's Goal Seek command can help you determine the maximum principal you can borrow if you want to keep your payments under a certain limit.

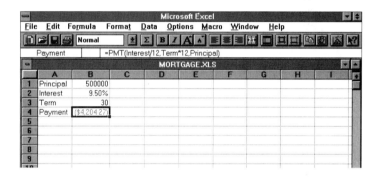

As you can see, a $500,000 mortgage would require monthly payments in excess of your $4,000 target. To find out how large a principal you can afford, first make B4 the active cell. (This isn't strictly necessary, but it simplifies the process.) Next, choose Goal Seek from the Formula menu. Excel displays the dialog box shown in Figure 11-17.

FIGURE 11-17.
To use goal-seeking, fill out this simple dialog box.

You want to make your Payment cell equal to –4000 by varying your Principal cell, so accept the value of $B$4 in the Set cell text box. Next, select the To value text box and type –4000. (Remember, Excel expects negative values for financial outflows.) Finally, select the By changing cell text box and type B1 — or point to B1 in the worksheet. (Alternatively, if you have assigned a name such as *Principal* to cell B1, you can type that name in the By changing cell text box.) Click OK or press Enter, and Excel displays the Goal Seek Status dialog box. Your answer — 475706.72 — appears in cell B1. To keep this value, click OK in the Goal Seek Status dialog box. To restore the value that was in B1 before you used the Goal Seek command, click Cancel.

Excel uses an iterative technique to perform goal seeking. It tries one value after another for the variable cell until it arrives at the solution you request. The mortgage problem we just looked at can be solved quickly. Other problems might take longer, and some might not be solvable at all.

While Excel is working on a complex goal-seeking problem, you can click Pause in the Goal Seek Status box to interrupt the calculation. You can then click Step to display the results of each successive iteration. A Continue button appears in the dialog box when you are solving a problem in this stepwise fashion. To resume full-speed goal seeking, click Continue.

Precision and multiple solutions

In Figure 11-18, we entered the formula =A2^2 in A1, and we asked the Goal Seek command to find the value of A2 that will make A1 equal to 4. The result, as shown in Figure 11-18, might be a little surprising. Excel seems to be telling us that the square root of 4 is 1.999917.

By default, the Goal Seek command stops when it has either performed 100 iterations (trial solutions) or found an answer that makes the goal cell come to

FIGURE 11-18.

By default, the Goal Seek command stops when the answer comes within 0.001 of your target value. You can use the Calculation command to make the results more precise.

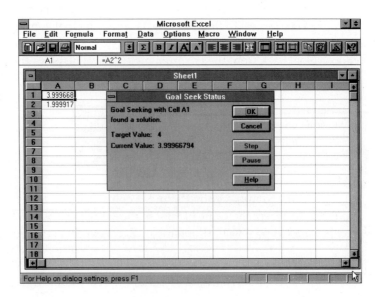

within 0.001 of your specified target value. If you need more precision than this, you can change the default limits by choosing the Calculation command from the Options menu. In the Calculations Options dialog box, you can change the Maximum Iterations value to a number higher than 100, the Maximum Change value to a number lower than 0.001, or change both values. For information about how Excel saves calculation options, see Chapter 3.

Figure 11-18 illustrates something else you should be aware of when you use the Goal Seek command. The Goal Seek command finds only one solution, even though your problem might have several. There are actually two square roots of 4: +2 and –2. In situations like this, the Goal Seek command tries to give you the solution with the same sign as the starting value. For example, in Figure 11-18, if we start with a value of –1 in cell A2, the Goal Seek command would report the solution as –2.0002, instead of +1.999917.

Introducing the Solver

The Goal Seek command is handy for problems that involve an exact target value that depends, ultimately or immediately, on a single unknown value. For more general problems, Microsoft Excel also includes a powerful optimizing tool called the Solver. The Solver can handle problems that involve many variable cells, can help you find combinations of variables that maximize or minimize a target cell, and lets you specify one or more constraints — conditions that must be met for the solution to be valid.

Like the Scenario Manager, the Solver is an add-in. If you performed a full installation of Excel 4, your Formula menu will include the Solver command. If

Differences between the Excel 3 and Excel 4 Solvers

The Solver was introduced with Excel 3. It has been rewritten completely to take advantage of the C application programming interface (API) provided with Excel 4. As a result, the new Solver can find solutions in as little as one-fourth of the time required by the Excel 3 Solver. In addition, the current version uses integer programming techniques when some or all of the variables must have integer outcomes. As of this writing, the Excel 4 Solver is the only spreadsheet optimizer that incorporates integer programming. Other improvements include a new sensitivity report, an automatic scaling option (useful for problems where variables and outputs differ by many orders of magnitude), and several ease-of-use features. Finally, the new Solver is conveniently integrated with the Scenario Manager.

you don't find that command on your Formula menu, you'll need to install the Solver by running the Excel Setup program again and choosing Custom Installation.

This section provides only an introduction to the Excel 4 Solver. A complete treatment of this powerful tool is beyond the scope of this book. For more details, including an explanation of the Solver's error messages, see the *Microsoft Excel User's Guide*. For background material on optimization, we recommend two text-books: *Management Science*, by Andrew W. Shogan (Englewood Cliffs, New Jersey: Prentice Hall, 1988) and *Operations Research, Applications and Algorithms*, by Wayne L. Winston (Boston: PWS-Kent Publishing Co., 1991).

For an example of the kind of problem that the Solver can tackle, imagine you are planning an advertising campaign for a new product. Your total budget for print advertising is $12,000,000, you want to reach at least 800 million readers, and you've decided to place ads in six publications — we'll call them Pub1 through Pub6. Each publication reaches a different number of readers and charges a different rate per page. (To keep this analysis simple, we'll ignore the issue of quantity discounts.) Your job is to reach the readership target at the lowest possible cost, while meeting the following additional constraints:

- At least six advertisements should run in each publication.

- No more than a third of your advertising dollars should be spent on any one publication.

- Your total cost for placing advertisements in Pub3 and Pub4 must not exceed $7,500,000.

Figure 11-19 shows one way to lay out the problem.

FIGURE 11-19.
We'll use the Solver to determine how many advertisements to place in each publication to meet our objectives at the lowest possible cost.

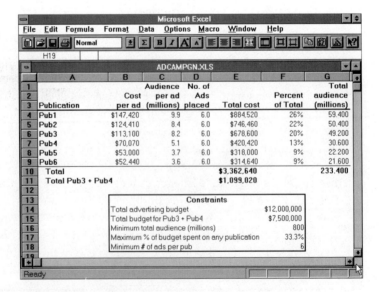

Publication	Cost per ad	Audience per ad (millions)	No. of Ads placed	Total cost	Percent of Total	Total audience (millions)
Pub1	$147,420	9.9	6.0	$884,520	26%	59.400
Pub2	$124,410	8.4	6.0	$746,460	22%	50.400
Pub3	$113,100	8.2	6.0	$678,600	20%	49.200
Pub4	$70,070	5.1	6.0	$420,420	13%	30.600
Pub5	$53,000	3.7	6.0	$318,000	9%	22.200
Pub6	$52,440	3.6	6.0	$314,640	9%	21.600
Total				$3,362,640		233.400
Total Pub3 + Pub4				$1,099,020		

Constraints	
Total advertising budget	$12,000,000
Total budget for Pub3 + Pub4	$7,500,000
Minimum total audience (millions)	800
Maximum % of budget spent on any publication	33.3%
Minimum # of ads per pub	6

You might be able to work this problem out by yourself by substituting many different alternatives for the values currently in D4:D9, keeping your eye on the constraints, and noting the impact of your changes on the total expenditure figure in G10. In fact, that's what the Solver will do for you — but it will do it much more rapidly, and it will use some analytic techniques to hone in on the optimal solution without having to try every conceivable alternative.

First, we'll choose the Solver from the Formula menu. The dialog box shown in Figure 11-20 appears. To fill out this dialog box, we must give the Solver three pieces of information: our objective (minimize total expenditure), our variables (the number of advertisements we'll place in each publication), and our constraints (the conditions summarized at the bottom of the worksheet in Figure 11-19).

FIGURE 11-20.
The Solver Para-
meters dialog box
prompts for three
items of information.

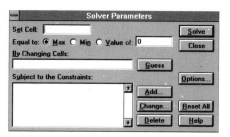

Stating the objective

In the Set Cell text box, you tell the Solver what you want to accomplish. We want to minimize our total cost figure, which is expressed in cell E10. Therefore, we specify our objective by entering E10 in the Set Cell text box and choosing the option button labeled Min. In Solver reports, the cell you specify in the Set Cell text box is called the *target cell.*

You can fill in the Set Cell text box by typing a cell's coordinates, typing a name that has been assigned to a cell, or pointing to a cell with the mouse. If you assign a name to the target cell, the Solver uses that name in its reports, even if you fill out the dialog box with the cell's coordinates instead of its name. Therefore, it's a good idea to name all the important cells of your model before you put the Solver to work. (If you don't name your cells, the Solver constructs names for the reports based on the nearest column-heading and row-heading text, but these names will not appear in the Solver dialog boxes.)

In our example problem, we want the Solver to set our objective cell to its lowest possible value, so we select Min. In other problems, you might want to raise a target cell to its highest possible value — for example, if your target cell expresses profits.

Alternatively, you can ask the Solver to find a solution that makes your objective cell equal to some particular value. To do that, you would select the Value option and enter an amount (or a cell reference) in the Value of text box. Note that, by selecting the Value option, specifying only one variable cell, and specifying no constraints at all, you can use the Solver as a glorified Goal Seek command.

You can also choose to specify no objective at all — that is, leave the Set Cell text box blank. By doing that and choosing the Show Iteration Results option (described in "The Show Iteration Results option," later in this chapter), you can use the Solver to step through some or all of the combinations of variable cells that meet your constraints. You will get an answer that solves the constraints but is not necessarily the optimal solution.

Specifying variable cells

The next step is to tell the Solver which cells to change — that is, you need to specify your variable cells. In our advertisement campaign example, the cells whose values can be adjusted are those that specify the number of advertisements to be placed in each publication. These cells lie in the range D4:D9. As usual, we can provide this information by typing cell coordinates, typing cell names, or pointing to cells on the worksheet. If the variables do not lie in an adjacent block, you should separate variable cells (or ranges) with commas. If you're pointing, hold down Ctrl while you select each cell or range.

You must specify at least one variable cell; otherwise, the Solver will have nothing to do. Also, if you specify a target cell (as you will in most cases), you must specify variable cells that are antecedents of the target cell. If the target cell's value does not depend on the variables, the Solver will not be able to solve anything.

Specifying constraints

The last step in filling out the Solver's dialog box is to specify constraints. You do that by clicking Add and filling out the Add Constraint dialog box shown in Figure 11-21.

FIGURE 11-21.
To specify a con-
straint, click Add and
fill out this dialog box.

As you can see, a constraint consists of three components: a cell reference, a comparative operator, and a constraint value. You specify your cell reference at the left side of the dialog box, choose a comparative operator from the drop-down list in the middle of the dialog box, and specify your constraint value at the right side of the dialog box. Figure 11-22 shows how we would express one of our constraints — that total advertising expenditure (cell E10 in our model) be less than or equal to

FIGURE 11-22.
We've told the Solver that our total advertising expenditure (E10) must not exceed budget (F14).

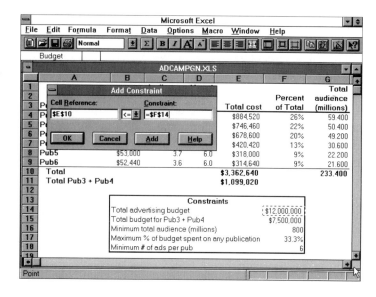

our total budget amount (cell F14). After specifying a constraint in this manner, you can either click OK to return to the Solver Parameters dialog box or click Add to express another constraint.

Figure 11-23 shows how the Solver Parameters dialog box looks after all our constraints have been named. Note that the constraints are listed in alphabetic order, not necessarily in the order in which you defined them.

FIGURE 11-23.
The Solver lists your constraints in alphabetic order and uses defined cell and range names wherever possible.

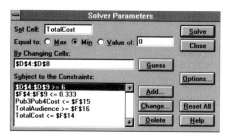

Also note that in two of our constraints, we've used range references on the left side of the comparative operator. We've used the expression $D$4:$D$9>=6 to stipulate that the value of each cell in D4:D9 must be 6 or greater, and the expression $F$4:$F$9<=0.333 to stipulate that the value of each cell in F4:F9 must be no greater than 33.3 percent. Each of these expressions is a shortcut for stating six separate constraints. If you use this kind of shorthand notation, the right-hand side of the constraint must either be a cell range of the same dimensions as the left-hand side, a single cell reference, or a constant value.

When you have filled out the dialog box, click Solve. As the Solver works, you'll see many messages flash across your status line. The Solver plugs trial values into your variable cells, recalculates the worksheet, and then tests the results. By comparing the outcome of each iteration with that of preceding iterations the Solver homes in on a set of values that meets your objective and satisfies your constraints. In our advertisement campaign example, the Solver stops before long and displays the dialog box shown in Figure 11-24.

You see the message in Figure 11-24 when the Solver arrives at an optimal value for your objective cell while meeting all of your constraints. When this message appears, the values displayed in your worksheet result in the optimal solution. You can leave these solution values in the worksheet by selecting the Keep Solver Solution option and clicking OK, or you can return the worksheet to its former state (the values that your variables held when you invoked the Solver) by pressing Esc, clicking Cancel, or selecting the Restore Original Values option and clicking OK. You also have the option of assigning the solution values to a named scenario; we look at that option in "Assigning the Solver results to named scenarios," later in this chapter.

The solution values shown in Figure 11-24 indicate that we can keep our advertisement campaign costs to a minimum by placing 6 ads in Pub1, 6 in Pub2, 33 in Pub3, 53.3 in Pub4, 34 in Pub5, and 6 in Pub6. This combination of placements will reach an audience of 800 million readers (assuming the publications' readership numbers are correct). Unfortunately, because it's not possible to run three-tenths of an advertisement, the solution is not practical. In fact, Pub4 is not the only publication for which the Solver is recommending a noninteger number of advertisement placements. The solution value for Pub3 is slightly more than 33, and that for Pub5 is slightly below 34, but these values appear to be whole numbers when displayed to one decimal point of precision.

FIGURE 11-24.
When the Solver succeeds, it presents this dialog box.

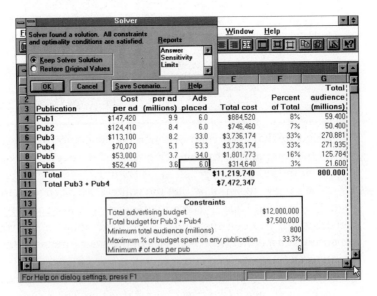

We can cope with the noninteger results in either of two ways — by rounding or by adding new constraints that force the results to be whole numbers. Rounding Pub4 upward produces a readership number of 803.2 million at a cost of $11,263,700, which appears to be an acceptable accommodation in this case. But let's see what happens if we constrain the Solver to give us an integer solution.

Specifying integer constraints

To stipulate that our advertisement placement variables be restricted to whole numbers, we invoke the Solver as usual and click the Add button. In the Add Constraint dialog box, we select the range that holds our placement numbers — D4:D9. Next, we open the drop-down list in the middle of the dialog box and select the last item, which is identified as *"int."* When we do that, the Solver adds the word *integer* to the right side of the constraint, as shown in Figure 11-25.

FIGURE 11-25.
To specify an integer constraint, select the item labeled "int" in the drop-down list.

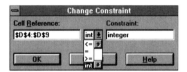

When we run the problem again with the new integer constraint, we discover that rounding the noninteger results was not the best we could do. It turns out that we can achieve a better whole-number solution by changing the Pub4 placements

Do you need integer constraints?

Adding integer constraints to a problem can increase geometrically the problem's complexity. In a problem like the one discussed in this chapter, the additional processing time that results from including integer constraints is insignificant because the problem itself is simple. In a more typical problem, however, forcing the Solver to handle integer constraints might result in unacceptable delays. If you don't have time to let the Solver complete an integer problem, you're probably better off removing the integer constraints and then using manual what-if methods to experiment with noninteger results.

Certain problems, however, can only be solved with integer methods. In particular, integer solutions are essential for problems in which decision variables can assume only two values, such as 0 or 1. If one of your variables records a yes-or-no decision, for example, you must constrain that variable to be an integer.

from 53.3 to 53.0 and increasing the Pub3 placements from 33 to 35. These figures generate a readership of 801.8 million at a cost of $11,246,630 — a savings of $17,070 over the simple round-up solution.

Saving and reusing the Solver parameters

When you save a worksheet after using the Solver, all the values you entered in the Solver's dialog boxes are saved along with your worksheet data. You will not need to respecify your problem at your next working session.

If you want to use more than one set of the Solver parameters with a given worksheet, however, you can use the Solver's Save Model option. To do this, invoke the Solver, click Options, and choose Save Model. Excel prompts you for a worksheet range on which to store the Solver's parameters. Specify a blank range by pointing or typing, and click OK. To reuse the saved parameters, click Options in the Solver Parameters dialog box, select Load Model, and specify the range to which you saved the Solver parameters.

You'll find it easiest to save and reuse the Solver parameters if you assign a name to each save range immediately after you use the Save Model command. That way, you can specify that name when you choose Load Model.

Generating reports

In addition to inserting optimal values into your problem's variable cells, the Solver can summarize its results in three reports. These reports are titled Answer, Sensitivity, and Limits. To generate one or more reports, select the names of the reports you want in the dialog box that appears when the Solver presents its solution. (See Figure 11-24.) Hold down Ctrl while you select each report that you want, and then click OK.

The Answer report

Figure 11-26 shows a portion of the Solver Answer report for our advertisement campaign problem. (To make more of the report visible in this screen shot, we've zoomed the window to 75 percent, hidden the toolbar, and deleted some blank rows.) As you can see, the report appears in a separate template window titled Answer Report 1. You can use the File Save command to turn this document into a normal worksheet file. Alternatively, you might want to create a workbook that consists of your original problem worksheet, plus this and any other Solver reports you produce.

The Answer report lists the objective cell (which it calls the target cell), each of your variables (adjustable cells), and each of your constraints. The Answer report also includes information about the status of and slack value for each of your

FIGURE 11-26.
*The Answer report
lists your object cell,
your variables, and
your constraints and
helps you distinguish
binding from non-
binding constraints.*

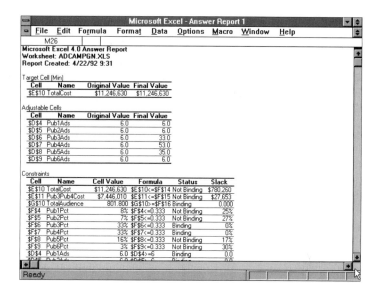

constraints. The status can be Binding, Not Binding, or Not Satisfied. The slack value is the difference between the solution value of the constraint cells and the number that appears on the right side of the constraint formula. For example, our constraint on total cost stipulated that total cost remain less than or equal to $12 million. The Solver's solution produced a total cost of $11,246,630. The slack value is $12 million minus $11,246,630, or $780,260.

A binding constraint is one for which the slack value is 0. A nonbinding constraint is a constraint that was satisfied with a nonzero slack value.

The Sensitivity report

The Sensitivity report provides information about how sensitive your target cell is to changes in your constraints. Figure 11-27 on the following page shows the Sensitivity report that the Solver produces for our advertising campaign if we delete the integer constraints. (The Sensitivity report is not available for problems that involve integer constraints.)

The Sensitivity report has two sections: one for your variable cells and one for your constraints. The right-hand column in each section provides the sensitivity information.

Each reduced gradient figure indicates how your target cell would be affected by a one-unit increase in the corresponding variable cell. For example, the reduced gradient of 5461.6 for the Pub1Ads variable (cell D4 in our model) means that if we constrained our solution to require the purchase of at least seven advertisements in Pub1, our total expenditure would increase by $5,461.60.

FIGURE 11-27.
*The Sensitivity report
provides information
about how changes in
your constraints
would affect your
target cell.*

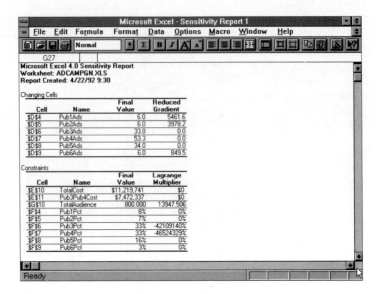

Similarly, each Lagrange multiplier number indicates how the target cell would be affected by a one-unit increase in the number to the left. For example, the Lagrange multiplier figure of 13947.506 on the third line of the Constraints section informs us that if we required the campaign to reach 801 million readers instead of 800 million, our total cost would increase by $13,947.51.

The Limits report

The Limits report tells you how much the values of your variable cells can be increased or decreased without breaking the constraints of your problem. Figure 11-28 shows the Limits report that the Solver produces for our advertising campaign if we delete the integer constraints. (The Limits report is not available for problems that involve integer constraints.)

For each variable cell, the Limits report lists the optimal value as well as the lowest and highest values that can be used without violating constraints. For example, the Limits report shown in Figure 11-28 shows that we can increase the number of advertisement placements in Pub1 from 6 to 11 without going over budget. Placing 11 advertisements in Pub1 would result in a suboptimal solution (meaning we need to spend more money than we might like) but would not run the campaign over budget.

FIGURE 11-28.

The Limits report tells you how much you can increase or decrease the value of variable cells without violating your constraints.

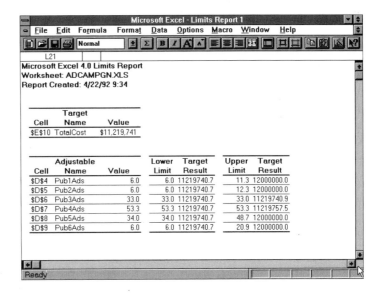

When the Solver is unable to solve

The Solver is powerful, but it's not miraculous. It might not be able to solve every problem you give it. If the Solver can't find the optimal solution to your problem, it presents an unsuccessful completion message, such as the one shown in Figure 11-29.

FIGURE 11-29.

If the Solver is unable to find the optimal solution to your problem, it presents this dialog box.

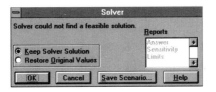

The most common unsuccessful termination messages are the following:

■ *The Solver could not find a feasible solution.* This means that the Solver is unable to find a solution that satisfies all your constraints. This can happen if the constraints are logically conflicting (for example, if in separate constraints you ask that Pub1 be greater than 5 and less than 3) or if not all of the constraints can be satisfied (for example, if you insist that your advertising campaign reach 800 million readers on a $1 million budget).

In some cases, the Solver also returns this message if your variable cells' starting values are too far from their optimal values. If you think your constraints are logically consistent and your problem is solvable, try changing your starting values and rerunning the Solver.

- *The maximum iteration limit was reached; continue anyway?* In order not to tie up your computer indefinitely with an unsolvable problem, the Solver is designed to pause and present this message when it has performed its default number of iterations without arriving at a solution. When you see this message, you can resume the search for a solution by clicking Continue or you can quit by clicking Stop. (You can also assign the current values to a named scenario. This option is described in "Assigning the Solver results to named scenarios," later in this chapter.)

  If you click Continue, the Solver begins solving again and does not stop until it finds a solution, gives up, or reaches its maximum time limit. If your Solver problems frequently exceed the iteration limit, you can increase the default by choosing the Solver command, clicking the Options button, and entering a new value on the Iterations line.

- *The maximum time limit was reached; continue anyway?* This message is similar to the iteration-limit message just discussed. The Solver is designed to pause after a default time interval has elapsed. You can increase this default by clicking Options and modifying the Max Time value.

The Assume Linear Model option

A linear optimization problem is one in which the value of the target cell is a linear function of each variable cell. That is, if you plotted an XY graph of the target cell's value against all meaningful values of each variable cell, your graphs would be straight lines. If some of your plots produced curves instead of straight lines, you would have a nonlinear problem.

The Solver can handle both linear and nonlinear optimization problems. But it can solve linear problems faster if you select the Assume Linear Model option. You can do this by clicking Options and selecting the check box labeled Assume Linear Model. If you use this option with a problem that is, in fact, not linear, the Solver presents an error message.

If you choose the Assume Linear Model option, the Solver produces a Sensitivity report in a slightly different form. For details, see the *Microsoft Excel User's Guide*.

The importance of using appropriate starting values

If your problem is nonlinear, you must be aware of one very important detail: Your choice of starting values can affect the solution generated by the Solver. Therefore, with nonlinear problems you should always do the following:

- Set your variable cells to reasonable approximations of their optimal values before running the problem.

- Test alternative starting values to see what impact, if any, they have on the Solver's solution.

The Show Iteration Results option

If you're interested in exploring many combinations of your variable cells, rather than only the combination that produces the optimal result, you can take advantage of the Solver's Show Iteration option. To do this, click Options and select the check box labeled Show Iteration Results. Then, after each iteration, you will see a dialog box like the one shown in Figure 11-30. After observing the status of the solution, you can continue by clicking Continue.

You should be aware that when you use this option, the Solver pauses for solutions that do not meet all your constraints as well as for suboptimal solutions that do.

FIGURE 11-30. *Choosing Show Iteration Results lets you explore suboptimal solutions and assign them to named scenarios.*

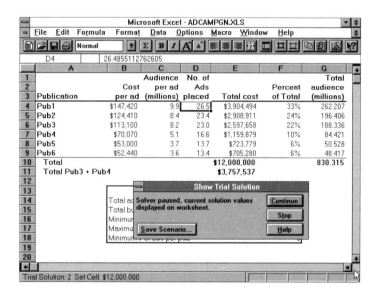

Assigning the Solver results to named scenarios

As you might have noticed, the Solver Show Trial Solution dialog box and various completion dialog boxes include a button labeled Save Scenario. If you click this button, the Solver invokes the Scenario Manager and lets you assign a scenario name to the current values of your variable cells. Choosing this option is an excellent way to explore — and perform further what-if analysis on — a variety of possible outcomes.

Letting the Solver work in the background

While the Solver is working, you can switch to other Windows applications. When the Solver has finished its work or needs input from you, it will sound your computer's bell and flash the Excel application window's title bar.

12

Printing and Presenting

Microsoft Excel makes it easy to produce polished, professional-looking reports from worksheets. This chapter explains how to use the Page Setup command to define the layout of your printed pages. It also explains how to restrict your print range, define print titles, control page breaks, and use Excel's Print Preview feature.

We'll also introduce two important new features of Excel 4, the Report Manager and the slide show facility. The Report Manager lets you assign names to particular combinations of print areas and print settings, making it easy for you to re-create a particular report at any time. The slide show facility lets you turn worksheet pages, charts, and imported graphics into impressive presentations, complete with visual and aural transitional effects.

This chapter concentrates on printing worksheet reports. However, all the techniques described here also apply to macro sheets. When we discuss charting in Chapter 13, we'll show you a few more tricks and techniques that will enhance the quality of your printed charts.

Printing an entire worksheet

Microsoft Excel automatically prints the entire populated area of your worksheet unless you tell it to do otherwise. Thus, if you simply want to print everything on the current worksheet, all you have to do is pull down the File menu and choose Print.

When you choose Print from the File menu, Excel presents the Print dialog box, as shown in Figure 12-1. You use this dialog box to tell Excel how you want your document printed. At the top of this dialog box is an important piece of information: the name of the printer to which Excel is about to print. If you have more than one printer driver installed in your Microsoft Windows system, it's a good idea to check this part of the dialog box to make sure you and Excel are in agreement about where the output is headed. If you need to change printer drivers, click Cancel, choose the File menu's Page Setup command, and then click the Printer Setup button. The Printer Setup dialog box includes a list of your installed printers, from which you can choose the printer you want to use.

FIGURE 12-1.
*The Print dialog box
lets you print a
specific range of pages
or ask for multiple
copies. It also
confirms the name of
the printer driver that
will process your
output.*

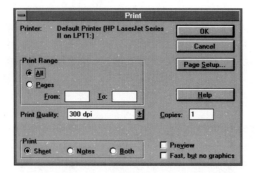

By default, Excel prints your worksheet only, omitting any notes you've attached to cells. You can use the option buttons at the bottom of the Print dialog box to print only the notes or to print both the worksheet and the notes. To restrict the printout to a specific range of pages, select the Pages option button and fill in the From and To text boxes.

Excel normally prints all graphic objects along with your worksheet data. To skip the graphics, select the check box labeled Fast, but no graphics. As its name suggests, this option can speed up the printing process considerably.

Printing multiple copies

Microsoft Excel normally prints one copy of whatever you ask it to print. If you want more than one copy, you have a choice. You can enter the number of copies you want in the Print dialog box (shown in Figure 12-1). Or you can choose Page Setup, click Printer Setup, select your printer from the Printer list, click Setup, and then specify the number of copies you want in the printer's setup dialog box. These two alternatives provide significantly different results.

Let's say you want to print two copies of a three-page document. If you ask for two copies by changing the Copies setting in the Print dialog box, Excel prints pages 1, 2, and 3 and then a second copy of pages 1, 2, and 3. If you ask for two copies by changing the setting in your printer's Setup dialog box, Excel prints two copies of page 1, followed by two copies of page 2, followed by two copies of page 3.

The first alternative may seem more convenient, but the second is often quicker. When you request multiple copies with the printer's setup dialog box, Excel treats the entire multi-copy printout as a single print job. It creates only one spool file for the Windows Print Manager, and it lets you return to your worksheet as soon as that spool file is created. Then the printer is responsible for printing multiple copies of each page it receives from your computer, a real timesaver.

On the other hand, if you request multiple copies by changing the setting in the Print dialog box, Excel treats each copy as a separate print job. That means it spends more time preparing spool files for Print Manager, and you have to wait longer before you can get back to work. And since the printer has to receive more pages from your computer, it moves slower too.

If you don't want to wait and you don't mind collating the output yourself, you might prefer to change the setting in the printer setup dialog box. Be aware, though, that a change in a printer driver's setup dialog box affects all subsequent printouts made with that driver, including those made from other Windows applications. If you change the printer's setup dialog box to make a multi-copy printout from Excel, you'll probably want to restore the default setting (one copy) at the end of your Excel session.

Printing with the Print tool

The shortest route to a default printout is to click the Print tool — the fourth tool from the left on an unmodified Standard toolbar. When you click the Print tool, Excel assumes that you want to reuse the last settings you made in the Print dialog box.

Printing a specific portion of a worksheet

Normally, when you choose the Print command, Microsoft Excel prints the entire populated area of your worksheet from cell A1 to the last cell, even if that means blank pages are printed. The Set Print Area command lets you print only selected sections of your worksheet. To define a print area, select the cells you want to print and choose Set Print Area from the Options menu.

Printing multiple ranges on the same page

Unlike Lotus 1-2-3 and Quattro Pro, Microsoft Excel automatically ejects the current page at the end of a print job. If you assign the name *Print_Area* to multiple nonadjacent regions, Excel also breaks pages between each region of your selection. Even if you combine different areas of a worksheet into a named report by using the Report Manager, Excel still starts each region on a new page.

Normally, the automatic page eject at the end of a print job is a convenience, because it means you don't have to worry about issuing Align and Page commands, as you do in Lotus 1-2-3. However, Lotus 1-2-3's approach has the virtue of letting you "gang" several print ranges on a single page.

If you want to print separate ranges together on one page in Excel, first try using Format menu commands to hide the intervening rows or columns. For example, you might print A1:D14 together with H1:K14 by hiding columns E:G and defining a print area that encompasses both ranges. If that approach isn't satisfactory (for example, because you want H1:K14 to be printed below A1:D14), you can use the Camera tool, found on the Utility toolbar. Take a snapshot of the second print range, paste it below the first range, and then define a print area that includes the first range plus the pasted snapshot.

Excel defines the print area you select as a range named *Print_Area*. You can edit or delete the range name by using the Define Name command from the Formula menu. If you delete the range *Print_Area*, Excel prints your entire worksheet the next time you use the Print command.

How Microsoft Excel breaks pages

When you print a large report, Microsoft Excel breaks that report into page-sized sections based on the current Page Setup settings. (We'll look at the Page Setup command in a moment.) The width of your columns, the height of your rows, and the size of the type you select also affect the number of rows and columns that can fit on each page.

If your print area is both too wide and too deep to fit on a single page, Excel normally works in "down, then over" order. For example, suppose your print area measures 120 rows by 20 columns, and given your Page Setup settings, Excel can fit 40 rows and 10 columns on a page. Using the "down, then over" order, Excel prints the first 40 rows and first 10 columns on page 1. Next, it prints the second 40 rows and first 10 columns on page 2, and then the third 40 rows and first 10 columns on page 3. On page 4, it prints the first 40 rows and second 10 columns — and so on. Using options in the Page Setup dialog box, you can change the printing order from "down, then over" to "over, then down."

Setting print titles

Although Microsoft Excel's automatic page-break capability is a big help, it can lead to a problem. Most of the time, the column and row labels that identify the contents of your worksheet are located in only the top few rows and leftmost columns of your worksheet. When Excel breaks a large report into pages, the column and row labels appear on the first page of the printout only. You can use the Page Setup command to assign headers and footers to your printout, so that a particular text string appears at the top or bottom of each page. Such text appears *only* on the printout, not on the worksheet.

The Set Print Titles command on the Options menu lets you print the contents of one or more rows, one or more columns, or a combination of rows and columns on every page of a report. Suppose you want to print the contents of rows 3 and 4 and column A on all pages of a lengthy report. To do this, choose Set Print Titles from the Options menu. Select the Titles for Columns box, and then select rows 3 and 4. Next select the Titles for Rows box, and then select column A. Then click OK to define your print titles. If you try to select nonadjacent rows or columns, Excel displays an alert box with the message *Select entire rows and/or columns before choosing Options Set Print Titles.*

Like the print area, the rows and columns you select for print titles are stored as a named range, this time with the name *Print_Titles.* You can edit or delete the *Print_Titles* range through the Define Name dialog box.

When you use the Set Print Titles command and the Set Print Area command, make sure your print titles don't lie within your print area. If they do, you might end up with two sets of row and column titles on the first page of your printed report.

Bear in mind that your print titles do not have to be adjacent — or even anywhere close — to your print area.

To cancel print titles, select the entire document by clicking the box at the intersection of the row and column headers, and then choose Remove Print Titles from the Options menu.

Setting manual page breaks

When you print a report that is too large to fit on a single sheet of paper, Microsoft Excel breaks that report into page-sized sections based on the current settings in the Page Setup dialog box. As you can see in Figure 12-2, Excel's automatic page breaks are indicated on the screen by dashed lines. (To make the page breaks easier to see, we've removed the worksheet gridlines from the display.)

FIGURE 12-2.
Automatic page breaks appear on the screen as light dashed lines.

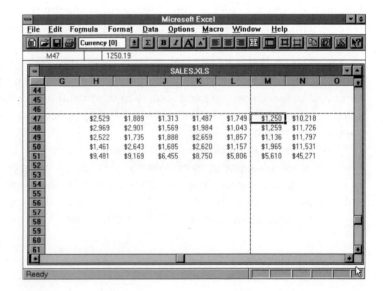

Frequently, you'll divide a report into pages yourself, rather than leave the decision to Excel. You can use the Set Page Break command on the Options menu to place vertical and horizontal page breaks in your printed report. The Set Page Break command tells Excel to force page breaks above and to the left of the current cell. When you add a forced page break, Excel adjusts the automatic page breaks in your document as well.

To distinguish manual page breaks from automatic ones, Excel marks manual page breaks with heavy dashed lines, as shown in Figure 12-3.

To add a horizontal page break without affecting the vertical breaks in your document, select the row with which you want to begin a new page, activate the cell in column A of that row, and choose the Set Page Break command. Excel inserts the horizontal page break just above the row you select. To insert a vertical page break without affecting the horizontal breaks, select the column with which you want to begin the new page, activate the cell in row 1 of that column, and choose the Set Page Break command. The page break will occur to the left of the column you select.

To delete a forced page break, select the cell below or to the right of the bold dashed line, and choose Remove Page Break, which now replaces the Set Page Break command on the Options menu.

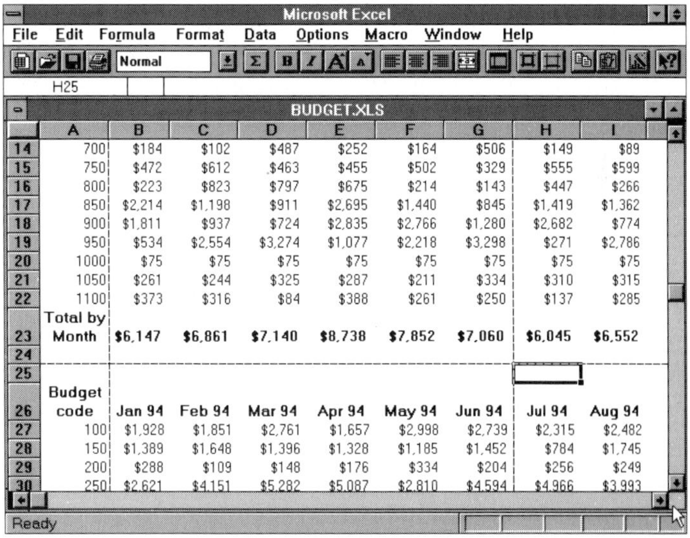

FIGURE 12-3.
Manual page breaks are indicated on the screen with bold dashed lines.

Controlling the appearance of your printed page

The Page Setup command on the File menu lets you specify a variety of factors that affect the appearance of your printed page. When you choose this command, you'll see a dialog box like the one shown in Figure 12-4. Microsoft Excel saves all the settings you select in this dialog box as part of your worksheet's data when you choose the File Save command. These settings override any corresponding settings in the printer's setup dialog box. For example, if you specify landscape orientation in the Page Setup dialog box, your worksheet prints in landscape orientation — even if you selected portrait orientation in the printer's setup dialog box.

FIGURE 12-4.
The Page Setup dialog box lets you specify margins, orientation, headers, footers, and other settings that affect the appearance of your printed page.

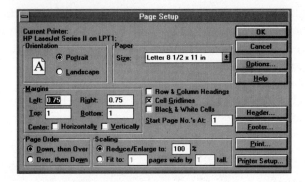

NOTE: *When you print a chart, the Page Setup dialog box presents a slightly different set of options. These options are described in Chapter 13.*

Creating headers and footers

A header is a single-line or multi-line block of text printed one-half inch from the top of each page. A footer is a single-line or multi-line block of text printed one-half inch from the bottom of each page. By default, Excel automatically creates a centered header and a centered footer on each page of your printouts. For the header, Excel uses the name of the document you're printing; for the footer, Excel prints the word *Page* followed by the current page number. You can change these default headers and footers to anything you choose.

To specify a header or footer (or to remove the default header or footer), choose the Page Setup command. Next, click either the Header button or the Footer button. Apart from the default text, the dialog box that appears is the same for both headers and footers. Figure 12-5 shows the Header dialog box.

FIGURE 12-5.
*Excel's Header and
Footer dialog boxes
make it easy to put
text at the top and
bottom of your printed
pages.*

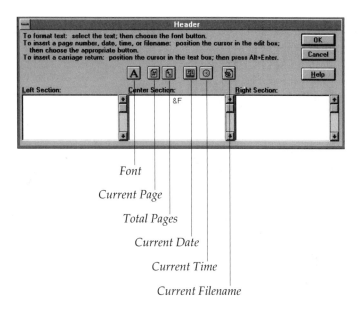

Font

Current Page

Total Pages

Current Date

Current Time

Current Filename

The symbol *&F* shown in the Center Section text box in Figure 12-5 is Excel's code for printing the current filename. Excel uses a number of codes, all of which begin with an ampersand, to represent information that you might want to put in your headers and footers — such as the current time, current date, and current page number. Fortunately, you don't have to learn these codes to create headers and footers. Simply click the appropriate section text box (left, center, or right), and then click the icons above the section boxes.

To specify text in your header or footer, click the appropriate section text box and type your text. If you want the text divided between two or more lines, press Alt-Enter at the end of each line. If you want to include an ampersand in your text, type two ampersands.

Suppose, for example, you want to create a header that contains three elements: the text *Smith & Jones,* flush left; the current filename in the center of the page; and the current date, flush right. Start by clicking the Left Section text box and typing *Smith && Jones.* The current-filename code, *&F,* already appears in the Center Section box, so you can leave that box alone. Finish the header specification by clicking the Right Section box, and then clicking the current-date icon — the one that looks like a miniature desk calendar. Your finished header specification looks like the one in Figure 12-6 on the following page.

FIGURE 12-6.
*The header specified
here would print*
Smith & Jones *on
the top left corner of
each page, the current
filename in the top
center, and the cur-
rent date in the top
right corner.*

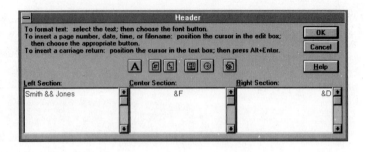

Changing fonts

Excel's default font for headers and footers is 10-point MS Sans Serif Regular. (In
Microsoft Windows version 3.0, this font is called Helv.) You can choose a different
typeface, point size, and style by clicking the Font icon — the capital *A* above the
section boxes. This action summons the Format Font dialog box, which works exactly the same way in headers and footers as it does in the worksheet. (To assign a
different font to text that you've already entered in a section box, first select that
text, and then click the Font icon.) Excel displays the header and footer text in your
chosen font and style. Note, however, that font commands apply to the current
section box only.

Deleting header and footer codes

Although Excel 4 relieves you of the need to learn its ampersand codes for entering
headers and footers, you might still need to know what the codes mean to be able
to delete material from header and footer strings. The following table lists the ampersand codes used by this version of Excel. To delete an element from a header or
footer string, select the code you want to remove, and then press Del.

Code	Action
&D	Current date
&F	Current filename
&N	Total number of pages in the current print area
&P	Current page number
&T	Current time

Setting margins

The Page Setup dialog box also lets you control the left, right, top, and bottom
margins of your printed reports. In Excel, margins are expressed in inches. As shown

in Figure 12-4, the default left and right margins are 0.75 inch, and the default top and bottom margins are 1 inch.

You can also adjust margin settings from within Excel's Print Preview feature. (See "Previewing the printout," later in this chapter.) You can center your report horizontally or vertically on the page as well. (See "Centering the printout," later in this chapter.)

Headings and gridlines options

The Page Setup dialog box includes options that determine whether row numbers, column letters, and gridlines appear in your printed report. As you learned in Chapter 4, you can suppress the display of these elements on your screen by deselecting them in the Display dialog box. Printing most of these elements, however, is independent of their display on the screen. Therefore, you must use the Row & Column Headings and Cell Gridlines options in the Page Setup dialog box to control their appearance in your printed report. (But if you remove gridlines from your screen display, Excel deselects Cell Gridlines by default in the Page Setup dialog box.)

Typically, you'll print your rough drafts with the Row & Column Headings and Cell Gridlines options active. These elements make it easy to locate entries in the worksheet. When you print the final version, however, you'll probably want to turn these options off.

Centering the printout

The Center Horizontally and Center Vertically options do what their names suggest: They position your report evenly between the left and right or the top and bottom margins. These options are particularly useful when you print a short or narrow report.

Note that centering takes place between the *margins,* not between the edges of the page. If your left and right margins are not equal, choosing the Center Horizontally option will not produce a report that appears centered.

Portrait versus landscape orientation

The Orientation option lets you choose between Portrait or Landscape printing. This setting in the Page Setup dialog box affects the current document only and takes precedence over the Orientation setting in the Printer Setup dialog box for your printer driver.

Paper size

The Paper Size option lets you select a paper size as a document-specific attribute. If your printer does not permit you to do this, the Paper Size option is dimmed.

Scaling and page fitting

Excel 4 lets you override the default size of your printouts in either of two ways — by specifying a scaling factor (from 10 percent through 400 percent) or by automatically fitting the report to a specified number of pages. These scaling options, which you access through the Page Setup dialog box, are available for any printer installed on your Windows system.

Be aware that Excel always applies a scaling factor in both the horizontal and vertical dimensions. For example, if your full-size printout is two pages deep by one page wide and you ask Excel to scale it to a single page, the resulting printout will be narrower as well as shallower.

If you want to return to a full-size printout after choosing one of the scaling options, choose the Page Setup command, select the Reduce/Enlarge option button, and type *100* in the percentage box.

Translating screen colors to black and white

If you've assigned background colors and patterns to your worksheet but you're using a black-and-white printer, you'll probably want to take advantage of the Page Setup command's Black & White Cells check box. Selecting this check box tells Excel to ignore any background colors and patterns when printing.

Previewing the printout

If you want to look at the page breaks, margins, and format of your report before you begin printing, choose the Print Preview command from the File menu. Microsoft Excel displays a picture of the printed page on the screen that reflects all the Page Setup and Print settings you've specified. Figure 12-7 shows an example of a previewed printout.

If you're not satisfied with the layout of your report, you can change the margins and column widths without leaving Print Preview. (You need a mouse to do this.) You can also display the Page Setup dialog box directly from within Print Preview and change any option that's available in that dialog box. For example, if after previewing your report you decide to use one of the centering options, you can call up the Page Setup dialog box and select the appropriate option. When you click OK in the Page Setup dialog box, you'll return to Print Preview, and be able to see the effect of your change.

FIGURE 12-7.

Print Preview shows where pages will break and lets you check the balance of white space and printed area.

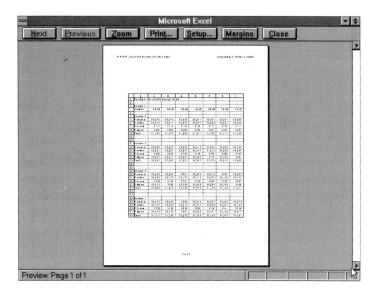

After you are satisfied with the appearance of your document, you can click the Print button to print the document. Or you can leave Print Preview and print using the File menu's Print command.

Moving from page to page

Print Preview displays one page at a time. You can move ahead or back a page at a time by clicking the Next or Previous button. You can also move directly to a particular page by dragging the box in the vertical scroll bar. As you move through the document, Excel displays the current page number (and the total number of pages in the document) in the lower left corner of the preview screen, as shown in Figure 12-7.

Zooming in on selected areas

Although you can get a general idea of the page layout using Print Preview, the image is too small to read. Fortunately, Excel provides a way to get a closer look.

Excel turns your mouse pointer into a magnifying glass while Print Preview is in effect so you can zoom in on any portion of the page you select. For example, to make sure your page header is formatted correctly, place the pointer at the top of the page and click. Your screen will look like the one in Figure 12-8 on the following page. If you want to see another area of the worksheet, you can use the horizontal and vertical scroll bars. Or you can return to the full-page preview by clicking the page again and using the mouse to move the magnifier to a new location.

FIGURE 12-8.
Using the mouse, you can magnify an area of the preview screen to check the contents and formatting of a report.

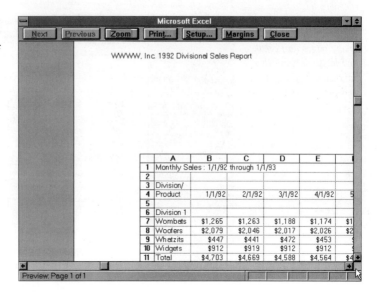

Adjusting margins and column widths

If you have a mouse, you can adjust any of the four margins or the width of any column from within Print Preview. Start by clicking the Margins button. As Figure 12-9 shows, when you click Margins, Excel displays dotted lines to represent the four margins. At the top of the preview display, you see "handles" that mark the right boundary of each column.

FIGURE 12-9.
The Margins button lets you change margin or column-width settings.

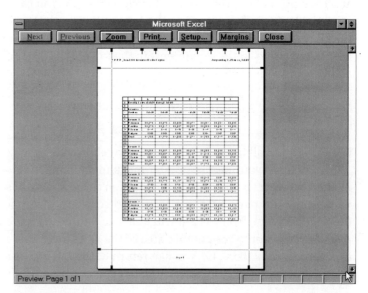

To adjust a margin, position the mouse on the appropriate dotted line; the pointer changes from an arrow to a double-pointed arrow. Hold down the mouse button and drag the dotted line to its new position. To assist you in this process, the page-number legend at the lower left corner of the screen changes to display the name of the margin and its current setting as you move the dotted line back and forth.

To adjust a column width, click the column's handle and drag it left or right. Here again, the pointer changes to a double-pointed arrow, and the legend at the bottom of the screen tells you the current column width as you drag.

Changing page setup options

In case you need to change one of the options offered in the Page Setup dialog box, Print Preview includes a Setup button. Click this button and you see the same dialog box you see when you choose Page Setup from the File menu. Click OK or Cancel to leave the Page Setup dialog box and return to Print Preview.

Using the Report Manager

The Report Manager lets you define a particular printout or collection of printouts as a named report, so that you can recreate that report by simply selecting the name and clicking the Print button. You'll find the Report Manager invaluable when you need to create two or more kinds of reports from the same worksheet or when you have to create a particular report on a recurring basis. Instead of constantly switching print settings (and hoping that you can recreate exactly the settings you used on a previous occasion), you define your report once and then regenerate it at will.

The Report Manager is an add-in that works hand-in-hand with two other add-ins — the View Manager and the Scenario Manager. If you did a full installation of Microsoft Excel, you can invoke the Report Manager by choosing the Print Report command (from the File menu), invoke the View Manager by choosing the View command (from the Window menu), and invoke the Scenario Manager by choosing Scenario Manager (from the Formula menu). If these commands do not appear on your system, you need to install the add-ins by rerunning the Excel Setup program and choosing Custom Installation.

Defining the report

A *report* consists of one or more elements, each of which can be either a view created with the View Manager or a scenario created with the Scenario Manager. (For details about using the View Manager, see Chapter 6. For details about using the Scenario Manager, see Chapter 11.) Let's look at a simple example.

Suppose that from the sales worksheet shown in Figure 12-10, you want to print five separate printouts at the end of each month — one for each of your four divisions and one of the entire worksheet. To define each of your regular printouts as a named report, start by using normal Excel procedures to prepare the first printout. That is, select the Division 1 data, and choose the Options Set Print Area command. Also specify the print titles, headers, footers, margins, and other print settings that you want to use for this report.

When you have set up Excel to print your Division 1 sales figures, choose the Window View command to invoke the View Manager, click the View Manager's Add button, and supply a name (such as Division 1) in the Add View dialog box. In the Add View dialog box, be sure the check box labeled Print Settings is selected. Note that it doesn't matter which part of your worksheet is visible when you create this named view; you're intending (presumably) to use the view only for the purpose of specifying a named report, so the current print settings are all that matters.

After you create a named view for your first divisional printout, repeat this procedure for each other division and for a printout of the entire worksheet. When you've finished, you'll have five named views, one for each combination of print settings that you commonly use.

Now choose the Print Report command from the File menu to invoke the Report Manager. The Print Report dialog box appears, as shown in Figure 12-11.

FIGURE 12-10.
*We can use the
Report Manager
to define each of
several divisional
sales printouts as
a named report.*

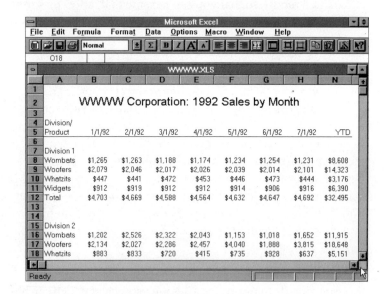

FIGURE 12-11.

When you first invoke
the Report Manager
with a new worksheet,
you'll see this empty
list box.

Because you haven't defined any reports yet, the Report Manager's initial dialog box presents an empty list. To define your first report, click Add and fill out the dialog box shown in Figure 12-12.

FIGURE 12-12.

To define a report,
supply a name at the
top of this dialog box.
Use the drop-down
lists to indicate the
named views and
scenarios you want
your report to include.

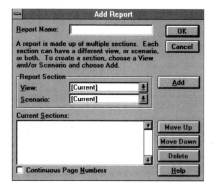

All you need to do is name the report in the text box at the top of the dialog box, open the drop-down list labeled View, and select the view that you want included in your report. Repeat these steps for each report you want to create. Now when you return to the Print Report dialog box, the list includes all your defined reports. To print one of them, you simply select a report name and click Print.

We've deliberately kept this example simple for illustrative purposes. But you can define reports that consist of as many views or scenarios — or both views and scenarios — as you please. When you create a report that consists of more than one element (view or scenario), think about how you want Excel to number pages. Excel begins printing each element of your report on a new page (you can't override that), but you can choose to have the pages numbered consecutively or to have each element begin with the same page number. Select the Continuous Page Numbers check box if you want the numbers to flow consecutively from the first element to the last.

Creating slide shows

Microsoft Excel 4 includes a facility for generating on-screen slide presentations, complete with visual and sound transitional effects. You can make a slide from any portion of any Excel worksheet, from any Excel chart, or from any graphic information that can be copied to the Windows Clipboard. You can specify an individual playback duration for each slide, or you can have your slides remain on screen until you press Spacebar or click the mouse button. You can also generate automatic slide shows that repeat continuously until you press Esc.

NOTE: *The slide show facility is an add-in. If you get an error message when you try to create a new slide show, choose the Add-ins command on the Options menu. Click the Add button, navigate to the EXCEL\LIBRARY\SLIDES directory, and choose SLIDES.XLA. If you don't find SLIDES.XLA, rerun the Excel Setup program, choose Custom Installation, and install the slide show add-in.*

To create a slide show, start by choosing the New command from the File menu. In the dialog box, select Slides. Excel loads the slide show add-in and presents a template file called slides. The slides template is illustrated in Figure 12-13.

Each row of the slides template can hold one slide. Excel uses the template's columns to record information about each slide, including any transitional effects you specify, whether you've selected manual or automatic advance, and so on.

To create a slide, first copy to the Clipboard whatever data you want the slide to contain. If the data is a worksheet range, select the range, and then choose the Copy command from the Edit menu. If you want to create a slide from an entire chart, first display that chart in a window. (See Chapter 13 for information about

FIGURE 12-13.
To create a slide show, use the File New command to open a new slides template.

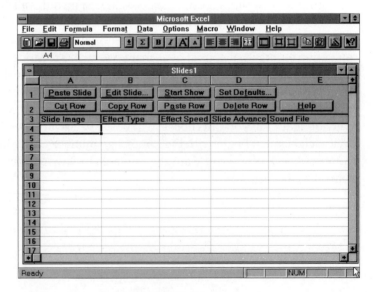

creating chart windows.) Then use the Select Chart command on the Chart menu, followed by the Copy command, to put the entire chart on the Clipboard. (If you want to make a slide from a portion of a chart, first copy the entire chart to the Clipboard. Then copy the Clipboard's contents into Paintbrush or another graphics program. In the graphics program, select the portion you want to use as your slide, and then copy that portion back to the Clipboard.)

NOTE: *For best appearances, choose scalable fonts for any text that will appear in your slides. One way to do that is to assign TrueType fonts to all your text. Other scalable font systems, such as Adobe Type Manager, also provide satisfactory results. You should avoid bit-mapped fonts, such as MS Serif and MS Sans Serif.*

With your slide data on the Clipboard, activate the slides template and click the button labeled Paste Slide, located in the upper left corner of the template. You don't have to select any particular cell before doing this. When you click Paste Slide, Excel pastes the Clipboard data into the first cell on the first available row of the slide template. At the same time, Excel displays the Edit Slide dialog box, shown in Figure 12-14.

FIGURE 12-14.
The Edit Slide dialog box lets you choose transitional effects and the duration of your slide's display.

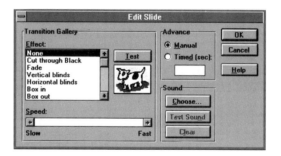

In the list box at the left side of this dialog box, you can choose among more than 40 visual transitional effects. To see what a particular effect looks like, select it and click the Test button. Note that your choice here determines the transition *into* the current slide.

If your computer includes Windows-supported sound hardware, you can also use the Edit Slide dialog box to choose an aural transition. To do this, click the button labeled Choose and select a WAV file from the ensuing dialog box. You return to the Edit Slide dialog box, where you can sample your sound effect by clicking the Test Sound button.

If you leave the Manual Advance button selected (as it is by default), Excel displays your slide until you click the mouse button or press Spacebar. If you'd rather have the slide advance automatically, select Timed and specify the number of seconds you want the slide to remain on screen.

When you click OK to leave the Edit Slide dialog box, Excel records your choices in the current row of the slides template. In the first column of this row, you'll find a scrunched-up approximation of the data you pasted from the Clipboard. You won't be able to tell much about how the slide will look by examining this cell, but you can display any particular slide by clicking the Start Show button.

Editing the slide show

To change any of the transitional or duration parameters assigned to a particular slide, select any cell in that slide's row, and click the Edit Slide button. You'll see the Edit Slide dialog box — the same dialog box you filled out when you created the slide.

To copy, delete, or change the order of your slides, use the buttons in the second row of the template. Note that you cannot insert new rows into the template file itself. If you want to add a new slide between slide 1 and slide 2, for example, you must move down all the slides from number 2 to the end of your show, and then use the Paste Slide button. The Paste Slide button always copies the Clipboard data into the first available row, so if you move slides 2 through 100 down one row, the next slide will be pasted into row 2.

Playing the slide show

To play your slides, click the Start Show button. Excel presents the Start Show dialog box shown in Figure 12-15.

FIGURE 12-15.
You can start the slide show at any slide, and you can also ask Excel to repeat the show

To start the slide show at some point other than your first slide, drag the scroll box at the bottom of the Start Show dialog box. If you want to set up a repeating slide show, select the Repeat check box. Excel will display your slides forever — or until someone presses Esc, turns the computer off, hits the computer's reset button, or presses Ctrl-Alt-Del.

If you do not select the Repeat check box, Excel returns you to the slides template after it has displayed your last slide. You can stop along the way by pressing the Esc key. When you do this, Excel displays another dialog box, similar to the one shown in Figure 12-15. You can use the scroll bar in this dialog box to skip to a particular slide, or you can click the Stop button to return to the slides template.

CHARTS

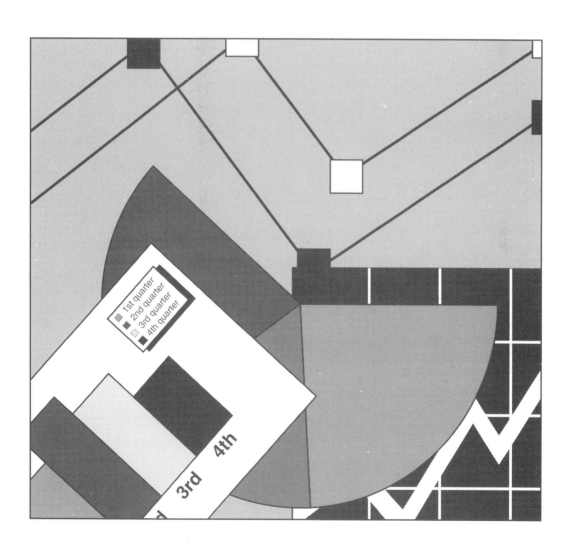

13

Basic Charting Techniques

Microsoft Excel offers a powerful and flexible charting facility that lets you create sophisticated graphics from your worksheet data. You can choose from eight two-dimensional and six three-dimensional chart types, each of which is available in several variations. For example, if you're creating a column chart, you can choose overlapped, clustered, stacked, or 100%–stacked columns. You can also combine the basic chart types. For example, you can lay a line chart over a column chart to plot a stock's price together with its sales volume. You can even create "picture" charts that use graphic images instead of ordinary bars and lines to represent values. All these chart types, combined with Excel's custom formatting options, provide you with a virtually endless variety of graphic presentations.

This chapter introduces you to the steps involved in creating a chart, adding a legend and title to the chart, saving the chart, and printing the chart. We also introduce the ChartWizard tool and examine the commands on Excel's Gallery menu, which depict all the available chart types.

In Excel, charts can reside either in separate document windows, called *chart windows,* or on the worksheet from which they're derived. A chart that appears directly on a worksheet is called an *embedded* chart.

An embedded chart is a type of graphic object. Like arrows, buttons, geometric shapes, pictures, and other graphic objects, embedded charts can be placed anywhere on the worksheet, even on top of your worksheet data. You can resize or reposition embedded charts, assign macros to them, and manipulate them in other ways, as described in Chapter 7.

In this chapter we show you how to create, save, and print both embedded charts and charts that reside in separate document windows. We discuss the procedures for customizing charts in Chapter 14. Chapter 15 will provide more details about working with chart data.

Creating an embedded chart with the ChartWizard tool

The Standard toolbar in Microsoft Excel version 4.0 includes a ChartWizard tool that makes creating graphs a straightforward process. To create an embedded chart with the ChartWizard tool, you simply select the data you want to plot, click the ChartWizard tool, tell Excel where you want to embed the chart, and fill out a series of interactive dialog boxes.

The ChartWizard tool looks like a fairy's wand about to anoint a column chart — or a falling smokestack, depending on your imagination. On the default (unmodified) Standard toolbar, the ChartWizard is the second tool from the right and appears just before the Help tool, as shown in Figure 13-1. You'll also find the ChartWizard tool on the default Chart toolbar — the toolbar that appears when you're working with a chart window.

FIGURE 13-1.   *ChartWizard*
The ChartWizard tool
appears on the default
Standard toolbar.

Creating an embedded chart without a mouse

If you do not have a mouse, you can still create an embedded chart. Start by creating a chart in a separate window, as described in the next section of this chapter. With the chart window active, choose the Select Chart command from the Chart menu. Next, choose the Copy command from the Edit menu. Return to your worksheet window, select the cell where you want the upper left corner of the chart to appear, and then choose the Paste command from the Edit menu. Excel embeds your chart in the worksheet, exactly as it appears in the chart window you copied it from.

Suppose you're working with the sales-target worksheet shown in Figure 13-2, and you want to embed a column chart from this data below the table, in rows 10 through 18. Start by selecting D3:F8 and clicking the ChartWizard tool. Excel draws

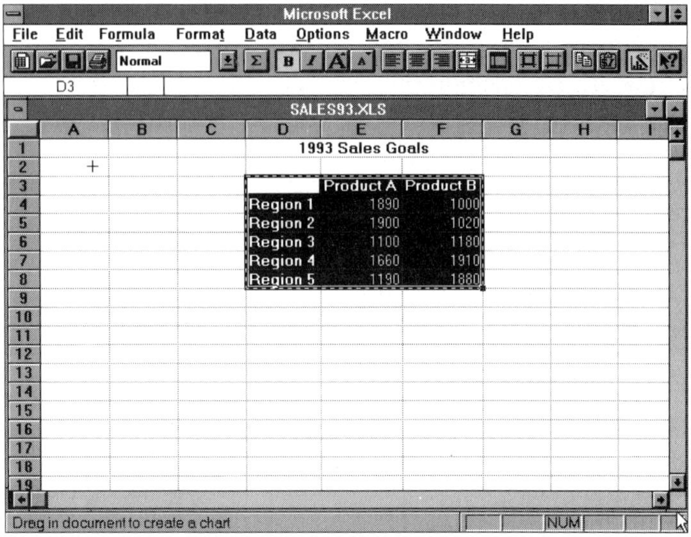

FIGURE 13-2.
After you click the ChartWizard tool, a message prompts you to define the area where you want to embed your chart.

Manipulating embedded charts

If you hold down Shift when drawing a rectangle to contain an embedded chart, Excel constrains your rectangle to a square. If you hold down Alt while creating the rectangle, the rectangle aligns with the gridlines of your worksheet.

You can make your embedded chart as large as you want. To make it extend beyond the limits of your screen, drag your mouse pointer across the border of your worksheet window as you create the rectangle.

Usually you'll want to place your embedded charts in blank worksheet areas. But you can put them anywhere, including directly over worksheet data or over other graphic objects.

To change a chart's position, first click the chart anywhere to select it. Next, position the mouse pointer anywhere within the chart and drag it in the direction you want to go. To change the chart's size, first select the chart and then drag one of the black handles outward to enlarge the chart or inward to reduce the chart.

To remove an embedded chart, select it and then use the Edit Clear command (or press Del).

a marquee around the selected data, changes the mouse pointer to a cross hair, and displays the message *Drag in document to create a chart* in the status bar.

Next, put the mouse pointer at one corner of the worksheet area where you want to embed the chart, drag to the opposite corner, and release the mouse button. As you drag, a dotted outline shows you where your chart will appear. (Don't worry about precision when staking out the chart area. You can always drag the chart to a new size and position after you've created it.) When you release the mouse button, you'll see a dialog box similar to the one shown in Figure 13-3.

FIGURE 13-3.
In the first of the
Chart Wizard's five
dialog boxes, you
confirm or specify the
data you want to plot.

As you can see from this dialog box's title bar, creating a chart with the ChartWizard is a five-step process. After completing each step, you move forward by clicking Next. At any time during the process, you also have the option of bailing out (click Cancel), returning to step 1 (click the second button from the left), or returning to the previous step (click Back). By clicking the fast-forward button at the right end of the button panel, you can also tell Excel to skip the remaining steps and draw a chart based on the information you've given it so far.

Specifying the data to plot

The ChartWizard's first dialog box asks you to confirm or specify the data you want to plot. In the example shown in Figure 13-2, you selected the data before clicking the ChartWizard tool, so the Range text box is already filled in correctly. You don't have to prespecify the data range, however; if you prefer, you can click the ChartWizard tool first and then tell the ChartWizard what you want to plot.

To fill out or change the contents of the Range line, you can either type a range reference, preceded by an equal sign, or simply point to the range with your mouse. If the ChartWizard's dialog box is in your way, drag its title bar to move it.

When you specify a plot range, it's a good idea to include any text that identifies the rows and columns of your data — such as the labels in column D and row 3 in Figure 13-1. The ChartWizard automatically incorporates such text into your graph, as you'll see in a moment. Unless you're plotting only a single column or row, however, don't include a chart title in the plot selection because the ChartWizard cannot tell a title from a data point. You can add the title later in one of the ChartWizard's dialog boxes.

Choosing a chart type and format

The ChartWizard's second dialog box presents the gallery of chart types shown in Figure 13-4. You want a column chart of your sales-target data, so select the third box in the top row.

FIGURE 13-4.
After telling the ChartWizard which data you want to plot, you select a basic chart type from Excel's 14 options.

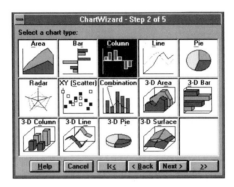

After you choose a chart type and click Next, the ChartWizard presents another gallery menu, this time showing you the built-in formatting variants available for your chart type. Figure 13-5 shows the format gallery for column charts.

FIGURE 13-5.
In the ChartWizard's third dialog box, you can select one of the built-in formatting variants for your chart type.

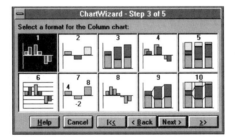

The default formatting variant for column charts, shown in picture 1 of this gallery menu, produces a nonoverlapping clustered chart with no gridlines. Other options produce various kinds of stacked and overlapping charts. For the purpose of this example, we'll stick with the default choice. (All the basic chart types and formatting variants are described in "Chart types," later in this chapter.)

Telling the ChartWizard how to interpret your data

In the ChartWizard's fourth dialog box, shown in Figure 13-6 on the following page, you specify how you want your data parsed, which depends on whether your data series are organized by row or by column, whether the first row and column contain data or labels, and so on. You don't have to spend a lot of time puzzling over these issues, however, because your choices are immediately reflected in the sample graph at the left side of the dialog box. In most cases, the ChartWizard anticipates your needs before you arrive at this step, so all you need to do is confirm its suggestions. (For more about Excel's data parsing options, see "Series and points," later in this chapter.)

FIGURE 13-6.
The ChartWizard's fourth dialog box concerns itself with data parsing.

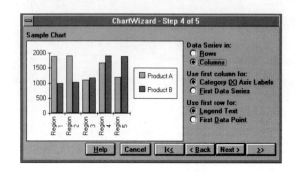

Adding text and a legend

Finally, in step 5, you add a title for the graph itself, titles for each axis, an overlay title (for combination graph types), and a legend. Here again, you can see the impact of your decisions before you leave the dialog box. Step 5 is shown in Figure 13-7.

FIGURE 13-7.
The ChartWizard's last dialog box lets you add titles and a legend.

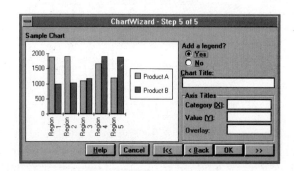

If you choose to include a legend, the ChartWizard positions it to the right of your chart, as shown in the example. You can change the legend's position later, but you can't move it around within the ChartWizard.

To add title text, simply type in the appropriate boxes. Any text you specify will be inserted in your chart as text rather than as a reference in the default font; if you want to change the content or appearance of the text, you can do so later with formatting commands. You cannot use the ChartWizard to link title text to worksheet cells. If you want your titles to change to reflect changes in underlying cells, you can link them after you've created the chart. (See "Linking a chart title to a worksheet cell," in Chapter 14.)

To dismiss the ChartWizard and embed your chart, click OK. (The OK button replaces the Next button in the step 5 dialog box.)

Modifying an embedded chart

After you have created an embedded chart, you might want to change its appearance. If you double-click the embedded chart, Excel creates a temporary chart window containing a copy of your embedded chart. You can modify the chart in any of the ways described in this chapter for modifying charts in chart windows. When you finish, close the chart window. Excel updates your embedded chart in the worksheet.

Creating a new chart in a chart window

To create a new chart in a separate window, first select the data you want to plot. Next, pull down the File menu, choose New, and then choose Chart. (As a shortcut for File New Chart, you can simply press F11 or Alt-F1.) Microsoft Excel displays your data in a new chart window, using the current default settings. (See Figure 13-8.)

FIGURE 13-8.
When you choose the New command from the File menu and select Chart, Excel plots the selected worksheet data in a separate chart window.

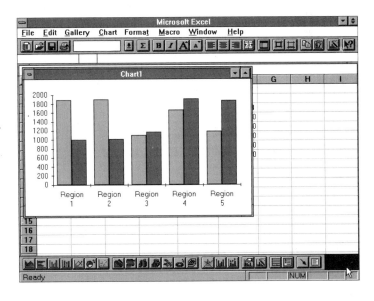

You can size, move, maximize, and restore your new chart window just as you can your worksheet window. Because the chart lives in its own window, you can also print it and save it independently of the source worksheet. Excel initially assigns the chart a dummy name, such as *Chart1*; you can name it whatever you like when you save it.

The chart window remains linked to the worksheet window, however. Excel uses linking formulas based on the SERIES function to connect the chart to its source worksheet. Thus, if you modify the underlying data, Excel updates the chart immediately to reflect the new source values. Excel creates the appropriate SERIES formulas for you when you select a range of data and open a new chart window, so you seldom have to deal with those formulas yourself. On occasion, however, you might want to edit a SERIES formula. We'll show you how to do that in Chapter 15.

When the active window is a chart window, Excel displays a Chart menu bar instead of a Worksheet menu bar. The Chart menu bar includes menus named File, Edit, Format, Macro, Window, and Help, but lacks the other menus that appear on the worksheet menu bar. The Chart menu bar contains two additional menus — Gallery and Chart — which only apply to chart making, however. Moreover, the Format menu on the Chart menu bar has an entirely different set of commands than its counterpart on the Worksheet menu bar.

Adding a legend and title to a chart in its own window

To add a legend to your new chart, pull down the Chart menu and choose Add Legend. Excel puts a legend near the right edge of the window and redraws the chart, as shown in Figure 13-9.

FIGURE 13-9.
To add a legend, open the Chart menu and choose Add Legend.

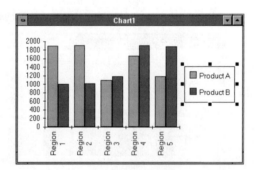

Notice that black squares, called *handles*, surround the rectangle in which the legend appears. You can use these handles to manipulate the legend. Excel uses two kinds of handles — black and white. Black handles denote objects that you can move, format, or edit; white handles denote objects that you can format or edit, but can't move. If either type of handle surrounds a rectangle, it is selected. When you finish with a legend, press Esc to remove the handles.

You might have noticed that when Excel redrew the chart, it rotated the text along the chart's x-axis to make room for the legend. If you enlarge this window significantly (by maximizing it, for example), Excel will have more room for the x-axis labels and will display them on a single line.

Now let's add a title to the chart. To do this, choose the Attach Text command from the Chart menu. Figure 13-10 shows the dialog box that appears when you choose Attach Text.

FIGURE 13-10.
The Attach Text command lets you assign titles to the x-axis and the y-axis, to individual data points, and to the chart itself.

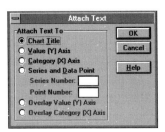

To add a title to the chart itself, select the first option in the dialog box, Chart Title. When you click OK, the word *Title* appears within a set of white handles, as shown in Figure 13-11. The word *Title* is Excel's default title text; you can edit it any way you like.

FIGURE 13-11.
When you add a chart title, Excel initially displays the default text Title.

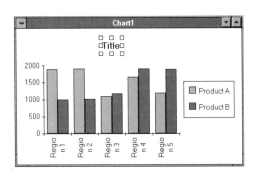

Notice that Excel reduced the height of the chart to make room for the title and incorrectly divided each of the x-axis labels into two lines. Excel attempts to make axis labels legible given the size of the chart window, but it doesn't always succeed. To restore order along the x-axis, simply increase the size of the chart window.

While the chart title is selected, you can modify its text in two ways. You can type a title and press Enter, or you can create a formula to link the title to the text in a cell on your worksheet.

Because we have a good title for this chart stored in cell D1 of the source worksheet, we'll modify the default title text by creating a formula. This approach means we don't have to retype the title. And if we subsequently change the text in A1, the title will also change.

What we need is a simple external-reference formula, like the ones discussed in Chapter 6. The formula reads

=SALES93.XLS!$D$1

To create the formula, make both the chart window and the worksheet window visible by choosing the Window menu's Arrange command. Next, while the chart window is still the active window, type an equal sign (=). Use the mouse to select cell D1 in the source worksheet and press Enter. Finally, press Esc to remove the white handles. Figure 13-12 shows the results. (In the figure, the x-axis labels are covered by the Chart toolbar. Rearranging the workspace will make the whole chart visible.)

FIGURE 13-12.
We used a formula to link the chart's title to cell D1 of the source worksheet.

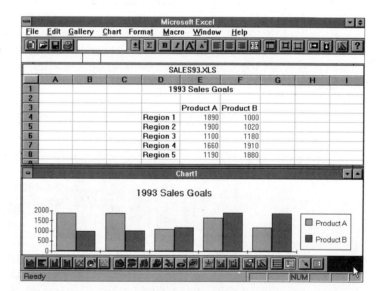

Series and points

A *series* is a group of related values, such as all the sales targets for a particular product. The individual members of a series are called *points,* or *data points.* The chart in Figure 13-12 includes two series, each of which consists of five points.

The range E3:F8 in SALES93.XLS (as shown, for example, in Figure 13-12) can also be plotted as five series, each of which consists of two points. In that case, it would look like the one in Figure 13-13.

FIGURE 13-13.
In this chart, we reversed Excel's normal series parsing, plotting E3:F8 as two series, each of which consists of five points.

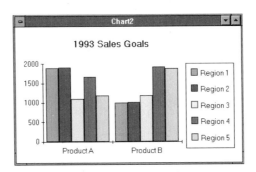

How does Microsoft Excel determine which way to plot? The program assumes you want fewer series than points per series. So, if you plot a range that has more columns than rows, Excel makes each row a series. If your selection has more rows than columns, Excel makes each column a series. If the selection has the same number of rows as columns, Excel treats the rows as series. Each series on a chart can have as many as 4000 data points. You can plot up to 255 series, but a single chart is limited to 32,000 total data points.

In determining which dimension should be a series, Excel ignores any text or dates included in the first row or column of your selection. It uses text cells or dates for axis or legend labels, but disregards them when parsing the chart data.

You can reverse the way Excel normally parses series by using the following procedure: First, select your data block and then choose the Edit menu's Copy command. Next, create a new, blank, chart window, and choose the Edit menu's Paste Special command.

Near the top of the Paste Special dialog box, you'll find a group of option buttons labeled *Values (Y) in*. The group presents two choices, Rows and Columns. Pick whichever one isn't currently selected. In other words, if Excel offers Rows as a default, choose Columns — and vice versa.

To reverse the normal series parsing in an embedded chart, first use Paste Special to create the chart in a separate window, as just described. Next, choose the Chart menu's Select Chart command, followed by the Edit menu's Copy command. Return to the worksheet, select the cell where you want the upper left corner of the chart to appear, and choose the Edit menu's Paste command.

Series and category names

When the selection you plot includes row and column labels, as D3:F8 in SALES93.XLS does in Figure 13-1, Excel automatically uses that text in your chart. The labels associated with your chart's series dimension become *series names* and appear in the chart's legend. The labels associated with the points dimension become *category names* and appear along the x-axis. For naming purposes, Microsoft Excel treats as text any date cells in the top row or left column of your selection.

For example, the selection D3:F8 has fewer columns than rows; therefore, columns represent the series dimension and rows represent the points dimension. The column headings, Product A and Product B, thus become series names and appear in the chart's legend. (See Figure 13-9.) The row headings — Region 1, Region 2, and so on — become category names and appear along the x-axis. Excel assigns each category name to a cluster of data points — one point from each series.

If your selection is parsed the opposite way, with rows as series and columns as points, the row labels become series names and the column labels become category names.

If you plot a selection without including labels for the series dimension, Excel assigns a dummy name to each series. The first series is called *Series1*, the second *Series2*, and so on. You can modify these names by editing the SERIES formulas used to create the chart. (See Chapter 14.)

If you plot a selection that includes no labels for the points dimension, Excel presents a dialog box like the one shown in Figure 13-14. In this example, columns represent the points dimension of the new chart, and Excel gives you the opportunity to treat the first column in the selection as a set of category names, rather than as data to be plotted.

FIGURE 13-14.
*If your plot selection
has more rows than
columns and the first
column has no text or
dates, this dialog box
appears.*

If the first column of your selection consists of numeric labels — budget or product numbers, for example — select the Category (X) Axis Labels option and click OK. Excel then plots only the remaining columns, and the numbers in the left column appear as category names along the x-axis.

If you choose either of the other two options in the dialog box — First Data Series or X-Values for XY Chart — Excel treats the first column as ordinary data to be plotted. In the first case (First Data Series), it creates a column chart like the one in Figure 13-8 and uses dummy category names. Excel names the first category 1, the second 2, and so on. (You can change these names later by modifying the SERIES formulas.) In the second case, it creates an XY chart and uses the left column as x-axis values. Each of the remaining columns then becomes a separate series of y-axis values. (See "XY (Scatter) charts," later in this chapter.)

Figure 13-14 shows the dialog box you see if your selection has more rows than columns and the left column contains no text or dates. If your selection has more columns than rows and the top row contains no text or dates, a similar dialog box asks you what you want to do with the top row. Your choices in these circumstances are just like the ones described for Figure 13-14. You can treat the top row as a set of category names (by selecting the second option in the dialog box) or you can plot it. If you select the first option in the dialog box, Excel applies dummy names to the x-axis. If you select the third option, Excel treats the top row as a set of x-axis values in an XY chart.

Plotting nonadjacent data

In all the examples so far, we plotted a single range of worksheet cells. In your own work, you might need to plot nonadjacent data. You can do this by outlining your worksheet, by hiding rows or columns that you want to exclude from the chart, by plotting a multiple selection, or by adding a new series to an existing chart.

Using outlining to plot nonadjacent data

Suppose you have an outlined worksheet that records financial data by quarters for the years 1989 through 1992. Following each set of quarterly columns is a yearly

column that totals the previous four quarters. You can collapse the column dimension of the outline so that only the year-end totals are visible. The resulting worksheet is shown in Figure 13-15.

Let's assume you want to create a chart of your cost-of-sales items by year. To
do this, first drag the mouse from C9 to W11. Next, choose the Formula menu's Select
Special command and click the option button labeled Visible Cells. Finally, create a
new chart as described above. Microsoft Excel plots your data just as it would if the
data lay in a contiguous block.

FIGURE 13-15.
*To plot nonadjacent
data, you can outline
your worksheet,
display only the
relevant levels, and
then select only the
visible cells.*

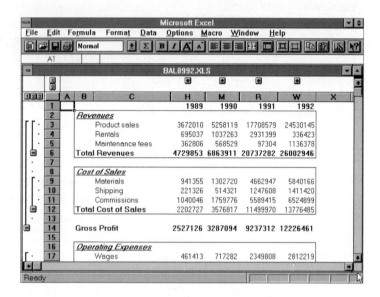

Excluding cells by hiding rows or columns

Another way to plot a nonadjacent data block is to hide the rows or columns that
contain the data you want to exclude. If your worksheet has columns for each month
of the year, for example, and you want to plot only the quarter-ending months, you
can use the Format menu's Column Width command to hide the columns for January, February, April, May, July, August, October, and November. You can then select
the remaining columns and select Visible Cells in the Select Special dialog box. Excel

plots the data in the columns you specify. Note that in this instance you cannot use outlining because all months of the year are at the same hierarchical level.

At times, you might find it helpful to combine the outlining technique with the column-hiding or row-hiding technique. In Figure 13-15, for example, if you want to include the year headings in your chart selection, you need to hide rows 2 through 8 (with the Format menu's Row Height command) and display only the top outline level in the column dimension. Once you do that, the required data appears on the screen in a contiguous block. (See Figure 13-16.) You can then select it, select Visible Cells in the Select Special dialog box, and create a new chart.

FIGURE 13-16.
To include the year headings in the plot selection, we hid rows 2 through 8 with the Format Row Height command.

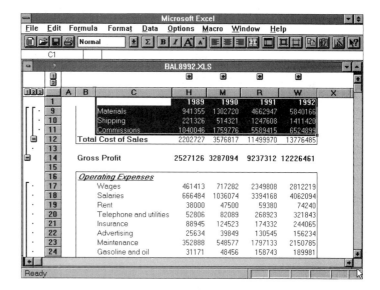

Plotting a multiple selection

Another way to plot nonadjacent data is to create a multiple selection. To do this, hold down Ctrl while you select each range you want to plot.

Figure 13-17 on the following page shows how you can plot your cost-of-sales figures for the four quarters of 1989. You can't use Select Special and Visible Cells in conjunction with a multiple selection, so this approach is less versatile than the outlining and hiding techniques previously described.

FIGURE 13-17.
*To plot the column
headings along with
the cost-of-sales data
on this worksheet, you
can use a multiple
selection.*

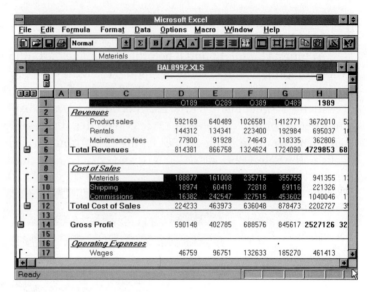

Adding series to an existing chart

Outlining, hiding rows and columns, and creating multiple selections are good
methods when you know exactly what you want to plot before you create your
chart. But if you want to add a data series to a chart you've already created, you
must select the new data series and then choose the Edit menu's Copy command.
Activate the chart window, pull down the Edit menu again, and choose Paste. Excel
adds the selected series to your existing chart.

Plotting data from more than one worksheet

When you use the Paste command to add a new block of data to a chart, Excel parses
that block the same way it would if you were creating a new chart. For example, if
the pasted block consists of five columns and two rows, Excel adds two series to
your chart, each of which consists of five points. To reverse the default parsing, use
Paste Special instead of Paste. In the Paste Special dialog box, you can indicate which
dimension should be series and which should be points.

Chart types

All of the examples we've seen so far are of vertically oriented bar charts, or *column
charts*. The column chart is Microsoft Excel's default, or *preferred*, chart type. You
can, however, use the Set Preferred command to specify a different default. (See
"Changing the default chart type," later in this chapter.)

Exploring the Gallery menu

The easiest way to change a chart's type is to click one of the chart icons on the Chart toolbar. Immediately, Excel changes your chart type. However, only a few of the chart types appear on the toolbar, so you will usually use the commands on the Gallery menu. The Gallery menu appears only when a chart window is active, and it includes one command for each of Excel's basic chart types: Area, Bar, Column, Line, Pie, Radar, XY (Scatter), Combination, 3-D Area, 3-D Bar, 3-D Column, 3-D Line, 3-D Pie, and 3-D Surface. When you select any of these commands, you see a graphical submenu from which you can pick a variant of the basic graph type. For example, Figure 13-18 illustrates the five kinds of area charts you see when you choose the Area command from the Gallery menu.

FIGURE 13-18.
You can choose variants of each basic chart type when you use the Gallery command.

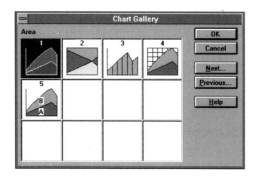

Choosing a chart type before formatting

You can think of the gallery as a large set of prefabricated chart formats — 90 to be exact. Choosing a format from the gallery is quick and easy. But if you apply certain formatting commands to your chart, and then you change the chart type with a command from the Gallery menu, the command might override your custom formatting. For example, if you change the colors and scaling of your axes, then use the Gallery menu to switch from a column chart to a bar chart, Excel restores the default axis scaling and colors.

Therefore, it's a good idea to select a chart type from the Gallery menu before you apply any custom formatting. If you need to change chart types after you've formatted your graph, you can use the Format menu's Main Chart and Overlay commands. (See Chapter 14 for details of these and other Format commands.)

To specify the style of graph you want, simply point to its picture and click, or type the number that appears above the picture. To move from one submenu to another, you can use the Next and Previous buttons. Alternatively, you can return to the Gallery menu and select another chart type.

Column and bar charts

As we explained earlier in this chapter, Excel calls vertically oriented bar charts column charts. Horizontally oriented bar charts are simply called *bar charts*. Figure 13-19 shows the gallery options for these two chart types.

FIGURE 13-19.
The Column gallery (top) and Bar gallery (bottom) include clustered, overlapping, and stacked options.

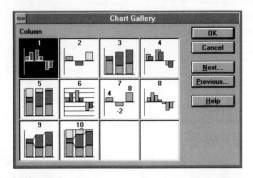

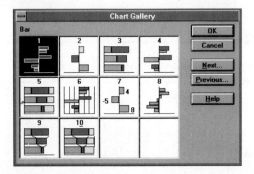

Column and bar charts are useful for comparing discrete values from two or more data series. Because the individual points in a series are not connected, these charts are less effective than line charts at showing trends.

Options 1 and 6 in the Column and Bar galleries display the points from each series in side-by-side clusters. Option 4 is similar, but the points in each cluster overlap, which means you can display more points in the same amount of space.

Options 3 and 9 stack the bars to give you a picture of each cluster's aggregate value. Options 5 and 10 produce *pie (100 percent)* bar charts. The values in each cluster are stacked and proportioned so that you can see what percentage each data point contributes to the cluster's total.

Option 2 is for single-series charts. If you choose this option, Excel draws each point in a different color. Option 7 is just like option 2, except that Excel displays numerals to indicate the value of each point. Option 8, which produces a *step chart*, is like option 1, except that the space between clusters is removed.

Line and high-low charts

Line charts are useful for showing the continuity between individual points in a series. You can use them to illustrate trends over time. *High-low charts* plot the value range over which events vary. For example, you might use a high-low chart to show average, high, and low rainfall figures by month. Excel also offers high-low-close and open-high-low-close charts, which you can use to track the prices of securities. Figure 13-20 shows the gallery options for line and high-low charts.

FIGURE 13-20.
The Line gallery includes high-low options as well as connected and disconnected line charts.

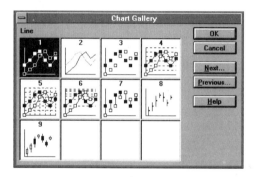

Option 1 results in a connected line chart, and option 3 results in an unconnected line chart. In these charts, a square marker identifies each point. Option 2 generates a connected line chart with no markers. Options 4 and 5 are like option 1, except that gridlines are included: horizontal gridlines only in option 4; gridlines in both directions in option 5. Option 6 applies logarithmic scaling to the y-axis.

Option 7 is a simple high-low chart in which all the points for each cluster are connected by a vertical line. The gallery picture shows only two points per cluster, but you can have as many as you need.

Option 8 is a high-low-close chart suitable for price tracking. To create this kind of chart, set up a data range in high-low-close order. That is, if your prices are arranged in columns, put high prices in the first column, low prices in the second, and closing prices in the third. Follow the same order if your data is arranged by row. This chart can display only three data series. No additional series you specify will appear in the chart, but they'll show up if you switch to a different kind of line chart or a different chart type.

Finally, option 9 creates an open-high-low-close chart. To use this chart type, arrange your data in four columns (or rows), in open-high-low-close order. Excel plots the high and low values for each point as a vertical line and the open and close values as a rectangle. One color (white by default) is used for periods when the close is higher than the open, and a contrasting color (black by default) for periods when the open is higher than the close.

Area charts

An *area chart* is a line chart in which the space between the line and the x-axis is filled. Figure 13-21 shows the gallery options for this chart type.

FIGURE 13-21.
The Gallery menu offers five kinds of area charts.

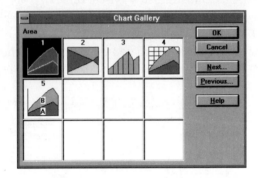

With options 1, 3, 4, and 5, Excel stacks the values for each cluster. Like a stacked column chart, this kind of chart can reveal trends assumed by aggregate values, while giving you a rough idea of each series' contribution to the whole. The area chart, however, emphasizes the continuity between points much more than the stacked column chart.

The differences between options 1, 3, 4, and 5 in the Area gallery are minimal. Option 3 adds vertical gridlines, option 4 adds horizontal as well as vertical gridlines, and option 5 displays series names within the chart (obviating the need for a legend).

Option 2 is quite another story, however. Like the pie-bar options in the Bar and Column galleries, option 2 shows what percentage each data point contributes to each cluster's total.

Pie charts

Unlike the other chart types discussed so far, a pie chart plots only one data series. Any additional series you specify are ignored, although they reappear if you switch to a different chart type.

Pie charts are designed to show the relative contribution of each data point to the series total. Figure 13-22 shows the six choices offered in the Pie gallery.

FIGURE 13-22.
Pie charts show the relative contribution of each member of a series to the series total.

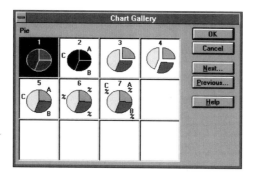

In option 1, the pie is fully assembled (all slices are in place), and no labels are assigned to the slices. In options 2 and 5, each slice is labeled. To create a labeled pie chart, select a column of labels and a column of numbers together (or a row of each). All the slices in option 2 are the same color (black, by default); each slice in option 5 is a different color. You can change the colors of slices individually using commands described in Chapter 14. For example, you might use option 2 to add color to one or two slices, while leaving the remaining slices dark.

In option 6, Excel computes the percentage contributions of all slices and displays them around the perimeter of the pie. In option 7, both labels and percentages are displayed.

Options 3 and 4 are exploded pies, which means slices are separated out. In option 3, only one slice — the first point in the data series — is exploded; in option 4, the entire pie is exploded. If you want more than one, but not all, slices exploded, or if you want to explode any single slice other than the first point in the data series, you can drag slices with the mouse. See Chapter 14 for more details about formatting pie charts.

Radar charts

In a radar chart, the value of each point is indicated by its radial distance from a central origin. The angle of the radius is determined by the point's position within the data series.

For example, the radar chart shown in Figure 13-23 on the following page plots a series of five points. The chart's value (y) axis is a vertical line drawn through the chart's origin. Each point in the series gets its own category (x) axis, and these category axes are spaced at equal angles. The magnitude of each point is represented by its distance from the origin. Note that the angular position of a data point is not particularly meaningful.

FIGURE 13-23.
In a radar plot, the value of each point is represented by its distance from the origin.

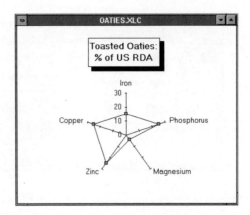

Radar charts are useful for showing or comparing the aggregate values of whole data series, rather than the values of individual points. Provided all values in a series have the same sign (positive or negative), the absolute value of the aggregate is proportional to the area enclosed by the plot.

Figure 13-24 shows the five options offered in the Radar gallery. Option 1, exemplified by the chart in Figure 13-23, produces a plot in which points along a series are marked and connected, and the category axes are displayed. Option 2 is like option 1, but without the point markers. Option 4 connects the category axes with gridlines. Option 5 is like option 4, except that the value axis is scaled logarithmically. Option 3 eliminates everything but the plot lines, so you can compare plot areas at a glance but you're left guessing about absolute values.

FIGURE 13-24.
The Gallery menu offers five kinds of radar charts.

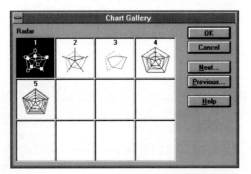

XY (Scatter) charts

Most of the chart types we've seen so far display values along one axis and category names along another. Usually the horizontal axis is the value axis and the vertical axis is the category axis. (The reverse is true with bar charts.) In an XY chart, both axes measure values.

XY charts are typically used to determine what kind of relationship — if any — exists between two data series. For example, Figure 13-25 shows a chart that plots the historical relationship between advertising expenditures and sales revenue for a company. A glance at this chart tells you that, historically, revenues rise with increasing advertising expenditures, but not in a strictly linear way.

FIGURE 13-25.
XY charts can help you determine if a predictable correlation exists between two or more sets of numbers.

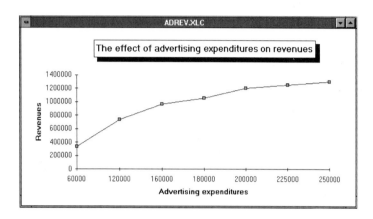

An XY chart plots each point using a pair of coordinates, one from an x series and one from a y series. The top row (or left column) of your data selection represents the x series, and each succeeding row (or column) represents a y series. You can have as many as 254 separate y series, each plotted against the common x series.

Figure 13-26 displays the five options available in the XY gallery. The chart in Figure 13-25 uses option 2, in which a straight line connects pairs of points. All the remaining options leave the points separated. Option 3 uses horizontal and vertical gridlines and linear scaling. Option 4 applies logarithmic scaling and gridlines to the y-axis. Option 5 uses logarithmic scaling and gridlines on both axes.

FIGURE 13-26.
XY charts are available in standard, semilogarithmic, and full logarithmic scaling.

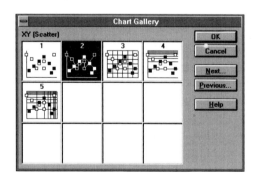

Combination charts

A combination chart is one that uses either two different chart types or has a secondary x-axis or y-axis. Combination charts comprising two chart types are useful for contrasting one or more series with the remaining series. For example, you might plot a salesperson's performance figures as a column chart together with quotas as a line chart. Combination charts that use a secondary x-axis or y-axis are valuable when some of your data series vary within one range of values and others vary within a markedly different range.

For some kinds of data, it is convenient to use two chart types and a secondary y-axis. For example, you might want to combine an open-high-low-close chart with a column chart to track stock prices and transaction volumes in a single graph. Because volumes can number in the millions and prices are likely to vary within a lower range, you need to plot the prices against one y-axis and the volumes against another. Figure 13-27 shows you the Gallery menu for combination charts.

FIGURE 13-27.
The Gallery menu includes six types of combination charts.

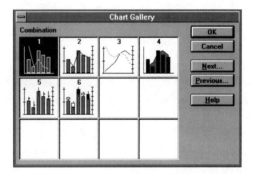

The Combination gallery offers six selections: a column/line chart with a single y-axis (option 1); a column/line chart with two y-axes (option 2); a line chart with two y-axes (option 3); a column/area chart with one y-axis (option 4); a high-low-close/volume chart (option 5); and an open-high-low-close/volume chart (option 6). In every case but the last two, Excel divides your data series evenly between the two chart types (or the two axes). For example, if you plot four data series using a column/line chart with two y-axes, your first two series are drawn as columns against the primary (left) y-axis, and the third and fourth series are lines plotted against the secondary (right) y-axis. In price/volume charts, Excel assumes that the volumes are in the first series and that your remaining series record prices.

As we'll see in Chapter 15, Excel lets you build many kinds of combination charts in addition to those that appear on the Gallery menu.

Three-dimensional column charts

The seven options in the 3-D Column gallery, shown in Figure 13-28, fall into two broad categories. Options 1 through 4 are similar to options 1, 3, 5, and 6 in the ordinary Column gallery, except that the columns appear as solid shapes. These charts display columns from each data series side by side in clusters, just as the two-dimensional column charts do.

FIGURE 13-28.
Four of the 3-D Column options plot solid bars in side-by-side clusters. The remaining three options plot each series on a separate plane.

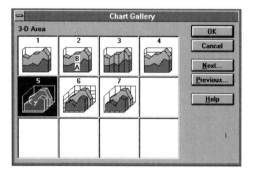

Options 5 through 7, on the other hand, display each data series on a separate plane. As Figure 13-29 on the following page shows, the differences between these two kinds of three-dimensional column charts are significant.

When Excel plots each data series on a separate plane, it adds a third axis to the chart. Category names then appear along one axis, series names along the second, and values along the third. The additional axis eliminates the need for a legend, although you can add one if you choose.

The only differences between options 5, 6, and 7 on the 3-D Column gallery have to do with gridlines. Option 5 has none, option 6 has gridlines along the floor and both walls of the chart, and option 7 has gridlines on its floor only.

Like the family portrait in a photo album, a three-dimensional chart such as the one on the right side of Figure 13-29 works best if the tall members stand behind the short ones. If you reverse the plotting order, the second data series becomes nearly invisible. However, as you'll see in Chapter 14, Excel makes it easy to modify the viewing angle of a three-dimensional chart, so in most cases you can avoid having one series obscure another.

FIGURE 13-29.
We plotted the same data using options 1 (left) and 5 (right) on the 3-D Column gallery.

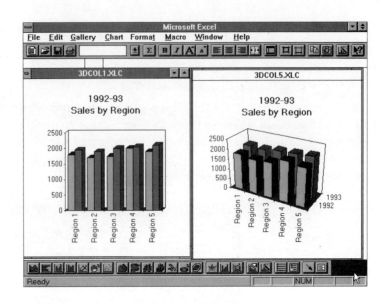

Three-dimensional bar charts

Bar charts are simply horizontal counterparts of column charts. Excel does not, however, allow you to create three-dimensional bar charts with each series plotted in a separate plane. The four options on the 3-D Bar gallery are illustrated in Figure 13-30.

FIGURE 13-30.
The 3-D Bar gallery does not include options for plotting series in separate planes.

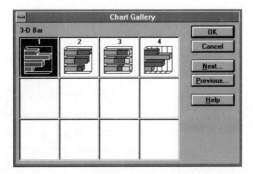

Three-dimensional area charts

The options in the 3-D Area gallery are similar to those in the 3-D Column gallery. The first four are solid-shape counterparts to four of the two-dimensional area choices, and the remaining three plot each data series in a separate plane. Figure 13-31 illustrates the 3-D Area options.

FIGURE 13-31.
Four of the 3-D Area options plot your data series in solid blocks. The remaining three options present each series on a separate plane.

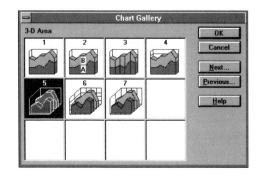

Three-dimensional line charts

In a three-dimensional line chart, each series is drawn as a "solid line," or "ribbon," and each appears in its own plane. Figure 13-32 shows the four 3-D Line gallery options.

FIGURE 13-32.
Each series in a 3-D line chart is drawn as a solid "ribbon."

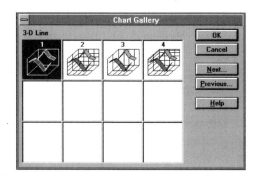

Your gallery selections in the 3-D Line gallery are based on the presence or absence of gridlines and logarithmic scaling. Option 2 includes wall and floor gridlines, and option 3 includes gridlines only on the floor. Option 4 is like option 2, except that the vertical (z-) axis is scaled logarithmically.

Three-dimensional pie charts

In a three-dimensional pie chart, your pie is drawn as a solid disk. By default, you look down on this disk from a 42-degree angle above the horizon, but formatting commands allow you to modify the viewing angle. (See Chapter 14.)

Figure 13-33 on the following page presents the seven 3-D Pie gallery options. When you compare Figure 13-33 with Figure 13-22, you can see that these options correspond exactly to the choices in the two-dimensional Pie gallery.

FIGURE 13-33.
*In a 3-D pie chart,
the pie is drawn as
a solid disk.*

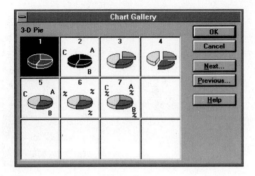

Changing the default chart type

Every chart you create initially appears in the Preferred format — a simple column chart. This initial format is equivalent to the first chart format in the Column gallery. If you modify the format of your chart and then decide you don't like the changes, you can choose Preferred from the Gallery menu to return to the initial format.

If you use another type of chart more often than the column type, you can change the Preferred (default) chart type. Simply select the format you prefer, and then choose Set Preferred from the Gallery menu. Until you issue another Set Preferred command, every new chart you create during the session initially appears in the new Preferred format. The new Preferred format, in turn, has every characteristic (even such details as line thickness, position of tick marks, and text formats) of the chart that was active when you chose Set Preferred. Of course the formats of existing charts do not change. To retain a Preferred format after a work session, you must save your charts and worksheets using the Save Workbook command. Then, when you want to begin a session using charts with that Preferred format, simply open the workbook file you saved. Otherwise, Microsoft Excel does not retain or recognize your Preferred format.

Usually, you'll want to set the Preferred format to match one of the basic options in Excel's Gallery menu. If none of Excel's chart formats meets your needs, however, you can tailor your own Preferred format. Format a chart with all the features you want, and then select Set Preferred from the Gallery menu. You can always return to the default Preferred format by choosing Column from the Gallery menu, selecting the first column-chart option, and choosing Set Preferred.

Saving and reopening chart files

To save a chart file for the first time, use the File menu's Save or Save As command. Either command prompts you for a file name. If you don't include an extension, Microsoft Excel uses XLC.

Charts are built with file-linking formulas. So, when you save a chart file, observe all the precautions for saving linked worksheets. (See "Saving linked worksheets" in Chapter 6.) In particular, be sure you name all source worksheets before you put away your charts.

Using template files to achieve consistency

If you regularly use several chart styles, you'll find template files a great convenience. By saving each of your favorite chart styles as a template file, you can easily achieve formatting consistency from chart to chart.

To create a chart template, first create a chart. You can choose a chart type from the Gallery menu and apply any additional formatting commands you want to include in the template. Then pull down the File menu, and choose Save As. In the File Name text box, enter the name you want to use for your template. Then select Template from the Save File as Type drop-down list, and click OK.

To reuse the template, select the data you need to plot. Then use the File Open command to open the template file. Excel automatically plots your worksheet selection in the template's chart type and with all the template's formatting settings.

Your new chart has a dummy name until you save it and supply a permanent file name. If your template is named LINE.XLT, for example, the new chart might be called Line1. To save the new chart, simply choose the Save or Save As command from the File menu and name the file.

If you want your template to apppear in the New dialog box, save your template in your EXCEL\XLSTART directory. If you are really pleased with your template and want to use it as your default chart type, save it under the name CHART in your EXCEL\XLSTART directory. Excel will use your chart template instead of Excel's default chart when you choose New from the File menu. Then you only need to copy your data and press F11 to create your favorite chart.

When you reopen a chart file using the File menu's Open command, Excel follows the procedures described in Chapter 6 for updating its formula links. For example, if the source worksheet isn't already open, Excel asks you whether you want to update references to unopened documents. If you answer no, Excel draws your chart using the same values it used when you last saved the chart.

Protecting a chart

After you create a chart, you can use the Protect Document command on the Chart menu to lock the chart and prevent anyone who views it from changing the chart's data series or formats. This command works the same way as the Protect Document command on the worksheet Options menu, discussed in Chapter 2.

You can also use the Password options in the Save As dialog box to prevent others from opening the chart file without the correct password.

Printing a windowed chart

Chapter 12 discussed the basic techniques for printing Microsoft Excel documents. Printing a windowed chart is the same as printing a worksheet, with a few minor differences.

The Page Setup command

To print a chart, first choose the Page Setup command from the chart window's File menu. This command lets you define the layout of the page on which you will be printing. Although your margin options are the same in both the chart and worksheet environments, three new options in the chart dialog box — Size on Screen, Scale to Fit Page, and Use Full Page — are added to the worksheet Page Setup dialog box. Scale to Fit Page, the default setting, tells Excel to print the chart as large as possible without losing the height-to-width ratio shown on the screen. If you want to control the dimensions of the printed chart manually, select the Size on Screen option. This option tells Excel to print your chart exactly as it appears on the screen. To vary the size of the screen image, you can resize the window just as you would resize a worksheet or macro sheet window. The Use Full Page option tells Excel to fill the entire page, regardless of the height-to-width ratio of the chart.

The Print Preview command

To see what your chart looks like before you print it, choose the Print Preview command (or select the Preview option in the Print command's dialog box). As in the worksheet environment, Excel displays the chart as it will appear on the printed page.

All the print preview features described in Chapter 12 work the same way with charts as they do with worksheets and macro sheets. You can zoom in for a close-up view, modify margin settings with the mouse, and return directly to the Page Setup dialog box to change any parameters you set there. To print, click Print.

When you click Print (or choose the File menu's Print command), you see a dialog box like the one you see when you choose the Print command in the worksheet environment, but without the options for printing the worksheet and notes.

The Pages option does not apply when you use the chart environment, because all your charts are one page long. However, you can use the Copies box to indicate the number of charts you want to print.

Printing an embedded chart

To print an embedded chart, follow all the procedures described in Chapter 12 for printing worksheets. If your chart lies within the range named *Print_Area* (or if no range named *Print_Area* exists), Microsoft Excel prints the chart together with your ordinary worksheet data.

You can also print an embedded chart independently of its worksheet. Double-click the embedded chart to open a chart window, and then print the chart as you would any windowed chart.

14

Customizing Charts

*I*n Chapter 13 we surveyed the steps involved in creating a chart and choosing a basic chart type. Now we'll look at the myriad ways in which Microsoft Excel can help you tailor the appearance of your charts to suit your tastes and presentation needs.

Customizing embedded charts

When you select an embedded chart, Microsoft Excel normally displays the Chart toolbar (unless you used the Toolbar command on the Options menu to tell it not to). This toolbar includes tools for several of the most commonly used formatting commands. For example, you can use Chart toolbar tools to switch from a column chart to a bar chart or to a pie chart.

In general, however, the first step in customizing an embedded chart is to double-click it. Excel presents a copy of the embedded chart in a separate window and displays the Chart menu bar. You can then customize your chart with any of the procedures described in the remainder of this chapter. Each change you make in the chart window is immediately reflected in the embedded chart. When you've finished customizing, simply close the chart window.

Changing chart types with the Main Chart command

As we explained in Chapter 13, when you use commands on the Gallery menu to change from one chart type to another, some of the custom formatting you applied to your chart might not be transferred. (For example, choosing any of the gallery options restores Excel's default series colors.) Therefore, if you have already done some custom formatting and you decide to switch to a different chart type, it's best not to use the Gallery menu. Instead, choose the Main Chart command from the Format menu, or use the right mouse button to click the chart and choose Main Chart from the shortcut menu that appears. When you do, you'll see the dialog box shown in Figure 14-1.

FIGURE 14-1.
When you change chart types with the Main Chart command, you preserve all your custom formatting.

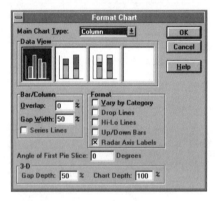

Near the top of the Format Chart dialog box is a drop-down list of Excel's chart types. Below that is a miniature gallery-style menu, from which you can choose basic variations. This mini-gallery has fewer variations than the main Gallery menu because it omits some variations that involve gridlines, data-point text, drop lines, and logarithmic scaling. You can apply these details with other formatting commands.

The Format Chart dialog box presents a number of choices including chart type. We discuss this dialog box again in "Formatting markers with the Main Chart command," later in this chapter.

Selecting chart objects

The term *chart object* refers to one of the components of a chart, such as an axis, a data point, a title, or a legend. Microsoft Excel divides a chart into the following classes of objects, each of which you can select and format:

- Chart area
- Plot area

- Floor (3-D chart types only)
- Walls (3-D chart types only)
- Corners (3-D chart types only)
- Legend
- Axes
- Text
- Arrows
- Gridlines
- First data series
- Second and subsequent data series
- Drop lines
- Hi-lo lines
- Upbars
- Downbars
- Series lines

Some object classes consist of two or more separate objects. For example, most charts have at least two axes, and data series consist of two or more data points. You can select and format the objects within a class separately.

With the mouse, you can usually select an object you want to format by simply clicking it. To change the scale of a chart's y-axis, for example, you can start by clicking that axis. In many cases, you can select an object and go immediately to a formatting dialog box by double-clicking the object. Double-clicking a legend, for example, takes you straight to the Patterns dialog box for legends, where you can specify a background color and pattern for the box that contains the legend, add a drop shadow, and so on.

Another easy way to format a particular kind of object is to click that object with the right mouse button. Excel displays a shortcut menu of formatting commands appropriate for the object that you clicked.

To select an object with the keyboard, use the arrow keys. Pressing the Up and Down arrow keys cycles you through the various object classes, and pressing the Left and Right arrow keys moves you from object to object within a class.

Whether you use a mouse or the keyboard, there are two ways to tell which object you selected: The object's name appears in the reference area (to the left of the formula bar), and the object itself is marked by *handles* (black or white squares) at its perimeter. Black handles indicate that you can move the object as well as format it. White handles indicate that you can format the object but not move it.

Excel abbreviates the names of some objects. For example, series are identified as S1, S2, and so on. The first data point in series 1 is called S1P1; the second data point in series 3 is S3P2; and so forth. If you find these abbreviations confusing, just ignore them and look at the handles to determine what's selected. For example, you might not remember which axis is axis 1; but when you see the white handles at the ends of your y-axis, you'll know which element of the chart you're about to format.

When you want to format an object, begin by selecting it (or double-clicking it to go straight to a formatting dialog box). When you finish formatting, the object remains selected in case you want to do anything further with it. To deselect the object, press Esc or click anywhere near the four edges of the chart window.

Adding attached and unattached text to charts

Microsoft Excel allows you to annotate your charts with several kinds of text. For example, you can add a title to the entire chart, descriptions beside the y-axis and below the x-axis, and words or numbers next to individual data points. Excel calls these annotations *attached* text because they're associated with particular chart elements.

You can also add "floating" annotations wherever you like. Such *unattached* text can be moved and placed anywhere.

Adding a chart title

To add a title to your chart, pull down the Chart menu, choose Attach Text, select the Chart Title option, and click OK. Excel responds by displaying the dummy text *Title* centered near the top of your chart. White handles appear around the dummy text.

To replace the dummy text, type your own title. Your words will appear on the formula line as you type, just like the characters of a worksheet cell entry. When you finish, press Enter. Excel displays your title but leaves the white handles in place in case you want to do anything further (such as choose a different font). Press Esc to delete the handles. (To learn how to change the font and other formatting characteristics, see "Formatting attached and unattached text," later in this chapter.)

Breaking a chart title into two or more lines

Excel normally displays your chart title on a single line. To break it into two or more lines, press Ctrl-Enter where you want a line break to occur. Be sure the title is selected, and click the formula bar or press F2. Then you can edit the title just as you would edit a worksheet cell entry.

Multi-line titles are centered by default, but you can select left or right alignment by clicking the appropriate tools on the Standard toolbar. You can also change the alignment of titles with menu commands. (See "Formatting attached and unattached text," later in this chapter.)

Automatic titles

In a few situations, Excel creates a title for you when you open a new chart window, rather than waiting for you to use the Attach Text command. This happens if the data to be plotted lies in a single worksheet column and you include a column heading in the chart selection or if the data to be plotted consists of a single row and you include a row heading.

For example, using the worksheet in Figure 13-1 (in the previous chapter), if you select D3:E8 and open a new chart window, Excel presents the column chart shown in Figure 14-2. If the chart had more than one series, the column heading *Product A* would be treated as a series name and included in the legend. Because the chart has only one series, Excel assumes that you don't need a legend and that the column heading *Product A* makes a suitable chart title. If you subsequently paste additional data series into this chart, Excel removes this title and uses the text as a series name in the chart's legend.

Linking a chart title to a worksheet cell

You can link a chart title to the contents of a worksheet cell so that cell changes are automatically reflected in the title. To do this, first create a dummy title, as described

FIGURE 14-2.
When your chart consists of a single series, Excel uses a column or row heading as a default chart title.

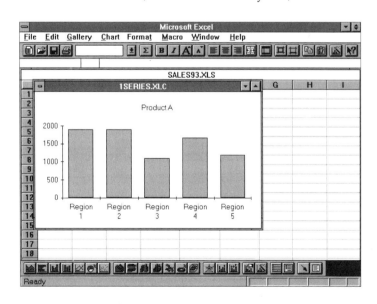

earlier in this chapter. Next, instead of typing the title text, create an external-reference formula. For example, to link the title of a chart to cell A1 in the worksheet named SALES93.XLS, enter the formula

=SALES93.XLS!$A$1

You can either type this formula or create it by pointing to the worksheet cell. If you subsequently cut the supporting cell and paste it somewhere else, Excel updates the external-reference formula so the text of the title remains the same.

You can link a title to a cell that contains numeric or text data. If you link it to a cell that contains numeric data, Excel uses the cell's current numeric format in your title.

When you link a title to a worksheet cell, remember these two rules: The worksheet must be open, and the reference must be to a single cell. (You can reference that cell by name or by address, however.)

Adding titles to chart axes

Adding a title to a chart axis is much like adding a title to the chart itself. Start by choosing the Chart menu's Attach Text command. In the dialog box that appears, you'll see option buttons for each of your chart's axes. Select the button for the axis you want to title, and then click OK.

In most two-dimensional charts, the horizontal axis is called the *category* or *x*-axis and the vertical axis is called the *value* or *y*-axis. The two exceptions are bar charts and pie charts. In bar charts, the category axis is vertical and the value axis is horizontal. Pie charts have no axes.

In three-dimensional charts (excluding 3-D pies, which have no axes), the value axis is still the vertical one, but now it's called the *z*-axis instead of the y-axis. The category axis remains the x-axis, and the *series* axis (if your chart plots separate data series in separate planes) is the y-axis.

Don't be concerned if you find this terminology hard to remember. When you select an axis option in the Attach Text dialog box, Excel displays a dummy title next to the axis, enclosed within white handles. Thus you can see immediately which axis you're about to title, and you can replace the dummy title with your own text or cell reference.

Excel centers axis titles between the endpoints of the axes. If you want the titles to appear somewhere else — above the y-axis, for example — use unattached text instead. (See "Adding unattached text," later in this chapter.)

Adding labels to data points

The easiest way to attach text to a data point is to select the data point and then choose the Attach Text command. For example, suppose you want to add labels that identify the low and high points for the year to the monthly earnings chart shown in Figure 14-3. The high point occurs in April, and the low point occurs in August. Start by selecting the April point by holding down Ctrl and clicking the chart line directly on the April data point. Excel marks the point with a handle and displays S1P4 (an abbreviation for series 1 point 4) in the reference area.

Next, pull down the Chart menu and choose Attach Text. As Figure 14-4 shows, Excel makes Series and Data Point the default choice in the Attach Text To group and fills out the text boxes to select Series Number 1 and Point Number 4. When you click OK, Excel displays the value of point 4, which is 9800, directly beside the data point. You can repeat these steps to annotate the August data point. Figure 14-5 on the following page shows how the chart looks with text attached to these two points.

The default text for a data-point label is the value of the data point. In most cases, that's the text you'll want to use, but you can edit the label if you like. Select the label, click the formula bar or press F2, and then make your changes.

In the procedure just described, we selected a data point before choosing the Attach Text command. If you prefer, you can choose Attach Text first, and then fill out the Series Number and Point Number text boxes yourself.

FIGURE 14-3.
You might want to attach text to the low and high points in a line chart.

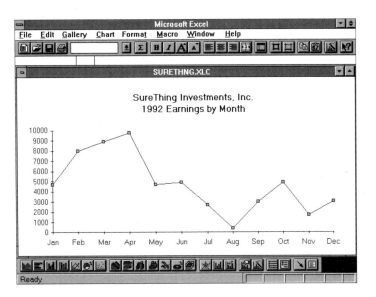

FIGURE 14-4.
When you choose Attach Text with a data point selected, Excel assumes you want to attach text to that data point.

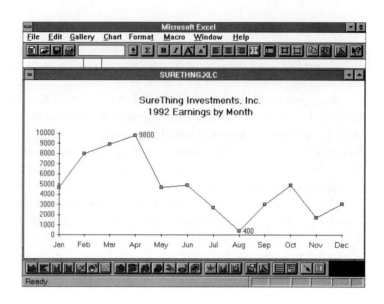

FIGURE 14-5.
We attached labels to show the value of the April and August data points. If the values of these points change, the labels change also.

Adding unattached text

So far, we've looked at three kinds of attached text — chart titles, axis titles, and data-point labels. Excel also allows you to annotate a chart with floating text. Such text is called *unattached* because you can move it anywhere on your chart.

To add unattached text to your chart, type the text in the formula bar. Press Ctrl-Enter to begin a new line of text, and press Enter to lock in your entry.

Before you begin typing, be sure no chart objects are selected. (In other words, no handles appear in the chart window, no text appears in the formula bar, and no object identifier appears in the reference area.) If a chart object is selected — particularly a data point or a text block — you can inadvertently destroy information in your chart when you create the unattached text. If you use a mouse, you can click near one of the edges of the chart window to ensure no chart object is selected. (Alternatively, if a toolbar that contains the Text tool is visible, you can click the Text tool. Excel will create a text block containing the word Text, which you can then edit.)

When you lock in your entry, the text initially appears in the middle of the plot area, making it difficult to read on the screen. You can move the unattached text to an empty area of the chart window so that it is more legible. To reposition the text with the mouse, drag the text block to the position you want. As you drag, a rectangular border called a positioning box replaces the black handles around the text block to show the new placement.

You can also change the proportions of the text block by dragging the black handles that appear around the block or by using the Size command on the Chart menu. To change the height or width of the text block with the mouse, drag one of the black handles at the sides of the text block; to change the height and width simultaneously, drag one of the corner handles.

When the positioning box is larger than the text block, the text is centered in the box area. When the positioning box is smaller than the text block, Excel displays as much text as it has room for. The effects of resizing a text block are particularly important when you use the Patterns command to place borders around your text. (See "The Patterns command," later in this chapter.) Figure 14-6 shows the line chart after we added some unattached text.

FIGURE 14-6.
We annotated the chart with unattached text.

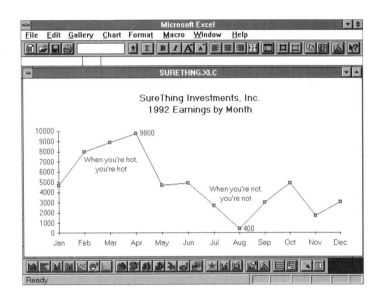

Editing and removing attached and unattached text

To change the contents of an attached or unattached text block, first select the block. Excel then displays the contents of the block in the formula bar. Press F2 or click the formula bar, and then follow the same procedures you use to edit a worksheet cell. When you finish, press Enter to lock in the modified text.

To remove a block of text, select it and press Del.

Formatting attached and unattached text

You can use three Format menu commands to change the appearance of attached and unattached text: Patterns, Font, and Text.

The Patterns command lets you add a border, with or without a shadow, around your text block. You can also use this command to apply a pattern or color to the block in which the text appears.

The Font command, like its counterpart on the worksheet Format menu, allows you to change the typeface, point size, style, and color of your text. (By *style*, we mean italics, underlining, bold, or strikeout; named styles are not available in charts.)

The Text command lets you change the alignment and orientation of your text. You can use it to switch from centered lines to left-aligned lines, or to rotate a label so that it reads vertically instead of horizontally.

A simple way to begin formatting a text block is to click it with the right mouse button. A shortcut menu appears that consists of the Patterns, Font, and Text commands, along with a Clear command. Alternatively, you can use "tunneling" buttons (shortcuts from one box to another), to get from one Format menu dialog box to another. In the Patterns dialog box, for example, you'll find command buttons labeled Font and Text. The Font dialog box includes buttons for Patterns, Text, and so on.

The Patterns command

The Patterns command lets you customize the appearance of the rectangle that contains a block of attached or unattached chart text. As Figure 14-7 shows, the Patterns dialog box has two main sections. The section on the left allows you to include a border around your text, with or without a shadow. The section on the right lets you add a color and pattern to the text area, which is the space within the perimeter of the text block. As we'll see later in this chapter, the Patterns command presents some different options when objects other than text blocks are selected.

FIGURE 14-7.
The Patterns com-
mand lets you add a
border and a back-
ground to text blocks
and other chart objects.

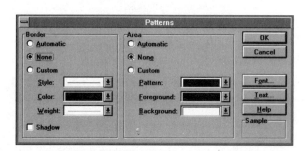

In the lower right corner of the dialog box is a rectangle marked Sample. As you work with the Border and Area options, the Sample box shows what your choices will look like.

The default setting for both Border and Area is None. To specify a border style, weight, and color, make selections from the three drop-down list boxes. Microsoft Excel changes the option-button setting from None to Custom as soon as you open one of these list boxes. To remove the border, click None.

To include a shadow along the bottom and right edges of your border, select the Shadow check box. Excel draws the shadow in black, regardless of what other colors you choose in the Patterns dialog box.

If you want your text to appear against a colored or patterned background, select options from the Area side of the dialog box. Here again, you have three drop-down list boxes to work with, and your option-button setting changes from None to Custom as soon as you open any one of these lists. To remove an Area setting, click None.

The Font command

The default chart fonts are 12-point MS Sans Serif bold for the chart title, 10-point MS Sans Serif bold for axis titles, and 10-point MS Sans Serif regular for all other text. (You can change these defaults by selecting the entire chart and using the Font command. See "Formatting background areas," later in this chapter.)

When you choose the Font command with a block of attached or unattached text selected, you see a dialog box like the one in Figure 14-8. (The fonts listed might be different on your system.) Many of the options in this dialog box are familiar to you because you've used them to format worksheet text. (See Chapter 4.)

FIGURE 14-8.
Use the Font dialog box to change the typeface, style, size, color, and background of your chart text.

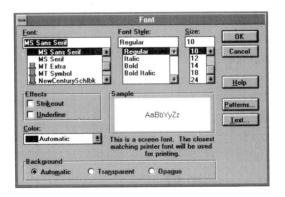

You use the Font, Size, and Style options to specify the typeface and format for the selected text. The Background options control the appearance of the area behind the text. If you use the default setting, Automatic, Excel selects a pattern for you. If you select Transparent, the area behind the text is "see-through," so any objects behind the text are visible — that is, the text appears as if it were simply typed on top of the chart. If you select Opaque, on the other hand, Excel blocks out an area behind each character of your text. The blocked-out area obscures any chart objects behind it, making your text stand out from the chart.

You can use the Color options in the Font dialog box to change the color of selected chart text for emphasis. Be sure to select a color for your text that contrasts sufficiently with the Area color you selected in the Patterns dialog box.

The Text command

The Text command controls the alignment of your chart text, its horizontal or vertical orientation, and the use of Excel's automatic labeling and sizing features. When you choose this command, Excel presents the dialog box shown in Figure 14-9.

FIGURE 14-9.
Use the Text dialog box to change the alignment and orientation of your text and to select automatic labeling and sizing.

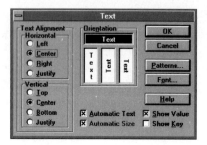

Unless you specify otherwise, Excel prints all attached and unattached text horizontally, except for titles attached to vertical axes. Text attached to a vertical axis on the left side of a chart is rotated 90 degrees counterclockwise. If you attach a title to a vertical axis positioned at the right side of your chart, Excel also rotates the title 90 degrees counterclockwise.

As you've seen in several examples, Excel also rotates category labels if they don't fit horizontally. You can override this setting, however. (See "Formatting and scaling axes," later in this chapter.)

To specify a different orientation for any block of attached or unattached text, select one of the options in the Orientation section of the Text dialog box.

The Automatic Text option

The Automatic Text option lets you restore the default contents of any attached text block. For example, when you select your main chart title, choose the Format menu's Text command, and select Automatic Text, Excel replaces your current title with the word *Title*.

You'll find the Automatic Text option convenient if you attach text to data points. The default text in this case is the value of the data point. If you subsequently change that text to something else and then decide you want to redisplay the data point's value, you can do so by selecting the data point, choosing the Format menu's Text command, and selecting the Automatic Text option.

The Automatic Size option

The Automatic Size option applies only to unattached text. Although Automatic Size is the default setting, Excel deselects it whenever you manually resize a text block. After you manually resize an unattached text block, you can use this option to revert to automatic sizing. When the Automatic Size option is in effect, the text block fits exactly around the text. The advantage of the Automatic Size option is that Excel adjusts the size of the text block as needed whenever you edit the text or use the Font or Text command to change the display characteristics of that text.

The Show Value and Show Key options

The last two options in the Text dialog box, Show Value and Show Key, appear only if the selected object is a block of text attached to a data point. The Show Value option works in conjunction with the Automatic Text option to determine the default text for your data-point labels. When Show Value is in effect, Excel labels your data markers by extracting the corresponding values from the worksheet. If you deselect this option, Excel uses the series name instead. If your chart contains only one data series, Excel labels the data marker with the category name when you deselect show value. If your data series contains no series name, Excel places the numbers 1, 2, 3, and so forth over each data-point marker.

The Show Key option tells Excel to display next to the data-point label a small square that reflects the pattern or color you've applied to the corresponding data marker. This option can be a handy alternative to a chart legend when you're short on space.

Adding, positioning, and formatting a legend

As discussed in Chapter 13, you can add a legend to a chart by using the Chart menu's Add Legend command. The legend appears on the right side of your chart, framed by a set of black handles. Microsoft Excel redraws the chart to make room for the legend. If the Chart toolbar is visible, you can also add (or remove) a legend by clicking the Legend tool (the third tool from the right on the default Chart toolbar).

Moving the legend

The easiest way to move a legend is to drag it to a new location. Another way to reposition a legend is to select it and then choose the Format menu's Legend command. Excel presents the dialog box shown in Figure 14-10 on the following page.

FIGURE 14-10.
*The Legend command
provides one way to
position a legend.*

If you select Bottom, Excel positions the legend as one line at the bottom of the chart, where it is less conspicuous and takes up less room. If you select Corner, Excel moves the legend to the upper right corner of the chart. If you select Top, Excel changes the legend to a horizontal format and centers it under the chart title. The Right and Left options center the legend along the right and left edges of the chart.

The advantage of dragging the legend with the mouse is that you're not limited to the five fixed-position options listed in the Legend dialog box. You can put the legend wherever you want it, even within the chart itself. Because displaying the legend alongside, above, or below the chart reduces the size of the chart's plot area, you might choose to place the legend within the chart. Figure 14-11 shows a legend positioned within a column chart.

When you first add a legend to a chart, Excel displays the series names above one another, in a vertical format. To switch to a horizontal layout, as in Figure 14-11, first drag or move the legend all the way to the top or the bottom of the chart. When

FIGURE 14-11.
*You can position a
legend inside the plot
area of your chart.*

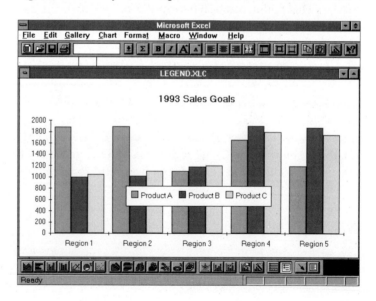

you release the mouse button, Excel redraws the legend in a horizontal format. Next drag the legend again to its final resting place. To return to a vertical layout, move the legend all the way to either side of the chart, and then move it to the desired location.

Changing the legend text

Excel does not allow you to edit the contents of the legend box. To alter the text in the legend box, you must edit the cells of the worksheet that contain the series labels. You can also use the Chart menu's Edit Series command to change the legend text. (See Chapter 15.)

If your chart doesn't include series names (that is, if you didn't include cells that contain labels in the columns or rows you selected for your data series), Excel displays Series1, Series2, and so on in the legend box. But you can change the legend to meaningful text using the Edit Series command.

Formatting the legend

You can use two Format menu commands to change the appearance of your legend: Patterns and Font. These two commands work the same way with legends as they do with attached and unattached text. You can use the Patterns command to add a background color and a shadow to the legend, and you can use Fonts to change the typeface, point size, and style. You can also apply bold and italics by selecting the legend and clicking the toolbar. (For details about the Patterns and Font commands, see "Formatting attached and unattached text," earlier in this chapter.)

Removing a legend

Deleting a legend is as easy as adding one. Add Legend is a toggle command, so as soon as you choose it from the Chart menu, its name changes to Delete Legend. To delete a legend you've created, choose the Delete Legend command (or click the Legend tool on the Chart toolbar). If the legend is positioned alongside, above, or below the chart, Excel expands the size of the plot area again to use the space occupied by the legend.

Working with arrows and lines

Arrows are an effective way to point out key information. When you choose Add Arrow from the Chart menu (or click the Arrow tool on the Chart toolbar), Excel places a black arrow on the screen, as shown in Figure 14-12 on the following page.

FIGURE 14-12.
*An arrow appears
when you choose the
Add Arrow command
from the Chart menu.*

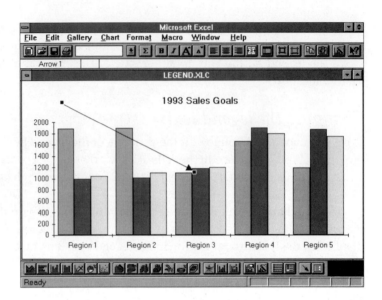

The arrow initially points to the center of the plot area and has a solid equilateral triangle for a head. You can change the length and position of the arrow, as well as the style and color of both the shaft and the head. You can even eliminate the arrowhead, turning the arrow into a simple straight line.

To adjust the length and position of the arrow, first select it if necessary, and then drag the handles with the mouse. When you drag the handle at one end, the handle at the other end remains anchored. By dragging either handle, you can easily adjust both the length and the angle of the arrow. You can also drag the entire arrow in any direction by starting with the mouse pointer on the shaft.

Changing an arrow's style, color, and weight

You can format your arrow by selecting it and choosing the Format menu's Patterns command. Figure 14-13 shows the Patterns dialog box.

FIGURE 14-13.
*The Patterns
command lets you
customize an arrow's
style, color, and
weight.*

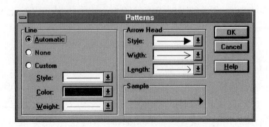

The left side of this dialog box looks and works much like the Patterns dialog box for text, which formats borders around text blocks and legends. The only differences are that the None option is dimmed — you can't have a disembodied arrowhead — and there's no Shadow check box. For details about choosing a style, color, and weight for the shaft of your arrow, see "The Patterns command," earlier in this chapter.

The drop-down lists on the right side of the dialog box let you pick a style, width, and length for the arrowhead. The color of the arrowhead is the same as that of the shaft.

Three styles are available: a filled head, an open head, and no head. You can combine either the open or the filled head with any combination of the length and width options; the results appear in the Sample section of the dialog box.

Choosing no head allows you to add straight lines to your chart. As Figure 14-14 shows, you can use this option to subdivide chart areas or pie slices. The pie chart in Figure 14-14 has only three data points — for electricity, natural gas, and other. We used headless arrows to break up the electricity slice. We then annotated the subdivisions with unattached text and additional headless arrows.

FIGURE 14-14.
The lines subdividing the electricity slice are headless arrows.

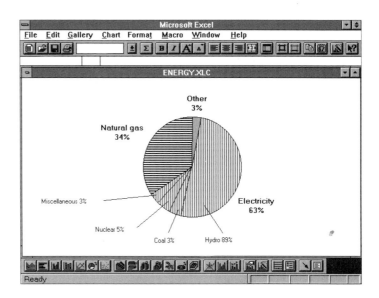

Deleting an arrow

To delete an arrow, first select it. Excel replaces the Add Arrow command on the Chart menu with the Delete Arrow command. Choose the Delete Arrow command to delete the selected arrow. (If an arrow is not selected, Excel redisplays the Add Arrow command on the Chart menu, allowing you to place additional arrows on the chart.)

Formatting data-point markers

In Microsoft Excel terminology, a *marker* is any symbol that represents a data point on a chart. In a column chart, for example, each column is a marker. In a line or radar chart, the little squares, triangles, and other symbols that appear along the lines of the chart are markers. Each slice of a pie chart is a marker, and so on.

You can change the color, pattern, and border of any marker by selecting a data point and choosing the Format menu's Patterns command. (You can also double-click the data point to call up the Patterns dialog box.) You can use the Format menu's Main Chart command to customize other aspects of a marker's appearance.

Selecting markers

In all chart types except area, 3-D area, pie, 3-D pie, and 3-D surface, you can select either an individual marker or all markers for a given series. When you click a marker while holding down Ctrl, Excel selects the individual marker. When you click a marker without holding down Ctrl, Excel selects that marker and all others in the same series.

To select an entire series of markers with the keyboard, press the Up arrow key or Down arrow key until you see the appropriate identifier in the reference area. The identifier for the first series is S1, for the second series S2, and so on. To select a single marker in a series, first select the series. Next, use the Right arrow key until the appropriate marker is selected.

Whether you use the mouse or the keyboard to make a selection, you can usually tell what's selected by looking at the handles. When you select an entire series, two or more of the series' markers have handles. When you select an individual marker, handles appear around only that marker. With line charts and XY charts, it can be hard to distinguish the handles from the markers themselves, however. In all cases, the reference area shows your selection. If you select a whole series, the reference area shows S1, S2, S3, or something similar. When you select an individual point, the identifier includes a P and an S. For example, if you select the second point in series 3, the reference area displays S3P2. (You should check the reference area after you use the Patterns dialog box, because the dialog box covers your chart, making it impossible to see the handles.)

In certain kinds of charts, when you select an individual marker, you'll see one black handle as well as a set of white handles. (In line charts and XY charts, you might see *only* a black handle.) The black handle in this case means that you can adjust the magnitude of the point with the mouse, and Excel will change the source cell to match. (See Chapter 15.)

Using the Patterns command

Figure 14-15 shows the Patterns dialog box for bar, column, and 3-D column charts. For area, 3-D area, 3-D line, pie, and 3-D pie charts, the dialog box looks the same, except that it lacks the Invert if Negative check box. The dialog box looks a little different when you format a line or an XY chart.

FIGURE 14-15.
This Patterns dialog box includes an Apply to All option, which lets you assign a marker format to every marker on your chart at one time.

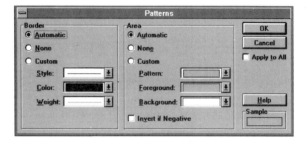

The dialog box in Figure 14-15 should look familiar. Most of the options provided in this dialog box are like those in the Patterns dialog boxes for text and legends. The Border section of the dialog box lets you select style, color, and weight for the line that surrounds your marker. The Area section lets you specify a color and pattern for the body of the marker.

The Apply to All option

If you select the Apply to All check box, Excel applies your formatting decisions to all markers in all series. You can use this option to draw a thick black border around all columns in a column chart, for example. Rather than selecting each series in turn, you can pick any series at random, specify a thick black border in the left side of the dialog box, and then select the Apply to All check box.

In most cases you'll want to avoid using the Apply to All check box when you've assigned a custom color to a marker or series of markers. Otherwise, Excel will apply the custom color to all series, making each series indistinguishable from the others.

If you make this error (or any other formatting error), you can use the Edit Undo command to restore the previous formats. You can also restore Excel's default formatting choices at any time by using the Patterns command and selecting the Automatic option in both the Border and Area sections of the dialog box.

The Invert if Negative option

If you select the Invert if Negative check box, Excel reverses the foreground and background color choices for markers with negative values. The foreground color becomes the background and vice versa. This option is available only with bar, column, and 3-D column charts.

Options for line, XY, and radar charts

If the current chart is a line, XY, or radar chart, Excel replaces the Border and Area sections of the dialog box with sections labeled Line and Marker. The Line section governs the appearance of the line that connects the various markers in a series; the Marker section specifies the appearance of the markers themselves. You can select the None option in the Line or Marker section of the dialog box to remove lines, segments, or markers in a series.

Exploding pie slices

To *explode* a pie slice means to pull it away from the center of the chart. You usually do this to emphasize particular slices.

To explode a pie slice, select it and drag it with the mouse. If you use the keyboard, select the slice and then choose the Format menu's Move command. Use the arrow keys to adjust the position of the slice, and then press Enter. You can explode as many slices as you like with both two-dimensional and three-dimensional pie charts.

Formatting markers with the Main Chart command

The Format menu's Main Chart command serves two purposes. It lets you change chart types without using the Gallery menu (thereby preserving your custom formatting), and it provides a handful of options that affect the positioning of data-point markers. The Format Chart dialog box is illustrated in Figure 14-1.

Positioning bars and columns

The Bar/Column options in the Format Chart dialog box let you increase or decrease the space between markers in a bar or column chart. The Overlap option controls the distribution of markers within a cluster, and the Gap Width option determines the space between clusters.

The default settings for the type of column chart illustrated in Figure 14-12 are 0% overlap and 50% gap width. This means that, within a cluster, Excel displays markers side by side with no overlap and no space between them. The space between clusters equals half the width of an individual marker.

To create a column or bar chart in which the markers overlap, enter a positive number (0 through 100) in the Overlap box. To separate markers within a cluster, enter a negative number (0 through –100) in the Overlap box.

Note that if you ask for 100 percent overlap, Excel displays all the markers in a given cluster on top of one another, but it doesn't stack them. To stack the markers, choose one of the gallery options (either from the Data View section of the Main Chart dialog box or from the Gallery menu) that depicts the markers stacked over one another.

Note, too, that if you choose a stacked column or bar chart, the default Overlap value is 100 percent. By entering a number less than 100, you can create bar or column charts that are stacked but also staggered.

To change the amount of space between clusters, enter a value between 0 and 500 in the Gap Width box. The smaller the gap width, the wider your columns or bars will be. By specifying a 0 gap width, you can create a step chart — a column or bar chart in which all markers are lined up next to each other, with no intervening spaces.

You can adjust the gap width for 3-D as well as 2-D column charts. The default spacing between clusters is 50 percent in both cases.

Rotating a pie chart

Excel normally draws both the 2-D and 3-D pie charts so that the first data marker begins with a line that radiates straight up from the center of the chart. Excel then draws the chart in a clockwise fashion. For example, if the first data point amounts to 25 percent of the series total, its slice begins with a line that points straight up (due "north") and ends with a line that points straight to the right (due "east"). Slice number 2 begins where slice number 1 ends, and so on.

By entering a value greater than 0 and less than 360 in the Angle of First Pie Slice box, you can rotate the graph to a different starting point. For example, to have the first slice begin with a horizontal radius that points to the right, enter 90 in the Angle of First Pie Slice box (in the Format Chart dialog box).

Adjusting the shape and spacing of three-dimensional markers

The shape and spacing of markers in three-dimensional column charts is determined by three settings: Gap Width, Gap Depth, and Chart Depth. Figure 14-16 on the following page illustrates the relationship between these three factors.

As the figure shows, Excel usually draws three-dimensional column markers so that the top of each column appears to be square — that is, each column's depth is equal to its width. To give the columns a flatter appearance, enter a value less than 100 in the Chart Depth box. (The minimum value is 20.) To make the columns thicker, enter a number greater than 100. (The maximum value is 2000.) You can also use the Chart Depth setting to modify the appearance of three-dimensional line and area markers.

Excel normally leaves a 50 percent space — a space equal to half a column's width — between columns along both the category and series axes. To change the spacing along the category axis, change the Gap Width setting. To change the distribution of space along the series axis, change the Gap Depth setting. You can choose values between 0 and 500 in both cases.

If your 3-D chart does not plot separate data series in separate planes, the default value for Gap Depth will be 0. You can increase that number, which will also increase the size of the floor on which the markers rest.

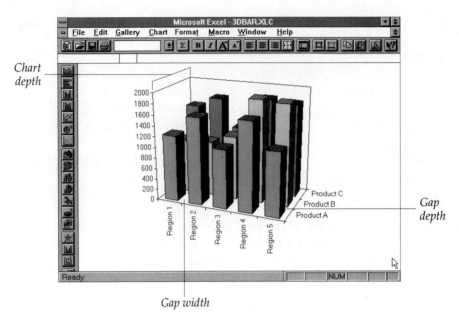

Chart depth

Gap depth

Gap width

FIGURE 14-16. *Gap Width and Gap Depth settings determine the space between markers, the former along the category axis and the latter along the series axis. The Chart Depth setting determines the shape of each marker.*

The Vary by Category option

Selecting the Vary by Category check box in the Main Chart dialog box tells Excel to display each marker of a single-series chart in a different color or pattern. Excel does this by default when you first create a pie chart, but it does not do it for other chart types. If you create a single-series column chart, for example, Excel normally displays all markers in the same color. You can adopt a multi-colored appearance by choosing a different Gallery menu option or by putting a check in the Vary by Category box.

Adding drop lines and hi-lo lines

Drop lines are straight lines that extend from a data point to the x-axis (category axis). You can add them to area, 3-D area, line, and 3-D line charts by selecting the Drop Lines check box.

Drop lines are most useful in 2-D or 3-D area charts. Markers in such charts blend together; the drop lines help clarify where one marker ends and the next begins. Figure 14-17 shows an example of a 3-D area chart with drop lines.

Hi-lo lines are straight lines that extend between the highest and lowest points in a cluster. You can use them for such things as drawing error bars or indicating the range over which a quantity varies. Figure 14-18 illustrates the use of hi-lo lines.

Hi-lo lines are available only in 2-D line charts. To use them, select the Hi-Lo Lines check box in the Main Chart dialog box.

FIGURE 14-17.
Drop lines can clarify area charts by showing where one marker ends and the next begins.

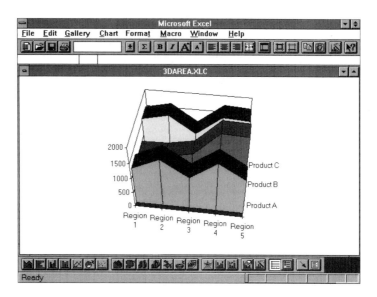

FIGURE 14-18.
Hi-lo lines show the range over which a quantity can vary.

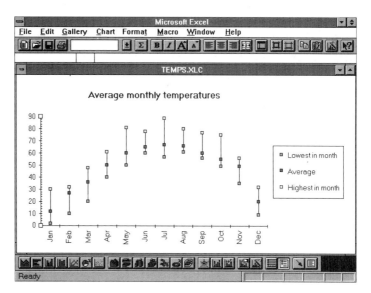

Adding upbars and downbars

Upbars and downbars are useful primarily in charts that track price movements. On the following page, Figure 14-19, a standard "open-high-low-close" chart, offers an example. The rectangles that bracket the opening and closing prices are the upbars and downbars. By default, Excel draws them in white when the closing price is higher than the opening price and in black when the opening price is higher than the closing price.

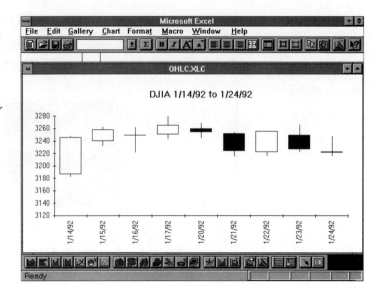

FIGURE 14-19.
*You can apply upbars
and downbars to the
first and last series in
a line chart. Excel
uses one color when
the last series is higher
than the first and a
contrasting color
when the opposite is
true.*

You can use the Main Chart command to add upbars and downbars to any line chart that includes at least two series of data. When the chart has more than two series, the upbars and downbars bracket the first and last series. Excel applies the upbar color when the last series has a higher value than the first.

Note that when you select the Up/Down Bars option in the Format Chart dialog box, Excel also lets you modify the gap width. This parameter is normally available only with bar and column charts, but Excel treats a line chart with upbars and downbars as a species of column chart. By increasing the gap width, you can make the upbar and downbar rectangles narrower, and by decreasing the gap width you can make the upbar and downbar rectangles wider.

Replacing markers with pictures

Another way to transform the appearance of markers is to replace them with graphic images, thereby creating a picture chart. Figure 14-20 gives you a basic idea of what you can do with this feature.

Any image that can be stored in picture or bit-mapped format on the Windows Clipboard can serve as the basis for a picture chart. You can create such images using Excel's drawing tools or with the help of many other Windows applications. (See Chapter 7.)

FIGURE 14-20.
*You can transform
column, bar, and line
graphs into picture
charts.*

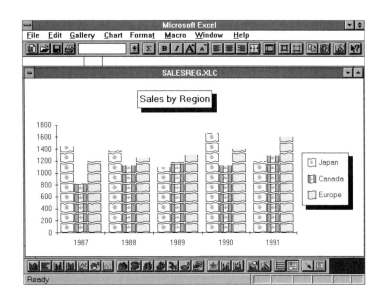

To create a picture chart, start by creating a bar, column, line, radar, or XY chart. Next, copy the graphic image you want to use to the Windows Clipboard.

Return to your Excel chart, select the individual marker or the series you want to replace, and use the Edit Paste command. Excel replaces either the individual marker or every marker in the series with your image.

If you replace markers in a line, radar, or XY chart, the image appears in its original size and shape. If you replace bar or column markers, the image initially stretches to fill the space formerly occupied by the marker. Using the Patterns command, you can use any of three sizing methods. Figure 14-21 shows the Patterns dialog box.

FIGURE 14-21.
*You can size pictures
in column and bar
charts using any of
three methods.*

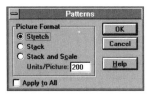

The default option, Stretch, stretches the image to fit the chart data. If you select Stack, Excel displays the image at its original size and uses as many copies as necessary to fill the bar or column. The last copy in the marker is usually cropped. (The Stack option is used in Figure 14-20.) Excel also repeats and stacks the image if you choose Stack and Scale, but in this case you can specify the magnitude of each unit in the stack.

Formatting and scaling axes

Microsoft Excel gives you a great deal of control over the format, position, and scale of your chart's axes. You can use the Patterns command to specify the color, weight, and style of axes, as well as the presence or absence of tick marks and tick labels. With the Font command, you can select the typeface, point size, and style that Excel uses for tick labels. The Text command lets you override Excel's default orientation for tick-label text (changing vertical labels to horizontal, for example). The Scale command lets you switch between normal and logarithmic scaling and lets you scale an axis manually.

These four commands — Patterns, Font, Text, and Scale — are available from the Format menu. You can also move from one to another by selecting command buttons in dialog boxes. For example, you can double-click an axis to get to the Patterns dialog box. From there, you can click the Text button to get to the Text dialog box, and so on. Thus, you can take care of all the axis-formatting details without ever using the Format menu.

Suppressing the display of an axis

The Axes command is located on the Chart menu. With this command, you can suppress the display of any axis. When you choose the Axes command, Excel displays one of the dialog boxes shown in Figure 14-22. (The one on the right appears if the current chart is three-dimensional.)

FIGURE 14-22.
If you don't need to display an axis, you can use the Axes command.

If you deselect an axis, Excel removes not only the axis lines but also any associated labels. Removing axes simplifies the display and gives Excel more space in which to draw the chart. When you want to call a viewer's attention to a single detail in a chart, you might want to delete one or more axes and then use a text block (with or without an arrow) to underscore your point.

Choosing line style, color, and weight

To format any axis line, double-click that line or select it and choose the Format menu's Patterns command. Either way, you see the Patterns dialog box shown in Figure 14-23.

FIGURE 14-23.
*This Patterns dialog
box lets you customize
an axis line and its
associated tick marks
and tick labels.*

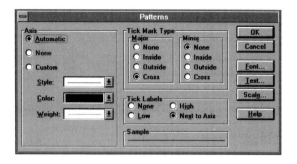

The left side of this dialog box presents the same options you used with text blocks and legends. You can use them to assign a style, weight, and color to the axis line. Note, however, that the None option is dimmed; if you want to remove the axis line altogether, use the Chart menu's Axes command rather than the Format menu's Patterns command.

Specifying the position of tick marks

Tick marks are short lines that either cross or abut an axis line at regular intervals. Like the lines that mark inches and fractions of inches along a ruler, they help define the axis scale. In Figure 14-18, there are *major* tick marks along the y-axis at 10, 20, 30, and so on. Along the x-axis, the major tick marks appear between the month names. The y-axis in this figure also has minor tick marks between each pair of major tick marks.

By default, Excel displays major tick marks on each axis but no minor tick marks. You can override these defaults (as in Figure 14-18) by selecting options from the Tick Mark Type section of the Patterns dialog box. If you decide to include tick marks, you can position them across, inside, or outside the axis line. In Figure 14-18, the major tick marks are across the axes and the minor tick marks are inside.

Using the Scale command, you can also control the interval at which both major and minor tick marks appear. (See "Scaling a value axis manually" and "Scaling a category axis manually," later in this chapter.)

Formatting tick labels

Tick labels are the text that appears beside or below major tick marks. In Figure 14-18, for example, the numbers 10, 20, and so on are tick labels; so are the chart's category names — Jan, Feb, Mar, and so forth. You can format tick labels in a variety of ways. With the Text and Font commands, you can adjust the tick labels' positions relative to the axis lines; change their fonts, sizes, and colors; and specify that Excel display them horizontally or vertically. You can also suppress the display of tick labels altogether. In addition, with the Scale command, you can alter the interval between tick labels.

Specifying position

The Tick Labels section of the Patterns dialog box (see Figure 14-23) determines the position of tick labels relative to axis lines. The default for all axes is the Next to Axis option.

If you select None, Excel suppresses the display of tick labels. You might find this option useful if you plot a block of data without associated column or row labels. In this case, Excel displays the dummy category names 1, 2, 3, and so on, below the x-axis. If you don't find those numbers meaningful, you can eliminate them with the None option.

The Low option is handy in charts that plot both negative and positive numbers. As Figure 14-24 shows, the default position of tick labels doesn't always produce the most satisfying results when the x-axis crosses the y-axis somewhere between the endpoints of the y-axis. In a case like this, you can select Low from the Patterns dialog box, and your chart will look more like the one in Figure 14-25.

The Low option ensures that your x-axis labels appear at the bottom of a chart and your y-axis labels appear at the left edge, regardless of where the axes cross. The High option does the opposite; it displays x-axis labels above the chart and y-axis labels along the right edge. (The exception is when you use the Scale command to reverse the direction in which axes are scaled. In that case, "high" labels appear to the left of or below the plot, and "low" labels appear to the right of or above the plot.)

FIGURE 14-24.
By default, Excel draws tick labels next to axes, even when point markers obscure the labels.

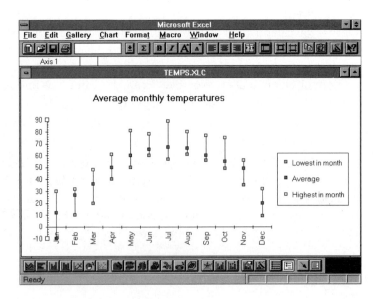

FIGURE 14-25.
You can eliminate the conflict between labels and markers by choosing the Low label position.

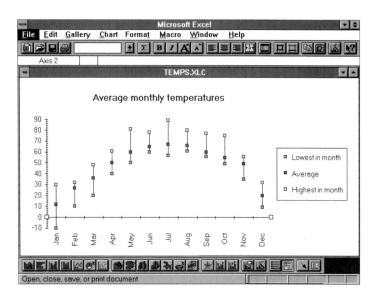

Changing the numeric format of tick labels

The numeric format of a chart's first data point — the first point in the first series — determines the display format used for tick labels along a value axis. The worksheet cells on which Figure 14-18 is based, for example, are all formatted as integers, so Excel uses that format on the chart's value axis. To change the tick labels' display format, simply reformat the worksheet cell that supplies the first data point.

Choosing a font and color

To assign a new typeface, size, color, or style to a set of tick labels, select the axis along which the labels appear, and then choose the Format menu's Font command. (Alternatively, use the right mouse button to click the axis and then click the Font command button.) The dialog box that appears operates exactly like the Font dialog box described earlier. (See "The Font command," earlier in this chapter.)

Adjusting the orientation

Excel displays tick labels horizontally whenever it can, and it rotates them 90 degrees counterclockwise when necessary to avoid overlapping. You can specify a nondefault orientation by selecting an axis and choosing the Format menu's Text command. You'll have the same four choices shown in the Orientation section of Figure 14-9.

Occasionally, Excel displays x-axis labels vertically when they could fit horizontally. In Figure 14-25, for example, Excel displays the month names vertically. By selecting the horizontal option in the Text dialog box, you can make this chart look like the one in Figure 14-26 on the following page.

FIGURE 14-26.
*We used the Text
command to restore a
horizontal orientation
to the month names.*

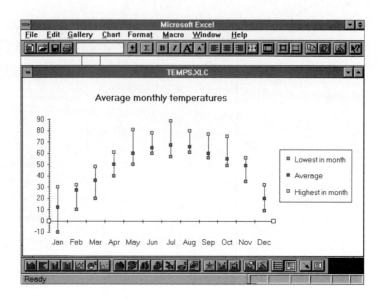

Scaling a value axis manually

Value axis is a generic term for any chart axis that is scaled by value (as opposed to by category or by series). Examples include the vertical axes in column, line, and area charts, and both axes in XY charts. Excel usually creates a satisfactory scale for your value axes automatically, but you can easily alter the default scale to suit your own needs.

To change the way a value axis is scaled, first select the axis. Next, use the Format menu's Scale command. The Scale dialog box for a value axis looks like Figure 14-27.

FIGURE 14-27.
*You can use this
dialog box to alter the
default scale for a
value axis.*

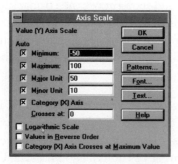

Minimum and maximum

When all the values in your chart data are positive, Excel's default value axis usually begins at 0 and ends at (or just above) the highest value in the chart. If all the chart values are negative, the scale normally begins at (or just below) the lowest value and ends at 0. If the chart includes both negative and positive values, the default scale starts at (or just below) the lowest value and ends at (or just beyond) the highest value.

In a chart with only positive values, you can "zoom" in on the plot by changing the minimum scale value from 0 to a number that approximates the lowest value in the chart. You can zoom in on a plot with only negative values by making a similar change to the maximum value. To change either endpoint of the scale, simply enter the value of your choice in the Maximum or Minimum text box.

When you change the Maximum or Minimum value, Excel deselects the Auto check box to the left of the word Maximum or Minimum. To restore the automatic maximum or minimum, reselect the appropriate Auto check box.

Changing the position of tick marks and gridlines

The Major Unit and Minor Unit values determine the position of major and minor tick marks. In the default chart, Excel displays major tick marks but not minor ones. However, if you use the Patterns command to display minor tick marks, they appear at the interval specified by the Minor Unit value.

The Major Unit and Minor Unit values also determine the position of major and minor gridlines if you choose to display them. You might occasionally need to display both major and minor gridlines but not want to display as many as Excel gives you by default. You can space out the gridlines by increasing the Major Unit value, the Minor Unit value, or both. Simply type new values in the Major Unit and Minor Unit text boxes. (See "Displaying and formatting gridlines," later in this chapter.)

X-axis tick labels

Sometimes Excel can't provide a satisfactory x-axis label display. The program doesn't know how to hyphenate, it won't automatically stagger labels or skip every other one, and it won't automatically switch to a smaller point size.

You can perform some of those tasks yourself, however. With the Font command, for example, you can select a smaller point size or a more compact typeface. With the Scale command, you can tell Excel to display every other label only — or every third, or fourth, and so on. (See "Scaling a category axis manually," later in this chapter.)

If all else fails, you can modify the text of the labels by changing the worksheet labels from which the x-axis labels were generated. Or you can specify new text altogether by editing the chart's SERIES formulas. We'll discuss this last option in Chapter 15.

When you change the Major Unit or Minor Unit value, Excel deselects the Auto check box to the left of the Major Unit or Minor Unit option. To restore automatic values, reselect the appropriate Auto check box.

Changing the intersection of the category axis

Normally, the category axis crosses the value axis at 0. To position it elsewhere, enter a value other than 0 in the text box labeled Category (X) Axis Crosses at. When you do this, Excel deselects the associated Auto check box. To restore the normal position of the category axis, reselect this Auto check box.

You can also modify the position of the category axis by selecting the check box labeled Category (X) Axis Crosses at Maximum Value. If you do this, Excel always displays your category axis at the high end of the value-axis scale, regardless of how the values in the chart change.

Using logarithmic scaling

A *logarithmic* scale is one in which each power of 10 is separated by the same distance. In a logarithmic scale that runs from 1 to 10,000, for example, the numbers 1, 10, 100, 1000, and 10,000 are equally spaced. Scientific and other kinds of technical charts often use logarithmic scaling.

To choose logarithmic scaling, select the Logarithmic Scale check box. To restore *linear* scaling, deselect that check box.

In a logarithmic scale, the lowest value is typically 1. Negative and 0 values cannot be plotted. If you apply logarithmic scaling to a chart that contains negative or 0 values, Excel displays an error message and removes those values from the chart. To restore them, simply restore linear scaling.

Reversing the value-axis scale

You can turn the value-axis scale upside down so that the highest values appear near the bottom of the chart and vice versa. This is a convenient option if all your chart values are negative and you're interested primarily in the absolute values of each point. To reverse the scale, select the Values in Reverse Order check box.

Scaling a category axis manually

Category axis is a generic term for any chart axis that is scaled by category (as opposed to scaled by value or series). Examples include the horizontal axes in column, line, and area charts. Excel usually creates a satisfactory scale for your category axes, but you can easily alter the default scale to suit your own purposes.

To change the scale of a category axis, first select the axis. Next, use the Format menu's Scale command. (Alternatively, use the right mouse button to click the axis, and then click the Scale command from the Shortcut menu.) The Scale dialog box for a category axis looks like the one in Figure 14-28.

FIGURE 14-28.
*You can use this
dialog box to alter
the default scale for
a category axis.*

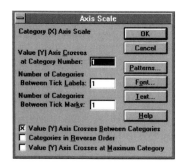

Changing the intersection of the value axis

Normally, the value axis crosses the category axis at the left side of the chart, to the left of the first category's data markers. You can position it elsewhere, however. Simply enter a value other than 1 in the text box labeled Value (Y) Axis Crosses at Category Number. To restore the normal position of the category axis, change the value back to 1.

You can also modify the position of the category axis by selecting the check box labeled Value (Y) Axis Crosses at Maximum Category. If you do this, Excel always displays your category axis at the right side of the chart (unless you also select the Categories in Reverse Order check box, described in "Reversing the category-axis scale," later in this chapter).

Changing the intervals between category labels

Category labels are labels displayed along a category axis to identify data clusters. In Figure 14-17, for example, the words *Region 1, Region 2,* and so on are category labels.

Excel often displays a category label for each cluster in your chart (or for each data point in a single-series chart). If you have many data points in each series, this default arrangement can make your labels hard to read. You can alleviate congestion along the category axis by choosing a value other than 1 in the Number of Categories Between Tick Labels box. If you put a 2 here, Excel displays a label for every other category. If you enter a 3, you get labels for every third category, and so on.

Changing the intervals between tick marks and gridlines

The box labeled Number of Categories Between Tick Marks determines the position of major tick marks along the category axis. In the default chart, major tick marks appear between every two category names. You can make them appear less frequently if you enter a value greater than 1 in this box.

By itself, the presence or absence of tick marks along the category axis doesn't have much of an impact on the appearance of your chart. But major gridlines emanate from major tick marks. If you display major category-axis gridlines, you can control the frequency at which they appear by altering the interval between tick marks.

(Excel draws minor category-axis gridlines halfway between each pair of major gridlines. You cannot customize this interval independently.)

The Value (Y) Axis Crosses Between Categories option

The check box labeled Value (Y) Axis Crosses Between Categories determines where the first point in each series appears, relative to the value axis. The default for this option is Yes (selected) for column and bar charts (both two-dimensional and three-dimensional charts) and No for everything else. As a result of these defaults, Excel draws line, XY, and area charts with their first markers flush against the value axis, and column and bar charts with a little "air" between the axis and the first marker.

You can try deselecting this check box in line, XY, and area charts to see if you prefer the results. You can also experiment with selecting the check box for bar and column charts, although the outcome will probably be unacceptable.

Reversing the category-axis scale

You can invert the category-axis scale so that the first category appears on the right side of the chart and the last appears on the left. This is a convenient option if you want to emphasize the last category. To reverse the scale, select the Categories in Reverse Order check box.

In bar charts, reversing the category-axis scale puts the first category at the top of the axis and the last category at the bottom. For example, if we display the chart shown in Figure 14-2 as a bar chart, Region 1 would normally appear at the bottom of the vertical axis, and Region 5 would appear at the top. If you dislike reading the axis in an upward direction, you can select the Categories in Reverse Order check box.

Scaling a series axis manually

A *series axis* is one that appears only in certain three-dimensional area, column, and line charts. When each series appears in a separate plane, Excel displays two axes along the floor of the chart and a third axis that rises straight up from the floor. One of the floor axes becomes the category (x) axis, and the other becomes the series (y) axis. The axis that rises out of the floor is the value (z) axis. Figure 14-29 shows these axes.

To modify the appearance of a series axis, select it and choose the Format menu's Scale command. (Or click it using the right mouse button and select the Scale command from the Shortcut menu.) The Axis Scale dialog box for a series axis looks like the one in Figure 14-30.

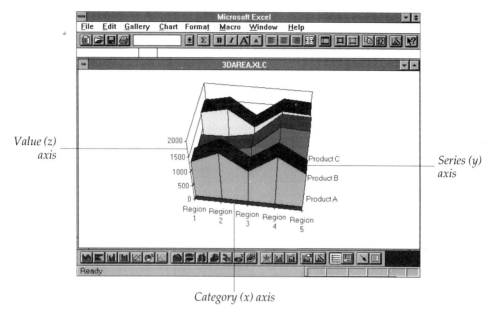

Value (z) axis

Series (y) axis

Category (x) axis

FIGURE 14-29. *Excel uses these terms to describe the axes of a three-dimensional chart.*

FIGURE 14-30.
When you scale a series axis, you see this dialog box.

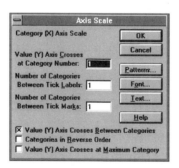

As you can see, your options for scaling the series axis are few and simple. To space out the series labels, enter a number greater than 1 in the Number of Series Between Tick Labels box. To space out the tick marks (and the gridlines, if you choose to display them), enter a value greater than 1 in the Number of Series Between Tick Marks box. To reverse the order in which Excel plots the series, select the Series in Reverse Order check box. This last option might be useful if the points in your first series obscure those in subsequent series. (You can also deal with that problem by rotating the chart, however. See "Changing three-dimensional viewing angles," later in this chapter.)

Displaying and formatting gridlines

Gridlines are horizontal or vertical lines that help clarify the position of data markers relative to axis scales. Figure 14-31 shows a chart with both category-axis and value-axis gridlines.

To add gridlines to your chart, choose the Chart menu's Gridlines command. You'll see a dialog box like one of the ones shown in Figure 14-32. Select the gridlines you want to see, and click OK.

Major gridlines emanate from major tick marks, and minor gridlines emanate from minor tick marks. You can change the position of both kinds of tick marks (and thus the number of gridlines that appear) by selecting an axis and using the Scale command. (See "Specifying the position of tick marks," earlier in this chapter.)

FIGURE 14-31.
Gridlines can clarify the meaning of a chart.

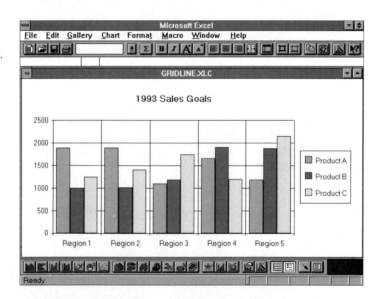

FIGURE 14-32.
Excel can display major and minor gridlines from each chart axis.

To format a set of gridlines, first select one of the gridlines, and then choose the Format menu's Patterns command. (Alternatively, double-click one of the gridlines you want to format.) The Patterns dialog box appears, allowing you to specify color, weight, and style for the selected gridlines.

Formatting background areas

Every chart has two background areas that you can format independently. The larger one is called the *chart area*, and the smaller one is called the *plot area*. Figure 14-33 shows the position of these two background areas. Three-dimensional area, line, and column charts have two additional background areas, called *walls* and *floors*, that can also be formatted. Figure 14-34 on the following page shows the locations of a 3-D column chart's walls and floor.

You can format any of these areas by selecting the area and choosing the Format menu's Patterns command. Alternatively, you can double-click the area and go straight to the Patterns dialog box.

The Patterns dialog box makes available to you many of the same options you've seen already in this chapter. You can add or remove a border (in any color, weight, and style) to or from any of the background areas, and you can fill in any area with a color and pattern of your choice.

FIGURE 14-33.
We used the Patterns command to format the chart area dark gray and the plot area light gray.

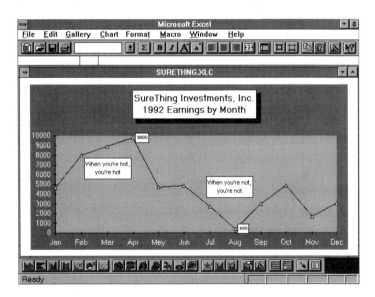

FIGURE 14-34.
We used the Patterns
command to format
the walls and floor of
this three-dimensional
chart.

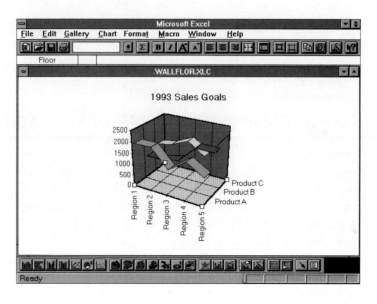

You have two additional options for the chart area. You can add a shadow to the right and lower edges of the border that surrounds the chart area, and you can choose the Font command button and change the default font for all text in your chart. Any font settings you make by selecting the chart area and using the Font command take precedence over any other Font command you used in the chart window. For example, if you change your legend text from 10-point MS Sans Serif to 12-point Courier bold, and you subsequently assign 10-point Arial to the chart area, Microsoft Excel displays all text — including the legend — in 10-point Arial.

Changing three-dimensional viewing angles

The simplest way to change the viewing angle of a three-dimensional chart is to start by selecting one of its corners. Microsoft Excel marks the corners with black handles and lets you manipulate the chart by dragging with the mouse. While you're dragging, Excel displays an outline of the chart.

This direct-manipulation approach is simple and quick, but it also lets you easily turn an intelligible chart into something quite the opposite. A mere flick of the wrist, for example, is all it takes to transform Figure 14-34 into Figure 14-35.

Fortunately, the Format menu's 3-D View command includes a Default button that you can use to return a graph to its original viewing angle. The 3-D View command also lets you fine-tune the appearance of your chart by modifying its elevation, rotation, and perspective and increasing or decreasing the ratio of its

FIGURE 14-35.
With direct manipulation, you can transform the appearance of three-dimensional graphs in dramatic ways. If your efforts prove too dramatic, as shown here, you can use the Default button in the 3-D View dialog box to restore the original view.

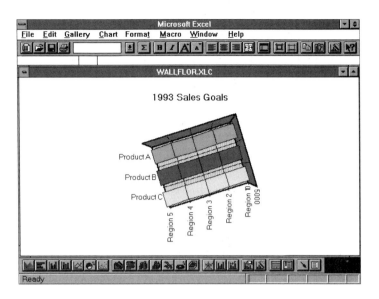

z-axis to its x-axis. Figure 14-36 shows the 3-D View dialog box. The 3-D View command also includes an Apply button that lets you see the effect of formatting changes before you leave the dialog box.

FIGURE 14-36.
The 3-D View command lets you rotate, tilt, and stretch your three-dimensional charts.

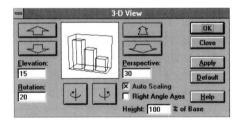

Elevation

The Elevation command changes your own viewing angle relative to the floor of the chart. The default setting is 25, and you can specify any value from –90 to 90. (With 3-D pie charts, you're limited to the range from 10 through 80.) A setting of 90 puts you directly above the chart, as if you were looking down on the tops of the markers. With a –90 setting, you'd be looking up through the chart's floor (which, incidentally, is transparent, regardless of how you format it). You can change the elevation either by typing a number in the Elevation text box or by clicking the two large arrows in the upper left corner of the dialog box.

Increasing a chart's elevation can help make all data series visible when some series would otherwise be hidden. The three-dimensional area chart in Figure 14-17 uses this technique. In this chart, we increased the elevation from the default of 25 to 46.

Rotation

Imagine that your chart is anchored to a turntable. The Rotation command spins the turntable. Technically, the rotation setting specifies the angle formed by the category axis and a line drawn horizontally across your screen. The default angle is 20 degrees (except for pie charts, where it's 0). You can specify any rotation value from 0 through 360 by entering a number in the Rotation text box or by clicking the buttons in the lower middle part of the dialog box (Figure 14-36). The Rotation command is especially useful if some markers are obscured by others at the default viewing angle.

Perspective

The Perspective command determines the apparent depth of a three-dimensional chart. (See Figure 14-36.) The default setting is 30, and you can specify any value from 0 through 100. Low values make the chart look flatter, as though you were looking at the chart through a telescope or a telephoto lens. High values have the opposite effect, as though you were looking through the wrong end of a pair of binoculars.

The default setting, 30, specifies that the far side of the chart is 30% smaller than the near side. This means that with a rotation of 0, the length of the back wall is 30% shorter than the front of the floor. Or if the elevation is 90, the bottom of a column in a 3-D column chart is about 30% smaller than the top of the tallest column.

To change the Perspective value, enter a new number in the Perspective text box or click the arrows near the upper right corner of the dialog box. You can also eliminate all perspective from the chart by selecting the Right Angle Axes check box.

Height

The height setting changes the ratio of a chart's value axis to its category axis. The default is 100 percent; you can select any value from 20 through 500. (See Figure 14-36.) The higher the value, the taller your chart becomes.

15

Working with Chart Data

*T*his chapter addresses the few remaining chart topics not covered in our discussions so far — combination charts, the Edit Series command, and Microsoft Excel's reverse "what-if" feature.

Combination charts

We touched briefly on combination charts in Chapter 13 in connection with the Gallery menu. The following sections provide additional details on combination charts and a step-by-step example.

A *combination chart* plots some data series in one chart type (column, for example) while plotting others in another chart type (line, for example). A combination chart can also plot some series against one axis and others against a different axis. Combination charts can help you emphasize a particular series — a trend line against a background of historical data, for example. They also let you plot series that occupy widely divergent numeric regions.

You can create a combination chart in either of two ways: You can use one of the Combination options available on the Gallery menu. Or you can create a simple (that is, noncombination) chart and then use the Add Overlay command to turn it into a combination chart.

Using Add Overlay to create a combination chart

Let's step through the creation of a combination column/line chart that displays a stock's closing prices and volumes for the date range January 2, 1991 through December 31, 1991. Figure 15-1 shows the first eight rows of data.

FIGURE 15-1.
We can create a combination chart based on these three columns of price and volume data.

	A	B	C	D	E	F	G	H	I
1	Date	Volume	Close						
2	1/2/91	793,950	49 53/64						
3	1/3/91	1,100,550	50 11/64						
4	1/4/91	1,218,450	50 37/64						
5	1/7/91	1,824,000	49 59/64						
6	1/8/91	1,593,000	49						
7	1/9/91	2,409,000	49 21/64						
8	1/10/91	2,581,500	52 11/64						
9	1/11/91	1,291,500	52						
10	1/14/91	1,333,500	51 11/64						

PRICEVOL.XLS

We begin by selecting all of the data we need to plot — in this case, cells A1:C254. Next, we press F11 to create a chart window. (Choosing the File New command and selecting Chart would accomplish the same thing.) Microsoft Excel responds by creating the column chart shown in Figure 15-2.

This chart actually plots both the volume figures and the closing prices. But the prices all fall within the range from $49 to $111.25, and the volumes are in the millions. With both series plotted against a single axis, the price columns are almost invisible. To remedy the problem, we'll choose Add Overlay from the Chart menu. Excel now displays something equally unintelligible, as shown in Figure 15-3.

FIGURE 15-2.
Excel plots the price information alongside the volume information, but the disparity in numeric ranges makes the price columns impossible to see.

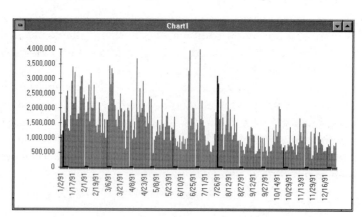

FIGURE 15-3.
The Add Overlay command turns Figure 15-2 into a combination column/line chart, but because of the scale, the price line is still invisible.

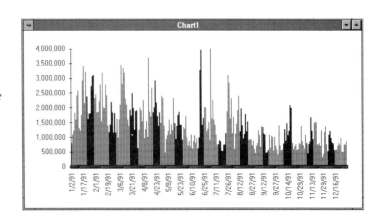

The Add Overlay command

The Add Overlay command splits your chart into two charts — a *main chart* and an *overlay chart*. Half of the original chart's data series remain in the main chart, and the other half go to the overlay chart. (If the original chart has an odd number of series, the main chart retains the larger share.) The default overlay chart type — the chart in which Excel first plots the overlay series — is a line chart.

In Figure 15-3, therefore, Excel has drawn the second series of the chart (the closing prices) as a line chart. If you look carefully, you can detect a thickening of the x-axis; that's the price line. Obviously, a scale problem still exists.

Adding axes for the overlay series

As you recall from Chapter 14, the Chart menu's Axes command lets you add and remove axes from the main chart. It also performs this service for overlay charts. To plot the prices in Figure 15-3 against a separate value axis, first choose the Axes command. Excel responds by displaying the dialog box shown in Figure 15-4.

FIGURE 15-4.
To add overlay axes, choose the Chart menu's Axes command.

As the figure shows, the Axes dialog box lets you add a category axis, a value axis, or both for the overlay series. In our price/volume chart, we don't need an overlay category axis because Excel plots both prices and volumes against the same range of dates. We do need a separate value axis, however. After adding the overlay value axis, our chart looks like the one in Figure 15-5 on the following page.

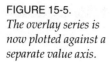

FIGURE 15-5.
The overlay series is now plotted against a separate value axis.

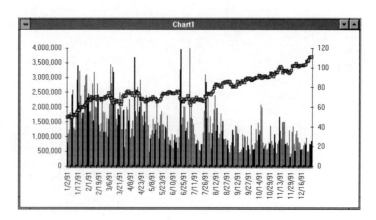

Formatting overlay series

Now we can see both series, but the chart still needs some formatting changes. With so many data points, the square markers along the overlay line give the line an unnecessarily gnarled appearance. We can remove the markers by double-clicking the line and selecting None in the Marker section of the Patterns dialog box.

Formatting an overlay series is much like formatting a main-chart series. First select the series, and then use the commands on the Format menu. Note that even though the combination chart is effectively one chart superimposed on another, Excel uses a single numbering system for all the chart objects. The series, for example, are numbered S1, S2, and so on, the same way as they are in a simple chart. To format the price series, we select series 2 (S2).

Changing the numeric format of tick labels

The three sets of tick labels in this chart can each benefit from a small formatting change. The volume figures along the left-hand value axis are all in the hundreds of thousands, so we can scale them down by a thousand to produce a trimmer-looking axis. The dates along the category axis all fall within the same year, so we can remove the 91's from their labels. Finally, the prices along the right-hand value axis might look better with dollar signs.

In a noncombination chart, Excel bases the numeric format of the value axis on the numeric format of the first number in the first data series. In a combination chart that has two value axes, Excel derives the numeric format of the second value axis from the numeric format of the first number in the first series plotted against that second axis.

Therefore, to modify the format of the left-hand axis labels, we need to change the format of cell B2. To scale the numbers down by 1000, we assign the format

0,

to cell B2. (To avoid a confusing appearance on the worksheet, we should assign that format to all the values in column B.) To add dollar signs to the numbers along the right-hand axis, we need to choose a currency format for cell C2. Our prices are expressed as fractions, so we use the techniques described in Chapter 4 to create and assign this custom numeric format:

$# ??/??

To drop the 91's from the dates along the category axis, we select all the values in column B and choose the date format

m/d

Figure 15-6 shows the effect of these formatting changes.

FIGURE 15-6.
We changed the tick-label display format of all three axes.

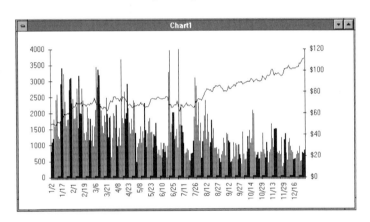

Scaling the left-hand value axis gives Excel more room to display the chart, but this chart still looks crowded. In many places, the volume markers seem to overlap one another, creating a black blur along the category axis. Fortunately, if you print this chart in landscape orientation, Excel can display all the data points cleanly.

Changing combination chart types

When you use the Add Overlay command to create a combination chart, Excel always plots the overlay series as a line chart. You can change the overlay series' chart type in either of two ways. You can select one of the options from the

Combination section of the Gallery menu, or you can use the Format menu's Overlay command. The Format Chart dialog box is shown in Figure 15-7.

FIGURE 15-7.
The Overlay com-
mand provides the
same formatting
options for overlay
series as the Main
Chart command
provides for
main-chart series.

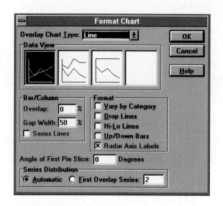

You can use the Overlay dialog box to change the overlay chart type without losing custom formatting. This dialog box looks and works much like the Format Chart dialog box you see when you choose Main Chart from the Format menu, as described in Chapter 14. The list of available chart types is shorter than the list you see when you format the Main Chart, however, because Excel does not permit you to plot overlay series in any of the 3-D chart types.

In fact, Excel doesn't allow either the main chart or the overlay chart to be three-dimensional. If you pull down the Chart menu while displaying a 3-D chart, you'll find that the Add Overlay command is dimmed. And if, while displaying a combination chart, you use the Main Chart command to change the main-chart series to a three-dimensional type, Excel displays the entire chart — overlay series and all — in the selected three-dimensional type.

Changing the distribution of series

Excel responds to the Add Overlay command by assigning half (or one fewer than half) of your data series to the overlay chart. If your chart has five series, for example, the first three remain in the main chart, and the fourth and fifth make up the overlay. You can use the Series Distribution section of the Overlay dialog box to change this distribution.

For example, if you have five series and need only the first series in the main chart, you can select the First Overlay Series option button and enter 2 in the associated text box. If you need the first four series to make up the main chart and only the fifth to be in the overlay type, you can select the First Overlay Series button and enter 5.

Note, however, that you cannot use the Overlay dialog box to plot series 1, 3, and 5 in one type and series 2 and 4 in another. To achieve a redistribution of that sort, you need to change the plot order of your series by using the Edit Series command. (See "Changing a series' plot order," later in this chapter.)

Turning a combination chart back into a simple chart

If you change your mind and decide you don't want a combination chart after all, pull down the Chart menu and choose Delete Overlay. Excel redisplays the overlay series as part of the main chart and removes any overlay axes you added.

Using the Edit Series command

The Edit Series command on the Chart menu presents a simple dialog box with which you can modify a chart's SERIES formulas. As described in Chapter 13, Microsoft Excel uses the SERIES formulas (formulas built with the SERIES function) to link charts to underlying worksheet cells. By modifying these formulas with the Edit Series command, you can add new series to a chart, delete existing series, add or delete data points, change the labels used in chart legends, change the labels assigned to the category axis, and change the order in which series are plotted.

Before we explore the Edit Series command itself, we need to take a quick look at the SERIES function.

The SERIES function

The SERIES function takes the form

=SERIES(*series name,categories reference,values reference,plot order number*)

The *series name* argument is the name of the data series being charted. The *categories reference* argument indicates where your category labels are located in the worksheet. The *values reference* argument indicates where the data-point values are located in the worksheet. The *plot order number* argument determines the order in which your data series appear on the chart.

Whenever you create a chart, Excel creates one SERIES formula for each data series in that chart. The chart in Figure 15-8 on the following page illustrates the

FIGURE 15-8.
This sample chart shows the SERIES function in the formula bar.

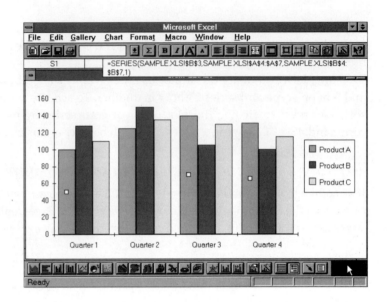

mechanics of the SERIES function. Excel drew this chart from cells A3:D7 of the worksheet shown in Figure 15-9. The formula bar shown in Figure 15-8 indicates that the SERIES formula for the first data series is

=SERIES(SAMPLE.XLS!$B$3,SAMPLE.XLS!$A$4:$A$7,
    SAMPLE.XLS!$B$4:$B$7,1)

FIGURE 15-9.
Excel plotted the sample chart in Figure 15-8 from this worksheet.

	A	B	C	D	E	F	G	H	I
1									
2									
3		Product A	Product B	Product C					
4	Quarter 1	100.00	128.00	110.00					
5	Quarter 2	125.00	150.00	135.00					
6	Quarter 3	140.00	105.00	130.00					
7	Quarter 4	131.00	100.00	115.00					
8									
9									

The *series name* argument in this formula is SAMPLE.XLS!$B$3. The *categories reference* and *values reference* arguments are SAMPLE.XLS!$A$4:$A$7 and SAMPLE.XLS!$B$4:$B$7. As explained in Chapter 6, Excel always uses the worksheet name followed by an exclamation point to indicate a reference to an external worksheet. Excel uses this same convention to define the arguments of a SERIES function. Excel also uses absolute cell references in its external references.

The *plot order number* argument in the example SERIES formula, 1, tells Excel to plot this data series before any of the others in this chart. As you'll see, you can change the order in which Excel plots data series simply by changing the *plot order number* argument at the end of the formula.

The *series name* and *categories reference* arguments don't always appear in the SERIES formula. Excel uses these arguments only if you select cells in your worksheet that contain category and series labels. For example, if you select only cells B4:D7 in the worksheet shown in Figure 15-9, Excel creates a chart like the one shown in Figure 15-10.

The SERIES formula for the first series in this chart is

=SERIES(,,SAMPLE.XLS!$B$4:$B$7,1)

Notice that the first two arguments — *series name* and *categories reference* — are missing from this formula. Because the formula includes no *series name* argument, Excel uses the dummy name *Series 1* in the legend. Because the formula has no *categories reference* argument, Excel supplies the dummy labels 1, 2, 3, and 4 for the category axis.

FIGURE 15-10.
*The SERIES formulas
in this chart include
neither series names
nor category labels.*

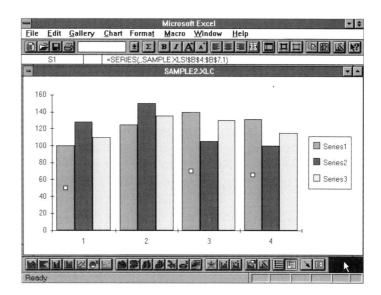

Editing *SERIES formulas*

You can edit formulas based on the SERIES function just as you would other kinds of formulas. For example, you can change the plot order of a chart series by selecting that series, pressing F2, and then modifying the last argument in the function. You can add a new series to a chart by typing a new SERIES formula, and delete a series from a chart by selecting it and then deleting its SERIES formula. You can even create a new chart by opening an empty chart window (choose the New command from the File menu with only a single worksheet cell selected) and then typing each SERIES formula by hand.

But because the SERIES function takes four arguments, three of which are likely to be external references, building or modifying SERIES formulas directly is tedious and difficult to do accurately. Thanks to the Edit Series command, it's also unnecessary. When you choose the Edit Series command, Excel presents a dialog box like the one shown in Figure 15-11.

FIGURE 15-11.
*The Edit Series dialog
box includes a
separate text box for
each of the SERIES
function's arguments.*

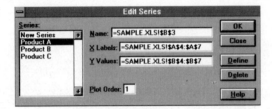

In the Edit Series dialog box, each of the SERIES function's arguments has its own text box. Thus, you can modify any component of a SERIES formula without inadvertently changing the rest of the formula. The left side of the dialog box presents a list of all your chart's series. To modify a series, select it in this list and then fill out the rest of the dialog box.

Changing a series' legend label

The contents of the Name box determine the label Excel uses in your chart's legend. To change the legend label for any series, type new text directly into the box, or enter a formula by hand or by pointing to a worksheet cell.

To enter text directly, type the text without an equal sign or quotation marks. For example, to assign the legend label *Product A* to the first series in Figure 15-10, you can select Series1 in the Series list, select whatever is currently in the Name text box (click that box if it's currently empty), and then type *Product A.*

To link the legend text to a worksheet cell, click the Name text box, pull down the Window menu and choose the name of your worksheet (the worksheet must be open when you do this), point to the cell you want to use, and then click OK or Define. (If you click OK, Excel removes the Edit Series dialog box and updates the chart. If you click Define, Excel updates the chart but leaves the dialog box on screen.) When you use the pointing method, you might need to drag the dialog box itself to one side of your screen so that you can see the cell you want to point to.

Changing a chart's category labels

The labels that appear along a chart's category axis are determined by the *categories reference* argument in the SERIES formula for the chart's first data series. If you omit that argument, Excel uses the dummy category names 1, 2, 3, and so on. Excel ignores the *categories reference* arguments for the second and subsequent data series, and they have no effect on the chart's appearance.

In spite of the fact that only the first series' *category reference* argument is significant, when you create a chart in the customary manner, Excel assigns the same *category reference* argument to each series. (By "customary manner," we mean selecting a worksheet range that includes column and row headings, as well as numbers, to be plotted.) Excel includes the argument in all series so that you can rearrange the series' plot order later on.

To change a chart's category labels, choose the Edit Series command. Next, select the chart's first series from the list at the left side of the dialog box. Click the X Labels text box and enter the text or worksheet reference for your new labels. If you enter text directly, type labels for each data point in the first series, separating the labels with commas. If you enter a worksheet range, the simplest method is to point to it — the same way you would to enter a legend label. The only difference is that in this case you point to a worksheet range instead of a single cell.

Adding points to a series

Some charts have a way of growing as time goes by. For example, if you plot stock prices in a chart like the one shown in Figure 15-6, you might want to add new data at the end of each day, week, or month.

The easiest way to do this is to include one blank row or column at the end of each series. You can then add new data by inserting new rows into your worksheet above the blank row (or new columns to the left of the blank column). If a series plots cells A2:A100, for example, and you insert new rows above row 100, the range reference in the SERIES formula automatically expands to include the inserted rows.

An alternative (and more difficult) way to add data to a series is to choose the Edit Series command, select the name of the series you want to modify, and then change the contents of the X Labels and Y Values text boxes.

Whichever method you use, you'll probably want to include the same number of data points in each of your chart's series. If you add points to the first series and not to the remaining series, for example, Excel fills out the remaining series with zeros when it plots the revised chart.

Changing a series' plot order

To change the order of a series in your chart, choose the Edit Series command, select the series you want to modify, and then change the value in the Plot Order box. Excel adjusts the plot orders of that series and any others affected by the change. For example, if you select the third series and assign it a plot-order number of 1, the first series becomes 2 and the second series becomes 3. As mentioned earlier in this chapter, changing the plot order of your series might be necessary if you want to alter the way Excel splits your data series for the main chart and overlay chart when it constructs a combination chart.

Using the Edit Series command with a three-dimensional chart

When you use the Edit Series command with a three-dimensional chart, the dialog box looks like the one in Figure 15-12.

FIGURE 15-12.
Excel presents this dialog box when the current chart is three-dimensional.

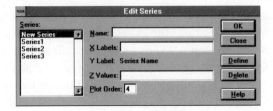

Although this dialog box has a slightly different appearance, it works exactly like its two-dimensional counterpart. To change legend labels (as well as the labels that appear along the series axis when Excel plots each series in a separate plane), use the Name text box. To change category labels, use the X Labels text box. To change the data plotted by a series, use the Z Values text box. To change the plot order, use the Plot Order text box.

Deleting a series

You can remove any series from a chart by selecting the series and deleting the SERIES formula from the formula bar. Alternatively, you can use the Edit Series command, select the series name in the list at the left side of the dialog box, and then click Delete.

Adding a new series

To add a series using the Edit Series command, select the New Series item in the list at the left side of the dialog box. Then fill out the remaining text boxes as described in the preceding paragraphs. Your new series assumes the highest plot-order number in the chart — unless, of course, you override that assignment.

Changing underlying worksheet values

Because charts are usually linked to worksheet cells, you can use them to play "what-if" with your data. If you set up a break-even analysis in a worksheet, for example, and plot fixed costs, variable costs, total costs, and gross margin in a chart, you can change fixed-cost assumptions and immediately see what effect your changes have on the gross-margin line.

Using Microsoft Excel, you can also reverse this process. You can drag chart data points upward or downward, and Excel will adjust the underlying worksheet. In the break-even analysis, for example, you can drag the gross-margin line upward (so that it crosses 0 at a different point) and find out exactly how much you would need to reduce your fixed costs to achieve that increase in profit. (You need a mouse or other pointing device to use this feature.)

Let's look first at a simple example and then at a slightly more complex one. Suppose that after looking at the chart shown in Figure 15-13, you decide that the fourth-quarter data doesn't look right. Product B appears to lag behind Products A and C in that quarter, but in fact, you expect it to do better than C — if not quite as well as A. Instead of going back to the worksheet and entering new numbers, you can change the chart directly.

First hold down Ctrl and click the fourth-quarter marker for Product B. Excel responds by displaying a single black handle on this marker, along with a set of white handles. Put the mouse pointer on the black handle, and drag the marker upward until its height is somewhere between that of Product A and Product C. As you do this, your display will look similar to the one in Figure 15-14 on the following page.

As you drag the marker, notice that both the reference area of the chart window and the value axis change to reflect the current value of the marker. That is, they tell you what the marker's value will be when you release the mouse button at any given point. In Figure 15-14, the reference area says 123, and a broad line appears on the value axis, one-fifth of the distance between the tick mark for 120 and the tick mark for 140. After you release the mouse button, the chart and worksheet look like the ones in Figure 15-15 on the following page.

FIGURE 15-13.
You can increase the fourth-quarter value for Product B by dragging the data marker upward.

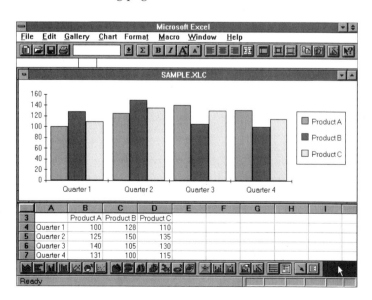

FIGURE 15-14.
*When you drag a
marker, the reference
area of the chart
window displays the
new value of the
marker.*

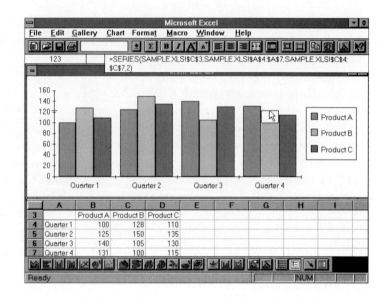

FIGURE 15-15.
*When you release
the mouse button,
Excel changes the
fourth-quarter value
for Product B to 123
on the supporting
worksheet, as well as
on the chart.*

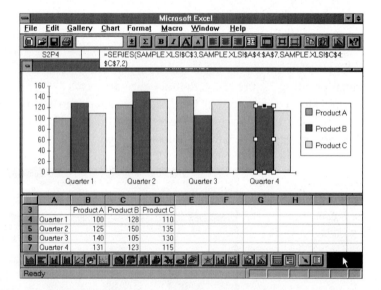

In this example, all Excel has to do to make the chart display the new value we requested is to modify cell C7 on the underlying worksheet. If C7 contains a formula instead of a constant, however, the situation becomes more complicated, as the following example illustrates.

The worksheet and chart shown in Figure 15-16 tell us that, given our fixed-cost and variable-cost assumptions, it will take sales of about 60,000 units to reach a break-even point. Suppose we want to know how much we have to reduce fixed

FIGURE 15-16.
To find out what our fixed costs must be to break even at 50,000 units, we will drag the gross-margin line upward.

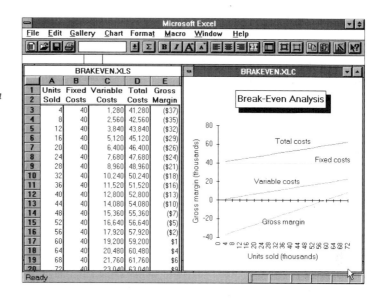

costs to break even at about 50,000 units. To find out, we hold down Ctrl and select a point on the gross-margin line just to the left of the category label 52. Next, we drag the line upward until it crosses the x-axis. Figure 15-17 shows what happens when we release the mouse button.

This time, the point we dragged is linked to a cell that contains a formula instead of a constant. The cell is E14, and its formula reads

    =A14–D14

FIGURE 15-17.
Because we dragged a data point that Excel linked to a formula cell, instead of to a constant, Excel presents the Goal Seek dialog box.

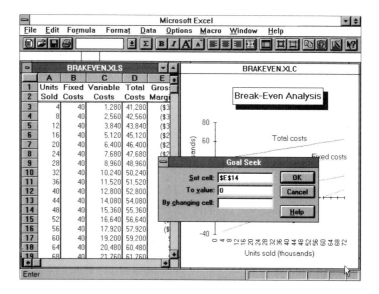

Excel understands that we want the result of E14's formula to be 0, but that we don't want to replace the formula with a constant. So it presents the Goal Seek dialog box — the same dialog box you see when you use the Formula menu's Goal Seek command. Now all we need to do is tell Excel what cell it can modify to produce the result 0 at cell E14.

In this example, we want to know by how much we need to lower our fixed costs, so we'll fill out the dialog box with a cell in column B. We've set up this worksheet so that B3 contains the constant 40,000 (formatted as 0,) and the remaining cells in column B contain formulas that refer, directly or indirectly, to B3. Cell B4 has the formula =B3, B5 contains the formula =B4, and so on. To complete the what-if reversal, we'll point to cell B3 and click OK.

Excel does some quick calculations and finds the answer: 33,000. Then, when we click OK again, it updates the worksheet and the chart. Figure 15-18 shows the resulting display.

Excel imposes a few limitations on this marker-dragging feature:

■ You can drag markers in bar, column, line, and XY charts only.

■ The marker you drag must be independently scaled; you cannot drag any part of a stacked column, stacked bar, or stacked line marker.

■ You cannot drag a marker beyond the endpoints of its value axis.

■ The supporting worksheet must be open.

You can drag "picture" markers (markers that have been replaced by graphic images, as described in Chapter 13), as well as ordinary markers.

FIGURE 15-18.
After we perform the goal-seeking operation and click OK to approve the result, Excel updates both the worksheet and the chart.

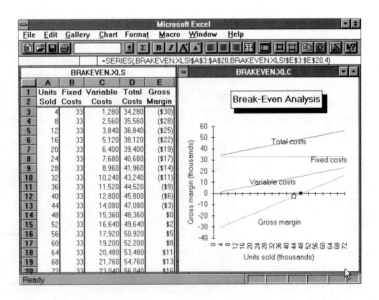

DATABASES

	A	B	C
1	Last	First	City
2			
3			

16

Database Management

You can use Microsoft Excel as an electronic spreadsheet and as a graphics program. In addition, you can use it as a database manager. This chapter explores the fundamentals of databases. To begin with, you will learn how to create, define, and format a database. Next, you will explore how to add, delete, and move records and fields, and then you will examine calculated fields.

What is a database?

A database is a structured collection of information. By structured, we mean that the information is arranged in a convenient, logical, consistent order. This structure makes it easy to quickly locate and retrieve individual items of information.

The kind of information you might put in a database can include anything from telephone numbers and names to part numbers and prices. You use simple databases every day; for example, a dictionary is a database of words and their definitions. Another commonly used database is the telephone book.

A telephone book contains thousands of listings, each of which generally includes four pieces of information: a last name, a first name, a street address, and a telephone number. The information in a telephone book is arranged in a rough tabular form. Each listing occupies one line, or row, in the book, and each item of information (last name, first name, and so on) occupies a single column. Excel databases use this same row-and-column structure. In database terminology, each of the listings in the telephone book is called a *record*. The individual items of information within a listing are called *fields*.

The usefulness of a database depends on how well the information it contains is organized and how easily it can be reorganized. For example, because the listings in a telephone book are arranged in alphabetic order based on the last-name entry of each listing, you can easily find the name (and thus the phone number) of any person you want to call.

However, the usefulness of a telephone book is limited. Because a telephone book is printed, the order of the information in it is fixed — you cannot reorder the records so that they're sorted by street or by number. For this reason, locating all the listings for people who live on a certain street or computing statistics for groups of listings (such as the number of people called Williams) would have to be done manually, which would be very difficult and time-consuming.

Excel stores information electronically, so the database is dynamic and can be manipulated easily. For example, if you enter the listings (records) from a telephone book into an Excel database, you can sort the records in that database in ascending or descending order based on any of the pieces of information (fields) in the listings. You can also locate, extract, and delete any information in the database that shares a common characteristic — for example, all the records for people who live on Elm Street or all the records for people named Jones.

Excel's database component can do more than sort a database and locate records. It also includes a set of functions that perform statistical calculations on records that meet specified criteria.

The structure of a database

Figure 16-1 shows a sample database that contains 10 records, each of which has six fields. This database is merely a rectangular range of worksheet cells. Within this range, each row contains a single record and each column is a separate field. For example, row 3 contains the record for John Johnson, and column D contains the Date of Birth field.

Notice that the top row of this database contains a series of field names. These names, which must always be entered in the top row of the database, identify the information that is stored in each field. For example, the entries in the First Name field are all first names, the entries in the Salary field are annual salary values, and so forth. These field names are the key to using selection criteria.

FIGURE 16-1.
*An Excel database
is a specially
organized group
of worksheet cells.*

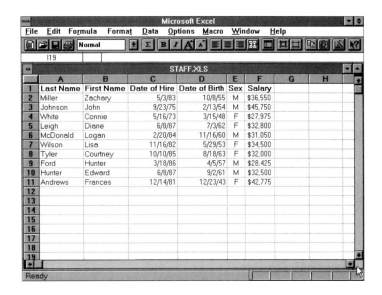

Creating a database

To create the database shown in Figure 16-1, begin by entering the field names *Last Name, First Name, Date of Hire, Date of Birth, Sex,* and *Salary* into any six adjacent cells on a single row of a worksheet. These field names are simple text entries. They can go in any row, but in this example we entered them in row 1.

You should keep the field names in your databases fairly short so that they're easy to remember and use. However, like all other text entries in Excel, field names can have as many as 255 characters and can contain any character, including blank spaces. Although field names are usually simple labels, they can wrap to more than one line, and they can be the results of functions that return text. You should not use numbers or formulas or functions that return values as field names.

After you organize the fields in your database, you can enter your records. You can make the same kinds of entries in a database that you make in a worksheet: text, numbers, formulas, and functions. After you create a database, you might want to change the format and alignment of the cells in selected fields and alter the width of certain fields. You can format and align the entries in a database in the same way you format and align the cells in a worksheet. Because all the entries in each field of most databases are of a similar type, you'll want to assign the same formats and alignment attributes to entire columns (fields) of the database. For example, in Figure 16-1, the m/d/yy format applies to all the date entries in the Date of Hire and Date of Birth fields.

Defining the database

Excel does not know the worksheet in Figure 16-1 is a database until you define it as one. To define a block of cells as a database, first select the entire rectangle that contains the database, including the field names. (In this case, you select the range A1:F11.) Next, choose the Set Database command from the Data menu.

The Set Database command assigns the range name *Database* to the selected block of cells. You can achieve the same effect by selecting the block of cells, choosing the Define Name command from the Formula menu, typing the name *Database*, and pressing Enter. However, choosing the Set Database command is faster and easier in most cases.

When you choose a database command, Excel looks for the range named *Database* to know on which area of the worksheet to operate. For this reason, a worksheet can have only one defined database at a time. (You can set up any number of databases in a worksheet, but only the database you're actively working with can be defined with the name *Database*.) To switch databases, you must redefine the database range.

Changing records and fields

After you create a database, you might want to add, delete, or move one or more records or fields. Because records are worksheet rows and fields are worksheet columns, adding, deleting, and moving records and fields is done the same way as adding, deleting, and moving rows and columns in the worksheet.

Adding records and fields

To add a record to the end of a database, enter each field of the new record in the first blank row below the last existing record. Next, select the entire range that contains the database (including the new record), and choose Set Database from the Data menu to include this new record in the database. Whenever you add one or more new records to the end of a database, you must use the Set Database or Define Name command from the Formula menu to redefine the range so that it includes the new records. If you omit this step, Microsoft Excel does not include the new records in the database.

To avoid this problem, you can add new records in the middle of the database rather than at the end. To add a record in the middle of a database, select the row where you want to add the record and choose the Insert command from the Edit menu. When you choose this command, Excel adds a blank row to the database above the selected row and pushes the existing rows down one row. Because the database range is a named range, Excel expands the range automatically when you add a new record in the middle of the database.

If you want to keep your database records in their order of entry, you might prefer to include an extra blank row at the bottom of the database. For example, if your database records currently occupy cells A1 through G50, you can define the database range as A1:G51. Then, whenever you want to add a new record, you can select the last row of the database, which is blank, and choose the Insert command. Excel adds a blank row to the database above the selected row and pushes the blank "dummy record" down one row.

You can also add new fields to existing databases. To add a new field at the right edge of a database, select the cell in the field-names row (the first row of the database range) immediately to the right of the last existing field name, and type the new field name. Next, make entries in the new field for the existing records in the database. Because the new field is outside the original database range, you must use the Set Database or Define Name command to include the new field.

You can also add a new field within an existing database range. Select the column where you want to add the new field and choose the Insert command. Excel inserts a blank column in the worksheet to the left of the selected column and pushes the existing columns one column to the right.

Deleting records and fields

To delete a record, select the row that contains the record and choose the Delete command from the Edit menu. Excel removes that record from the database, shifts all the rows below the removed record up one row to fill in the "empty" space, and contracts the database range to reflect the deletion.

To delete a field, select the column that contains the field and then choose the Delete command. Excel removes that column from the database and contracts the database range to reflect the deletion, regardless of the position of the field.

Reordering records and fields

You can reorder records and fields within an Excel database by moving the rows and columns of the worksheet.

To move a record within the database range, insert a new row where you want the moved record to appear, select the row that contains the record you want to move, and choose Cut. Next, select the newly inserted row and choose Paste. Finally, delete the row from which the record was cut. To move a field to a new location within the database range, first insert a new column where you want the moved field to appear. Next, select the column that contains the field you want to move, choose Cut, select the newly inserted column, and choose Paste. Then delete the column from which the field was cut. Excel adjusts the database range to reflect the movement of records and fields.

Calculated fields

Most of the field entries you make are text, numbers, and dates. However, you can also make formula entries. Fields whose entries are the result of formulas or functions are called *calculated* fields.

The database shown in Figure 16-2 contains an example of a calculated field. This database is the same as the one in Figure 16-1 except for the addition of the Age field. To add this field to the database, we entered the text *Age* into cell G1 and then expanded the database range by selecting cells A1:G11 and choosing Set Database from the Data menu. Next, we entered the formula

=INT((NOW( )–D2)/365)

into cell G2. This formula tells Excel to subtract the serial date value in cell D2 (the Date of Birth entry for the first record) from the current date (the result of the NOW function). To calculate the Age field for the remaining records, simply replicate this formula in the range G3:G11.

The entries in calculated fields result from individual formulas in the cells of that field. Whenever you add a new record to a database, you can copy and paste the formula into the new record so that Excel can calculate a value for it. If you're entering a group of records, you can save time by entering all the records first, selecting the cells where the calculated field is to appear, and then using the Copy and Paste commands or Fill Down to enter the formula into the calculated field of all the new records at once.

FIGURE 16-2.
We added the calculated field Age to this employee database.

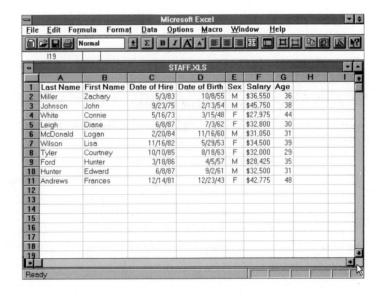

Data forms

It is often convenient to view your databases as lists. However, you can also view the contents of a database through a simple one-page form, called a *data form*. Using data forms, you can add records to a database, delete records from a database, and edit existing records. You can even specify criteria in the data form dialog box and use those criteria to help you locate database records.

The primary advantage of data forms is that they let you view all the fields of a record at once. When you view a database in list form, only a few fields are visible at a time and you see several records at once on the screen. (The number of fields that are visible depends on the width of the columns displayed on your screen.) The following section discusses Microsoft Excel's default data form.

Creating a data form

Before you can create a data form, you must use the Data menu's Set Database command to define a database range in your worksheet. Be certain to include the cells that contain the database's field names in the database range; Excel uses these names to identify each of the fields in your data form. After you define your database range, choose the Form command from the Data menu. Excel tailors a data form for your database and displays it in a special dialog box.

For example, to create a data form for the database shown in Figure 16-2, select the range A1:G11, and choose the Set Database command from the Data menu to define the database range. Next, choose the Form command from the Data menu to create a data form like the one shown in Figure 16-3.

FIGURE 16-3.
The Form dialog box appears when you select Form from the Data menu.

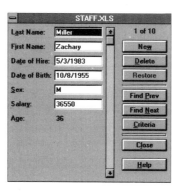

At the top of the data form, Excel displays the name of the worksheet that contains the database on which the data form is based. Immediately under this title bar are all the field names from the first row of the database. If you've already entered some records into your database, you'll see the field entries for your first record to the right of the field names.

At the upper right corner of the dialog box is a notation in the form x of y that tells you which record is currently displayed and how many records are currently located in the database range. For example, the *1 of 10* that appears in the dialog box in Figure 16-3 indicates that the displayed record is the first record of 10 records. If you haven't entered any records, the text boxes to the right of the field names will be blank, and you'll see the notation *New Record* at the upper right corner of the dialog box.

At the right side of the data form are several command buttons that let you work with the database records. We discuss these options later in this chapter.

Fields whose entries are displayed in text boxes — in our example, Last Name, First Name, Date of Hire, Date of Birth, Sex, and Salary — are called *editable fields* and can be edited. Fields whose entries do not appear in a text box — Age, in our example — are called calculated fields. Calculated fields display the result of a function or formula and cannot be edited. If you use the Cell Protection and Protect Document commands to lock and protect any of the cells in the database, your data form might contain protected fields. Excel displays the contents of a locked field on the data form, but without a text box, indicating that you can't edit it.

To close a data-form dialog box, you can choose the Close command from the dialog-box Control menu (or press Alt-F4), click the Close button near the lower right corner of the dialog box, or press Esc. The data form disappears from view. If you want to reopen the form, choose the Form command from the Data menu again.

If you need to look at the worksheet while you're working in the data form, you can move the form aside by dragging the title bar with the mouse.

You must close the data-form dialog box before you can activate another window or issue any commands.

Navigation techniques

The scroll bar in the center of the data-form dialog box lets you scroll through the records in your database. You can move backward or forward through the database one record at a time by clicking the up or down scroll arrow. You can move through the database 10 records at a time by clicking the gray area of the scroll bar above or below the scroll box. You can also drag the scroll box to the approximate position of a record. For example, if your database contains 10 records and you drag the scroll box to the middle of the scroll bar, the fifth record appears in the form. If you drag the scroll box to the bottom of the scroll bar, Excel displays a set of empty fields, ready for a new database record.

You can also use Excel's navigation keys to move through the database. To move from one record to the next or previous record, press the Up arrow key or the Down arrow key. To move to the first record in the database, press Ctrl-Up arrow; to move to the end of the database so that you can enter a new record, press Ctrl-Down arrow. To move through the database 10 records at a time, press PgUp or PgDn.

You can use any of several techniques to move from field to field in a record in a data form. With the mouse, you can move to a new field by clicking that field. If you prefer to use the keyboard, use Tab to move forward to the next field or Shift-Tab to move backward to the previous field. Alternatively, to move to a field in the current record, press Alt and type the underlined letter in the name of that field. (Because Excel tailors each data form to reflect the underlying worksheet, two or more fields might contain the same underlined letter. If this happens, continue to press Alt and the letter until Excel highlights the correct field.)

The following table summarizes the selection and navigation techniques you'll use to move around in a data form.

Action	Technique
Select an option	Click the option button you want.
	Press Alt in conjunction with the underlined letter.
Move to the same field, next record	Click the down scroll arrow.
	Press the Down arrow key.
Move to the same field, previous record	Click the up scroll arrow.
	Press the Up arrow key.
Move to the next field	Click the field.
	Press Tab.
Move to the previous field	Click the field.
	Press Shift-Tab.
Move to the first field, next record	Click the first field, and then click on the down scroll arrow.
	Press Enter.
Move to the same field, 10 records forward	Click below the scroll box in the scroll bar.
	Press PgDn.
Move to the same field, 10 records backward	Click above the scroll box in the scroll bar.
	Press PgUp.
Move to the last record	Drag the scroll box to the bottom of the scroll bar.
	Press Ctrl-PgDn.
Move to the first record	Drag the scroll box to the top of the scroll bar.
	Press Ctrl-PgUp.
Move/edit within field	Click to set the insertion point.
	Use Home, End, and the Left and Right arrow keys to position the insertion point.

Editing records

To edit a record in a form, use the navigation keys or the scroll bars to bring the record you want to edit into view, and then use the Tab key or the mouse to move to the desired field. To add characters to an entry in a field, position the insertion point in that field and type the additional characters. To delete characters, highlight the characters you want to delete and press Del. To replace characters with new characters, highlight the characters you want to replace and type the new characters. To lock in your change, press Enter, move to another record or another field, or click the Exit button.

Suppose you want to edit the record for employee McDonald. You want to raise his salary from $31,050 to $50,000. To begin, bring this record (number 5) into view in the form, as shown in Figure 16-4. To display the record, press the Down arrow key four times, drag the scroll button, or click the down scroll arrow. When you see the record, select the Salary field by using the Tab key, clicking the field, or pressing Alt-Y. (Notice that the letter Y is underlined in the field name *Salary* on the left side of the dialog box.) Next, type *50000* and press Enter to lock in your change. Figure 16-5 shows the changed record.

FIGURE 16-4.
You can use data forms to edit records.

FIGURE 16-5.
The entry in the Salary field changes from 31050 to 50000.

As soon as you make a change in a record, the Restore button on the right side of the dialog box becomes available. If you make a change in an existing record and then discover a mistake before you move to another record, you can click Restore to return the record to its original condition.

You can edit only those fields that are displayed in boxes. You cannot edit calculated or protected fields nor move to a calculated or protected field in a form.

Adding records

To add a record to a database using the data form, click New or drag the scroll box to the bottom of the scroll bar. Excel scrolls to the first blank record at the end of the database and displays New Record at the upper right corner of the data form. You can now add a new record by entering the information into the fields of the form. If you make an error, you can edit the field entries in the data form just as you would edit an existing entry. When you're finished, lock in the new record by moving to another record, clicking New or Close, or pressing Enter. Excel adds the new record to the database.

Suppose you want to add a new record to the example database. To begin, click New, press Ctrl-Down arrow, or drag the scroll box to move to the first blank record at the end of the database. Next, add the new record by making entries in the fields of the form. Figure 16-6 shows a new record in the form and in the worksheet. When we entered the record, Excel added the record to the end of the database range, filled in the calculated Age field, and formatted the numeric entries in columns C, D, and F.

FIGURE 16-6.
*We used the data form
to add a new record
for Barbara Harrison.*

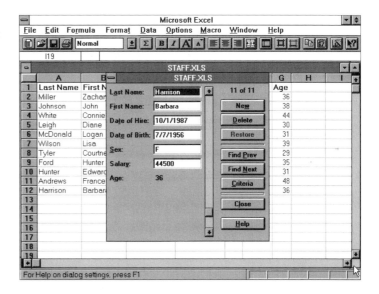

When you use the data form to add new records to your database, Excel adds those new records to the bottom of the database and extends the database range to include your additions. If the last record in the database includes calculated fields, Excel "copies" the formulas from those fields into the new record. Always be sure you have sufficient room for new records below the database range. If Excel can't find room to expand the database, you'll see the alert message *Cannot extend database* when you try to create a new record.

Deleting records

To delete a record through a data form, bring that record into view in the form and click Delete. Excel presents an alert box that reminds you that the current record will be permanently deleted from the database. If you click OK, the record vanishes from both the data form and the worksheet. Any records below that record in the worksheet are shifted upward to fill the resulting gap. If you click Cancel, the record is not deleted.

Defining criteria and selecting records

You also can use a form to define selection conditions (called *criteria*) and to find records in the database based on the criteria you define. This capability is useful when you need to move from one record to another that contains a particular entry. We explain criteria and show how you can define and use criteria in forms in Chapter 17.

Custom data forms

You can develop your own custom form dialog boxes to collect input from the user and display information in any format and arrangement you choose. Chapter 21 describes how to create custom forms.

17

Queries and Extracts

*S*o far, we've looked at the way Microsoft Excel stores information in a database. After you create and define a database range, Excel can also help you locate and manipulate the information stored in that range. This chapter discusses three Data menu commands that operate on the records in a database: Find, Extract, and Delete. The Find command instructs Excel to locate, one at a time, those records in the database that match the criteria in the criteria range. The Extract command lets you copy the entries from those records that match the criteria to another location in the worksheet. The Delete command lets you delete from the worksheet all the records that match the criteria.

Excel also offers twelve special database functions: DAVERAGE, DCOUNT, DCOUNTA, DGET, DMAX, DMIN, DPRODUCT, DSTDEV, DSTDEVP, DSUM, DVAR, and DVARP. These functions return information about the records that match the criteria you define. Before you can use these commands and functions, however, you must specify selection criteria.

Selection criteria

Selection criteria are the tests Microsoft Excel uses to determine which database records it should act upon when you use a database command or function. For example, you might use a criterion such as "all the people who live on Main Street" to extract information from a telephone book database.

565

Like database records, selection criteria are simply entries in a worksheet. In the same way that you define a database, you need to define a range of cells, known as the *criteria range,* in which to store your selection criteria.

Creating and defining a criteria range is a three-step process: First, you enter one or more field names across one row of a worksheet; second, you enter selection criteria into the cells below the field names; third, you select the cells that contain the field names and the criteria, and you choose Set Criteria from the Data menu. The Set Criteria command assigns the range name *Criteria* to the selected cells, which tells Excel that those cells are the criteria range. Each worksheet can have only one range at a time with the name *Criteria.*

Cells A15:G16 in Figure 17-1 contain a sample criteria range that you can use to select records from the employee database above it. As you can see, the structure of a criteria range is much like that of a database range. The first row of a criteria range must contain one or more of the field names from the database with which the criteria range is associated. The first row of the criteria range in Figure 17-1 contains all the field names from the database. The entries in the row or rows immediately below these field names are the criteria themselves. You can think of each row as a "criteria record."

The field names in the criteria range must be identical to the corresponding field names in the database. If a field name in the criteria range does not exactly match one in the database (except for capitalization differences), Excel cannot use the criteria you enter in that field.

To construct the criteria range in Figure 17-1, select cells A1:G1 (the cells of the database range that contain the field names) and choose the Copy command. Then select cell A15 and choose the Paste command to place a copy of those entries in

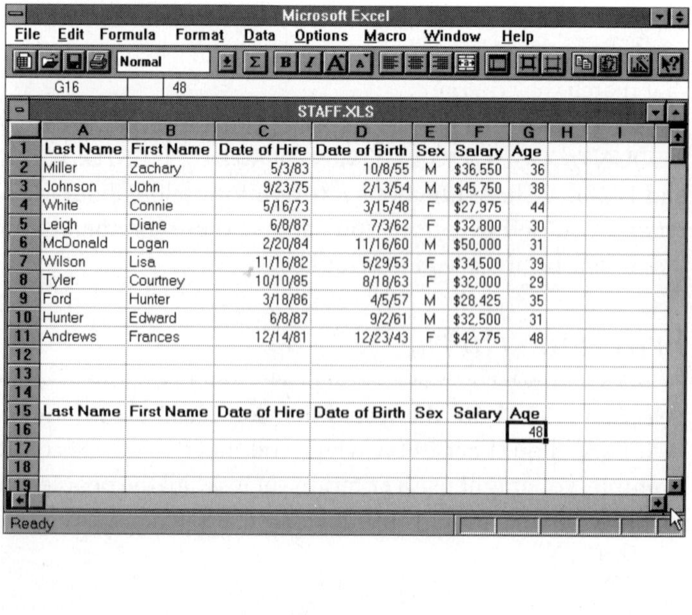

FIGURE 17-1.
*Cells A15:G16
contain the criteria
range.*

cells A15:G15. (Alternatively, you can hold down Ctrl while dragging a copy of A1:G1 to row 15.) Next, select cells A15:G16 and choose the Set Criteria command from the Data menu to define that block of cells as the criteria range. Finally, enter the selection criteria into the cells in row 16.

Although the example criteria range includes every field name from the database, your criteria ranges don't have to include every field name. You need include only the name of one field in the criteria range — the field you want to use to select records. For instance, if you want to select records only on the basis of the entries in the Age field, the criteria range can include only the name of that one field. If you need to make selections based on the entries in more than one field, you must include all those field names in your criteria range. In general, we recommend that you include the names of all the fields from your database in a criteria range to make it easy to specify criteria for any field.

Database criteria fall into two broad categories: comparison criteria and computed criteria. Comparison criteria compare the entries in one field to a numeric or text value — for example, "Is the entry in the Salary field greater than $50,000?" Computed criteria are more complex because they use the values in two or more fields — as in the criterion "Is Salary divided by Age greater than 1000?" — or they use Excel functions to act on field entries. Most of the examples in this chapter use comparison criteria.

Comparison criteria

Comparison criteria compare the entries in a field of an Excel database to text, numbers, or the results of formulas. The comparison can be an equality (=) or one of Excel's five relational operators (>, <, >=, <=, or <>).

In Figure 17-1, the criteria range encompasses cells A15:G16. The top row of the criteria range contains the field names to which the criteria relate. The entries below the field names tell Excel which entries to look for in each field when it selects records from the database. In this example, the number 48 below the field name *Age* in the criteria range is an *exact-match number criterion*. When you use commands or functions that depend on this criterion, Excel operates on only those records that contain the number 48 in the Age field.

Instead of simply entering the value you want Excel to match, you can preface that value with an equal sign. For example, you can enter

=48

in cell G16 and achieve the same result as when you enter only the number 48.

You can also use the >, <, >=, <=, and<> signs in numeric comparison criteria. For example, if you enter the criterion

>35

in cell G16, Excel operates on only those records with an Age entry greater than 35.

Text criteria

You can also use comparison criteria in text fields. For example, suppose you want Excel to select each record in the database shown in Figure 17-1 that has a Sex entry of *M*. You can enter the single letter *M* in cell E16 (the cell immediately below the field name *Sex* in the criteria range).

When you enter a simple number in a cell of the criteria range, Excel selects only those records that have that exact number in the specified field. However, when you use a simple text entry as a criterion, Excel selects each record that has an entry in the specified field that begins with the text string you specified. For example, the criterion *M* matches not only records that have the entry *M* in the Sex field, but all records that have Sex entries that begin with *M*, such as *Male* or *man*. (Excel doesn't differentiate between uppercase and lowercase letters when evaluating text criteria.)

Suppose you want to select all the records that have a Last Name entry that begins with *M*. To do this, you can erase the current contents of the criteria record and enter the letter *M* in cell A16 (below the field name *Last Name* in the criteria range). Based on this criterion, Excel selects each record with a Last Name entry that begins with *M*. In our example, Excel selects two records: the one in row 2, *Miller*, and the one in row 6, *McDonald*.

If you want to make the criterion more selective, you can replace the single letter *M* in cell A16 with the letters *Mc*. Using this criterion, Excel selects each record that has a Last Name entry that begins with *Mc* — in this case, only the record in row 6, which contains the Last Name entry *McDonald*.

You can also use the >, <, >=, <=, and <> signs in a text criterion. These operators act upon the "value" of the text entry, where *A* is less than *B*, *B* is less than *C*, and so on. Uppercase and lowercase forms of the same letter are equal; that is, *Z* and *z* have the same value. For example, you can enter

    <N

in cell A16 of our example criteria range to select all records whose Last Name entry begins with a letter before *N* (the first half of the alphabet). Or you can enter

    <>M

in cell E16 to select all records whose Sex entry does *not* start with *M* (or *m*).

Exact-match text criteria

You can force Excel to select only those records with an entry that exactly matches your criterion in the specified text field. To do this, you must enter the criterion in the form

    ="=*text*"

where *text* is the string you want to match. You should always use this alternative form when you want Excel to match a text criterion exactly. For example, if you enter the criterion

="=White"

in cell A16 (under Last Name in the criteria range), Excel selects only those records that have a Last Name entry of *White* — not records that have a Last Name entry like *Whiteman, Whitehall,* and so on.

Wildcards

Excel lets you use the wildcard characters ? and * as part of any text criterion. The ? symbol takes the place of any single character. For example, the criterion

="=Sm?th"

matches the names *Smith* and *Smyth*. You can also use multiple question marks within the same criterion. For example, the entry

="=H??t"

matches the names *Hart, Hurt, Heit,* and so forth.

The * symbol can replace any number of characters. For example, the exact-match criterion

="=S*n"

matches, among others, the names *Stevenson, Svenson,* and *Smithson*. You can also use the wildcard * at the beginning of an exact-match text criterion. When you do this, Excel selects every entry that ends with the letters that follow the *. For example, the criterion

="=*th"

matches the names *North, Smith, Roth,* and any others that end with the letters *th*.

Similarly, you can use the * wildcard at the end of an exact-match text criterion to make Excel select all entries that begin with the specified text but end with any characters. Thus, the criterion

="=St*"

matches the names *Stevenson, Stack,* and any others that begin with the letters *St*. (You can also use the text criterion *St* to select any entries that begin with the letters *St*.)

You can use wildcards in text criteria that are not exact-match criteria. However, you might get unexpected results. For example, the criterion

Sm?th

will match the names *Smith* and *Smyth,* but it will also match the names *Smythe, Smithson,* and *Smithsonian.* Similarly, the criterion

   *th

matches not only the names *Smith* and *Roth* but also the name *Smithson.*

(To find an actual asterisk or question mark in your data field, precede the character in the criteria range with a tilde [~]. For example, ~? matches any entry that begins with a question mark.)

Combining criteria

In many cases you might want Excel to select records that meet several different criteria, or that meet at least one of several criteria. For example, you might want to select every record in a database that has a Salary value greater than $30,000 and a date of hire before January 1, 1980. Or you might want to select every record with a Salary value less than $20,000 and a date of hire after December 31, 1983. In these cases, you have to make entries in more than one cell below the criteria field names.

Logical AND. When you make two or more entries in the same row of a criteria range, Excel selects only those records that meet both (or all) of those criteria. This condition is called a *logical AND.* For example, suppose you want to select only the males who are over 36 years of age from the database shown in Figure 17-2. To do

---

Using several criteria ranges

You can set up many criteria ranges in a worksheet, but Excel can work with only one at a time. The range that is selected when you use the Set Criteria command is the only criteria range that Excel uses. Excel assigns the name *Criteria* to that range. If you then select a different range and use the Set Criteria command again, Excel assigns the name *Criteria* to the second range and removes it from the first range.

If you find yourself using several criteria ranges regularly with the same database, you might want to assign each range a name other than *Criteria.* That way, you can easily switch between criteria ranges using the Formula Goto command (or its keyboard shortcut, F5). For example, suppose you have assigned the name *Less_Than_40* to one criteria range and the name *Between_40_and_50* to another. After you perform a query using *Less_Than_40,* you can switch to *Between_40_and_50* by pressing F5 and selecting *Between_40_and_50* in the Formula Goto dialog box. Excel then selects the range named *Between_40_and_50.* Now you can use the Set Criteria command to define this range as your criteria range.

FIGURE 17-2.
*We combined two
criteria with a logical
AND to select only
the males who are over
36 years of age.*

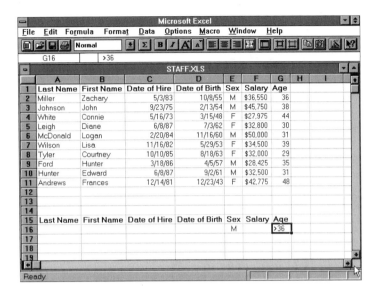

this, type *>36* in cell G16 and type *M* in cell E16. Because both of these criteria are
on the same line of the criteria range (which we defined as cells A15:G16), Excel
operates on only those records that meet both criteria. In our example database, it
operates only on the record for Johnson when you use a criterion-dependent command or function. The record for Miller in row 2 does not meet these criteria unless
you change the entry in cell G16 of the criteria range to *>=36*.

You might sometimes want to match records with an entry that falls between
two values in a particular field. To do this, you must combine two criteria that relate
to the same field into a logical AND form. For example, suppose you want Excel to
select those records from the database shown in Figure 17-2 that have an Age entry
between 40 and 50, inclusive. To do this, you need to specify two criteria that relate
to the Age field: *>=40* and *<=50*. Because both of these criteria relate to the Age field
but you have only one cell to put them in, you must add another Age column to the
criteria range to accommodate the extra Age entry. To do this, select cell H15 and
type *Age* (or copy that entry from cell G1 or G15). Next, type *>=40* in cell G16 and
<=50 in cell H16 (or vice versa). Finally, include column H in the criteria range by
selecting cells A15:H16 and choosing Set Criteria. When you finish, your criteria
range should look like the one in Figure 17-3 on the following page.

Because these two entries are on the same row of the criteria range and both
are beneath an Age header, Excel combines them with a logical AND and conse-
quently selects only those records with Age entries that are both greater than or
equal to 40 and less than or equal to 50. In this example, Excel selects the records
in rows 4 and 11.

FIGURE 17-3.
We added an extra
Age entry to the
criteria range to select
those records whose
Age entries fall
between two criteria.

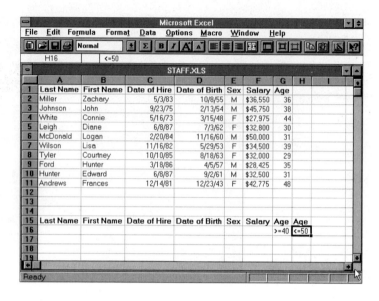

Logical OR. In some cases, you might want Excel to select records that meet either of two (or any of several) criteria. This condition is called a logical OR. Whenever you make entries in more than one row below the criteria field names and then include those rows in the criteria range, Excel selects records that match the specified criteria in any one or more of the rows.

For example, suppose you want to select from the employee database all records with an Age entry less than or equal to 30, as well as all records with an Age entry greater than or equal to 40. To do this, type <=30 in cell G16 and >=40 in cell H17 (or vice versa), as shown in Figure 17-4. Next, expand the criteria range to include row 17. Because these entries are on two separate rows of the worksheet and both rows are within the criteria range, Excel selects any record that meets either condition. In this example, it will select rows 4, 5, 8, and 11.

Combining logical AND and OR. You can also combine logical AND's and OR's by making more than one entry in one or more rows of a multi-row criteria range. For example, suppose you want to select the females over 40 years old and the males over 35 years old from the employee database. Figure 17-5 shows the criteria range that you must create to do this.

In this criteria range, the entries in row 16 tell Excel to select only those females whose age is greater than 40. The entries in row 17 instruct Excel to select only those males whose age is greater than 35. Because the logical AND pairs are on separate rows of the criteria range, Excel combines them with a logical OR. The result is that Excel selects each record that meets both of the criteria on either line — that is, each record that has an Age entry over 35 *and* a Sex entry of *M* (rows 2 and 3) *or* that has an Age entry over 40 *and* a Sex entry of *F* (rows 4 and 11).

FIGURE 17-4.
We combined two criteria with a logical OR to select those records with Age entries that are 30 or less or 40 or more.

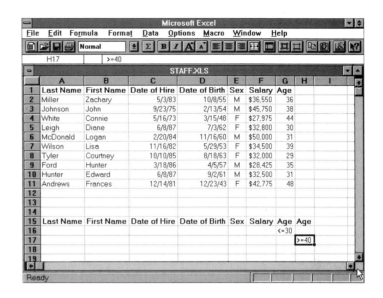

FIGURE 17-5.
We combined logical AND's and OR's to select females over 40 years old and males over 35 years old.

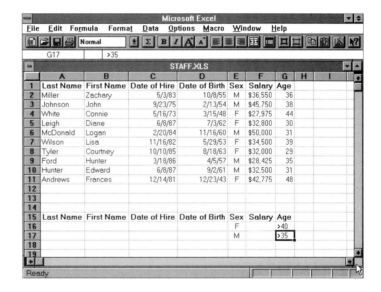

Blank cells. In each of the previous examples, we left some blank cells in each row of the criteria range. When Excel encounters a blank cell underneath any field name in a criteria range, it selects whatever entry is in that field. Excel interprets the criteria shown in Figure 17-6 on the following page like this: *Select all records that have any entry in the Last Name, First Name, Date of Hire, Date of Birth, Salary, or Age field, and an* M *in the Sex field.*

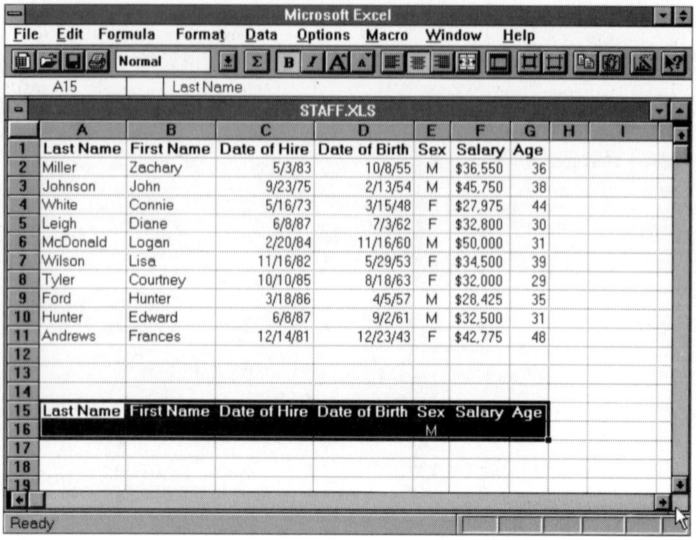

FIGURE 17-6.
The blank cells in the criteria range match any entry in that field.

As long as at least one of the cells in each row of a criteria range contains an entry, blank cells do no harm. If you include a totally blank row in the criteria range, however, the criteria will match every record in the database instead of the subset of records you intended. Suppose you make the entry

=M

in cell E16, as shown in Figure 17-6, intending to select only the males from the database in cells A1:G11. Instead of specifying cells A15:G16 as the criteria range, however, you specify cells A15:G17. Because a blank row makes Excel select any entries in any fields, and a multi-row criteria range makes Excel select records that meet the criteria in any row, this criteria range tells Excel to select all records that have the text *M* in the Sex field — and all records that have any entry in any field! As a result, Excel selects every record in the database. This mistake is particularly damaging when you use the Delete command from the Data menu to delete all records that match the current criteria.

Formulas and functions in comparison criteria

Most of your comparison criteria will compare the entries in a field of a database to a simple text or numeric entry. However, these criteria can also compare the entries in a field to the result of a formula or function.

Suppose you want to locate in the sample database any employee who was hired on May 16, 1973. To do this, enter the criterion

=DATE(73,5,16)

in cell C16. Using this criterion, Excel selects each record with a Date of Hire entry equal to 26800 (the serial date equivalent of May 16, 1973). In the example shown in Figure 17-7, the only employee with this date of hire is Connie White.

Cell references in comparison criteria

Sometimes you might want to operate on records that have an entry in a certain field that matches the contents of a cell located outside the database and criteria ranges. For example, suppose you want to operate on the records with an Age entry equal to a number in cell G18. To do this, enter

=G18

into cell G16. (Be sure your criteria range includes only rows 15 and 16.) Now, when you use a criterion-dependent command or function, Excel checks the current value in cell G18 and then acts on any records with Age entries equal to that value. For example, if cell G18 contains the number 29, Excel operates only on the record in row 8.

Comparison criteria determined by cells outside the database range can also be in the form of formulas. For example, you can enter the criterion

=G18*G19

into cell G16 to select those records with Age entries equal to the product of the numbers in these two cells. You can also use the formula

=G18+25

in that cell to select records with Age entries equal to the number in cell G18 plus 25.

FIGURE 17-7.
We used the DATE function in our comparison criterion.

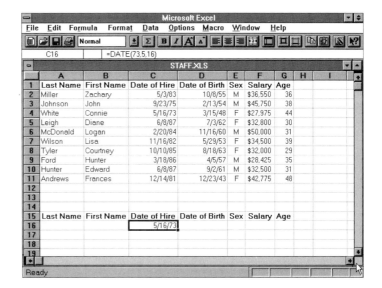

Computed criteria

Suppose you want to select from a database every record with an Age entry less than the value in cell G18. You might attempt to do this by entering the criterion

>   <G18

in cell G16 of the criteria range. Unfortunately, this would not work. Instead of selecting those records with an Age entry less than the number in cell G18, Excel selects those records with the text *<G18* in that cell. Whenever you begin comparison criteria that contain cell references with the symbols >, <, >=, <=, and <>, Excel treats the entry as text.

To instruct Excel to select the records with Age entries less than the value in cell G18, you must use a computed criterion. To create the criterion for this example, enter the formula

>   =G2<$G$18

in cell G16, select the range G15:G16, and choose the Set Criteria command from the Data menu to define the criteria range. Figure 17-8 shows the worksheet at this point; cell G18 contains the value 40.

Notice that we placed this simple computed criterion in a cell under a blank cell. You always enter a comparison criterion beneath a cell that contains a field name, but you must enter a computed criterion beneath a blank cell or beneath a cell that contains a label other than a field name. If you try to use a computed criterion beneath a cell that contains a field name, the computed criterion does not work as you intend it to. For the sake of convenience, enter the computed criterion

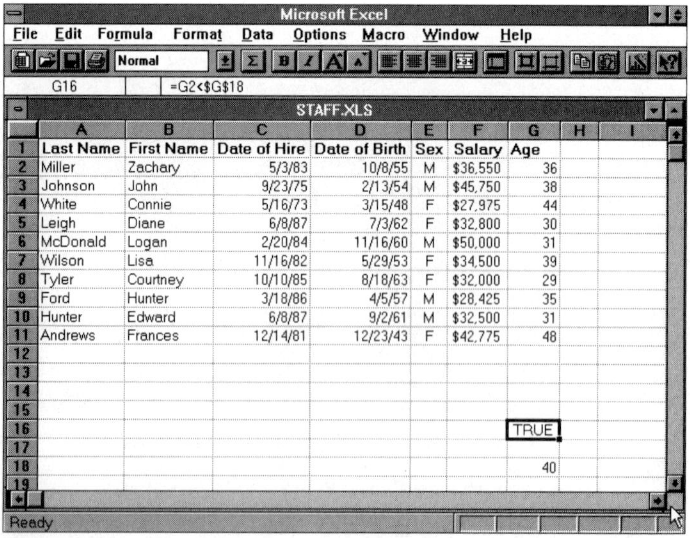

FIGURE 17-8.
This computed criterion makes Excel select those records with an Age entry less than the value in cell G18.

	Last Name	First Name	Date of Hire	Date of Birth	Sex	Salary	Age
1	Last Name	First Name	Date of Hire	Date of Birth	Sex	Salary	Age
2	Miller	Zachary	5/3/83	10/8/55	M	$36,550	36
3	Johnson	John	9/23/75	2/13/54	M	$45,750	38
4	White	Connie	5/16/73	3/15/48	F	$27,975	44
5	Leigh	Diane	6/8/87	7/3/62	F	$32,800	30
6	McDonald	Logan	2/20/84	11/16/60	M	$50,000	31
7	Wilson	Lisa	11/16/82	5/29/53	F	$34,500	39
8	Tyler	Courtney	10/10/85	8/18/63	F	$32,000	29
9	Ford	Hunter	3/18/86	4/5/57	M	$28,425	35
10	Hunter	Edward	6/8/87	9/2/61	M	$32,500	31
11	Andrews	Frances	12/14/81	12/23/43	F	$42,775	48

in the same row as your other criteria but in the column to the right of the last field in the existing criteria range. If you do make a text entry above the computed criterion, you'll probably want it to be a description of the criterion's purpose.

Also, the computed criterion in our example includes a reference to cell G2, the first cell in the database under the field name *Age*. This reference tells Excel that the criterion applies to the Age field. Every computed criterion must include a reference to the cell immediately below a field name in the database. This reference tells Excel which field the criterion applies to. In our example database, computed criteria that apply to the Age field must refer to cell G2. Similarly, computed criteria that apply to the Salary field must refer to cell F2.

Computed criteria must usually refer to the cells in the second row of the database; they cannot refer to the fields of a database by name. The criterion

=Age<$G$18

causes Excel to return the error message #NAME?

As Figure 17-8 shows, Excel displays TRUE as the result of the computed criterion in cell G16. This criterion refers directly to the entry in cell G2, so Excel uses the number in that cell when it evaluates the criterion's formula. Because cell G2 contains the number 36, and 36 is less than 40 (the value in cell G18), the test is true for that record and Excel displays the logical constant TRUE. If the entry in cell G2 were 41, or the entry in cell G18 were 35, Excel would display the result FALSE in cell G16.

The result of any computed criterion is either TRUE or FALSE. However, the result that Excel displays in the criteria range only tells you whether or not the criterion matches the first record in the database. When Excel evaluates a computed criterion, it calculates the criterion's function or formula once for every record in the database, using the entries in the referenced fields of the current record. If the result of the evaluation is TRUE, Excel selects the record; if the result is FALSE, zero, or a text or error value, Excel ignores the record. In this example, Excel selects all records except those in rows 4 and 11.

Notice also that the reference to cell G18 in this formula is absolute. Whenever you create a computed criterion that refers to a cell outside the database range, you must make the reference to that cell absolute (or at least mixed, with the row reference absolute). Unless the reference is fixed in terms of rows, Excel moves down one cell each time it tests a new record.

Let's consider another example of a computed criterion. Suppose you want to act on those records for which the result of dividing the Salary entry by the Age entry is a value greater than 1000. To do this, use the criterion formula

=F2/G2>1000

Notice that this criterion refers to more than one cell in the database, which demonstrates another property of computed criteria: They let you compare the contents of one field with the contents of another field in the same record. Whenever you create a criterion that applies to more than one field in a database, the criterion must refer to the first cell under the field name of each of those fields. In this case, the criterion applies to the Age and Salary fields, so it must refer to both cells G2 and F2. (This formula selects rows 2, 3, 5, 6, 8, and 10.)

Using functions in computed criteria

You can use computed criteria to test the result of a function that operates on the entries in a database field. For example, suppose you want Excel to select only those records from your sample database with a Last Name entry five characters long. To do this, enter the function

=LEN(A2)=5

in cell G16 (or any blank cell with another blank cell above it), and define the criteria range to include that cell. In this case, Excel selects only the records in rows 4, 5, and 8.

Logical AND and OR in computed criteria. Functions in computed criteria also provide an alternative way to create logical AND's and OR's, all within a single cell. For example, the criterion

=AND(F2>40000,F2<50000)

matches every record with a Salary entry between $40,000 and $50,000. This is equivalent to entering >40000 and >50000 in separate cells with the field name *Salary* in the same criteria row. The criterion

=OR(F2<20000,F2>60000)

also matches every record whose Salary entry is less than $20,000 or greater than $60,000. This is equivalent to entering 20000 and 60000 in the same column under the field name *Salary*.

Comparing entries in different records

You can also use a computed criterion to compare the entry in a field of one record with the entry in the same field of the record above it. For example, suppose you want to select every record in the employee database with an Age entry at least five years greater than the record above it. (You use this type of criterion most often after you sort the database.) The criterion

=G2>G1+5

accomplishes this result. This criterion explicitly compares the entry in cell G2 with the entry in cell G1. As with all other computed criteria, however, Excel evaluates this criterion formula once for every record in the database, comparing each entry in the Age field to the entry immediately above it in that field.

You can extend this technique to compare an entry in any record to the record that is two, three, four, or more records above it. Simply be sure that enough blank rows exist above the database to set up comparison criteria for the first few records. In this database, for example, you can use the criterion

=G3>G1

to compare each entry in the Age field to the entry two records above it.

Creating linked references to a database

Although you can have only one active database and criteria range in each worksheet, Excel lets you create criteria that act on a database located in another worksheet by using a linked external reference to that database range. This technique is useful when you work with a very large database. Calculation time can be slow when you work with large files. You can alleviate this problem by storing your database records in one worksheet and maintaining your database calculations and reports in one or more separate, linked worksheets. The worksheet that contains your database is the *supporting main worksheet,* and the worksheets that contain your reports and other calculations are the *dependent worksheets.* This way, you only need to open the linked worksheets when you want to update your calculations.

For example, suppose you're preparing a report and you want to create a separate worksheet that contains a subset of the data in your main database. You can set up a criteria range in another worksheet and then use the Extract command to draw the needed data from the main database. (See "The Extract command," later in this chapter.) Similarly, suppose you want to create a summary worksheet that lists statistical information about the records in a database. Rather than clutter your database with these statistics, you can set up your criteria range in a second worksheet, and then use the database statistical functions to perform the needed calculations. (See "Database functions," later in this chapter.)

Using different windows for database and criteria ranges

In this chapter, we intentionally keep our sample database small so that we can display both the database and the criteria range at the same time on the screen, within the same window. When you work with larger databases, it's a good idea to use two windows: one for the database itself and one for the criteria range. That way, you can easily switch back and forth between the database and the criteria range by switching windows instead of by scrolling to distant parts of the worksheet in a single window.

As we explained in Chapter 16, the Set Database command on the Data menu defines a named range called *Database*. The cells that are highlighted in the active worksheet when you choose the Set Database command are the cells that Excel considers when you perform database operations. However, to create a linked reference to a database stored in another worksheet, you must use the Define Name command. In the Define Name dialog box, type *Database* in the Name text box. Next, activate the Refers to box and enter an external reference to the worksheet and range that contain the database. For example, if the database range is stored in cells A1:G11 of the worksheet named STAFF.XLS, you would type the reference

=STAFF.XLS!$A$1:$G$11

When you use cell references to define the database range in a remote worksheet, keep in mind that Excel does not update those cell references when you add records to or delete records from the database. You can work around this updating problem by using the range name *Database* in the Refers to text box instead of cell references. For example, if you apply the name *Database* to cells A1:G11 in the worksheet STAFF.XLS, you can use the remote reference

=STAFF.XLS!Database

to create a linked database definition. Excel updates the definition of *Database* in your dependent worksheet when you change the definition of *Database* in the main (supporting) worksheet.

After you create this linked name reference, you can proceed as usual to set up your criteria range. Of course, the criteria range you define should include one or more field names from the database in the remote worksheet. Next, you can use the Extract command or any of Excel's database functions to create your database report.

For example, Figure 17-9 shows a criteria range in a new worksheet, Sheet1, that refers to the database stored in STAFF.XLS. This criteria range instructs Excel to act on all the records in the STAFF.XLS database with entries greater than $35,000 in the Salary field and entries greater than 30 in the Age field.

To create this criteria range, we opened a new worksheet and used the Move and Size commands to create non-overlapping windows. Then we selected cells A1:G1 in the STAFF.XLS worksheet, chose the Copy command, activated cell A1 in the Sheet1 worksheet, and then chose the Paste command. After we entered the criteria in row 2 of Sheet1, we selected cells A1:G2 and chose the Set Criteria command. Finally, we chose the Formula menu's Define Name command and created a linked reference to STAFF.XLS to define the linked database range.

FIGURE 17-9.
*We entered our
database criteria in a
separate, linked
worksheet.*

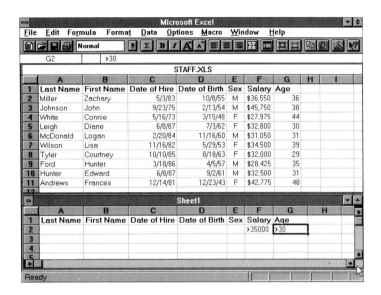

Using selection criteria

Now that you know how criteria work, let's take a look at some uses for them. This section discusses the three Microsoft Excel commands that work with criteria: Find, Extract, and Delete. These Data menu commands instruct Excel to locate, copy, and erase records that match criteria in a database range.

The Find command

The Find command instructs Excel to select, one at a time, the records in a database that match the criteria in the criteria range. For example, suppose you want Excel to find every record in the database in Figure 17-10, shown on the following page, that has the entry *M* in its Sex field. To begin, highlight the range A1:G11 and use the Set Database command on the Data menu to define the database range. Next, enter the field name *Sex* in cell E15 and the letter *M* in cell E16, select both cells, and choose the Set Criteria command. Now you're ready to use the Find command. When you choose this command from the Data menu, Excel selects the first record in the database that matches the current criterion. In our example, Excel selects the record in row 2, the first record in the database.

The record Excel finds first when you use the Find command depends on which cell of the worksheet is active when you choose the command. If, as will often

FIGURE 17-10.
We used the Find command to locate the first record in the database with M *in its Sex field.*

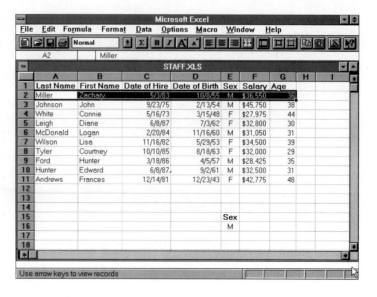

be the case, a cell outside the database range is the active cell, Excel finds the criteria-matching record closest to the top of the database, as in the example shown in Figure 17-10. If, however, a cell within the database is active when you choose the Find command, Excel locates the first criteria-matching record that lies below the record that contains the active cell. (If you press Shift when you choose the Find command, Excel locates the first matching record above the active cell.) If no records in the database meet the stated criteria, Excel beeps and displays the alert message *Could not find matching data.*

As soon as you choose the Find command, Excel changes the name of that command to Exit Find. When you want to move freely between database records again, choose this command from the Data menu. Alternatively, you can exit from Find mode by selecting any worksheet cell outside the database range, issuing another command, pressing Esc, or editing a cell entry.

If your database does contain criteria-matching records, the scroll bars at the right side and bottom of the window change to a different color (or a striped pattern) indicating that the actions of these tools are restricted. In Find mode, you can use the scroll arrows to move up and down through the database but only to locate those records that meet the stated criteria. For example, to move to the next criteria-matching record, click the down scroll arrow. Excel selects the record in row 3. If you click the down scroll arrow again, Excel skips to row 6, and then to row 9, and finally to row 10. If the last record that matches the criteria is selected and you again click the down scroll arrow, Excel beeps and remains at the current record.

To move backward through the database, click the up scroll arrow. Excel moves to the next record above the current active record that matches the criteria.

In addition to the scroll arrows, you can use the scroll bars to move more quickly between records when you use Find in a large database. When you move the scroll box in Find mode, Excel selects the record that meets the criteria whose position in the database is proportional to the position of the scroll box in the scroll bar. By clicking the gray area of the scroll bar above or below the scroll box, you can move to the next criteria-matching record that is at least one screen up or down from the current selection.

Although the horizontal scroll bar remains active while you're in Find mode, Excel does not let you scroll the last column in the database out of view; the scrolling action locks when the last column of the database reaches the left edge of the screen. To scroll further, you must leave Find mode by choosing Exit Find from the Data menu or by selecting a cell outside the database range.

You can also use the keyboard to move from one criteria-matching record to the next. Use the Up and Down arrow keys to move forward or backward one record at a time. Use the Left and Right arrow keys to bring additional columns of the database into view. (As with the horizontal scroll bar, however, you can't scroll past the boundaries of the database range with the Left and Right arrow keys.) You can also use PgUp and PgDn to move to the next criteria-matching record that is at least one screen above or below the current selection.

Editing in Find mode

While Excel is in Find mode, you can use the Cut, Copy, and Clear commands to move, copy, and delete any criteria-matching record. First choose the Find command and use the selection techniques already described to locate the record you want to cut, copy, or clear. When this record is highlighted, choose the Cut, Copy, or Clear command from the Edit menu.

If you choose Cut, Excel removes that record from the database the next time you use the Paste command. If you choose Copy, Excel saves the cell references of that record on the Clipboard, but doesn't remove the record from the database immediately. (If you clear a record by mistake, use the Edit Undo command to restore it.)

As soon as you choose any of these commands, Excel leaves Find mode. To find the next record, use the Data Find command again.

The Extract command

The Extract command lets you copy, as a group, records that meet specified criteria. Extracting records is a three-step process: First, you use the Set Criteria command to define a criteria range; second, you define the area where you want Excel to place the records it extracts (the *extract range*); and third, you choose Extract from the Data menu.

Specifying criteria

Suppose you want Excel to extract the entries from the Last Name and Salary fields in the employee database for only those records with a Salary entry between $30,000 and $40,000, inclusive. First, enter the criterion

=AND(F2>=30000,F2<=40000)

in your worksheet, as shown in the formula bar in Figure 17-11. Next, select the criteria range (cells F13 and F14 in our example) and issue the Set Criteria command.

Defining the extract range

Now you must define the area where you want Excel to copy the selected records. First enter the names of the fields you want Excel to extract in a row of cells in a blank portion of the worksheet. In this example, shown in Figure 17-11, we want to extract entries from the Last Name and Salary fields, so we need to include only those two field names at the top of the extract range. Although we could place these field names anywhere in the worksheet, we'll put them in cells A16 and B16.

The field names in the extract range must be in a single row. When you choose the Extract command, Excel places the extracted information in the cells below these names.

If you type the field names in the top row of the extract range, be sure to enter them exactly as they appear in the database range. A field name in the extract range must exactly match its counterpart in the database (except for capitalization differences), or Excel will not recognize the field name in the extract range. You can avoid typographical errors by using the Copy and Paste commands to copy the field names from the top row of the database to the extract range.

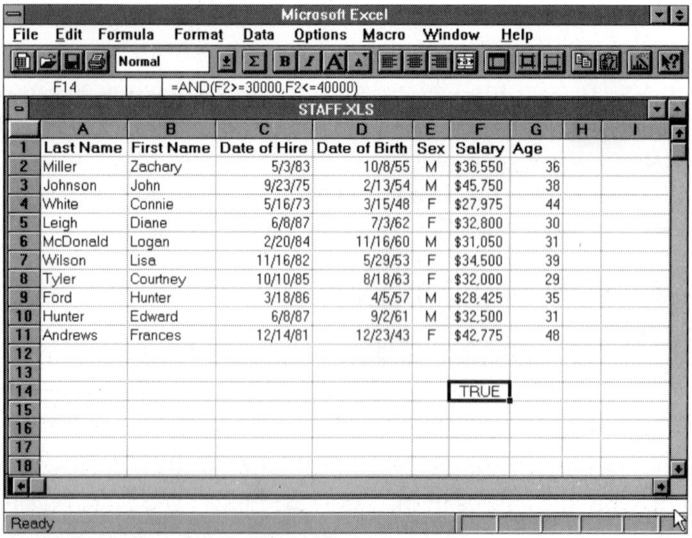

FIGURE 17-11.
We want to extract the Last Name and Salary entries for employees with incomes between $30,000 and $40,000.

Although you recognize the entries you made in cells A16 and B16 as headers for the extract range, Excel doesn't know where you want it to place the extracted field entries until you tell it. To define the extract range, simply select it.

You can define the extract range as only the cells that contain the field names (in this case, cells A16:B16) or as a block of cells headed by those field names (such as the range A16:B30). Your choice affects the number of records Excel can extract. If you define only the field-name entries as the extract range, Excel extracts the specified fields of every record in the database that matches the current criteria. If you select a multi-row block of cells, however, Excel extracts only as many matching records as can fit into the selected area. For example, if you select cells A16:B18 as the extract range, Excel extracts a maximum of two records, because the range has only two blank rows. If Excel fills up the extract range before it can copy every criteria-matching record, it beeps and displays the message *Extract range is full*.

Extracting information

After you specify the criteria, decide which fields you want to extract, and select the extract range, you're ready to extract the records that match your criteria. With the extract range still selected, choose the Extract command from the Data menu. Excel displays the dialog box shown in Figure 17-12. To extract only those records with entries in the extracted fields that are not duplicates of entries in other records, select the Unique Records Only check box. To extract all the records that match the criteria, leave the check box unselected.

FIGURE 17-12.
Select this check box to extract unique records only.

In most cases, you'll want Excel to extract every criteria-matching record to the extract range. To do this, simply click OK. Excel copies the criteria-matching records to the extract range (after first erasing the previous contents of the extract range). Only the fields that have headings in the extract range are copied. Figure 17-13 on the following page shows the result of our example extraction.

The Unique Records Only option

Perhaps your database contains several duplicate records, and you want to extract only one record from each set of duplicates. If you select the Unique Records Only option in the Extract dialog box, shown in Figure 17-12, Excel copies only one record from each set of duplicates to the extract range.

A record does not have to be identical in all fields to be omitted from the extraction. Only the entries in the extracted fields need match the entries of a previously extracted record for that record to be considered identical.

FIGURE 17-13.
Excel extracted the records that match the criteria.

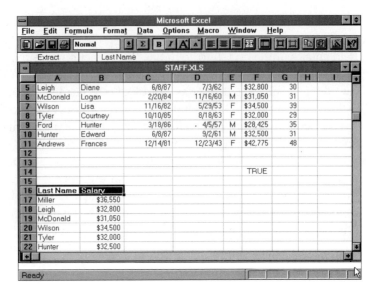

For example, suppose we add a record for Robert McDonald to our sample database. Let's assume that, like Logan McDonald, whose record appears in row 6, Robert McDonald earns $31,050. Figure 17-14 shows the result of performing a unique extraction on the employee database. Even though the database now includes two McDonalds, each earning $31,050, only one of those records is extracted, because we selected the Unique Records Only option.

Erasing the extract range

As previously mentioned, when you use the Extract command, Excel erases the contents of the extract range before it begins extracting records. This can lead to problems if you designed a one-row extract range. If you define only the row of field names as the extract range, Excel considers that the extract range extends from that row to the bottom of the worksheet. The program, therefore, erases any entries in the cells below the field names, all the way to the bottom of the worksheet, whenever you issue the Extract command. Any information in those cells is permanently erased and cannot be recovered with the Undo command.

When you define a multi-row extract range, however, Excel considers the extract range to be only that block of selected cells. The contents of the entire extract range are still erased when you choose the Extract command, but because the range is limited, you don't risk erasing valuable information unintentionally.

FIGURE 17-14.
When we used the
Unique Records Only
option, Excel didn't
extract the record in
row 12.

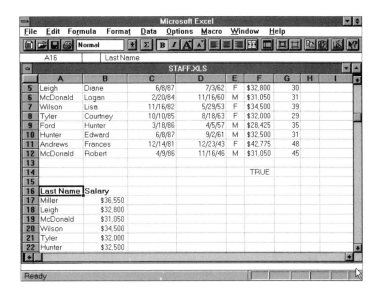

The Delete command

The Data menu's Delete command lets you delete all the records that match the current criteria. For example, suppose you want to delete from the employee database every record that has the entry *M* in the Sex field. First enter the criterion *M* in cell E16 and the field name *Sex* in cell E15. Next, define the criteria range by selecting cells E15:E16 and choosing the Set Criteria command. Finally, choose the Delete command from the Data menu. When you choose this command, you see the warning message *Matching records will be deleted permanently*. If you don't want to delete the records that match the current criterion, select Cancel to terminate the command. If you do want to delete those records, click OK. When you do this, Excel deletes the entries in every field of every criteria-matching record and then shifts the remaining records up.

Figure 17-15 on the following page shows the result of using the Delete command with the criteria in our previous example. As you can see, Excel removed the records from rows 2, 3, 6, 9, and 10 of the original database, and it moved the remaining records up so that the database remains in an adjacent block.

Because the effects of the Delete command can be disastrous, you should use it with extreme caution. You can't use Undo on a Delete command from the Data menu. When you delete records, you can't retrieve them. You can minimize the effects of unintentionally deleting records from a database in two ways. First, use the Save or Save As command immediately before you choose the Delete command. That way, you'll have a copy of the database as it existed before the deletion, and you can recover the lost information by opening the same worksheet again. When you choose the Open command from the File menu and select the worksheet name

FIGURE 17-15.
*We used the Delete
command to delete all
the records in the
database with M in
the Sex field.*

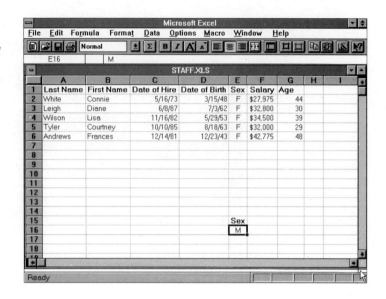

from the list box, a dialog box appears and asks if you want to revert to your last saved version. (You'll lose any changes you made since you last saved the database.)

For additional security, before you use the Delete command, use the Extract command to make a copy of every field of each record that matches the current criteria. This technique lets you view the records that Excel will delete before it deletes them; it also stores a backup copy of the deleted entries within the worksheet. We strongly recommend that you always use Save, Save As, or Extract before you use Delete.

CAUTION: *Do not use the Delete command when your criteria range contains a totally blank row. A criteria range that contains a blank row matches every record in the database. Therefore, if you choose the Delete command when the criteria range contains a blank row, Excel erases the entire database.*

Using criteria in forms

You can also use criteria to select database records from within the Form dialog box. The Form dialog box includes three options that let you define and use criteria: Criteria, Find Next, and Find Prev. The Criteria option lets you define criteria in a form. The Find Next and Find Prev options let you use those criteria to find matching records: Find Next searches down through the database for the next matching record; Find Prev searches up through the database for the previous match.

To define criteria from within a form, first use the Data Form command. Next, select the Criteria option in the Form dialog box. Microsoft Excel clears the contents of all text boxes in the data form, allowing you to enter your criteria. As you can see in Figure 17-16, the word *Criteria* appears in the upper right corner of the form, and the *Criteria* button has changed to read *Form*. When you finish entering the criteria for selecting records, you can select the Form option to return to the data form.

FIGURE 17-16.
Use the Criteria
option to enter
selection criteria in
the Form dialog box.

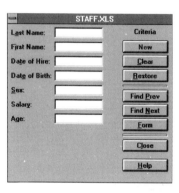

Suppose you need to create a criterion that finds the record for employee Logan McDonald in the database in Figure 17-11. Open the worksheet and use the Set Database command to define the database range as A1:G11. Next select the Form command from the Data menu to create the data form. When the data form appears, it displays the first record in the database. To define the criterion, select the Criteria option button. Excel erases the fields on the data form and changes the Criteria option to Form, as shown in Figure 17-16. Now select the Last Name field, and then enter the criterion *McDonald*. (See Figure 17-17.) Finally, select the Find Next option. Excel displays the record for employee McDonald in the data form on the right, as you can see in Figure 17-17.

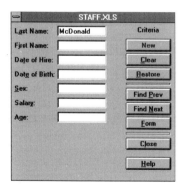 

FIGURE 17-17. *To define a criterion, we made an entry in one of the fields of the form (left). We chose Find Next to display the matching record (right).*

You can use most of the selection criteria we discussed in data-form criteria. You can ask Excel to match a series of characters by entering text, numbers, or logical values. If you want to compare a quantity, you can enter =, >=, >, <=, <, or <>. You can also use the wildcard characters ? and * in your selection criteria. Remember, if you search for a literal ? or *, you must precede the character with a tilde (~). You cannot use computed criteria to search in the data form. For example, you can't enter a criterion that uses the values in two or more fields.

If you have several records that share one or more characteristics, you can combine criteria to narrow your search. For example, suppose our database contained several employees named McDonald. To search for a specific record, we would enter *McDonald* in the Last Name field and a name in the First Name field, or an *F* or *M* in the Sex field, to further restrict the search for employee McDonald. Excel beeps if it finds no records that match your criteria.

Database functions

Microsoft Excel offers 12 functions — DAVERAGE, DCOUNT, DCOUNTA, DGET, DMAX, DMIN, DPRODUCT, DSTDEV, DSTDEVP, DSUM, DVAR, and DVARP — that operate on the records in a database. DGET returns the value of a particular field in a particular record. The other 11 functions are related closely to the worksheet statistical functions described in Chapter 8. Except for DCOUNTA and DGET, you can use the database functions only on fields that contain numeric entries. The following table describes the results of each function.

Function	Action
=DAVERAGE	Returns the average value from the specified field of the criteria-matching records.
=DCOUNT	Returns the number of numeric entries in the specified field of the criteria-matching records.
=DCOUNTA	Returns the number of non-blank cells in the specified field of the criteria-matching records.
=DGET	Returns the value of the field argument in the record that satisfies the criteria-range argument. (If no record satisfies the criteria, the function returns #VALUE! If more than one record satisfies the criteria, the function returns #NUM!)
=DMAX	Returns the greatest value from the specified field of the criteria-matching records.
=DMIN	Returns the smallest value from the specified field of the criteria-matching records.
=DPRODUCT	Returns the product of the values from the specified field of the criteria-matching records.

(Continued)

Function	Action
=DSTDEV	Returns the sample standard deviation of the values in the specified field of the criteria-matching records.
=DSTDEVP	Returns the population standard deviation of the values in the specified field of the criteria-matching records.
=DSUM	Returns the total of the values in the specified field of the criteria-matching records.
=DVAR	Returns the sample variance of the values in the specified field of the criteria-matching records.
=DVARP	Returns the population variance of the values in the specified field of the criteria-matching records.

All 12 database functions have the same syntax:

=DFUNCTION(*database,field,criteria*)

The first argument specifies the database range upon which the function acts. This can be either a range name or the coordinates of a range. If you use the Set Database command to name your database range, you can use the range name *Database* as the first argument of these functions. In all cases, the range you specify must be an Excel database.

The second argument tells Excel which field of the database contains the entries the function should evaluate. You can enter the name of the field, enclosed in quotation marks. For example, if you want a function to work on the Salary field of a database, you can enter the second argument as

"Salary"

Except for capitalization, *field* must be identical to the field name in the database range. If the name you use in the function is not identical to the name of one of the fields in the database, the function returns the error value #VALUE!

Alternatively, you can specify *field* as the position of the field within the database. To use the entries in the leftmost column of the database, enter the field index number 1 as the second argument of the function; to use the entries in the second column of the database, enter the number 2; and so on. When you specify *field* in this manner, you don't need to enclose the number in quotation marks.

The third argument of any database function identifies the criteria range the function uses to select the records on which it operates. You can use either a range name or cell coordinates to specify this range. If you use the Set Criteria command to define your criteria range, you can use the name *Criteria* as the third argument of the database function. The range you specify must be an Excel criteria range.

Let's use a database function to calculate the average value in the Age field for the females in our example employee database. As the first step, create a criterion in cell E16 that will select only records with the entry *F* in the Sex field. Next, use the Set Criteria command to define cells E15:E16 as the criteria range. Finally, be sure the proper block of cells (in this case, A1:G11) is defined as the database range. Now enter the formula

=DAVERAGE(Database,"Age",Criteria)

in any empty cell of the worksheet outside the database and criteria ranges. In this case, enter the function in cell G16, as shown in Figure 17-18. Excel calculates its result by summing the entries in the Age field for those records that meet the selection criterion and by dividing the sum by the total number of records that meet the criterion. In this case, Excel adds the Age values of the records in rows 4, 5, 7, 8, and 11 (total 190), divides by the number of criteria-matching records (5), and returns the value 38.0.

You can state this formula in other ways. For instance, you can replace the second argument, "Age", with a field index number that indicates the position of the Age field within the database:

=DAVERAGE(Database,7,Criteria)

In this example, you use 7 for the second argument, because the Age field is in the seventh column of the database (the leftmost column is column 1).

You can also replace the range names *Database* and *Criteria* with the coordinates of the database range and the criteria range:

=DAVERAGE(A1:G11,7,E15:E16)

After you enter this formula, you can use it to calculate the average age for other groups of records simply by changing the entries in the criteria range. For example, if you replace the *F* in cell E16 with an *M*, the function calculates the average age of the males in the database. Or, if you want to calculate the average income of the females in the database, you can replace the second argument, "Age", with "Salary".

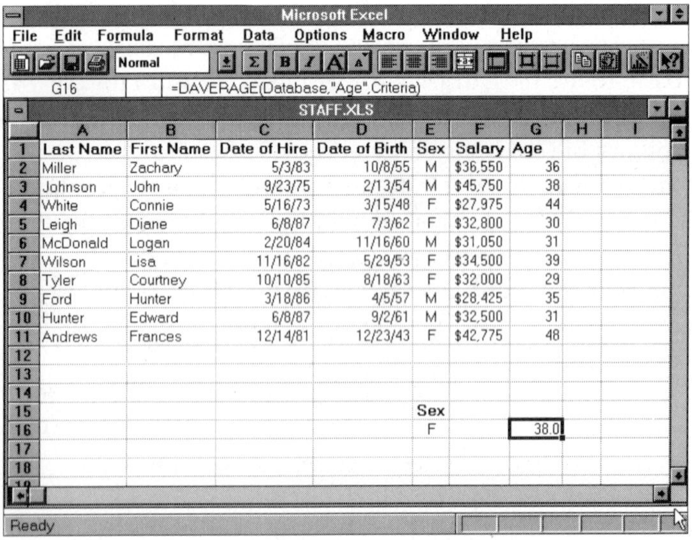

	A	B	C	D	E	F	G	H	I
1	Last Name	First Name	Date of Hire	Date of Birth	Sex	Salary	Age		
2	Miller	Zachary	5/3/83	10/8/55	M	$36,550	36		
3	Johnson	John	9/23/75	2/13/54	M	$45,750	38		
4	White	Connie	5/16/73	3/15/48	F	$27,975	44		
5	Leigh	Diane	6/8/87	7/3/62	F	$32,800	30		
6	McDonald	Logan	2/20/84	11/16/60	M	$31,050	31		
7	Wilson	Lisa	11/16/82	5/29/53	F	$34,500	39		
8	Tyler	Courtney	10/10/85	8/18/63	F	$32,000	29		
9	Ford	Hunter	3/18/86	4/5/57	M	$28,425	35		
10	Hunter	Edward	6/8/87	9/2/61	M	$32,500	31		
11	Andrews	Frances	12/14/81	12/23/43	F	$42,775	48		
12									
13									
14									
15					Sex				
16					F		38.0		
17									
18									

FIGURE 17-18.
We used the DAVERAGE function to calculate the average age of the females in the employee database.

18

Using the Crosstab ReportWizard

A crosstab is a table that summarizes particular fields of information from a database. The Crosstab ReportWizard is an add-in that makes it extremely easy to create crosstabs from Microsoft Excel databases. The Crosstab ReportWizard uses a series of dialog boxes to find out what information you want and how you want it organized. As you fill out the dialog boxes, the ReportWizard shows you a graphic representation of the table you're asking it to build. It then creates the table of information for you, either in a separate worksheet or in the same worksheet as the database.

In this chapter, we'll show you what a powerful tool the Crosstab ReportWizard is and how easy it is to use it to analyze your data.

NOTE: *The Crosstab ReportWizard is an add-in. If you did a complete installation of Microsoft Excel, you'll find a Crosstab command on your Data menu. If that command is not there, you'll need to install the Crosstab ReportWizard add-in. You do this by rerunning the Excel Setup program and choosing Custom installation.*

Introducing the ReportWizard

Suppose you recorded transactions for a small business in the database shown in Figure 18-1. As the year comes to an end, you want to know how much you have spent per quarter in each of the expense categories that appear in your Category field. You can get this information in a variety of ways. Using the methods described in Chapter 17, for example, you can set up a criteria range and perform a series of extracts on your database. Or you can use a criteria range and the DSUM function. But using these methods to get the totals for each of your expense categories requires a considerable amount of labor. With the Crosstab ReportWizard, you can quickly turn the raw data of Figure 18-1 into the report shown in Figure 18-2.

TIP: While the Crosstab ReportWizard creates your crosstab table, you can't do other work in Excel. You can work in other applications, but on some systems, the standard Alt-Esc, Ctrl-Esc, and Alt-Tab methods of switching between Excel and other applications might be ineffective while the ReportWizard works. To be sure you can switch to a different program, restore Excel to an unmaximized window before you choose the Crosstab command. Then if you get tired of waiting for the ReportWizard to finish, you can use the mouse to move to a different program.

Let's look at the steps involved in creating the table shown in Figure 18-2.

The first thing you need to do is define the data shown in Figure 18-1 as a Microsoft Excel database. If you use the Crosstab command in a worksheet that does not include a range named *Database*, you will get an error message. (If your

FIGURE 18-1.
The Crosstab ReportWizard can tell us how much we spent per quarter in each expense category.

FIGURE 18-2.
We used the Crosstab ReportWizard to tabulate quarterly expense totals by category.

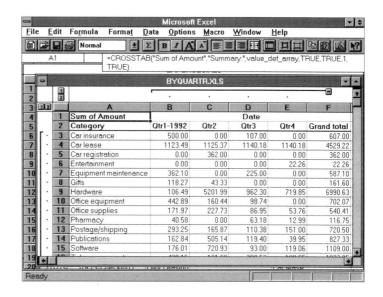

database includes a criteria range, the ReportWizard analyzes only the records that meet the current criteria. Therefore, when you're first experimenting with the ReportWizard, you might want to clear your criteria range or delete the name *Criteria*.)

Next, pull down the Data menu and choose Crosstab. The ReportWizard presents its introductory dialog box, shown in Figure 18-3.

FIGURE 18-3.
Each of the ReportWizard dialog boxes consists of a right panel, where you take some action, and a left panel that provides graphical feedback about what you're doing.

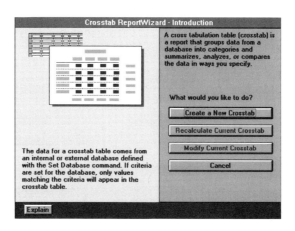

Each of the ReportWizard's dialog boxes is structured in a similar way to the one shown in Figure 18-3. In the panel on the right, you tell the ReportWizard what you want to do. In the panel on the left, the ReportWizard shows a graphic representation of the table you're constructing. At the bottom of the left panel is an Explain button. You can get more information about what the ReportWizard is asking you by clicking this button. (Click Explain a second time to return the left panel to its original state.) Figure 18-4 shows the introductory dialog box after you click Explain.

FIGURE 18-4.
When you click
Explain, the left side
of the ReportWizard's
dialog box provides
more information
about what you're
currently doing.

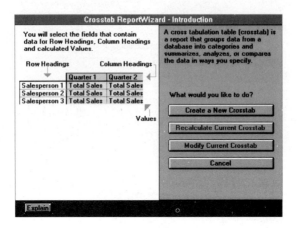

As the left side of Figure 18-4 shows, to create a crosstab you supply three items of information: what database field or fields will be used for row headings; what field or fields will be used for column headings; and what kind of data you want in the body of the table — at the intersections of the row and column headings. The ReportWizard uses three dialog boxes to collect these three elements of your table specification.

To begin, click the button labeled Create a New Crosstab. The ReportWizard presents the Row Categories dialog box, shown in Figure 18-5.

FIGURE 18-5.
First tell the
ReportWizard which
field or fields you
want to use for the
row dimension of your
crosstab.

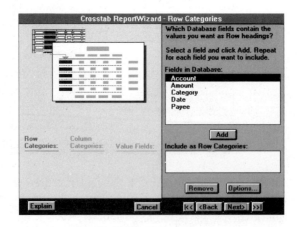

In this dialog box, you tell the ReportWizard which database field to use for the row dimension of the crosstab. We want expense categories to appear as row headings. (See the table in Figure 18-2.) Expense categories belong to the field labeled *Category* (as in Figure 18-1), so we select Category and click Add. The ReportWizard responds by displaying the selected field name in the list box at the bottom of the right panel.

We're creating a relatively simple table that uses only one field for the row headings and one for the column headings. As we'll see later, the Crosstab Report-Wizard can also handle tables that use more than one field for either the row or the column dimension (or both).

The column dimension is specified correctly, so we tell the ReportWizard to move on now by clicking Next. The Next button is one of four controls that appear below the right panel. You can click the Next button at any time to move to the subsequent dialog box, the Back button to return to the previous dialog box, the button to the right of Next to "fast-forward" to the last dialog box, or the button to the left of Back to return to the first dialog box. Clicking Next now takes us to the Column Categories dialog box, shown in Figure 18-6.

FIGURE 18-6.
After indicating which field or fields to use for the row dimension, tell the ReportWizard which field or fields to use for the column dimension.

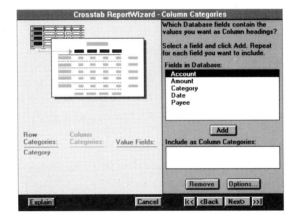

We want the column dimension of the finished table to list time periods, so we select Date in the field list and click Add. This specification is a little different from the row specification, however. In the case of the row dimension, we want each value of the Category field to appear in a separate row. In the case of the column dimension, we definitely don't want the ReportWizard to create a separate column for each date. Even if a breakdown by day were useful for some reason, a table with a separate column for each day would exceed Excel's 256-column width limit. Rather, we want the ReportWizard to give us one column per quarter.

To specify one column per quarter, we select Date in the list at the bottom of the right dialog box panel, and then click the Options button. The ReportWizard presents the Column Category Options dialog box, shown in Figure 18-7 on the following page.

FIGURE 18-7.
*In this dialog box,
we can tell the
ReportWizard to
group the columns
by quarter instead
of by day.*

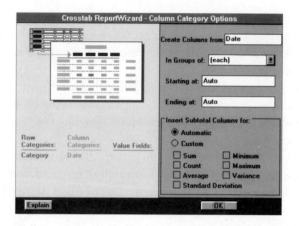

To group the columns by quarter, simply open the drop-down list labeled In Groups of. There you'll find all the time intervals you're most likely to need, from seconds to years. For this example, select Quarters and click OK. That takes you back to the Column Categories dialog box, where you can now click Next to move on.

The Value Fields dialog box appears, where you tell the ReportWizard what to put in the table. In our simple example, we want the amount of money spent for each column and time period to appear at the intersection of each category row and date column. So we select Amount as our value field, click Add, and then click Next once more. That brings us to the ReportWizard's Final dialog box, shown in Figure 18-8.

FIGURE 18-8.
*In the left panel of
the Final dialog box,
you can review the
setup of your crosstab
table before the
ReportWizard
creates it.*

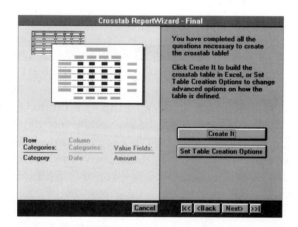

This last dialog box gives you a chance to review the structure of your table (in the left panel) before you put the ReportWizard to work. (It also offers an Options button; we'll look at what's behind that button in a moment.) If the table setup looks right, all you need to do is click Create It. In a few moments, the ReportWizard produces the new worksheet shown in Figure 18-9.

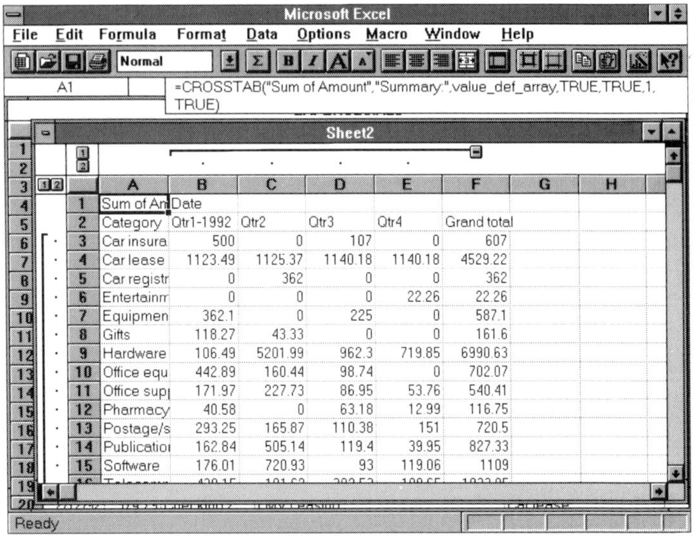

FIGURE 18-9.
By default, the ReportWizard puts your crosstab in a new, outlined worksheet.

As you can see, the ReportWizard creates your table in a separate, outlined worksheet, but it doesn't concern itself with such matters as column widths and numeric formatting. To turn the output into something readable, you can begin widening individual columns with the mouse. Or, more simply, select cell A1, hold down Shift, and click the AutoFormat tool until you find a format that pleases you.

Finding the details behind aggregate values

Suppose that on inspection of the table in Figure 18-9, you find yourself wondering how you happened to spend nearly $7,000 on hardware in 1992. You could go back to the database and use the Data Extract command to pull out the records in which the Category field contains the value *Hardware*. But the Crosstab ReportWizard offers a simpler alternative: Double-click cell F9, the Grand Totals cell for the Hardware row. In a moment, the ReportWizard presents the new worksheet shown in Figure 18-10 on the following page.

FIGURE 18-10.
*The detail used to
create summary data
on the crosstab table is
a double-click away.*

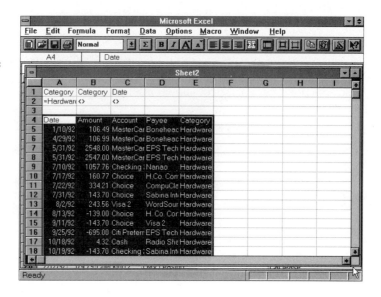

Provided you don't change the ReportWizard's default output options (discussed later in this chapter), you can get the details for any aggregate value in your crosstab worksheet using this technique.

Recalculating the table

Notice the formula area of the worksheet shown in Figure 18-9. The current cell is A1, and the Crosstab ReportWizard has used the CROSSTAB function to generate the contents of that cell. If you explore the crosstab worksheet, you'll find that all the headings are produced by formulas that involve the CROSSTAB function, but all the numbers are constants. Does this mean the table is *static* (not subject to change as the underlying database changes) or *dynamic*?

The table is either, depending on what you choose to do with it. Like a worksheet that has recalculation set to manual, the crosstab table is "updatable," but Microsoft Excel doesn't update it unless you ask it to.

To recalculate a crosstab table, first be sure that the database worksheet is open. Next, select any part of the crosstab worksheet and choose the Crosstab command again. In the Introduction dialog box (shown in Figure 18-3), click the Recalculate Current Crosstab button.

For recalculation to work, you must leave all the CROSSTAB formulas in place. If you want to change the appearance of your row and column headings, do so by applying formatting commands or by modifying the first argument of the headings' CROSSTAB formulas, not by replacing the formulas with static labels.

Modifying the table definition

If you change your mind about the parameters of your crosstab table, you don't have to start over from scratch or modify CROSSTAB formulas and recalculate. Simply select any part of the table, choose the Crosstab command again, and click Modify Current Crosstab. (The database worksheet must be open when you do this.) Then step through the ReportWizard's dialog boxes until you come to the part of the table definition that you want to change.

For example, suppose you decide you'd like to see monthly expense totals, rather than quarterly totals. Select a cell in the crosstab table, choose the Crosstab command, click the Modify Current Crosstab button, and then click Next once. You'll see the Column Categories dialog box where you can click the Options button and change the grouping from quarters to months. After you fix the column definition, click the fast-forward button, and then click the Create It button. The Crosstab ReportWizard responds by overwriting the current table worksheet with your modified table.

CAUTION: *If you modify a table in a way that makes it larger, be sure the area to the right of and below the current table is clear. The ReportWizard does not issue a warning before it overwrites non-crosstab data.*

Modifying the table linkage

If you select any cell in the crosstab worksheet and choose the Links command from the File menu, you will see a dialog box like the one shown in Figure 18-11. This dialog box provides the only evidence of the database worksheet that supplied your crosstab's data.

FIGURE 18-11.
The Links dialog box shows the name of a crosstab add-in sheet as well as the name of the database worksheet that supplied the crosstab's data.

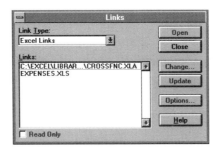

Normally, you don't need to concern yourself with the Links dialog box. When you save your crosstab worksheet (either separately or as part of a workbook), it "remembers" the worksheet to which it's linked. Provided the database worksheet is open, the next time you use either the Recalculate Current Crosstab or the Modify Current Crosstab procedure, the ReportWizard will know where to look for data. If you change the name of the database worksheet while both the database worksheet and the crosstab worksheet are open, the linkage record is adjusted accordingly.

However, if you change the name of the Excel database worksheet from another application, from Microsoft Windows, from MS-DOS, or from a file-management utility, or if you rename it while the crosstab worksheet is not open, the linkage will no longer be correct. In that case, you can repair the link using the Change button in the Links dialog box. (For more about the File menu's Links command, see Chapter 6.)

Invalid file links are most likely to occur when you move files between directories or servers. The best way to avoid mishaps is to save associated files together in workbooks.

Aggregating values with functions other than SUM

In our expense crosstab, we asked the ReportWizard to give us the total expense figures for each category by quarter. The ReportWizard responded by aggregating the appropriate value sets and applying the SUM function. SUM is only one of seven functions you can use, however. The others are AVERAGE, COUNT, MAX, MIN, STDEV, and VAR. To choose a function other than SUM, click the Options button in the ReportWizard's Value Fields dialog box. In the next dialog box that appears, open the Calculation Method drop-down list and choose the function you want to perform.

If you just want a count of the records in your database, broken down by a specific row field and column field, leave the Value Fields dialog box blank. For example, suppose you're working with the database shown in Figure 18-12, and you'd like a simple head count of employees broken down by division and department. By choosing Division as your row field and Dept. as your column field and then skipping right past the Value Fields dialog box, you can obtain the crosstab shown in Figure 18-13.

Using multiple row or column fields

All the examples so far in this chapter have used a single database field for row headings and another single database field for column headings. The ReportWizard also handles multiple row and column fields. For example, from the database shown in Figure 18-12, you might want to generate a crosstab that shows the average

FIGURE 18-12.
To generate an employee count by division and department, specify Division for the row field, Dept. for the column field, and nothing for the value field.

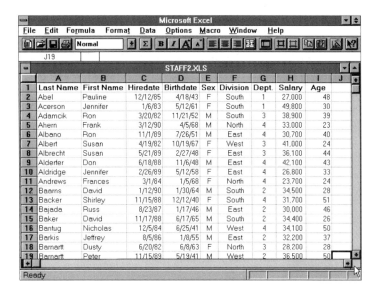

FIGURE 18-13.
When you omit the value field, the Crosstab ReportWizard produces a count at the intersection of each row and column heading.

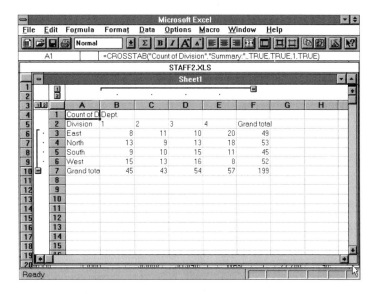

salary for men and for women broken down by departments within divisions. To do this, you can specify Division as your first row category and Dept. as your second row category. For the column dimension of your table, specify the Sex field. For the values field, specify Salary and ask the ReportWizard to aggregate Salary values using the AVERAGE function. Figure 18-14 on the following page shows the crosstab that results.

FIGURE 18-14.
The Crosstab
ReportWizard can
handle multiple row
and column fields.
This table uses two
row fields — Division
and Dept.

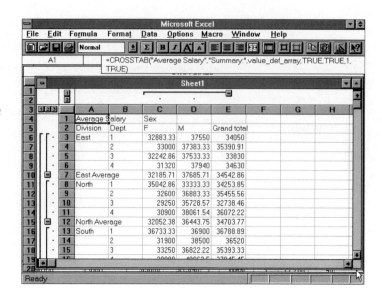

Because you specified the Division row first and then the Dept. row, the ReportWizard treats departments as subcategories of divisions. If you named the fields in the opposite order, the resulting table would list divisions as subcategories of departments instead.

You can also arrange for the table to have more than one field in the column dimension. For example, the table in Figure 18-15 presents the same information as the one in Figure 18-14, but it uses a different row-and-column layout. In

FIGURE 18-15.
This table presents the
same information as
the one in Figure
18-14, but it uses a
different layout.

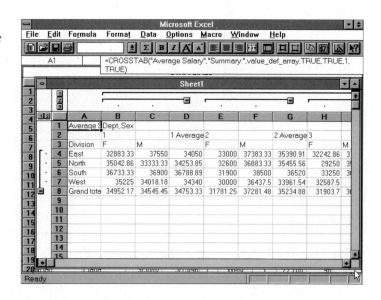

Figure 18-15 we have assigned two fields (Dept. and Sex) to the column dimension and only one (Division) to the row dimension. You might want to experiment with some of these options to find the layout that best serves your own needs.

Subtotaling options

Notice that after each set of departmental rows, the table in Figure 18-14 includes a row that gives averages for the current division. Row 7, for example, shows that the average salaries for all departments of the East Division are $32,185.71 for women, $37,685.71 for men, and $34,542.86 for all employees. This is the ReportWizard's default, or automatic, approach to subtotaling. You can apply a variety of other kinds of subtotaling as well.

For example, suppose that at the bottom of each division's information you want to include rows that show the number of employees by sex, the total salaries by sex, and the average salaries by sex. Starting from the crosstab shown in Figure 18-14, select any cell in the crosstab worksheet, choose the Crosstab command from the Data menu, and click the Modify Current Crosstab button. The ReportWizard presents its Row Categories dialog box. In the lower right corner of the dialog box, you will see the names of your two row fields — Division and Dept. Select Division and click the Options button. The dialog box shown in Figure 18-16 appears.

FIGURE 18-16.
*The Row Category
Options command lets
you choose alternative
subtotals.*

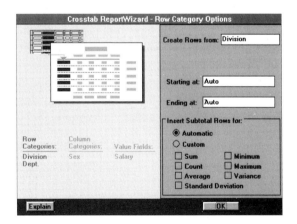

In the bottom section of this dialog box, click the Custom option button. Next, select the check boxes for the subtotaling functions you want to use — Sum, Count, and Average. (Note that if you want no subtotals at all, you can choose the Custom option button and deselect all the check boxes.) Click OK, click the fast-forward button, and then click the Create It button. The ReportWizard displays the table shown in Figure 18-17 on the following page.

FIGURE 18-17.
*We used the Row
Category Options
command to add
two more subtotal
lines to the table.*

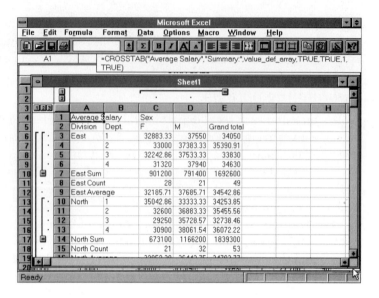

More aggregation options

Earlier in this chapter we saw that clicking the Options button in the Values Field dialog box lets you choose an aggregation function — for example, to change sums to averages or counts. The dialog box that appears when you click the Options button is shown in Figure 18-18. Near the center of the dialog box is a set of check boxes that let you analyze your aggregated data in various other ways. If we select the box labeled Percent of Row, for example, the ReportWizard creates the table shown in Figure 18-19. In this table we can see, among other things, that women in Department 1 of the East Division make, on average, 96.57 percent of the average salary earned by all employees.

FIGURE 18-18.
*The check boxes in the
center of this dialog
box let you analyze
your aggregate data
in various ways.*

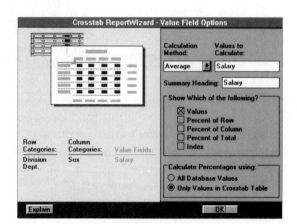

FIGURE 18-19.
We selected Percent of Row in the Value Field Options dialog box. The additional information in the table tells us, for example, that the average of women's salaries in Department 1 of Division East is 96.57% of the average salary for all employees of that division.

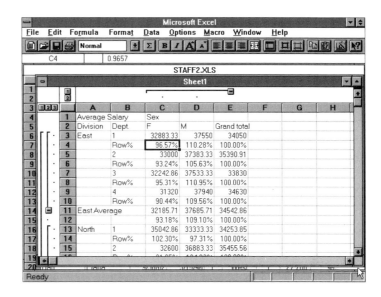

If you choose any of the percentage aggregation options, be sure also to use the option buttons at the bottom of the dialog box to indicate whether percentages should be calculated with respect to the entire database or only with respect to those records included in the crosstab. In the examples we've considered so far, the crosstab has included all the records in the database, so this choice is irrelevant. In other cases, however, you might crosstabulate only part of the original data. (See "Crosstabulating a subset of the database," later in this chapter.)

Using multiple value fields

In all the examples so far in this chapter, our crosstab tables have used either no value field or one value field. In Figures 18-2 and 18-9, for example, the value field is the Amount field from an expense database. In Figures 18-14, 18-15, 18-17, and 18-19, the value field is the Salary field from a personnel database. The crosstab in Figure 18-13, meanwhile, uses no value field at all; the table merely shows the number of records in the database, broken down by the table's row and column headings.

The Crosstab ReportWizard can also handle multiple value fields. From your personnel database, for example, you might be interested in seeing a table that reports average age as well as average salary for employees of each sex, with the figures organized by departments within divisions. Figure 18-20 on the following page shows how such a table might look (after formatting).

To include additional value fields in your table specification, simply select the fields you want in the Value Fields dialog box. Select the first field and click Add,

FIGURE 18-20.
In this table, we've used two value fields, Salary and Age, and applied the AVERAGE function to both aggregates.

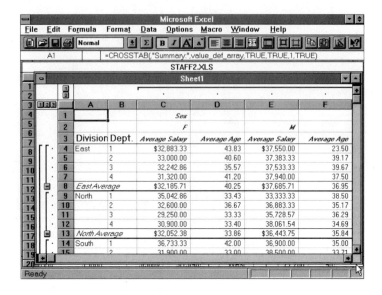

select the second field and click Add, and so on. If you want to use a nondefault form of aggregation (for example, if you want to use the AVERAGE function instead of the SUM function), select the field name to which you want to apply the nondefault aggregation. Next, click Options, open the drop-down list box, and choose your function. Be sure to do this with each value field if you want nondefault aggregations for each.

When you use multiple value fields, the Crosstab ReportWizard presents a dialog box, shown in Figure 18-21, in which you can specify the layout of the table.

FIGURE 18-21.
When you use multiple value fields, you need to choose from this menu of layout options.

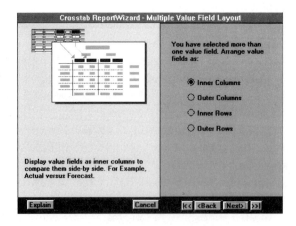

We've used the default option, called Inner Columns, in Figure 18-20. For each combination of row and column fields, this option puts our two value fields side by side on the same row.

Grouping numeric and date fields

In the first example we looked at in this chapter, the report of expense amounts by expense category (see Figures 18-2 and 18-9), we used a date field as our column field and grouped the output by quarter. Grouping options such as the one used in this example are available for any date or numeric field. By default, the ReportWizard treats each value in each field as a separate case and gives it its own column or row (depending on whether you've specified the field as a row field or a column field). To override this default, first select the field name in the lower list box of the Row Fields or Column Fields dialog box. Then, click the Options button and specify your grouping preference on the second line of the dialog box that appears.

Crosstabulating a subset of the database

All the examples we've considered so far crosstabulate entire databases. In some cases, you might be interested in analyzing particular records only. You can filter the data supplied to the ReportWizard in either of two ways — by creating a database criteria range or by specifying Starting at and Ending at values in the ReportWizard's own dialog boxes.

Creating a criteria range is the more powerful of the two methods because it lets you specify computed criteria. (See Chapter 17.) But you might find that specifying end points in the ReportWizard's dialog boxes is as effective and quicker under most circumstances. You can also combine the two methods.

To specify end points in a ReportWizard dialog box, select the appropriate field name in the lower list box of the Row Fields or Column Fields dialog box. Next, click the Options button. In the Options dialog box, you'll find text boxes labeled Starting at and Ending at. The default value in these boxes is *Auto*, which tells the ReportWizard to begin with whichever record would appear first in Excel's sorting order and stop at the record that would appear last. Figure 18-22 on the following page shows how the dialog box would look for an Age field if you wanted the ReportWizard to exclude records whose Age values were less than 20 or greater than 50. In this dialog box, we've also asked the ReportWizard to group the remaining records in bunches of five years.

FIGURE 18-22.
*We've used the
Options dialog box to
limit the crosstab to
records whose Age
values fall between 20
and 50 and asked the
ReportWizard to
analyze the remaining
records in groups of
five years.*

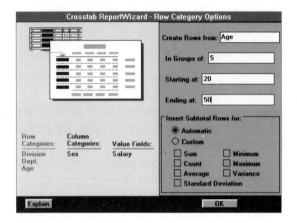

Other table creation options

By default the Crosstab ReportWizard creates crosstab tables in a new worksheet (not in your database worksheet), outlines the resulting table, assigns range names to the table's columns and rows as well as to the table itself, and stores pointers that let you "drill down" (incrementally go to the next level of detail) for a detailed view of any aggregate value. When you ask the ReportWizard to modify an existing crosstab, by default it overwrites the current crosstab (the one you're modifying), rather than creating another brand-new worksheet.

If you want to change any of these defaults, click the Set Table Creation Options button in the ReportWizard's Final dialog box. Bear in mind, though, that you can have only one crosstab in a worksheet. If you ask the ReportWizard to create a crosstab in the same worksheet as your database, and you subsequently decide to create a new crosstab (still in the same worksheet), the new table overwrites the old. Therefore, we recommend letting Excel create separate sheets for each of your crosstab reports. If you want to keep crosstabs closely associated with their underlying data, you can bind separate database and crosstab worksheets together in a workbook. If you want to see them on the same worksheet, you can create crosstabs in separate worksheets, and then use the Copy and Paste Picture Link commands to put an image of each crosstab in the database worksheet.

MACROS

19

Macro Basics

A macro is a series of formulas and statements that instruct Microsoft Excel to take an action or perform a calculation for you. Macros are like computer programs, but they run completely within Excel. You can use them to automate tedious or frequently repeated tasks, standardize tasks that you want performed exactly the same way every time, or collapse long sequences of menu commands and mouse movements into convenient keyboard shortcuts.

Macros are divided into two broad categories: *command macros* and *function macros*. Command macros are macros that you initiate to carry out sequences of actions much more quickly than you could do yourself. For example, you can create a command macro that enters a series of dates across a row of the worksheet and then centers those dates in the cells. Or you can create a command macro that defines print settings in the Page Setup dialog box and then chooses the Print command. Command macros can be very simple or extremely complex. They can even be interactive; that is, you can write macros that request information from the user and then act upon that information.

Function macros are initiated in the same way as built-in functions (when Excel calculates the formulas on a worksheet or macro sheet). Function macros make calculations and return values without performing actions in the workspace. Once you create a function macro, you can use it like any other function (except for minor differences that we'll discuss in "Function macro rules," later in this chapter). Often, function macros let you condense into one cell calculations that would otherwise occupy a large amount of space in a worksheet.

We'll cover both command and function macros in this chapter. Chapter 20 presents an overview of Excel's many macro functions. Chapter 21 discusses advanced techniques for creating interactive command macros.

Macro sheets

In Microsoft Excel you create and store macros on macro sheets, which are very similar to worksheets. In many spreadsheet programs, macros are stored in the cells of the related worksheet. Because you create and store Excel macros independently of any specific worksheet, you can create one macro and use it with many worksheets. In fact, you can store several macros on one macro sheet and use that sheet as a macro library. Storing macros in a separate file also helps prevent accidental deletions or other errors that might damage the macro or the worksheet data.

Creating a macro sheet

To create a macro, you first need to open a macro sheet. You do this by choosing the New command from the File menu and selecting the Macro Sheet option. A blank macro sheet like the one in Figure 19-1 appears. As you can see, a macro sheet, like a worksheet, is divided into rows and columns, with numbers and letters as headings. The menu bar above a macro sheet is identical to the one above a worksheet.

Macro sheets do differ from worksheets, however. For instance, the columns in the macro sheet appear wider than those in the worksheet. (Actually, this difference exists because the Formulas option in the Display dialog box is selected by default.

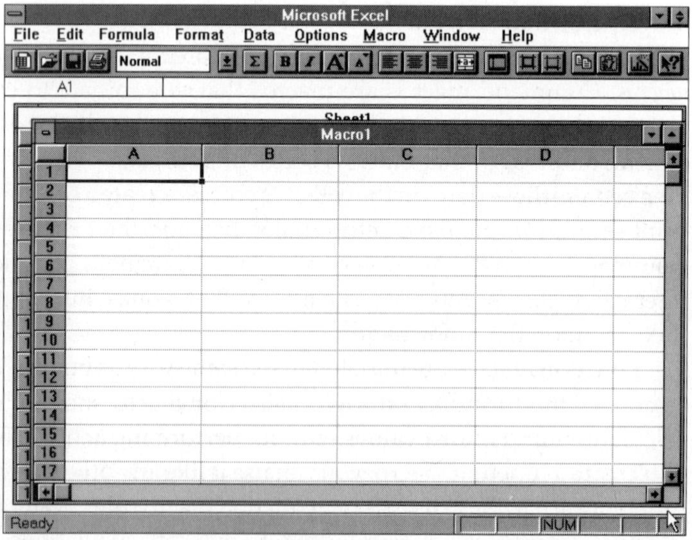

FIGURE 19-1.
A macro sheet looks very much like a worksheet.

Thus, you'll see the formulas in the cells in the macro sheet instead of the results of those formulas.) In addition, Excel calculates macro formulas only when you execute the macro, and then always in strict top-down, linear order. For this reason, you don't have the same control over recalculation or iteration in a macro sheet that you have in a worksheet. Also, as you'll see, the Define Name command works a bit differently in macro sheets.

Except for these differences, macro sheets are nearly identical to worksheets. You make and edit entries, copy and move entries, and insert and delete rows the same way you do in a worksheet. Similarly, you use the same commands and techniques to save and open macro files that you use to save and open worksheets and charts.

Functions available for creating macros

When you choose Paste Function from the Formula menu in a macro sheet, you'll see the dialog box shown in Figure 19-2. If you scroll through the list of functions, you'll immediately see the most important difference between worksheets and macro sheets: You can use many more functions in a macro sheet than you can in a worksheet. These functions are the building blocks you use to construct command and function macros.

FIGURE 19-2.
The Paste Function
dialog box.

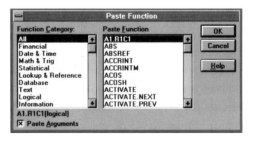

You can use any of the standard worksheet functions (discussed in Chapter 6) in the macros you create. These functions return values to a formula in a macro sheet the same way they do to a formula in a worksheet. You can use the remaining functions, which are part of Excel's *macro language,* only on macro sheets. These functions fall broadly into five groups, which correspond loosely to the categories displayed under the Function Category list in the Paste Function dialog box:

■ *Command-equivalent functions,* which take the place of commands on menus in Excel. For example, the CLEAR function is the macro equivalent of the Clear command on the Edit menu; it allows you to create macros that erase cells. This group corresponds to the functions in the Commands category.

■ *Action-equivalent functions,* which simulate the process of using the mouse or keyboard to perform an action. For example, the FORMULA function is equivalent to entering text into a cell of a worksheet. The ACTIVATE function is equivalent to bringing a specified window to the front or choosing the window's name from the Window menu. Other action-equivalent functions allow you to select ranges (SELECT), scroll through a worksheet (VSCROLL and HSCROLL), manipulate an outline (PROMOTE and DEMOTE), and perform similar tasks from within a macro. This group corresponds to the functions in the Commands category.

■ *Customizing functions,* for creating menus, commands, and dialog boxes, and for working with the toolbar. When you create a command macro, you can use customizing functions to automate a process even further. For example, you can use the ADD.MENU and ADD.COMMAND functions to add the name of a macro to a menu so that you can choose it like a standard command. Or you can use the MESSAGE function to have a macro report on its progress during a complicated procedure. Using the DIALOG.BOX function, you can create dialog boxes that request information and then use that information to modify the way the macro behaves. You can even create custom help screens that provide on-line documentation by using the HELP function. This group corresponds to the functions in the Customizing category.

■ *Control functions,* for performing a variety of programming tasks. You can use control functions to create loops and branches in macros (for example, FOR, NEXT, and WHILE), and for other purposes, including working with text files (for example, FOPEN, FCLOSE, FREAD, FWRITE). This group corresponds to the functions in the DDE/External category.

■ *Information functions,* also known as *value-returning functions,* which take no explicit action other than returning various types of information to an executing macro. For example, the ACTIVE.CELL function returns the reference of the active cell in a worksheet; the DOCUMENTS function returns an array of all the open documents in the workspace; and the GET.FORMULA function returns the contents of a cell. This group corresponds to the functions in the Information category. Many of the functions in this category are also available to worksheets.

You'll see examples of many of these functions in this and subsequent chapters as we show you how to create and use macros. First, let's delve into the process of developing a macro.

Creating command macros by hand

Creating a command macro is a three-step process. First, you create a new macro sheet or open an existing macro sheet. Second, you enter the functions that make up the macro within a single column in the macro sheet. Third, you use the Define Name command to assign a name to the macro, identifying it as a command macro and perhaps assigning a shortcut key to invoke it. To run the macro, you can use either the Run command on the Macro menu or the assigned shortcut key.

A simple text-entry macro

Let's investigate this process by creating a simple macro for entering text into the currently selected cell in a worksheet.

Entering the macro

If you haven't already done so, begin by creating a new macro sheet and save it as MACRO1.XLM. (See "Creating a macro sheet," earlier in this chapter.) In cell A1, type the text entry *First*. Although this title is not required, it helps you name and maintain the macro. Next, move to cell A2 and enter the formula

=FORMULA("This is my first Microsoft Excel macro!")

Then select cell A3 and enter the formula

=RETURN()

Your screen should look like Figure 19-3. (We widened column A so that you could view the entire FORMULA statement.)

FIGURE 19-3.
*We entered a label and
two functions to
create a simple macro.*

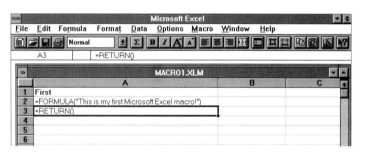

FORMULA and RETURN are two of the functions from Excel's macro language. FORMULA allows you to enter text, numbers, or formulas into cells of the worksheet. In this case, the FORMULA function in cell A2 enters the label

This is my first Microsoft Excel macro!

into the currently selected cell when you invoke the macro.

The information in the argument of FORMULA could also be a formula or a value. For example,

=FORMULA("=SUM(A1:A20)")

enters the formula =SUM(A1:A20) in the active cell.

The RETURN function signals the end of the macro. All macros end either with a RETURN function or a HALT function. (We'll discuss HALT in Chapter 20.) If you don't end a macro with one of these functions, when you try to run the macro, Excel displays the alert message *Did not encounter RETURN() or HALT() on macro sheet.*

Defining the macro

Now that the macro is in place, give it a name. The name of a macro is simply a range name assigned to the first cell in the macro. You name macros the same way you name cells in a worksheet — by selecting the cell and choosing Define Name from the Formula menu.

For example, to name this sample macro, select cell A1 and choose the Define Name command. You'll see a dialog box like the one in Figure 19-4. Notice that Excel has entered the reference of the selected cell, A1, in the Refers to text box and has entered the text from the same cell, *First,* in the Name text box. (Recall from Chapter 3 that when you use the Define Name command, Excel always looks for a possible name in the active cell, the cell above, or the cell to the left.)

FIGURE 19-4.
Use the Define Name dialog box to identify your macros.

Before you click OK or press Enter to accept the suggested name, tell Excel that the macro you've created is a command macro. To do this, select the Command option at the bottom of the dialog box. If you forget to select this option, Excel assigns the name *First* to cell A1, but it doesn't know that cell A1 is the first cell in a command macro.

When you select the Command option, the Key option becomes available. This option allows you to assign a shortcut key to the macro so that you can run it by pressing Ctrl along with the shortcut key. You can assign only single letters (not numbers or other characters) to shortcut keys, but Excel distinguishes between uppercase and lowercase letters; for example, the name *A* is different from *a*. To assign a shortcut key to our macro, click the text box and enter a letter. (We'll use the letter *f*.)

If you want, you can assign a category to the macro; *First* is a command macro, so you could select the Commands category. The next time you call up the Paste Function dialog box, *First* will be listed under that category. Finally, click on the Add button to define the macro's name and shortcut key, or click OK to define the macro and close the dialog box.

Running the macro

Now let's run the macro. To do this, move back to a worksheet window and select any empty cell. Choose Run from the Macro menu. You'll see a dialog box like the one in Figure 19-5.

FIGURE 19-5.
You can use the Run dialog box to invoke macros.

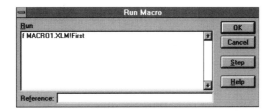

The list box on the left side of the Run dialog box displays the names of all the command macros that reside in all open macro sheets. Because you've created only one macro, only one name appears in the list. Notice that the name has three parts: the shortcut key you've assigned, the name of the macro sheet that contains the macro, and the name of the macro. As with all external references in Excel, the two parts of the name are separated by an exclamation point.

To run the macro, select its name in the Run dialog box and click OK or press Enter, or simply double-click the name. Watch what happens in the worksheet.

To run the macro using its assigned shortcut key, simply select any cell in the worksheet and press Ctrl-f. The macro should run immediately, entering the text in the cell you selected.

In effect, this simple command macro is a storehouse for a series of keystrokes. After you've created this macro, you need never type these keystrokes again. Instead, to enter these characters in a cell, simply select the cell and run the macro.

Although this macro is trivial, it illustrates all the basic characteristics of macros: They are stored in a macro sheet; they are made up of functions; they have names, which are simply range names assigned to the first cell in each macro; and they are executed by selecting a name from the list in the Run dialog box. Every command macro we create follows these basic rules.

A more complex text-entry macro

Suppose you're creating a monthly report and want to enter abbreviations for the names of the months (Jan, Feb, Mar, and so on) into the range B4:M4. If you create reports like this fairly often, you could write a macro to perform this task for you. You can use a macro like the one in Figure 19-6 to create these headers. Let's walk through this macro one line at a time.

NOTE: This macro is given as an example only. Remember that you can use Excel 4's AutoFill feature to accomplish the same task.

Entering the macro

The label in cell A5, *Header,* serves as the name of the macro. The formula in cell A6 is

=SELECT(!B4)

The SELECT function, one of the most commonly used functions in the Excel macro language, is action-equivalent; it corresponds to the action of selecting a cell. In our example, the result of this function is identical to selecting cell B4. Notice that the reference to cell B4 is preceded by an exclamation point, marking it as an external reference. Because the exclamation point is not preceded by a document name, Excel assumes you're referring to cell B4 in whichever worksheet is currently active. By not linking the action to a specific worksheet, you can use this macro on any active worksheet.

The FORMULA statement in the next line of the macro tells Excel to enter the text *Jan* into the selected cell.

The formula in cell A8

=SELECT(!C4)

FIGURE 19-6.
This command macro creates a series of column headings.

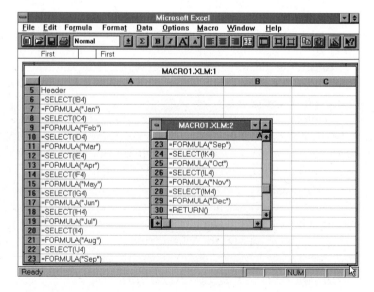

selects cell C4, and the FORMULA statement in cell A9 enters the text *Feb* into that
cell. The macro continues in this way to cell A30, which marks the end of the macro
with a RETURN function.

You can type each formula individually, but a faster way to create the macro
is to enter only the first two formulas in the range A6:A7. Next, choose Copy from
the Edit menu, select the range A8:A29, and choose Paste from the Edit menu.
Finally, go back and edit each formula until the macro looks like the one shown in
Figure 19-6.

Naming the macro

Before you use this macro, you should give it a name. Select cell A5 and choose the
Define Name command. The Define Name dialog box appears, and the label from
cell A5, *Header*, is suggested as the macro's name. After you name the macro, select
the Command button to define it as a command macro, enter *h* as the shortcut key,
and then click OK or press Enter.

Running the macro

To run the Header macro, activate an open worksheet and select any cell. Then press
Ctrl-h. Figure 19-7 shows the result. (We narrowed the columns so that you could
see all the label entries in columns B through M.)

FIGURE 19-7.
*This worksheet shows
the results of the
column-heading
macro.*

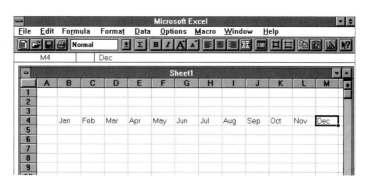

Macro sheet rules

When you run a macro, Excel begins by calculating the formula in the first cell in
the macro. Then it moves down one row and calculates the formula in the next cell
in that column, and then the next, and the next, and so on. Macro calculation continues in this linear fashion until Excel comes across a RETURN or a HALT function
(which stops the macro) or a GOTO or a *ref()* function (which causes execution to
branch to the macro routine that *ref()* names), or until an error occurs.

Macros can include formulas that return values, functions that take actions, and constant values, such as numbers or text. If a cell contains a function that takes an action, the macro takes that action immediately when the cell is calculated. If a cell contains a formula that produces a value, Excel calculates the value of the formula, which can then be used by other formulas later in the macro. If a cell contains a constant value — a text entry or number — or is blank, Excel skips over that cell and proceeds to the next cell.

Although the macros we've built so far have been in column A, you can put a macro anywhere in a macro sheet. We could easily have entered our first macro in cells AZ100:AZ102. But convention — and sound practice — dictates that macros be entered only in the first few columns of your macro sheets. If you create macros in faraway corners, you might have a difficult time finding them when you need to edit them.

You can run any macro from within any worksheet. Keep in mind, though, that you can run only those macros that are stored in open macro sheets, and your computer's memory limits the number of macro sheets you can have open at any time. As soon as you open a macro sheet, Excel adds the names of the macros in that sheet to the list in the Run dialog box, with each name preceded by the name of the macro sheet in which the macro is stored. When you close a macro sheet, Excel removes the names of the macros in that sheet from the list.

Excel assigns the name *Macro1* to the first macro sheet you create in a given work session, the name *Macro2* to the second sheet you create, and so on. You can always use the Save As command to save a macro sheet under any name you desire.

One macro sheet can hold many macros. To enter a new macro in an existing sheet, select a blank portion of the sheet and enter the macro. As soon as you name a new macro in an existing macro sheet, its name appears in the list box of the Run dialog box.

Each macro in a macro sheet should have a unique name. If you assign a name to a macro in a macro sheet that already contains a macro with that name, the reference attached to the name changes from its old location to the new one, which might cause unexpected results when you run the macro. If two macros on different sheets have the same name, the Run dialog box lists both, and you can choose the one you want. If two macros have the same shortcut key, Excel executes the first one in the Run dialog box that has that shortcut key.

Macro subroutines

When you create complex macros, you may want one macro to call another, using the *ref()* syntax mentioned earlier. To illustrate this, we'll create a command-macro routine you could use by itself. Then we'll update the *Header* macro to take advantage of the new routine.

The *ref()* syntax lets you create *subroutines*. A subroutine is a program that contains a set of instructions; you can use these instructions by calling the name of the subroutine in another program rather than repeating the instructions. Subroutines simplify macros because they let you write a set of frequently used instructions once, instead of repeating the instructions everywhere they're needed.

Creating the subroutine

The *Dater* macro, shown in Figure 19-8, enters the label *Last Revision* into the currently selected cell and the NOW function into the next cell to the right. It displays the resulting number in the *m/d/yy* format.

FIGURE 19-8.
The Dater *macro
enters the revision
date of a worksheet.*

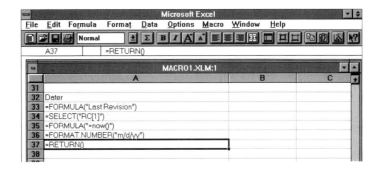

As before, we've entered the name of the macro, *Dater*, in the first cell of the macro. The second cell of the macro, A33, contains the formula

=FORMULA("Last Revision")

which enters the text *Last Revision* into the cell that is active when the macro is run. The formula in cell A34

=SELECT("RC[1]")

selects the cell one cell to the right of the active cell using the R1C1 method for describing relative cell locations. The formula

=FORMULA("=now()")

in cell A35 enters the formula *=NOW()* into that cell. Notice that the NOW function in this statement is enclosed in quotation marks. These quotation marks are required — they tell Excel to enter the specified text as a formula into the active cell.

The formula in cell A36

=FORMAT.NUMBER("m/d/yy")

is a command-equivalent function that instructs Excel to assign the *m/d/yy* number format to the selected cell. Finally, the RETURN function in cell A37 tells Excel that this is the end of the macro.

After naming the macro (*Dater*, with shortcut key *d*), test it by selecting cell A3 and pressing Ctrl-d. Figure 19-9 shows the result. Notice that the macro has entered the text *Last Revision* in cell A3 and the NOW formula in cell B3, resulting in the current date (in the format *m/d/yy*).

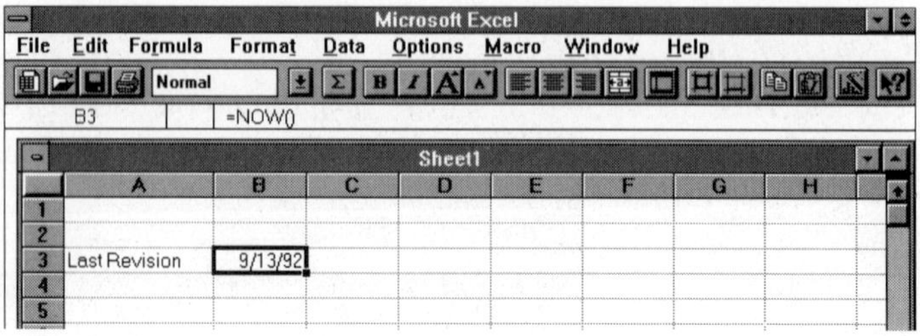

FIGURE 19-9.
This worksheet shows the results of the Dater macro.

This simple but useful macro illustrates how you can use the FORMULA function to enter formulas into a cell, as well as how you can use a command-equivalent function to choose a menu command from within a macro. It also demonstrates that you can easily use a command macro intended as a subroutine (that is, intended for use within another macro) as a stand-alone routine.

Updating the Header macro

Excel lets you run one macro from within another by including the name of the second macro as a function in the first macro. This is called the *ref()* syntax. For example, if the formula

=Test()

is executed in a macro, the formula immediately activates and runs the macro that begins at the cell named *Test*. Alternatively, you can use a cell reference to direct Excel to the appropriate starting cell:

=B50()

When Excel encounters the RETURN function at the end of the second macro, it returns to the cell below the one that contains the calling statement and resumes execution of the first macro.

Now let's modify the *Header* macro slightly, so that the header created by the macro also includes the revison date. To do this, select rows 6 and 7 and choose Insert from the Edit menu, opening up two empty cells in the macro, below the macro's title. Next, enter the following two formulas, as shown in Figure 19-10:

=SELECT(!A2)

=Dater()

The SELECT formula moves the active cell to cell A2. The second formula uses the *ref()* syntax to call the *Dater* macro as a subroutine. When *Dater* is executed, it

FIGURE 19-10.
We've modified the
Header *macro to*
include the revision
date.

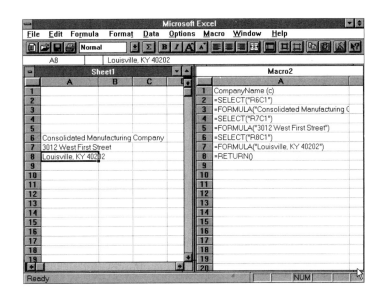

enters *Last Revision* into the active cell (A2) and then enters *=NOW()* into the cell one cell to the right. It then returns control to cell A8 in the *Header* macro. Finally, *Header* enters the rest of the labels in the header.

Creating command macros with the Recorder

Instead of typing command macros character by character into the cells of a macro sheet, you can instruct Microsoft Excel to create command macros simply by using the Recorder to record the keystrokes you type and the commands you issue.

After you've recorded a set of commands, you can ask Excel to "play back" those commands, duplicating exactly the actions you performed. As you might expect, this playback capability is most useful for writing macros that automate long or repetitive processes, such as entering and formatting tables or printing a certain section of a worksheet.

Creating a command macro with the Recorder is usually a four-step process:

1. Select a range in an open macro sheet and choose Set Recorder from the Macro menu to specify where you want the new macro placed. The Set Recorder command defines a range in the macro sheet. (This step is optional.)

2. Return to your document and choose Record from the Macro menu to turn the Recorder on and start recording. If you did not use the Set Recorder command in step 1 to establish a location for the macro, Excel opens a new macro sheet and requests a macro name and shortcut key before beginning to record your actions.

3. With the Recorder on, choose the commands and type the keystrokes you want to record.

4. When you finish, choose Stop Recorder from the Macro menu to turn the Recorder off.

Let's investigate this process by creating a simple macro that inserts a company name and address in a worksheet. Begin by saving and closing all open worksheets and macro sheets, and then open a new worksheet. Next, choose Record from the Macro menu. (We'll cover the use of the Set Recorder command in the next section.) Excel displays a dialog box like the one shown in Figure 19-11. Here, you can assign a name and shortcut key to the new macro. You can either accept Excel's suggested name (*Record1*, *Record2*, *Record3*, and so on) or enter a name in the Name text box — we'll use *CompanyName* and *c*. You can also select an option for storing the macro in a global macro sheet. A global macro sheet is visible after you use it if you choose Unhide from the Window menu after recording the macro. In this case, be sure that the Macro Sheet option is selected.

FIGURE 19-11.
The Record Macro
dialog box appears
when you issue the
Record command.

When you click OK, Excel opens a new macro sheet to hold the Recorder entries, enters the macro's name and shortcut key in the first column, and then waits for you to perform the steps you want to record. (The new macro sheet appears behind the active document window so that it won't interfere with your recording actions.) Excel displays the message *Recording* in the status bar.

As you enter keystrokes and issue commands in the worksheet, the Recorder stores each action in the next available cell of the macro sheet. You can watch this process, if you like, by choosing Stop Recorder and Arrange from the Window menu (select the Tiled option), and then Start Recorder, so that both the worksheet and the macro sheet are visible. For the purposes of this example, select cell A6 and enter

Consolidated Manufacturing Company

Move to cell A7 and enter

3012 West First Street

Then move to cell A8 and enter

Louisville, KY 40202

Then turn off the Recorder by choosing Stop Recorder from the Macro menu. This step is very important. If you leave the Recorder on accidentally, it records keystrokes and commands that you don't want in the macro.

Now switch back to the macro sheet. As you entered your company's name in the worksheet, Excel recorded your keystrokes in the macro sheet. Depending on how you've arranged your windows, the sheet should now look like Figure 19-12.

The entries that appear in cells A2 to A8 are the macro versions of the keystrokes you typed when you entered the address. For example, the statement in cell A4

    =SELECT("R7C1")

is the macro equivalent of selecting worksheet cell A7. Notice that Excel has recorded the references in the SELECT formulas as absolute references in the R1C1 format.

Excel can now insert your company's name and address into a worksheet whenever you run this macro. For a demonstration, activate the worksheet and clear cells A6:A9. Select any cell and press Ctrl-c. The macro inserts your company name and address in the worksheet.

FIGURE 19-12.
Excel records your keystrokes as you make entries in the worksheet.

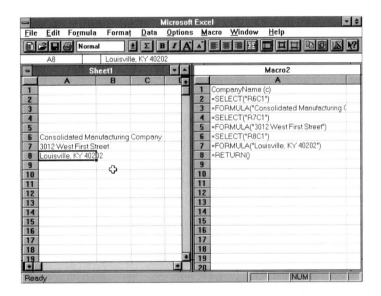

Setting the Recorder range

In the last example, the Recorder recorded your macro starting in the first cell of the first blank column. But what if you want to position a macro elsewhere in a macro sheet or add to an existing macro? For example, suppose you want macro statements to begin in cell C20 of an existing macro sheet. You can select cell C20 and then choose Set Recorder from the Macro menu. If you then choose Define Name and select *Recorder*, you'll see that the range assigned is C20. Next, instead of using the Record command, use the Start Recorder command and proceed as before. (You'll probably want to activate the window you'll be working in before you choose Start Recorder. Otherwise, the window activation will be recorded, too.)

Let's recreate the simple date-header macro from Figure 19-6 using the Recorder. To begin, define the *Recorder* range in the macro sheet.

Excel offers two options for selecting the *Recorder* range. If you select one cell in the macro sheet and choose Set Recorder from the Macro menu, Excel uses the entire column below that cell as the *Recorder* range. If, on the other hand, you select a range of cells, Excel uses only that range. It is difficult to predict how long a macro will be when you create it with the Recorder. Because the one-cell option allows your macros to be as long as necessary, we prefer it.

To set the *Recorder* range in our example, open MACRO1.XLM (the macro sheet in which we created the first Header macro), select cell A50, enter the title of the macro, *Header2*, and then choose the Set Recorder command. Next, open a new worksheet and select Start Recorder. Now select cell B4 in the worksheet and type *Jan,* press Tab, type *Feb,* press Tab, type *Mar,* press Tab, and so on. When you reach *Dec,* press Enter instead of Tab; pressing Tab would be recorded as another SELECT formula at the end of the macro.

When you finish, choose Stop Recorder from the Macro menu. Now switch back to the macro sheet. It should contain the macro shown in Figure 19-13.

Because you used the Set Recorder and Start Recorder commands, you haven't assigned a name or shortcut key to your macro. Select cell A50 and choose Define

FIGURE 19-13.
After you record the commands and entries in the worksheet, the macro sheet contains this macro.

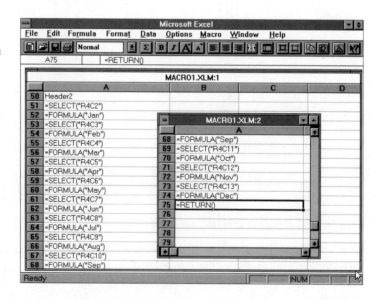

Name from the Formula menu. Confirm the name (*Header2*) in the Name field, select the Command option, enter *C* (capital *C*) in the Key text box, put the macro in the Commands category, and click OK.

Now use the New command to create a new worksheet. When the new worksheet is ready, select any cell and press Ctrl-C. As soon as you do this, the macro selects cell B4 in the new worksheet and enters the labels *Jan, Feb,* and so on in cells B4:M4.

Adding to the macro

Now suppose you want to change the *Header2* macro so that it not only enters the headers into row 4 but also centers them. To make this change, select the worksheet in which you just used the macro, choose the Start Recorder command, and select the range of cells you want to format — B4:M4. Next, click the Center Alignment button in the toolbar, and then choose the Stop Recorder command. Figure 19-14 shows the result.

Notice that the entries in cells A75 and A76 are now

=SELECT("R4C2:R4C13","R4C13")

and

=ALIGNMENT(3,FALSE,3,0)

and that the RETURN function that was once in cell A75 is now in cell A77. Here's why: When you start the Recorder without first resetting the *Recorder* range, the

FIGURE 19-14.
We added SELECT and ALIGNMENT functions to this macro using the Recorder.

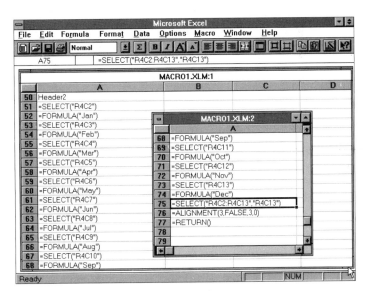

Recorder writes over the RETURN statement and adds the new commands to the end of the macro. As long as you haven't reset the *Recorder* range and blank cells remain within the range, you can stop and restart the Recorder as often as you like. This lets you make changes to the worksheet or execute commands and then restart the Recorder without having to reset the range. (Your version of the SELECT function may have only one argument; we selected the range from M4 to B4, leaving M4 the active cell. Because we did this, Excel added the second argument, which specifies the active cell if it isn't the top left cell in the recorded range.)

If you've reset the *Recorder* range but want to add to a previously created macro, select the title of the macro and use the Set Recorder command. The recorder begins recording at the last RETURN command in the column. If there's a macro below the one to which you want to add, the new commands are added to that macro. To prevent this, simply insert a range of several cells where you want the recorded formulas to go, select the range, and then choose the Set Recorder command to define the *Recorder* range to the open area.

Using absolute and relative references

When you pulled down the Macro menu, you may have noticed the Relative Record command. Relative Record and Absolute Record let you specify whether you want cell references to be recorded as relative references or absolute references. If you choose Relative Record, the menu selection changes to Absolute Record, allowing you to switch back to absolute references later. (You can toggle back and forth between Relative Record and Absolute Record at any time — even in the middle of recording a macro.) No matter which option you select, the Recorder records any cell references in the R1C1 format. In the preceding example, we accepted the default, Absolute Record.

Let's recreate the macro we just created, this time using Relative Record instead of Absolute Record. Select cell B52 in MACRO1.XLM and choose the Set Recorder command. Now create a new worksheet and select cell B4 in that worksheet. Next choose the Relative Record command to change the recording method to relative. Choose the Start Recorder command. Type *Jan*, press Tab, type *Feb,* press Tab, type *Mar,* press Tab, and so on until you've entered labels for the entire year. When you finish, choose the Stop Recorder command.

Figure 19-15 shows the macro sheet after you create this macro. Because we started the new macro in cell B52, it appears side by side with the corresponding

FIGURE 19-15.
We recorded this macro using relative references.

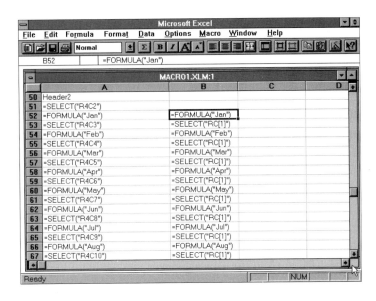

commands in the absolute-reference version. As you can see, the new version of the macro in column B uses only relative references. For example, the statement in cell A53 is

=SELECT("R4C3")

but the entry in cell B53 is

=SELECT("RC[1]")

The first macro always puts the column headings in the range B4:M4, no matter which cell is active when the macro is run. The second macro, on the other hand, puts the column headings in the current row, beginning with the active cell. This version allows you to enter these headings anywhere in any worksheet.

Obviously, the position of the active cell makes a great deal of difference when you use a macro that was recorded with relative references. Before you run the macro, always select the cell in which you want to start the series. Otherwise, the series will begin wherever the active cell happens to be.

Which form is better — relative or absolute? It depends. Absolute cell references are useful when you want to perform the same action in exactly the same spot in several worksheets, or when you want to perform the same action repeatedly in the same part of one worksheet. Relative cell references are useful when you want to perform an action anywhere in a worksheet.

More about recording

Excel's macro recorder runs more smoothly than most. In some spreadsheet programs, if you type a word incorrectly or choose the wrong command, both the mistake and your efforts to correct it are recorded. Excel's macro recorder does not record an action until you complete it. For example, the Recorder does not record a cell as being selected until you take some action in it, such as invoking a formatting or an editing command. Similarly, the Recorder does not record a menu command that calls up a dialog box until you complete it. If you choose such a command and then click Cancel, the Recorder does not include the command in the macro.

You'll find this feature of the Recorder very helpful because you'll end up with fewer errors in your recorded macros. Even so, the Recorder records your commands literally, so be careful to limit your actions to choosing commands, selecting cells, and making entries you want to record. Also, remember to turn the Recorder off when you've finished recording or when you need to correct a mistake.

If you choose to use a range instead of a single cell as the *Recorder* range, it might become full before you finish recording the macro. If this occurs, Excel stops recording and displays an alert box with the message *Recorder range is full*. If you see this error and want to continue recording, activate the macro sheet and select a new and larger *Recorder* range that includes the incomplete macro. If no blank cells are available below the *Recorder* range, you could define a new *Recorder* range in a different part of the macro sheet and use a GOTO function to join the two macros together. (The GOTO function is discussed in the next chapter.) However, because this leads to complex macro sheets, it's generally better to cut and paste macros to rearrange them in the macro sheet, use the Insert command to open up more space, or break your macros into smaller routines and use the *ref()* syntax to link the subroutines together.

Debugging macros

Macros don't always work correctly. They can fail because of syntax errors or because of function arguments that don't make sense. For example, the formula

    =COLUMN.WIDTH(–1)

causes an error because the argument –1 is not acceptable. Similarly, the formula

    =SELECT(nextRight)

where *nextRight* is defined as

    ="!B1"

causes an error because its argument is invalid: the SELECT function requires either a reference in the active worksheet (such as !B1) or a text argument in the R1C1 format (such as ="RC[1]").

One thing is certain: If you create macros, you'll make mistakes. Like all programmers, you'll spend a good deal of time correcting, or debugging, macros. Fortunately, Microsoft Excel makes this task relatively easy. When you run a macro and Excel encounters an error, it stops calculating the macro and displays an alert box like the one in Figure 19-16. This alert box tells you that an error has occurred, shows you the location of the error, and gives you four options: Halt, Step, Continue, or Goto. (The fifth, Help, leads you to the macro error topic in Excel's Help system.)

FIGURE 19-16.
This alert box tells you where an error has occurred.

The Halt option simply stops the macro. You could then use the reference given in the dialog box to trace the problem, but it's usually easier to click the Goto button to both stop the macro and jump to the cell that contained the error.

The Continue option causes Excel to ignore the error and continue to the next statement in the macro. You won't usually select this option, because an error in one cell of a macro often results in accumulated errors in subsequent cells. If you click the Continue option, you'll likely encounter more errors before the macro is finished.

The Step option causes Excel to continue processing the macro one step at a time, beginning with the line after the line that caused the error. As Excel executes each line of the macro, it stops, displays the Single Step dialog box, shown in Figure 19-17 on the following page, and waits for your instructions. Because the macro proceeds step by step, you can easily locate errors.

"Deactivating" a formula in a macro

The primary difference between a formula, which is executed, and a constant value, which isn't, is that formulas are always preceded by an equal sign. Therefore, if you're building a lengthy macro and enter a particular formula, but you want to run the macro without executing that formula, simply remove the equal sign, converting the formula into text. When you run the macro, Excel skips past the deactivated formula as if it weren't there.

FIGURE 19-17.
Use the Single Step
dialog box to walk
through a macro one
line at a time.

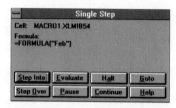

The Step Into button carries out the next instruction; if the formula in the next cell contains a reference to another macro, Excel steps through that macro as well. The Step Over button carries out the next instruction, but doesn't step through macro subroutines. The Halt and Continue buttons in the Single Step dialog box behave as you would expect. If you click on the Pause button the Step dialog box disappears, so you can, for example, check the contents of certain cells.

When you choose Resume from the Macro menu, Excel displays the Step dialog box again and returns to the last instruction carried out. The Evaluate button is very useful for debugging because it calculates each expression within a formula, one part at a time, displaying each intermediate result as it goes.

Clicking either the Step Into or the Step Over button after an error has occurred is usually not very helpful, because Excel begins stepping from the cell that follows the cell that contains the error. You're better off selecting the Halt option and then rerunning the macro from the beginning using Step mode.

Excel provides four ways to invoke Step mode before an error occurs. First, you can start the macro from the Run dialog box by selecting the name of the macro and then clicking on the Step button. When you do this, Excel displays the Single Step dialog box.

Keeping an eye on the macro sheet

If you want to see what's going on in the macro sheet as the macro runs, try using the Display command from the Options menu to display values rather than formulas. Then use the Arrange command to resize and reposition the macro sheet and other documents in your workspace so that you can see all the action. (It's a good idea to close any extraneous documents before you test a macro; that way, you can avoid accidental destruction of data.) Activate the document on which you want the macro to operate and then run the macro. (If the macro operates on more than one document, activate the first document in the sequence.) When you run the macro, you'll be able to see the results of the macro formulas as they are calculated. At the same time, you'll be able to see the effects of those calculations on the active document(s).

Second, you can interrupt a macro that's running at any time by pressing Esc. Again, you can stop the macro, use Step mode, or continue. If you use Esc to halt a macro as soon as it begins and then select Step, you can step through all but the first few lines of the macro.

Third, you can insert one or more STEP functions in the form

=STEP()

into your macro at the point(s) where you want to begin using Step mode. When it runs into a STEP function, Excel presents the Single Step dialog box, letting you walk through the macro one formula at a time. If your macro contains more than one STEP function, you can use the Continue button in the Single Step dialog box to tell Excel to run the macro as usual until it locates another STEP function, whereupon the program enters Step mode again.

Fourth, you can choose the Step Macro tool on the Macro toolbar for stepping through a macro routine, beginning with the active cell. To display the Macro toolbar, choose Toolbars from the Options menu, select the Macro toolbar, and click the Show button.

A different kind of error

So far, we've considered only those errors that make it impossible for Excel to compute the macro. However, errors that occur when a macro runs properly but doesn't do what you expect can be even more troublesome. Because Excel doesn't recognize this type of error, it doesn't stop the macro when such an error occurs. As a result, the error can be very destructive. If the macro includes such functions as CLEAR or EDIT.DELETE, your worksheet might be ruined before you know it.

To avoid this type of error, build your macros one routine at a time, test each routine before you go on to the next, and use the *ref()* syntax to connect the parts of a large macro system together. These tactics allow you to debug the macro a few lines at a time, which is easier than debugging the entire system at once. We also suggest that you use a "dummy" worksheet, whenever possible, to test macros. Either use a blank worksheet or create a copy of the worksheet in which you plan to run the macro, so that your original worksheet is safe from damage.

Formatting and documenting macros

As you can imagine, even relatively simple macros can be difficult to read. You can make your macros easier to understand, however, by entering explanatory text in the cells next to a macro in the macro sheet. For example, Figure 19-18 on the following page shows a modified *Dater* macro. We've adopted a three-column format, eliminated the gridlines by deselecting the Gridlines option in the Display dialog box, and added borders to mark the various parts of the macro. The second column holds the formulas of the macro itself, beginning with a title that describes the name of the macro and its associated shortcut key, if any. The text in the third column explains the purpose of each line in the macro.

FIGURE 19-18.
The Dater *macro, formatted and with comments.*

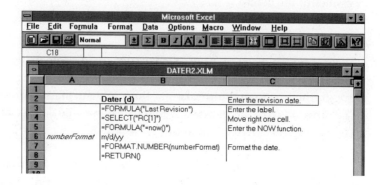

The first column holds the labels for named cells, such as the *numberFormat* label in cell A6. An easy way to create this arrangement of named cells in a macro sheet is to select columns A and B, choose the Create Names command from the Formula menu, select the Left Column option, and then click OK. In this case, the *numberFormat* label names cell B6, which contains the number format to be used in the next formula, B7.

Because Microsoft Excel ignores any text values it encounters in the process of calculating a macro, you can also include documentation between the statements in your macros. For example, in Figure 19-18 you could insert identifying phrases between the lines of the macro to flag named cells or subroutines.

Another way to document your macros is to give them descriptive names. The more descriptive the name, the better. For example, instead of naming your macro *Header*, you could name it *RelMonthsHeader*, where *Rel* indicates that the macro uses relative references and *MonthsHeader* describes the type of header the macro creates. Because you don't have to type the name of a command macro to run it, you need not keep its name short (although if the name is too long, it won't be completely visible in the Run scroll box). Using descriptive names for your macros is essential when you create many macros, and particularly if you create macros that have similar, but not identical, purposes.

How you document your macros is a matter of personal preference. It doesn't matter which method you select, as long as you do include documentation. Documentation is most important for long and complex macros, for macros that you look at only once in a while, and for macros you must explain to others.

You don't have to name command macros in Excel (although you must name function macros). If you don't give a command macro a name, you can still run it by choosing the Run command from the Macro menu. Of course, the macro you want to use will not appear in the list of macros in the Run dialog box. You have to enter its location in the Reference field at the bottom of the dialog box. For example, suppose you've created a macro that begins at cell G40 of the macro sheet named HEADERS, and you haven't given it a name. To run that macro, choose the Run command, type

=HEADERS!G40

and click OK or press Enter.

Similarly, if you don't tell Excel that a macro you've created is a command macro, it won't include the name of that macro in the Run list. Therefore, always specify the macro type each time you create a macro.

Creating custom functions

Custom functions, also known as user-defined functions, are one of the most innovative and exciting features of Microsoft Excel. These functions, implemented by function macros, accept information from the worksheet, perform calculations, and then return the result to the worksheet. The types of information-handling and calculation tasks that you can simplify, generalize, or streamline with custom functions are nearly unlimited.

Although Excel includes a multitude of built-in functions, you probably have specific sets of calculations that you perform regularly that could easily be condensed into functions. Suppose your company uses a complex mathematical formula for computing sales commissions. Wouldn't it be convenient if you had a function called *Commis* that would perform this calculation for you? Or suppose your company has a stepped discount schedule. Wouldn't it be helpful if you had a function called *Discount* that could compute the discount for you on any order? In this section, we'll show you how to create such functions using function macros.

You can also add custom functions to Excel and use them in exactly the same way you would any of the built-in functions, by saving the macro sheet in the special Add-In format, discussed in Chapter 21.

A simple commission function

To create a custom function, you typically use two macro functions — ARGUMENT and RETURN — as well as a series of formulas that calculate the value or values you want the function to return. The ARGUMENT function allows you to define the arguments the custom function uses. (We'll discuss the ARGUMENT function in "Functions available to function macros," later in this chapter.) The RETURN function returns the result of the custom function to the worksheet.

To see how these functions work, let's build a simple function macro. Suppose your company pays a commission of 10 percent on all sales. Each week, the payroll department computes each salesperson's commission for that week. The worksheet in Figure 19-19 shows the weekly sales of four salespeople. Let's create a function macro to compute their commissions.

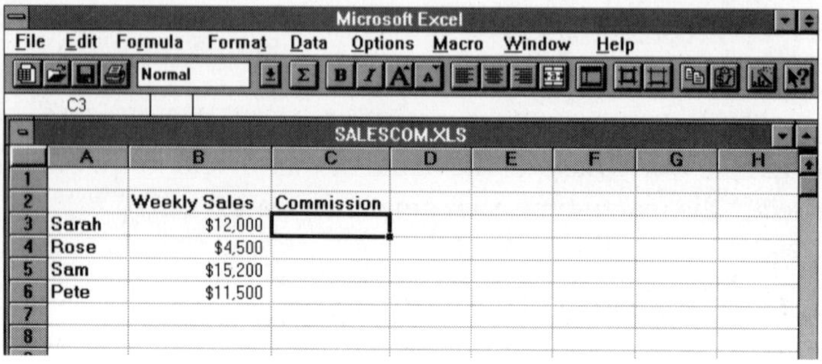

FIGURE 19-19.
We want to calculate each salesperson's commission.

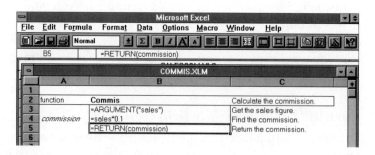

To begin, create a new macro sheet. In the macro sheet, enter the name of the function, *Commis*, in cell B2. Now save the macro sheet as COMMIS so that it has an XLM extension. Next, in cells B3:B5 enter the formulas

=ARGUMENT("sales")

=sales*0.1

=RETURN(commission)

Finally, enter the cell label *commission* in cell A4, select A4:B4, and choose Create Names from the Formula menu to assign the label to cell B4. Figure 19-20 shows the formatted macro sheet at this point. You can format the macro and add comments as shown in the figure, or in any way you want.

FIGURE 19-20.
This function macro calculates sales commissions.

Next, give the function macro a name. As with all other macros, this name is a label you assign to the first cell in the macro. The first cell in this macro is technically cell B3, but it's usually helpful to make the macro's title the first cell Excel executes when it runs the macro. If you do this, you can easily insert another formula between the title and the first line of the macro if you need to, without having to redefine the macro's starting point.

To name the macro, select cell B2 and choose Define Name from the Formula menu. Notice that the Refers to text box contains the reference of the selected cell, $B$2, and the Name text box contains the label from cell B2, *Commis.* Specify that the macro you're naming is a function macro by selecting the Function button. From the Category list, select the Financial option. (Although it's also a good idea to put all your functions in the User Defined category at first so you can find them easily.) To accept the default name, *Commis,* click OK or press Enter.

Now you're ready to use the new custom function. To do this, return to the worksheet shown in Figure 19-19 and select cell C3. Now enter

=COMMIS.XLM!Commis(B3)

in that cell. Notice that the name of this custom function consists of two parts: The first part, COMMIS.XLM!, identifies the macro sheet that contains the function; the second part is simply the macro name, *Commis.* The function's argument, B3, identifies the cell that contains the data you want the function to use. When you press Enter, it calculates and returns the correct commission for the sales amount in cell B3: $1,200.

Let's consider how Excel interprets the macro. When you press Enter, Excel immediately looks on macro sheet COMMIS.XLM for the cell named *Commis* (cell B2). Because the cell does not contain a formula, execution moves on to the formulas in cells B3, B4, and B5 of the macro sheet, one at a time. The ARGUMENT formula in cell B3 assigns the name *sales* to the value passed to the function, which is $12,000 from cell B3 of the worksheet. (If you activate the macro sheet and choose Define Name from the Formula menu, you see the name *sales* in the list of names in the dialog box. If you select this name, the last value passed to the function is displayed in the Refers to text box.)

Next, the formula in cell B4 multiplies the value of sales by 0.1. Finally, the RETURN formula in cell B5 passes the value of the formula in cell B4, 1200, back to C3, the worksheet cell that contains the *Commis* function.

Next, assign a dollar format for the cell, and then copy the formula from cell C3 into cells C4:C6, as shown in Figure 19-21 on the following page. To do this, drag the AutoFill handle down three more cells. Because the reference to cell B3 in the original formula is a relative reference, it changes as the formula is copied into the new cells, so that the formula in cell C4 is

=COMMIS.XLM!Commis(B4)

and so forth.

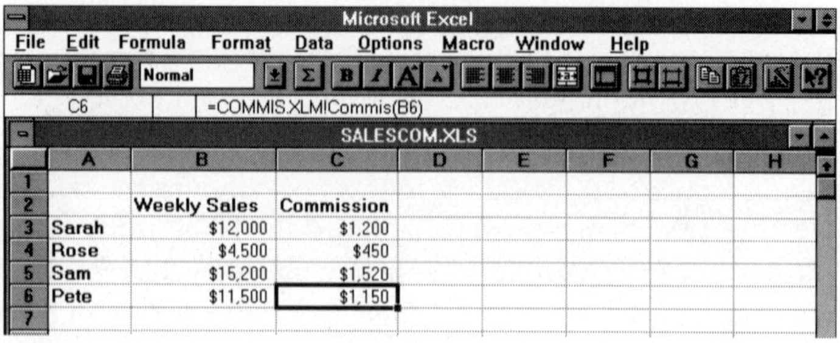

FIGURE 19-21.
The worksheet shows
the result of the
custom function
Commis.

Now suppose you need to change the values in cells B3:B6. As you might expect, the custom function updates the commission calculations in cells C3:C6 as you enter the new sales figures.

This first example is simple, but when the computations become more complex, custom functions can be real time-savers. Later in this chapter, we'll expand on this example to make the advantages of custom functions clear.

Function macro rules

The simple example we just looked at illustrates many of the characteristics of function macros. First, a function macro must include a RETURN function and almost always includes at least one ARGUMENT formula. (Technically, you can create a custom function that uses no data from a worksheet but returns a value; for example, you could create a macro that contains the NOW function to get the current time and date and return it as a specially formatted text string.) Most function macros also include one or more formulas that perform calculations using the arguments.

The order of the formulas in a function macro is important and follows this format:

FunctionTitle

=ARGUMENT("name1")

=ARGUMENT("name2")

=ARGUMENT("nameEtc")

:

(your formulas)

:

=RETURN()

The macro begins with one or more ARGUMENT functions (up to 30 arguments) and ends with the RETURN function. The formulas that actually do the work of the function lie between the ARGUMENT functions and the RETURN function.

You can use only those function macros that are located in open macro sheets. If you close a macro sheet that contains a function macro you want to use in open worksheets, the values returned by that function change to #REF! To regenerate these values, you must reopen the macro sheet.

Naming custom functions

As a rule, you should give a custom function the shortest name that describes its purpose and yet sets it apart from other functions. For example, you might call a function that computes federal income taxes *FederalIncomeTax*, but it would be better to shorten that name to *FedIncTax* or *FedTax*. However, don't make the names of your custom functions so short that they aren't descriptive. For example, you probably wouldn't want to call your federal income tax function *Tax*, because this name doesn't tell you what kind of tax the function computes. In addition, do not give your functions names that conflict with the names of Excel's built-in functions, such as PV, SUM, LINEST, or IF.

Similarly, you must specify the name of a macro sheet every time you use a custom function, so get in the habit of using short descriptive names for your macro sheets. (Functions from add-in macro sheets are an exception discussed in Chapter 20.) For example, you might want to use a name such as CF1 (for *Custom Functions 1*) for the first macro sheet in which you create custom functions, CF2 for the second such sheet, and so on. Alternatively, you can combine short macro-sheet names with short custom function names that provide more detail when taken together. For example, you might have a federal income tax function named *Fed* stored in a macro sheet named TAX.XLM. To use the function, you would type

=TAX.XLM!Fed()

To change the name of a macro sheet, use the Save As command. If you've used in a worksheet any of the custom functions in the macro sheet you're saving, and the worksheet is still open, the names of those functions will change when you save the macro sheet. For example, suppose a worksheet cell contains the formula

=MACRO1.XLM!Commis(C5)

If you use Save As to change the name of MACRO1 to SALES, the formula changes to

=SALES.XLM!Commis(C5)

The Paste Function command

Instead of entering the macro-sheet and custom function names into a worksheet by hand, you can use the Paste Function command to enter the function in the same way you do for standard worksheets and macro formulas. After you've created a custom function, Excel adds the name of the function to the list in its assigned category in the Paste Name dialog box. Custom functions appear in alphabetic order at the end of the category list. (Functions that reside in add-in macro sheets appear without the filename, in alphabetic order with standard worksheet and macro sheet functions. We'll describe add-in macros in Chapter 21.)

Select the name of the custom function you want and click OK; the macro-sheet name and the function name appear in the formula bar. You can enter the function's arguments by hand, but if the Paste Arguments check box is selected, Excel also pastes in the list of arguments the function expects, using the same argument names you specified when you created the function.

The Paste Function dialog box lists the names of all the custom functions contained in every open (hidden or unhidden) macro sheet. When you open a macro sheet, Excel adds the names of any custom functions in that sheet to the Paste Function list; when you close a macro sheet, Excel removes all the names in that sheet from the list.

Editing a custom function

Let's expand our simple commission calculation to see how function macros can be edited. Suppose your company uses a more complex commission formula: Salespeople receive a 10 percent commission if they sell up to $5,000 worth of goods, an 11 percent commission if they sell more than $5,000 worth of goods but not more than $15,000 worth, and a 12 percent commission if they sell more than $15,000 worth of goods.

To modify our custom function to perform this new calculation, select the macro sheet COMMIS.XLM, select cell B4 (the cell that contains the commission calculation), and enter the formula

=IF(sales>15000,sales*0.12,IF(sales>5000,sales*0.11,sales*0.1))

That's all there is to it. The custom function now computes commissions using the new formula.

Recalculating custom functions in a worksheet

If you switch back to the worksheet, you'll see that the values in cells C3 to C6 haven't changed — you can even choose Calculation from the Options menu and click the Calc Now button, but the formulas still aren't recalculated. Excel doesn't update the custom functions in a formula when you make a change to its function macro, but only when the worksheet cell is edited or any cell it refers to needs to be recalculated. To update the results in the worksheet, you could manually reenter the formulas in cells C3:C6 by selecting each cell and retyping the formula in it. Fortunately, however, Excel provides an easier method. Select each of the cells in the range, one by one, and, while the cell is selected, click the formula bar and then immediately click the Enter box or press Enter. "Editing" each cell in this way causes Excel to recalculate it.

If you want a custom function to be updated every time a calculation occurs anywhere in the worksheet and anytime you choose the Calculate Now command, you can insert the VOLATILE function immediately after the last ARGUMENT formula in the function macro. The VOLATILE function takes no arguments.

Using more than one argument

Now let's consider a more complex example. Suppose your company sells three products and each product carries a different discount schedule. Salespeople earn a 10 percent commission on all sales of Product 1 and an 8 percent commission on sales of Product 2. They earn a commission on Product 3 of 10 percent on sales to $5,000 and 12 percent on sales of more than $5,000. Any salesperson who sells more than $25,000 total for all three products in a period earns an additional 1 percent bonus commission.

Let's create a new function macro to make this computation. Move to cell B8 in the COMMIS.XLM sheet and enter the name *Commis2*. Then enter the macro shown in Figure 19-22 on the following page into cells A8:C17. When you finish, select cell B8 and choose Define Name from the Formula menu. Excel suggests the name *Commis2*. To accept this name, select the Function button, put the custom function in the Financial category (or wherever you put the first *Commis* function), and then click OK or press Enter. Finally, select cells A13:B16 and use the Create Names command from the Formula menu to name the cells in the range B13:B16.

Recalculating custom functions

Another way to trick Excel into updating custom functions is to select the range of formulas that contain the custom functions you want to update, and then use the Replace command to replace the equal sign at the beginning of each formula with an equal sign. Even though the formulas don't change, Excel updates the formulas in the range as if they were edited. You can also create a command macro that does this replacement automatically over the selected range or for the entire worksheet.

FIGURE 19-22.
*This function macro
computes more
complex commissions.*

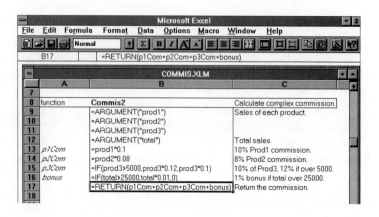

This new function macro is considerably more complex than the other two we've built. First, notice that it includes four ARGUMENT functions to store the values passed to the function as names. When we use the function in the worksheet, it will take the form

=COMMIS.XLM!Commis2(prod1,prod2,prod3,total)

where *prod1* is the sales of Product 1, *prod2* is the sales of Product 2, *prod3* is the sales of Product 3, and *total* is the total sales for the period. The order of the arguments in the custom function matches that of the ARGUMENT formulas in the macro. This is critical; if you enter the arguments in the function in a different order, the function will not compute the correct result. Of course, you're free to define the order of the arguments in any way you wish by changing the order in which the ARGUMENT formulas are presented in the macro sheet.

The three formulas in the range B13:B15 compute the commissions on sales of Product 1, Product 2, and Product 3. The formula in cell B16 computes the bonus commission on sales over $25,000. The RETURN formula in cell B17 calculates the total commission by summing the results of the preceding four formulas and returns the result to the cell in the worksheet that contains the custom function.

Notice that this macro follows the rules outlined earlier regarding the order of the terms in a function macro: ARGUMENT functions first, followed by the computing formulas, followed by the RETURN function.

We've called this function *Commis2* instead of *Commis*, because you cannot have two custom functions with the same name in the same macro sheet. Excel would let you name this new macro *Commis*, but it would then remove that name from cell B2 and, hence, from the simpler macro.

Now let's put this custom function to work. Create the new commissions worksheet shown in Figure 19-23, using the SUM function to total the sales in column E. Then select cell F3 and enter

=COMMIS.XLM!Commis2(B3,C3,D3,E3)

FIGURE 19-23.
Entering the
Commis2 *custom*
function in cells F3:F6.

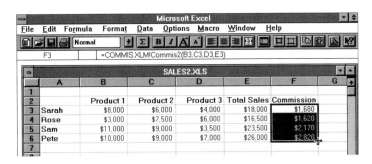

When you press Enter, Excel executes the *Commis2* macro and displays the commission for Sarah in cell F3. To complete the job, use the Fill Down command to copy the formula from cell F3 into cells F4:F6.

Omitting arguments

Some of Excel's built-in functions let you omit certain arguments. For example, you can omit the *type* and *future value* (*fv*) arguments from the PV function and Excel still computes the result. If you omit an argument from a custom function, however, Excel assigns the value #N/A to that argument. As you learned in Chapter 3, any formula that refers to a cell or a name that contains the value #N/A generally assumes the value #N/A as well. Thus, if you omit an argument from your custom function, it will probably return the value #N/A. You can avoid this problem by using the IF function to test the value of each of the arguments you might omit from the custom function to see if they have the value #N/A.

Suppose you want to create a simple function, called *Triangle*, that uses the Pythagorean theorem to compute the length of any side of a right triangle, given the lengths of the other two sides:

$$a^2 + b^2 = c^2$$

where *a* and *b* are the short sides, and *c* is the hypotenuse. The function macro shown in Figure 19-24 performs this task.

FIGURE 19-24.
This function macro
computes the length of
any side of a right
triangle, given the
lengths of the other
two sides.

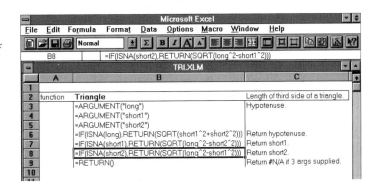

The first three formulas consist of ARGUMENT formulas that define *long*, *short1*, and *short2*. The next three lines contain IF formulas that test the values of these arguments for possible #N/A errors; if an argument evaluates to #N/A, then it hasn't been supplied in the calling formula in the worksheet, and our macro must calculate it. The formula in cell B6

=IF(ISNA(long),RETURN(SQRT(short1^2+short2^2)))

tests the value of *long*. If *long* evaluates to #N/A, Excel computes the square root of the sum of the squares of the lengths of the two short sides and returns that value to the worksheet. If not, Excel processes the formula in cell B7

=IF(ISNA(short1),RETURN(SQRT(long^2−short2^2)))

which tests the value of *short1*. If *short1* evaluates to #N/A, Excel computes the square root of the difference of the square of the length of the long side and the square of the length of the other short side and returns that value to the worksheet. If not, Excel processes the formula in cell B8

=IF(ISNA(short2),RETURN(SQRT(long^2−short1^2)))

which tests the value of *short2*. If *short2* equals #N/A, then Excel computes the square root of the difference of the square of the length of the long side and the square of the length of the other short side and returns that value to the worksheet.

To name this function, select cell B2, choose Define Name from the Formula menu, select the Function button, put the custom function in the User Defined category, and click OK or press Enter to accept the default name, *Triangle*.

Now let's use the function in a worksheet. The formula

=TRI.XLM!Triangle(5,4,)

returns the value 3, the length of the missing short side. Similarly, the formula

=TRI.XLM!Triangle(5,,3)

returns 4, the length of the other missing short side. And finally, the formula

=TRI.XLM!Triangle(,4,3)

returns 5, the length of the hypotenuse.

In this macro, we were able to avoid using the omitted argument in any calculations. For this reason, we didn't have to worry about an #N/A value being passed from formula to formula in the macro. If you need to use an omitted argument in a calculation, you can use the SET.NAME function to assign that argument the value 0 or 1, so that it has no effect on the calculation.

Of course, we're assuming in this macro that whoever is using the custom function is supplying only two of the three arguments. If all three are supplied, then none of the ISNA functions in the IF formulas evaluate to TRUE, the function does not return a value to the worksheet, and #N/A appears in the cell that contains the calling formula.

Similarly, if only one argument is supplied, the first IF formula whose ISNA function evaluates to TRUE is executed. Assume you've supplied the *long* argument alone; if you don't supply *short1*, it has the value #N/A in the function macro, and Excel executes the formula in B7. However, because *short2* isn't supplied either, it also has the #N/A value, and the formula returns #N/A to the worksheet.

There's one more problem. What if a user enters cell references as arguments to the *Triangle* function in the worksheet? Suppose a user enters the following function in cell D4 on a worksheet:

=TRI.XLM!Triangle(A4,B4,C4)

intending that the lengths of two of the triangle's sides will be entered in the referenced cells instead of in the function directly. If cells A4 and B4 contain the lengths of the hypotenuse and one of the short sides, and C4 is empty, you might expect *Triangle* to return the length of the unsupplied third side. However, using the reference to the empty cell, C4 evaluates to 0, not #N/A; and, because all three arguments have numeric values, the function returns #N/A.

One way to deal with this is to change the IF formulas so that they test for zero values as well as #N/A. It's not possible for a right triangle to have a side of zero length, so if an argument evaluates to zero, it must mean that the argument wasn't supplied. Here's a new set of IF formulas that take zero arguments into account:

=IF(OR(ISNA(long),long=0),RETURN(SQRT(short1^2+short2^2)))

=IF(OR(ISNA(short1),short1=0),RETURN(SQRT(long^2−short2^2)))

=IF(OR(ISNA(short2),short2=0),RETURN(SQRT(long^2−short1^2)))

This problem highlights one of the major issues that faces the designer of custom functions: how to design a function that can accommodate users who might use it in unexpected ways.

Validating arguments supplied to custom functions

Suppose your company uses the following discount schedule for the products it sells to wholesalers and retailers:

Quantity purchased	Wholesale discount (%)	Retail discount (%)	
0 through 5	0	0	
6 through 10	0	40	
11 through 20	50	41	
21 through 50	51	43	
51 or more	52	45	

You want to create a custom function that returns the correct discount, given the type of customer you're selling to and the quantity purchased.

Figure 19-25 shows a simple invoice worksheet. Cell B4 contains a code that describes the type of customer: W for wholesale, R for retail. Select the cell, and use the Define Name command to assign it the name *type*. Cell C11 contains the total quantity ordered by the customer; select it and assign it the name *totalQuant*. The values in these cells will become arguments for the custom function we're going to create.

To define the function, create a new macro sheet (we'll call it DISCOUNT.XLM) and enter the macro shown in Figure 19-26. Don't forget to define the macro as a function macro (using the Define Name command), and name cells B5 and B6 *type* and *disc* (using the Create Names command).

Cell B2 of the macro sheet contains the name of the macro, *Discount*. Cells B3 and B4 contain ARGUMENT formulas that define *quant* and *type*. Notice that we

FIGURE 19-25.
This worksheet is set up to calculate the correct discount for the type of customer and the quantity ordered.

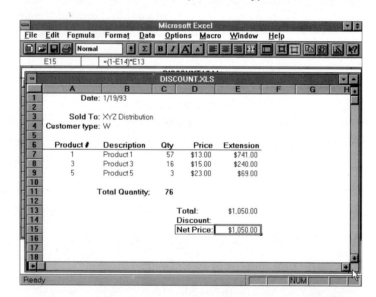

FIGURE 19-26.
The Discount *function macro calculates customer discounts.*

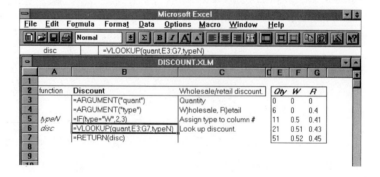

don't have to do anything special to define type as a text argument: The ARGU-MENT function can accept either numeric or text arguments. The formula in cell B5

=IF(type="W",2,3)

tests the value of *type*; if "W", the IF formula returns 2, and if not, 3. The cell is named *type*, and it effectively converts *type* into a number code for looking up the discount in the lookup table in the range E3:G7. The formula in cell B6

=VLOOKUP(quant,E3:G7,typeN)

uses the value of *quant* and *type* to look up the appropriate discount from the lookup table. This value is returned to the cell; the cell is named *disc*. Finally, the RETURN function returns the value of *disc* to the worksheet.

Now let's use the *Discount* function. Activate the worksheet, select cell E14, and enter

=DISCOUNT.XLM!Discount(totalQuant,type)

Notice that the arguments supplied to the custom function are defined in the worksheet, not the macro sheet. Figure 19-27 shows the result. As you can see, *Discount* has looked up the correct discount from the table in the macro sheet and returned that value to cell E14 of the worksheet. The formula in cell E15

=(1−E14)*E13

uses this result to compute the net price of the order. Of course, if you change either the entry in cell B4 or the total in cell C11, the result of the function changes.

FIGURE 19-27.
We used the Discount *function to calculate the discount on this customer's order.*

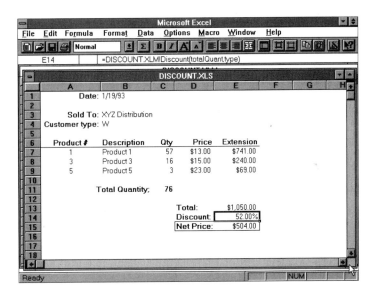

But what happens if the user makes an entry other than *W* in cell B4? The way the macro is now structured, the function returns the retail discount no matter what else is entered in cell B4. To overcome this problem, you can modify the formula in cell B5:

=IF(type="W",2,IF(type="R",3,RETURN("#VALUE!")))

This change prevents the kind of error we described. The new formula tests the value of *type:* if "W", the formula returns 2; if "R", the formula returns 3; if anything else, the formula stops the macro and returns #VALUE! to the worksheet.

The basic concept presented in this macro — storing a lookup table in a macro sheet and using a function macro to look up values from that table — can be applied to many different types of custom functions. For example, you can use this technique to create functions that perform complicated tax computations based on tax tables you store in a macro sheet.

So far, we've discussed two types of errors that relate to arguments: missing or optional arguments, and supplied arguments that are not allowed. There are others: for example, if a function macro expects a value of a certain data type, such as a logical value, and a user supplies a value of another type. One way to deal with this is to use the *dataType* argument in the ARGUMENT function to specify allowable data types, as discussed in the next section. Excel attempts to convert a number expressed as text into a number if a number is requested, for example; but if it is not successful, the macro returns a #VALUE! error. If, however, you want the macro to accept and handle more than one data type, you can use the type argument to determine the data type associated with an argument and process the argument as needed. You can also use a naming convention to indicate to the user the allowable data types; for example, appending *T* for text values, *L* for logical values, and so on.

Functions available to function macros

The range of functions you can use in function macros is somewhat smaller than the range you can use in command macros. All of the standard worksheet functions are allowed, of course, but command-equivalent and action-equivalent functions are not. Of the macro functions, you can use only those functions that return information but do not take any action in the workspace. You can use all the functions described in the next chapter that accept, convert, and return references, for example, as well as all the information, programming, and control functions.

In this section, we'll focus on three macro functions — the ARGUMENT, RESULT, and CALLER functions — and discuss their use in custom functions.

The ARGUMENT function

The ARGUMENT function takes two forms:

=ARGUMENT(name,dataType)

=ARGUMENT(name,dataType,reference)

where *name* is the name of the argument, *dataType* is a number that specifies the type of the argument, and *reference* is the cell in which you want Excel to store the value of the argument. The first form is for assigning the incoming value to a defined name that has no cell in the macro sheet. The second form is for storing the incoming value in a cell on the macro sheet; *name*, if supplied, then names the cell or range that contains the argument.

Each argument in a function macro must have a unique name. If you use the same name for two arguments in a function macro, Excel replaces the first definition of the name with the second definition.

For instance, suppose you've written a macro named *Quiz* that takes arguments for a test's name and numerical weight relative to other tests and begins with the formulas

=ARGUMENT("test")

=ARGUMENT("test")

When you enter the formula

=MACRO1.XLM!Quiz(A1,A2)

in a worksheet, the first ARGUMENT formula stores the value from cell A1 in the worksheet under the name *test*. Then the second formula stores the value from cell A2 under the same name, replacing the prior definition of *test*.

For the same reason, avoid using the SET.NAME function to define range names that conflict with argument names or the names attached to cells in the macro sheet. If, however, two function macros in a macro sheet assign the same name to different items, the names usually will not conflict because macros are executed sequentially instead of simultaneously. If you look in the Define Names dialog box, you'll see only one name, but the name is only referenced by the running macro. However, if a macro uses a name and calls a second macro that uses the same name, the value assigned to the name will likely be changed when control returns to the first macro. If you want to make sure that names will always be unique, try adding the name of the macro itself to the argument, as in *discountType*.

The *dataType* argument lets you use different types of entries as arguments in your custom functions. The possible values for *dataType* and their meanings are shown in the following table:

dataType	Expected data type
1	Number
2	Text
4	Logical
8	Reference
16	Error
64	Array

You can also use the sum of any two or more of these codes as the *dataType* argument. If you do this, Excel accepts any of the constituent data types in the values passed to the argument. For example, if you use the number 3, which is the sum of codes 1 and 2, Excel accepts either a number or text as the argument. The default *dataType* value is 7, which is the sum of codes 1 (number), 2 (text), and 4 (logical).

You'll rarely, if ever, need to specify any type but the default, 7. In fact, about the only time you'll use the *dataType* argument is when you want to use an array as an argument.

The *reference* argument used in the second form of the ARGUMENT function lets you specify a cell in the macro sheet in which to store the incoming value (or values). For example, the formula

=ARGUMENT("test",7,D1)

stores the value that is passed to the argument *test* in cell D1 in the macro sheet and then assigns the name test to that cell.

If you use *reference* to enter an array in the macro sheet, be sure that it defines a range large enough to accommodate the array. Otherwise, only as many elements of the array as fit in the defined space will be passed to the macro sheet. To be safe, use a reference argument that defines a range you know is larger than the array. The ARGUMENT function assigns the designated name to only those cells in the range that are used, not to the entire range.

Most of the time, you won't want to store the values you pass to a macro sheet in the cells of that sheet. The main benefit of storing values in a macro sheet is that it makes it easier to work with the individual elements in an array. This capability also comes in handy when you're debugging a function macro. If you enter each value that is passed to the function macro into one of the cells in the macro sheet, you'll be able to tell at a glance if all the values have been received correctly.

The RESULT function

Just as a function macro can accept different types of arguments, it can also return different types of results. The type of result a function macro returns is determined by the RESULT function. This function has the form

=RESULT(type)

where *type* specifies the type of result. The numeric codes for RESULT are the same as those for ARGUMENT, and, as with the ARGUMENT function, *type* can be the sum of two or more codes. The default type is also 7, which allows for number, text, and logical results. The required position for this function is immediately after the macro's title, before the ARGUMENT formulas.

You don't have to include the RESULT function in a function macro unless you want the function to return a result that is not text, a number, or a logical value. You probably won't use RESULT very often, but if you want to create a function that returns an array, you'll need to include it at the beginning of your function macro.

The CALLER information function

The CALLER function returns a reference, filename, or ID belonging to the cell, range, sheet, or object that contains the formula that started the currently running macro. It is useful when you want a macro to process information differently, depending on how the custom function is called. The CALLER function can only be used in a function macro, an Auto_Open macro, or an Auto_Close macro. (Auto_Open and Auto_Close macros are discussed in Chapter 20.) This function takes no arguments.

If a cell contains a call to a custom function, and that function contains the CALLER function, then CALLER returns the reference of the cell. If the CALLER function is in an array formula that you entered in a range in a worksheet, then it returns the reference of the range. If the custom function that contains the CALLER function is called by an Auto_Open or Auto_Close macro, then the CALLER function returns the name of the macro sheet that contains the Auto_Open or Auto_Close macro. If you assign a macro to an object (discussed in Chapter 21) and that macro contains the CALLER function, then CALLER returns the ID of the object. Finally, if you run a command macro and that macro contains the CALLER function, CALLER returns #REF!

For example, suppose you have two macros in a macro sheet: *Test* and *Test1*. Cell A10, which is part of the macro *Test*, contains the formula

=Test1()

If *Test1* contains the formula

=CALLER()

that function returns the address R10C1.

20

Overview of
Macro Functions

Chapter 19 introduced the concept of macro functions and gave you a few examples of how you can use these functions to create command and function macros of your own. In this chapter, we'll take a tour of Microsoft Excel's many macro functions, with the exception of a few specialized functions covered in Chapters 19 and 21. (Chapter 21 presents a group of functions you can use to create a user interface for your macro applications.)

You can duplicate most of the commands available on Excel's menus with a macro. For example, to issue the Paste Special command with a macro, use the PASTE.SPECIAL function. (You might find it useful to refer to additional information on individual menu commands elsewhere in this book.)

You can enter most commands that use dialog boxes (that is, commands followed by an ellipsis on the menus) in either of two forms. In the first form, you set dialog-box options by specifying the appropriate arguments in the function. In the second, you add a question mark (?) after the function name to have Excel display the dialog box, letting the user select the desired options. When you use the question-mark form of a command-equivalent function, you can enter the function's arguments or omit them. If you omit them, you see the default entries in the dialog box when it is displayed on the screen. If you include the arguments, Excel sets the specified options in the dialog box but leaves the dialog box open so that the user can change or confirm the selections.

A few functions, such as SIZE and MOVE, do not represent commands that display dialog boxes. Instead, they are action-equivalent functions that require instructions.

Many macro functions don't require arguments. However, as with standard worksheet functions, such as PI and RAND, you must include the parentheses when you enter any function into a macro sheet. For example, to issue the Copy command from within a macro, enter the formula

=COPY()

In addition, most macro functions contain optional arguments. If you omit these arguments from your formulas, be sure to include the comma that separates the omitted argument from the one after it. The commas serve as placeholders; they preserve the order in which the arguments are presented. You need not enter commas beyond the last argument specified.

Certain macro functions — often called *information functions* — let you obtain information about conditions and analyze that information from within a macro. These functions are not command-equivalent or action-equivalent. You'll frequently use these functions with the logical functions IF, AND, and OR. Often, the actions you want a macro to perform depend on certain conditions. For example, you might want to branch to one of several subroutines, depending on the information contained in the active cell.

Generally, a value supplied as an argument can be either a constant or an expression or defined name that evaluates to the type cited. For example, if an argument must be a logical value, you can use an expression instead of TRUE, such as *2 < 4* or *testFlag* (assuming *testFlag* is TRUE).

It's no longer possible to provide detailed information about each of the macro functions in Excel — there are simply too many of them to cover in this book. Therefore, as you read the following sections, refer to your *Microsoft Excel Function Reference* for information regarding the arguments that belong to each of the functions. Arguments cited in this chapter correspond to the arguments Excel presents in the Paste Function list box when you select the Paste Arguments option.

Document-management functions

The functions described in this section let you carry out file-management and document-management commands from within a macro. Most of these functions are command-equivalent functions from the File menu, but some are information functions. (You can also use a series of functions to create, open, read from, write to, and close text files; these functions are discussed in Chapter 23.)

Many of these functions require filenames as arguments. Unless otherwise noted, you can substitute a simple filename for the full pathname when the file is stored in the current directory. For example, if the file EXAM.XLS is in the directory C:\WORK and the current directory is C:\WORK, you can use either C:\WORK\EXAM.XLS or EXAM.XLS.

The NEW function

The NEW function lets you create a new Excel document or workbook, or open a template. It is equivalent to the New command on the File menu.

The NEW function takes a numeric code that describes the kind of document you want to create, or, in the case of a template, the name of a template that resides in the start-up directory, XLSTART. If you've selected a range of cells and you want to create a chart, you can also specify the arrangement of data in the chart. Finally, you can both create a new document and add it to the current workbook with the new *add_logical* argument.

The OPEN function

The OPEN function lets you open an existing document or workspace. It is equivalent to the Open command on the File menu.

The OPEN function takes the filename of the document you want to open, including a drive and pathname, if desired; if a path is not specified, Excel assumes the document resides in the current directory. If the document you want to open is not located in the current directory, use the full pathname:

=OPEN("C:\MYDIR\MYSUBDIR\TEST",1)

Alternatively, if you want to change the default directory, use a DIRECTORY function (described later in this chapter) before you use the OPEN function.

In the question-mark form of this function, you can use the * and ? wildcard characters to select files to open. For example, if you want to open a macro sheet, you might use the formula

=OPEN?("*.XLM")

This procedure is equivalent to typing *.*XLM* in the File Name text box of the File Open dialog box to display those files in the current directory that carry the XLM filename extension.

When the user opens a linked worksheet file, Excel asks whether to update references to supporting documents; you can use the *update_links* argument to eliminate this message. Similarly, your macro can use the *read_only* argument to open a document as Read Only.

If the document is not in the specified directory, Excel displays an alert message and asks whether to Retry or Cancel. If the user chooses Cancel, Excel returns a macro error message, because subsequent commands in the same macro will undoubtedly assume the file has been opened. If you do not specify the document name, as when you use the question-mark form of this function, the user can click Cancel without receiving the error message.

The FILE.CLOSE function

The FILE.CLOSE function closes the active document. It is equivalent to the Close command on the File menu. With this function you can either close a document without saving it, or save it first. When its *save_logical* argument is omitted and the file has been changed, Excel asks whether to save the document.

The CLOSE.ALL function

The CLOSE.ALL function is equivalent to the Close All command on the File menu. (To see this command, press Shift before you drag down the File menu.) This function, which takes no arguments, closes all unprotected windows currently open in the workspace. If the user has made any changes to the document or documents to be closed, Excel asks the user whether to save those changes.

The SAVE and SAVE.AS functions

The SAVE function saves the active document to disk. It is equivalent to the Save command on the File menu. It takes no arguments. The SAVE.AS function is equivalent to the Save As command on the File menu. With its *document_text* argument you can specify the filename under which you want to save the document; if you don't include the full pathname of the file, Excel saves it in the current directory. If a document of the same name already exists, Excel asks the user whether to overwrite the previous version.

The *type_num* argument identifies the file format for saving the document, which adds the appropriate file extension to the file's name. If you want Excel to use a file extension other than the default XLS, XLM, or XLC, include your own file extension in the *document_text* argument. Not every file format applies to each type of document you can create in Excel.

To protect the document with a password, use the *prot_pwd* argument, which is text of no more than 15 characters. To create a backup file, set the *backup* argument (equivalent to the Create Backup File check box in the File menu's Save As dialog box) to TRUE.

For example, if the current document is a macro sheet, the formula

=SAVE.AS("Test",1,"Secret",TRUE)

saves the active document in a file named TEST.XLM. Excel protects the file with the password *Secret* and automatically backs it up.

If you want to control the user's ability to write to a file, supply a password in the *write_res_pwd* argument.

The FILE.DELETE function

The FILE.DELETE function deletes a file from disk. It is equivalent to the Delete command on the File menu. With this function you specify the filename of the document you want to delete. Include the file's full pathname, if desired. For example, the statement

=FILE.DELETE("Test")

deletes the file *Test* from the current directory. If the specified document is not in the current directory, Excel displays an error message.

When you use the question-mark form of this function, you can also use the * and ? wildcard characters to control which files Excel displays in the File Delete dialog box.

The QUIT function

The QUIT function terminates the Excel session. It is equivalent to the Exit command on the File menu. The QUIT function takes no arguments.

If you have any unsaved files, Excel asks the user whether to save them before quitting — unless a macro has turned off error checking by setting ERROR(FALSE).

The DIRECTORY function

The DIRECTORY function sets the current drive and directory and returns the name of the current directory to the macro sheet. Its action is equivalent to choosing a new directory from the Directory list box in the Open or Delete command dialog boxes.

In this function, you specify as text the pathname of the drive and directory you want to make current. If you omit the drive name from the argument, Excel assumes you want to use the current drive. If you omit the argument altogether, Excel returns the name of the current directory.

For example, the formula

=DIRECTORY("A:\1993\PROFITS")

changes the current directory and returns the text value *A:\1993\PROFITS*. If you omit the drive specifier, Excel assumes you're using the current drive and includes that specifier in the path text it returns to the worksheet. For example, if the current drive is C, the formula

=DIRECTORY("\1993\PROFITS")

returns the text value *C:\1993\PROFITS* to the macro sheet.

The DOCUMENTS function

The DOCUMENTS function returns in a horizontal array an alphabetic list of all open documents. The first argument, a number code, specifies whether add-in documents (also known as *embedded objects*) are included. See Chapter 21 for information about embedded objects.

For example, suppose four windows appear on the screen: Sheet1:1, Sheet1:2, Sheet2 (which has one embedded chart), and Chart1. The formula

=DOCUMENTS(3)

returns the horizontal array *{"Chart1","Sheet1","Sheet2", "Sheet2 Chart1"}*. The second Sheet1 window is not included in the list, because it is not a separate document.

It's often helpful to use DOCUMENTS with the SET.NAME or SET.VALUE function. For example, the formula

=SET.NAME("Documents",DOCUMENTS())

stores the list of document names as a horizontal array under the name *Documents*. The formula

=SET.VALUE(C1:Z1,DOCUMENTS())

enters the list into cells C1:Z1 in the macro sheet. The problem with this statement is that you generally don't know how many documents are open in the workspace. The macro shown in Figure 20-1 solves this problem.

First, *TestDOC* gets a list of all open documents and stores it in a horizontal array called *docs*. Next, it finds the number of elements in the array; this number is stored in cell B3. (Use the Create Name command to assign the name *numDocs* to cell B3.) The formula in cell B4 creates a text string for selecting a range in column D, which is used to store the array after the formula in cell B5 converts it to a vertical array. The TEXTREF function in cell B5 takes the text string and converts it to a reference; the TRANSPOSE function converts the horizontal array into a vertical array, and the SET.VALUE function actually puts the array in column D on the macro sheet. We've marked cell B5 with italics to indicate that you must press Ctrl-Shift-Enter to enter the formula as an array formula.

FIGURE 20-1.
You can use the TestDOC macro to enter a vertical array of open documents in the macro sheet.

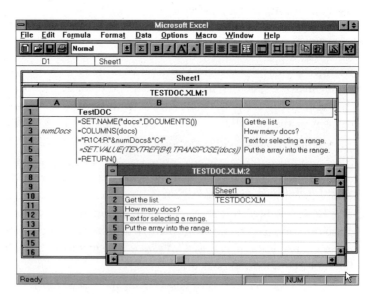

The second argument, *match_text*, allows you to specify which documents you want included. You can use the ? and * wildcard characters to limit your selection.

The GET.DOCUMENT information function

The GET.DOCUMENT function returns information about a document. The function's *type_num* argument is a numeric code that specifies the item of information you seek. The *name_text* argument is the name of a document that is currently open; if it's omitted, Excel returns information about the active document.

The FILES information function

The FILES function returns the filenames of all files in a directory as a horizontal array of text values. This function takes one argument — the directory name; if the argument is omitted, Excel returns a list of the files in the current directory. You can also use the ? and * wildcard characters to search for files.

As with the DOCUMENTS function, described earlier in this chapter, you can use the COLUMNS function to determine the number of items in the array, the INDEX function to find items in the array, and the TRANSPOSE function to convert the horizontal array into a vertical array.

The PROTECT.DOCUMENT function

The PROTECT.DOCUMENT function controls whether cell protection (set using the Format menu's Cell Protection command) takes effect, and it determines whether you can size or move windows. It is equivalent to the Protect Document command on the Options menu or the Chart menu.

You can set the *contents* or *windows* arguments to either TRUE or FALSE to specify whether these types of protection are on or off. Setting both arguments to FALSE is equivalent to selecting the Unprotect Document command. The *password* argument sets a password for protecting or unprotecting the file, and *objects* corresponds to the Objects check box in the Options menu's Protect Document dialog box; if this argument is TRUE or omitted, Excel protects all locked objects; otherwise they are not protected.

Add-in functions for working with documents

The FILEFNS.XLA file contains four functions that extend the range of operations you can perform on documents and files: DELETE.DIRECTORY, CREATE.DIRECTORY, DIRECTORIES, and FILE.EXISTS.

The DELETE.DIRECTORY add-in function deletes an empty directory, given its pathname; if you don't specify the full pathname, Excel assumes you mean to delete a subdirectory of the current directory. If the specified directory isn't empty, the function returns the value FALSE.

The CREATE.DIRECTORY add-in function creates a directory, given its pathname; if you don't specify the entire pathname, Excel creates the directory inside the current directory.

The DIRECTORIES add-in information function is like the FILES information function, but it returns as a horizontal array the names of every directory contained in the specified directory. If you don't specify a directory, Excel assumes you mean the current directory.

Finally, you can use the FILE.EXISTS add-in information function to determine whether the specified file or directory exists; if it does, the function returns TRUE.

Formulas for working with links

Excel provides the following formulas for working with links. Both links to files and Dynamic Data Exchange (DDE) links are managed by these functions. Throughout this section, the term *name* refers to filenames and DDE links. See Chapter 22 for more information on DDE links.

The LINKS information function

The LINKS function returns a horizontal text array of the names (including the full pathnames) of all external references for a specified document. The first argument it takes is the name of the document whose links you are seeking. If you omit this argument, Excel returns information about the active document. If the document isn't open, LINKS returns #N/A. The *type* argument specifies the type of linked document to return.

For example, suppose the current document is a chart named Chart1, developed from data in worksheets named PROFITS.XLS and LOSSES.XLS, which are stored in your C:\FINANCES directory, and from column 2 in the QE Query named HISTORY.QEF in the same directory. The formula

=LINKS("Chart1")

returns the array

{"C:\FINANCES\PROFITS.XLS","C:\FINANCES\LOSSES.XLS"}

whereas

=LINKS("Chart1",2)

returns the array

{"QE|C:\FINANCES\HISTORY.QEF!C2:C2"}

You can use LINKS with the SET.NAME or SET.VALUE function in the same way you do with the DOCUMENTS information function, discussed earlier in this chapter. For example, the formula

=SET.NAME("Profits",LINKS())

stores the list of pathnames of worksheets used as external references as an array under the name *Profits,* and the formula

=SET.VALUE(F1:J1,LINKS())

enters the array into cells F1:J1 in the macro sheet.

After you create an array of linked names, you can use the INDEX function to select the name of the document you want to use. You can also use the TRANSPOSE function to transform the horizontal array returned by LINKS into a vertical array, in the same way we did with the DOCUMENTS information function earlier in this chapter.

The OPEN.LINKS function

The OPEN.LINKS function opens the documents linked to the active document. It is equivalent to the Links command on the File menu.

You can specify the filenames of up to 12 linked documents, set the documents to read-only status, and specify the type of link you want information about.

For example, the formula

=OPEN.LINKS("EXAM.XLS","EXAM2.XLS","EXAM3.XLS")

opens three worksheets. If any of the linked documents contain external references to a supporting file, Excel updates both the external and remote references.

You can make the OPEN.LINKS function more flexible by using the LINKS function as its argument. LINKS returns a horizontal array of the pathnames of all the documents linked to the active document. Thus, the formula

=OPEN.LINKS(LINKS())

opens all the documents linked to the active document.

The CHANGE.LINK function

The CHANGE.LINK function changes the supporting documents that serve as external references for the active document. It is equivalent to choosing the Links command from the File menu, selecting the document whose link you want to change from the Links list box, selecting the Change button, and selecting from the Files list box the name of the document you want to include in the link.

You can specify the name of the supporting document you want to change, the name of the document you want to link to the active document, and the type of link you want to change (either standard Excel links or DDE links).

The PASTE.LINK function

The PASTE.LINK function pastes data from a supporting document into the active document and creates a link between the two documents. It is equivalent to the Paste Link command on the Edit menu.

The PASTE.LINK function takes no arguments. You use it in conjunction with the COPY function. For example, the formulas

    =ACTIVATE("Sheet1")

    =SELECT(!A1)

    =COPY()

    =ACTIVATE("Sheet2")

    =SELECT(!B1)

    =PASTE.LINK()

instruct Excel to select cell A1 in the worksheet Sheet1, issue the Copy command, activate Sheet2, select cell B1, and enter the linked reference

    =Sheet1!A1

The supporting document can also be from another application that supports Dynamic Data Exchange (DDE), which is discussed in Chapter 22.

The GET.LINK.INFO information function

The GET.LINK.INFO function returns information about the specified link. You can specify both the pathname and the type of link you want information about.

The SET.UPDATE.STATUS function

The SET.UPDATE.STATUS function switches between manual and automatic updating of a link. You can specify the pathname of the linked file for which you want to change the update status and whether you want automatic updating or manual updating.

The UPDATE.LINK function

The UPDATE.LINK function updates a link to the specified document, and is equivalent to clicking the Update button in the File menu's Links dialog box. If you omit the name of the link, Excel updates only the links to other Excel documents from the active document.

Windowing functions

Most windowing functions are command-equivalent or action-equivalent functions for using the mouse to change the size and position of a window, split the window into panes, open and close windows, and so on. They take the place of the scroll bars, document-window Control menu commands, and other tools that let you navigate through worksheets and macro sheets and manipulate document windows.

The WINDOW.SIZE function

The WINDOW.SIZE function, which replaces the older SIZE function, changes the size of the specified document window, regardless of whether the window is active. If you don't specify the window to be resized, Microsoft Excel assumes you want to resize the active window.

You can set the width and height of the specified window in points, a unit of measurement equal to $\frac{1}{72}$ of an inch. WINDOW.SIZE moves the lower right corner of the window as necessary to achieve the desired width and height, but it does not move the upper left corner. (To move the upper left corner, use the WINDOW.MOVE function, described next.)

If you use the question-mark form of the function, the window changes size (if specified), and the pointer changes to a four-headed arrow so that the user can manually resize the window. If you have maximized or minimized the window, WINDOW.SIZE returns an error. To avoid this error, use the WINDOW.RESTORE function beforehand.

The WINDOW.MOVE function

The WINDOW.MOVE function changes the position of the specified document window on the screen without activating it or changing its size. It is equivalent to dragging the title bar of a document window or choosing the Move command from the document-window Control menu.

You can set the desired horizontal and vertical positions of the upper left corner of the window. As with WINDOW.SIZE, both arguments are expressed in points, measured from the left edge of the workspace to the left edge of the window and from the top edge of the workspace to the top edge of the window.

If you use the question-mark form of the function, Excel changes the pointer to a four-headed arrow so that the user can manually reposition the window.

The WINDOW.MAXIMIZE, WINDOW.MINIMIZE, and WINDOW.RESTORE functions

The WINDOW.MAXIMIZE function expands the specified document window to fill the workspace. It is equivalent to clicking the Maximize icon, choosing the Maximize command from the Control menu of the active document window, or pressing Ctrl-F10. Similarly, the WINDOW.MINIMIZE function minimizes the specified window, and the WINDOW.RESTORE function restores the specified window to its previous state.

The WINDOW.TITLE function

The WINDOW.TITLE function replaces the title of the active window with the specified text. When you use the WINDOWS function after renaming the window, Excel returns the new name rather than the name of the document. This function is particularly useful when you're creating a macro application for others and want to hide the filenames of supporting documents or make window titles more readable.

The ZOOM function

The ZOOM function lets you magnify or reduce the contents of the active window to the specified scale. It corresponds to the Zoom command on the Window menu.

The NEW.WINDOW function

The NEW.WINDOW function opens a new window to a worksheet or macro sheet. It is equivalent to the New Window command on the Window menu. This function applies only to worksheets and macro sheets. If you run a macro that contains this function when the active window is a chart or a member of a workgroup, the function returns an error.

The HIDE and UNHIDE functions

The HIDE and UNHIDE functions conceal or redisplay the specified window. They are equivalent to the Hide and Unhide commands on the Window menu.

Excel does allow you to use the ACTIVATE function (described next) and perform other actions on hidden windows from within a macro. Thus, you can use HIDE to suppress the display of windows while a macro is running. This procedure speeds macro processing because the screen isn't updated until you tell Excel to UNHIDE the window.

The ACTIVATE function

The first argument of the ACTIVATE function specifies a window to be activated. The second specifies the pane in a split document window to be activated. It is equivalent to pressing F6 or Shift-F6 to move between windows or panes or to clicking a window to bring it to the front. If you specify only a pane number, Excel activates the requested pane in the current document.

If you've opened more than one window in a document and don't specify which window you want to work with, Excel activates the first window that belongs to the document. Suppose a document has two windows, Sheet1:1 and Sheet1:2. The formula

    =ACTIVATE("Sheet1")

activates the Sheet1:1 window, the first window in which the document is displayed. If you want to work with the second window, you must use the complete argument *Sheet1:2*.

The ACTIVATE.NEXT and ACTIVATE.PREV functions

The ACTIVATE.NEXT and ACTIVATE.PREV functions activate either the next window or the previously active window in the stack. They are equivalent to pressing the Ctrl-F6 and Ctrl-Shift-F6 key combinations. If you specify the name of a workbook, Excel activates the next or previous document in the workbook.

These two functions don't work quite the way you might expect. If you look at the stack of windows on your screen, you see that the second window on the stack is the window you used last. So when you ask for the next window, you get the window you used last, and when you ask for the previous window, Excel reaches to the bottom of the stack and gets the window that has been inactive longest.

Suppose three windows are currently open: Sheet1, Sheet2, and Sheet3. Sheet1 is the active window and Sheet3 is the previously active window. The formula

=ACTIVATE.NEXT()

activates Sheet3. The formula

=ACTIVATE.PREV()

activates Sheet2.

The CLOSE function

The CLOSE function closes the active document window. It is equivalent to the Close command on the document window's Control menu.

The function takes one argument to indicate whether you want to save changes to the document; TRUE saves the changes and FALSE leaves the document unchanged. If you omit the argument and the document contains changes, Excel presents an alert message asking whether to save the changes.

The SPLIT function

The SPLIT function divides a worksheet window vertically, horizontally, or both. It is equivalent to dragging the split bars or choosing the Split command from the document window's Control menu.

You use this function's two arguments to specify where to split the document window vertically and horizontally, with the topmost row and leftmost column numbered 1. To remove a split, enter 0 for the appropriate argument. (If you omit an argument, the split controlled by the argument doesn't change.) When you enter the SPLIT function for a window with frozen panes, Excel returns a macro error.

For example, the formula

=SPLIT(,4)

produces a horizontal split below the fourth row of the document window. If you've already split the window vertically, the vertical split remains unchanged. The formula

=SPLIT(2.5,0)

creates a vertical split in the center of the third column in the active window and removes any horizontal split.

The FREEZE.PANES function

The FREEZE.PANES function freezes the top pane, the left pane, or both in the active document window. It is equivalent to the Freeze Panes and Unfreeze Panes commands on the Options menu.

The ARRANGE.ALL function

The ARRANGE.ALL function arranges all open document windows to make the most efficient use of your workspace. It is equivalent to the Arrange command on the Window menu. You can specify the arrangement pattern of windows in Excel's workspace, whether to arrange only the windows that belong to the active document or all open windows, and whether open windows that belong to the same document should have synchronized scrolling.

The SHOW.INFO function

The SHOW.INFO function displays the Info window. It is equivalent to the Show Info command on the Window menu. The function takes only one argument, which, if TRUE, displays the Info window. If the argument is FALSE and the Info window is the active window, Excel activates the document associated with the Info window.

The WINDOWS information function

The WINDOWS function returns a horizontal text array of all windows, whether hidden or unhidden; you can exclude add-in documents, if you want, and specify a text string for selecting certain window names.

The first name in the list returned by WINDOWS is the name of the active window. The names of the remaining windows appear in the same order in which the windows are stacked on the screen. For example, suppose three windows are stacked on the screen in the following order: *Sales:2, Sales:1,* and *Data1.* The formula

=WINDOWS(1,"SALES*")

returns the horizontal array {"Sales:2","Sales:1"}.

You are most likely to use WINDOWS with the SET.NAME, SET.VALUE, and TRANSPOSE functions, as described in "The DOCUMENTS function," earlier in this chapter.

The GET.WINDOW information function

The GET.WINDOW function returns a wealth of information about the specified window, such as the window's name, location, size, and display options. If you don't specify the document's name, Excel returns information about the active window.

The VLINE, VPAGE, and VSCROLL functions

VLINE, VPAGE, and VSCROLL scroll vertically through a worksheet. They change the view on the worksheet but do not change the active cell.

Using VLINE is equivalent to clicking the scroll arrows in the vertical scroll bar or pressing Scroll Lock and then using the Up and Down arrow keys.

Using VPAGE is equivalent to clicking the gray area of the scroll bar or pressing Scroll Lock and then PgUp or PgDn to bring a new screenful of information into view. As when you click the scroll bar or press PgUp or PgDn, the actual distance you move depends on the size of the active window. For example, if the current window is 20 rows deep, the formula

=VPAGE(1)

scrolls the next 20 rows into view.

Using VSCROLL is equivalent to dragging the vertical scroll box to position the window over the desired cells in the worksheet. You can use either a row number or a percentage to represent the relative position of the rows you want to view. The bottom row (row 16,384) represents 100%. For example, the following formulas all tell Excel to scroll to row 4096 of the 16,384-row worksheet (one-quarter of the way down the worksheet):

=VSCROLL(4096,TRUE)

=VSCROLL(.25,FALSE)

=VSCROLL(25%,FALSE)

=VSCROLL(4096/16384)

The HLINE, HPAGE, and HSCROLL functions

The HLINE, HPAGE, and HSCROLL functions scroll horizontally through a worksheet and are analogous to VLINE, VPAGE, and VSCROLL. These functions change your view of the worksheet but do not change the active cell.

As with VLINE and VPAGE, the arguments of the HLINE and HPAGE functions are numbers that tell Excel how many columns or screens to scroll and in which direction. Like VSCROLL, the HSCROLL function can take either a number-of-columns value or a percentage of the distance between column A (or 1) and column IV (or 256).

Printing functions

The following nine functions carry out printing commands from within a command macro.

The PAGE.SETUP function

The PAGE.SETUP function defines printing parameters such as the header, footer, margins, and so on. It is equivalent to the Page Setup command on the File menu, and it has two forms. One prints a worksheet or macro sheet; the other prints a chart.

The function's arguments correspond to options set in the Page Setup dialog box, such as options for setting the contents of the header and footer, the size of the margins, whether you want to print row and column headings or gridlines, the size of the paper on which the document is to be printed, and so on. If you omit an argument, Microsoft Excel retains the previous setting for that option.

The PRINTER.SETUP function

The PRINTER.SETUP function selects a printer. It is equivalent to the Printer Setup command on the File menu. You must specify the name of the printer exactly as it is listed in the File menu's Printer Setup dialog box. For example, the formula

=PRINTER.SETUP("Epson 9 pin on LPT1:")

selects a 9-pin Epson printer attached to LPT1. To ensure that the printer name is entered correctly, it's best to use the macro recorder to enter this function in the macro sheet.

The SET.PRINT.AREA and SET.PRINT.TITLES functions

The SET.PRINT.AREA function defines the range of cells for Excel to print. It is equivalent to the Set Print Area command on the Options menu, which defines the Print_Area name on the active worksheet or macro sheet. You'll usually use a SELECT statement to select the range you want to work with before you use the SET.PRINT.AREA function.

The SET.PRINT.TITLES function creates print titles in your documents. It is equivalent to the Set Print Titles command on the Options menu, which defines the Print_Titles name on the worksheet. You can also specify references for columns and rows to be used as titles.

The SET.PAGE.BREAK and REMOVE.PAGE.BREAK functions

The SET.PAGE.BREAK and REMOVE.PAGE.BREAK functions create and delete page breaks in your documents. They are equivalent to the Set Page Break and Remove Page Break commands on the Options menu.

Neither of these functions takes an argument. You'll usually use a SELECT statement to select the place where you want the page break inserted or removed before you use these functions. For example, the formulas

=SELECT(!F10)

=SET.PAGE.BREAK()

create page breaks between columns E and F and between rows 9 and 10. The formulas

=SELECT(!F10)

=REMOVE.PAGE.BREAK()

remove the page break.

The PRINT.PREVIEW function

The PRINT.PREVIEW function calls up the Print Preview window so that the user can see how the document will look when printed. It is equivalent to the File menu's Print Preview command, and it does not take an argument.

The PRINT function

The PRINT function sends your document to the printer. It is equivalent to the Print command on the File menu. The function supports arguments for specifying the range of pages to be printed, the number of copies, and the quality of printing, if supported by the destination printer.

The LINE.PRINT function

The LINE.PRINT function sidesteps the printer drivers available in Windows, and takes direct control of the printer. You use this function if your printer prints characters in a single fixed width and uses control codes for creating simple formatting effects such as bold and underlining. Unless your printer is not supported by Windows or you want to send special control codes to your printer, use the PRINT function instead.

Add-in functions for creating printed reports

The REPORT.XLA file contains four add-in macros for formatting and printing reports. These add-in macros work with the View Manager and the Scenario Manager to generate a report that has the formats specified for a series of named views and scenarios that together define the report.

The REPORT.DEFINE function is equivalent to clicking Add in the File menu's Print Report dialog box; you specify the name of a report to add, and an array that contains one or more rows of view/scenario pairs that collectively define the report.

The REPORT.DELETE function is equivalent to clicking Delete in the File menu's Print Report dialog box to delete the specified report.

The REPORT.GET information function returns various types of information about the reports associated with the active document, such as an array of the named reports and an array of the view/scenario pairs defined in the specified report.

The REPORT.PRINT function is equivalent to clicking Print in the File menu's Print Report dialog box. Use the name of the report in the Print Report dialog box as the first argument for generating the associated series of printed reports.

Editing functions

The functions in this section are mostly command-equivalent functions that correspond to items on Microsoft Excel's Edit menu. These functions let you copy and paste the contents and formats associated with cell ranges, insert and delete cell ranges, and so on.

The UNDO function

The UNDO function reverses the effects of the previous command. It is equivalent to the Undo command on the Edit menu. The UNDO function takes no arguments.

The EDIT.REPEAT function

The EDIT.REPEAT function is equivalent to the Repeat command on the Edit menu; it repeats most Excel commands and actions. The EDIT.REPEAT command takes no arguments.

The CUT function

The CUT function lets you move the contents of a cell or range to another location via the Clipboard. It is equivalent to the Cut command on the Edit menu.

There are two ways to use the CUT function. The first is to use CUT in conjunction with the SELECT function or some other cell-selection function, such as FORMULA.GOTO. As with the Cut command, the range moved must be a single rectangular range. For example, to cut the range A1:A5 you can use the formulas

=SELECT(!A1:A5)

=CUT()

If you previously used the Define Name command to assign the name *Totals* to cells A1:A5, you can also use the formulas

=FORMULA.GOTO("Totals")

=CUT()

to accomplish the same purpose. After you've cut the selected range, use the PASTE or PASTE.SPECIAL function to paste the contents of the cut range elsewhere in the document.

The second method is to use the CUT function's *from_reference* and *to_reference* arguments to specify the range of the material to be moved, and the destination for the material. If *from_reference* is omitted, Excel assumes you want to cut the current selection. If *to_reference* is omitted, you can use the PASTE or PASTE.SPECIAL function to paste the material back into the sheet. PASTE.SPECIAL gives you the option of pasting only the formulas, values, or formats from the source material.

The COPY function

The COPY function lets you copy the contents of a cell or range to other locations via the Clipboard. It is equivalent to the Copy command on the Edit menu.

Using the COPY function is very similar to using CUT. You can use COPY in conjunction with the SELECT function or some other cell-selection function, such as FORMULA.GOTO, and then you can paste the contents of the copy range elsewhere in the document using the PASTE or PASTE.SPECIAL function. You can also specify the source and destination range of the material you want to copy, as with the CUT function.

The CANCEL.COPY function

The CANCEL.COPY function clears the marquee after you copy or cut a cell or range. It is equivalent to pressing Esc. The CANCEL.COPY function takes no arguments.

The COPY.PICTURE function

The COPY.PICTURE function copies the selected range to the Clipboard as a picture. It is equivalent to holding down Shift while choosing the Copy command from the Edit menu. You can specify whether you want to copy the picture as it appears on the screen or as it will appear when printed.

The function's *size_num* argument applies only to charts. If you want to copy the picture in the size it appears on the screen, use 1. If you want to copy the picture in the size it will appear when printed, use 2.

Finally, you can also set the type of graphic that is copied to the Clipboard — either a bit map (which you can edit in the Windows Paintbrush application, for example) or a picture that contains a defined shape for every object in the graphic (which you can edit in the Microsoft Draw program, for example).

The PASTE function

The PASTE function places the contents of the Clipboard in another location. It is equivalent to the Paste command on the Edit menu.

You use PASTE in conjunction with the CUT or COPY function and the SELECT function or some other cell-selection function, such as FORMULA.GOTO. For example, you can use the formulas

    =SELECT(!A1:A5)

    =CUT()

    =SELECT(!B1)

    =PASTE()

to cut the contents of cells A1:A5 and paste them into the range B1:B5.

Like CUT and COPY, the PASTE function now supports a *to_reference* argument, which means you do not have to select the destination range before pasting.

The CLEAR function

The CLEAR function erases the contents, the formats, the notes, or all three from the selected cells in the worksheet. It is equivalent to the Clear command on the Edit menu.

Depending on whether you've selected elements of a worksheet, macro sheet, or chart, you can specify which component of the selected entries you want to delete: formats, values, formulas, or the notes attached to cells.

For example, the formulas

    =SELECT(!A1:C10)

    =CLEAR(1)

clear all parts of the entries in cells A1:C10 in the active worksheet.

The PASTE.SPECIAL function (form 1)

The PASTE.SPECIAL function is equivalent to the Paste Special command on the Edit menu. It has different forms, depending on whether you're using it in a worksheet or a chart, or pasting data from another application into an Excel document.

If you're working in a worksheet, the PASTE.SPECIAL function pastes the contents of the cut or copied cells into the selected paste range using certain special parameters.

You can specify what you want to paste into the selected range — formulas, values, formats, or cell notes — and whether you want to add, subtract, multiply, or divide the pasted material into the values contained in the destination range.

Additionally, you can specify whether you want to skip blank cells when you paste, and whether you want to switch the orientation of the pasted data from horizontal to vertical.

The EDIT.DELETE function

The EDIT.DELETE function deletes the current selection from the worksheet. It is equivalent to the Delete command on the worksheet's Edit menu.

You can specify the direction you want to shift the cells in the worksheet to fill the space left by the deletion. For example, the formulas

=SELECT(!1:3)

=EDIT.DELETE(2)

delete rows 1, 2, and 3 from the worksheet and shift the remaining rows up to fill in the space.

If you omit the argument, Excel guesses at the direction in which to shift the cells, based on the range you select. For instance, the formulas

=SELECT(!A1:E1)

=EDIT.DELETE()

select the range A1:E1 for deletion and, because this range is wider than it is tall, shift the remaining cells up.

The INSERT function

The INSERT function inserts cells into a worksheet. It is equivalent to the Insert command on the worksheet's Edit menu. If you have recently cut or copied material to the Clipboard, new cells are inserted and the material pasted into the new cells.

As with the EDIT.DELETE function, you can specify the direction you want Excel to shift the cells in the worksheet when it inserts new cells. For example, the formulas

=SELECT("R3")

=INSERT(2)

insert a blank row above row 3 of the worksheet and shift the old row 3 and the rows below it down.

The FILL.RIGHT, FILL.DOWN, FILL.LEFT, and FILL.UP functions

The FILL.RIGHT, FILL.DOWN, FILL.LEFT, and FILL.UP functions copy an entry across, down, or up several adjacent cells. They are equivalent to the Fill Right and Fill Down commands and, if you hold down Shift, the Fill Left and Fill Up commands on the Edit menu.

None of these functions takes an argument. You usually use them in conjunction with the SELECT function. For example, the formulas

=SELECT(!F3:F6)

=FILL.DOWN()

copy the entry and formats from F3 (the first cell in the selected range) into cells F4, F5, and F6.

The FILL.GROUP function

The FILL.GROUP function fills the current selection into the same range in every worksheet in a group. It is equivalent to choosing the Fill Group command from the Edit menu. You can specify the type of information to be filled: formulas, formats, or both. To create a workgroup, you use the WORKGROUP function, discussed later in this chapter.

The FILL.AUTO function

The FILL.AUTO function corresponds to Excel's AutoFill feature. The function takes the reference of the cell to which the fill selection handle is dragged, starting from the current selection. You'll run into problems with this if the reference doesn't follow the rules for the AutoFill feature. For example, suppose the current selection consists of one cell and your macro contains the formula

```
=FILL.AUTO("RC:R[4]C[2]",FALSE)
```

This formula results in an illegal reference error, because you're trying to autofill one cell into an entire range. Instead, use the following two formulas:

```
=FILL.AUTO("RC:R[4]C",FALSE)
=FILL.AUTO("RC:R[4]C[2]",FALSE)
```

The SPELLING and SPELLING.CHECK functions

The SPELLING function is equivalent to choosing the Spelling command from the Options menu, and operates on the currently selected range. You can specify the name of a custom dictionary, whether to ignore words that are in uppercase, and whether to always suggest corrections.

If you want to check a specific word, use the SPELLING.CHECK information function; given the word as an argument, the function returns TRUE if the word is found in either the default or custom dictionary, and FALSE if not.

Formula functions

The functions in this section let you automate the commands on Microsoft Excel's Formula menu.

The SELECT function (form 1)

The SELECT function has three forms: one for a worksheet or macro sheet, one for an object on a worksheet or macro sheet, and another for a chart. In this section, we'll discuss the form that applies to worksheets and macro sheets. We'll discuss the other two forms later in this chapter.

The SELECT function for a worksheet or macro sheet selects a specified cell or range. If you're selecting a range, you can also set the active cell within that range.

You can enter these references in two ways: as absolute references to the active worksheet, such as *!A4:A7* or *!Total,* or as R1C1-style relative references in the form of text, such as *"R[1]C[1]:R[–1]C[–1]"*. Use the R1C1 style when you need to make a selection relative to the current active cell in the worksheet or macro sheet.

For example, if you want to select the range B5:B10 from within a macro, you can use the formula

=SELECT(!B5:B10,!B10)

No matter where the active cell is located when this instruction is executed, the function selects cells B5:B10 in the active worksheet and activates cell B10.

Suppose cell A1 is the currently active cell and you want to select the range one column to the right that begins four rows below the active cell and ends nine rows below the active cell. You also want the last cell in that range to become the active cell. In this case, you can use the formula

=SELECT("R[4]C[1]:R[9]C[1]","R[5]C")

Like the first formula, this instruction selects cells B5:B10 and activates cell B10. However, if cell C5 is the active cell when this instruction is executed, Excel selects cells D9:D14 and activates cell D14.

The SELECT.LAST.CELL function

The SELECT.LAST.CELL function selects the last cell in the active area of the worksheet. It is equivalent to pressing Ctrl-End. The SELECT.LAST.CELL function takes no arguments.

For example, if your worksheet is 26 columns wide and 100 rows deep, the SELECT.LAST.CELL function selects the cell at the intersection of column Z and row 100, which is cell Z100.

The SELECT.END function

The SELECT.END function moves the active cell to the edge of the next block of entries in your worksheet or macro sheet. It is equivalent to pressing Ctrl in conjunction with one of the arrow keys. You can specify the direction Excel moves the active cell.

The SELECT.SPECIAL function

The SELECT.SPECIAL function corresponds to setting options in the Select Special dialog box to select cells that have specific characteristics. The function takes a numeric argument for specifying what you want to select: constants, formulas, blank cells, and so on. If you're selecting constants or formulas, you can also specify whether to select numbers, text, logical values, error values, or some combination of these values.

For example, the statement

=SELECT.SPECIAL(2,1)

selects all cells in the worksheet that contain constant numeric values.

The SHOW.ACTIVE.CELL function

The SHOW.ACTIVE.CELL function brings the active cell into view. It is equivalent to choosing the Show Active Cell command from the Formula menu or pressing Ctrl-Backspace. When you're using a macro to work in a remote area of your worksheet, this function offers a handy way to bring the active cell back into view in the current window. The SHOW.ACTIVE.CELL function takes no arguments.

The UNLOCKED.NEXT and UNLOCKED.PREV functions

The UNLOCKED.NEXT and UNLOCKED.PREV functions select either the next or the previous unlocked cell in a protected worksheet. They are equivalent to pressing Tab or Shift-Tab. The UNLOCKED.NEXT and UNLOCKED.PREV functions take no arguments.

The ENTER.DATA function

The ENTER.DATA function lets you turn on Data Entry mode, which permits the user to enter data only into the unlocked cells in the current selection or to view an area on the worksheet without moving the active cell. Turning on Data Entry mode restricts the movement of the active cell to the unlocked cells in the worksheet, and makes available only those operations that Excel enables for protected worksheets.

The FORMULA.GOTO function

The FORMULA.GOTO function moves directly to the specified cell in your worksheet or macro sheet. It is equivalent to choosing the Goto command from the Formula menu or pressing F5.

The specified cell can be an external reference to a worksheet or another macro sheet. To select a cell in the current worksheet, you must precede the name or reference of the cell with an exclamation point. To select a cell in another worksheet, you must include the name of that worksheet, followed by an exclamation point, followed by the name or reference of the destination cell.

For example, the formula

=FORMULA.GOTO(!$A$1)

selects cell A1 in the current worksheet, and the formula

=FORMULA.GOTO(EXAM2.XLS!$A$10)

selects cell A10 in EXAM2.

You can also put the reference in the R1C1-text form. For example, the formula

=FORMULA.GOTO("EXAM2.XLS!R2C2")

selects cell B2 in EXAM2.

To return to the cell or range that was active before Excel carried out your last FORMULA.GOTO instruction, enter a second FORMULA.GOTO statement with no reference argument.

The FORMULA function

The FORMULA function makes entries in cells from within a macro. It is equivalent to selecting a cell and entering data or a formula into the cell. If the specified text is a formula, all references in the formula must be in the R1C1-text form. You can also specify where to make the entry; if you omit this argument, Excel puts the entry in the active cell.

For example, the formula

=FORMULA("This is a string")

enters the label *This is a string* in the active cell.

If you're working in the chart environment, you can use the FORMULA function to add and edit text labels and SERIES formulas. The effects of the FORMULA function depend on what type of chart object you've selected. For example, if you select a SERIES function in a chart and use FORMULA to create a SERIES function, Excel overwrites the existing SERIES function. If, however, you select some other chart object and use FORMULA to create a SERIES function, Excel adds the new SERIES formula to the chart. FORMULA works similarly with other chart objects, overwriting the existing object if the new object and the selected object are of the same type, or creating a new object if the new object and the selected objects are of different types.

The FORMULA.FILL function

The FORMULA.FILL function is like FORMULA, but it fills a range with an entry. It is equivalent to pressing Ctrl while you lock in a formula.

The FORMULA.ARRAY function

The FORMULA.ARRAY function lets you enter an array formula into a range of cells. It is equivalent to pressing Ctrl-Shift-Enter.

The GET.FORMULA information function

The GET.FORMULA function returns the contents of the upper left cell in the specified range. If the referenced cell includes a formula containing cell references, that formula is returned in the R1C1 style.

For example, if cell A1 in the current worksheet contains the value 100, the formula

=GET.FORMULA(!A1)

returns 100.

If cell B3 is the active cell and contains the formula =B2, the formula

=GET.FORMULA(ACTIVE.CELL())

returns the string =R[−1]C.

The NOTE function

The NOTE function adds or edits notes attached to cells. It is equivalent to the Note command on the Formula menu. The function takes as arguments text of up to 255 characters, and the reference of the cell to which you want to add the note; the default is the active cell. You can also specify the starting character and number of characters to remove in an existing note when you want to add text; if you omit these arguments, Excel assumes you want to start at the beginning of the note.

For example, to add a note that says *Next dental appointment in June* to cell G477 in a worksheet, use the formula

=NOTE("Next dental appointment in June",G477)

Later, after the note has expired, delete it with the formula

=NOTE(,G477)

or change it to *Next dental appointment in December* with the formula

=NOTE("December",G477,28,4)

The GET.NOTE information function

The GET.NOTE function returns the text from a note attached to a specified cell. The string returned can start with a position other than the first character in the note and continue for a specified number of characters.

The FORMULA.FIND, FORMULA.FIND.NEXT, and FORMULA.FIND.PREV functions

The FORMULA.FIND function searches for a specified text string throughout the worksheet or macro sheet. It is equivalent to the Find command on the worksheet's Formula menu.

You can specify in the function the text for which you want to search; you can use wildcard characters to find strings that might vary. For example, if the names *Jensen* and *Jansen* appear in your worksheet, you can use *J?nsen* as the *text* argument to find both entries. The ? wildcard represents a single character; the * character represents any sequence of characters. To search for the literal * and ? characters, precede them with a ~ (tilde).

As in the Find dialog box, other arguments specify the parameters for the search: whether to locate the text string in the worksheet formulas, displayed values, or cell notes; whether to use the Whole option or the Part option; whether to look for exact matches; whether to search by row or by column; and so on.

For example, the formula

=FORMULA.FIND("=A1",1,2,1)

looks for the text =A1 within any formula in the cells of the active worksheet. The search is conducted by rows. If Excel finds the string, it selects the cell that contains the string and moves on to the next line in the macro. If it can't find the string, it displays an alert box and doesn't proceed with the next line in the macro until the user clicks OK.

When you use the FORMULA.FIND.NEXT and FORMULA.FIND.PREV functions after you've used the FORMULA.FIND function, Excel searches for the next occurrence, or the previous occurrence, of whatever you specified in the *text* argument. These functions are the macro equivalents of the F7 and Shift-F7 keyboard commands, and they take no arguments.

For example, the formulas

=FORMULA.FIND("=A1",1,2,1)

=FORMULA.FIND.NEXT()

cause Excel to look for the text =A1 in the contents of the cells of the active worksheet. When Excel finds the first occurrence, it selects the cell that contains the value and moves on to the second line of the macro, to search for the next occurrence.

The FORMULA.REPLACE function

The FORMULA.REPLACE function finds text in a formula or a cell and replaces it. It is equivalent to the Replace command on the Formula menu.

You can specify the text you want to search for and the text you want to substitute. If you omit either of these arguments, Excel uses the last known values used in the Replace dialog box or with this command as the default. As with FORMULA.FIND, you can use the wildcard characters ? and * to find variant spellings.

For example, the formula

=FORMULA.REPLACE("Sales","Gross Sales")

replaces the string *Sales* with *Gross Sales* throughout a worksheet if you've selected a single cell, or throughout a selection if you've selected a range.

The GOAL.SEEK function

The GOAL.SEEK function calculates the values needed in a formula to make the formula evaluate to a specific number. It is equivalent to choosing the Formula menu's Goal Seek command.

The function takes as an argument the reference of the cell that contains the target formula you want the function to evaluate, which corresponds to the Set Cell text box in the Goal Seek dialog box. You can also specify the number you want the formula to return, which corresponds to the To Value text box. You can also specify the cell that contains the variable that Excel should modify to make the formula return the target value.

Functions for working with outlines

The following functions let you create and manipulate worksheet outlines. They are mostly action-equivalent functions that correspond to clicking the outlining icons on a toolbar and expanding and collapsing outline levels when the worksheet displays the outline.

The OUTLINE function

The OUTLINE function specifies settings for creating or formatting an outline. It is equivalent to choosing the Formula menu's Outline command. The function's arguments correspond to check boxes in the Outline dialog box: whether the automatic styles are activated for the outline, whether summary rows are below the subordinate rows, whether summary columns are to the right of the subordinate columns, and so on.

The PROMOTE and DEMOTE functions

The PROMOTE and DEMOTE functions promote or demote selected parts of an outline by one level. They are equivalent to clicking the Promote or Demote buttons on a toolbar.

The SHOW.LEVELS function

The SHOW.LEVELS function displays the specified number of rows and/or column levels. It is equivalent to clicking a level button in the upper left corner of a worksheet that contains an outline.

The SHOW.DETAIL function

The SHOW.DETAIL function expands or collapses the rows or columns under a specified summary row or column. It is equivalent to clicking a level bar or icon when an outline is displayed.

Functions for working with names and references

The following functions work with names and references: naming ranges, listing them, getting information about them, manipulating references, and converting references from one type to another.

The DEFINE.NAME function

The DEFINE.NAME function lets you name cells, ranges, formulas, and values in your worksheets and macro sheets. It is equivalent to the Define Name command on the Formula menu.

Arguments to the function specify the name you want to define and the reference, formula, number, text, or logical value to which you want to assign the name. If you're defining a command or function macro, you can specify a single letter that defines the Ctrl-key equivalent you want to assign to the name, if any, and a category for the macro. Finally, you can also determine whether Excel hides the name. (If the name is seldom used, confusing, or temporary, you might want to hide it from users.)

For example, the formula

=DEFINE.NAME("Test",100)

creates the name *Test* in the active worksheet and assigns that name to the value 100. The formula

=DEFINE.NAME("Test",!A1:A10)

creates the name *Test* in the active worksheet and applies that name to cells A1:A10. The formula

=DEFINE.NAME("Test","=R1C1+100")

assigns the name *Test* to the formula

=R1C1+100.

If you omit the argument that specifies the reference to be named, the name you specify is assigned to the currently selected range. For example, the formulas

=SELECT(!A1:A10)

=DEFINE.NAME("Test")

assign the name *Test* to the range A1:A10 in the active worksheet.

The DEFINE.NAME function creates the specified name in the active worksheet or macro sheet. You can't create a name in a sheet other than the active sheet. However, you can use a formula such as

=DEFINE.NAME("Test",Sheet2!A1)

to create a remote reference to a cell in another worksheet. This formula creates the name *Test* in the active worksheet, not in Sheet2, and assigns that name to the formula

=Sheet2!A1

The CREATE.NAMES function

The CREATE.NAMES function uses the labels in the top or bottom row or left or right column of a selected range as names for the cells in adjacent rows or columns. It is equivalent to the Create Names command on the worksheet's Formula menu.

The LIST.NAMES function

The LIST.NAMES function creates a list of all the named cells, ranges, values, and formulas in your worksheet or macro sheet. It is equivalent to clicking Paste List in the Paste Name dialog box. The LIST.NAMES function takes no arguments.

Before you use this function, be sure to select an empty region of your document large enough to accommodate the list. Otherwise, the new data overwrites any existing data in that region. When you use the LIST.NAMES function in a worksheet, the list occupies a range two columns wide, listing each name and its definition. When you use the function in a macro sheet, the list occupies a range five columns wide, listing each name, its definition, and 1 for a function macro, 2 for a command macro, or 0 for anything else. The fourth column contains the shortcut key, if any, and the fifth column contains a name or numeric code that represents the category of the macro.

The NAMES information function

The NAMES function returns, as a horizontal text array, all names defined in the document specified by *document_text,* or the active document if the argument is omitted. You can optionally include hidden names in the array, and you can use wildcard characters to return a list of names that match a certain pattern.

You can manipulate the list of names returned by the NAMES information function just as you can with the FILES, DOCUMENTS, and WINDOWS functions, discussed earlier in this chapter.

The GET.NAME information function

The GET.NAME function returns the definition of the specified name of a cell, range, value, or formula. The definition returned is the same as that in the Refers to text box of the Define Name dialog box: the reference of the named cell or range, or a string in the R1C1-text format that contains the named value or formula.

For example, if you've assigned the name *Test* to cell A1 in the active worksheet, the formula

    =GET.NAME("!Test")

returns *R1C1.* If the name *Number* describes the value 100 in the macro sheet, the formula

    =GET.NAME("Number")

returns 100.

The DELETE.NAME function

The DELETE.NAME function removes the specified name from the list of names defined for the active worksheet or macro sheet. It is equivalent to clicking Delete in the Define Name dialog box.

The APPLY.NAMES function

The APPLY.NAMES function tells Excel to search for a name definition in a formula array and replace the definition with the specified name. It is equivalent to the Apply Names command on the Formula menu and options in the Apply Names dialog box.

The ACTIVE.CELL information function

The ACTIVE.CELL function returns the reference of the active cell in the worksheet as an external reference. This function takes no arguments.

For example, if Sheet1 is the active worksheet and B2 is the active cell, the ACTIVE.CELL function returns the reference *Sheet1!B2*.

ACTIVE.CELL is frequently used in combination with the DEFINE.NAME function. For example, if cell B2 in Sheet1 is the active cell, the formula

=DEFINE.NAME("Active",ACTIVE.CELL())

assigns the name *Active* to cell B2.

Generally, when you use ACTIVE.CELL in another function, the reference is translated into the contents of the reference. To be sure you are working with the actual reference instead of what the reference refers to, use REFTEXT (discussed later in this chapter) to convert the cell reference to text.

The SELECTION information function

The SELECTION function returns the reference of the selected cells in the worksheet as an external reference, or returns the object identifiers of the selected objects. This function takes no arguments.

For example, if the active window is named Sheet1 and cells A1:A10 in that document are selected, the formula

=SELECTION()

returns *Sheet1!A1:A10*.

The SELECTION function is handy when you need to refer to the current worksheet range from within a macro. Suppose you want to assign the name *TestRange* to the selected range of cells in your worksheet. You can embed the SELECTION function in a DEFINE.NAME function, like this:

=DEFINE.NAME("TestRange",SELECTION())

The GET.DEF information function

The GET.DEF information function returns the name that corresponds to the specified definition, whether it is a cell, range, value, or formula. References for *def_text* must be in R1C1 style. If GET.DEF finds more than one name for a definition, it returns the first name it finds.

For example, if cell A1 in EXAM2 has the name *Test*, the formula

=GET.DEF("R1C1","EXAM2.XLS")

returns *Test*.

The ABSREF information function

The ABSREF function returns the address of the cell or range at the position described by the relationship to the reference cell or range.

For example, the formula

=ABSREF("R[–1]C[–1]",B2)

returns the reference *A1*. If C3 is the active cell, the formula

=ABSREF("R[2]C[1]",ACTIVE.CELL())

returns the reference *D5*.

Generally, you should use the OFFSET function, discussed in Chapter 8, to compute relative references. Usually, the reference returned by the ABSREF function is converted to the contents of the referenced cell, but not if the reference is used as an argument to another function that expects a reference. To work with the actual reference, use the REFTEXT function discussed later in this chapter.

The RELREF information function

The RELREF function returns a relative reference, in R1C1- text form, that describes the relationship between two cells. The direction of evaluation is from the second reference to the first. For example, the formula

=RELREF(A1,B2)

returns the relative reference *R[–1]C[–1]*.

The REFTEXT and TEXTREF information functions

The REFTEXT function changes a reference to an absolute reference in text form, in either the A1-text or R1C1-text form. Generally, you embed the REFTEXT function in other functions that require you to present cell and range reference arguments in text form.

The TEXTREF function converts references in text format to standard references, given the type of reference you're converting, either an A1-style reference or an R1C1-style reference.

The DEREF information function

The DEREF function returns the value of a specified cell or range. For example, if cell A1 contains the value 100, the formula

=DEREF(A1)

returns 100. If the supplied argument refers to a range, the DEREF function results in an array of values. For example, if cells A1:A3 contain the values 10, 20, and 30, the formula

=DEREF(A1:A3)

returns the array {10;20;30}.

In most Excel formulas, you can use either a value or a reference to a cell that contains that value. For example, if A1 contains the value –100, the formulas

=ABS(A1)

and

=ABS(–100)

return the same result. However, in some cases there is a big difference between using the reference and using the value. For example, the formula

=SET.NAME("Test",C13)

stores the formula =$C$13 under the name *Test*. If you want to store the *value* from cell C13 under the name *Test*, you must use the formula

=SET.NAME("Test",DEREF(C13))

The FORMULA.CONVERT function

The FORMULA.CONVERT function converts the references in a formula from A1 to R1C1 style and vice versa, and returns a text string that contains the new formula.

The function takes as arguments the formula to be converted, the type of reference given, whether in A1 or R1C1 style, the type of reference you want returned, and whether you want the function to return relative references.

The EVALUATE function

The EVALUATE function takes as an argument a text string that represents a legal expression (or the reference of a cell that contains such a string), and returns the result of the expression. For example, the formula

=FORMULA(EVALUATE(OFFSET(ACTIVE.CELL(),0,–1)&"(PI())"))

assumes the text in the cell to the left of the active cell is the name of a function that can be evaluated with the single argument *PI()*, and inserts the result in the active cell. Figure 20-2 on the following page shows the results of applying the macro to the SIN, COS, LN, TAN, and TANH functions.

FIGURE 20-2.
The TestEVALUATE
macro enters a result
based on the function
in the cell to the left of
the active cell.

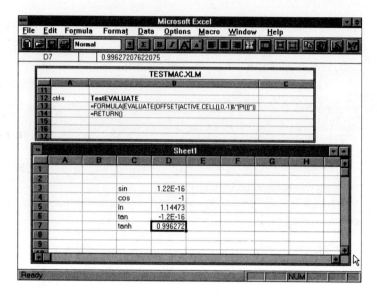

The SET.NAME function

The SET.NAME function creates a name in the macro sheet from within a macro and assigns a value to that name. For example, the formula

=SET.NAME("Test",100)

stores the value 100 under the name *Test*. If, after running the macro that contains this line, you pull down the macro-sheet Formula menu and choose Define Name, you see the name *Test* listed in the Define Name dialog box. If you select this name, you see that it refers to the value 100.

The value argument is usually a number, but it can also be a formula, a text string enclosed in quotation marks, an array, or a cell reference. For example, if you've already created the name *Test* and assigned it the value 100, the formula

=SET.NAME("Test",Test+1)

increases the value of *Test* by 1. Because *Test* is currently assigned the value 100, this function stores the number 101 under the name *Test*.

The formula

=SET.NAME("Test","Credit")

stores the text string *Credit* under the name *Test*.

The formula

=SET.NAME("Test",{1;2;3;4;5})

stores the vertical array *{1;2;3;4;5}* under the name *Test*.

If you want to assign a cell's value to a name you must use the DEREF function within the SET.NAME function. Otherwise, the name will refer to the cell itself. For example, if cell C1 contains the value 100, the formula

=SET.NAME("Test",DEREF(C1))

stores the value 100 under the name *Test*.

The SET.NAME function is very similar to the DEFINE.NAME function; however, DEFINE.NAME creates a name only in the active worksheet. The SET.NAME function is best used for storing temporary values during macro execution.

You can use an equal sign as an alternative syntax for the SET.NAME function; this corresponds to the assignment operators used in other programming languages. For example, the formulas

=SET.NAME("Test",100)

=Test=100

are equivalent.

The SET.VALUE function

The SET.VALUE function assigns a value to a cell in the macro sheet. For example, the formula

=SET.VALUE(C1,100)

enters the number 100 in cell C1 in the macro sheet.

The supplied argument is usually a number, but it can also be a text string, a formula, or an array. For example, the formula

=SET.VALUE(C2,"Test")

enters the text value *Test* in cell C2. The formula

=SET.VALUE(C1,C1+1)

increases the value in cell C1 by 1. If C1 contains the value 100, this function enters the number 101 in cell C1.

The formula

=SET.VALUE(C1:C5,{1;2;3;4;5})

enters the value 1 into cell C1, the value 2 into cell C2, and so on. If the second argument specifies an array that doesn't fit in the range set by the first argument, the function fills the specified range with as much of *values* as will fit.

Formatting functions

Most of the formatting functions correspond to options on the Format menu or are derivatives of these commands. You can use these functions to assign numeric formats, alignments, fonts, patterns, borders, and so on.

The FORMAT.NUMBER function

The FORMAT.NUMBER function lets you assign a numeric format to any cell in the worksheet. It is equivalent to the Number command on the Format menu. For example, the formulas

=SELECT(A1:C10)

=FORMAT.NUMBER("0%")

assign the built-in 0% format to cells A1:C10, and the formulas

=SELECT(A1:C10)

=FORMAT.NUMBER("0.000%")

create a new format, 0.000%, and assign it to the range A1:C10.

The DELETE.FORMAT function

The DELETE.FORMAT function lets you delete custom formats. It is equivalent to selecting a custom number format in the Format Number dialog box and clicking Delete. (You can't delete Excel's 27 built-in formats.) For example, if you created the custom format $#,##0.000, you can use the formula

=DELETE.FORMAT("$#,##0.000")

to delete the format.

The ALIGNMENT function

The ALIGNMENT function lets you change the alignment of the entries in the selected range in the worksheet. It is equivalent to the Format menu's Alignment command. The arguments to the function specify the alignment you want to assign to the selected range, whether text in the cell wraps, and how the text is oriented in the cell.

For example, the formulas

=SELECT(A1:C10)

=ALIGNMENT(2)

left-align all the entries in the range A1:C10.

The JUSTIFY function

The JUSTIFY function arranges the text in each cell of the selected range so that each line fits within the cell gridlines. It corresponds to the Justify command on the Format menu. The JUSTIFY function takes no arguments.

For example, suppose cell A1 in your worksheet contains the label *The rain in Spain falls mainly on the plain, except when it falls elsewhere.* The formulas

=SELECT(!A1:A4)

=COLUMN.WIDTH(20)

=JUSTIFY()

select cells A1:A4, set the width of column A to 20 characters, and distribute the label in cell A1 into cells A1:A4, like this:

The rain in Spain falls

mainly on the plain,

except when it falls

elsewhere.

The FORMAT.FONT function (forms 1 and 2)

The FORMAT.FONT function lets you select the font and type size that Excel uses to display the contents of a worksheet, text box, or chart. It is equivalent to the Font command on the Format menu.

The FORMAT.FONT function has three forms: one for worksheet and macro sheet cells, one for the text in text boxes and buttons, and another for charts. We'll discuss the form for charts in "Chart Format menu functions," later in this chapter. The arguments to the function let you specify the name of the font, the font size, style characteristics, effects, and color of the text.

For example, when Excel encounters the formula

=FORMAT.FONT("Arial",10,TRUE,TRUE)

it changes the worksheet font to Arial 10-point bold italic.

Form 2 of the FORMAT.FONT function applies only to the text in text boxes and buttons, and adds three more arguments: the ID of the text box or button you want to format; the starting character of the text in the box to be formatted; and the number of characters to format from that point.

The REPLACE.FONT and STANDARD.FONT functions

The REPLACE.FONT function changes the current font. It is equivalent to choosing the Font command from the Format menu, clicking the Fonts button, choosing a new font, and selecting the Replace option. It is supplied so that macros written for versions 2.1 and earlier of Microsoft Excel for Windows will work in versions 3.0 and later; in versions 3.0 and later, use FORMAT.FONT instead.

The STANDARD.FONT function sets the standard font for the worksheet. It is supplied only to provide compatibility with earlier versions of the macro language; in the current version of Excel, use DEFINE.STYLE and APPLY.STYLE instead. The arguments of the STANDARD.FONT function are the same as those of the FORMAT.FONT function.

The BORDER function

The BORDER function adds borders or shading to the selected cell or range. It is equivalent to the Border command on the Format menu. Its arguments specify the Border options you want to use: the edge to have the border, the type of border and its color, and whether the cell is shaded.

For example, the formula

=BORDER(,2)

draws a medium line at the left edge of every cell in the selected range, and the formula

=BORDER(6,,,,,,3)

outlines the selected range with a red double line.

The PATTERNS function (forms 1, 2, and 3)

The PATTERNS function sets patterns for a variety of worksheet and chart objects: cells, lines, text boxes, plot areas, pie slices, and so on. It has eight forms, but only the first three forms apply to items found in worksheets and macro sheets: Form 1 of the function applies to the text in cells; Form 2 applies to lines or arrows on worksheets or charts; and Form 3 applies to text boxes, rectangles, ovals, arcs, and pictures. The remaining forms apply only to charts, which we'll discuss in "Charting functions," later in this chapter.

The arguments to the various forms of the function let you specify the pattern of the shading applied to the selected range, the foreground and background colors of the pattern, the line weights used in lines and borders, the characteristics of arrowheads, and so on.

You can apply pattern characteristics to more than one selected object on a worksheet at a time, but not on a chart. If you need to do this, use the form that has the most options; Excel won't use the options that don't apply to an object.

The CELL.PROTECTION function

The CELL.PROTECTION function controls access to and viewing of the cells in your worksheet by activating or deactivating the locked and hidden formats. It is equivalent to the Cell Protection command on the Format menu.

The ROW.HEIGHT function

The ROW.HEIGHT function changes the height of selected rows in your worksheet or macro sheet. It is equivalent to the Row Height command on the Format menu.

You can specify how high you want the rows to be, in points, and the reference of the rows to be changed as either an external reference to the active worksheet or an R1C1-style text reference; if you don't specify a row reference, Excel changes the row height in the current selection.

You can also set the row height according to the height of the fonts used in the specified rows. Finally, you can also hide the row, unhide the row by setting the height to whatever it was before it was hidden, or set the row height to the tallest cell in the row.

The COLUMN.WIDTH function

The COLUMN.WIDTH function lets you change the widths of selected columns in a worksheet or macro sheet. It is equivalent to the Column Width command on the Format menu.

The arguments to the function set the width of the specified columns; if omitted, Excel sets widths for the columns in the current selection. You can also set the width to the default width and change the value of the default width.

For example, the formula

=COLUMN.WIDTH(15,!A:C)

changes the widths of columns A, B, and C in the active worksheet to 15. If A1 is the active cell, the formula

=COLUMN.WIDTH(25,"C:C[+3]")

changes the widths of columns A, B, C, and D to 25.

The GET.CELL information function

The GET.CELL function returns information about a cell's formatting, location, or contents.

You can specify the type of information you seek and the cell about which you want that information; if the type of information is omitted, Excel returns information about the upper left cell of the current selection.

The FORMAT.AUTO function

The FORMAT.AUTO function corresponds to selecting a collection of number, font, alignment, border, pattern, and column width formats that belong to one of the samples shown in the AutoFormat dialog box. For example, the formula

=FORMAT.AUTO(2,FALSE,TRUE,TRUE,TRUE,FALSE)

formats the current selection in the "Classic 2" table format, but uses only the font, alignment, border, and pattern characteristics of the style.

Functions for working with styles

The following four functions are for creating, applying, and deleting styles and for merging styles from another open document into the active document.

The DEFINE.STYLE function

The DEFINE.STYLE function corresponds to options set in the Define Style dialog box and has two major formats. Form 1 is for defining a style by example, from the formats that belong to the selected cells. You define (or redefine) a style with

Form 1 by using the other formatting functions on a selection, and then using Form 1 of the DEFINE.STYLE function to define the number, font, alignment, border, pattern, or protection formats for the style.

For example, the following formulas set up a new style called *heading,* which is defined as being in 12-point bold Courier New, blue, with a medium bottom border, and a foreground color of light blue:

=FORMAT.FONT("Courier New",12,TRUE,FALSE,FALSE,FALSE,5)

=BORDER(0,0,0,0,2,,,,,,0)

=PATTERNS(1,8,0)

=DEFINE.STYLE("heading",FALSE,TRUE,FALSE,TRUE,TRUE,FALSE)

=APPLY.STYLE("heading")

The first three formulas establish the formats of the cell. The DEFINE.STYLE formula uses these formats to define the *heading* style, and the APPLY.STYLE function (discussed next) applies the formats back to the selection.

Forms 2 through 7 are for directly changing the formats associated with a specified style, without first formatting a sample cell. Each form supports one component of the style you want to define. The remaining arguments correspond to the arguments of the functions that format the components of the new style, according to the following table:

Attribute	Formatting arguments
2	FORMAT.NUMBER
3	FORMAT.FONT
4	ALIGNMENT
5	BORDER
6	PATTERNS
7	CELL.PROTECTION

For example, the following formulas define the *heading* style, without first formatting a sample cell:

=DEFINE.STYLE("heading",FALSE,TRUE,FALSE,TRUE,TRUE,FALSE)

=DEFINE.STYLE("heading",3,"Courier New",12,TRUE,FALSE,FALSE,FALSE,5)

=DEFINE.STYLE("heading",5,0,0,0,2,,,,0)

=DEFINE.STYLE("heading",6,1,8,0)

The first formula defines which attributes belong to the style, and the three formulas after it add the font, border, and pattern attributes to the style.

The APPLY.STYLE function

The APPLY.STYLE function applies a defined style to the selected range. It is equivalent to choosing the Format menu's Style command, choosing a style and then clicking OK, or selecting a style from the Standard toolbar's style drop-down list.

The MERGE.STYLES function

The MERGE.STYLES function merges styles from a specified open document into the active document. It is equivalent to clicking the Merge button in the Format menu's Style dialog box.

If any of the names in the list of styles to be merged are the same as style names in the active document, a dialog box appears that asks if the user wants to replace the names. If the user clicks Yes, Excel replaces all the corresponding style definitions.

The DELETE.STYLE function

The DELETE.STYLE function deletes a style from the active document. It is equivalent to clicking Delete in the Format menu's Style dialog box.

Functions for working with objects

The following functions are for creating, deleting, moving, grouping, and rearranging worksheet and macro sheet objects.

The CREATE.OBJECT function

The three forms of the CREATE.OBJECT function govern creating an object by selecting an icon in one of the toolbars and dragging in a worksheet. Form 1 creates a new line, rectangle, oval, arc, picture, text box, or button that contains the specified text at the specified location. Form 2 creates a new polygon. Form 3 creates a new embedded chart. All three forms return as text the ID of the new object, such as *Text 2* for the second text box on your worksheet.

The FORMAT.SHAPE function

The FORMAT.SHAPE function corresponds to clicking the Reshape tool in the drawing toolbar and adding, subtracting, or moving vertices in a selected polygon. You can specify the number of the vertex, whether you are adding or removing it, and the location of the vertex relative to the cells in the worksheet.

For example, let's say you've used the macro shown in Figure 20-3 on the following page to create the triangle shown in the worksheet.

If you want to add a vertex, you can use the formula

=FORMAT.SHAPE(4,TRUE,,25.5,17)

FIGURE 20-3.
We used this macro to
create a triangle at a
specific location in the
worksheet.

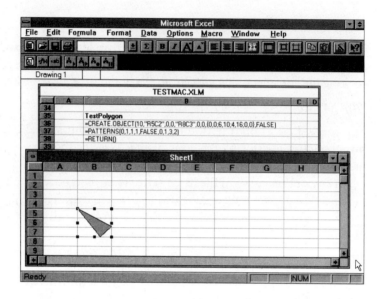

This formula makes what was the fourth vertex the fifth, and adds a new fourth vertex at the location specified, as shown in Figure 20-4.

The EXTEND.POLYGON function

The EXTEND.POLYGON function adds vertices to a shape created with the CREATE.OBJECT or FORMAT.SHAPE function. The EXTEND.POLYGON function takes an array of up to 1024 coordinate pairs that describe the position of each point relative to the upper left corner of the polygon's bounding rectangle.

FIGURE 20-4.
We used a formula to
add a new fourth
vertex.

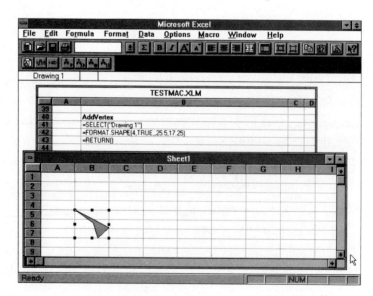

The SELECT function (form 2)

Form 1 of the SELECT function, discussed earlier in this chapter, is for selecting ranges on a worksheet or macro sheet. Form 3 is for selecting items on a chart and is presented with the other charting functions.

Form 2 of the SELECT function is for selecting objects on a worksheet or macro sheet, given a text string that consists of the ID's of the objects you want to select, separated by commas. These ID's correspond to the text returned by the CREATE.OBJECT function, discussed in the previous section. The last item in the list becomes the active object. You can also specify whether or not you want to add the specified object to a collection of objects already selected, which is equivalent to pressing Shift while selecting additional objects with the mouse.

The FORMAT.MOVE function (form 1)

After you've used form 2 of the SELECT function to select one or more objects in a worksheet or macro sheet, you can move them with the FORMAT.MOVE function, which is equivalent to moving an object with the mouse.

The FORMAT.SIZE function

The FORMAT.SIZE function is similar to FORMAT.MOVE in that you first use form 2 of the SELECT function to select one or more objects. This function takes two forms. In form 1, which also works with chart items, the dimensions of the object are set regardless of their position relative to a cell. In form 2, the dimensions of the object are set relative to a cell.

The OBJECT.PROPERTIES function

The OBJECT.PROPERTIES function sets the attachment of a selected object relative to the grid of cells beneath it. It is equivalent to choosing the Format menu's Object Properties command. This function replaces the PLACEMENT function in earlier versions of Excel.

You can specify how to attach the selected object so that Excel moves and sizes the selected object with the underlying cells, moves the object with the underlying cells but does not resize the object, or neither moves nor resizes the object. You can also specify whether the object is printed.

The DUPLICATE function

The DUPLICATE function duplicates the selected worksheet or macro sheet object. This function takes no arguments.

The TEXT.BOX function

The TEXT.BOX function replaces specified characters in a text box with new text. It is equivalent to clicking a text box to select it and editing the text manually. You can specify the text you want to add, the text box to which you want to add the text, and the starting character and number of characters to replace. The default is the currently selected text box.

The GROUP function

The GROUP function groups the currently selected objects. It is equivalent to choosing the Format menu's Group command. The GROUP function takes no arguments and returns the object ID of the group.

The UNGROUP function

The UNGROUP function breaks a set of grouped objects into separate objects. It is equivalent to choosing the Format menu's Ungroup command. This function takes no arguments.

The BRING.TO.FRONT function

The BRING.TO.FRONT function brings the selected object to the front. It is equivalent to choosing the Format menu's Bring to Front command. This function takes no arguments.

The SEND.TO.BACK function

The SEND.TO.BACK function moves the selected object behind all other objects. It is equivalent to the Format menu's Send to Back command. This function takes no arguments.

The HIDE.OBJECT function

The HIDE.OBJECT function hides or unhides the selected or specified object. You specify the object identifier of the object you want to hide, as displayed in the reference area when you select the object, or as returned by the CREATE.OBJECT function when you create the object. You can also supply a list of objects separated by commas.

The OBJECT.PROTECTION function

The OBJECT.PROTECTION function sets the protection status for the selected object. It is equivalent to clicking the Locked check box in the Format menu's Object Protection dialog box.

The GET.OBJECT information function

The GET.OBJECT function returns a wealth of information about the specified object, or the currently selected object if not specified. The items of information returned include the type of the object, its location, the name of a macro assigned to the object (such as a button), the text contained within it, the text's style attributes, and so on.

Workspace functions

These Microsoft Excel functions let you determine and set workspace display and calculation options, and manage workgroups and workbooks.

The A1.R1C1 function

The A1.R1C1 function changes the method of referencing cells from the A1 method to the R1C1 method and vice versa. Using this function is equivalent to choosing the Workspace command from the Options menu and selecting the R1C1 check box.

The PRECISION function

The PRECISION function controls the form of a value used in calculations. It is equivalent to choosing the Calculation command from the Options menu and selecting the Precision as Displayed check box in the Sheet Options group.

The DISPLAY function

The DISPLAY function has two forms. The first form lets you control the screen display. It is equivalent to choosing the Display command from the Options menu and setting the options in the resulting dialog box.

The arguments to the function specify the display options you want to turn on or off, such as the color to apply to the gridlines and headers, whether outline symbols are displayed, whether automatic page breaks are displayed, and so on.

Form 1 of the function lets you bypass the Display dialog box and specify display parameters directly. For example, the formula

=DISPLAY(,FALSE)

turns off the display of gridlines in the worksheet, and the formula

=DISPLAY(TRUE)

turns on the display of formulas.

Form 2 of the DISPLAY function lets you control what Excel displays in the Info window. It is equivalent to the commands on the Info menu when Show Info is activated.

The SAVE.WORKSPACE function

The SAVE.WORKSPACE function provides macro compatibility with Excel 3 macro sheets. When Excel 4 opens a macro sheet that contains this function, it converts the function to SAVE.WORKBOOK.

The WORKSPACE function and the GET.WORKSPACE information function

The WORKSPACE function specifies how Excel sets up your workspace. It is equivalent to the Workspace command on the Options menu. Omitting an optional argument in this function does not change the status of the settings, except where noted otherwise. You can specify a variety of options: whether the status bar, info window, scroll bars, and note indicators are displayed; an alternate menu key; whether Excel's Drag-and-Drop option is turned on; and others.

The GET.WORKSPACE function returns information about the workspace as displayed in the Workspace Options dialog box. Optionally, it also returns the name of the environment running this copy of Excel (very useful if you're developing a macro that should work well with both the Windows and Macintosh versions of Excel); Excel's version number; the amount of free memory available; whether a math coprocessor is present; the name of the owner of this copy of Excel; the pathname of the startup directory; and so on.

The COLOR.PALETTE function

The COLOR.PALETTE function replaces the color palette of the active document with that of another open document. It is equivalent to selecting a document in the Copy Colors From drop-down list box in the Options menu's Color Palette dialog box.

The EDIT.COLOR function

The EDIT.COLOR function sets an existing color to the levels of red, green, and blue specified as numbers from 0 to 25. It is equivalent to clicking Edit in the Options menu's Color Palette dialog box.

The CALCULATION function

The CALCULATION function lets you control the method of recalculation of your worksheets, as well as the number of iterations. It is equivalent to the Calculation command on the Options menu. Arguments to this function determine the type of calculation you want (automatic, automatic except tables, or manual), whether iteration is used and the maximum number of iterations you want to perform each time the worksheet is calculated, whether remote references are updated, and so on.

The CALCULATE.DOCUMENT function

The CALCULATE.DOCUMENT function causes Excel to calculate the active document. It is equivalent to clicking the Calc Document button in the Calculation Options dialog box.

The CALCULATE.NOW function

The CALCULATE.NOW function causes Excel to recalculate all open documents. It is equivalent to clicking the Calc Now button in the Calculation Options dialog box.

Functions for working with workbooks and groups

The following Excel functions let you create, manage, and delete workgroups and workbooks.

The WORKGROUP function

The WORKGROUP function creates a workgroup from the specified documents. It is equivalent to choosing the Window menu's Workgroup command and selecting a series of open documents to be in the group. Every document must be open and unhidden. After you've added documents to the group, you can use the EDIT.GROUP function, discussed earlier in this chapter, to work on the group as a whole.

The WORKBOOK.ACTIVATE function

The WORKBOOK.ACTIVATE function activates a document in a workbook. It is the equivalent of double-clicking the name of a specified document in a workbook window. You can specify the name of the document, and whether to open the document in a new window rather than having the document take over the workbook window.

The WORKBOOK.ADD function

The WORKBOOK.ADD function adds one or more documents to a workbook. It is the equivalent of clicking Add in a workbook window. You can specify as arguments an array of document names, the name of the workbook to which you're adding the documents, and the position number of the first document added.

The WORKBOOK.COPY and WORKBOOK.MOVE functions

The WORKBOOK.COPY function copies one or more documents from one workbook to another. It is the equivalent of pressing Ctrl while dragging one or more selected documents from one workbook to another. You can specify an array of document names, the name of the workbook to which you're copying the documents, and the position number of the first document in the series. You can move a document out of a workbook to create an independent document by omitting the name of the destination workbook.

The WORKBOOK.MOVE function is similar to WORKBOOK.COPY, but it moves the specified documents instead of copying them; you can also change the order of a document in a workbook by giving the document a new position number.

The WORKBOOK.OPTIONS function

The WORKBOOK.OPTIONS function binds or unbinds the specified document in a workbook. It is the equivalent of clicking the Options button in a workbook window and selecting the Workbook File or Separate File options in the Document Options dialog box.

The WORKBOOK.SELECT function

The WORKBOOK.SELECT function selects one or more documents in an open workbook. It is the equivalent of pressing Ctrl while clicking a series of documents in the workbook window. You can specify as arguments an array of the names of the documents to select, and the name of the active, or last-selected, document.

The GET.WORKBOOK information function

The GET.WORKBOOK function returns several items of information about the specified workbook, such as an array of the names of every document in the workbook, the name of the active document in the workbook, an array of the selected documents in the workbook (if any), and the number of documents in the workbook.

The SAVE.WORKBOOK function

The SAVE.WORKBOOK function saves an open workbook. It corresponds to choosing the File menu's Save Workbook command. You can specify the name of the workbook, its file type, password, and so on, just as you can for the SAVE.AS function.

Data menu functions

These Microsoft Excel functions let you use commands from the Data menu without opening that menu.

The SET.DATABASE function

The SET.DATABASE function defines the current database. It is equivalent to the Set Database command on the Data menu. To define a database from within a macro with SET.DATABASE, you must first use the SELECT function to select a range of cells. For example, the formulas

    =SELECT(!A10:E275,!A10)

    =SET.DATABASE()

define the range A10:E275 in the active worksheet as the database range.

The SET.CRITERIA function

The SET.CRITERIA function defines a database criteria range. It is equivalent to the Set Criteria command on the Data menu. To define a criteria range from within a macro with SET.CRITERIA, you must first use the SELECT function to select a range of cells. For example, the formulas

    =SELECT(!A1:E3,!A1)

    =SET.CRITERIA()

define the range A1:E3 in the active worksheet as the criteria range.

The DATA.FIND, DATA.FIND.NEXT, and DATA.FIND.PREV functions

The DATA.FIND function locates records in your database that match specified criteria. It is equivalent to the Find command on the Data menu. The function takes one argument, a logical value that specifies whether to execute the Find or Exit Find command.

After you use the DATA.FIND function in a macro to select the first record that matches the selection criteria you've defined, you can use the DATA.FIND.NEXT and DATA.FIND.PREV functions to select the next and previous matching records. These functions are the macro equivalents of pressing the Up or Down arrow key after choosing the Find command from the Data menu.

The SET.EXTRACT function

The SET.EXTRACT function defines an extract range for a database. It is equivalent to the Set Extract command on the Data menu. To define an extract range from within a macro with SET.EXTRACT, you must first use the SELECT function to select a range of cells. For example, the formulas

    =SELECT(!A280:E545,!A280)

    =SET.EXTRACT()

define the range A280:E545 in the active worksheet as the extract range.

The EXTRACT function

The EXTRACT function copies records from a database into an extraction range. It is equivalent to the Extract command on the Data menu. The function takes one argument that, if TRUE, extracts only the unique records from the database.

The DATA.DELETE function

The DATA.DELETE function deletes records from a database. It is equivalent to the Delete command on the Data menu. If you use the question-mark form of the function, Excel presents an alert box to warn the user that the records will be permanently deleted from the database. If you don't want the alert message to appear, use the standard form of the function.

The DATA.FORM function

The DATA.FORM function displays a dialog box arranged as a database form. It is equivalent to the Form command on the Data menu.

The SORT function

The SORT function arranges the rows or columns of the current selection in an order defined by the arguments. It is equivalent to the Sort command on the Data menu. Arguments to the function indicate whether you want to sort by rows or by columns, which columns to use as sort keys, and the order of the sort.

The DATA.SERIES function

The DATA.SERIES function creates a series of evenly spaced numbers in your worksheets. It is equivalent to the Series command on the Data menu. Arguments to the function specify the orientation of the series, the type of series, the date unit you're working with if you're creating a date series, the interval you want between each number in the series, and the maximum value in the series.

The TABLE function

The TABLE function lets you create a what-if table. It is equivalent to the Table command on the Data menu. Arguments to the function specify the reference of the row input cell and the reference of the column input cell.

The PARSE function

The PARSE function distributes the contents of a selected single-column range across the columns to the right, overwriting any information in those columns. It is equivalent to the Data menu's Parse command. Arguments to the function specify the parse line to be used and the reference of the destination.

The CONSOLIDATE function

The CONSOLIDATE function consolidates data from multiple worksheets. It is equivalent to the Data menu's Consolidate command. Arguments to the function specify a horizontal text array of external references to worksheet areas you want to consolidate, a numeric code that specifies a function for consolidating the data, whether data is consolidated by position in the worksheet, and whether a link is created to the source data.

Charting functions

The functions described in this section let you automate the process of creating, editing, and formatting Microsoft Excel charts. Many of the standard Excel functions also work on charts and chart documents; many have alternate forms that apply to charts.

Chart Gallery menu functions

The following functions let you select a chart type from the same options presented on the Gallery menu.

The GALLERY functions

Excel offers a group of seven functions — one function for each chart type — that are the macro equivalents of the various two-dimensional Gallery menu options. For example, the GALLERY.PIE function is equivalent to the Pie option on the Gallery menu. Other functions in this group are GALLERY.COLUMN, GALLERY.AREA, GALLERY.BAR, GALLERY.LINE, GALLERY.SCATTER, and GALLERY.RADAR. You can specify the type of chart from the gallery presented when you choose that chart command, and you can delete any overlays before formatting the chart.

For example, the formula

=GALLERY.PIE(1)

changes the chart in the active window to the first pie-chart format in the gallery — a basic pie chart.

The COMBINATION function

The COMBINATION function sets the type of the active chart to one of Excel's six combination chart types. It is equivalent to the Combination command on the Gallery menu.

The GALLERY.3D functions

Excel also offers a group of functions that are the macro equivalents of the various GALLERY.3D menu options. For example, the GALLERY.3D.PIE function is equivalent to the 3-D Pie option on the Gallery menu. Other functions in this group are GALLERY.3D.AREA, GALLERY.3D.BAR, GALLERY.3D.COLUMN, GALLERY.3D.LINE and GALLERY.3D.SURFACE.

The PREFERRED and SET.PREFERRED functions

The PREFERRED function changes the current chart format to the format you define with the Set Preferred command. It is equivalent to the Preferred command on the Gallery menu. If you haven't changed the preferred chart type, Excel uses the default chart type — a simple column chart.

The SET.PREFERRED function sets Excel's Preferred chart format to the type of the current chart. It is equivalent to the Set Preferred command on the Gallery menu.

Chart menu functions

The following functions let your macros access the commands and dialog boxes on the Chart menu.

The ATTACH.TEXT function

The ATTACH.TEXT function adds text to various parts of a chart. It is equivalent to the Attach Text command on the Chart menu. Arguments to the function specify what to attach the text to, depending on whether the chart is two- or three-dimensional.

If you're attaching text to a series or data point, you can specify the numbers of the series and the data point within the series you want to work with. Because this function doesn't actually work with text, you must follow this function with a FORMULA function to assign the new text to the item selected by ATTACH.TEXT.

The ADD.ARROW and DELETE.ARROW functions

The ADD.ARROW and DELETE.ARROW functions add an arrow and remove a selected arrow from a chart. They are equivalent to the Add Arrow and Delete Arrow commands on the Chart menu. After you've added an arrow, it remains selected so you can apply formatting functions to it.

The LEGEND and FORMAT.LEGEND functions

The LEGEND function adds a legend to or deletes a legend from a chart. It is equivalent to the Add Legend and Delete Legend commands on the Chart menu.

The FORMAT.LEGEND function changes the position of the legend on a chart. It is equivalent to the Legend command on the Format menu.

The AXES function

The AXES function specifies which axes Excel displays in the current chart. It is equivalent to the Axes command on the Chart menu. This function has two forms: one for 2-D charts, and one for 3-D charts. Arguments to both forms of the function represent the choices in the Axes dialog box.

The GRIDLINES function

The GRIDLINES function specifies which gridlines Excel displays in the current chart. It is equivalent to the Gridlines command on the Chart menu. Arguments to the function represent the choices in the Gridlines dialog box.

The ADD.OVERLAY and DELETE.OVERLAY functions

The ADD.OVERLAY and DELETE.OVERLAY functions divide the current chart into a main chart and an overlay chart or delete an existing overlay chart. They are the equivalents of the Add Overlay and Delete Overlay commands on the Chart menu.

The EDIT.SERIES function

The EDIT.SERIES function creates, edits, and deletes data series on charts. It is equivalent to the Chart menu's Edit Series command. Arguments to the function specify the number of the series you want to edit, the name of the series, external references to the ranges that contain the x-axis, y-axis, and z-axis data to be turned into a chart, and the plotting order for the series in the chart.

The SELECT function (form 3)

The SELECT function lets you select an item on a chart. It is equivalent to clicking an item on a chart. You can specify the object you want to select by using an appropriate identification string. For example, the formula

    =SELECT("Text Axis 1")

selects the label for the main chart value axis.

The SELECT.CHART and SELECT.PLOT.AREA functions

The SELECT.CHART and SELECT.PLOT.AREA functions are equivalent to the Select Chart and Select Plot Area commands on the Chart menu. These functions are provided primarily for compatibility with Excel macros written for the Macintosh. These functions have the same effect as the formulas

    =SELECT("Chart")

and

    =SELECT("Plot")

which are described in the previous section.

The MAIN.CHART, MAIN.CHART.TYPE, OVERLAY, and OVERLAY.CHART.TYPE functions

These four functions are included for compatibility with earlier versions of Excel. For MAIN.CHART and MAIN.CHART.TYPE, use the FORMAT.MAIN function. For

OVERLAY and OVERLAY.CHART.TYPE, use the FORMAT.OVERLAY function. Both functions are described later in this chapter.

Chart Format menu functions

The following functions correspond to commands found in Excel's Format menu when a chart is the active document.

The PATTERNS function (forms 4, 5, 6, 7, and 8)

The PATTERNS function changes the patterns and colors of the selected object. It is equivalent to the Patterns command on the Format menu.

The PATTERNS function as it applies to charts has five forms, depending on the object you select. Form 4 affects chart plot areas, bars, columns, pie slices, and text labels. Form 5 affects chart axes. Form 6 affects chart gridlines, hi-lo lines, drop lines, lines on a picture line chart, and picture charts. Form 7 affects chart data lines. Form 8 affects picture-chart markers.

The FORMAT.FONT function (form 3)

This form of the FORMAT.FONT function is specifically for charts. It changes the font in which the selected chart object is displayed and is equivalent to the Font command on the chart environment's Format menu. Arguments to the function let you specify the color of the text, the type of background you want to use, the name of the font you want to use, its font size, and the style of the text.

The FORMAT.TEXT function

The FORMAT.TEXT function changes the text settings of a selected chart object. It is equivalent to the Text command on the Format menu. Arguments to the function specify, for example, the alignment and orientation of the text.

The FORMAT.MOVE function (form 2)

Form 2 of the FORMAT.MOVE function moves the selected chart object. It is equivalent to moving an item with the mouse. You can specify the horizontal and vertical position of the object. If Excel can't move a chart object, FORMAT.MOVE returns FALSE.

The SCALE function

The SCALE function controls the appearance of the axes. It is equivalent to the Scale command on the Format menu. This function has five forms. Form 1, for example, is for category axes on a 2-D chart. You can specify the category at which you want the value axis to cross, how many categories you want to put between tick-mark labels, the number of categories between tick marks, whether the value axis crosses the category axis between categories, whether the value axis crosses the category axis at the maximum category, and whether categories are displayed in reverse order.

Form 2 is for value axes on a 2-D or XY (scatter) chart, form 3 is for the category (x) axis on a 3-D chart, form 4 is for the series (y)axis on a 3-D chart, and form 5 is for the value (z) axis on a 3-D chart.

The GET.CHART.ITEM information function

The GET.CHART.ITEM information function returns the horizontal or vertical position of a point on a selected object in a chart. You can specify which coordinate you want, which point, and a string that identifies the item, such as that used in the SELECT function; if no item is specified, Excel returns information about the currently selected item.

The FORMAT.MAIN function

The FORMAT.MAIN function formats a chart using your arguments, rather than the automatic formats of the Gallery functions. It is equivalent to choosing the Format menu's Main Chart command. You can specify the type of chart you want, the overlap of its bars or columns, if applicable, and so on.

The FORMAT.OVERLAY function

The FORMAT.OVERLAY function is equivalent to choosing the Format menu's Overlay command and setting options in the Overlay dialog box. The arguments to this function are the same as those to the FORMAT.MAIN function, except that the range of chart types is more limited.

The VIEW.3D function

The VIEW.3D function adjusts the view on the active 3-D chart. It is equivalent to choosing the Format menu's 3-D View command and setting options in the resulting dialog box. You can specify the elevation of the viewer's location, the rotation of the chart, the height of the chart expressed as a percentage of the length of the base, and so on.

Other Chart functions

The following functions complete the set of Excel's charting functions.

The PASTE.SPECIAL function (forms 2 and 3)

When used with a chart, PASTE.SPECIAL has two forms: One lets you paste from a worksheet or macro sheet to a chart, and the second lets you paste from one chart to another.

To copy data from a worksheet or macro sheet into a chart, use form 2. In this form, you can specify whether the values are in rows or columns, whether you want to use the entries in the first row (or column) of the selection as series names, whether you want to use the entries in the first column (or row) of the selection as category labels, and whether to apply the category names to all series in the chart.

To copy data between chart windows, use form 3 of the function, in which you can specify which parts of the copied chart you want to paste into the active chart window.

The CHART.WIZARD function

The CHART.WIZARD function corresponds to clicking the ChartWizard tool in the Standard toolbar, which leads the user through the process of creating a chart from selected data in a worksheet or macro sheet, in either the five-step or the two-step versions. You can specify the reference of the source data, the type and style of chart you want to create from Excel chart galleries, the titles attached to the chart's axes, and so on. It's often best to record your use of the ChartWizard with the macro recorder, then cut and paste the results into your own macro.

Macro programming functions

In this section, we'll cover functions unique to Microsoft Excel's macro programming environment. This group includes functions that take actions, make decisions, repeat actions, run macros, and test macros.

The ref() syntax

The *ref()* syntax tells Excel where to go to execute a subroutine macro. You simply enter the cell reference, followed by a pair of parentheses. For example, to route macro processing to cell B20 (which is named *OpenTemplate*), you can use either

    =B20()

or

    =OpenTemplate()

Obviously, the second syntax is much easier to understand and document. If *ref()* is a range, execution moves to the upper left corner of the reference. If you want to run a macro on another macro sheet, *ref()* can be an external reference. In addition, *ref()* can be a formula that returns a reference.

As we'll discuss in Chapter 21, you can enter arguments in the parentheses; if the receiving routine has corresponding ARGUMENT functions at the beginning of the macro subroutine, the subroutine can use them in its execution.

The RUN function

The RUN function lets you start one macro from within another macro. It is equivalent to the Run command on the Macro menu.

The form of the RUN function is

=RUN(*reference,step*)

=RUN?(*reference,step*)

where *reference* is either an external reference to the macro sheet that contains the macro you want to run, or an R1C1 external reference in the form of text. The *reference* argument can also take the value 1 to run all Auto_Open macros on the active macro sheet, 2 to run all Auto_Close macros on the active macro sheet, 3 to run all Auto_Activate macros on the active macro sheet, or 4 to run all Auto_Deactivate macros on the active macro sheet. If you omit this argument, execution proceeds from the active cell.

The *step* argument, if TRUE, runs the macro in single-step mode; if FALSE or omitted, the macro runs normally.

For example, the formula

=RUN(Macro1!A15)

runs the macro at cell A15 in the macro sheet Macro1, as does the formula

=RUN("Macro1!R15C1")

If cell A15 in Macro1 is named *Test*, the formula

=RUN(Macro1!Test)

also runs the macro.

The HALT function

The HALT function stops all currently running macros. It takes the form

=HALT(*cancel_close*)

If an Auto_Close macro contains the HALT function with the *cancel_close* argument set to TRUE, Excel does not close the macro sheet. If the argument is FALSE or omitted, the macro sheet closes normally.

For example, the formula

=IF(Test>100,HALT())

stops the macro immediately if the value of the name *Test* is greater than 100. If the macro that contains this statement is embedded in another macro, the calling macro also stops. If the macro that contains this statement is an Auto_Close macro, it closes normally.

The RETURN function

The RETURN function ends the execution of a specific macro or subroutine, and takes the form

=RETURN(*value*)

The *value* argument in a function macro tells the macro to return *value* to the calling cell. You can't use *value* in a command macro that the user initiates, but you can use it in a command macro called by another command macro (a command macro subroutine).

If the macro was started with the Run command from the Macro menu or with a shortcut key, the macro ends with the RETURN function. If the RETURN function is embedded in a subroutine, Excel returns to the cell immediately after the cell that called the subroutine.

The GOTO function

The GOTO function lets you redirect the calculation of a macro. You can use GOTO to branch from one macro to another or to create a loop within a macro. This function takes the form

=GOTO(*reference*)

where *reference* is the reference or name of the cell that contains the next macro function you want Excel to execute. After the macro branches to *reference,* execution continues with the cells below *reference* until the macro encounters a RETURN function, a HALT function, a subroutine call using the *ref()* syntax, or another GOTO function.

Generally, it is a good idea to avoid using the GOTO function. Excessive use of GOTO can lead to confusing macro structures that are very difficult to debug and document. Instead, use the looping functions or the macro IF function, or break your macro into smaller subroutines threaded together by a larger routine.

The WAIT function

The WAIT function suspends the execution of a macro until a specified time, and takes the form

=WAIT(*serial_number*)

where *serial_number* is the serial-number time to resume execution. For example, to pause execution until 2:00 AM, you can use the formula

=WAIT(0.08333)

To pause execution for a specified amount of time, you can include an embedded NOW function in the *serial_number* argument. Keeping in mind that Excel calculates time relative to midnight, you can calculate the value of a second by entering 12:00:01 AM in cell C3 of your macro sheet (equal to 1.15741E–05, or the value of 1 day divided by 24*60*60 seconds). Use the formula

=WAIT(NOW()+C3*5)

to suspend a macro for five seconds. (You can also resume execution by pressing Esc, unless you've disabled the Esc key with a CANCEL.KEY function.)

The RESTART function

The RESTART function modifies the action of the next RETURN function, which lets you return control to whatever macro level you want. This function takes the form

=RESTART(*level_num*)

When you include this function without a *level_num* argument in a subroutine macro and Excel subsequently encounters a RETURN statement, the macro stops and does not return control to the parent macro. The *level_num* argument specifies the number of preceding macros to jump over before returning control. For example,

=RESTART(1)

returns control not to the macro that initiated the current macro, but to the macro that precedes the initiating macro.

The RESTART function does not take the place of a HALT or RETURN function.

The STEP function

The STEP function starts Excel's step mode and begins executing the current macro one step at a time. This function takes no arguments. For more on the STEP function, see Chapter 21.

The PAUSE and RESUME functions

The PAUSE function pauses the macro in which it occurs; you can then debug the macro, enter or work with data in a worksheet, or even run another macro. You can specify whether Excel's Resume toolbar appears when the macro pauses, so that you can debug the macro and then start it again.

To start the macro running again from the point at which the macro was paused, click the Resume tool in the toolbar or run a macro that contains the RESUME function.

The ASSIGN.TO.OBJECT function

The ASSIGN.TO.OBJECT function assigns a macro to the selected object, to be run when you click the object. It is equivalent to choosing the Macro menu's Assign to Object command.

This function takes the form

=ASSIGN.TO.OBJECT(*macro_ref*)

=ASSIGN.TO.OBJECT?(*macro_ref*)

where *macro_ref* is the macro you want to run when you click the object. You can "unassign" a macro by selecting the object and using the function without an argument. You can also change the assigned macro by selecting the object and substituting the name of a different macro.

Decision-making functions

The macro programming functions in this group let your macros test for conditions and change the way they behave based on those conditions.

The IF–END.IF block

The IF and END.IF functions work as a pair to mark out a section of a macro that executes if a certain condition is met.

The structure of an IF-END.IF block is as follows:

=IF(*logical_Test*)

:

(formulas to be executed if logical_Test *is TRUE)*

:

=END.IF()

The END.IF function takes no arguments.

When you format and document an IF-END.IF block (as well as the other types of blocks and looping structures we'll discuss in this section), for legibility you can indent lines by inserting spaces between the equal sign at the beginning of a formula and the formula itself.

For example, suppose you want to write a set of macros that will, among other things, print a new set of calendar sheets on a certain date. The following routine accomplishes this task:

=IF(thisDate>=timeToPrint)

= PrintCalendars(numMonths)

=END.IF

If the serial date stored in *thisDate* is greater than or equal to the serial date stored in *timeToPrint*, then the logical test evaluates to TRUE, and Excel executes the formula between the IF and END.IF functions. In this example, the formula is a macro subroutine (using the *ref( )* syntax) for printing calendars for the number of months stored in *numMonths*.

The IF–ELSE–END.IF block

An IF-ELSE-END.IF block is similar to the IF-END.IF block, but it also provides for a routine to be executed if *logical_Test* evaluates to FALSE. Using the same example, if the time to print new calendars hasn't arrived, we want the macro to update a list of tasks to be printed on the calendars:

=IF(thisDate>=timeToPrint)

=   PrintCalendars(numMonths)

=ELSE()

=   UpdateTasks()

=END.IF

The ELSE function takes no arguments and must occupy a line by itself.

The IF–ELSE.IF–END.IF block

What if you want the list of tasks to be updated only on Mondays, instead of every time the macro is run? To do this, we need to alter the macro so that it makes a second test:

=IF(thisDate>=timeToPrint)

=   PrintCalendars(numMonths)

=ELSE.IF(WEEKDAY(thisDate)=2)

=   UpdateTasks()

=END.IF

Looping functions

Macro loops let you repeat a set of calculations. Loops come in handy for two reasons: First, they save space in the macro sheet because you can "recycle" a set of instructions instead of repeating it several times. Second, the number of times a set of calculations should be repeated can vary from one situation to the next. By creating conditional tests, you can vary the number of executions.

You can use the next five functions — FOR, WHILE, NEXT, BREAK, and FOR.CELL — in a macro to repeat a calculation or action. To do this, you create FOR-NEXT, WHILE-NEXT, and FOR.CELL loops.

FOR–NEXT loops

The FOR function repeats a set of calculations a specific number of times, and takes the form

=FOR(*counter_text,start_num,end_num,step_num*)

The *counter_text* argument identifies the named value that Excel uses to keep track of how many times it has executed the loop. The *start_num* argument, which defaults to 0, is the value you want to begin with; the *end_num* argument, which defaults to 1, specifies when you want Excel to stop repeating the calculation or action. The *step_num* argument determines the increment Excel uses each time it executes the loop. If you omit *step_num*, Excel assumes it is 1.

You need not use the Define Name command to define your named *counter-text* before running the macro. Excel creates this named value as the macro is executed and resets it to its initial *start_num* value each time it encounters the loop.

The NEXT function marks the end of FOR-NEXT loops and WHILE-NEXT loops. This function takes no arguments.

The FOR-NEXT loop tells Excel to repeat a calculation or action a specified number of times before continuing with the next macro function. You designate a counter name, a start value, a stop value, and, if you want, a step value to increment the counter. After each pass through the loop, Excel adds the value in *step_num* to the current value of *counter_text*. If *counter_text* is not greater than *end_num*, Excel goes through the loop again. When the counter value is greater than the stop value, Excel stops the loop and continues with the macro function that follows NEXT.

For example, the series of formulas

=FOR("Test",1,10)

=   SET.VALUE(B1,B1*2)

=NEXT()

doubles the value in cell B1 of the macro sheet 10 times. Suppose cell B1 initially contains the value 2. On the first pass through this loop, Excel sets cell B1 to 4. On the second pass, *Test* is set to 2 and the SET.VALUE formula doubles the value in the active cell again, setting cell B1 to 8. This process continues until *Test* is greater than 10. In fact, if you issue the Define Name command after this loop is completed, you see that *Test* equals 11. (At this point, B1 equals 2048.) The next time you run the macro, *Test* is reset to the value set by the *start_num* argument, which is 1.

WHILE–NEXT loops

A WHILE-NEXT loop lets you repeat a set of calculations until a specified condition is met, and takes the form

=WHILE(*logical_test*)

:

(formulas to be executed if logical_test *is TRUE)*

:

=NEXT()

where *logical_test* determines whether Excel executes the macro again. Generally, this argument is an embedded logical test that results in a TRUE or FALSE value. When *logical_test* is TRUE, Excel continues to execute all statements up to the NEXT statement until *logical_test* becomes FALSE. If *logical_test* is FALSE the first time the macro reaches WHILE, Excel skips the loop entirely and continues with the first formula after the NEXT function.

For example, consider this simple macro loop:

=WHILE(B1<2048)

=   SET.VALUE(B1,B1*2)

=NEXT()

This routine works much like the FOR-NEXT loop you saw earlier. It doubles the value in cell B1 of the macro sheet. This time, however, the macro continues until cell B1 is greater than or equal to the test value 2048.

The BREAK function

The BREAK function lets you escape from a FOR-NEXT or WHILE-NEXT loop and continue with the function immediately after the NEXT function. The BREAK function takes no arguments.

The BREAK function stops either a FOR-NEXT loop or a WHILE-NEXT loop before completion. Often, you'll want to embed the BREAK function in your loops to help avoid error conditions. For example, in the series of statements

=WHILE(B1<2048)

=   IF(B1<0,BREAK())

=   SET.VALUE(B1,B1*2)

=NEXT()

we used a logical function to ensure that cell B1 contains a positive value. If cell B1 is less than or equal to 0, then Excel breaks the loop and continues with the macro formula immediately after the NEXT function.

FOR.CELL–NEXT loops

The FOR.CELL function runs a FOR-NEXT loop once for each cell in the specified range. It differs from a standard FOR-NEXT loop in that there is no conditional test. The FOR.CELL-NEXT structure takes the form

=FOR.CELL(*ref_name,area_ref,skip_blanks*)

:

(formulas to be executed once for each cell)

:

=NEXT()

The *ref_name* argument is a name that Excel applies to the cell currently being operated on. The *area_ref* argument specifies the group of cells to be processed, and it can be a multiple selection. If you omit *area_ref*, Excel assumes *area_ref* to be the current selection. If *skip_blanks* is TRUE, Excel does not apply the formulas in the loop to empty cells; if this argument is FALSE or omitted, Excel applies the formulas in the loop to every cell in the selection, even if they are empty.

For example, you can develop a simple routine that converts text to uppercase letters in every cell that contains text in a selected range by using the following macro:

```
Uppercase
=FOR.CELL("thisCell",TRUE)
=    IF(TYPE(thisCell=4))
=        FORMULA(UPPER(thisCell),,thisCell)
=    END.IF()
=NEXT()
=RETURN()
```

The FOR.CELL loop in the *Uppercase* macro assigns the name *thisCell* to each cell in the current selection, sequentially; blank cells are skipped. The IF formula checks whether the content of the cell is text; if so, the FORMULA formula in the next line converts the text into uppercase and puts the text back into the cell named by *thisCell*. When all the cells have been processed, Excel reaches the RETURN formula and the macro ends.

21

Building a
User Interface

Chapters 19 and 20 described how to build and create command macros and function macros. This chapter presents some advanced techniques you can use to create customized applications. The functions and techniques discussed in this chapter help you develop a user interface for a Microsoft Excel application. A Microsoft Excel application is a unified system of worksheets, charts, or other files driven by macros that can present information to users in ways that are different from Excel's standard menus and dialog boxes.

The user-interface issues discussed in this chapter include the following:

- Creating custom alerts, dialog boxes, and data forms

- Developing custom menus and menu commands

- Attaching macros to objects

- Creating custom tools and toolbars

- Responding to events, such as the opening or closing of a worksheet or macro sheet, the passing of an interval of time, the activation of a particular window, or the entry of data in a worksheet

- Saving command and function macros in the Add-In format so that they seem to belong to the standard Microsoft Excel environment

- Hiding worksheets and macro sheets that provide supporting information or serve as temporary work areas for documents so the user isn't overwhelmed with information

- Providing help for the users of an application: written documentation, help screens, templates, and comments in the macro sheets themselves

Throughout this chapter, we describe how to use functions to create a user interface. For complete details about the syntax of these functions, see the *Microsoft Excel Function Reference*.

Presenting information to the user

This section describes the functions that notify the user of conditions in the workspace and get information from the user. These functions build simple notification dialog boxes and complex custom dialog boxes, and even play recorded text or music.

The ALERT function

You can create alert boxes with the ALERT function. You can supply the message you want to display in the alert box and specify the type of alert box you want to create. For example, the first ALERT formula in the macro shown in Figure 21-1 displays the alert box in the lower right corner of the screen. If you click OK, the macro displays the alert box shown in Figure 21-2.

FIGURE 21-1.
This macro tests alert boxes.

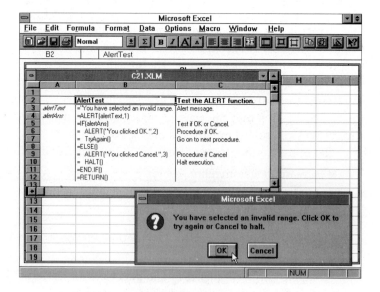

FIGURE 21-2.
*If you click OK, the
macro displays an
information alert box.*

You might use this kind of ALERT function to provide users with a "second chance" to correct an error condition. If the user clicks OK, the ALERT function returns TRUE. If the user clicks Cancel, the function returns FALSE. Often, you can use these logical results to branch to different parts of the macro.

You can also create alert boxes that contain only an OK button; the user must click OK to acknowledge the message before the macro continues. You can display an *i* symbol instead of a question-mark symbol to present information, or an exclamation point to notify the user of an error condition. As a rule, when you notify the user of an error condition, you follow the ALERT function with a HALT or RETURN, or branch to a macro subroutine that handles the error.

The MESSAGE function

The MESSAGE function lets you display custom messages in the status area at the lower left corner of the application window while your macro is running. You can specify the message and whether to turn off your control of the message area, thus resuming Microsoft Excel's normal reporting of the descriptive text associated with actions and commands. If you omit the message text, Excel displays a blank message line, which hides the normal Excel messages that usually appear in this area.

You can use the MESSAGE function to display reminder or status information to inform the user when one of your macros is about to perform a protracted calculation. For example, the formula

=MESSAGE(TRUE,"Please wait. Report being generated.")

creates a message like that shown in Figure 21-3 to let the user know the delay is caused by the macro.

FIGURE 21-3.
*Use the MESSAGE
function to display
status messages.*

When you use a MESSAGE function in a macro, be sure to include the formula

=MESSAGE(FALSE)

in the macro. Otherwise, when you halt the macro, Excel continues to display the last message you created until the user ends the current session.

Also, you can send a message to the status area even when you have told Excel not to display the status bar. (You control display of the status bar with the Workspace command on the Options menu or with the Workspace function.) When you reset the option to display the status bar, the message appears.

The INPUT function

The INPUT function displays a dialog box that prompts the user for information. You can specify the text you want to appear as a prompt in the dialog box, such as *Select the records to include in your report.* You can add a title to the dialog box; if you do not supply a title, Excel displays the word *Input* in the title bar. You can also set a default value for the text box in the dialog box; to accept this default, the user can click OK or press Enter.

Optionally, you can use a numeric code to specify the correct data type for the information to be entered. If the user doesn't enter data in the correct type, Excel tries to convert it. (For example, a single-cell reference might convert to the contents of the cell.) If Excel cannot successfully convert the data type, it displays an error message. By adding these numeric codes together, you can create an INPUT function that accepts two or more kinds of entries. For example, if the data type code is 3, the input dialog box will accept both numbers and text. If the data type code is 8, INPUT returns an absolute reference to the cell or range indicated by the user.

If the data type code is 0, the function returns the formula that the user enters in the dialog box as text. Excel converts references in the formula to R1C1-text style. For example, if the user enters the formula

=SUM($A$1:$A$10)

Excel converts that formula to *=SUM(R1C1:R10C1)*.

Finally, you can specify where to position the dialog box horizontally and vertically on the screen. These arguments should be expressed in points and are measured relative to the upper left corner of the application window. (A point is $\frac{1}{72}$ of an inch.)

Suppose you create a report-generator macro, and you want to select a group of records to include in the report. You can use an INPUT formula such as

=INPUT("Select the records to put in the report.",8,"Custom Report",
    "=Database",,)

to create a dialog box like the one in Figure 21-4. This input dialog box accepts cell references. Notice, however, that we used the range name *Database* as the default argument. If the user doesn't select another range, the INPUT function returns the address of the range named *Database*. For example, if the worksheet named *Clients* is active when the user runs the macro and the Clients database is defined as A1:F100, this INPUT function results in the reference Clients!$A$1:$F$100.

FIGURE 21-4.
This dialog box prompts the user for a range reference.

Instead of typing references in the dialog box, the user can also select cells with the mouse or the keyboard. This technique is equivalent to pasting cell references into the worksheet formula bar.

When the user clicks OK or presses Enter, Excel returns the contents of the dialog-box text box to the macro sheet. Thus, you can refer to the results of the INPUT function in later formulas to select, format, or otherwise manipulate the specified range. If, however, the user clicks Cancel, the INPUT function returns FALSE.

The BEEP function

The BEEP function sounds the computer's bell or plays a sound file; you can supply a number from 0 to 4 that specifies the type of sound the function produces. The tone your computer delivers for each number depends on your system. On some computers, the tone for all four numbers is the same. On others, the values represent the Default Beep, Critical Stop, Question, Exclamation, and Asterisk events as defined in the Sound dialog box of Windows Control Panel.

You can use BEEP to signal the user that some important event has occurred in the processing of a macro. For example, you can use BEEP to alert the user that some input is required or to signal the end of the macro.

The SOUND.NOTE and SOUND.PLAY functions

The SOUND.NOTE function lets you record, delete, or copy a sound from another file. This function requires that you have a suitable device for acquiring sound installed in your computer. (If you're using Windows 3.0, SOUND.NOTE also requires the Multimedia Extension.) This function can take two forms: In one form, you record or erase sounds and must specify the cell that you want the sound added to or deleted from; in the other form, you use previously recorded sounds and must specify the name of the file that contains the sound you want to use. If you're recording a sound from a device directly into a cell note, Excel presents the Record dialog box so the user can manage the recording process.

To play the sound, use the SOUND.PLAY function. This function corresponds to selecting a sound attached to a cell and clicking the Play button in the Note dialog box, or clicking the Import button, selecting a file and sound, and then clicking Play. Together, SOUND.NOTE and SOUND.PLAY let you add various types of sound effects to a worksheet or dialog box. For example, you can record brief suggestions to help inexperienced users of your application.

The ECHO function

The ECHO function controls the updating of the screen during execution of a macro. This function takes only one logical argument for turning screen updating on and off. By turning off screen updating, you can dramatically increase the speed of a macro. You need not include an ECHO formula at the end of a macro routine to turn on updating; when the macro stops running, Excel turns on screen updating automatically. Excel also turns on screen updating when an error message interrupts macro processing. Turning off screen updating does not prevent the display of dialog boxes.

Building a custom dialog box

At times, you might need to create complex dialog boxes that prompt the user for several items of information at a time or that offer more than one option. For example, you might want to create a dialog box that contains two or more text boxes, a list box, a group of option buttons, or a series of check boxes. Using the DIALOG.BOX function, you can create custom dialog boxes to meet these needs.

To create a dialog box, you can either build a definition table in a macro sheet, or use the Dialog Editor and paste the resulting table into your macro sheet. (See "Using the Dialog Editor," later in this chapter.) To display the dialog box, use a DIALOG.BOX formula in a macro that specifies the location of the definition table. The DIALOG.BOX function takes only one argument, which specifies a reference to the definition table. The reference can be a cell range or a defined name that evaluates to a cell range.

Building a definition table

Figure 21-5 shows a dialog box created by the definition table entered into cells I2:O40 of the macro sheet in Figure 21-6.

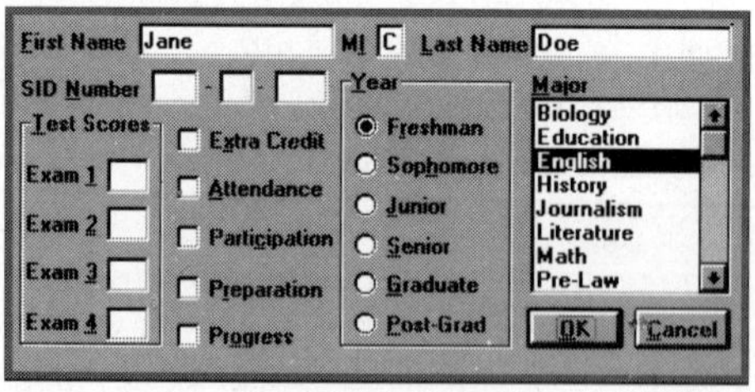

FIGURE 21-5.
This custom dialog box collects information about students.

FIGURE 21-6.
This definition table creates the dialog box shown in Figure 21-5.

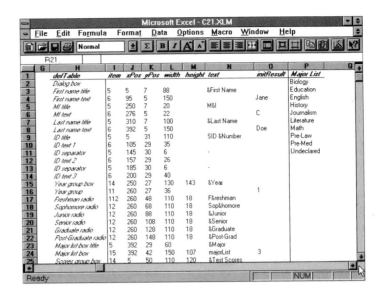

defTable	item	xPos	yPos	width	height	text	initResult	Major List
Dialog box								Biology
First name title	5	5	7	88		&First Name		Education
First name text	6	95	5	150			Jane	English
MI title	5	250	7	20		M&I		History
MI text	6	276	5	22			C	Journalism
Last name title	5	310	7	100		&Last Name		Literature
Last name text	6	392	5	150			Doe	Math
ID title	5	5	31	110		SID &Number		Pre-Law
ID text 1	6	105	29	35				Pre-Med
ID separator	5	145	30	6		.		Undeclared
ID text 2	6	157	29	26				
ID separator	5	185	30	6		.		
ID text 3	6	200	29	40				
Year group box	14	250	27	130	143	&Year		
Year group	11	260	27	36			1	
Freshman radio	112	260	48	110	18	F&reshman		
Sophomore radio	12	260	68	110	18	Sop&homore		
Junior radio	12	260	88	110	18	&Junior		
Senior radio	12	260	108	110	18	&Senior		
Graduate radio	12	260	128	110	18	&Graduate		
Post-Graduate radio	12	260	148	110	18	&Post-Grad		
Major list-box title	5	392	29	60		&Major		
Major list box	15	392	42	150	107	majorList	3	
Scores group box	14	5	50	110	120	&Test Scores		

A definition table consists of seven columns — in this case, columns I through O — and at least two rows. The titles entered in row 1 are optional; we added the labels in column H to help identify the entries in the definition table. You can use any columns in the definition table beyond the first seven essential ones to store entries for list boxes within the dialog box; we've used column P to store one list.

After you enter the definition table, it's useful to format it, so that the table stands out on the macro sheet and is easier to use in your macros. For example, you can put a border around the definition table and name it. (In this case, we called it *studentDialog*.)

The first row of the definition table (row 2) describes the height and width of the entire dialog box, as well as its position on the screen. If you don't make any entries in this row, Excel centers the dialog box and adjusts the size to accommodate the contents of the box. If you create a help file to explain the dialog-box options (see "Providing help for users," later in this chapter), you can include the name of that file in the first cell of the definition table (cell I2 in the example); otherwise, leave the cell blank. Subsequent rows of the definition table describe each item you want to display in the dialog box.

It is important to reserve space for each of the seven columns in the definition table and arrange them in the following order: *item, xPos, yPos, width, height, text,* and *initResult*. The following table offers a brief description of each of the seven columns, and a table of *item* description codes follows that.

DEFINITION TABLE COLUMNS

Column	Type	Description
item	number	The type of each object in the dialog box. (See the table of item codes that follows this table.)
xPos	number	The horizontal position, measured in points, of the dialog box on the screen or of each item within the dialog box. If you omit *xPos* in the first row of the definition table or enter a zero in this row, Excel centers the dialog box between the left and right edges of the application window. If you omit *xPos* from an item description, the program positions the item for you. When used to define the position of a dialog box, *xPos* is measured from the left edge of the application window to the left edge of the dialog box. When used to define the position of an item within a dialog box, *xPos* is measured from the left edge of the dialog box to the left edge of the item.
yPos	number	The vertical position, measured in points, of the dialog box on the screen or of each item within the dialog box. (A point is $\frac{1}{72}$ of an inch.) If you omit *yPos* in the first row of the definition table or enter a zero in this row, Excel centers the dialog box between the top and bottom edges of the application window. If you omit *yPos* from an item description, the program positions the item for you. When used to define the position of a dialog box, *yPos* is measured from the bottom edge of the menu bar to the top of the dialog box. When used to define the position of items within a dialog box, *yPos* is measured from the top of the dialog box to the top of the item.
width	number	The width of the item, measured in horizontal screen units ($\frac{1}{8}$ of the width of the characters used in the dialog boxes). The *width* values are optional; if you omit them, Excel sizes the item for you.
height	number	The height of the item, measured in vertical screen units ($\frac{1}{12}$ of the height of the characters used in the dialog boxes). The *height* values are optional; if you omit them, Excel sizes the item for you.

(Continued)

Column	Type	Description
text	text	The text associated with the item: title, name in a button, name of a radio button or check box, and so on. In most built-in dialog boxes, one character is underlined in titles, check-box names, option-group names, list-box names, and text-box names. You can move to that item by pressing Alt in conjunction with the underlined character. To achieve the same effect in a custom dialog box, place an ampersand (&) before the desired access character entered in this column.
initResult	any value	The default selections and text-box entries you want to appear when the dialog box is first displayed. In the first line of the definition table, you can enter a number in this column to specify which item is highlighted when the dialog box is displayed. Items are numbered sequentially, starting with the second row of the definition table.

ITEM DESCRIPTION CODES

item	Object	Description
1	OK button	(Default) If the *item* code is 1, the resulting OK button appears with a thick black border and is chosen when the user presses Enter. This button closes the dialog box, enters the data from the dialog box into the *initResult* column, and continues processing the macro with the next cell after the DIALOG.BOX formula. The entry in the *text* column of the definition table becomes the button's label; you can use the standard text, *OK*, or something different, such as *Enter Record*.
2	Cancel button	(Not default) Closes the dialog box without entering the data from the dialog box into the *initResult* column. Macro-sheet processing continues with the next cell after the DIALOG.BOX formula. The entry in the *text* column of the definition table becomes the button's label; you can use the standard text, *Cancel*, or something different, such as *Halt* or *Escape*.

(Continued)

item	Object	Description
3	OK button	(Not default) Same as item 1, except that the OK button is not selected when the user presses Enter.
4	Cancel button	(Default) Same as item 2, except that the Cancel button appears with a thick black border and is automatically chosen when the user presses Enter.
5	text	Descriptive labels, explanatory text, or any other message or symbol you want to display in the dialog box. Generally, however, the text items label a text box or list box. When this is the case, the text becomes associated with the item that immediately follows it in the definition table.
6	text edit box	A box into which the user can enter text. Excel accepts any kind of entry in this type of text box (in contrast with items 7 through 10). Excel ignores the *text* column for this item; to label the text box, include a text item (type 5) in the definition table. To set an initial value for the edit box, enter the desired text in the *initResult* column.
7	integer edit box	Same as item 6, except that the user can enter only integer values between −32765 and +32767. If the user makes an invalid entry, Excel beeps, displays an alert message, and highlights the contents of the edit box.
8	number edit box	Same as item 7, except that the user can enter decimal as well as integer values.
9	formula edit box	Same as item 6, except that the user can enter formulas only. Excel converts any references in the formula to R1C1 style when it transfers the formula to the *initResult* column; however, when it reopens the dialog box, Excel converts these references back to the reference style selected in the Workspace dialog box. If the user enters a number, an equal sign is inserted before it; text is enclosed in quotation marks.
10	reference edit box	Same as item 6, except that the user can enter references only. References entered in A1 style notation are converted to text in the R1C1 style when transferred to the *initResult* column. Range names are also accepted and converted to text in the R1C1 style. To define an initial value, enter the R1C1-style text in the *initResult* column.

(Continued)

item	Object	Description
11	option-button (or radio-button) group	This is the first line in an option-button group description. Designate the default option-button selection by entering the option number in the *initResult* column. Options are numbered sequentially, beginning with the row immediately below the option-button group definition. If the *initResult* column is empty, the first button is selected. Only one button in a group can be selected at a time. After the user makes a dialog-box selection, the number of the selected button is returned in the *initResult* column. The *text column* can contain a label for the group. To draw a box around the option-button group, include a group-box definition (item 14) in the row immediately above the option-button group definition.
12	option button	Displays an option button with accompanying label. Unlike edit boxes, you can label option buttons by entering the text in the *text* column. Excel ignores the contents of the *initResult* column. To activate an option button, make an entry in the *initResult* column of the preceding option-button group definition.
13	check box	Displays a check box with accompanying label. As with option-button options, label a check box by entering text in the *text column*. A TRUE value returned in the *initResult* column indicates that the check box is selected; a FALSE value or a blank cell indicates that it is deselected; an #N/A value indicates that the check box is dimmed.
14	group box	Draws a box around a group of related items. Label the group by entering a descriptive phrase in the *text* column. Enter the group-box item definition in the descriptor-range row immediately above the items you want to group.
15	list box	Displays a list box that contains a list of items defined in a range on the macro sheet. To specify the items you need to list, enter the list in a range outside the definition table, define the range, and then enter the name in the *text* column, or specify the range as R1C1-style text. Designate the default list-box selection by entering the option number in the *initResult* column. Excel numbers the options in the list sequentially, beginning with the first row of the specified range.

(Continued)

item	Object	Description
15	list box *(Continued)*	If you don't make an entry in the *initResult* column, the first list item is initially selected; if you enter #N/A, no list item is selected. After the user makes a selection, the number of the selected list item appears in the *initResult* column.
		If you want to let users select more than one item in the list at a time, enter a name in the *initResult* column. If the name is already defined on the macro sheet as a one-dimensional array, the array of numbers becomes the selected list items. If the name isn't defined, Excel defines the name. When the user clicks OK, an array that consists of the selected items in ascending order is returned as the name's new definition.
		To label the list box, include a *text item* (item 5) in the descriptor-range row above the list-box definition.
16	linked list box	Same as item 15, except that Excel enters the selected list-box item into a text box. The text edit box (item 6) must be defined in the descriptor-range row immediately above the linked list-box definition or in the row above that if the row above contains a text item (item 5) used to label this linked list box.
17	icon	Displays one of three icons that are identical to those that appear in dialog boxes created by the ALERT function. (See "The ALERT function," earlier in this chapter.) A 1 in the *text* column displays a question mark, a 2 displays an *i* icon (i), and a 3 displays an exclamation point (!).
18	linked file list box	Similar to item 16, except that this option displays a list of files in a directory. Unlike the linked list box (item 16), you don't need to specify a list of items to appear; instead, the list of filenames in the current directory is displayed. You must precede this item with a text edit box (item 6), which displays the name of the file that is currently selected in the file list box. You may also use a text item (item 5) just before this item as a label. The user can also use this text edit box to restrict the filenames that appear in the list box.

(Continued)

item	Object	Description
19	linked drive-and-directory list box	Similar to item 18, except that this option lists the available drives and directories. Excel automatically supplies the drive-and-directory names in the list box. You must precede this item with a linked file list-box definition (item 18). To change directories, enter the desired pathname in the text box that precedes that linked file list-box definition. If a fixed text item (item 5) appears after the linked drive-and-directory definition, Excel displays the name of the current drive and directory. This name is updated if the drive or directory is changed.
20	directory text	Displays the name of the current directory, which doesn't change when the user chooses a new drive or directory. To update the drive-and-directory text, use a fixed-text item (item 5) and a linked drive-and-directory list box (item 19).
21	drop-down list box	Displays a box containing the specified item of a list of items, followed by a downward-pointing arrow. The *text* column contains a reference that specifies a list stored on the macro sheet, as in the list-box item (item 15), and the reference can also be to a named array. The *height* column sets the height of the drop-down list, and the *initResult* column sets the default selected item, or contains the number of the selected item returned by the dialog box.
22	drop-down combination list box	Displays a list like the drop-down list box, but the user can edit the entry in the box like a text box. When the user clicks OK, Excel returns either the number of the list entry or the edited entry in the *initResult* column. Must be preceded by a text edit box (item 6). (For an example of this item see the Style box on the Standard toolbar.)
23	Picture button	Creates a button from a graphic object you created with the Excel drawing tools. The button acts like the item 3 OK button. To place a graphic object in a dialog box without having it act like a button, use the code 223 in place of 23.
24	Help button	Displays a button that presents the custom help topic for the dialog box. For information about creating custom help topics, see "Providing help for users," later in this chapter.

Using the intersection operator to reference cells

You can use the Create Names command to generate a set of references in a macro sheet to specify any cell in the definition table. Select both the top row and the row to the left of the definition table, which contain the identifying labels for the rows and columns in the definition table. In the example in Figure 21-6, this is the range H1:O40. Next, choose Create Names from the Formula menu and select both the Top Row and Left Column check boxes. Excel uses the names assigned to each row to name that row in the definition table, and the column headings to name each column. For example, the name of the row that defines the *Major list box* becomes *Major_list_box*. Similarly, the name attached to the *initResult* column becomes *initResult*. Finally, the name entered in the upper left cell in the range becomes the name of the definition table itself, which you can use as the *dialogRef* argument in the DIALOG.BOX function.

Make sure that each row and column identifier is unique, so that Excel does not replace the range assigned to a name with another range. The *ID separator* labels in cells H11 and H13 are examples of this (but we wouldn't usually need to differentiate between these two rows).

To access any cell in the definition table, use the intersection operator (a space character) to return the cell reference that lies at the intersection between a specified row and column. For example, if you want to find the number of the item the user chose in the Major list box, use this reference:

=Major_list_box initResult

To find the item in the list that has that number, you can use this formula:

=INDEX(majorList,Major_list_box initResult)

When you use this method, you do not have to look up and edit each direct cell reference in a system of macros if you change the structure of the definition table.

Finally, if you have more than one dialog-box definition table on a macro sheet, you can repeat the column titles for each definition table and change the definition associated with each title name so that the name refers to the entire column instead of only the portion of the column within the first definition table. To do this, select the entire range of columns, choose the Create Names command, and select the Top Row option. Doing this in our example replaces the previous definition of *initResult*, $O$2:$O$40, with $O$2:$O$16384, letting you specify references within the definition tables for every dialog box on the macro sheet with only one set of column names.

Now we examine a few of the items in our custom dialog box:

■ The text item defined in row 3 (*First name title*) of the sample definition table in Figure 21-6 becomes a label for the text edit box defined in row 4 (*First name text*).

■ Row 16 (*Year group*) describes the option-button group specified in rows 17 through 22 (*Freshman radio* through *Post-Graduate radio*). We entered a 1 in the *initResult* column for the *Year group* to preselect the Freshman option as the default.

■ The *Major* list box is specified in row 24 of the definition table. We entered the Major list in cells P2:P11, named the range *majorList,* and entered the name in the *text* column of row 24.

■ We sprinkled ampersands (&) throughout the *text* column so that the user can move among the various options in the dialog box by pressing Alt with the indicated character. To set the Year to Junior, for example, the user can press Alt-J.

Suppose you've created this dialog box as a user interface for a student database; a macro presents the dialog box that displays the initial defaults specified in the *initResult* column. The user makes entries in the text boxes, selects items from the list, selects options from the option-button and check-box groups, and then clicks OK to accept the entries. When the user clicks OK (item 1), the entries overwrite the previous entries in the *initResult* column, and the number of the item clicked is returned in the cell that contains the DIALOG.BOX function. If those results aren't changed, the next time the dialog box is displayed, the user's most recent entries and selections appear again in the dialog box.

If, however, the user clicks the Cancel button, then the DIALOG.BOX function returns FALSE and the contents of the *initResult* column remain unchanged.

Therefore, to use the information entered in the dialog box, you must access the cells in the *initResult* column. You can do this by writing a *ProcessEntry()* macro, which you call from the line after your DIALOG.BOX formula. You can also use a series of SET.VALUE functions in a *ResetDialog()* macro to reset some or all of the default values in the *initResult* column. (Another way to reset these defaults is to copy the original *initResult* column somewhere, and then have a macro use PASTE.SPECIAL to paste back the values.)

Using the Dialog Editor

To create a custom dialog box, you can set up a table as described in the preceding section, manually specifying the numeric location of each element in the dialog box. Or you can use the Dialog Editor to create a custom dialog box, and then insert a table that contains the specifications for the dialog box in the macro sheet.

A good way to proceed is to rough out the look of the dialog box using the Dialog Editor, transfer its definition table to a macro sheet, and then refine the positions of the items in the dialog box by manually adjusting numbers in the table. If you want a column of check boxes to line up, for example, they should all have the same starting value in the *xPos* column.

Creating a dialog box

First, start the Dialog Editor by choosing the Control menu's Run command, selecting the Dialog Editor option, and then clicking OK. The Dialog Editor starts, and you see an empty dialog box in the middle of the screen, as shown in Figure 21-7.

Transferring the dialog box to a macro sheet

To add an item, choose it from the Item menu; if ellipses follow the command, another dialog box appears that offers other options. After you've added the item, you can drag it around within the confines of the dialog box. To enlarge the item, place the mouse pointer over a border and drag in the direction you want the item to grow. To delete an item, select it and choose Clear from the Edit menu.

At first, you can't change the size or position of some items (such as the position of the dialog box itself) because the Dialog Editor assigns them an automatic format. You can change this by selecting the object and choosing Info from the Edit menu, or by double-clicking the item. The Info dialog box appears and lists the same information for the item that you would enter in the definition table if you were to

FIGURE 21-7.
The Dialog Editor.

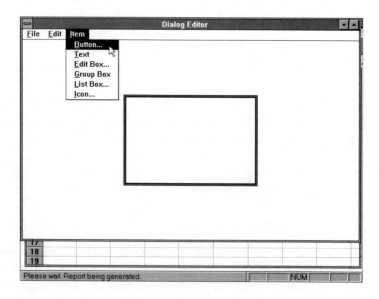

create it manually. Deselect the Auto option for the object's size or position, and then enter the numbers manually or click OK and use the mouse to resize or reposition the object.

To place a series of items inside a group box, first choose the Group box command from the Item menu; a new group box appears. While the group box is selected, choose from the Item menu the items you want to appear in the group box. As a shortcut, you can press Enter to create a new option button. Type the name of the button, and then press Enter to create the next option button. Option buttons that you add in this way are linked together; their size and position are set by the Auto format, and if you drag the top button in the group, all the buttons move.

You can also insert a new option button between two buttons or at the end of the list. To do this, select the button after which you want to insert the new button, press Enter, and then type the new button's name.

When you've arranged the contents of the new dialog box to your liking, you can transfer the definition table for the dialog box to a macro sheet. The Dialog Editor doesn't support its own file format for saving dialog box definitions, so the only way you can preserve your work, even temporarily, is to convert the dialog box into a definition table and paste the definition table into a macro sheet.

To do this, select the dialog box, either by choosing Select Dialog from the Edit menu or by clicking a border that belongs to the dialog box. Choose Copy from the Edit menu. Excel converts the dialog box into a definition table and stores it in the Clipboard. Next, switch to Excel and open or activate the macro sheet to which you want to add the definition table, select the cell where you want to place the upper left corner of the definition table, and then choose Paste from the Edit menu. Excel adds one row for each item in the definition and one row for the dialog box as a whole, so be sure there is enough room for it on your macro sheet. Finally, with the entire table selected, name the table by choosing Define Name from the Formula menu and supplying a name.

Transferring a dialog box from a macro sheet to the Dialog Editor

Although it's often easier to make minor positioning adjustments by editing numbers in the definition table, you can also use the Dialog Editor to rearrange, add, or delete items in a dialog box.

First, select the definition table. A good way to do this is to choose the Formula menu's Goto command and double-click the table's name in the Goto dialog box. Next, choose the Copy command. Finally, switch to the Dialog Editor, choose the Paste command, and make the changes you want.

When you return the changed definition table to the macro sheet, don't forget to redefine the name associated with the table, because adding or deleting items in the definition changes the length of the table.

Dynamic custom dialog boxes

You can create dialog boxes that change when the user selects certain options or clicks certain buttons. Examples of such dynamic dialog boxes in the Excel program itself are the Series, Define Name, Calculation, Workspace, Apply Names, and Style dialog boxes. In the Define Name dialog box, for example, when you define a new command macro and select the Command option, the Key text box becomes available. The action taken with one option changes the condition of another option.

In standard dialog boxes, only buttons of types 1 through 4 (corresponding to what are typically named the OK and Cancel buttons) can dismiss a dialog box. In dynamic dialog boxes, other items, called *triggers*, can return information to the cell that contains the DIALOG.BOX function and the *initResult* column of the definition table, but without dismissing the dialog box. The macro that brings up the dialog box can then respond to the information returned, modify the definition table, and redisplay the dialog box with the new configuration. Alternatively, it can use DIALOG.BOX(FALSE) to dismiss the dialog box.

You turn an item into a trigger by adding 100 to its code. You can change the following types of objects into triggers:

item	Description
1	OK button (default)
2	Cancel button (not default)
3	OK button (not default)
4	Cancel button (default)
11	option-button group
12	option button
13	check box
14	group box (option-group boxes only)
15	list box
16	linked list box
18	linked file list box
19	linked drive-and-directory list box
21	drop-down list box
23	picture button

For example, to turn a particular option button into a trigger, you add 100 to its item code, 12, and enter 112 in the *item* column for that option button. Trigger option buttons supersede an option-button group that is a trigger.

A dimmed object is, in a sense, the opposite of a trigger; you can't take any action on it. You dim an object by adding 200 to its item number.

The pattern of a macro that manages a dynamic dialog box is as follows. Returning to Figure 21-6, assume that the range of the definition table is assigned the name *studentDialog*, and you use the Create Names command to assign names to both the objects in the dialog box and the column titles, as described in the sidebar earlier in this chapter. If you want the Graduate option button, the twentieth item in the dialog box, to activate the Progress check box, use the following series of formulas:

=SET.VALUE(Graduate_radio item,112)

=SET.VALUE(Progress_check item,213)

=DIALOG.BOX(studentDialog)

=IF(up1=19)

= SET.VALUE(Progress_check item, Progress_check item–200)

= DIALOG.BOX(studentDialog)

=END.IF

:

(macro formulas that process the returned information)

:

where *up1* is defined as the relative reference R[–1]C. However, the user can select the trigger option button again, and execution will continue with the next formula after the END.IF formula, regardless of whether the user finished entering text and setting options in the dialog box. In practice, you can put all the DIALOG.BOX functions that display or redisplay the dialog box in a WHILE-NEXT loop, recycling the dialog box until the user actually clicks OK or Cancel. It would also help to develop a macro that does the equivalent of toggling the dimming or undimming of the item, depending on whether the trigger object is selected again.

Building custom data forms

As discussed in Chapter 16, you can replace Excel's built-in data form with a custom data form. Building a custom data form for a database is similar to specifying a custom dialog box, but Excel adds its own buttons to the data form and limits the number of possible items. However, you can define a custom data form in the worksheet that contains the database instead of on a macro sheet. This process doesn't involve macros, but it does provide another way for you to refine the user interface for the Excel applications you develop.

To create a data form, first create a definition table for it in the same worksheet that contains the database (or use the Dialog Editor and paste the definition table into the worksheet). Set up this definition table like the one we created in Figure 21-6, but use only item 5 for static text and item 6 for the text box where the user will type the entries to add to the database. You need not include items to create the standard buttons that appear in a data form (New, Delete, Restore, Find Prev, Find

Next, Criteria, and Exit); Excel creates these buttons automatically. Excel also creates the record-number designation in the upper right corner of the data form (such as *1 of 10*) and the scroll bar used to move among records.

After setting up your definition table, select all of it and name it *Data_Form*. Your custom data form will now appear whenever you choose Form from the Data menu.

Excel does not link the custom data form to your database range, however. To link each field in the data form to a database field, you must enter the database-field name in the *initResult* column of the definition table in the same row as the item that defines the text box for that field's data. This field name must exactly match the name that appears in the field header row of the database; otherwise, Excel will not transfer the contents of the form window to the database correctly.

Although the field names in the *initResult* column must exactly match the field names in the header row of the database, the text you use to label each text box in the form need not match the database-field names. For example, your database might contain a field named *FName*, but in the custom data form the corresponding text box can be labeled *First Name*. In addition, the fields in the custom data form need not appear in the same order as the fields in your database; however, every field you create in the data form must correspond to one of the fields in the database range.

You don't need to include all the database fields in the data form. If you include locked or calculated fields, they will appear in the form window without boxes and will not be available for editing.

Customizing menus

In addition to dialog boxes and data forms, you can create custom menu bars, menus, and commands. When the user chooses a custom command, Microsoft Excel runs the associated macro. You can add new commands to Excel's built-in menus, rename existing commands, dim them, put check marks next to them, and remove them. You can even create menus to add to a built-in menu bar (such as the Chart menu bar) or to appear on a new menu bar of your own design.

We classify the functions for customizing menus in three groups, depending on whether they affect commands, menus, or menu bars.

Creating new commands

The first group comprises the following functions:

- The ADD.COMMAND function lets you add new menu commands.
- The ENABLE.COMMAND function lets you dim and undim commands.

- The CHECK.COMMAND function lets you add a check mark before the command or remove it.

- The RENAME.COMMAND function lets you rename commands.

- The DELETE.COMMAND function lets you delete commands.

- The CUSTOM.REPEAT function lets you set the REPEAT command.

- The CUSTOM.UNDO function lets you set the UNDO command.

Many of Excel's custom-menu functions require an argument that identifies the menu bar you want to work with. The program's nine built-in menu bars are numbered from 1 through 9:

bar number	Menu bar
1	Macro and worksheet (full menus)
2	Chart (full menus)
3	Nil (contains File and Help menus only; appears when no documents are open in the workspace)
4	Info
5	Macro and worksheet (short menus)
6	Chart (short menus)
7	Cell, toolbar, and workbook shortcut menus
8	Object shortcut menu
9	Charting shortcut menu

You can use the GET.BAR function to find the number of the current menu bar. (See "The GET.BAR function," later in this chapter.) If you create a custom menu bar, the ADD.BAR function returns a new bar number for the added menu bar.

Many of the menu functions also require that you identify the menu with which you want to work, either by numerical position (1 is the leftmost menu), or by name, as text. Thus, in the worksheet environment, you can use an argument of 3 or "Formula" to refer to the Formula menu, the third menu in a worksheet document. If you add a command to one of the shortcut menus, you can also specify the exact shortcut menu that you want to appear when the user presses the right mouse button with the pointer over the various active areas on the screen.

Some functions require an argument that points to an entry in a table of menu commands on the macro sheet, called a *menu definition table*. A good place to put a menu definition table is to the right of the columns that encompass the dialog box definition tables. Using the dialog box example presented earlier in this chapter (see Figure 21-6), the menu definition table could begin in column R of the macro sheet.

The menu definition table consists of five columns, which we can name *commandName, macroName, shortcut, statusMessage,* and *helpTopic.*

Column	Description
commandName	The name of the command, or a single hyphen for a separator line. You can also use the ampersand (&) to aid in choosing commands using the keyboard.
macroName	An external reference to a name or to an external reference in the R1C1 style to the first cell of the command macro you want to invoke when the command is chosen. The macro can be on the same or another open macro sheet.
shortcut	Ignored for the Windows and OS/2 versions of Excel, but serves as a placeholder for compatibility with the Macintosh version of Excel.
statusMessage	An optional label that describes the menu or command. When the user selects the command, this label appears in the status bar at the lower left corner of the window. For example, when the user selects the Cut command from the Edit menu, the message *Move selected cells to the Clipboard* appears in the status bar.
helpTopic	An optional help topic, described in "Providing help for users," later in this chapter. If you create a custom help file to explain a menu or command, you can identify that help file in this column.

Many of the menu functions include an argument that specifies where on the menu you want the command to appear — either a number that reflects the position of the command on the menu or the command name as text. The separator lines that appear between some commands count in the numbering. For example, the Save command on the File menu has a position value of 6 because it is preceded by four commands (New, Open, Close, and Links) and one separator line. In general, use names rather than numbers, because you can't always be sure that the number of a command will remain the same if you delete another command. Using names also makes your macros more readable.

The ADD.COMMAND function

The ADD.COMMAND function lets you place a new command on a menu. If ADD.COMMAND succeeds, Excel adds the command to the appropriate menu and returns the new command's position number. You can supply a position number above which Excel adds the new command; if the number is omitted, Excel adds the command to the bottom of the menu.

Suppose you've created a command macro called *Totals* that assigns selected cells a bold font, centered alignment, an outline border, and the $#,###.00 numeric format. Let's add a command to the Format menu that invokes this macro. We'll name the command *Totals* and separate it from the rest of the menu. We'll assume that the *Totals* macro is located in a macro sheet named FORMATS.XLM.

We can use the formula

=ADD.COMMAND(1,"Format",R4:V5)

to add the Totals command to the Format menu. This formula refers to a definition table located in cells R4:V5 of the macro sheet. (See Figure 21-8.)

The first row in this definition table (other than the column headings) contains only a single hyphen character in cell R4, indicating that you want a separator line to appear between the new command and the previous command on the menu. The second line of the definition table defines the Total command. In cell R5, we entered the command name, preceded by an ampersand. The ampersand underlines the *T*, allowing the user to select the command by pressing */TT*; the first *T* selects the Format menu, and the second chooses the new Totals command.

In cell S5, we entered the external reference text *FORMATS.XLM!Totals*. This entry specifies that the FORMATS.XLM macro sheet contains the command macro associated with the Totals command, and that the macro starts in the cell named *Totals*. When the user chooses the Totals command, Excel runs this macro.

The third column, column T, acts as a placeholder and is ignored. The fourth column contains the message we want to appear in the status bar. As you can see in Figure 21-9 on the following page, this message appears at the lower left corner of the application window when the command is selected.

FIGURE 21-8.
The macro and definition table used to create the Totals command.

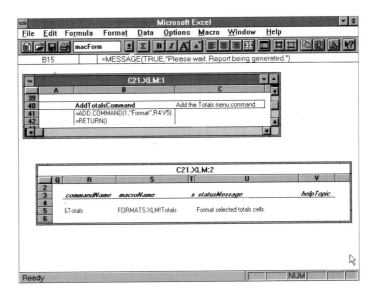

FIGURE 21-9.
*The separator line and
Totals command now
appear on the Format
menu.*

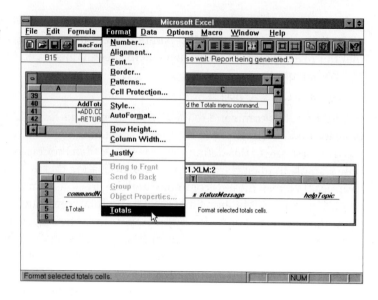

We omitted the fifth column from our definition table in this example. If you've created a custom help file to guide the user, however, you can use this column to include a reference to that help file.

The ENABLE.COMMAND function

On occasion, you might need to disable a command. The ENABLE.COMMAND function lets you enable and disable custom commands. You can specify the command to enable — either the position number or the name of the command. If you use 0 (zero), the entire menu is enabled or disabled. You cannot disable the built-in commands, but you can delete them with the DELETE.COMMAND function. (See "The DELETE.COMMAND function," later in this chapter.)

To dim the Totals command in our example, you can use the formula

=ENABLE.COMMAND(1,"Format","Totals",FALSE)

The CHECK.COMMAND function

The CHECK.COMMAND function places or removes a check mark before a command. Check marks are useful for showing that some condition is in effect. For example, if you created a command and accompanying command macro to display formulas on a worksheet, you can use a check mark to indicate when formula viewing is in effect.

Because the action of a built-in command is internal to the program, if you put a check mark before a built-in command, the check mark often disappears mysteriously.

The RENAME.COMMAND function

The RENAME.COMMAND function assigns a different name to a specified command on a menu, whether a built-in or custom command, or the name of a menu itself. In addition to arguments that describe the menu name and position in a menu bar, you can also specify the new name you want to assign to the command. For example, suppose you want to change the Open command on the File menu to *Get Document*. You can use the formula

=RENAME.COMMAND(1,"File","Open","&GetDocument")

To change the name of a menu rather than a command, use 0 (zero) as the *command* argument.

The DELETE.COMMAND function

The DELETE.COMMAND function removes a command from a specified menu; you can delete both built-in and custom commands.

Suppose you want to prevent the user from selecting the Delete command on the Data menu. You can use the formula

=DELETE.COMMAND(1,"Data","Delete")

to remove the command altogether. Make sure you don't delete the Exit command on the File menu unless you provide a command macro for quitting Excel (or unless you want users to reboot their machines).

You can delete the list of recently opened files that appears at the bottom of the File menu by setting the command argument to *File List*. You can delete the Window menu's list of open windows by using *Window List* as the command argument. When you delete a command, all the commands below the deleted command move up one position — another reason to avoid specifying commands by position.

The DELETE.COMMAND function returns an ID number. If you need to restore a deleted command, use this ID number as the command argument in an ADD.COMMAND formula.

The CUSTOM.REPEAT function

You insert the CUSTOM.REPEAT function inside a command macro associated with a menu command when you want to provide a means for repeating the command. When executed, this function creates a Repeat command that is customized for a menu command.

You can specify the name of the macro you want to run when the user chooses the Repeat command. Generally, this is the name of the command macro itself. You can also specify the wording of the Repeat command that appears in the Edit menu, as well as the text recorded when the user records the associated menu command with the recorder.

Suppose you want to create a custom Repeat command for the Totals menu command described earlier and to provide a formula to be recorded. To do this, insert the following formula into the Totals command macro:

=CUSTOM.REPEAT("Totals","&Repeat Totals", "=FORMATS.XLM!Totals()")

The CUSTOM.UNDO function

Like the CUSTOM.REPEAT function, you insert the CUSTOM.UNDO function inside the command macro associated with a particular menu command. You can specify the name of the command macro that undoes the action performed by the menu command, and you can also specify the exact wording of the Undo command. For example,

=CUSTOM.UNDO("RemoveTotals","&Undo Totals")

specifies that a command named *RemoveTotals* runs if the user chooses the Undo Totals command.

Creating new menus

This section describes how you can create new menus. You can add these menus to built-in menu bars or to custom menu bars. (See "Creating new menu bars," later in this chapter.)

The ADD.MENU function

To add a custom menu to a built-in menu bar or to a custom menu bar, use the ADD.MENU function. You can specify the number of the menu bar to which you're adding the menu, the location of the menu definition table, and the position of the menu relative to the other menus in the menu bar. If ADD.MENU succeeds, Excel returns the new menu's position number to the macro sheet.

With one exception, the menu definition table you use is identical to the one used to create new commands on pre-existing menus. Figure 21-10 shows a sample definition table, the macro used to create the menu, and the Student menu itself, to the left of the Help menu.

The difference is that in the first cell of the definition table you enter the name of the menu, preceded by an ampersand. Excel underlines the *S* in the menu, and the user can select the menu by pressing Alt-S. Cell U8 holds the descriptive text that appears in the status bar when the user selects the menu name.

Rows 9 through 11 of the definition table list the menu's new commands: *Add New Student, Edit Record,* and *Create Report.* Column S contains external references

FIGURE 21-10.
The definition table and macro create a custom Students menu that contains three commands.

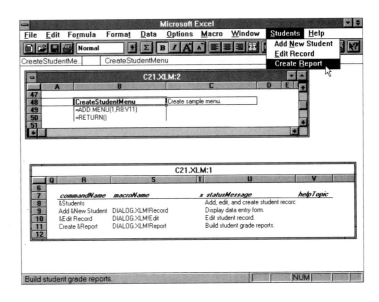

to the command macros invoked when the user selects the commands. Column U contains the command descriptions. You can use the fifth column to identify a custom help topic for each command.

Notice that the ADD.MENU formula in the *CreateStudentMenu* macro specifies the first two arguments, but not the third; if you omit *position,* the new menu becomes the new rightmost menu, except for the ubiquitous Help menu. (You can, however, delete the Help menu if needed.)

The DELETE.MENU function

The DELETE.MENU function removes a built-in or custom menu and takes as arguments the location of the menu to be deleted from the specified menu bar.

After you remove the menu, Excel decreases the menu position numbers by one for all menus to the right of the deleted menu. If you try to delete a nonexistent menu, DELETE.MENU returns a #VALUE! error. To restore a built-in menu without its custom commands, use the ADD.MENU function, supplying the menu name as an argument.

Creating new menu bars

If you want to develop an entire application within Excel, you can create up to 15 completely new menu bars for custom menus and commands. You can add, remove, hide, show, and get information about menu bars by using the ADD.BAR, SHOW.BAR, DELETE.BAR, and GET.BAR functions. As described earlier, Excel's nine built-in menu bars have the following menu bar IDs:

bar number	Menu bar
1	Macro and worksheet (full menus)
2	Chart (full menus)
3	Nil (contains File and Help menus only; appears when no documents are open in the workspace)
4	Info
5	Macro and worksheet (short menus)
6	Chart (short menus)
7	Cell, toolbar, and workbook shortcut menus
8	Object shortcut menu
9	Charting shortcut menu

The ADD.BAR function

The ADD.BAR function lets you create a menu bar. It takes no arguments. ADD.BAR returns the bar number of the new menu bar. If more than 15 custom menu bars are defined at one time, this function returns #VALUE! You might find it helpful to use the Create Names command to create a named cell reference for the cell that contains the ADD.BAR formula, or use the SET.NAME function to assign a descriptive name to the number returned by the ADD.BAR function, which you can then use in other formulas.

The SHOW.BAR function

The ADD.BAR function does not display the menu bar. To make the bar appear, you must use the SHOW.BAR function. First, however, you need to use one or more ADD.MENU functions to add menus and commands to the bar, using the result of the ADD.BAR function as the *bar_num* argument.

To display your menu bar and new menus, use the SHOW.BAR function. To redisplay a built-in menu, set *bar_num* to the appropriate number (1 through 9). If the specified menu bar is not appropriate for the active document, SHOW.BAR returns an error and stops the macro. If you omit the bar number, Excel displays the appropriate menu bar for the active document.

The *CreateStudentBar* macro in Figure 21-11 shows a definition table and macro that create the custom menu bar at the top of the screen.

FIGURE 21-11.

This macro uses the menu definition tables to create the menu bar at the top of the screen.

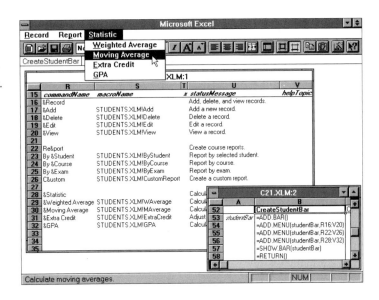

As you can see, the three ADD.MENU functions after the ADD.BAR function use the reference *studentBar* as their *bar_num* arguments and refer to the definition tables shown in Figure 21-11. These definition tables are set up exactly like the ones shown in Figure 21-10. Finally, the SHOW.BAR function displays the menu bar on the screen.

The DELETE.BAR function

To eliminate a menu bar, use the DELETE.BAR function. Its single argument must be the number of a menu bar returned by the ADD.BAR function. You cannot delete a built-in menu bar (bars 1 through 9). Nor can you use the bar number of a currently displayed menu bar as the argument of a DELETE.BAR function. Before deleting a bar, use the SHOW.BAR command to display another menu bar.

The GET.BAR function

The GET.BAR function returns information about menu bars, menus, and commands. This function has two forms. Use the first to find the ID number of the current menu bar. You use this form when you create a custom menu bar and need to include the bar number as an argument in a function. For example, to add a command to the current menu bar, you can embed a GET.BAR function as the *bar_num* argument.

Use the second form of this function to find the name or position number of a specified menu or command, given the menu bar number, and either the menu's name or position number in the menu bar. If you specify the name of the command, Excel returns the position number of the command on the specified menu; if you specify the position number, then Excel returns the name of the command.

Customizing toolbars

We discuss interactively customizing toolbars in Appendix A, but even if you've skipped ahead and read that section, you'll need a few definitions. A *tool* is an action or operation that you can request from Microsoft Excel, such as an action normally attached to any of Excel's menu commands. It can also be a procedure defined by a macro. Excel supports over 130 built-in tools, which are listed in Appendix A. Each built-in tool has a default image, and an associated name and identification (ID) number.

The image attached to a tool that the user sees on a toolbar is called a *tool face*. You can use any of the built-in tool faces or create your own tool faces in a painting or drawing program, such as the Windows Paintbrush application shown in Figure 21-12. The tool face on the left is the Excel printer tool face; the one on the right we drew. Figure 21-13 shows the tool face we drew displayed on a toolbar. Tool faces should fit within a rectangle 16 pixels wide and 15 pixels tall. Otherwise, Excel scales the image to these dimensions, which usually distorts the image.

FIGURE 21-12.
You can create custom tool faces in a paint program such as Windows Paintbrush.

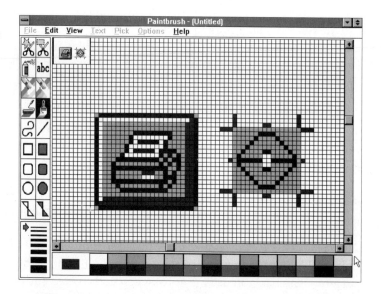

FIGURE 21-13.
The resulting tool face displayed on a toolbar.

A *toolbar* is a type of window in which the user can access available tools, and move tools and their assigned tool faces. A toolbar can be hidden or visible, docked against any of the four edges of the Excel workspace, or floating somewhere in the middle of the workspace. Excel supports nine built-in toolbars, which have their own ID numbers, as shown in the following table:

number	Toolbar
1	Excel's standard toolbar: file, style, and formatting tools
2	Formatting: style, font, and numeric formatting tools
3	Utility: editing, sorting, outlining, and other tools
4	Chart: tools for creating and formatting charts
5	Drawing: tools for creating graphic object such as lines, arcs, circles, and text boxes
6	Excel 3: tools which match those found in Excel 3
7	Macro: tools for pasting names and functions, and for recording and running macros
8	Stop Recording: the Stop Recording tool
9	Macro Paused: the Macro Paused tool, which is also available on the Macro toolbar

Working with tools and toolbars through macros is very similar to working with menus: In the same way that you can add commands to Excel's built-in menus, add menus to menu bars, and add menu bars to the set of built-in menu bars available to Excel, you can add tools to toolbars, create new tools, assign them to tool faces, and bring together collections of tools into custom toolbars.

First, we'll look at the range of macro functions you can use to work with tools, and then the macro functions you can use to work with toolbars.

Creating new tools

The first group comprises functions for working with the tools on a toolbar, such as adding a tool to a toolbar, assigning a macro routine to a tool, enabling and clicking a tool, and moving a tool face between tools.

The ADD.TOOL function

The ADD.TOOL function adds a tool to a toolbar. You can specify the number (or in the case of a custom toolbar, the name of a toolbar), the position of the tool on the toolbar, and the reference of a toolbar description table or the ID of a built-in tool.

For example, to add the Stop Recording tool to the Macro toolbar, you can use the formula

=ADD.TOOL(7,8,99)

The 7 specifies the Macro toolbar, the 8 sets the position of the tool to the rightmost tool but one (the gap between the third and the fourth tool counts as one position), and the 99 specifies the Stop Recording tool and tool face. If your macro executes this formula on the default Macro toolbar, the resulting toolbar looks like the second one shown in Figure 21-14.

FIGURE 21-14.
*The toolbar before and
after adding the Stop
Recording tool.*

The ASSIGN.TO.TOOL function

The ASSIGN.TO.TOOL function assigns the specified macro to a tool; it corresponds to using the Assign to Tool command on the Macro menu or the Assign Macro To Tool command on the Tools shortcut menu. You can supply as arguments the ID number or name of a toolbar, the position of the tool to which you want to assign the macro, and the name or reference of a macro to run when the user clicks the tool.

For example, Excel doesn't offer a tool that is equivalent to the Set Recorder command. If you want to create a custom tool, you can create a MySetRecorder macro on a macro sheet called MACROMGR.XLM, create a custom tool face, add the tool face to the Macro toolbar (in the tenth position, let's say), and use the following formula to assign the macro to the custom tool:

=ASSIGN.TO.TOOL(7,10,"MACROMGR.XLM!MySetRecorder")

The ENABLE.TOOL function

It's often inappropriate to use a tool under certain conditions. For example, it doesn't make sense to add a chart legend to a macro sheet — when you click the tool, Excel only beeps. The ENABLE.TOOL function is analogous to the ENABLE.COMMAND function. It lets a macro control whether clicking a tool initiates an associated macro routine. You can specify the toolbar and position of the tool on the toolbar, and whether the tool is enabled or disabled.

The PRESS.TOOL function

The PRESS.TOOL function changes the appearance of a tool on the specified toolbar. You can use this to give the user information about the state of a format or process during the execution of a macro. For example, you can create a tool that is linked to a macro routine for transferring information from another application to an Excel worksheet: the user clicks the button, and the button stays "depressed" until the process is complete.

The COPY.TOOL and PASTE.TOOL functions

The COPY.TOOL function corresponds to using the Copy Tool Face command from the Edit menu or the Tools shortcut menu to copy a tool face to the Clipboard. You can specify the number or name of a built-in or custom toolbar and the position of a tool on the toolbar whose face you want to copy. After you do this, you can use the PASTE.TOOL function to duplicate the process of choosing the Paste Tool Face command from the Edit menu to replace the image of the specified tool with the image on the Clipboard.

The MOVE.TOOL function

The MOVE.TOOL function copies or moves a tool, including its face and associated macro, from one bar to another. This function corresponds to the action of dragging a tool from one toolbar to another while the Customize dialog box is active. You can specify the source and destination toolbar ID and tool position, whether to copy the specifed tool, which results in two tools, or whether to move the tool, which results in one tool.

The DELETE.TOOL function

The DELETE.TOOL function corresponds to dragging a tool off a toolbar or choosing the Delete Tool comand from the Tools shortcut menu to delete the tool. You can specify the number or name of a toolbar and the position of a tool on the toolbar.

The GET.TOOL function

Given the position of a tool on the specified toolbar, the GET.TOOL function returns a range of items of information about the tool. This information includes the tool's ID number, the name or reference of its associated macro routine, and whether the tool is up, down, enabled, or disabled.

For example, you can use the PRESS.TOOL function with GET.TOOL to reverse the state of a button in a toolbar, creating the ability to toggle the tool from the pressed state to the unpressed state.

The RESET.TOOL function

The RESET.TOOL function is equivalent to selecting a built-in tool, choosing the Reset Tool Face command from the Tools shortcut menu, removing the assignment of a macro to a built-in tool, and restoring its original assignment. You can specify the ID of the toolbar and the position of a tool.

Creating new toolbars

Working with toolbars is similar to working with menu bars. First, you create the toolbar, usually through a structured definition table, adding a list of built-in and custom tools to the toolbar. Next, you display the toolbar, either in one of the docked positions or in a floating window in the Excel workspace.

Figure 21-15 shows the standard structure for a toolbar definition table in cells X2:AE6; each row in the table specifies either a built-in or a custom tool. You can specify the following items in the table, indicated in the figure by the labels at the top of the sheet:

Item	Description
toolID	Either a number that specifies one of the built-in tools (if 140 or less) or a custom tool (if greater than 140), or a name that you can use to identify the tool, as shown in the fifth row of the table.
macroName	The name of a macro to run when the user clicks the tool.
down	Whether the tool usually appears in the pressed state.
enabled	Whether the tool is enabled.
face	The tool face displayed for the tool. In Figure 21-15, we pasted the object in the right side of the cell that contains the name that identifies the tool face.
helpText	The help text displayed in the status bar when the user first clicks the tool.
balloon	In the Macintosh version of Excel, balloon text that appears when Balloon Help is turned on and the mouse pointer is positioned over the tool.
helpTopic	A reference to a topic in the specified Help file.

FIGURE 21-15.
A toolbar definition table.

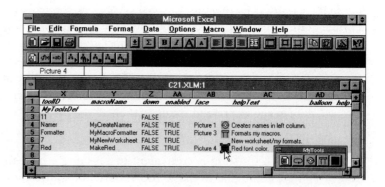

The ADD.TOOLBAR function

The ADD.TOOLBAR function creates a toolbar that contains zero or more tools. You can specify the ID of a built-in or custom toolbar and a reference area that describes the toolbar. If you use this function to create a new toolbar but don't specify any tools, you can use ADD.TOOL to populate the toolbar. In Figure 21-15, we've shaded the definition table and used the Define Name dialog box to give the table the name *MyToolsDef*. To add the toolbar and name it *MyTools*, you can use the formula

=ADD.TOOLBAR("MyTools",MyToolsDef)

The SHOW.TOOLBAR function

The SHOW.TOOLBAR function lets you display or hide the specified toolbar. It corresponds to selecting the name of a toolbar in the Toolbars dialog box and clicking the Show button, or selecting the name of a toolbar in the Tools shortcut menu.

For example, the formula

=SHOW.TOOLBAR("MyTools",TRUE)

displays the toolbar created in the last example.

The CUSTOMIZE.TOOLBAR function

The CUSTOMIZE.TOOLBAR function corresponds to using the Option menu's Toolbar command or the Customize command on the Tools shortcut menu to bring up the Customize Toolbar dialog box. Because everything you can do in this dialog box is represented by other macro functions, the CUSTOMIZE.TOOLBAR function is available only in the question-mark form.

The DELETE.TOOLBAR function

The DELETE.TOOLBAR function corresponds to selecting and then deleting a custom toolbar in the Toolbar dialog box. You cannot delete built-in toolbars.

The GET.TOOLBAR function

The GET.TOOLBAR function is like the GET.TOOL function, but returns items of information about the specified toolbar. This information includes an array of the ID number of every tool on the specified toolbar, the position and size of the toolbar, and whether the toolbar is visible or hidden.

For example, the formula

=SET.NAME("toolsArray",GET.TOOLBAR(1,"MyTools"))

assigns the name *toolsArray* to the list of all tool ID numbers or names on the *MyTools* toolbar defined with the ADD.TOOL function. (See "The ADD.TOOL function," earlier in this chapter.)

The RESET.TOOLBAR function

The RESET.TOOLBAR function is similar to the RESET.TOOL function, but it resets a built-in toolbar to its default state, removing any tools that were added and restoring all the tools in the toolbar to their original assignments. If your macro attempts to reset a custom toolbar, the function returns FALSE and takes no other action.

The SAVE.TOOLBAR function

The SAVE.TOOLBAR function saves one or more toolbars in the specified file. If you omit the filename, Excel saves the toolbar in the EXCEL.XLB file. You can supply the ID of one toolbar, or an array of IDs for a series of toolbars.

Attaching macros to objects

You can initiate a command macro in several ways: through the Run dialog box; by using a keyboard shortcut; by choosing a menu command assigned to a macro; by clicking a tool in a toolbar; by associating a macro with an event in the workspace; and by specifying that a macro be run when you take an action in a custom dialog box. You can also have Microsoft Excel run a macro whenever the user clicks a graphic object on a worksheet or macro sheet.

Protecting the macro sheet

After you finish entering one or more macros into a macro sheet, you might need to protect the macro sheet to prevent any accidental changes or destruction of data. You can apply all the same protection techniques to macro sheets that are available for worksheets. For example, you can protect the document by entering a password in the Save As dialog box.

You can also lock the cells in the macro sheet by applying the Locked setting in the Cell Protection dialog box and then using the Protect Document command on the Options menu. You can also use the Windows option in the Protect Document dialog box to prevent the user from activating the macro sheet. You can even hide the macro sheet from view by using the Hide command on the Window menu.

If you design your macro to work with a worksheet template, you can apply many of the same protection measures to the template as well. For example, you can lock all the cells in the template except for the specific input cells in which you want the user to enter data.

You can use any of the following to initiate macro execution:

- Buttons, created with the Button tool in the toolbar. You can even hide buttons in the rows of an outline, revealing nested sets of buttons that offer a range of commands.

- Lines, rectangles, ovals, arcs, and pasted pictures.

- Text boxes. After you assign a macro to a text box, when a user clicks the text box, Excel activates the macro instead of setting an insertion point in the text.

- Embedded charts. You can create a macro, for example, to update a chart in a particular way when the user clicks the chart.

To assign a macro to an object, select the object, either by pressing Ctrl and clicking the object, or by using the Selection tool in the toolbar and dragging an outline around the object. Next, choose Assign to Object from the Macro menu, and either select a macro from the open macro sheets listed in the dialog box or enter an external reference to the command macro.

When the user clicks an object assigned to a macro, the macro runs. If the macro sheet that contains the macro isn't open, Excel opens it and then runs the macro.

To remove a macro assigned to an object, select the object, choose the Assign To Object command, and delete the reference to the macro in the Reference text box.

Responding to events in the workspace

If you want Microsoft Excel to run a macro every time the user opens or closes a document, you can identify that macro as an *autoexec* macro — a special type of macro executed automatically, without a Run, menu, or Ctrl-key command from the user. A macro can identify and respond to other types of events as well: the activation of a window, the recalculation of a worksheet, the passage of time, the occurrence of an error on a macro sheet, and so on.

Auto-open macros

To run a macro automatically when you open a document, begin by activating the document. Next, choose Define Name from the Formula menu, and enter a name that starts with *Auto_Open* in the Name text box, such as *Auto_Open_Macros*. In the Refers to text box, enter the reference of the first cell of the macro you want to run, such as *MACLIB.XLM!StartStudentApp*. If you enter an external reference, Excel first opens the macro sheet and then runs the macro. If you don't use an external reference, Excel assumes that the macro sheet is already open. Finally, click OK or press Enter.

From now on, whenever that document is opened, Excel runs the specified macro. If you want to open the document and bypass the auto-open macro, choose the Open command from the File menu, select the filename from the list box, and hold down Shift while you click OK. Also hold down Shift while clicking OK in any other dialog box (such as one requesting a password) that appears before the document opens.

If you use an auto-open macro to open a macro sheet that has an auto-open macro of its own, Excel won't run the second macro. To avoid this problem, you can include a RUN formula in the first auto-open macro.

Also, you can run a succession of auto-open macros from one document, each starting with the text *Auto_Open*. For example, to start a complicated Excel application you've developed, you can create macros named *Auto_Open_InitMenus*, *Auto_Open_LoadTemplates*, *Auto_Open_AddIns*, and *Auto_Open_InitDialog*.

You can specify that a certain document, such as a macro library, open automatically each time the user starts Excel, by putting the document in Excel's STARTUP directory. If that document specifies one or more auto-open macros, you can start an entire Excel application automatically.

Auto-close macros

To run a macro automatically whenever a document is closed, follow the procedure described for creating an auto-open macro, but enter a name that starts with *Auto_Close* in the Name text box of the Define Name dialog box. The macro sheet that contains the auto-close macro must be open when the document is closed. To close the document without executing the macro, press Shift as you issue the Close command.

You can prevent a document from being closed, if needed, by putting the formula

=HALT(TRUE)

in an auto-close macro.

Responding to other types of events

Excel offers several additional functions that let you execute macros automatically whenever certain events occur. For example, you can have Excel run your macro whenever the user selects a certain window or double-clicks the mouse.

The ON.RECALC function

Use the ON.RECALC function when you want a specified macro to run when the user, rather than a macro, recalculates the worksheet. The macro runs whenever the specified document is recalculated. If you do not specify the document, the macro runs whenever any document is recalculated.

To turn off the recalculation macro for a document, use the formula

=ON.RECALC(*sheet_text*)

To turn off a recalculation macro that runs for every document unspecified in a previous ON.RECALC formula, use the formula

=ON.RECALC()

The ON.KEY function

The ON.KEY function runs a macro when the user presses a specific key. You can specify the key the user presses to run the specified macro as any single key or any key combined with Shift and/or Ctrl and/or Alt.

If you use " " (a null string) instead of specifying a macro, Excel does nothing when a user presses the specified key. If you omit the argument, the key returns to its normal use. Be sure the macro sheet that contains the macro is open; if it's closed, Excel returns an error when the user presses the key.

The DISABLE.INPUT and CANCEL.KEY functions

You can use the DISABLE.INPUT function to stop all keyboard and mouse input. This is useful if you want to dedicate a macro application to a single purpose for a period of time, such as when performing a lengthy series of calculations, or if you don't want anyone to interrupt a process. If another macro doesn't re-enable input to the computer, all further interaction with Excel is disabled, and the user might have to reboot the machine.

The CANCEL.KEY function specifies a macro to run when the user presses the Esc key to interrupt a macro.

The ON.TIME function

The ON.TIME function runs a macro at a specified time. You supply as an argument a serial date value that represents the date and time when you want the macro to run. If the number is less than 1, the specified macro runs every day. You can also specify a tolerance period — how long you're willing to wait for Excel to run the macro.

Under some circumstances, Excel does not respond to the ON.TIME function as expected. If the macro sheet that contains the macro isn't in memory when the correct time arrives, Excel ignores the request. Similarly, if Excel isn't in Ready mode at the specified time or during the tolerance period, it waits until the tolerance period elapses and then cancels the macro's run.

The ON.WINDOW function

The ON.WINDOW function runs a macro when a user activates a certain window. If you don't specify a window, Excel runs the macro when a user activates *any* window, except for those windows included in other ON.WINDOW formulas. For example, you can use this function in a custom application with the menu bar and menu command functions, to switch menu bars when a user activates a certain document.

The ERROR and LAST.ERROR functions

As you learned in Chapter 19, Excel usually displays an alert box when it encounters an error during the calculation of a macro. The ERROR function lets you use a more advanced form of error checking in your macros, by branching to a specified macro routine when an error occurs. If you don't specify a macro, Excel displays the standard error-alert box and doesn't branch to any routine.

You can also turn off error handling altogether; if the program encounters an error in this situation, it ignores the error and continues with the macro. Be sure you don't turn off error checking until your macro is completely and thoroughly debugged.

The LAST.ERROR information function returns the reference of the most recent error encountered in the execution of a macro. You can use this function when you're using one macro to handle more than one type of error, or errors in more than one routine, and you want to determine exactly where the error occurred.

The ON.DOUBLECLICK function

You can use the ON.DOUBLECLICK function to run a macro when the user double-clicks any cell or object in an Excel document. For example, you can use this function to prevent the display of notes in a worksheet.

The ON.ENTRY function

You can use the ON.ENTRY function to run the specified macro when the user enters data into a cell through the formula bar in the specified worksheet or macro sheet.

Working with add-in macros

When you create a series of command and function macros that work well and are thoroughly debugged, you can convert them into a form that makes them appear as if they are part of Microsoft Excel itself. To do this, use the Save As command to save the macro in the Add-in format. Excel responds by saving the macro sheet with an XLA extension.

When you open the add-in macro sheet, it is hidden but cannot be revealed through the Unhide dialog box. Also, the names of function macros appear in the Paste Name dialog box with the standard functions, in alphabetic order, but the names of command macros don't appear in the Run dialog box.

In addition, the Close All command doesn't close the add-in macros, and the Exit command doesn't prompt for changes to add-in macro sheets; to save them, you must include the SAVE function in an auto-close macro for each sheet.

You can auto-open an add-in macro sheet, or put it into the startup directory so Excel opens it automatically. Using auto-open add-in macros, you can create an application that completely changes the standard appearance of Excel, replacing all the built-in menus with those of your choosing.

To open an add-in macro sheet as a regular macro sheet again, press Shift as you click OK in the Open dialog box.

Providing help for users

There are many ways to provide help for users of a Microsoft Excel application you create. The following are some ideas:

- You can prepare printed documentation, from crib sheets to manuals.

- You can create screens of text and use the VSCROLL or FORMULA.GOTO function to present various screens in the document under macro control.

- You can attach a macro to a button or other graphic object for requesting help, and present help information in a text box on the worksheet or macro sheet.

- You can build documentation into templates, perhaps templates that contain text boxes or buttons.

- Your macros can detect error conditions and notify the user through dialog boxes, alert boxes, and text screens.

- If your users need to work with the macros themselves, you can develop and follow standard conventions for naming variables, macro program formatting, and providing comments in the listings.

- You can add your own help topics to Excel's Help feature and call context-sensitive Help topics up through menu commands and actions in a dialog box. To implement custom help topics in Excel, you need the *Microsoft Excel Custom Help Development Kit*, available from Microsoft.

MICROSOFT EXCEL & OTHER APPLICATIONS

22

Integrating
Applications with
the Clipboard,
OLE, and DDE

*A*s you work with Microsoft Excel, you might need to transfer information from Excel to another program or from another program to Excel. For example, you might want to import a macro from the Macintosh version of Excel or transfer a chart picture or a table from Excel to a report you're writing in Microsoft Word for Windows or in Ami Pro.

Excel offers several methods of exchanging data with other programs. You can convert a file by using the Save As command to save it in a format other programs can read. Or you can share data with other programs that run under Windows via the Clipboard. You can also use Object Linking and Embedding (OLE) or Dynamic Data Exchange (DDE) to create links between documents created in different programs.

In this chapter and in Chapter 23, we'll show you some techniques for transferring information between Excel and other programs. We begin this chapter with a discussion of the Windows Clipboard, OLE, and DDE. In Chapter 23, we focus on methods for converting Excel's files to other formats and for importing documents that were created in other spreadsheet and database programs. In both chapters, we discuss manual data-exchange techniques and techniques that use macro programming.

Data formats and the Clipboard

Using the Clipboard to copy or move information between Microsoft Excel and another Windows application is much the same as using it to replicate data within Excel. In the same way as you use the Edit menu's Copy and Paste commands to reproduce a cell or range within an Excel worksheet, you can use Excel's Copy command and some other application's Paste command to reproduce a section of the worksheet in another program's document — a report you write in a word processor, for example. Or you can use another program's Copy command and Excel's Paste command to import some data — a block of text, a table, a graphic image, or even a sound annotation — from another Windows application into Excel.

In all these cases, the Windows Clipboard acts as a way station for information in transit. The Copy command stores information on the Clipboard. (The Cut command does the same but also removes it from the source document.) And the Paste command fetches whatever the Clipboard currently is storing.

The only complexity in all of this arises from the fact that the Clipboard typically stores data in several formats at the same time. When you move information within or between Excel documents, you usually don't need to concern yourself with the format of the data you're moving. But when you use the Clipboard as a transfer medium between applications, it can be useful to know what formats are available.

When you copy a worksheet range from Excel to the Clipboard, Excel normally stores your data there in 16 separate formats. You can see the names of these formats by copying some data, opening the Windows Clipboard Viewer, and pulling down the Display menu. (You can open the Clipboard Viewer from within Excel by choosing Run from Excel's Application Control menu.) As Figure 22-1 shows, the Clipboard's Display menu lists the available formats.

The Clipboard Viewer's window initially displays a simple text string that reads something like *Copy 15R x 2C*. (The numbers depend on how many rows and

FIGURE 22-1.
Excel's Edit Copy command puts your data on the Clipboard in a multitude of formats.

columns you copied.) By selecting items on the Display menu, you can see what some of the alternative formats look like. (The names listed in gray identify formats that the Viewer is unable to display.)

When you use another application's Paste command — or, for that matter, Excel's — which format will the pasted data be in? It depends.

The application whose Paste command you use chooses what it considers to be the most appropriate of the available formats. (If none of the available formats is appropriate, the application dims its Paste command.) Often the format chosen by the receiving application is just the one you want, but it might not always be.

In some cases, the receiving application can only receive data in one particular format, so the issue of which format to paste does not arise. For example, if you copy data from Excel and paste it into Notepad (an application that deals only with the simplest form of text), Notepad requests the Text format; you have no choice in the matter. Similarly, if you paste Excel data into a non-Windows program running under Windows, the non-Windows program pastes *OEM* text — a format similar to text except that it uses the IBM PC extended-ASCII character set instead of the ANSI character set.

Many Windows programs can handle data in more than one format, however. For example, Microsoft Write, the executive word processor shipped with Windows, can accept information in both textual and graphic formats.

Choosing formats with the Paste Special command

Most Windows programs that can paste data in more than one format have a Paste Special command on the Edit menu. (In some applications, the command might have a slightly different name, such as Paste Format.) Whenever the Clipboard holds information in more than one usable format, such applications make their Paste Special commands available. If you choose the Paste command, the application pastes the data in its default format. If you choose the Paste Special command, a dialog box appears that lists all the available formats (including the default), so you can take your pick.

You're probably accustomed to using Paste Special in Excel for pasting the formats assigned to a worksheet range without pasting the range's values, or for pasting the values without the formats. This form of Excel's Paste Special command operates quite differently from the Paste Special command of other programs. (See Chapter 5.)

When the Clipboard holds data that originated outside Excel, however, Excel's Paste Special command changes. Like the Paste Special of other applications, it lets you choose among the available Clipboard formats. Figure 22-2 shows how Excel's Paste Special dialog box looks if the Clipboard holds text copied from Microsoft Word for Windows.

FIGURE 22-2.
Excel's Paste
Special command
lets you choose among
the formats offered
by the originating
application.

Here are some basic guidelines to help you choose among the options you're most likely to encounter.

Microsoft Excel and OLE

Microsoft Excel supports the Windows Object Linking and Embedding specification in both client and server modes. If the application to which you're pasting supports OLE as a client, your Excel data (whether from a worksheet, a macro sheet, or a chart) is an object you can embed. In many cases, the receiving program's normal Paste command will automatically embed the Excel data. If that isn't the case, you can embed your data by choosing the program's Paste Special (or equivalent) command and selecting the format whose description includes the word *object*. (See "Object linking and embedding," later in this chapter.)

If the application you're copying from supports OLE as a server application, the copied data can be embedded in your Excel worksheet or macro sheet. (Chart documents do not accept embedded data.) Depending on the server application, the Paste command might embed the Clipboard's data automatically. If the Paste command doesn't work, you can embed by choosing Excel's Paste Special command and pasting the format that includes the word *object* in its description. (For more information, see "Object linking and embedding," later in this chapter.)

Pasting from Microsoft Excel into text-oriented programs

Windows programs that handle text, such as word processors and text editors, can paste Microsoft Excel worksheet and macro sheet data in either Text or Rich Text Format. In either case, any formulas in your worksheet are converted to their results.

When you paste in Text format, formatting characters such as dollar signs or percent signs are included in the paste. But font, size, alignment characteristics, column widths, shading, borders, and color are omitted. The original columns of your Excel data are separated by tab characters, but unless all the entries in each column happen to be of the same width, you will probably need to adjust the tab settings in the receiving application to make the columns line up evenly.

When you paste in Rich Text Format (which is also sometimes identified as *RTF* or *formatted text*), virtually all of your formatting characteristics are preserved. Typically, the receiving application responds to Excel data in Rich Text Format by setting up a table. If you paste RTF data into Microsoft Word for Windows, for example, you get a table in your Word document, which you can then manipulate further with commands on Word's Table menu.

Unlike most other formats that include formatting information, Rich Text Format is a 7-bit format, which means that you can telecommunicate it using 7-bit communications parameters. Thus, for example, if you send an Excel document to a colleague via an electronic mail service, such as MCI Mail, you might look for a communications package that will let you paste data in the Rich Text Format.

Many Windows word processors can paste graphic information as well as text. Thus, for example, you can paste an Excel chart (a graphic) into a Word for Windows document, as easily as you might paste a table of numbers from an Excel worksheet. The word processor in this context behaves like a graphics-oriented program. (For more information on this kind of paste, see "Pasting from Microsoft Excel into graphics-oriented programs," later in this chapter.)

Pasting from text-oriented programs into Microsoft Excel

Microsoft Excel pastes text from the Clipboard in various ways, depending on context.

Pasting text into worksheet or macro sheet cells

If the current selection is a worksheet cell or range, the Paste command imports words and numbers as unformatted text. In other words, it handles characters received from the Clipboard much as it would if you typed them at the keyboard. Each line of text copied to the Clipboard is pasted into Excel on a separate worksheet row, beginning at the current cell selection. If the current selection encompasses a single column and multiple rows, Excel pastes only as many lines as the selection includes rows. If the selection encompasses multiple columns, in most cases you will be warned that the paste area is not the same shape as the data on the Clipboard — and you will be asked to confirm your intentions. If you make a mistake, you can use the Undo command.

Despite the fact that Excel can copy text to the Clipboard in Rich Text Format, it does not paste text in Rich Text Format. Therefore, text formatted in a word processor must be reformatted after you import it into Excel.

Excel normally treats a tab character in Clipboard text as a signal to move to the next column. Thus, for example, you can copy a table from a word processor into Excel and typically have it correctly parsed into columns on the first try. You can also select a different "column delimiter" character by choosing the Open command from the File menu and clicking the Text button. The dialog box that appears is shown in Figure 22-3.

FIGURE 22-3.
The Text option of the File Open command lets you specify a column delimiter character. The default delimiter is the tab character.

The Text File Options dialog box is most commonly used to govern the way Excel parses textual data read in from a disk file. But it affects Clipboard transfers in exactly the same way. Thus, for example, if you have comma-separated data in a word processor merge file, you can copy that to the Clipboard and set Excel's column delimiter to Comma so each field of the copied text will appear in a new column. To change the delimiter character, select the Column Delimiter character you want to use, click OK, and then click Cancel in the Open dialog box. Note that the Column Delimiter section of the dialog box shown in Figure 22-3 also lets you specify a custom delimiter (any single character) or no delimiter at all.

When you paste text into a worksheet cell or range, Excel does not, by default, treat the text as an embeddable object, even if its source is an OLE server program such as Word for Windows. If you want the text to be embedded, use the Paste Special command. (See "Object linking and embedding," later in this chapter.)

Pasting text onto worksheet objects

If you paste text that originated in an OLE server program and if the current selection is a worksheet graphic object other than a text box, Excel's Paste command embeds the text as an object. Otherwise, Excel imports the text into a new text box. If the current selection lies within a text box, Excel pastes the text into the box, even if it came from an OLE server.

Pasting text with the Paste Picture command

If you hold down Shift while you open the Edit menu on Excel's worksheet menu bar, the Paste command is replaced by a Paste Picture command. The action of this command depends on the contents of the Clipboard at the time you use it. If the Clipboard contains text only, the Paste Picture command causes Excel to behave exactly as though you selected a graphic object and used the ordinary Paste command. For example, if the current worksheet selection is a cell and the Clipboard contains text only, the Paste Picture command creates a new text box that contains the Clipboard's text.

Pasting text onto a chart document

You cannot paste text directly into a separately windowed chart, but you can paste text into a chart window's formula bar. Thus, for example, if you want to use a heading from a word processor document as unattached text for a chart, you can copy that text to the Clipboard, click the chart window's formula bar, and use the Chart menu bar's Edit Paste command.

Pasting from Microsoft Excel into graphics-oriented programs

Microsoft Excel's Copy command puts two graphic formats on the Clipboard, called Picture and Bitmap. Most programs that handle graphics information accept either format from the Clipboard but use the picture format by default. In most cases, you must use the Paste Special (or equivalent) command to paste bit-mapped data.

The essential difference between the Picture and Bitmap formats is that the Bitmap format is an exact reproduction, bit for bit, of the pixels that make up the visual presentation of your data in Excel. The Picture format is a translation of the image into commands. For example, a straight line formatted as Bitmap includes a specification of each individual point along the line. Formatted as Picture, the same image includes only the end-point specifications and other characteristics of the line.

The principal advantage of the Picture format is that it is designed to be scalable. You can also scale Bitmaps, but they usually suffer serious distortion in the process. In particular, you are much more likely to get a satisfactory printout from an image in Picture format than from one in Bitmap format. You will probably find little reason to use the Bitmap format to paste an image into a program that can accept the Picture format.

You should be aware of one important difference in the way Excel handles the two graphics formats, however. By default, a bit-mapped image of worksheet data includes the worksheet frame and essentially creates an image of your data as it appears on screen. The Picture format normally reproduces the worksheet range as it might appear in a printout — and hence does not include the worksheet frame unless you use the File menu's Page Setup command and select Row & Column Headings.

The Copy Picture command

If you want data in Picture format to mirror the screen exactly, including screen colors and the sculpted appearance of the worksheet frame, use Excel's Copy Picture command to put your selection in the Clipboard. The Copy Picture command replaces the normal Copy command when you hold down Shift before you open the Edit menu. The Copy Picture command presents the dialog box shown in Figure 22-4. In this dialog box you can specify As Shown on Screen as your appearance option and Picture as your format option.

FIGURE 22-4.
When you choose
Copy Picture in an
Excel worksheet, you
see this dialog box.

You might also find the Copy Picture command useful under two other circumstances. In a macro-driven application, you can use it to restrict the macro's user to pasting a particular format into the Clipboard. And you can use the Copy Picture command as a way to paste a "snapshot" of a worksheet range into another (or the same) Excel document. In effect, you can use Copy Picture as a substitute for the Camera tool. (The Camera tool is discussed in Chapter 7 and Appendix A.)

Pasting from graphics-oriented programs into Microsoft Excel

Excel can also paste two kinds of graphic formats, Picture and Bitmap. As with copying from Excel, you'll generally get the best results when you choose Picture format.

Pasting from Microsoft Excel into Lotus 1-2-3 for Windows

You must exercise caution when pasting worksheet data from Microsoft Excel into Lotus 1-2-3 for Windows (version 1.0a). 1-2-3 for Windows does not include a Paste Special command, so you can paste data only in the Clipboard format it chooses, which is WK1.

Pasting WK1 format data into a worksheet has one advantage over pasting text. The WK1 format includes your formulas. Thus a SUM() formula copied from Excel into Lotus 1-2-3 for Windows will become an @SUM formula in the 1-2-3 worksheet.

This advantage comes at a price. All cells pasted from Excel into 1-2-3 for Windows are offset from the cell-pointer position by an amount that reflects their position in the Excel worksheet. For example, suppose you copy the range C1:C3 from an Excel worksheet to the Clipboard. Next, you open a 1-2-3 for Windows worksheet, position the cell pointer at C1, and paste. The incoming data arrives in column E! What's worse, any data that happens to lie between your cell-pointer position (C1 in this example) and the actual paste destination (column E) is obliterated.

The best advice we can give about transferring worksheet data from Excel to 1-2-3 for Windows is to avoid the Clipboard. Instead, use the File Save As command to save your worksheet as a WK1 file, and then use 1-2-3 commands to open the file in 1-2-3 for Windows or to combine it with an existing 1-2-3 for Windows worksheet.

You can copy graphic objects or charts safely from Excel to 1-2-3 for Windows. Lotus 1-2-3 for Windows pastes the graphic in Picture format into the current cell selection. (It identifies Picture format by its synonym, *metafile*.) You should therefore select an area large enough to accommodate the graphic before you use the Paste command.

Object linking and embedding

All the Clipboard transfers described so far produce what might be called static results. A block of text copied into a Microsoft Excel worksheet from Notepad, for example, simply becomes a range of words or numbers on the receiving worksheet, just as if you had entered the data directly from the keyboard. In particular, the pasted data has no link to its source application. If the document in which those words and numbers were first generated happens to change, you have to repeat the Copy and Paste procedure to keep the Excel worksheet in step.

Excel also supports the Windows Object Linking and Embedding (OLE) protocol, however, which lets you copy and paste data in such a way that the data remains associated with its source. OLE is a superset of an earlier transfer protocol called Dynamic Data Exchange, or DDE. Excel 4 still supports DDE and includes a number of DDE-oriented macro comands, which are described in "Using DDE with macros," later in this chapter. DDE macros written for earlier versions of Excel still work in Excel 4, and Copy and Paste Link procedures that involve Excel and other DDE-supporting applications still work as well. But OLE gives you some valuable new ways to integrate data across applications.

Linking versus embedding

As its name indicates, OLE has two components, *linking* and *embedding*. The difference between them is crucial. When you *link* Excel data into another program, that other program stores a set of pointers to the data's source in Excel; it does not store the data itself. If the source data changes, the document into which it is linked is updated — either automatically or on demand. In contrast, when you *embed* Excel data into another application, a copy of the embedded data is incorporated into the receiving document, and this embedded information is not updated as a result of changes to the data source.

Clients and servers

OLE involves an exchange of information between two parties, called a *server* and a *client*. The server is the program in which the data originates. The client is the one that receives the data. If you embed an Excel chart in an Ami Pro document, for example, the server is Excel and the client is Ami Pro.

Excel and some other Windows programs support OLE as both server and client. A variety of other programs, including several of the accessories shipped with Microsoft Windows version 3.1, support OLE in only one mode or the other. (Paintbrush, Sound Recorder, and Object Packager are OLE servers; Cardfile and Write are OLE clients.) Some programs do not support OLE at all.

Many Windows programs that have been on the market for a while support DDE but do not yet support OLE. When using such programs with Excel, you can link but not embed.

Data objects

The *object* in an OLE transaction can be any data item managed by an OLE server application — for example, a block of text from Microsoft Word for Windows, a sound annotation recorded in Sound Recorder, or an image created in Paintbrush. One of the ways in which OLE represents an advance over earlier methods of data exchange is that the client application doesn't have to know how to render the embedded or linked data object. If you embed a sound object in an Excel worksheet, for example, Excel displays an icon to represent the embedded object. When you want to "play" the annotation, the OLE mechanism invokes the server program (Sound Recorder, for example), and the server renders the object.

Why and how to embed

You should embed, rather than link, when you want the server data in its current form to become a permanent part of the client document, or when the client document will be going "off line" from the server document. For example, suppose you plan to create a report in Ami Pro that incorporates several Excel tables and charts. You need to take this report on the road. On your portable computer's hard disk, you have Excel and Ami Pro, but you keep your Excel data files on a file server at the office. In this case it is appropriate to embed the Excel material in your Ami Pro document. While on the road, if you want to reformat or edit the Excel data, all you'll need to do is double-click it in your Ami Pro document.

You might also want to use embedding when you want to call on an OLE server for some simple ad hoc procedure. Microsoft Word for Windows, for example, is shipped with an equation editor that can act as an OLE server program. While you work in Excel, you might want to use this equation editor to create a text box that shows some Excel formula in traditional (non-spreadsheet) mathematical notation.

With embedding, you don't need to go out to Program Manager (or Word), invoke the equation editor, create the equation, copy it to the Clipboard, and paste or link it into Excel. Instead, you can invoke the equation editor with Excel's Insert Object command (which we'll describe next), create your equation, and then use the editor's Update command to embed your work in the Excel document. You need not save the equation itself as a data file.

You can embed an object in two ways — by using Copy and Paste (or Paste Special) or by using the Insert Object (or equivalent) command.

To embed a data object with the Copy and Paste commands, begin by copying the data from the server program to the Clipboard in the usual way. Next, use the client program's Paste or Paste Special command. In many situations, if the data on the Clipboard originated in an OLE server, the client program's Paste command will automatically embed the object. But this is not always the case. To be sure that you're actually embedding the data, you might want to use Paste Special, instead of Paste. In the list of formats that appears, choose the one that includes the word *object*.

Most OLE client programs (including Excel) offer an Insert Object command, typically on their Edit menus. When you choose this command, a dialog box appears that lists all the types of embeddable data objects known to your system. (Windows gets this information from the Windows *registration database*.) For example, if you use Excel's Insert Object command, you might see a listing similar to the one shown in Figure 22-5.

FIGURE 22-5.
You can use the Insert Object command to invoke an OLE server, create a data object, and embed that object in an OLE client.

By selecting the name of the object you want to embed and clicking OK, you can invoke the server program associated with that kind of object. After you create your object in the server program, you can use the server's Update command (typically on the File menu) to embed the data in your client document. (You can also embed the data by simply quitting the server program and answering Yes to an update prompt.)

So, for example, if you want to use Paintbrush to create a visual adornment for your Excel worksheet, you can start by choosing Excel's Insert Object command. Next, select Paintbrush Picture and click OK, create your graphic, use Paintbrush's Update command, and then quit Paintbrush. The Paintbrush image is embedded as a picture at the current cell location in the Excel worksheet.

When you embed any form of data into Excel, Excel renders it as a graphic object and identifies it with a formula based on the EMBED function. Figure 22-6, for example, shows an Excel worksheet with two embedded objects — a block of text from Microsoft Word for Windows and a sound annotation created in the Windows Sound Recorder accessory. The Word object is selected. As you can see, the reference area identifies this object as Picture 1, and the formula bar displays the object's EMBED formula. Note that the designation *Picture 1* does not imply that the embedded data is in any way graphic. Rather it means that the data is represented in the Excel worksheet by a graphic token (an icon). This token is in every way a normal Excel graphic object. You can size it, move it, attach a macro to it, and manipulate it just as you would other worksheet objects. (For more about worksheet objects, see Chapter 7.)

If you're embedding information from Excel into a document created in a different OLE application, whether or not that data is represented as an icon depends entirely on the abilities and predilections of the client application.

Strewing your Excel worksheet with icons that represent embedded data won't do you much good if you can't "play" that data. To see or hear what's behind the icon, simply double-click the icon. This action causes the server program to render the embedded data. In some cases, you might be "transferred" to the server in the process. For example, if you double-click an embedded Word icon, you'll actually find yourself in Word for Windows looking at the embedded data. You can then return to Excel using any of the normal Windows procedures — by pressing Alt-Tab or quitting Word, for example. In other cases, such as with an embedded Sound Recorder object, you'll never see the server program. The server simply arrives behind the scenes, plays the object, and departs.

FIGURE 22-6.
This Excel worksheet has two embedded objects, a block of text from Word for Windows and a sound annotation from Sound Recorder.

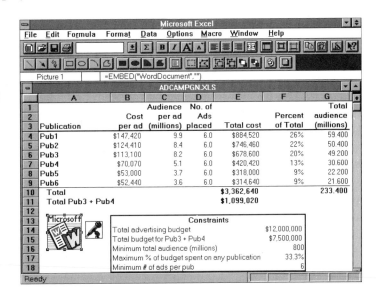

If double-clicking the embedded object actually takes you to the server program, you can easily edit the embedded data there. This, in fact, is one of the principal advantages of embedding over static pasting. When the data is embedded, you don't need to worry about forgetting where it came from. When you want to edit it, simply double-click. When you're finished, use the server's Update command.

If double-clicking does not take you to the server, you can still edit the object. Begin by selecting it and pressing the right mouse button. You'll see a shortcut menu similar to the one shown in Figure 22-7. Selecting Edit Object on this menu will take you to the server program, where you can edit the embedded object.

Procedures for playing and editing objects in OLE clients other than Excel vary somewhat from program to program. If you're having difficulties, consult the documentation that came with your client program.

FIGURE 22-7.
*To edit some objects,
press the right mouse
button and then select
Edit Object from the
shortcut menu.*

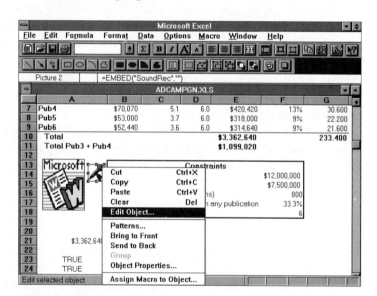

Why and how to link

You should link, rather than embed, when you want to use a data object in several client documents and you need to ensure that the data will be identical in each; when the data object is likely to change over time and you want to maintain it in its source application; or when you simply want to avoid enlarging the client document. For example, suppose you want an Excel worksheet to use sales information recorded in an OLE server document that's stored on a network file server. As time goes by, this data is frequently updated in the source document, and you want your Excel worksheet always to have access to the current values. In this case, you can create a link. As we'll see, you can designate the link as either *automatic* or *manual*.

If it's automatic, changes to the data source are always reflected in the Excel worksheet. If it's manual, the changes are read into the Excel document only when you ask for them.

As mentioned earlier, you can create links either with server programs that support OLE or with older Windows programs that support DDE but not OLE. The procedures for creating and maintaining the links are the same in both cases. And whether the programs involved support OLE or only DDE, the document that supplies the data is called a server, and the document into which the data is linked is called the client.

To create a link, first make sure that the server document has been saved. Most server programs will not copy a linkable format to the Clipboard from a document that has never been saved because such a document does not have a filename.

Start by copying the data you want to link to the Clipboard, just as you would if you were performing a static transfer. Next, go to your client document and use either the Paste Link command (if one is available) or the Paste Special (or equivalent) command. If you use Paste Link, the link is created with default parameters — that is, with the default data format and either automatic or manual, according to the default set by the client program. (Most client programs, Excel included, create automatic links by default.) If you use Paste Special, you might be able to choose the data format, and possibly the automatic/manual status of the link. When you select a format that can be linked, a Paste Link (or simply Link) command button will be available.

If you link data from Excel to another program, it's highly advisable to name the Excel range that contains your linked data before you create the link. If you do not name the range and you subsequently rearrange your worksheet, the odds are good that your client application will no longer be linked to the correct data. If a worksheet rearrangement causes the client document to be linked to an entirely new set of numbers, you might not realize that the link had, in effect, become corrupted.

Even when you do name the Excel range before you create the link, the client program may or may not identify the server range by its name. Some programs — Lotus 1-2-3 for Windows (version 1.0a), for example — insist on using the row and column coordinates even when the range has a name. Fortunately, you can use the client program's link-editing procedure (described in "Editing links," later in this chapter) to see how the link is identified and to change it if necessary.

Automatic versus manual links

As mentioned earlier, links are either automatic (updated whenever data changes) or manual (updated on demand). In some programs you will see other terminology, such as *hot* and *cold, hot* and *warm,* or *active* and *inactive.* But the concepts are the same in all cases; no other forms of linkage exist.

To update a manual link, you typically choose a Links command from a File menu. (In some programs, this command has a similar but different name.) The dialog box that appears will list all links to the current document and provide a set of command buttons. One of those buttons will be called Update, Activate, or something similar. (In Excel, the button is called Update.) Click this button to get the latest values for your link.

In most programs, the same dialog box that lets you update a manual link also lets you change a link's status from manual to automatic or vice versa. In Excel, you do this by choosing Links, selecting the link to be changed, and clicking the Options button. The next dialog box that appears lets you toggle the status of the link.

How links are identified in Microsoft Excel

Linked data is identified by three elements: the server application, the server filename, and the location of the data within the server file. In formal DDE parlance, you will see these elements referred to as *application, topic,* and *item.* When you link data into an Excel worksheet, Excel creates a formula to identify the link. The formula looks like this:

=Application | Topic!Item

This formula effects what is called a *remote reference.* Note that a vertical bar separates the application from the topic, and an exclamation point separates the topic from the item. You can create links manually by entering such a formula yourself into any worksheet cell. But the only practical reason for creating a link manually is if you want to set up a link at a time when the server program or document isn't available. Otherwise, you'll probably find it simpler to use the Copy and Paste Link technique.

Activating a link

If the server program happens to support OLE, you can "activate" the link by double-clicking it. (If the client is Excel, be sure to double-click the cell where the link formula is stored.) Windows responds by launching the server application (if it isn't already running). The server in turn loads the server document and presents the linked item.

As an alternative to double-clicking — one that works with non-OLE programs as well as with OLE servers — you can pull down the File menu and choose Links. (In some programs, this is called Edit Links or something similar.) In the dialog box that appears, you should see a list of all linked items as well as some command buttons. Select the item you want to activate, and then look for a command button called Open, Activate, or something along those lines. In Excel, the button is called Open.

The *window_num* argument is a numeric code that determines the size of the application window as follows:

Code	Description
1	Normal
2	Minimized
3	Maximized

If you omit the *window_num* argument, it is assumed to be 2; thus, the newly opened application appears as an icon at the bottom of the screen.

The EXEC function returns a task ID number to the macro sheet. You can use this number in later macro functions, such as INITIATE, to identify the application you want to work with.

The APP.ACTIVATE function

The APP.ACTIVATE function lets you activate an open application.

The APP.ACTIVATE function takes the form

=APP.ACTIVATE(*title_text,wait_logical*)

The *title_text* argument represents the name of the application window you want to activate. This argument, which must appear in quotation marks, should be the exact text that appears in the application window's title bar. If you omit the *title_text* argument, the macro activates Excel.

The *wait_logical* argument is a logical value that determines whether Excel should suspend macro processing until Excel is activated. If *wait_logical* is TRUE (the default), Excel waits to be activated before it activates the specified application. If *wait_logical* is FALSE, Excel activates the specified window immediately.

The APP.SIZE function

The APP.SIZE function is similar to the SIZE function; it changes the size of Excel's application window. (See Chapter 20.) The action of the APP.SIZE function is equivalent to dragging the application window's border or choosing the Size command from the application window's Control menu.

The APP.SIZE function takes the forms

=APP.SIZE(*x_num,y_num*)

=APP.SIZE?(*x_num,y_num*)

where the *x_size* and *y_size* arguments are the desired width and height of the window. As with the SIZE function, you must express these arguments in points, a unit of measurement equivalent to $\frac{1}{72}$ of an inch.

If you use the question-mark form of the APP.SIZE function, Excel changes the mouse pointer to an arrow shape so that you can manually resize the application window.

The APP.MOVE function

The APP.MOVE function is similar to the MOVE function; it changes the position of the Excel application window. The action of this function is equivalent to dragging the application window's title bar or choosing Move from the application window's Control menu.

The APP.MOVE function takes the forms

=APP.MOVE(x_num,y_num)

=APP.MOVE?(x_num,y_num)

where the x_num and y_num arguments represent the desired horizontal and vertical positions of the upper left corner of the window relative to the top and left edges of the screen. These arguments are expressed in points.

The APP.MINIMIZE, APP.MAXIMIZE, and APP.RESTORE functions

The APP.MINIMIZE function reduces Excel's window to an icon. Its action is equivalent to choosing the Minimize command from the application window's Control menu or clicking the Minimize icon. APP.MINIMIZE takes no arguments.

The APP.MAXIMIZE function maximizes Excel's window. Its action is equivalent to choosing the Maximize command from the application window's Control menu or clicking the Maximize icon. APP.MAXIMIZE takes no arguments.

The APP.RESTORE function restores the size of the Excel application window to its previous size after you have used the Maximize or Minimize command. Its action is equivalent to choosing the Restore command from the application window's Control menu. APP.RESTORE takes no arguments.

The SHOW.CLIPBOARD function

The SHOW.CLIPBOARD function displays the Microsoft Windows Clipboard Viewer. Its action is equivalent to choosing the Run command on Excel's application Control menu and selecting Clipboard from the Run Application dialog box. To close the Clipboard Viewer, use the macro function CLOSE.

You can also activate the Clipboard Viewer by using the APP.ACTIVATE function or the EXEC function. (Excel's SHOW.CLIPBOARD function is designed to make Excel macros written for Windows compatible with Excel macros written for the Macintosh.)

If the Clipboard Viewer is already running in Windows, SHOW.CLIPBOARD activates the viewer. If it is not running, the function starts it but you must call the function a second time to activate the Clipboard Viewer.

The SEND.KEYS function

After you activate an application, you can use the SEND.KEYS function to issue commands, navigate, and make entries in a document created in another application. As its name implies, this function lets you send a series of keystrokes to the active application.

The SEND.KEYS function takes the form

=SEND.KEYS(*key_text,wait_logical*)

The *wait_logical* argument is a logical value that determines whether Excel suspends macro processing until the keystrokes you've sent are processed. The default value, FALSE, instructs the macro to continue processing without waiting for the keystrokes to be processed.

The *key_text* argument represents the keys you want to "press." This argument, which must be a text string enclosed in quotation marks, can include any keyboard characters—letters, numbers, and symbols—as well as special function keys. To enter a standard keyboard character, simply type the character you want to use. To enter special function keys such as Backspace and Enter, use one of the codes listed in the following table.

Key	Code
Backspace	{BACKSPACE} or {BS}
Break	{BREAK}
Caps Lock	{CAPSLOCK}
Clear	{CLEAR}
Delete	{DELETE} or {DEL}
Down arrow	{DOWN}
End	{END}
Enter	{ENTER} or ~ (tilde)
Esc	{ESCAPE} or {ESC}
Help	{HELP}
Home	{HOME}
Ins	{INSERT}
Left arrow	{LEFT}
Num Lock	{NUMLOCK}
PgDn	{PGDN}
PgUp	{PGUP}

(Continued)

Key	Code
PrtSc	{PRTSC}
Right arrow	{RIGHT}
Tab	{TAB}
Up arrow	{UP}
F1, F2,...F15	{F1}, {F2},...{F15}
Shift	+
Ctrl	^
Alt	%

As you know, some keyboard commands and actions require that you press Shift, Ctrl, or Alt while pressing another key. To indicate that a key should be held down while another key is pressed, enclose the second set of key codes in parentheses. For example, you might hold down Alt while pressing the W and A keys to issue the Arrange All command on the Windows menu. This sequence would be written as %(WA).

Because the +, ^, and % characters serve special functions, you must use braces whenever you want to enter these characters as literal text. For example, if you want to type a plus sign, you must enter that character as {+}.

You might want to repeat the same key sequence several times. For example, to move down 10 lines in a document, you would press the Down arrow key 10 times. Fortunately, you don't have to repeat the {DOWN} code 10 times in your macro. To repeat a key sequence, specify the number of repetitions inside the braces, like this:

{code number}

You must include one blank space between the *code* and *number* arguments. For example, to move down 10 lines in a document you would use {DOWN 10}.

Let's look at a practical example. The macro

=SELECT(!Results)

=COPY()

=EXEC("C:\WINDOWS\WRITE.EXE",1)

=APP.ACTIVATE("Write - (Untitled)",FALSE)

selects a range of cells named *Results* in your Excel worksheet, issues the Copy command, and then activates the Write word processing program. You might then use the SEND.KEYS function

=SEND.KEYS("The results of our survey are summarized in the table below.
    {ENTER 5}%(EP)",TRUE)

This function types the characters *The results of our survey are summarized in the table below*, presses the Enter key five times to start a new paragraph, and then issues the Paste command. (The %(*EP*) is equivalent to choosing the Paste command from the Edit menu.)

Using DDE to control macros in other programs

Often you'll want to get full access to all the commands available in programs that have a macro language, such as Microsoft Word for Windows — not only the ones available by using the SEND.KEYS function. The INITIATE and EXECUTE functions let you send commands directly to other programs.

The INITIATE function

To set up a DDE conversation to send commands directly to other programs, use the INITIATE function. As its name implies, the INITIATE function initiates a full DDE conversation between Microsoft Excel and another Windows application that can be controlled by DDE.

The INITIATE function takes the form

=INITIATE(*app_text,topic_text*)

The *app_text* argument is a text string that identifies the application that Windows is to start. The *topic_text* argument is the name of that application's document. If the application is not currently running, Windows asks the user whether to start the application.

The function returns the channel number used by Excel to communicate with the application. This number is used for every subsequent communication with the application.

The EXECUTE function

The EXECUTE function sends command messages to another application via DDE. The command messages often represent menu or macro commands. For example, to tell Word for Windows to print the current file, you would send a FilePrint command.

This function takes the form

=EXECUTE(*channel_num,execute_text*)

The *channel_num* argument is the channel number received by the INITIATE function. The *execute_text* argument is a text string consisting of the required commands enclosed in brackets.

The following example is part of a DDE conversation between Excel and Word for Windows. The macro selects a range of cells named Results, issues a copy command, activates Word for Windows, pastes the Results range into the file TEST.DOC, prints the document, closes the file, and then closes Word for Windows.

=SELECT(!Results)

=COPY()

=INITIATE("WINWORD","TEST.DOC")

=EXECUTE(C5,"[EditPaste][FilePrint][FileSave]")

=EXECUTE(C5,"[FileExit]")

The EXECUTE function refers to cell C5, which contains the INITIATE function.

The TERMINATE function

It is important to terminate any DDE conversation you start. In the previous example, we terminated the conversation by closing Word for Windows. However, several DDE conversations can be open in different applications, or you could be editing a document in Word for Windows while your Excel macro is running in a different window. The TERMINATE command lets you close a DDE conversation without terminating the other program.

The TERMINATE function has the form

=TERMINATE(*channel_num*)

The *channel_num* argument is the number returned by the INITIATE command.

23

Importing and
Exporting

*I*n this chapter we take up the topic of foreign relations. We'll look at the procedures for exchanging information with Lotus 1-2-3, the various flavors of dBASE, text files, and other versions of Microsoft Excel. Although Microsoft Excel version 4.0 is a far more versatile file exchanger than any of its predecessors, diplomacy is never entirely uncomplicated. If you're moving to Excel from another spreadsheet program, such as 1-2-3, you'll be pleased to know that most of your worksheets and macros will work immediately in Excel. But 1-2-3 and Excel are different programs in many respects. This chapter will explain some of the differences and how they affect the process of importing and exporting worksheets and charts.

Earlier versions of Excel relied on a macro translation utility to convert 1-2-3 macros. The current version includes that translator but no longer requires it. The new 1-2-3 macro *interpreter* executes 1-2-3 macros directly — without translating them first. We'll discuss both the macro interpreter and the macro translator in this chapter as well.

Using the Save As command to export

To export a Microsoft Excel worksheet, macro sheet, or chart document to another program's format (or a format used by an earlier version of Excel), use the File menu's Save As command. In the drop-down list labeled Save File as Type, you can specify the file format you want to use. With worksheets, you have 18 choices: Normal, Template, Excel 3.0, Excel 2.1, SYLK, Text, CSV, WKS, WK1, WK3, DIF, DBF 2, DBF 3, DBF 4, Text (Macintosh), Text (OS/2 or MS-DOS), CSV (Macintosh), and CSV (OS/2 or MS-DOS). With charts and macro sheets, you have somewhat fewer choices. For all document types, the default choice is Normal — the standard Excel format for worksheets, macro sheets, and charts.

Note that to export your file you must select a format from this list. You can't turn your Excel worksheet into one that 1-2-3 can read, for example, by simply changing the extension from XLS to WK1. When you pick a format from the drop-down list, Excel changes the extension for you.

Many Microsoft programs can produce SYLK (symbolic link format) files. You'll want to save Excel worksheets in the SYLK file format when you plan to share data with early versions of Multiplan. When you choose this option, Excel saves the file with the SLK filename extension.

Some programs, such as VisiCalc, require you to save files in the DIF (data interchange) format. This file-format option saves values only, not the formulas that produce them. When you use this option to save a worksheet, Excel saves the file with the DIF filename extension.

As you'll see later in this chapter, the WKS, WK1, and WK3 file formats let you share data with Lotus 1-2-3 and Lotus Symphony. The DBF 2, DBF 3, and DBF 4 formats let you exchange information with dBASE, and the Text and CSV formats let you convert documents to ASCII text format for exchange with a variety of programs. The Excel 3.0 and 2.1 formats let you share with users of earlier Excel versions.

Certain of the formats supported by Excel can act as go-betweens for programs with which Excel does not maintain diplomatic relations. For example, to transfer a file from Excel to Quattro Pro, you can save it as a WK1 (1-2-3) file. Quattro Pro can read files in the WK1 format, so you can import the WK1 file into Quattro Pro — and then save it in Quattro Pro's native (WQ1) format.

Unfortunately, other programs cannot read certain data in your Excel worksheet. For example, if the program to which you're exporting does not have an equivalent for one of Excel's built-in functions, Excel's export routine replaces the formula with its current value.

When Excel's export routine can't translate a formula, it pauses and displays an alert box like the one in Figure 23-1, which shows the location of the cell that contains the error. The alert box asks if you want Excel to signal you each time it can't convert a formula. If you choose Yes, Excel displays this box each time it can't convert a formula. If you choose No, Excel does not pause until it has completed conversion of the whole worksheet. It then displays an alert box that shows the total number of formulas it could not convert.

FIGURE 23-1.
If Excel can't convert a formula, it displays an alert box.

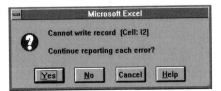

Your choice of Yes or No depends on the worksheet you're converting. If the worksheet contains many similar formulas and Excel can't convert the first one, you might want to choose No to avoid seeing the alert box over and over and to speed the conversion process. If, however, you think your worksheet contains only a few formulas that can't be converted, choosing Yes allows you to note the location of each problem.

If you're exporting a file to a program that can import Excel files, you might want to try using both applications' conversion facilities. For example, suppose you want to convert an Excel worksheet into the WK3 format, so that you can use it in 1-2-3 for Windows. If you're using a version of 1-2-3 for Windows that can import Excel 4 XLS files, try exporting the file from Excel as a WK3 file and also importing it directly into 1-2-3 for Windows. The two programs might handle incompatibilities differently. You can compare results to see which approach is more satisfactory.

Using the Open command to import

To import a file, simply use the File Open command, the same as you would to open a Microsoft Excel file. You can use the drop-down list at the lower left corner of the File Open dialog box to "filter" the file list so that it displays only files of a given type — such as WK* files. But this isn't required. Nor is the file you import required to have its program's default extension. Excel determines the format of any file you open by looking at the content of the file.

Excel 4 can import files in any of its export formats, plus the WR1 format used by Lotus Symphony. For a description of Excel's export formats, see the previous section of this chapter. If the import routine does not recognize a file format, it treats the file as plain text. (See "Importing text files," later in this chapter.) But if the file appears to be a binary file (something other than plain text), the alert message shown in Figure 23-2 appears. This message warns that the file is probably full of unintelligible code. You can bail out with the Cancel button.

FIGURE 23-2.
The File Open
command presents
this message if it
encounters an
unfamiliar file format.

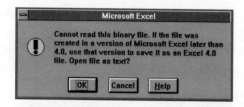

Like the export routine, the import routine displays an alert message when it encounters an untranslatable spreadsheet formula. You can ask to see a separate message for each such formula if you want, but you'll probably find it more convenient to skip the messages. Excel's import routine flags each untranslatable formula with a note. You can then use the Select Special command to find all the cells with attached notes.

When you open a file in a foreign format, Excel assumes you want to keep it in that format. For example, if you use File Open to load a WK1 worksheet into Excel and subsequently use the File Save command, Excel saves the file in WK1 format. In this circumstance, you don't need to use Save As, because you aren't really changing the format. You can use Save As and select the Normal option if you want to store the imported file as an Excel 4 XLS file.

Exporting WK1 files

Microsoft Excel 4 can convert worksheets to the WK1 format used by Lotus 1-2-3 Release 2.x. Numeric formats (those supported by 1-2-3), text alignment, and defined range names are preserved in the exported WK1 file. Panes in the Excel file, whether frozen or not, are translated into frozen titles.

The WK1 export routine also creates an FMT file, which is used to record other formatting information — such as fonts, borders, shading, and colors. If you use Lotus 1-2-3 Release 2.3 or 2.4, you can preserve most of your Excel formatting by attaching the Lotus-supplied add-in WYSIWYG, which reads the FMT file. If you use 1-2-3 Release 2.01 or 2.2, you can read this formatting information by attaching a third-party add-in called Impress. (Impress, from PC Publishing, is identical in most respects with the WYSIWYG add-in.)

You can export Excel charts, but only if they're embedded in the Excel worksheet. You cannot export charts in separate windows to 1-2-3. If you use WYSIWYG or Impress, your embedded Excel charts will appear in the 1-2-3 worksheet. But with or without WYSIWYG or Impress, you'll be able to display your Excel charts using 1-2-3's /Graph Name Use command. The first chart on your Excel worksheet is exported as *Chart 1;* the second as *Chart 2,* and so on.

Excel does not write (or read) Allways files.

Format conversion

Most built-in Excel numeric formats have Lotus 1-2-3 counterparts and convert properly. Those Excel formats that do not have 1-2-3 equivalents (the fractional formats, for example) are given the General format in the WK1 file. Note that these untranslatable formats do *not* acquire the 1-2-3 global default format. If you use /Worksheet Global Format to change the global default — say from General to one of 1-2-3's Currency formats — your untranslatable Excel formats remain in the General format.

If you've defined your own formats in your Excel worksheet, Excel attempts to convert those formats to 1-2-3 formats. For example, Excel converts the custom format $#,##0.000_);($#,##0.000) to currency with three decimal places. However, if Excel can't convert the format, the cell becomes General format in the 1-2-3 worksheet. For example, the custom format dddd, mmmm d, yyyy displays Excel dates in the following form: Friday, January 1, 1904. This format has no counterpart in 1-2-3, however, so the resulting cell in the 1-2-3 worksheet is formatted as General.

External-reference formulas

Lotus 1-2-3 Release 2.2, Release 2.3, and Release 2.4 support only the most rudimentary form of external-reference formulas. In those programs, you can reference a single external cell, but you cannot perform calculations within the external-reference formula. If you restrict your external-reference formulas similarly in Excel, you can translate them to the WK1 format. (Note, however, that 1-2-3 Release 2.01 does not support any form of external referencing, so even correctly translated external-reference formulas return ERR in Release 2.01.) Before you export an Excel worksheet that contains external-reference formulas, be sure to save all the supporting worksheets in WK1 format.

Differences and incompatibilities

Any Excel formula that involves arrays or that uses a nonadjacent selection as an argument is converted to its current value. Also, some Excel functions and their 1-2-3 equivalents don't work in exactly the same way. In most of these cases, Excel overcomes the differences during translation. In a few cases, however, the conversion might not work. For example, the Excel PV, FV, and PMT functions can take as many as five arguments, but 1-2-3 doesn't support the fourth (*future value*) and fifth (*type*) arguments. If you translate an Excel worksheet that contains these functions, Excel converts them properly if they have no more than three arguments. If you translate a PV, FV, or PMT function that has more than three arguments, Excel replaces the formula with a constant.

The Excel NPV function is similar to the 1-2-3 @NPV function, except that the Excel function accepts as many as 29 *cash flow* arguments, whereas the 1-2-3 function accepts only one. If your Excel NPV function has more than one *cash flow* argument, Excel converts the formula to a constant. Formulas that involve functions without a 1-2-3 counterpart are also converted to constants.

When you transfer an Excel worksheet to 1-2-3, all AND, OR, and NOT functions change to #AND#, #OR#, and #NOT# operators. For example, the Excel function

=AND(A1>100,A1<200)

converts to the 1-2-3 operator

(A1>100#AND#A1<200)

This change does not affect the formula's behavior.

Excel supports seven error values: #VALUE!, #REF!, #DIV/0!, #NAME, #N/A, #NULL!, and #NUM! These values can appear as constants in cells and formulas and also as the result of formulas. 1-2-3 supports only two error values — ERR and NA — both of which appear only as the result of formulas. When you export an Excel worksheet to 1-2-3, the error value #N/A translates to NA. Any other error value translates to ERR. When you import a 1-2-3 worksheet to Excel, any NA value translates to the #N/A error constant, and any ERR value translates to the #VALUE! error constant.

Excel offers two other reference operators that 1-2-3 does not support: union (,) and intersection (space). Excel translates any formula that contains a union or intersection operator to a value.

The Excel worksheet includes 16,384 rows. Lotus 1-2-3 Release 2.0 and later worksheets include only 8192. If your Excel worksheet includes data beyond row 8192, break it up before you export it. The export routine does not generate warning messages when it translates references outside 1-2-3's 8192-row limit.

In Excel, you can assign names to cells or ranges in the worksheet or to constant values and formulas that aren't entered in cells. Lotus 1-2-3, on the other hand, lets you assign names only to cells or ranges and not to multiple areas, constant values, or formulas. Any formula that contains a reference to a named cell or range converts properly from Excel to 1-2-3. If you convert a worksheet that contains formulas that use named constants or formulas, however, Excel converts those named constants and formulas into constant values. For example, suppose you've assigned the name *Test* to the constant 100 in an Excel worksheet and then used that name in the formula

=Test*A1

When Excel converts this formula, the name *Test* changes to the value 100.

Lotus 1-2-3 and Microsoft Excel both support Manual and Automatic calculation. However, 1-2-3's Automatic calculation is the same as Excel's Automatic Except Tables. When you transfer worksheets from Excel to 1-2-3, Automatic remains

Automatic, Manual remains Manual, and Automatic Except Tables becomes Automatic. Although 1-2-3 accepts Excel's Maximum Iterations setting, it ignores the Maximum Change setting when the file is converted.

When your Excel worksheet contains a data table, the table formula and the input values (variables) are usually converted properly for 1-2-3. Keep in mind that 1-2-3 requires your input values to appear in the first column of the table range, however. The results in an Excel data table are array formulas; these formulas are changed to constant values during the conversion. In addition, you must redefine the table range and the input cell or cells before you use the table in 1-2-3.

Excel and Lotus 1-2-3 both support cell protection. In Excel, however, a cell can be both locked (protected from accidental change) and hidden. In 1-2-3, cells can only be locked. Thus, when you export an Excel worksheet to 1-2-3, all locked cells are locked in the 1-2-3 worksheet; however, cells that are hidden in Excel are not hidden in 1-2-3 unless you used Excel's Hidden number format.

WK1 files can use only eight fonts. Therefore, only the first eight fonts you use are translated to equivalent WYSIWYG formatting.

Finally, outlines and graphic objects (other than embedded charts) are not translated. And Excel macros cannot be translated to 1-2-3.

Importing WKS, WK1, and WR1 files

When you open a WKS, WK1, or WR1 file, Microsoft Excel translates the file, converting Lotus 1-2-3 formulas, formats, and names to Excel formulas, formats, and names. If the imported file includes graphs, Excel automatically creates new chart windows for each graph. The current graph appears in a chart window named CURRENT.XLC. Named graphs also appear in separate chart documents; Excel assigns names to them based on the first eight characters of their 1-2-3 names.

Most formatting that you assign to a 1-2-3 file with the Impress or WYSIWYG add-in is translated to equivalent Excel formatting, provided that Excel finds an FMT file in the same directory as the WK1 file. (The FMT file must have the same filename as the WK1 file.) Excel does not translate Allways formatting.

A few WYSIWYG and Impress formatting commands cannot be translated correctly into Excel. Format codes within cell entries (such as codes to change the font for particular words in a label) appear as unreadable characters in Excel; you'll need to edit such codes out of the imported file and substitute the appropriate Excel commands by hand. Drop shadows and objects drawn on top of charts are not translated. Double underlines and wide underlines are converted to single underlines.

By default, Excel displays imported 1-2-3 files without gridlines and uses 10-point Courier as the font assigned to Excel's Normal style. Font assignments made with WYSIWYG and recorded in the FMT file are converted to the closest equivalents available on your Windows system.

Excel translates most 1-2-3 numeric formats into standard or custom Excel formats. The only 1-2-3 formats it can't translate are +/− and Text; these it converts to General.

When you import a 1-2-3 worksheet, Excel locks all protected cells and displays them in a contrasting color.

Formula conversion

The precedence of mathematical operators in Excel is different from that in Lotus 1-2-3. In Excel, the negation operator takes precedence over the exponentiation operator. In 1-2-3, the exponentiation operator takes precedence over the negation operator. Thus, the formula =−2^2 returns 4 in Excel but −4 in Lotus 1-2-3. You can overcome this difference by careful use of parentheses.

Excel supports only natural-order calculation. In addition to natural-order calculation, 1-2-3 supports by-row and by-column calculation. When you import a 1-2-3 worksheet to Excel, recalculation is set to Natural.

All 1-2-3 functions have counterparts in Excel. Some functions have slightly different names, but they are otherwise identical. For example, the function that computes the average of a set of values is =AVERAGE in Excel and @AVG in 1-2-3. When you convert one of these functions, Excel automatically changes the name of the function.

In a few cases, an Excel function and its 1-2-3 equivalent don't work in exactly the same way. Usually, Excel overcomes the differences during translation. Some of these transformations are quite sophisticated. For example, both 1-2-3 and Excel have CHOOSE functions. In Excel, the function has the form

=CHOOSE(*index,value1,value2,...*)

In 1-2-3, this function has the form

@CHOOSE(offset,*value0,value1,...*)

The difference between these functions is that the first value in the Excel function has an index value of 1, whereas the first value in the 1-2-3 list has an offset (index) of 0. In other words, the function

=CHOOSE(1,100,200,300)

will return 100 in Excel, but the function

@CHOOSE(1,100,200,300)

will return 200 in 1-2-3.

Excel overcomes this difference by subtracting 1 from the index when it converts an Excel CHOOSE function to 1-2-3 or by adding 1 to the offset when it loads a 1-2-3 worksheet into Excel. Excel uses the same technique with the VLOOKUP and HLOOKUP functions and with all database statistical functions (DSUM, DAVERAGE, and so on).

In Excel, the *payment* and *principal* arguments of the PV, FV, and PMT functions are negative. In 1-2-3, the same arguments are positive. For this reason, when Excel translates one of these functions from Excel to 1-2-3, or from 1-2-3 to Excel, it changes the sign of the *payment* and *principal* arguments.

The 1-2-3 @IRR function has the form

@IRR(*guess,values*)

whereas the Excel IRR function has the form

=IRR(*values,guess*)

To account for this difference, Excel always transposes the *values* and *guess* arguments when it translates an IRR or @IRR function.

Linked files

1-2-3 formulas that reference external worksheets are translated into external-reference formulas in Excel. After Excel translates a file that contains such formulas, it presents a dialog box that asks if you want to update your external references. If you choose No, the program uses the formulas' most recent values. If you choose Yes, Excel reads the supporting documents on disk and updates the external-reference formulas.

Dates

Excel and 1-2-3 use the same serial date system for calculating date and time values. However, the Excel DATE function accepts *year* arguments from 0 through 178, whereas the 1-2-3 @DATE function accepts *year* arguments from 0 through 199. As long as the *year* argument of a 1-2-3 @DATE function you import is less than 179, Excel converts the function correctly. If the *year* argument of a 1-2-3 @DATE function is outside this range, Excel does not recognize it as a date value.

Tables and databases

If your 1-2-3 worksheet contains a data table, Excel imports the input values, table formulas, and results of the table. However, the definition of the table is lost. You must use the Table command on the Data menu to redefine the table in Excel.

Excel data tables are slightly different from those in 1-2-3. First, the results of an Excel data table are defined by an array formula; arrays are not supported in 1-2-3. In addition, Excel data tables are calculated automatically whenever you calculate the worksheet, just like other formulas. In 1-2-3, you must issue a command or press a function key to calculate your data tables. Finally, Excel allows more flexibility with the input values in a one-input table: They can be in either the first column or the first row of the table. In 1-2-3, they must be in the first column.

Excel database commands are similar to 1-2-3 commands. When you import a 1-2-3 database, Excel preserves the database range, the input range, the criteria range, and the output range.

The Alternate Expression Evaluation and Alternate Formula Entry options

Certain other differences between Excel and 1-2-3 present more difficult translation issues. For example, in most contexts, 1-2-3 (Release 2.01 and later) treats both blank cells and label cells as equivalent to 0. Excel treats blanks as equivalent to 0, but it regards text as a separate data type that cannot be referenced with a numeric operator. These differences can cause the same worksheet to produce divergent results in the two programs.

Suppose, for example, that you have text in cell A1 and the value 100 in cell A2. The following formulas produce one set of results in Excel and something quite different in 1-2-3:

Excel formula	Returns	Equivalent 1-2-3 formula	Returns
=2*A1	#VALUE!	+2*A1	0
=MIN(A1:A2)	100	@MIN(A1..A2)	0
=AVERAGE(A1:A2)	100	@AVG(A1..A2)	50
=COUNT(A1:A2)	1	@COUNT(A1..A2)	2

Excel and 1-2-3 also differ in the way they handle text as the first argument to a VLOOKUP or HLOOKUP function. If you're going to use text values in the first column of a vertical lookup table or first row of a horizontal lookup table, Excel requires that you order the text values alphabetically. Excel then searches through the first column or first row until it finds a value "greater than" the text supplied as the first argument of the function. When it finds such a value, it backs up to the previous item in that column or row and uses that item as an index to the lookup table. Lotus 1-2-3, in contrast, does not insist on an alphabetically ordered index column (or row), but if the first argument of the lookup function doesn't match an index value exactly, the function returns *ERR*.

For example, suppose your lookup table (named TABLE) looks like this:

Johannesburg	10
New Delhi	90
Rangoon	45

The formula =VLOOKUP("Madras",TABLE,2) would return 10, the value opposite Johannesburg. If you had the same table in 1-2-3, the function @VLOOKUP("Madras",TABLE,1) would return ERR, because the argument "Madras" does not exactly match an entry in the index column of the table.

Other small differences between the two spreadsheet programs affect the outcome of INT and MOD functions, the behavior of computed criteria in database criteria ranges, and the values returned by logical formulas.

Excel 4 includes an option called Alternate Expression Evaluation, which causes Excel to interpret worksheet formulas in exactly the same way the comparable formulas would be interpreted in a 1-2-3 worksheet. If you regularly work with both native Excel files and imported files from any version of 1-2-3, it is vitally important that you be aware of the state of this option. As you can see, turning this option on or off can change the values returned in your worksheet.

Excel's import routine automatically turns Alternate Expression Evaluation on for any imported 1-2-3 file — WKS, WK1, WR1, or WK3. If you want to change the setting of this option for the current worksheet, pull down the Options menu, choose Calculation, and select or deselect the check box labeled Alternate Expression Evaluation. Your setting affects the current worksheet only and is saved as an attribute of that worksheet.

Another option provided for compatibility with 1-2-3 is called Alternate Formula Entry. This option, described in Chapter 3, primarily affects the way range names are handled. With Alternate Formula Entry on, range names are automatically applied to formulas. If you subsequently delete a range name, any formula references to that name revert to the underlying cell coordinates. (This is 1-2-3 Release 2.x's normal behavior, not Excel's. In Excel, formulas that reference deleted range names normally return #REF!)

Excel's import routine, by default, turns Alternate Formula Entry on for imported worksheets that include one or more backslash-named ranges (ranges with names such as \A), because such ranges are customarily assigned to macro code, and your macros might depend on 1-2-3's default behavior. Alternate Formula Entry is normally left off with imported worksheets that do not include a range name that begins with a backslash. You can change the state of this option for the current worksheet by choosing the Options menu's Calculation command and selecting or deselecting the check box labeled Alternate Formula Entry. Your selection affects the current worksheet only and is saved as an attribute of that worksheet.

If you want to change the way Excel handles Alternate Formula Entry, you can edit the file EXCEL4.INI in your WINDOWS subdirectory. Look for the line AFE=0, which tells Excel to turn Alternate Formula Entry off by default. Change it to AFE=1 if you want Excel to always turn on Alternate Formula Entry when it reads a Lotus 1-2-3 worksheet. Change it to AFE=2 if you want Excel to turn on Alternate Formula Entry only when it reads a Lotus 1-2-3 worksheet that contains a backslash-named range.

If you regularly work with both imported WK1 and native XLS files, it is vitally important that you be aware of the state of both the Alternate Expression Evaluation and Alternate Formula Entry options. Prudence also suggests that you adopt a consistent policy regarding these options! Note that Excel does not display the status of these options in the message area at the bottom of the application window. If you're not sure whether an option is on or off, look at the Calculation Options dialog box — choose Calculation from the Options menu — to find out.

Exporting WK3 files

To export a file in WK3 format for use in 1-2-3 Release 3.x or 1-2-3 for Windows, use the File Save As command and choose WK3 from the Save File as Type drop-down list. If the file you're saving is not part of a workbook, the export routine creates a single-sheet WK3 file. If the current file is a workbook, Microsoft Excel exports a multi-sheet WK3 file. The first file in your workbook becomes sheet A of the translated file, the second becomes sheet B, and so on. The table-of-contents page of your Excel workbook is not translated.

Like the WK1 export routine, the WK3 routine also records formatting information in a WYSIWYG file. This file has the same name as the worksheet file but gets the extension FM3. Charts embedded in your Excel worksheets appear as embedded charts in 1-2-3 Release 3.x, provided you have WYSIWYG attached. (This is not an issue in 1-2-3 for Windows, which has WYSIWYG functionality built-in.)

Lotus 1-2-3 for Windows and 1-2-3 Release 3.x support a few functions (for example, @SUMPRODUCT) that are not available in Release 2.x. Therefore, if you plan to use your Excel worksheets in one of these versions of 1-2-3, you should definitely export a WK3 file, not a WK1 file, even if your Excel files are not workbooks.

Importing WK3 files

Microsoft Excel imports single-sheet WK3 files as ordinary XLS worksheets and multiple-sheet WK3 files as workbooks. WYSIWYG formatting is imported and converted to Excel formatting, provided Excel can find a like-named file with an FM3 extension in the same directory as the WK3 file. A few formatting commands assigned with WYSIWYG might not be translated. (See "Importing WKS, WK1, and WR1 files," earlier in this chapter.) Graphs embedded on the 1-2-3 worksheet appear as embedded charts in Excel. Any 1-2-3 graph to which you assign a name is converted to a separate Excel chart document, whether it's also embedded or not. The current 1-2-3 graph also appears in a separate chart window, under the name CURRENT.XLC. Comments embedded in WK3 formulas following semicolons are converted to notes in Excel.

Limitations of WK3 file import

Lotus 1-2-3 Release 3.x and 1-2-3 for Windows are true three-dimensional spreadsheets. Excel 4 is not three-dimensional, although its workbook feature lets it simulate three-dimensionality in many respects. For example, a three-dimensional reference such as

@SUM(A:A1..C:A1)

can be translated successfully from a WK3 file to an Excel workbook file. Certain other three-dimensional features cannot be translated, however. The following is a summary:

- Range names that span two or more WK3 sheets are not translated.
- Graph series that span two or more WK3 sheets are not translated.
- Sensitivity tables with three inputs are not translated.

Graphs that include both single-sheet data series and cross-sheet series are translated, but the cross-sheet series are omitted from the resulting charts!

Using the 1-2-3 macro interpreter

Microsoft Excel 4's Lotus 1-2-3 macro interpreter lets you run most macros written for 1-2-3 Release 2.01 without change and without a separate translation step. Simply import your WK1 or WK3 file into Excel. If Excel's import routine sees a 1-2-3 range name that consists of a backslash (\) followed by a single letter, it creates a similar name on the translated Excel worksheet, turns the Alternate Formula Entry and Alternate Expression Evaluation options on, and makes the macro interpreter available. To run your 1-2-3 macro, press Ctrl plus the letter associated with the macro's range name. For example, if your 1-2-3 macro is stored in a range named \a, you would run this macro by pressing Ctrl-a. Note that the letter you press with the Ctrl key must be lowercase, even if you assigned the name in 1-2-3 using an uppercase letter.

While your 1-2-3 macro is running, you will see the designation MI (for *macro interpreter*) in the lower right corner of your Excel application window. In response to interactive macro commands, such as {GETLABEL}, the interpreter will display a dialog box. Custom 1-2-3 menus will also appear in dialog boxes.

In response to the {?} command, the interpreter simply pauses and displays *MI PAUSE* in the message area at the bottom of the application window. Macro execution resumes when you press Enter. While the macro is suspended, all Excel menus are dimmed, except for the application and document control menus. Thus, you can move and size an imported 1-2-3 document while its macro awaits input from you. (You can even close the document or quit Excel.) But you can't use any Excel-specific features that require access to the menu bar.

You can interrupt a 1-2-3 macro by pressing Ctrl-Break, even if that macro includes a {BREAKOFF} command. Single-step execution of 1-2-3 macros is not available.

Excel's Alternate Expression Evaluation feature is automatically enabled whenever you import a 1-2-3 worksheet that contains a backslash-named macro range. Even if you turn this option off after importing, however, Excel turns it back on for you while the macro is running. Thus, 1-2-3 macro expressions such as

    {wait @now+@time(0.0.5)}

will work correctly, regardless of how you set Alternate Expression Evaluation. For sanity's sake, however, you'd do well to leave the option in one mode or the other.

Limitations and caveats

If worksheet translation is a perilous enterprise, interpreting another program's macros is even more fraught with traps and pitfalls. Be sure to test all your imported macros carefully before you commit your data to them. Here are some issues to be aware of as you work with imported 1-2-3 macros:

- The interpreter lets you invoke only those macros in ranges named with a backslash and a single letter. You cannot use Alt-F3 to invoke other macro ranges. Backslash-named macros can, however, call subroutines and other macros that do not have backslash names.

- The macro interpreter cannot import macros from Lotus MLB (macro-library) files.

- Macros on imported WK3 files run only if they don't reference ranges on other sheets. Therefore, after you import a WK3 file, you might need to copy macros from a dedicated macro sheet to the sheets on which you want the macros to run.

- Navigation commands in imported macros work as they do in 1-2-3, regardless of how Excel's Alternate Navigation Keys option is set. However, the effects of commands such as {BIGRIGHT} and {BIGLEFT} are measured relative to the current window dimensions. Before you run an imported macro, you might want to make sure that the window displays 20 rows by 8 columns, the size of the normal 1-2-3 display.

- Macros that depend on 1-2-3 add-ins, including Allways and WYSIWYG, will not work.

- An imported macro must not end in a menu.

- The macro interpreter supports the menu system of 1-2-3 Release 2.01. Thus, for example, a macro can use /FR (File Retrieve) but not /FO (File Open). This is true because /FR is included in the Release 2.01 command set, while /FO was not introduced until Release 3 — despite that fact, /FR has no direct equivalent in Excel but /FO does!

- Some 1-2-3 commands, such as /File Combine and /File Admin, do not work in Excel because Excel cannot mimic them.

- If your macro turns the worksheet frame off with {BORDERSOFF} or {FRAMEOFF}, you must turn it back on it again with {BORDERSON} or {FRAMEON}. Unlike 1-2-3, Excel's macro interpreter does not automatically redisplay the frame at the end of a macro run.

- The following 1-2-3 macro commands are not supported and generate a syntax error: {APPENDBELOW}, {APPENDRIGHT}, {FORM}, {FORMBREAK}, and {MENU}.

Editing imported 1-2-3 macros

Excel normally does not permit you to assign range names that begin with the backslash character. Therefore, you cannot create additional 1-2-3–style macros in an imported WK1 file. If you need new macros and want to use the 1-2-3 macro language, you can reopen the file in 1-2-3; do your programming there, and then import the file back into Excel.

You can, however, change or add to existing 1-2-3 macros. Simply edit those macros the same way you would in 1-2-3. You can also create new subroutines using names that don't start with the backslash character.

You can also invoke normal Excel macros from 1-2-3 macros. The commands to do this are

{XLCALL *excel_macro_name*}

and

{XLBRANCH *excel_macro_name*}

{XLCALL} invokes an Excel macro as a subroutine for a 1-2-3 macro. {XLBRANCH} transfers control from a 1-2-3 macro to an Excel macro. Both commands require a single argument, which is an external reference to a name or cell on an Excel macro sheet.

Using the 1-2-3 Macro Translation Assistant

Microsoft Excel 4 also includes the Macro Translation Assistant, a utility designed to convert 1-2-3 macros to equivalent Excel macros. To use the Macro Translation Assistant, use Excel's File Open command to open the 1-2-3 file that contains the macro or macros you want to translate. The macro is displayed in its original form in a standard Excel worksheet. Next, choose the Run command on the Control menu (or press Alt-Spacebar-U). When the Run Application dialog box appears, select Macro Translator and click OK. Excel displays the Macro Translation Assistant dialog box shown in Figure 23-3.

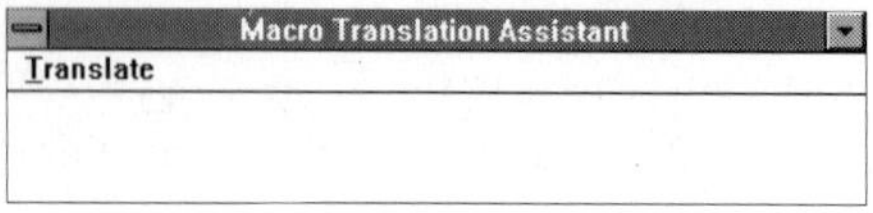

FIGURE 23-3.
Use this dialog box to convert macros from other applications.

Next, select the Lotus 1-2-3 command from the Translate menu. Excel lists the names of all open documents. Select the name of the worksheet or worksheets you want to translate, and then click OK or press Enter. Now Excel displays a dialog box that lists defined range names, so that you can specify which macros you want to translate. (You can select more than one macro by holding down Shift and using either the arrow keys or the mouse.)

The Verbose option lets you place the 1-2-3 macro statements next to the corresponding Excel statements in the macro sheet. If you don't want to see the 1-2-3 commands, turn off the Verbose check box. (Comments in your 1-2-3 macro text are not carried over to the translated macro sheet unless they are embedded in the 1-2-3 macro commands.)

The Macro Translation Assistant opens a new Excel macro sheet and begins to convert the Lotus 1-2-3 macros to Excel macros. The Assistant displays its progress inside the dialog box. If it encounters any problems translating the 1-2-3 macros, you'll see an alert message in the Macro Translation Assistant window and a translation comment in bold characters above or below the problem on the new macro sheet. To continue the translation, click OK. To stop the translation process, press Esc.

When the translation is complete, Excel asks if you want to close the Macro Translation Assistant. If you have no more macros to translate, click Yes. The program then presents a dialog box that lets you open TRANS123.XLM to run the translated macros.

TRANS123.XLM is a macro sheet that contains routines that Excel needs in order to run certain (but not all) macros translated from 1-2-3. All macro sheets created by the Macro Translation Assistant include an *Auto_open* macro that opens TRANS123.XLM. Thus, in the future, whenever you use the File Open command to open a macro sheet that contains one or more translated macros, TRANS123.XLM will also be opened. If you plan to run your translated macros now, however, the *Auto_open* macro won't yet have had a chance to run, and TRANS123.XLM won't yet be open. Therefore, you should answer yes to the prompt about whether you want to open TRANS123.XLM.

Before you work with translated macros, check the Macro Translation Assistant's work carefully. Be sure to read any warning messages that appear in the translated macro sheet and make any necessary adjustments.

Sharing data with Microsoft Excel for the Macintosh

The Windows and Macintosh versions of Microsoft Excel share data easily. All numbers and text values — and most formulas and cell formats — are converted without problems. A document's protection status and calculation, iteration, and display settings are also converted.

To exchange data with a user of Excel for the Macintosh, simply transfer those files from one computer to the other. (You can accomplish this with a special cable or with a modem.) If your computer uses a disk drive that accepts 3½-inch disks, you can also use a utility program to transfer data between Windows and the Macintosh. If you're connected to a network that supports both Windows and the Macintosh, you'll probably be able to transfer files from one computer to another without any extra equipment or software.

Although we discuss transferring worksheets in this section, the same instructions apply to transferring macro sheets and charts.

Importing Macintosh files

The first step in importing a Macintosh file is to transfer the file to your PC. Next, start the Windows version of Excel, choose the Open command from the File menu, and type the name of the document you want to open. Because the Macintosh does not add filename extensions when you save a file, you will be able to zero in on your Macintosh files by typing a wildcard and the null filename extension, such as

*.

When you click OK or press Enter, Excel lists all available files without an extension. When you select the appropriate worksheet from the Open dialog box, Excel automatically identifies the selected file as it loads it.

Exporting Windows Excel files

Transferring data from the Windows version of Microsoft Excel to the Macintosh is just as easy. First, transfer the file from the PC to the Macintosh. Next, start Excel on the Macintosh and use the Open command to load the file.

Adjusting date values

Although the Windows and Macintosh versions of Excel share many characteristics and capabilities, they do not use the same date system. In Excel for the PC, the base date is January 1, 1900. In Excel for the Macintosh, the base date is January 2, 1904. When you transfer worksheets either to or from the Macintosh, Excel maintains the date type by changing the 1904 Date System check box in the Calculation Options dialog box. Although this is usually acceptable, it can cause problems when a date from a Macintosh worksheet is compared with a date from a PC worksheet. For this reason, we suggest that you use the same date setting on all worksheets on all machines you use.

Other differences

The PC and Macintosh versions of Excel are nearly identical, but there are a few commands unique to each version. For example, there is no mail system on the PC, so the function OPEN.MAIL() creates an error message when executed in a PC macro. For more information on particular functions, refer to the *Microsoft Excel Function Reference*.

Sharing data with Microsoft Multiplan

In many respects, Microsoft Excel worksheets and Microsoft Multiplan worksheets are similar. A few important differences exist, however. This discussion applies primarily to transferring data to and from Multiplan versions 2.0 and later. Although you can share data with earlier versions, the exchange is not as complete.

Importing Multiplan files

If you use Multiplan version 3.04 or earlier, load Multiplan and open the document you want to transfer. Choose the Transfer Options command and select the Symbolic option. To save the document, choose Transfer Save. Multiplan saves the file in the SYLK format.

To import a Multiplan file saved in the SYLK format, start Excel, choose the Open command from the File menu, and type the filename. To see a list of all available SYLK files, type *.SLK in the File Name text box and click OK. Excel displays the names of all your SYLK worksheets in the list box. When you select the appropriate worksheet from this list, Excel automatically identifies the selected file as a SYLK file and converts the file as it loads it.

Multiplan versions 4.0 and later can read and write Excel version 2.1 files. Therefore, simply save the Multiplan file in Excel 2.1 format and then open it in Excel.

Exporting Multiplan files

To export an Excel file to Multiplan 4.0 or later, use the File Menu's Save As command and select the Excel 2.1 format. To export to Multiplan 3.04 or earlier, use Save As and select the SYLK format.

Conversion details

Excel does a good job of importing Multiplan worksheets. Most of the basic data in the Multiplan worksheet, including all numeric and text entries, names, formats, and protection status, are converted correctly. Multiplan formulas are converted to Excel formulas. To convert Multiplan macros, use the Macro Translation Assistant. (See "Using the 1-2-3 Macro Translation Assistant," earlier in this chapter.)

Sharing data with dBASE

Microsoft Excel can also exchange database ranges with dBASE II, dBASE III, or dBASE IV.

Importing dBASE files

To import a dBASE file into Excel, choose the Open command from the File menu and type the name of the file you want to open. To see a list of available dBASE files, select dBASE Files (*.DBF) from the List Files of Type drop-down list box. When you select the appropriate database from the list of dBASE files, Excel automatically converts the file as it loads it.

Excel places the dBASE field names in the first row of a new worksheet, and then uses them as the field names in the Excel database. Each dBASE field name appears in a different worksheet column. The dBASE records appear in rows immediately under the field names. Excel sets the worksheet column width to match the width of the dBASE fields. Columns that contain data from dBASE character and numeric fields are the same width as their corresponding fields in dBASE.

Exporting Excel files to dBASE

Before you save an Excel document in the DBF format, be sure you've defined the database. Next, to convert the file, choose the Save As command from the File menu, click the Options button, and choose the appropriate file format: DBF 2 if you're transferring to dBASE II, DBF 3 if you're transferring to dBASE III, or DBF 4 if you're transferring to dBASE IV. Excel saves the file with the DBF filename extension. After you leave Excel, you can load dBASE and the DBF file.

Exporting text files

You can save Microsoft Excel documents in any of six text formats: Text, Text (Macintosh), Text (OS/2 or MS-DOS), CSV, CSV (Macintosh), and CSV (OS/2 or MS-DOS). With all these options, Excel preserves any formatting assigned with the Format Number command but removes all other formatting.

With any of the three Text options, Excel separates the cells of each row with tab characters. Carriage-return and line-feed characters appear at the end of each line. Any cell in which a comma appears is surrounded by quotation marks. The Text options are preferable to the CSV options if you're planning to import the resulting text file to a word processing program as a document.

With any of the three CSV options, Excel separates the cells of each row with commas. (CSV stands for *comma-separated values*.) As with the Text options, Excel adds carriage returns and linefeeds at the end of each row of the file, and it surrounds cells that contain commas with quotation marks. CSV files are preferable to Text files for importing into database management programs. (Many database management programs can accept either form of text file, but some accept only CSV files.) CSV files can also be used by many word processing programs that store the information for form letters in comma-delimited files.

The differences between the normal, Macintosh, and DOS-OS/2 variants of each file type have to do only with characters that lie outside the normal 7-bit ASCII range. The Text and CSV options use the ANSI character set. You should select one of these options if you intend to import your text file into a Windows application, such as Word for Windows or Ami Pro. The Macintosh options use the Macintosh character set; select one of these options if you intend to transfer your file to a Macintosh application. The MS-DOS and OS/2 options use the PC-8 character set — the same character set your computer uses when it's not running Windows. (The documentation for some Windows programs or for Windows itself might refer to this character set as OEM text.) Select one of these options if you intend to import your text file into a non-Windows application, such as XyWrite, or into an OS/2 application.

Importing text files

To import a text file, either select Text Files (*.TXT;*.CSV) in the List Files of Type drop-down list box or (if the file has some different extension) select All files (*.*) in the List Files of Type box. If Excel doesn't recognize the file as an Excel document, a supported Lotus document, or a supported dBASE document, it considers the file to be text.

The File Open dialog box includes a button labeled Text. The dialog box that appears when you click that button was shown in Figure 22-3 in the previous chapter.

In the top part of this dialog box, you tell Excel how the data in your text file is organized. In the lower part, you specify whether the text was generated in a Windows application (ANSI), a Macintosh application, an MS-DOS (non-Windows) application, or an OS/2 application. The default choices are Tab-delimited and ANSI.

If you specify Tab-delimited, each line of your text file appears as a single cell in a row by itself, unless the line includes tab characters. Excel interprets a tab character as a signal to move to the next cell in the same row.

If you specify comma-delimited, each line of your text file appears as a single cell in a row by itself, unless the line includes commas. Excel interprets a comma as a signal to move to the next cell in the same row. (If a comma appears between quotation marks, Excel ignores it.)

The Parse command

The easiest way to import a text file is to be sure in advance that either tabs or commas appear wherever you want Excel to skip to a new column. Text files often are not so neatly laid out, however. For example, if you need to import a Lotus PRN file (a file "printed to disk"), Excel will probably store each line of the imported file in a single cell in column A. That's because PRN files use spaces rather than commas or tabs to achieve column alignment. You typically encounter the same kind of problem if you download stock prices from an on-line information service, and then import those prices into Excel. Fortunately, Excel's Data menu provides a Parse command to help you reorganize long text cells into neat columns.

Figure 23-4 on the following page shows an imported file that contains five fields. It might look like the headings in row 1 are distributed across five columns, but if you glance at the formula bar you'll see that row 1 really contains a single label in column A. The same is true of each row in this worksheet.

The first step in breaking this data into a usable form is to select the entries you want Excel to parse. Excel places no limit on the number of rows it can parse, but your selection must be only one column wide. In our example, we'll begin parsing at row 3; we can come back and fix the headings later. We want to parse all the labels in column A from row 3 downward, so we'll select everything from A3 to the bottom of the column.

NOTE: *When Excel parses records, it places each piece of information in a separate cell to the right of the selected column. Before you begin, be sure your worksheet has room to expand. In our example, the data will be redistributed into columns A through E.*

After you've highlighted the entries to be parsed, select the Parse command from the Data menu. You'll see the dialog box shown in Figure 23-5 on the following page. As you can see, the contents of the first selected cell (A3) appear in the Parse Line text box at the top of the dialog box. You use this parse line to indicate how you want Excel to divide the field entries.

FIGURE 23-4.
*All five data fields in
this sample worksheet
are lumped together in
column A.*

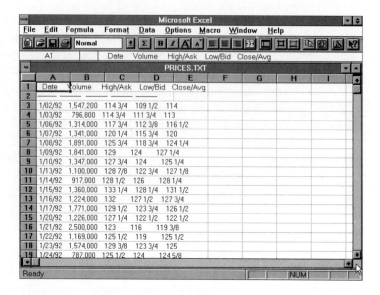

FIGURE 23-5.
*Use the Parse dialog
box to break entries
into separate fields.*

Use brackets to indicate the number of fields (columns) you want to create and the number of characters in each field. An open bracket ([) marks the beginning of a field and a close bracket (]) marks the end. You can insert as many pairs of brackets as you like. (If you omit an open or close bracket, Excel warns you with an *Error in parse line* message.) If you want to exclude some of the data from your worksheet when you parse, don't include those characters in brackets.

The Guess button at the bottom of the dialog box tells Excel to make a guess as to how the selected entries should be divided. Excel bases its guess on the type of data it finds in the parse line — text or numbers, for example — and on the position of blank characters. If necessary, you can adjust the position of the brackets that Excel inserts.

To specify the length of each field manually, position the insertion point at the spot where you want to type a bracket, or use the Left and Right arrow keys to move through the parse line, and then insert the brackets.

If you want to remove all the brackets from the parse line and make a fresh start, click Clear. To remove individual brackets, use the Left and Right arrow keys to position the insertion point, and then press the Backspace or Del key.

Figure 23-6 shows the position of the brackets in our sample parse line. When you click OK or press Enter, Excel separates all the selected entries into the five fields you delineated with the brackets. Figure 23-7 shows the results.

Obviously, the Parse command is most effective when all the parsed rows are structured in approximately the same way. When you have lines that don't fit the common pattern (such as the headings in our example), you can either edit them manually or use the Parse command again.

FIGURE 23-6.
We have separated the parse line into five fields.

FIGURE 23-7.
Using the brackets as its guide, Excel split the entries in column A into five fields.

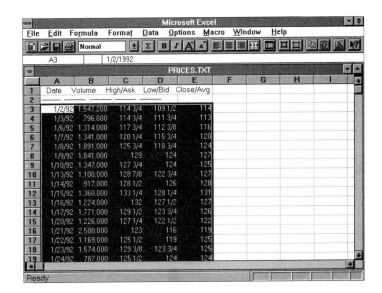

Using macros to manipulate text files

Microsoft Excel also offers a set of macro functions you can use to work with text files. These functions let you open, read, and write text files. They also let you determine the size of the file and control your position in the file.

The FOPEN and FCLOSE functions

The FOPEN function lets you open an existing text file or create a new text file. This function takes the form

=FOPEN(*file_text, access_num*)

The *file_text* argument, which is the name of the text file you want to open, must be a text value enclosed in quotation marks. Excel assumes the text file you're opening or creating is located in the current directory. If you want to open or store a file in another directory, include the full pathname in your *file_text* argument.

The *access_num* argument is a numeric code that specifies the type of access you want to use with the document:

Code	Type of access
1	Read file and write to it
2	Read file but do not write to it
3	Create a new file with read and write access

If the file you specify doesn't exist and you've specified an *access_num* argument of 1 or 2, the FOPEN function returns an #NA! error value.

When Excel executes the FOPEN function, it returns a document ID value that you use to refer to the text file in subsequent macro functions.

When you finish working with a file, you should use the FCLOSE function to close it. This function takes the form

=FCLOSE(*file_num*)

The *file_num* argument is the document ID that Excel returned when you used the FOPEN function to open or create the text file. This argument can be a constant value or a reference to the cell that contains the FOPEN function.

The FPOS function

The FPOS function lets you specify a character position in a text file. For example, before you use the FWRITE function to write a series of characters to a text file, you can use FPOS to specify the location at which you want Excel to insert those characters.

The FPOS function takes the form

=FPOS(*file_num,position_num*)

where *file_num* is the file ID Excel returned when you opened the file with the FOPEN function. If the *file_num* argument is not valid, Excel returns #VALUE!

The *position_num* argument is a numeric value that specifies the desired character position in a file. The first character in a file is numbered 1, the second is numbered 2, and so forth. If you omit *position_num*, Excel returns the current position.

The FSIZE function

The FSIZE function returns the number of characters in a text file. This function takes the form

=FSIZE(*file_num*)

where *file_num* is the file ID Excel returned when you opened the file with the FOPEN function. If the *file_num* argument is not valid, Excel returns #VALUE!

You can use the FSIZE function in conjunction with FPOS to move to the end of a file.

The FREAD and FREADLN functions

The FREAD and FREADLN functions let you retrieve data from a text file. The FREAD function lets you read a specified number of characters. This function takes the form

=FREAD(*file_num,num_chars*)

where *file_num* is the file ID Excel returned when you opened the file with the FOPEN function. If the *file_num* argument is not valid, Excel returns #VALUE! *Num_chars* is the number of characters you want to read.

Excel begins reading the file at the current position and returns the specified number of characters to the macro sheet. Excel then updates the current position so that a subsequent read of the file will start at the next character. (You can use the FPOS function, described earlier, to specify a different starting position.) If Excel reaches the end of the file before this function is called or for some reason can't read the file, the function returns #NA!

The FREADLN function is similar to FREAD, except that it reads an entire line of text rather than a specified number of characters. This function returns to the macro sheet all the characters from the current position up to but not including the carriage-return and linefeed at the end of the line.

The FREADLN function takes the form

=FREADLN(*file_num*)

The FWRITE and FWRITELN functions

The FWRITE function lets you write text to a text file. The FWRITE function takes the form

=FWRITE(*file_num,text*)

where *file_num* is the file ID Excel returned when you opened the file with the FOPEN function. If the *file_num* argument is not valid, Excel returns #VALUE!

Excel begins writing the text at the current position. (You can use the FPOS function, described earlier, to specify your starting position.) If Excel can't write to the file, the function returns #NA!

The FWRITELN function is similar to FWRITE. This function also writes text to a text file, beginning at the current position. However, FWRITELN also adds a carriage-return and linefeed character at the end of the text string.

The FWRITELN function takes the form

=FWRITELN(*file_num,text*)

If the FWRITE and FWRITELN functions execute successfully, they return to the macro sheet the number of characters written to the text file.

SECTION SEVEN

APPENDIXES

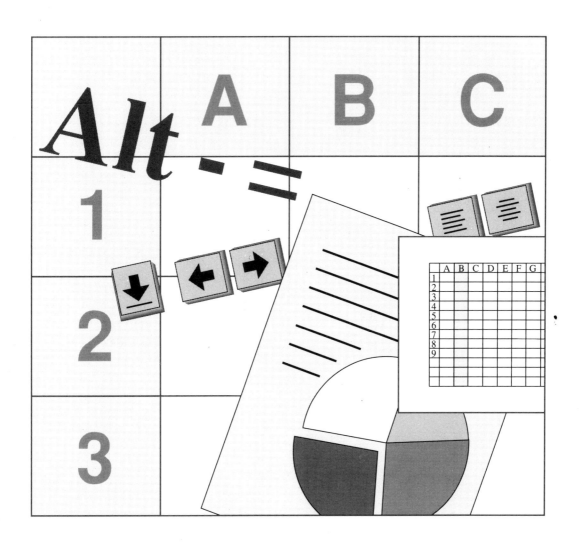

A
Toolbars

*M*icrosoft Excel 3 introduced the toolbar, which made frequently used commands available at the click of a mouse. Microsoft Excel 4 takes the next step by offering a smorgasbord of toolbars to simplify repetitive operations even further. You can build your own toolbars, choosing from nearly 150 predefined tools or using tools that you create yourself. In this appendix we'll describe each tool, explore the new toolbars, and show you how to customize tools and toolbars to fit your own work patterns.

Customizing toolbars

Microsoft Excel comes with nine predefined toolbars that contain 98 tools. Forty-five other tools, which are not on any of the predefined toolbars, are also available for use on the toolbars. You can also create your own tools to add to the list. In this section, we'll tell you how to remove tools from toolbars, add tools to toolbars, create new toolbars, and create new tools.

Removing and adding tools

To remove a tool from a toolbar, choose the Toolbars command from the Options menu and click the Customize button. Alternatively, you can choose the Customize command from the Toolbar shortcut menu. (To display the Toolbar shortcut menu, move the mouse pointer anywhere over a displayed toolbar and click the right mouse button.) When the Customize dialog box appears, click the tool that you want to remove in the toolbar (don't click in the dialog box), drag it anywhere outside the toolbar, and release the mouse button.

For example, to remove the Decrease Font Size tool (the tool with the small *A* in it) from the Standard toolbar, first display the Customize dialog box, and then drag the Decrease Font Size tool off the toolbar. Figure A-1 shows this process.

Notice that when you click any tool, either in the Customize dialog box or on a displayed toolbar, the tool's outline changes to gray, and the tool's description appears in the Tool Description area of the Customize dialog box. This way, you can make sure that you selected the correct tool for removal.

To add a tool, select the category of tool you want to add from the Categories list in the Customize dialog box. Excel displays all the tools available in that category in the Tools area of the dialog box. Next, click the tool you want to add and drag it to the position on the toolbar where you want it to appear. Any existing tools move to the right to accommodate the new tool. Be aware that it is possible to add more tools to a toolbar than can be displayed while the toolbar is docked, depending on the size of your screen. (We discussed docking and undocking toolbars in Chapter 1.)

For example, let's add the Underline tool to our modified toolbar. With the Customize dialog box displayed, select the Text Formatting category from the Categories list. Next click the Underline tool (with the capital *U* on it), and drag it to the Standard toolbar, between the Italic tool (with the capital *I* on it) and the Increase Font Size tool (with the large *A* on it). The result looks something like the toolbar in Figure A-2.

FIGURE A-1.
We are removing the Decrease Font Size tool from the Standard toolbar.

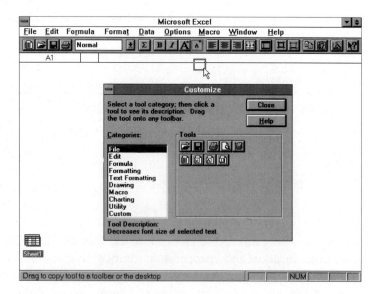

FIGURE A-2.
*We added the
Underline tool to the
right of the Italic tool
on the Standard
toolbar.*

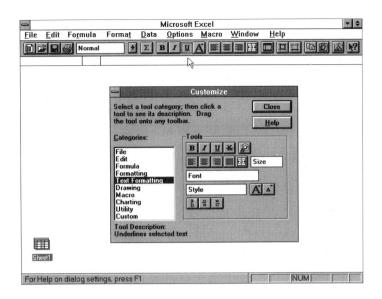

Rearranging toolbars

You can also rearrange tools on a toolbar while the Customize dialog box is displayed. Using our Standard toolbar example, drag the Underline tool we just added to the left until the tool's drag outline half overlaps the left side of the Bold tool (with a capital *B* on it). The result looks something like Figure A-3.

FIGURE A-3.
*We moved the
Underline tool to the
left of the Bold tool.*

You can also rearrange the spaces between tools by removing spaces or adding new ones. It takes a little practice, but the basic techniques are simple. To add a space, drag the tool beside which you want a space until it half overlaps the adjacent tool. Drag the tool to the right if you want to create a space on the left; drag the tool to the left if you want to create a space on the right. Similarly, you can remove a space by dragging an adjacent tool over the space until the tool is approximately centered over the space.

You can also rearrange toolbars by dragging tools between displayed toolbars. For example, with both the Standard and Formatting toolbars displayed, choose the Customize command from the Toolbar shortcut menu. After the Customize dialog box appears, drag any tool from one toolbar to the other. The tool disappears from its original location and reappears in the new location. You can also copy tools between toolbars in this way. Hold down Ctrl when you click the tool you want to copy, and drag it to the new location. The tool remains on the original toolbar, and a duplicate tool appears in the new location. If you change your mind, simply drag the duplicate off the toolbar.

Restoring default toolbars

If you decide you want to return your modified toolbar to its original condition, choose the Toolbars command from either the Options menu or the Toolbar shortcut menu. Select the name of the toolbar you want to restore from the Show Toolbars list, and then click the Reset button. The toolbar returns to its default configuration.

Creating new toolbars

It's easy to create your own customized toolbars. First, choose the Toolbars command from the shortcut menu. When the Toolbars dialog box appears, type the name of the toolbar you want to create in the Toolbar Name text box. Next, click the Add button. The Customize dialog box appears, along with a small, floating, empty toolbar, as shown in Figure A-4.

Now you can add tools to your custom toolbar by dragging tools from the Customize dialog box, or by copying or moving tools from other toolbars. After you define a custom toolbar, its name appears in the Show Toolbars list in the Toolbars dialog box, as well as in the Toolbar shortcut menu. You can choose to display, hide,

FIGURE A-4.
When you type a new name in the Toolbars dialog box, an empty toolbar that you can customize appears.

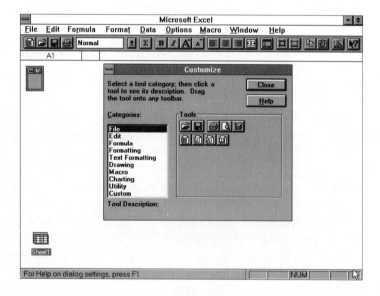

and dock a custom toolbar just like any predefined toolbar. If you select the custom toolbar name from the Show Toolbars list, the Reset button changes to the Delete button, which lets you remove a custom toolbar.

Another way to create a new toolbar is to drag a tool from the Customize dialog box. If you release the mouse button anywhere except on an existing toolbar, Excel automatically creates a new toolbar and names it Toolbar1.

Creating your own tools

Not only can you create your own toolbars, but you can also create your own tools. You can do this by assigning macros to one of the custom tools in the Custom category, by assigning macros to your own tool (using a graphic image created in another application), or by redefining one or more of Microsoft Excel's existing tools to use a specific macro.

Assigning macros to tools

Assigning macros to tools is similar to assigning macros to objects, as discussed in Chapter 7. You can assign a macro to any tool, even to a tool that performs a pre-defined action or command. To do so, first choose the Customize command from the Toolbar shortcut menu. When the Customize dialog box appears, click any tool on any visible toolbar with the right mouse button to display the Tool shortcut menu, shown in Figure A-5. Next, choose the Assign Macro To Tool command to display the Assign To Tool dialog box, shown in Figure A-6 on the following page.

FIGURE A-5.

To paste a custom tool face on a selected custom tool, click the right mouse button to display the Tool shortcut menu, and choose the Paste Tool Face command.

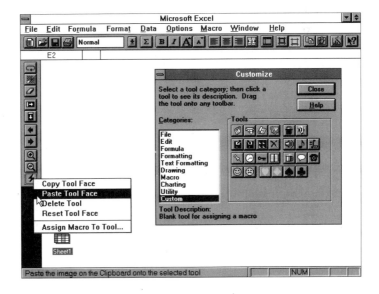

FIGURE A-6.
The Assign To Tool
dialog box lets you
attach macros to
any tool.

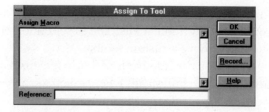

Like the Assign To Object command, the Assign Macro To Tool command gives you the option of selecting an existing macro from an open macro sheet or recording a macro that you want to attach to the selected tool.

If you choose to redefine the action of an existing tool, only the copy of the tool on that toolbar is affected. If the same tool exists on another toolbar, it still operates as before, as does the same tool that appears in the Customize dialog box. If you delete a tool that you redefined, you can replace the original tool using the Customize command, but you need to reassign your macro to the original tool using the Assign Macro To Tool command.

Custom tools

The Customize dialog box contains a category named Custom. In it are a number of tool faces, or buttons with images on them, to which you can assign macros to create custom tools. You can use the tool faces in the Custom category as they are if the image seems appropriate for your needs. You can also use them as building blocks to create your own tools. You can create a tool-face image in a separate Windows graphics application, such as Windows Paintbrush, and then copy and paste the image onto one of the custom tools (or any tool, for that matter). The image you create should be 16 pixels wide and 15 pixels high for optimum resolution. If you have an existing image that does not conform to this size, the image is scaled to fit within the tool, which may cause distortion.

For example, first create a 16 by 15 pixel image in Paintbrush, select it, and copy it. Next, switch to Excel, choose the Customize command from the Toolbar shortcut menu, and then drag the tool to the toolbar where you want to place it. (If you are assigning an image to a custom tool, you will be prompted to assign a macro to the tool, as described in the previous section.) With the new tool selected, click the right mouse button to display the Tool shortcut menu, as shown in Figure A-5.

Choose the Paste Tool Face command from the Tool shortcut menu. Your custom graphic image replaces the original image on the selected tool. The original tool face is still available from the Customize dialog box, however. Note that unlike a custom toolbar name, which appears in the list of toolbars, a custom tool face exists only on a toolbar; it does not appear as a custom tool in the Customize dialog box.

After you drag a predefined custom tool onto a toolbar, the Assign To Tool dialog box appears automatically. You use this dialog box to record a macro or attach it to your new tool.

If you reconsider your customization efforts, you can always restore the original tool face using the Reset Tool Face command on the Tool shortcut menu, as shown in Figure A-5.

The Switching tools

Three tools in the Custom tools category are called *switching tools*. These tools let you switch to Microsoft Word, Microsoft Project, or Microsoft PowerPoint. Before you can use one of these tools, you must open the SWITCH.XLA add-in macro sheet, which is located in the Library directory in your Excel directory. For more information about add-ins, see Chapter 19.

To add the switching tools, choose the Open command on the File menu, switch to the EXCEL\LIBRARY subdirectory, highlight the SWITCH.XLA file, and click OK. A dialog box appears that allows you to select the toolbar to which you want to add each switching tool. Note that you cannot add switching tools to custom toolbars at first. You must install them on another toolbar and then drag them to a custom toolbar using the customization techniques described in "Creating new toolbars," earlier in this chapter.

The first tool for which SWITCH.XLA asks you to select a toolbar is the Microsoft Word tool. Select a toolbar from the list box and click the Add button, or if you don't want to install this tool, click the Skip button. Next, you are asked to specify toolbars for the Microsoft PowerPoint and Microsoft Project tools, each of which you can either add to a toolbar or skip. If you simply click the Add button each time, all three tools are added to the Standard toolbar. After you finish with the Microsoft Project tool, the dialog box disappears, and you can move the newly installed tools or test their operation. If you want to move them to different toolbars, first make sure that the Standard toolbar and the toolbars to which you want to move the switching tools are visible. Then choose the Toolbars command from the Options menu, click the Customize button, and drag each tool to the desired toolbar.

Once you have used the SWITCH.XLA add-in macro sheet to install the switching tools, you need not concern yourself with it again. Thereafter, when you click one of the switching tools, the associated application is activated. If the application is not open, the switching tool opens it and makes it the active application. Note that you must have the application installed on your computer, and the full path to the application files must be specified in the PATH command in your AUTOEXEC.BAT file. To return to Excel, press Ctrl-Esc to activate the Task List, and double-click Microsoft Excel.

Saving toolbar settings

When you quit Microsoft Excel, any changes you made to the predefined toolbars, or any custom toolbars you created, are saved in the condition and position they were in when you quit. Each time you start Excel, your custom and modified toolbars are ready for use. If you want to create different combinations of toolbar settings, you can save modified and custom toolbar variations by renaming the EXCEL.XLB file.

The EXCEL.XLB file saves the toolbar configuration whenever you quit Excel. If you make changes to the toolbars during an Excel session, these changes are recorded in the EXCEL.XLB file. But suppose you want to save your current settings so you can make further modifications but still be able to restore the last custom configuration. You can do this by switching to the Windows File Manager and changing the name of the EXCEL.XLB file, which is located in the directory that contains your Windows files. The settings that were active the last time you started Excel are saved under the new filename, and any modifications you make during the current session are saved in a new EXCEL.XLB file when you quit Excel. You can subsequently rename this new EXCEL.XLB file, if you want. In this way, you can create any number of different toolbar configurations. To use any of these toolbar configuration files, simply open EXCEL.XLB using the Open command on the File menu.

Reference to tools and toolbars

The Standard toolbar, shown in Figure A-7, includes the following tools, from left to right: New Worksheet, Open File, Save File, Print, Style box, AutoSum, Bold, Italic, Increase Font Size, Decrease Font Size, Left Align, Center Align, Right Align, Center Across Columns, AutoFormat, Outline Border, Bottom Border, Copy, Paste Formats, ChartWizard, and Help.

FIGURE A-7.
The Standard toolbar.

The Formatting toolbar, shown in Figure A-8, includes the following tools, from left to right: Style Box, Font Name Box, Font Size Box, Bold, Italic, Underline, Strike-out, Justify Align, Currency Style, Percent Style, Comma Style, Increase Decimal, Decrease Decimal, Light Shading, and AutoFormat.

FIGURE A-8.
The Formatting toolbar.

The Utility toolbar, shown in Figure A-9, includes the following tools, from left to right: Undo, Repeat, Copy, Paste Values, Paste Formats, Zoom In, Zoom Out, Sort Ascending, Sort Descending, Lock Cell, Promote, Demote, Show Outline Symbols, Select Visible Cells, Button, Text Box, Camera, Check Spelling, Set Print Area, and Calculate Now.

FIGURE A-9.
The Utility toolbar.

The Chart toolbar, shown in Figure A-10, includes the following tools, from left to right: Area Chart, Bar Chart, Column Chart, Stacked Column Chart, Line Chart, Pie Chart, XY (Scatter) Chart, 3-D Area Chart, 3-D Bar Chart, 3-D Column Chart, 3-D Perspective Column Chart, 3-D Line Chart, 3-D Pie Chart, 3-D Surface Chart, Radar Chart, Line/Column Chart, Volume-Hi-Lo-Close Chart, Preferred Chart, ChartWizard, Horizontal Gridlines, Legend, Arrow, and Text Box.

FIGURE A-10.
The Chart toolbar.

The Drawing toolbar, shown in Figure A-11, includes the following tools, from left to right: Line, Arrow, Freehand, Rectangle, Oval, Arc, Freehand Polygon, Filled Rectangle, Filled Oval, Filled Arc, Filled Freehand Polygon, Text Box, Selection, Reshape, Group, Ungroup, Bring to Front, Send to Back, Color, and Drop Shadow.

FIGURE A-11.
The Drawing toolbar.

The Microsoft Excel 3 toolbar, shown in Figure A-12, includes the following tools, from left to right: Style Box, Promote, Demote, Show Outline Symbols, Select Visible Cells, AutoSum, Bold, Italic, Left Align, Center Align, Right Align, Selection, Line, Filled Rectangle, Filled Oval, Arc, Preferred Chart, Text Box, Button, and Camera.

FIGURE A-12.
The Microsoft Excel 3 toolbar.

The Macro toolbar, shown in Figure A-13, includes the following tools, from left to right: New Macro Sheet, Paste Function, Paste Names, Run Macro, Step Macro, Record Macro, and Resume Macro.

FIGURE A-13.
The Macro toolbar.

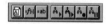

The Macro Paused toolbar, shown in Figure A-14, includes only the Resume Macro tool.

FIGURE A-14.
The Macro Paused toolbar.

The Stop Recording toolbar, shown in Figure A-15, includes only the Stop Recording Macro tool.

FIGURE A-15.
The Stop Recording toolbar.

Table of tools in alphabetic order

The following table is an alphabetic list of each tool included with Microsoft Excel, along with its name, the name of the toolbar on which it resides (or *None,* if it appears only in the Customize dialog box), the tool category or categories it belongs to, a brief description of its operation, and if applicable, a brief description of how its operation changes if you press Shift while clicking the tool. Also listed is the Code Number for the tool, which is the number used to refer to the tool in macro formulas. (The Font Name box, Font Size box, and Style box are listed here but not illustrated.)

Tool	Tool name	Toolbar	Category	Code	Description
	3-D Area Chart	Chart	Charting	109	Creates a default 3-D area chart.
	3-D Bar Chart	Chart	Charting	110	Creates a default 3-D bar chart.
	3-D Column Chart	Chart	Charting	111	Creates a default 3-D column chart.
	3-D Line Chart	Chart	Charting	113	Creates a default 3-D line chart.
	3-D Perspective Column Chart	Chart	Charting	112	Creates a default 3-D perspective column chart.
	3-D Pie Chart	Chart	Charting	114	Creates a default 3-D pie chart.
	3-D Surface Chart	Chart	Charting	116	Creates a default 3-D surface chart.
	Arc	Drawing/ Excel 3	Drawing	85	Draws an arc. Shift-click draws a filled arc. Press Shift after click to create a semicircle.
	Area Chart	Chart	Charting	103	Creates a default area chart.
	Arrow	Chart/ Drawing	Charting/ Drawing	77	Draws a line with an arrow at the point you release the mouse button. Press Shift to constrain along horizontal, vertical, or diagonal lines.
	AutoFormat	Standard/ Formatting	Formatting	52	Applies last-used table format from the Format AutoFormat command list. Shift-click cycles through formats.
	AutoSum	Standard/ Excel 3	Formula/ Utility	39	Inserts the SUM function and automatically selects a range.
	Bar Chart	Chart	Charting	104	Creates a default bar chart.
	Bold	Standard/ Formatting /Excel 3	Text Formatting	58	Applies bold text format to selection.

(Continued)

Tool	Tool name	Toolbar	Category	Code	Description
	Bottom Border	Standard	Formatting	47	Applies border to the bottom edge of selection.
	Bottom Double Border	None	Formatting	48	Adds or removes a double border at the bottom edge of selected cells.
	Bring to Front	Drawing	Drawing	95	Moves selected objects to foreground. Press Shift-click to send to back.
	Button	Utility/ Excel 3	Utility/ Drawing	80	Creates a button to which you can attach a macro.
	Calculate Now	Utility	Utility	126	Recalculates all open documents.
	Camera	Utility/ Excel 3	Utility	125	Makes a linked copy of selection.
	Center Across Columns	Standard	Text Formatting	67	Centers text across selected cells.
	Center Align	Standard/ Excel 3	Text Formatting	64	Center-aligns text in selection.
	ChartWizard	Standard/ Chart	Charting	121	Starts the ChartWizard, which steps you through the process of creating a new chart.
	Check Spelling	Utility	Utility	127	Checks spelling of document or text in the active formula bar.
	Clear Formats	None	Edit	16	Deletes only formats from selection.
	Clear Formulas	None	Edit	15	Deletes only formulas and values from selected cells, or deletes selected objects.
	Colon	None	Formula	35	Inserts a colon (:) at the insertion point in the formula bar.
	Color	Drawing	Drawing	97	Changes foreground color of selection to the next color in the palette. Shift-click for previous color.
	Column Chart	Chart	Charting	105	Creates a default column chart.
	Comma	None	Formula	36	Inserts a comma at the insertion point in the formula bar.
	Comma Style	Formatting	Formatting	55	Applies comma style to selection.

Tool	Tool name	Toolbar	Category	Code	Description
	Constrain Numeric	None	Formula	42	Restricts handwriting recognition for Pen Windows to digits and punctuation.
	Copy	Standard/ Utility	Edit	13	Copies selection to the Clipboard.
	Currency Style	Formatting	Formatting	53	Applies currency style to selection.
	Cut	None	Edit	12	Cuts the selection and places it on the Clipboard.
	Dark Shading	None	Formatting	49	Adds dark shading pattern to selection.
	Decrease Decimal	Formatting	Formatting	57	Removes a decimal place from the number format of selection. Shift-click to add a decimal place.
	Decrease Font Size	Standard	Text Formatting	72	Changes text in selection to the next smallest built-in font size. Shift-click for next largest font size.
	Delete	None	Edit	19	Removes selected cells and shifts adjacent cells to fill in the space. Shift-click inserts cells.
	Delete Column	None	Edit	21	Removes selected columns. Shift-click inserts columns.
	Delete Row	None	Edit	20	Removes selected rows. Shift-click inserts rows.
	Demote	Utility/ Excel 3	Utility	130	Assigns selection to next lowest level in an outline. Shift-click assigns next highest level.
	Division Sign	None	Formula	31	Inserts a slash (/) at the insertion point in the formula bar.
	Dollar Sign	None	Formula	38	Inserts a dollar sign at the insertion point in the formula bar.
	Drop Shadow	Drawing	Drawing	51	Adds drop-shadow effect to selected cells or objects.
	Equal Sign	None	Formula	27	Inserts an equal sign at the insertion point in the formula bar.
	Exponentiation Sign	None	Formula	32	Inserts a caret (^) at the insertion point in the formula bar.

(Continued)

Tool	Tool name	Toolbar	Category	Code	Description
	Fill Down	None	Edit	26	Copies values, formats, and formulas in the top row of the selection down, to fill selection. Shift-click copies from the bottom up.
	Fill Right	None	Edit	25	Copies values, formats, and formulas in the leftmost column of selection to the right, to fill selection. Shift-click copies from right to left.
	Filled Arc	Drawing	Drawing	90	Draws a filled arc. Shift-click draws an unfilled arc. Press Shift after click to create a filled semicircle.
	Filled Freehand Polygon	Drawing	Drawing	92	Draws filled combination freehand/straight line solid objects. Click the beginning point to complete the drawing. Shift-click to draw an unfilled polygon.
	Filled Oval	Drawing/Excel 3	Drawing	89	Draws a filled oval. Shift-click draws an unfilled oval. Press Shift after click to create a filled circle.
	Filled Polygon	None	Drawing	91	Draws filled solid objects using straight lines. Click the beginning point to complete the drawing. Shift-click to draw an unfilled polygon.
	Filled Rectangle	Drawing/Excel 3	Drawing	88	Draws a filled rectangle. Shift-click draws an unfilled rectangle. Press Shift after click to create a filled square.
	Font Name box	Formatting	Text Formatting	68	Lists all available fonts.
	Font Size box	Formatting	Text Formatting	69	Lists all available font sizes.
	Freehand	Drawing	Drawing	78	Draws a freehand line.
	Freehand Polygon	Drawing	Drawing	87	Draws combination freehand/straight line solid objects. Click the beginning point to complete the drawing. Shift-click to draw an unfilled freehand polygon.

Tool	Tool name	Toolbar	Category	Code	Description
	Freeze Panes	None	Utility	137	Freezes windows that are already split into panes, or splits and freezes panes above and to the left of the active cell.
	Group	Drawing	Drawing	93	Joins selected objects together as a single object. Shift-click separates grouped objects.
	Help	Standard	Utility	128	Click this tool, and then click item about which you want help to display on-line help topic. Double-click to display Help search dialog box.
	Horizontal Gridlines	Chart	Charting	122	Adds or removes major gridlines on the value axis.
	Increase Decimal	Formatting	Formatting	56	Shift-click removes a decimal place. Adds a decimal place to the number format of selection.
	Increase Font Size	Standard	Text Formatting	71	Changes text in selection to the next larger built-in font size. Shift-click for next smaller size.
	Insert	None	Edit	22	Inserts cells at the selected location and shifts adjacent cells to accommodate insertion. Shift-click deletes cells.
	Insert Column	None	Edit	24	Inserts columns at the selected location and shifts adjacent columns to accommodate insertion. Shift-click deletes columns.
	Insert Row	None	Edit	23	Inserts rows at the selected location and shifts adjacent rows to accommodate insertion. Shift-click deletes rows.
	Italic	Standard/ Formatting /Excel 3	Text Formatting	59	Applies italic text format to selection.
	Justify Align	Formatting	Text Formatting	66	Aligns text in the selection flush right and flush left, adding space between words where necessary.
	Left Align	Standard/ Excel 3	Text Formatting	63	Aligns text in selection flush left.

(Continued)

Tool	Tool name	Toolbar	Category	Code	Description
	Left Border	None	Formatting	44	Adds or removes a border at the left edge of selected cells.
	Left Parenthesis	None	Formula	33	Inserts an open parenthesis at the insertion point in the formula bar.
	Legend	Chart	Charting	124	Adds or removes a chart legend.
	Light Shading	Formatting	Formatting/ Drawing	50	Adds light shading pattern to selection.
	Line	Drawing/ Excel 3	Drawing	76	Draws a straight line. Press Shift to constrain along horizontal, vertical, or diagonal lines.
	Line Chart	Chart	Charting	107	Creates a default line chart.
	Line/Column Chart	Chart	Charting	118	Creates a default line/column chart.
	Lock Cell	Utility	Utility	136	Applies locked protection format to selection.
	Microsoft PowerPoint	None	Switching	N/A	Switches to Microsoft PowerPoint. SWITCHTO.XLA must be installed.
	Microsoft Project	None	Switching	N/A	Switches to Microsoft Project. SWITCHTO.XLA must be installed.
	Microsoft Word	None	Switching	N/A	Switches to Microsoft Word. SWITCHTO.XLA must be installed.
	Minus Sign	None	Formula	29	Inserts a minus sign at the insertion point in the formula bar.
	Multiplication Sign	None	Formula	30	Inserts an asterisk (*) at the insertion point in the formula bar.
	New Chart	None	File	8	Creates a new chart document.
	New Macro Sheet	Macro	File	6	Creates a new macro sheet.
	New Workbook	None	File	9	Creates a new workbook document.
	New Worksheet	Standard	File	7	Creates a new worksheet.
	Open File	Standard	File	1	Displays File Open dialog box.

Tool	Tool name	Toolbar	Category	Code	Description
	Outline Border	Standard	Formatting	43	Applies border to the outside edges of selection.
	Oval	Drawing	Drawing	84	Draws an oval. Shift-click to draw a filled oval. Press Shift after click to create a circle.
	Paste	None	Edit	14	Pastes the contents of the Clipboard.
	Paste Formats	Standard	Edit	17	Pastes only the formats of copied cells. Shift-click pastes only values.
	Paste Function	Macro	Formula/ Macro	40	Displays Paste Function dialog box.
	Paste Names	Macro	Formula/ Macro	41	Displays Paste Name dialog box.
	Paste Values	Utility	Edit	18	Pastes only the values of copied cells. Shift-click pastes only formats.
	Percent Sign	None	Formula	37	Inserts a percent sign at the insertion point in the formula bar.
	Percent Style	Formatting	Formatting	54	Applies percent style to selection.
	Pie Chart	Chart	Charting	108	Creates a default pie chart.
	Plus Sign	None	Formula	28	Inserts a plus sign at the insertion point in the formula bar.
	Polygon	None	Drawing	86	Draws solid objects using straight lines. Shift-click draws a filled polygon. Click the beginning point to complete the drawing.
	Preferred Chart	Chart/ Excel 3	Charting	120	Creates a chart in the format currently defined with the Chart Gallery Set Preferred command.
	Print	Standard	File	3	Prints active document. Shift-click for print preview.
	Print Preview	None	File	4	Displays the Print Preview window. Shift-click to print the active document.
	Promote	Utility/ Excel 3	Utility	129	Assigns selection to next higher level in an outline. Shift-click for next lower level.

(Continued)

Tool	Tool name	Toolbar	Category	Code	Description
	Radar Chart	Chart	Charting	117	Creates a default radar chart.
	Record Macro	Macro	Macro	98	Records your actions as a new macro.
	Rectangle	Drawing	Drawing	83	Draws a rectangle. Shift-click draws a filled rectangle. Press Shift after click to create a square.
	Repeat	Utility	Edit	11	Repeats the last command or action.
	Reshape	Drawing	Drawing	82	Lets you adjust the shape of polygons and freehand lines.
	Resume Macro	Macro Paused	Macro	102	Resumes running a paused macro.
	Right Align	Standard/ Excel 3	Text Formatting	65	Aligns text in selection flush right.
	Right Border	None	Formatting	45	Adds or removes a border at the right edge of selected cells.
	Right Parenthesis	None	Formula	34	Inserts a close parenthesis at the insertion point in the formula bar.
	Rotate Text Down	None	Text Formatting	75	Rotates text vertically, reading from top to bottom.
	Rotate Text Up	None	Text Formatting	74	Rotates text vertically, reading from bottom to top.
	Run Macro	Macro	Macro	100	Runs the selected macro starting at the active cell. Shift-click to step through macro.
	Save File	Standard	File	2	Saves active document.
	Select Current Region	None	Utility	133	Selects all adjacent cells in a rectangular area, bounded by blank rows and columns.
	Select Visible Cells	Utility/ Excel 3	Utility	132	Selects visible cells in selection, ignoring hidden cells.
	Selection	Drawing/ Excel 3	Drawing	81	Selects groups of objects.
	Send to Back	Drawing	Drawing	96	Moves selected objects to background. Shift-click to bring objects to foreground.

Tool	Tool name	Toolbar	Category	Code	Description
	Set Print Area	Utility	File	5	Defines selection to the range you want to print.
	Show Outline Symbols	Utility/ Excel 3	Utility	131	Displays or hides outline symbols. If no outline exists, asks if you want to create one.
	Sort Ascending	Utility	Utility	134	Sorts selected cells in alphabetic order, using the active cell as sort key. Shift-click to sort in descending order.
	Sort Descending	Utility	Utility	135	Sorts selected cells in reverse alphabetic order, using the active cell as sort key. Shift-click to sort in ascending order.
	Stacked Column Chart	Chart	Charting	106	Creates a default stacked column chart.
	Step Macro	Macro	Macro	101	Displays the Single Step dialog box. Steps through the selected macro starting at the active cell. Shift-click to run the macro.
	Stop Recording	Stop Recording	Macro	99	Stops the macro recording.
	Strikeout	Formatting	Text Formatting	61	Applies the strikeout format to text in the selection.
	Style box	Standard/ Formatting /Excel 3	Formatting/ Text Formatting	70	Lists all defined cell styles. Define a new style by selecting a formatted cell, typing new style name, and pressing Enter.
	Text Box	Chart/ Utility/ Drawing/ Excel 3	Charting/ Drawing/ Utility	79	Inserts a floating text box object to a worksheet, or an unattached text box to a chart.
	Text Color	None	Text Formatting	62	Changes text color in selected cells to the next color in the palette. Shift-click for the previous color.
	Top Border	None	Formatting	46	Adds or removes a border at the top edge of selected cells.
	Underline	Formatting	Text Formatting	60	Applies the underline format to text in the selection.
	Undo	Utility	Edit	10	Undoes the last command or action.

(Continued)

Tool	Tool name	Toolbar	Category	Code	Description
	Ungroup	Drawing	Drawing	94	Separates previously grouped objects. Shift-click to group objects.
	Vertical Gridlines	None	Charting	123	Adds or removes major gridlines on the category axis.
	Vertical Text	None	Text Formatting	73	Stacks text vertically in cells.
	Volume-Hi-Lo-Close Chart	Chart	Charting	119	Creates a default volume-hi-lo-close chart.
	XY (Scatter) Chart	Chart	Charting	115	Creates a default XY (scatter) chart.
	Zoom In	Utility	Utility	138	Increases the Window Zoom command's magnification one step. Shift-click to zoom out.
	Zoom Out	Utility	Utility	139	Decreases the Window Zoom command's magnification one step. Shift-click to zoom in.

B

The 30 Most Valuable Keyboard Shortcuts

*E*ach new release of Microsoft Excel adds a wealth of new features — and a raft of new keyboard shortcuts. The *Microsoft Excel User's Guide* devotes no fewer than 19 pages to tables of keyboard shortcuts. Provided you can remember them, they're all valuable — particularly if you're using Excel on a laptop without an effective pointing device. But most of us don't have time to remember 19 pages' worth of shortcuts. In this appendix we offer a subset — the 30 shortcuts we think are most worth the trouble to learn.

Shortcut	Action
Data entry	
Ctrl-;	Enter current date on formula bar
Ctrl-:	Enter current time on formula bar
Ctrl-"	Copy value (but not formula) from cell above
Ctrl-'	Copy formula from cell above (without update of relative references)
Ctrl-Enter	Fill selection with current formula

(Continued)

Shortcut	Action
Data entry (*Continued*)	
Shift-F3	Paste function
Ctrl-A	Paste arguments (Type the function name. Then press Ctrl-A to see the function's arguments.)
Editing	
Alt-Enter	Repeat last action
Alt-Backspace	Undo
Ctrl-Z	Undo
Alt-=	AutoSum
Ctrl-R	Fill Right
Ctrl-D	Fill Down
Ctrl-X	Cut
Ctrl-C	Copy
Ctrl-V	Paste
Formatting	
Ctrl-B	Toggle bold on or off
Ctrl-I	Toggle italic on or off
Ctrl-U	Toggle underscore on or off
Ctrl-1	Apply normal font
Ctrl-F	Choose a font
Ctrl-S	Choose a style
Ctrl-$	Format as currency
Ctrl-%	Format as percent
Files	
F11	New chart
Ctrl-F11	New macro sheet
Ctrl-F12	File Open
Shift-F12	File Save
Display	
Ctrl-7	Toggle Standard toolbar
Ctrl-`	Toggle formula display

Index

E

Craig Stinson

Craig Stinson is a contributing editor of *PC Magazine* and *PC/Computing*. He edits the Spreadsheets column for *PC Magazine* and writes the Windows Help column for *PC/Computing*. An industry journalist since 1981, Stinson was formerly editor of *Softalk for the IBM Personal Computer*. Stinson is the author of *Running Windows 3.1* (Microsoft Press, 1992) and coauthor of *Microsoft Excel 4 Companion* (Microsoft Press, 1992). In addition to his numerous computer publications, he has written music reviews for publications such as *Billboard*, the *Boston Globe*, the *Christian Science Monitor*, and *Musical America*. He lives with his wife and children in Eugene, Oregon.

Mark Dodge

Mark Dodge is a technical writer and editor whose previous experiences include cost accounting and small-business management. He has received awards from the Society for Technical Communication as technical editor of *Working with Word* (Microsoft Press, 1989) and *PowerPoint Presentations by Design* (Microsoft Press, 1991). As a freelance technical writer, he has produced documentation, on-line help, and marketing materials, and is coauthor of the *Microsoft Excel 4 Companion*, (Microsoft Press, 1992). He is currently senior technical writer for Microsoft's Excel User Education Group.

Chris Kinata

Chris Kinata graduated from the University of California at Irvine, with a major in psychology and a minor in computer science. He worked for Microsoft Corporation from 1984 through 1989 — as a technical editor, writer, and Microsoft Word guru. He is the author of the award-winning *Working with Word* (Microsoft Press, 1989) and coauthor of *Complete Guide to Microsoft Excel Macros* (Microsoft Press, 1992). He now lives in the Ballard section of Seattle, balancing the arts of writing, homeschooling, and toddler physics.

The Cobb Group

The Cobb Group, a leader in computer training and support, is well known for its bestselling, high-quality computer books and for its series of critically acclaimed newsletters that cover popular software.

The manuscript for this book was prepared and submitted to Microsoft Press in electronic form. Text files were processed and formatted using Microsoft Word.

Principal word processor: Sean Donahue
Principal proofreaders: Joan Goldsworthy and Karen Segal
Principal typographer: Debra Marvin
Interior text designer: Kim Eggleston
Cover designer: Rebecca Geisler
Cover color separator: Color Service Inc.

Text composition by Editorial Services of New England, Inc. in Palatino with display type in Palatino, using Xerox Ventura Publisher and the Compugraphic 9600 imagesetter.

Printed on recycled paper stock.

Great Resources for Windows™ 3.1 Users

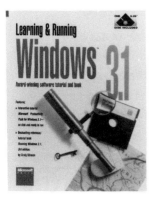

LEARNING & RUNNING WINDOWS™ 3.1
Includes *Microsoft® Productivity Pack for Windows* and *Running Windows 3.1, 3rd ed.*

Microsoft Corporation and Craig Stinson

This is the ideal blending of software and book instruction for users of all levels of experience. If you want to be up and running with Windows 3.1 quickly and easily, this is the place to start. *The Microsoft Productivity Pack for Windows 3.1* (regularly $59.95) combines disk-based lessons with hands-on exercises. RUNNING WINDOWS 3.1 (regularly $27.95) will continue to answer day-to-day questions about Windows long after you've learned the basics from the software tutorial. An unbeatable package at an unbeatable price. Sold separately for $87.90.
560 pages, softcover with one 5 ¹/₂-inch (HD) disk $39.95 ($54.95 Canada)

RUNNING WINDOWS™ 3.1, 3rd ed.

Craig Stinson

Build your confidence and enhance your productivity with Microsoft Windows, quickly and easily, using this hands-on introduction. This Microsoft-authorized edition—for new as well as experienced Windows users—is completely updated and expanded to cover all the new exciting features of version 3.1. You'll find a successful combination of step-by-step tutorials, helpful screen illustrations, expert tips, and real-world examples. Learn how to install and start using Windows 3.1, use applications with Windows, and maximize Windows performance.
560 pages, softcover $27.95 ($37.95 Canada)

WINDOWS™ 3.1 COMPANION

The Cobb Group:
Lori L. Lorenz and R. Michael O'Mara with Russell Borland

This bestseller is now completely updated to cover the important new features of version 3.1. Both a step-by-step tutorial and a comprehensive reference, this book is specifically designed to help you quickly find the information you need—moving from the basics to more advanced information. Learn to take advantage of all the extraordinary improvements and added features of version 3.1, including the new, *faster* File Manager; TrueType font; support for multimedia; the improved Program Manager; the faster Printer Manager; automatic network reconnections; the new "drag and drop" feature. The authors include a wealth of expert tips and tricks and great examples to show you how to use Windows more efficiently.
550 pages, softcover $27.95 ($37.95 Canada)

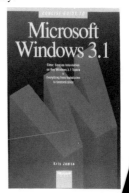

CONCISE GUIDE TO MICROSOFT® WINDOWS™ 3.1

Kris Jamsa

Instant answers to your Windows 3.1 questions! Clear, concise information on all the key Microsoft Windows 3.1 features. For beginning to intermediate users. A great complement to *Windows 3.1 Companion.*
192 pages, softcover $12.95 ($17.95 Canada)

STEP BY STEP SERIES
The Official Microsoft® Courseware

Tried-and-tested, these book-and-disk packages are Microsoft's official courseware.
Complete with follow-along lessons and disk-based practice files, they are ideal self-study
training guides for business, classroom and home use. Scores of real-world business examples make
the instruction relevant and useful; "One Step Further" sections for each chapter cover advanced uses.
These courseware products are the perfect training guide for business, classroom, or home use.

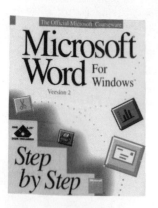

MICROSOFT® WORD FOR WINDOWS™
STEP BY STEP
Version 2

Microsoft Corporation
Learn to produce professional-quality documents with ease.
Covers Microsoft Word for Windows version 2.
296 pages, softcover with one 3.5-inch disk
$29.95 ($39.95 Canada)

MICROSOFT® WINDOWS™ 3.1
STEP BY STEP

Catapult, Inc.
Learn Microsoft Windows the easy way with
MICROSOFT WINDOWS 3.1 STEP BY STEP.
272 pages, softcover with one 3.5-inch disk
$29.95 ($39.95 Canada)

MICROSOFT® POWERPOINT®
FOR WINDOWS™ STEP BY STEP

Steven M. Johnson
The fastest way to get up and running with Microsoft
PowerPoint! Covers Microsoft PowerPoint version 3.
300 pages, softcover with one 3.5-inch disk
$29.95 ($39.95 Canada)

MICROSOFT® EXCEL MACROS
STEP BY STEP
For Windows™ and the Macintosh®
Version 4

Steve Wexler and Julianne Sharer
The ideal way for proficient Microsoft Excel users to
learn how to use macros to save time and simplify their work.
Scores of examples.
**272 pages, softcover with one 720-KB 3.5-inch PC disk and
one 800-KB 3.5-inch Macintosh disk**
$34.95 ($47.95 Canada)